MAXWELL

THE FINAL VERDICT

ALSO BY TOM BOWER

Blind Eye to Murder
Klaus Barbie: Butcher of Lyons
The Paperclip Conspiracy
Maxwell: The Outsider
Red Web
Tiny Rowland: The Rebel Tycoon
Heroes of World War II
The Perfect English Spy: Sir Dick White

Tom Bower

MAXWELL

THE FINAL VERDICT

HarperCollins*Publishers*

HarperCollins*Publishers*
77–85 Fulham Palace Road,
Hammersmith, London W6 8JB

Published by HarperCollins*Publishers* 1995
1 3 5 7 9 8 6 4 2

A catalogue record for this book
is available from the British Library

ISBN 0 00 255564 6

Set in Linotron Sabon by
Rowland Phototypesetting Ltd,
Bury St Edmunds, Suffolk

Printed in Great Britain by
HarperCollinsManufacturing Glasgow

To Sophie

You are my teacher and all my life you have tried to demonstrate the principles underlying every action or inaction ... Above all, you have given me the sense of excitement of having dozens of balls in the air and the thrill of seeing some of them land right.

KEVIN MAXWELL, written to his father in 1988

The Maxwell Foundation will be one of the richest of its kind in the world.

JOE HAINES, 1988

Contents

Dramatis Personae

Aboff, Shelly: Robert Maxwell crony based in New York
Anselmini, Jean-Pierre: deputy chairman, MCC; director LBI
Baker, Richard: deputy managing director, MCC
Brookes, Basil: finance director, MCC
Bunn, Robert: treasurer, later finance director, MCC
Burrington, Ernest: managing director, MGN
Carson, Stuart: compliance officer and director, LBI
Clark, Sir Robert: non-executive director, MGN
Cook, Trevor: manager, director and compliance officer, BIM
Cowling, John: Coopers auditor for BIM
Donoughue, Lord: executive vice-chairman, LBI
Ford, Jonathan: finance director, LBI
Freedman, Ellis: Robert Maxwell's personal lawyer, New York
Fuller, Albert: treasurer, RMG
Gould, John: accountant, BIT; assistant to Robert Bunn
Guest, Lawrence: financial director, MGN
Halloran, John: manager, BPCC
Harry, Bill: tax adviser, Macmillan
Highfield, Jeffrey: deputy manager, BIM
Laister, Peter: non-executive director, MCC
McInroy, Alan: chairman, First Tokyo
Martin, Andrea: Robert Maxwell's secretary
Mishcon, Lord: Robert Maxwell's solicitor
Morgenstern, Philip: Robert Maxwell's solicitor
Richardson, Sir Michael: chairman, Smith New Court
Rippon, Lord: non-executive director, MCC
Roberts, Jane: treasurer, RMG; later assistant to Robert Bunn
Russell, Dick: Kevin Maxwell's brother-in-law; solicitor
Shaffer, David: president, Macmillan Inc; director, MCC

Smith, Andrew: director, LBI, LBI Inc
Stephens, Alan: company secretary for over 200 Maxwell companies
Stoney, Michael: accountant; deputy manager, MGN
Taberner, Neil: Coopers auditor for MCC
Tapley, Mark: managing director, LBI
Trachtenberg, Larry: director, LBI; later director, BIM and RMG
Vogel, David: Maxwells' solicitor
Walker, Peter: chairman-designate, MCC
Walsh, Peter: Coopers auditor for RMG
Willet, George: director, LBI
Lord Williams of Elvel: formerly director Ansbacher Bank: director, MGN, PHL and LBI
Woods, Ron: tax specialist and director, MCC
Wootten, Stephen: Coopers auditor for RMG

Glossary of Abbreviations

ACT	advance corporation tax
AGB	privately owned research company, owner of *Daily News*
BIM	Bishopsgate Investment Management
BIT	Bishopsgate Investment Trust
BPC	British Printing Corporation
BPCC	British Printing & Communication Corporation
CDA	Call Deposit Account
CEO	chief executive officer
CIF	Common Investment Fund
GAS	Global Analysis Systems
HIL	Headington Investments Ltd
IBI	Maxwell private company
IMRO	Investment Management Regulatory Organization
KGB	Soviet intelligence service
LBG	London & Bishopsgate Group
LBH	London & Bishopsgate Holdings
LBI	London & Bishopsgate Investments
LBII	London & Bishopsgate International Investment
LBIIM	London & Bishopsgate International Investment Management
MAMI	Marine & Aviation Management International
MCC	Maxwell Communication Corporation
MI5	British domestic counter-intelligence service
MI6	British external intelligence service
MGN	Mirror Group Newspapers
MGPT	Mirror Group Pension Trust
OAG	Official Airline Guides

Ph (US) Inc.	Pergamon Holdings (US) Inc.
PHL	Pergamon Holdings Ltd
RMG	Robert Maxwell Group
SFO	Serious Fraud Office

Acknowledgements

Researching and writing this book would have been impossible without the generous assistance provided by numerous people who sacrificed their time. Many did so on condition of their anonymity (especially the lawyers, bankers and accountants) while others, providing information which has made this book unusually rich in detail, were willing to be quoted.

My first thanks are to Bob Cole, Maxwell's former press spokesman. In 1987, when I first embarked upon the research of *Maxwell the Outsider*, I cheekily telephoned Cole and asked whether his employer was minded to cooperate. The reply was a letter warning of a writ. Seven years later, after his employer's sudden passing, Bob Cole honestly and passionately sought to put the record right. This book offers him some consolation for devoting himself to a man who roundly abused his unconditional trust.

Secondly I am grateful to Steve Hewlett, Olivia Liechtenstein and especially Paul Hamann at BBC TV's Documentaries department who allowed me a latitude which has become quite exceptional in Britain's media, to pursue a story which requires time and expense. With Clare Duggan, who as director was a tremendous help, I was able to begin pulling together the extraordinary story of Maxwell's last year which resulted in a television documentary and this book.

Among those who kindly provided information were Jean-Paul Anselmini, Lord Archer, Brian Basham, Rolf Beeler, John Bender, Larry Bloom, Rudi Bogni, Tony Boram, Peter Boyer, Carol Bragoli, Desmond Bristow, Doug Bristow, Basil Brookes, David Burnside, Ernie Burrington, Oscar Buselink, John Campi, Clive Chalk, Martin Cheeseman, Robert Clark, Julius Claverie, Alan Clements, Brian Cole, Dick Cowley, Trevor Cook, Tim Daily, Ellis Freedman, John

Featley, Ray Fox, Lawrence Guest, Marshall Genger, Terry Gilmour, Yuri Gradov, Douglas Harrod, Bill Harry, President Chaim Herzog, Judah Hiss, Jim Hoge, Jeff Highfield, Bill Hull, Joe Jacobs, Bill Kay, Mark Killick, Peter Laister, Carlos Lamela, George McDonald, Alan McInroy, David Meggit, Sir John Morgan, Robert Pirie, John Pole, Gus Rankin, Roger Rich, Sir Michael Richardson, Dr Alfred Rosenbaum, Arik Sharon, Eric Sheinberg, Barry Shepherd, Grahame Shorrocks, the late Susan Silverman, Dr Iain West, George Wheeler, David Whiteman, Ron Woods.

I am also grateful to those who helped my research: Tim Brown in Spain; Karen Blanchard and Karl McLaughlin in Tenerife; Israel Goldvitch in Israel; Suzanne Lowrie in Paris; Ksenia Shergova and Elena Koralova in Moscow; and especially to Robert Fink in New York, a tireless and generous associate.

Daily, over six months, I sat in Court 22 reporting the Maxwell trial for the *Observer*, alongside John Steele of the *Daily Telegraph* and John Mason of the *Financial Times*. Both were good companions and I am grateful for their help.

At HarperCollins I was enthusiastically and efficiently assisted by Michael Fishwick and Rebecca Lloyd. My editor Peter James was more than magnificent – I am embarrassed by the magnitude of my debt towards him.

Michael Shaw of Curtis Brown was as steady and helpful as always and David Hooper of Biddle & Co provided a sure guide through the libel laws.

My greatest thanks are naturally to Veronica, a great friend and supporter, and my four children.

Preface

On 12 May 1989, Peter Jay signed a short letter marked 'Private and Confidential' addressed to George Potter OBE, a director of Control Risks, one of Britain's leading private detective agencies. Jay, the chief of staff to Robert Maxwell, thanked Potter, a former police officer, for 'your letter and for the time you gave to meeting me and preparing it'.

Potter's letter had described his surveillance of 'the location and the levels of background radiation in the area'. Potter was referring in cryptic fashion to a surreptitious reconnaissance mission which he had undertaken around my home in Hampstead, north-west London. He continued: 'Extremely sophisticated equipment does exist which might overcome the technical problems. Its acquisition would cost an estimated £50,000.' The private detective was describing a scanner which would emit rays capable of penetrating my home and 'reading' the contents of my computer's hard disc.

Wisely, Potter cautioned Jay about the problems. First, the detective wanted to be paid in advance the £50,000 for the equipment and also some fees. Secondly, Potter warned, he had 'reservations as to the possibility of obtaining the evidence you require and the ability to keep the operation covert'. The detective's concerns were understandable. A van carrying the scanner would be parked at the bottom of my garden in a narrow service road used by the Hampstead postal sorting office. Remaining unobtrusive for long periods would be difficult.

Jay, who had once basked in the glorious description as one of Britain's 'cleverest men', was not slow to grasp Potter's cautionary tone but was sensitive to the dissatisfaction that this report would cause his demanding employer. Little had been achieved since, one month earlier, he had received a briefing from Tony Frost, an assistant editor of the *Daily Mirror*, following his investigation around my Hampstead home.

Frost had accurately noted my address and identified my car, before reporting that 'neighbours say his working hours are "rather erratic" with frequent trips away' and that I 'spent "a full working week" at the offices or studios of the various TV companies who commission his work'. Curiously, he noted that my newsagent 'seemed to know Bower quite well'. After alluding to my financial status, Frost observed that my road is 'typical of the more up-market parts of Hampstead' and flatteringly noted, 'the house looked to be tastefully and expensively decorated inside'.

Copies of Frost's memorandum were also sent to Eve Pollard (then editor of the *Sunday Mirror*), Ernest Burrington, (then editor of the *People*) and Joe Haines (then a *Daily Mirror* columnist and a director of the Mirror Group) – all owned by Maxwell's Mirror Group Newspapers.

Jay filed Frost's report in his bulging 'Bower File', which was marked in large letters 'Private and Confidential', reflecting the heading of every document it contained. Each letter on the topic signed by the chief of staff urged its recipient to treat the matter with utmost secrecy. Jay had become rather proficient in conducting the operation.

Ever since his employer had heard in summer 1987 that I was planning to write *Maxwell: the Outsider*, an unauthorised biography of himself, Peter Jay had been employed as his chief of intelligence to gather and co-ordinate information about my activities and identify those people whom I was interviewing. On one occasion, detectives had clearly followed me to a meeting with Anne Dove, Maxwell's former secretary, with whom he had enjoyed a close relationship in the 1950s. The results of their work were formalised under Jay's supervision in sworn statements which would be used to back the avalanche of writs and court hearings, costing £1 million, which obsessed Maxwell until his death.

Initially, Maxwell tried to prevent the book's publication in February 1988, at the same time publishing his own version written by Joe Haines. When my book hit the top of the bestseller list, Maxwell sought through individual cajolery and writs to prevent every bookshop in Britain selling the title. Eventually he was successful in this endeavour, but he nevertheless continued to hound me and the publishers by pursuing various writs for libel. Jay's task was to co-ordinate and supervise the unprecedented legal battle.

By spring 1989, one year after publication, when the first of three publishers had agreed to publish the paperback version only to retreat rather than face the subject's wrath, Maxwell's anger was increasing in parallel to the secretly developing insolvency of his empire. His fury had shifted from the book's accurate description of his unaltered dishonesty to something which in his view was more sinister. He believed that I had become a focus for his enemies and a receptacle of damaging information. Just as he was finalising a deceptive annual financial report for the Maxwell Communication Corporation, of which he was chairman, he embarked upon a new venture to humiliate the book's publisher and bankrupt its author.

Four lawyers were Maxwell's principal advisers. Lord Mishcon and Anthony Julius were his solicitors and Richard Rampton QC and Victoria Sharp were the barristers. During their frequent court appearances, they betrayed no hint of doubt about their client's virtues. On the contrary, they pursued his mission with depressing vigour, commitment and pitilessness.

Their client's anger had by then increased still further. The book had been published in France and his defamation action there had failed. To his fury, a court had ordered that he pay me FFrs 10,000 in costs. The threat that the book might also be published in his beloved New York galvanised him to resort to more draconian measures.

Maxwell had become convinced, in the words of Stephen Nathan, another barrister hired for advice, that I had 'compiled (and continued to compile) an extensive record of information concerning Mr Maxwell and has put the distillation of that information on to a computer which he keeps at home'. Maxwell's source was Frost, who, during his gumshoe expedition around Hampstead, had picked up from an 'unidentified source' the notion that my study had become a centre for subversive activities against the Chairman.

Nathan had been asked to advise whether I could be prosecuted for failing to register as a data-user under the Data Protection Act 1984 or, better still, whether Maxwell might approach the Director of Public Prosecutions. The DPP, the Chairman hoped, would direct the police to seize the computer without warning. That course, advised Nathan, would be possible only if Maxwell could persuade the DPP of the allegedly dangerous contents of the computer.

Frustrated by Nathan's wishy-washy advice, Maxwell ordered Lord Mishcon to seek the seizure of my computer on the orders of a judge under an Anton Piller order. Naturally Jay passed on the instruction to Julius. Such an order, suggested Jay, would enable 'Bower's computer records to be seized under warrant, without advance notice being given, therefore without Bower having an opportunity to destroy or conceal such records'. In retrospect, the irony of Maxwell mentioning Anton Piller was manifest. The order, as Mishcon explained, is used to obtain the seizure of documents for the investigation of fraud or systematic dishonesty. And Jay, in passing on Mishcon's advice to the Chairman in another 'Intermemo' on 7 April 1989 headed 'Bower's Computer' and marked 'Strictly Confidential', noted mournfully, 'Legally speaking, this is not (quite) the situation with Bower.'

Mishcon urged his client to adopt the customary course and apply to the court for the computer records. But, he cautioned, 'Our evidence that these records exist is thin.' Therefore, advised the peer, 'I recommend that investigations should continue.' Hence Maxwell ordered Jay to seek the evidence required, and this was why Jay was inspired to ask the detective to place the scanner at the bottom of my garden. But after receiving Potter's disappointing news, Jay concluded, 'It is not really practical to proceed along the lines we discussed.'

That was by no means the end of the battle. Until October 1991, Maxwell regularly held meetings with lawyers and with his personal security staff to propel the battle towards my bankruptcy and his vindication. The readiness of Peter Jay, a journalist and former British ambassador, to function as his willing tool was sadly not unique in Britain or elsewhere. He merely epitomised a cravenness common among a horde of self-important personalities and powerbrokers whose self-esteem was boosted by the Chairman's attentions and deep purse.

Unfortunately, the sort of campaign directed against my book acted as a disincentive for most newspapers against exposing Maxwell in his lifetime. Many blame Britain's libel laws and lawyers' fees for protecting him, yet the law and its expense were not the sole reason for British newspapers' reluctance or inability to uncover his crimes. More important was the environment in which newspapers now operate.

Few newspaper editors and even fewer proprietors nowadays relish causing discomfort to miscreant powerbrokers. By nature anti-Establishment, the so-called 'investigative' reporter finds himself working for newspapers which are increasingly pro-Establishment. Only on celluloid, it seems, does an editor smile when listening to a screaming complainant exposed by his journalists.

Proper journalism, as opposed to straightforward reporting or the columnists' self-righteous sermonising, is an expensive, frustrating and lonely chore. Often it is unproductive. Even the rarity of success earns the 'investigative' journalist only the irksome epitaph of being 'obsessional' or 'dangerous'. The final product is often complicated to read, unentertaining and inconclusive. No major City slicker has ever been brought down merely by newspaper articles. Like the Fraud Squad, financial journalists usually need a crash before they can detect and report upon the real defects. Often, only with hindsight does the crime seem obvious. Even though in Maxwell's case his propensity to commit a fraud had been obvious since 1954, it was almost impossible for any journalist to produce the evidence contemporaneously.

Moreover, many of those who reported Maxwell's affairs during the 1980s were only vaguely aware of the details of the Pergamon saga in 1969, when his publishing empire had disintegrated amid suspicions of dishonesty which appeared to have terminated his business life. After three damning DTI reports, no one expected Maxwell's resurrection. However, the DTI inspectors, having found the evidence of fraud and voiced a memorable phrase about his unfitness to manage a public company, had not directly accused him of criminality. It was the inspectors' cowardly reluctance to publish their real convictions and the police failure to prosecute which permitted Maxwell during the 1980s, when explaining his life, to distort the record of the Pergamon saga.

Accordingly, by 1987, Buckingham Palace, the City, Westminster and Whitehall had forgotten or forgiven the past. In the year in which Maxwell's final frauds began, most journalists reflected the prevailing sentiment and were willing to afford him the benefit of the doubt.

To have broken through Maxwell's barrier required not only a brave inside source who was willing to steal documents but also someone who would risk the Chairman's inevitable writ. But, unlike in America, whistleblowers are castigated in Britain, where secrecy is a virtue. To break those barriers also required expertise and a lot of money, increasingly unavailable to newspapers and to television. So almost until his end Maxwell enjoyed a relatively favourable press, although journalists were not to blame for the canker's survival.

The real fault for Maxwell's undiscovered fraud belongs to the policemen employed in the Serious Fraud Office, to the civil servants, especially in IMRO and the DTI, who are empowered to supervise Britain's trusts and corporations, and to the accountants at Coopers and Lybrand who were his companies' auditors. As with most of Britain's financial scandals, those arrogant, idle and ignorant bureaucrats, having failed in their duties, were not embarrassed nor dismissed, because they were protected by self-imposed anonymity. It was their good fortune that many blamed Britain's libel laws for the failure to expose Maxwell's fraud. But that was and remains too easy. Maxwell prospered because hundreds of otherwise intelligent people wilfully suspended any moral judgment and succumbed to their avarice and self-interest. To suggest that much will be learned from Maxwell's story is to ignore past experience, but his story is an extraordinary fable, not least because only now can one read the final verdict.

ONE

The Autopsy

– 9 November 1991

The corpse was instantly recognizable. The eye could follow the jet-black hair and bushy eyebrows on the broad Slav head down the huge white torso towards the fat legs. Until four days earlier, the puffy face, recorded thousands of times on celluloid across the world, had been off-white. Now it was an unpleasant dark grey. The body was also disfigured. An incision, 78 cm long, stretched from the neck down the stomach to the crotch. Another incision crossed under the head, from the left shoulder along the collar bone. Firm, black needlework neatly joined the skin to conceal the damage to the deceased's organs.

Lying on a spotless white sheet in a tiled autopsy room, the corpse was surrounded by eight men and one woman dressed in green smocks. An unusual air of expectancy, even urgency, passed among the living as they stood beneath the fierce light. It was 10.25 on a Saturday night and there was pressure on them to complete their work long before daybreak. Over the past years, thousands of corpses – the victims of the Arab uprising – had passed through that undistinguished stucco building in Tel Aviv. But, for the most part, they had been the remains of anonymous young men killed by bullets, mutilated by bombs or occasionally suffocated by torture.

This cadaver was different. In life, the man had been famous, and in death there was a mystery. Plucked from the Atlantic Ocean off the Canary Islands, he had been flown for burial in Israel. Standing near the corpse for this second autopsy was Dr Iain West, the head of the Department of Forensic Medicine at Guy's Hospital, London. His hands, encased in rubber gloves, were gently touching the face: 'He's been thumped here. That looks genuine. You don't get that falling just over the edge of a boat. You don't get this sort of injury.' West's Scottish-accented voice sounded aggressive. Retained by the British insurance companies who would have to pay out £21 million if the cause of death were proved to have been accident or murder, he found his adrenalin aroused by a preliminary autopsy report signed two days earlier by Spanish pathologists. After twenty-one years of experience – and 25,000 autopsies – he had concluded that there were no more than two Spanish pathologists who deserved any respect: the remainder were 'not very good'. The conclusion of Dr Carlos Lopez de Lamela, one of that remainder, that the cause of death was 'heart failure' was trite and inconsequential. West was thirsting to find the real cause of death. His first suspicion was murder. Yet he knew that so much of pathology relied upon possibilities or probabilities and not upon certainties. Mysteries often remained unresolved, especially when the evidence was contaminated by incompetence.

The Briton's position at the autopsy was unusual. Under the insurance companies' agreement with the Israeli government, he could observe but not actively participate. West regretted that he would not be allowed to follow the contours and patterns of any injuries which might be discovered and privately felt slightly disdainful of his temporary colleague, Dr Yehuda Hiss. He recalled the forty-five-year-old Israeli pathologist – then his junior – learning his craft in Britain in the mid-1980s. He had judged him to be 'competent', although unused to the traditional challenges of autopsy reports in Britain. West was nevertheless now gratified to learn that his lack of confidence in the Spaniards was partially shared by Hiss. In the Israeli's opinion, Dr Lamela's equivocation about the cause of death was unimpressive.

West watched Hiss dictate his visual observations. Touching the body gently, even sensitively, the Israeli noted small abrasions around the nostrils and rubbed skin under the nose and on the ear, but no signs of fresh epidermal damage anywhere on the head or neck. There were no recently broken bones. Although the body had apparently floated in the sea for up to twelve hours, the skin showed no signs of wrinkling or sunburn. 'We'll X-ray the hands and the foot,' ordered Hiss.

His dictation was interrupted by West: 'I wonder if they've looked at his back?'

'No, no,' replied Hiss, going on to note a small scar, thin pubic hair and circumcision.

Again he was interrupted: 'The teeth are in bad condition.'

'The dental treatment is poor,' agreed another Israeli.

'Very poor', grunted West, 'for a man who was so rich.'

'Are you sure it's him?' asked an Israeli. 'We'd better X-ray the teeth for a dental check.'

'Well, it looks like him,' snapped West. 'The trouble is we're up against time. He's being buried tomorrow. I think we'll take fingerprints.' Again, he criticized the Spaniards: 'The fingernails haven't been cut off. They said they'd done it.'

Midnight passed. It was now the day of the burial. The corpse was turned over. 'We'll cut through and wrap it back,' said West impatiently. The two pathologists had already concurred that the Spanish failure to examine the deceased's back was a grave omission – it had been a common practice in Britain since the 1930s, as a method of discovering hidden wounds.

There was no sentiment as two scalpels, Hiss's and an assistant's, were poised over the vast human mound. None of the doctors contemplated its past: the small baby in the impoverished Czech *shtetl* or ghetto whose soft back had been rubbed after feeding; or the young man whose muscular back had been hugged by admiring women; or the tycoon whose back five days earlier had been bathed in sunshine on board a luxury yacht worth £23 million. Their scalpels were indiscriminate about emotions. They thought only of the still secret cause of death.

After the scalpels had pierced the skin and sliced through thick, yellow fat on the right side, West's evident anticipation was initially disappointed: 'I'm surprised that we didn't find anything.' A pattern of bruises was revealed to be only on the surface, the result of slight pressure, but not relevant to the cause of death. More dissections followed, mutilating the body tissue, slitting the fat, carving the flesh inch by inch in the search for the unusual. Minutes later there was a yelp.

'Do you see that?' exclaimed Hiss.

'It's a massive haematoma!' gasped West, peering at the discovery. There, nestling among the flesh and muscle in the left shoulder was a large, dark-red blob of congealed blood.

'Nine and a half by six centimetres,' dictated Hiss in Hebrew, 'and about one centimetre thick.'

West prodded the haematoma: 'There's a lot of torn muscles – pulled.' It was those tears which had caused the bleeding.

Here was precisely the critical clue missed by the Spaniards: since there were no suspicious bruises on the skin, they had lazily resisted any probing. Now the new doctors were gazing at violently torn fibres. Yet Hiss was not rushing to the conclusion he sensed was already being favoured by West. 'The trouble is, it's also an area where you often hit yourself,' he observed.

'It's not a hit,' growled West.

There was, they agreed, no pattern of injuries of the kind which usually accompanies murder – no tell-tale grip, kick or punch marks, no small lacerations on the skin which at his age would easily have been inflicted in the course of a struggle or by dragging a heavy, comatose body.

'There's tearing,' insisted West, peering into the corpse. 'Violent along the muscle.' The dissecting continued. Another muscle tear was found near the base of the spine and a third haematoma deep in the muscle in the front abdomen. The blood was so localized, they concluded, that the tears must have occurred shortly before death.

By 12.30, as the cadaver steadily ceased to resemble a human being, West became quite certain: 'The muscle fibres were torn in a desperate attempt to grab something.' Hiss did not reply. As the legs and each finger were cut open to scour for other secrets, he remained reserved. The embalmer's formalin, he realized, had destroyed any chance of finding conclusive evidence. 'It's well worth doing, isn't it?' repeated West as they drank coffee.

'Yes,' replied Hiss, still looking for a pattern of injuries and still feeling restrained by a Health Ministry official's edict that he should be cautious (the edict was possibly a consequence of the friendship between the deceased and the serving minister of health).

The corpse was turned over on to its shredded back. The Spanish stitches were cut by a sharp scalpel. It was just past one o'clock in the morning and the pathologists were about to enter already trodden ground. Swimming in formalin within the distastefully brown chest cavity were the remains of the Spaniards' handiwork.

Dr Lamela, the senior Spanish pathologist, had carried out his duties in circumstances very different from those enjoyed by the Israelis. Working in a cramped, ill-lit autopsy room, he had lacked important instruments, and had afterwards been denied any laboratory in which to conduct essential scientific tests. Aged thirty-five, he was a reluctant pathologist, obtaining little satisfaction from his task. In his three-and-a-half-hour investigation of the virgin corpse, he had noted that there were no external marks, bruises or perforations of the skin, the obvious signs of murder or violent death. Later tests had confirmed that no poisons were present.

Lamela's next theory was drowning. But he had noticed no water in the respiratory tracts leading to the lung, which ruled out death by drowning. Nor had he found much water inside the lung tissue. The single, reliable test for judging whether the deceased was alive or dead when he fell into the sea had been frustrated by nature. That proof depended upon traces of the sea's diatoms (microscopic algae) in the bone marrow. If the person had fallen living into the sea and swallowed water, the diatoms would have entered the bone marrow, providing irrefutable evidence of drowning. Subsequent tests revealed that at the point in the Atlantic where the corpse had been discovered and hoisted into a helicopter, the seawater contained no diatoms. The 'little' water in the lungs Lamela ascribed to pulmonary oedema, water which could arise through a heart attack. He therefore relied upon speculation rather than scientific proof when, mistakenly believing that the deceased was a strong swimmer, he excluded drowning and suicide as a cause of death.

Instead, Dr Lamela had concentrated upon the coronary arteries to the enlarged heart. Both were 70 per cent constricted. The evidence of a heart attack seemed strong. The twenty-two-stone man had lived with only one functioning lung and a diseased heart, and the right ventricular muscle of the stricken heart was acutely enlarged. His widow had disclosed a medical report written some years earlier which had noted a lack of oxygen in the blood, a common cause of sudden death. Taking into account the deceased's complaints to the ship's crew just before his death about the temperature in his cabin, Lamela concluded that the fatality had been caused by a heart attack. But, by scientific criteria, he was again speculating. He had failed to test whether there was an infarction of the heart muscle (a noticeable scar in the heart tissue), a certain indicator of an attack. Instead he had relied upon the small blemishes which revealed slight attacks in the past. His short-comings were manifest.

At 1.20 on Sunday morning in Tel Aviv, eight men and one woman peered into the evidential debris bequeathed by Lamela, the stench from the formalin irritating their eyes and noses. As an assistant ladled the liquid out of the cadaver, Hiss complained, 'There are some bits here you don't recognize as a human being's.' The Spaniards had butchered the evidence. Dissected organs had been thrown into the corpse rather than sealed in a plastic bag. What remained of the lungs was full of water, but whether natural fluids, seawater or formalin was impossible to determine. The dissection of a remnant of the lung revealed some froth. 'Consistent with both heart attack and drowning,' the pathologists agreed. Examination of the liver revealed acute sclerosis, consistent with alcoholism. What remained of the other organs was practically worthless.

'There's no heart, nothing,' complained West.

'I think we should send the bill for this one to the Spanish,' laughed West.

'To the King, Juan Carlos,' agreed the Israeli.

Suddenly, another assistant excitedly announced the discovery of a blood clot in the head. Further examination revealed no bruising. It was just accumulated blood fixed with formalin, West and Hiss agreed, a relic of Lamela's butchery. A deep bruise near the right ear also contributed nothing to establishing the cause of death but was probably contemporaneous with the tearing of the muscles. The British pathologist's earlier excited conclusion that 'He's been thumped' had been jettisoned, along with his initial assumption of murder.

At 2.30 a.m., their work was completed. 'I think it's been a very bloody dissection,' mourned West as he lit a cigarette. Stepping into the warm air outside, he walked towards his car. He would drive back to Jerusalem, where he had landed just twelve hours earlier on a Gulfstream jet formerly owned by the man whose corpse he had just abandoned. 'I'll look at Jerusalem before I go home,' he decided as he sat back in the car for the fifty-minute journey to the Holy City.

The body would soon be transferred to the same destination for its funeral after a mortician had performed some rapid repairs. It would be buried with a mystery. Three pathologists – British,

Spanish and Israeli – had ruled out murder but disagreed on the cause of death. Both Hiss and West discounted Lamela's dismissal of drowning. The ambivalent evidence prevented any definite decision. But Hiss supported the Spaniard's theory of a heart attack.

In the Israeli's scenario, the deceased had suffered the preliminaries of the attack, left his cabin and walked to the rail overlooking the sea. Either stumbling or in the early stages of the attack, he had fallen forward, toppling over the ship's rail or under a steel cord in the stern. At the last moment, he had grabbed at the rail, torn his muscles and, in pain, had plunged into the dark wilderness where the heart attack had come to a swift conclusion. 'I think he drowned with an epidural haematoma,' said Hiss.

Suicide was ruled out by the Israeli. In those circumstances, he argued, suicides never cause themselves violent harm before their death. Nor do those contemplating suicide jump naked to their death, and the deceased's body had been found without the nightshirt which he had worn that night.

On reflection, West was dismissive of Lamela and Hiss. The Briton's conclusions were determined by the torn muscles and coagulated blood. Lamela would say in retrospect that the muscles had torn during the convulsions of the heart attack. Both West and Hiss rejected that as 'ridiculous'. Both agreed that the muscles had been ripped by a sudden jerk after the deceased's left hand had grabbed something. The pain in those seconds would have been intense. West discounted a heart attack, although 'he had a heart disease which was potentially lethal'. He had two reasons: first, because 'I would expect him to have fallen on to the deck'; second, even if he had toppled over the railing, 'He would have been acutely breathless, convulsing and unable to grab anything.'

West favoured the theory that the muscle tears were caused in the deceased's passage towards suicide or by an intervening accident. He had left his cabin and walked to the railing of his yacht. After climbing over, he had held on pondering his fate. Either he had accidentally slipped or he had deliberately jumped. In either event, in a sudden reaction, he had grabbed for the rail to save himself. His twenty-two stone combined with the fall's momentum had ripped his muscles and within seconds forced him to release his grip. He had fallen into the dark sea where he had drowned. But even that was supposition: 'I think that probably death was due to drowning. I can't prove it. Nor can I prove the opposite.' In an English court, 'The verdict would be an open verdict.'

Distillation of the pathologists' opinions leads towards the most reliable conclusion. Feeling unwell, the deceased had been on deck for fresh air. Stumbling, probably from a minor heart attack, he had fallen forward, passing under the steel cord or over the rail and, as he had twisted to grab it, had hit the side of his head against the boat. In double agony, he had lost his grip and dropped into the sea. There he died, some time later, from exhaustion or a heart attack.

But two critical issues remained unresolved. First, the cabin door had apparently been locked from the outside. If true, it pointed either to suicide or to murder, because anyone feeling unwell would be unlikely to lock a door. Secondly, the corpse had been found in seas notorious for strong currents. Twelve hours had elapsed between the deceased's disappearance and his discovery. In the frequent occurrences of drowning around the Canary Islands, bodies are rarely found if missing for more than nine hours. Dr Lamela, with years of experience of drownings in that area, was puzzled by the condition of this particular corpse, which had allegedly spent twelve hours in the sea. 'The body', he recorded, 'appeared to have been dead longer than it was in the water.'

Lamela's conjecture spawned tales of intrigue, unidentified frogmen, a mystery ship, satellite photographs, radio intercepts, intelligence-service rivalries, unauthorized weapons deals, stolen gold, secret bank accounts, money laundering, untraceable poisons and ultimately murder. Given the identity of the corpse, nothing was unimaginable. At four o'clock in the morning of 10 November 1991, it was *en route* to Jerusalem to be fêted by the world's most enigmatic government as a national hero.

In his lifetime, the deceased had boasted of his final bequest. 'Billions of pounds', he had crowed, 'will be left to charity. My children will inherit nothing.' The reality, he knew, was very different. He had bequeathed a cataclysm, but the full nature of his criminality was still known only to his youngest son.

TWO

The Secret

– 5 November 1990

The plan was finalized precisely one year before he mysteriously died.

Concorde landed at New York's JFK airport six minutes late on 5 November 1990. Among the forty-nine passengers gliding self-assuredly off the supersonic flight from London at 9.26 a.m. was Ghislaine Maxwell, the twenty-eight-year-old daughter of the media billionaire. Elegantly dressed and wearing a distinctive hat, Ghislaine was blessed as Robert Maxwell's youngest and favourite child. But even to her father's most loyal employees, the thin, would-be socialite was condemned as arrogant and a beneficiary of her father's fame and power. 'She'd ask for a cigarette and walk out with the packet,' complained Carol Bragoli, a secretary.

That morning she seemed more purposeful than usual. Robert Maxwell had entrusted her with a mission to carry an envelope across the Atlantic. Stepping into a chauffeured limousine, she was whisked to 200 Park Avenue in Manhattan. Awaiting her on the twenty-eighth floor was Ellis Freedman, an elderly lawyer who worshipped her father and had served his interests for nearly forty years. Ushered into the waiting room, the messenger handed over the envelope. There was no reason for the young woman to be suspicious. Yet, unknowingly, she had become enmeshed in a plan, initiated by her father, to steal $200 million.

Eleven days earlier, at 8 a.m. on 25 October, Kevin Maxwell, the thirty-one-year-old joint managing director of the Maxwell empire, had met Albert Fuller, the thirty-nine-year-old accountant responsible for the empire's treasury. Like all of Maxwell's most trusted employees, Fuller's qualification for his well-paid position was his tolerance of abuse dispensed around the clock by the tycoon.

Deliberately, even cynically, Maxwell had gathered in his inner sanctum apparatchiks who were not only beholden to him but even adulated him. Although technically competent, they were weak men attracted to a father-figure. Fuller was especially grateful to Maxwell. Two years earlier, he had been involved in the loss of a banker's draft worth £4.7 million but had been exonerated and allowed to resume work after several weeks' suspension.

Fuller did not query Kevin's instruction to fly immediately to New York. His tasks seemed simple. From one office he was to retrieve a share certificate numbered B1001, bearing 10.6 million shares in Berlitz, the famous international language school. Then he was to travel to another office and there exchange the single document, worth over $200 million, for nine certificates of varying denominations. There was little cause for Fuller to be suspicious about that effortless transaction. Kevin's request was not illegal and his need for discretion was understandable. Berlitz was owned (with 56 per cent of the shares) by the American Macmillan publishing company, which in turn was owned by Maxwell Communication Corporation (MCC) – the public company, still 60 per cent owned by the founder himself, which aspired to dominate the world's exploding media industry. By 30 October, Fuller had returned to London, his mission accomplished.

Six days later, an hour before Ghislaine's arrival in New York, Robert Maxwell telephoned Ellis Freedman, his lawyer. The instructions again seemed straightforward. Ghislaine, said Maxwell, would be bringing an envelope with nine share certificates showing Macmillan's ownership of the Berlitz shares. Freedman was to secure their reissue in twenty new certificates of 500,000 shares each and one for 600,000 shares. But, said Maxwell, there was to be one significant variation. The new certificates should not mention Macmillan's ownership. Instead, each certificate was to be issued showing the owner as Bishopsgate Investment Trust (BIT), with the inscribed caveat 'Purely as a nominee'. Even in Maxwell's strictly compartmentalized world, Freedman ought to have been suspicious. For BIT was a private company owned by Maxwell. To the inquisitive, the laundering would not have been well disguised.

The legal authority for that exchange was to be an executive committee board meeting to be held in Freedman's office later on the same day. The participants were three Macmillan directors:

Robert and Kevin Maxwell, and David Shaffer, Macmillan's American president and its chief operating officer in New York. None of the three men, however, was in Manhattan.

The 'meeting' occurred at 11.15 a.m. New York time. The two Maxwells were 'present' by telephone from London while Shaffer spoke from Stouffers' Hotel in Westchester, New York State. According to the telephone records, the conference call lasted eleven minutes. One year later, Shaffer would claim to have been duped and would dispute Freedman's official record. 'Either I was not told the true purpose of the board meeting,' he protested, 'or there was a telephone connection but I was not involved.'

At the end of that day, 5 November 1990, Ellis Freedman handed the twenty-one new share certificates to Ghislaine. By then the youngest Maxwell had varied her plan. Robert Maxwell had agreed that his daughter, instead of flying immediately back to London, could stay in New York overnight. After indulging herself in Manhattan's shops, Ghislaine met friends for dinner. The following morning, she boarded a Jumbo 747 for the return flight. That night, the envelope was deposited in Robert Maxwell's personal safe, located in the bathroom of his penthouse apartment on the tenth floor of Maxwell House, adjacent to the Daily Mirror building in Holborn (he had bought the Mirror Group in 1984). He now possessed $200 million, the property of unsuspecting shareholders, for his personal use. That had been precisely his intention.

Two days later, on 8 November, Kevin Maxwell sat in his office, smiling at Julie Maitland, a thirty-year-old banker employed by Crédit Suisse. Over the previous months, Kevin had been assiduously wooing the dark-haired woman, who some would judge in retrospect to be naive and lacking imagination. Like most of the banking fraternity in London, Maitland had eagerly offered her services to the Maxwells and had succumbed to flattery when invited to join what Kevin called the 'inner circle' of core banks acting for the family group. Like other bankers, she understood that the Maxwell companies were suffering a financial squeeze. But the truth, cleverly disguised by the Maxwells from the star-struck woman, was worse. The empire was hovering on the verge of bankruptcy and Kevin was hunting for gigantic loans to tide it over. His smiles for Julie Maitland, a wilful adjustment to his customary cold demeanour, were designed to perpetuate that deception and to entice the Swiss bank to lend the Maxwells even more money.

Naturally, the young woman could not act independently. Every discussion with Kevin had been carefully noted and reported in detail, first to her London superiors and then to the bank's head office in Zurich. 'The Maxwells want us to understand the private companies,' Maitland had written plaintively six months earlier about the web of 400 different corporate names through which the Maxwells operated. And there was so much to understand.

Robert Maxwell had always yearned to manage a publicly quoted company, not just for the prestige but, more pertinently, to enable him to play with other people's money. The Maxwell Communication Corporation was that tool, marred though it was for him by a colossal defect: the legal requirement for public accountability. For a man whose love of publicity went hand in hand with a pathological desire for secrecy, the desire for a publicly quoted company seemed illogical. But the sophist's empire was designed to fool the honest inquirer. MCC sat at the centre of an utterly confusing and ever changing matrix of private and therefore secret companies. At the very top were a group of Liechtenstein trusts, anonymous and unaccountable owners of the majority of MCC's shares. In reality, they were controlled by Maxwell. Beneath those Liechtenstein trusts and surrounding MCC like a constellation were 400 private companies of varying sizes and activity, trading with MCC and among themselves, not only in all matters of publishing, communications, printing and technology, but also in property, currencies, gilts and shares.

MCC was the corporate name adopted in 1987, replacing the British Printing and Communications Corporation. The reason, said Maxwell's spokesman, was to shed the image of 'dark northern printing halls', but it was not, claimed Maxwell unconvincingly, 'an ego trip. It was a decision reluctantly taken.' To boost MCC's value, Maxwell had incorporated Pergamon Press, his privately owned and profitable international scientific publishing company which was the foundation of his fortune, into the public company. Maxwell's own shares in MCC were owned by Pergamon Holdings, which in turn was a subsidiary of the Maxwell Foundation, a private Liechtenstein company which in turn also controlled the privately owned Mirror Group, and which in 1991 was renamed the Robert Maxwell Group. In parallel, there was another Maxwell family company called Headington Hill Investments, ultimately owned by Liechtenstein trusts, which controlled the family's shares in other private companies.

Maxwell's purpose in creating this constellation of companies was indisputable. Beyond public scrutiny, he could move shares, assets, cash and debts to satisfy any need, increasingly regardless of rules and laws. So long as MCC was recording gigantic profits in its annual glossy brochure, the City experts did not query his netherworld. But recently a new phrase, its implicit rebuke stirring unease, had entered into the experts' vocabulary – 'the quality of MCC's profits'. There was a suggestion that the empire's finances were not as sound as their conductor desired the world to believe.

The deliberate confusion created by Robert Maxwell had now become a barrier against the sympathy he required. Maitland's initial proposal for a loan had been rejected by Zurich. There was more than passing concern about the Maxwells' 'rush' for money and there was some doubt about their ability to repay. The astute feared that they might be ambushed by the confusion.

'Speculative characteristics' were mentioned in Zurich and were blamed for the recent drop in MCC's credit rating from BBB to BB, a warning to banks that their loans were marginally less secure. The doubts which this decline reflected had been fuelled by disparaging newspaper reports about Maxwell's awkward repayment deadlines and the 'juggling acts' he was performing in order to pay off $415 million of debt. To find the cash, he had begun dismantling his empire. Businesses worth $500 million had been quickly sold, arousing suspicion and uncertainty and prompting newspaper comments about strange deals set up to channel money from his private companies to MCC. The very bankers who had rubbed their hands in glee at the prospect of earning fees by helping to finance the creation of the Maxwell empire were being approached to earn more money in arranging sales. In return for commission awarded for selling Maxwell businesses, the banks were expected to lend more money. But, increasingly, they wanted safer security for their loans. That was the reason for Kevin's smiles at Julie Maitland, the banker.

For years, Robert Maxwell had publicly prided himself on the education of his children. In numerous interviews he had extolled the virtues of the 'Three Cs' – concentration, consideration and conciseness. But there was an extra, unpublicized lesson he gave Kevin: the unique importance of a businessman's relationship with his bankers. For Maxwell, it was said, there were only two relationships: master and servant, and customer and supplier. While most suppliers could be treated with disdain, even contempt, Kevin had been nurtured by his father to cultivate and charm those whose money he wanted to use. Banks, he had learnt, survived and prospered by cultivating a certain trick of confidence, lending more money than they possessed. His father responded by perpetrating a succession of confidence tricks.

So Kevin reacted promptly when he heard from Maitland about her superiors' reluctance to lend money. Oozing apparent sincerity, he promised: 'We can provide ample security for the loans.' The names and quantities of the shares he mentioned as a guarantee for the repayments persuaded Maitland's superiors to abandon their doubts. He was offering shares in the most prestigious companies – seemingly a testament to Maxwell's personal wealth hoarded in Liechtenstein. On 7 September Crédit Suisse accordingly granted a £50 million loan for six months. The loan was not to Maxwell Communication Corporation, the publicly quoted company, but to the biggest of Maxwell's private companies, the Robert Maxwell Group (RMG). Simultaneously, Kevin ordered the appropriate share certificates to be hand-delivered to Maitland's bank. But there was good reason for the bank to be suspicious of these. On each share certificate, the registered owner was shown as Bishopsgate Investment Management (BIM).

BIM was a private company established by Maxwell to manage the nine pension funds of his 23,400 employees pooled in the Common Investment Fund (CIF) and worth about £727 million. In theory, BIM was the trustee of CIF, which included the Mirror Group Pension Trust (MGPT), but because MGPT's sixteen directors at the beginning of 1991 included Robert, Kevin and Ian Maxwell (and four trade union representatives), who were also directors of BIM, the self-governance of BIM never existed. Under the regime imposed by Robert and Kevin Maxwell, who were respectively chairman and finance director of BIM, the purchase and sale of BIM's investments and, equally important, the registration of its share certificates and the location of their physical custody were determined by them rather than by Trevor Cook, the company's manager (who was also a director).

On the Maxwells' directions, Cook would either loan BIM's cash to the Robert Maxwell Group or deposit the money in the account of Bishopsgate Investment Trust (BIT), which the Maxwells could draw at their convenience. BIT had been specially created by Maxwell to act as a private nominee owner of shares without any legal relationship to the pension funds, blurring the actual ownership in the eyes of outsiders. As directors of BIM, BIT and RMG, the Maxwells could effectively constitute themselves a board of directors and transfer the ownership of shares from the pension funds to their private company, using them as collateral for private loans without the knowledge of anyone else. That easy access to loans depended on the size of the pensions' Common Investment Fund.

Ever since the CIF had been created, Maxwell had sought to persuade, cajole and even threaten his employees not to opt out of their employer's pension funds. A special twenty-one-minute video, fronted by Maxwell himself seated on a large black leather chair, promised them that the pension schemes would 'provide good benefits, are financially sound and well run'. To his relief, few had dared to withdraw their money. He could continue to use their millions as his own. No company's affairs received greater attention from Maxwell than BIM's.

Maitland ought to have appreciated that BIM managed the pension funds of Maxwell's empire, but she felt no need to make special inquiries. With each share certificate was a transfer form signed by Kevin and others, including Ian, his thirty-four-year-old brother, showing that ownership of the shares had been transferred to RMG. Maitland did not query why the pension funds should agree to that transfer. Indeed, when on one occasion she saw that a share certificate sent by Kevin was still owned by BIM, she returned it for RMG's name to be inserted on the transfer form. So, by 8 November 1990, £70 million of pension fund shares had been used to raise money for Maxwell personally. On that same day, Kevin asked Maitland for another private loan. She seemed unsurprised when he offered as collateral a share certificate for 500,000 Berlitz shares. It was, he said, 'owned by the private side'. Again, Maitland and her superiors had reason to be suspicious.

To repay MCC's debts in December 1989, 44 per cent of Berlitz had been sold to the public for $131 million. No one had ever suggested that the Maxwells themselves had bought any of those Berlitz shares as a private investment. Nor was their name listed among Berlitz's registered shareholders. But Maitland would insist that no hint of suspicion ever passed through her mind when Kevin said, 'These Berlitz shares are privately owned.' The paperwork for transferring the Berlitz certificate to Maitland had been completed by one of Maxwell's treasury officials. The Berlitz shares, owned by MCC, the public company, were being used by the Maxwells for their private purposes. By any reckoning, it was highly improper.

Robert Maxwell of course understood the impropriety. Later that week, he signed documents promising not to use the Berlitz share certificates brought back by Ghislaine in any manner without Macmillan's explicit agreement. His indecipherable scribble would adorn many such documents over the next year. In each case, after he had signed, he would more or less forget the deception. Dishonesty did not trouble him. Throughout his life, he had ignored the norms of morality. Indeed his fortune had been constructed, lost and rebuilt by deliberate transgressions, outwitting and outrunning his opponents regardless of any infringement of the laws. According to the ethics he had learnt as a child, watching smugglers in his Ruthenian border town, the goal was survival and profit, and the consequences to the losers were irrelevant. For Maxwell, the Berlitz transaction had been a minor sideshow at the beginning of another hectic week, working in a moral vacuum within a surreal world.

The atmosphere in the citadel of his empire, the £2 million penthouse apartment on the tenth floor of Maxwell House, was suffocatingly imperious. Polished, double doors led across marble floors into a high-ceilinged hall supported by brown marble Doric columns and lit by glass chandeliers. Beyond, the spectacle of a huge living area decked out with expensive mock-Renaissance tapestry-covered furniture and with carpets patterned in a vast 'M' design cautioned any visitor who might be contemplating criticism or challenge. Access to the apartment, in common with all the buildings on the Holborn site, could be gained only by coded plastic cards. Even between neighbouring offices movement was monitored by video cameras. Rigorous security was imposed to protect Robert Maxwell's secrecy and cushion his paranoia.

The twenty-two-stone proprietor, clothed in bright-blue shirts and dazzling ties, intimidated visitors by his gestures as much as his words, his gargantuan performance humbling those physically and financially less well endowed. The theatricality, the egocentricity and the vanity of the man were unsurpassed. Servile staff offered refreshments, earnest secretaries announced incoming calls from the world's leaders, and bankers, lawyers and accountants did everything they could to please their client, while his deep, gravelly voice issued curt instructions, allowing no questions. Those who attempted to understand his psychology invariably failed, because both his motives and his reasoning were unique. Utterly consumed by his own self-portrayal as a great man, he was certain of his invincibility, sure that his abilities would overcome the natural consequences of any decision he took. 'Bob believed he was bigger than the City,' lamented Johnny Bevan, one of his many brokers. To Maxwell's gratification, enough of his visitors accepted his self-appraisal. Even his most bitter enemies used the sobriquet 'Cap'n Bob' – thereby recognizing, as he saw it, his supreme importance.

On the floor below, the communications centre of his universe, other compliant men and women toiled in the service of the Publisher, otherwise known as the Chairman or RM. Visitors knew that, as in a medieval court, the official job descriptions of these employees often bore little similarity to their actual task. And, again as in a medieval court, dozens of those visitors and employees waited patiently for the opportunity of an audience. From outside, invitations arrived hourly. Most were rejected with the standard computer-template reply that the Chairman regretted that his diary was full for two years. The world's newspapers, television and radio were constantly monitored for every mention of the man, the precise words faithfully reported in regular faxes. Constantly updated handbooks listed the telephone numbers of every employee, business contact and powerbroker across the world – town home, country house and office – and the speed-dial numbers of those included on a special list. The Publisher delighted in calling employees at the most inopportune moments, demanding not only their attention but their immediate presence. Television screens displayed the trade of MCC shares in seven stock exchanges across Europe and Canada – and were the object of his intense scrutiny. The image was intended to match the substance: not a second could be wasted as the workoholic billionaire controlled his worldwide enterprise.

The empire was run on similar lines to those of Nicolae Ceausescu and Todor Zhivkov, the autocratic communist presidents of Romania and Bulgaria whom Robert Maxwell expensively nurtured. His employees knew only a small part of the scenario, unaware of the implications and the background to the letters and telephone calls flowing to and from their master in those nine languages he claimed to speak. None of the secretaries was allowed to remain employed too long – not even the very pretty ones whose employment the Publisher had particularly requested. No one would be permitted to learn too much, despite the effect on the office's organization. Nevertheless, their loyalty, devotion and discretion were bought by unusually high salaries, and by fear: fear of Maxwell and fear of losing their jobs and being unable to find similarly lucrative employment. Verbal brutality crushed any opposition. In return for exceptional remuneration, they agreed to sing to their employer's song sheet. The sole exception, and only a partial one, was Kevin. Fear of Robert Maxwell had been instilled in him from childhood, but by November 1990 his father's passion for secrecy had been offset by the need for an ally. Kevin had become the cog in the machine essential for his father's survival.

Bankers, brokers and businessmen in London and New York almost unanimously agreed that Kevin was clever, intelligent, talented, astute and, most importantly, not a bully like his father. Eschewing tantrums and verbal abuse, he had at a young age mastered the intricacies, technicalities and jargon of the financial community. But, with hindsight, the perceptive would be struck by the image of a dedicated son: of medium height, thin, dark, humourless, ruthless, efficient, manipulative, cold and amoral. Kevin acknowledged the source of other qualities in a written appreciation sent to his father: 'You are my teacher and all my life you have tried to demonstrate the principles underlying every action or inaction even if we were playing roulette or Monopoly . . . you have given me the sense of excitement of having dozens of balls in the air and the thrill of seeing some of them land right.' Willingly submitting to the Chairman's daily demand to vet both his diary and his correspondence for approval and alteration, Kevin would tolerate anything from that quarter for the chance to indulge his love of the

Game based upon money and power. 'I don't think anyone would ever describe me as being a member of the Salvation Army,' he would later crow, echoing his father's statement to truculent and threatening printers in the early 1980s.

For the previous three years he had worked under his father's supervision, accepting his rules as gospel, not least the injunction never to give up. 'He enjoyed fighting and enjoyed winning,' Kevin admiringly observed of Maxwell's achievement in creating an empire within one generation, while Rothermere, Sainsbury and Murdoch had relied upon inherited money. Kevin positively glowed, relishing both his own family's wealth and the servility shown towards him.

Yet, despite his power and privilege within the organization, Kevin shrank in his father's presence. Conditioned by the beatings – psychological rather than physical – which he had received as a child, his eyes would dart agitatedly around, nervously sensing his father's approach, and sometimes at meetings he would slightly raise his hand to stop someone interfering: 'Let the old man finish.' Kevin may well have thought that he could manage the family business honestly, but within recent months either he had veered towards dishonesty or his remaining scruples had been distorted by Robert Maxwell. Many would blame his father's lifelong domi-nance for that change, while others would point to his mother's failure to imbue her youngest son with the moral strength to resist her husband's demands.

Robert Maxwell had become a collector rather than a manager of businesses. Size, measured in billions of pounds, was his criterion. The excitement of the deal – the seduction, the temptation, the haggling, the consummation and the publicity – had fed his appetite for more. By November 1990, he owned interests in newspapers, publishing, television, printing and electronic databases across the world estimated to be worth £4.2 billion. But the cost of his greed was debts of more than £2.2 billion, and the coffers to repay the loans were empty. This was the background to Ghislaine's flight to New York to bring back the Berlitz share certificates.

The principal cause of indebtedness was the $3.35 billion spent by Maxwell in 1988 on the 'Big One', as his excitable American banker Robert Pirie called it. The money had bought Official Airline Guides (OAG) for $750 million and, more importantly, after an intense and successful public battle with Henry Kravis, the famous pixie-like arbitrageur, the Macmillan publishing group for $2.6 billion. Pirie had throughout stoked Maxwell's burning sense of triumph.

Pirie, the chief executive of Rothschild Inc., had played on Maxwell's weaknesses. 'If you want to be in the media business,' advised the Rothschild banker, 'you've got to be prepared to pay the price.' He did not add that he would earn higher fees if Maxwell won. Telling his client, 'You're paying top dollar,' Pirie did not discourage him from going for broke. Maxwell's self-imposed deadline for joining the Big Ten League, alongside his old rival Rupert Murdoch, would expire in just thirteen months. Intoxicated by the publicity of spending $3 billion, he crossed the threshold without considering the consequences. 'Plays him like a puppet,' sniped one who was able to observe Pirie's artful sycophancy. To Pirie, Maxwell had not overpaid. There were, in the jargon of that frenetic era, 'enormous synergies' and the Publisher himself did not even consider his plight as a debtor owing $3 billion. After all, Pirie boasted, 'Maxwell had no credibility problem with the lending banks.' But the Rothschild banker disclaimed any responsibility for the other deal. 'He paid too much for OAG,' he later volunteered, adding unconvincingly, 'The deal was done by Maxwell, not me.'

Forty-four banks had lent Maxwell $3 billion, hailed by all as proof of his return to respectability. Astonishingly, the giant sum was not initially secured against any assets. He could lose all that cash without more than a blink. The interest rates, moreover, were a derisory 0.5 per cent over base rate. The deal was a phenomenal bargain negotiated through Crédit Lyonnais and Samuel Montagu by Richard Baker, MCC's gruff deputy managing director, who had been born in Shepherds Bush, west London. Maxwell had inherited Baker when he bought the British Printing Corporation (BPC), Britain's biggest printers, in an exquisite dawn raid in 1980.

Maxwell's victory was more than commercial. Despite his infamous branding as a pariah by British government inspectors in 1971, which had cast him into the wilderness, Maxwell had reestablished his respectability and acceptability among most in the City. Here was the reincarnation of what had long ago been unaffectionately dubbed 'The Bouncing Czech'. Leading the supporters was the NatWest Bank, his bankers since 1945, who were impressed by the way their client had crushed the trade unions at BPC, restoring the company to robust profitability. Now the 'Jumbo Loan' was the world financial community's statement of faith in Maxwell. 'All the banks were clamouring to join the party,' recalled Ron Woods, Maxwell's soft-spoken Welsh tax adviser and a director of MCC. Bankers judged MCC to be not only an exciting but a safe company. Former enemies had become allies – and over the years he had collected many enemies. Their numbers had multiplied after 1969 when he had sold Pergamon Press, his scientific publishing company, to Saul Steinberg, a brash young New York tycoon. Since Maxwell was a publicity-seeking, high-profile Labour member of parliament, the deal had attracted unusual attention. Pergamon, Maxwell's brainchild, was a considerable international success, elevating its owner into the rarefied world of socialist millionaires.

But within weeks the take-over was plunged in crisis. Steinberg's executives had discovered that Maxwell's accounts were fraudulent, shamelessly contrived to project high profits and conceal losses. In the ensuing storm of opprobrium, Maxwell was castigated by the Take-Over Panel, lost control of Pergamon and was investigated by two inspectors appointed by the Department of Trade and Industry. In their first report published in 1971, the inspectors, after reminding readers that Maxwell had been censured in 1954 by an official receiver for trading as a book wholesaler while insolvent, revealed that his confidently paraded finances were exercises in systematic dishonesty. Their final conclusion was to haunt Maxwell for the rest of his life:

He is a man of great energy, drive and imagination, but unfortunately an apparent fixation as to his own abilities causes him to ignore the views of others if these are not compatible. . . . The concept of a Board being responsible for policy was alien to him.

We are also convinced that Mr Maxwell regarded his stewardship duties fulfilled by showing the maximum profits which any transaction could be devised to show. Furthermore, in reporting to shareholders and investors, he had a reckless and unjustified optimism which enabled him on some occasions to disregard unpalatable facts and on others to state what he must have known to be untrue. . . .

We regret having to conclude that, notwithstanding Mr Maxwell's acknowledged abilities and energy, he is not in our opinion a person who can be relied upon to exercise proper stewardship of a publicly quoted company.

Even before that excruciating judgment was published, most City players had deserted Maxwell or refused his business. Ostracized, he did not begin to shrug off his pariah status until July 1980, when he succeeded in his take-over bid for the near-bankrupt British Printing Corporation (partly financed by the National Westminster bank). Within two years, his brutal but skilful management had transformed Britain's biggest printers into a profitable concern, laying the foundations for his purchase of the Mirror Group in 1984.

Building on that apparent respectability, the financial community had cast aside their doubts and contributed to the Jumbo Loan. Among his closest advisers were Rothschilds, his bankers, who had shunned him after 1969; his accountants were Coopers and Lybrand, one of the world's biggest partnerships; and among his lawyers was Bob Hodes of Wilkie Farr Gallagher, who had led the litigation against him in 1969. For Hodes, a scion of New York's legal establishment, Maxwell had become 'a likeable rogue who appeared to enjoy the game'. Like all the other professionals excited by the sound of gunfire, Hodes was confident that he could resist any pressure from Maxwell to bend the rules.

A celebration lunch when the Jumbo Loan had been rearranged was held at Claridge's on 23 October 1989 by Fritz Kohli, of the Swiss Bank Corporation. The champagne had flowed as successive toasts and speeches showered mutual congratulations upon Maxwell and his banks. The Publisher had been gratified, especially by the presence of Senator John Tower and Walter Mondale, the former US vice-president, both of them anxious to become his paid lobbyists. Everyone was excited by the star because he was a dealmaker and deals generated headlines and income. Few bothered to consider that behind the deals there was little evidence of any considered strategy or of diligent management. But even then, unknown to the bankers, the consequences of that weakness were already apparent and Maxwell's grandiose ambitions were faltering. Unexpectedly high interest rates, a worldwide recession and a fall in stock market prices were gradually devastating his finances.

One option for salvation was to adopt Rupert Murdoch's solution. Maxwell's bugbear had confessed his financial problems to his banks and had renegotiated the repayment of his $7.6 billion loans. Maxwell rejected that remedy. The wilfully blind would blame his vanity but, in retrospect, others understood his secret terror of having the banks inspect his accounts. The result would have been not a sensible rearrangement but merciless castration. Ever since 1947 when he had first launched himself into business, Maxwell had massaged profits, concealed losses and siphoned off cash by running several companies in parallel and organizing spurious deals within his empire. This manipulation was possible because only he, at the centre of the web, saw the total picture. Renowned as a master-juggler, he was blessed with a superb memory, perfectly focused amid the deliberate confusion, ordering obedient and myopic accountants to switch money and companies through a bewildering jungle of relationships.

By 1990, those trades had come to infect the interlocking associations between the complex structure of the tycoon's 400 private companies and Maxwell Communication Corporation, the publicly quoted company. The disease was his insatiable ambition. He wanted to be rich, famous, powerful, admired, respected and feared. His empire was to reflect those desires. The means to that end were MCC's ever increasing profits, which in turn determined the company's share price. That relationship was the triple foundation of his survival, his dishonesty and his downfall. Whenever the profits were in danger, Maxwell resorted to a ruse which exposed his instinct for fraud: he pumped his personal money into the public company. Since 1987, he had bought with private funds bits of MCC at inflated prices to keep its profits and share price high. Invariably, he was buying the unprofitable bits.

To pay for that extravagance, Maxwell had borrowed money. By 1989, his private empire – unknown to outsiders – was on the verge of insolvency. As security for the loans, he had pledged to banks his 60 per cent stake in MCC. Unfortunately for him, by November 1990 growing suspicion of his accounts and critical newspaper reports had triggered a slide in the value of MCC shares, which over three years had fallen from 387p to a new low of 142p. The latest discontent in early October intensified Maxwell's crisis.

As his financial problems grew and MCC's share price fell, the banks demanded more security for their loans. Maxwell's solution was radical and initially secret. To keep the share price high, he had undertaken two bizarre and contradictory strategies. First, MCC was paying shareholders high dividends to make the shares an attractive investment. But the Publisher's insoluble problem was that the dividends which MCC paid out were actually higher than the company's profits. In 1989, the dividend cost £112.3 million, while the profits from normal trading were £97.3 million. Among the necessary costs of maintaining that charade was payment of advance corporation tax which in 1989 amounted to £17.6 million. The extraneous tax cost for the same ruse in 1990 was £98.8 million on adjusted trading profits of £71.1 million.

Maxwell's second strategy to keep the share price high was to buy MCC shares personally. Since 1989 he had quietly spent £100 million in that venture. The solution bred several problems, not least that he soon ran out of cash. His response was to borrow more money to buy his own shares.

To their credit, both father and son could still rely upon the large residue of goodwill among leading bankers in all the major capitals – London, New York, Tokyo, Zurich, Paris and Frankfurt – and upon those bankers' conviction that MCC's debts were manageable. Their guarantee, they believed, was the vast private fortune of Robert Maxwell's privately owned companies secreted in Liechtenstein. Although none of those bankers had ever seen the accounts of his Liechtenstein trusts, they believed they had no reason to doubt the Publisher's boasts. Maxwell continued to encourage their credulity, while using banks in the Dutch Antilles and Cayman Islands as the true, secret receptacles of his wealth.

Among that army of bankers was Andrew Capitman, an ambitious manager of Bankers Trust, the American bank. Two years earlier, Capitman had purposefully moved to London to earn his fortune pleasing Maxwell in the course of completing thirty-eight separate transactions. Not surprisingly, he enjoyed the Concorde and first-class flights across the world, the heaps of caviar and champagne, all funded by his client. He too assumed that the Liechtenstein billions were the source of Maxwell's cash for another unusual transaction to be completed at noon on 5 November 1990, just three hours before the seizure of the Berlitz shares.

Descending from his office on the ninth floor, Maxwell hurriedly chaired an extraordinary general meeting of MCC in the Rotunda on the mezzanine floor of the ugly Mirror headquarters in Holborn. The topic was one of Maxwell's more expensive inter-company deals. Two Canadian companies, owned by MCC, were to be sold. And, because the recession meant that the price offered by others would be low, Maxwell proposed himself (or rather the Mirror Group, which he still privately owned) as the purchaser. Capitman understood that Maxwell's strategy in that bizarre arrangement was to boost MCC's profits and he had independently valued the two Canadian paper and print companies, Quebecor and Donohue, at a high £135 million. In return for offering a 'slam-dunk' generous valuation, the banker pocketed a cool $700,000 fee.

Capitman's assumption that the £135 million was drawn from the Liechtenstein billions was erroneous. The true source of the £400 million Maxwell required to buy a succession of companies in similar deals from MCC during the following year was his own private loans – an unsustainable burden on his finances.

Among his most important lenders was Goldman Sachs, the giant New York bank. Of the many Goldmans executives with whom Maxwell spoke, none seemed more important that Eric Sheinberg, a fifty-year-old senior partner and graduate of Pennsylvania University. Sheinberg arrived in London in 1987 after a profitable career in New York and Singapore. For the hungry young traders in Goldman Sachs' London office, which was sited near Maxwell's headquarters, Sheinberg not only provided leadership but inspired trust. Trained by Gus Levy, a legendary and charismatic Wall Street trader, he was renowned for having made a killing trading convertible equities. 'Eric's a trader's trader,' was the admiring chant among his colleagues. Eric, it was said, had once confided that Goldmans was his first love: his formidable wife had to take second place. After losing successive internal political battles and suffering some discomfort after a colleague had been indicted for insider trading, Sheinberg, an inventor of financial products for the unprecedented explosion in the bull market, was now seeking the business of London's leading players in the wake of the City's deregulatory Big Bang. Few were bigger than Maxwell.

Goldmans already enjoyed a relationship with Maxwell. In 1984, the bank had rented office space from him in Holborn, and

Sheinberg had organized the financing of his purchase of the Philip Hill Investment Trust in 1986. Despite some misgivings, Goldmans had also welcomed the business of floating 44 per cent of Berlitz in 1989, although the negotiations over the price had provoked deep antagonism, especially against Kevin. To prove his macho credentials, the son had telephoned the banker responsible at 4 a.m. New York time, to quibble about the price. 'Both Maxwells behaved appallingly,' recalled one of those involved. 'Kevin worst of all. We soon hated them.'

Yet Maxwell's business was too good to reject. The echo of the lawyers' cries in Maxwell House – 'Bob's been shopping!' – whenever the Chairman's settlement agreements arrived from stockbroking firms, encouraged brokers like Sheinberg to seek his lucrative business. Although Sheinberg was renowned for his dictum, 'There are no friends in the business, and I don't trade on the basis of friendship,' his staff in London noticed an unusual affinity between him and Maxwell. Some speculated that the link lay in their mutual interest in Israel, while others assumed it was just money. Maxwell was a big, brave gambler, playing the markets whether with brilliant insight or recklessness for $100 million and more a time, and Sheinberg was able to offer expertise, discretion and – fuelling his colleagues' gossip – the unusual practice of clearing his office whenever Maxwell telephoned. Their kinship extended, so the gossip suggested, to Sheinberg's readiness to overnight in Maxwell's penthouse, to ride in Maxwell's helicopter and even to use Maxwell's VIP customs facilities at Heathrow airport – suggestions which Sheinberg denied.

Acting as a principal and occasionally as an adviser, Sheinberg had already undertaken a series of risks which had pleased Maxwell. On the bank's behalf, the broker had bought 25 million MCC shares and, in controversial circumstances in August 1990, as MCC's price hovered around 170p, he had bought another 15.65 million shares as part of a gamble with Maxwell that the price would rise. Maxwell had channelled the money for that transaction through Corry Stiftung, one of his many Liechtenstein trusts. In the event, the Publisher had lost his gamble and Goldman Sachs had been officially reprimanded for breaking the City's disclosure regulations. That, however, Sheinberg blamed upon Goldmans' back office, since fulfilling the legal requirements was not his responsibility. Nevertheless, by November 1990, the bank was holding 47 million MCC shares, a testament of faith which could be judged as either calculated or reckless.

As the pressure on Maxwell increased, rival traders in London watched on their screens as, at precisely 2.30 p.m. every afternoon, Goldman Sachs 'hoovered up all the available MCC shares'. The bank's commitment went further than was normal for a market-maker. In gratitude for the vast speculative foreign exchange deals bestowed by Maxwell on John Lopatin, a Goldman Sachs foreign exchange executive, and for Maxwell's considerable share trading, the bank's loans were mounting. 'I don't promise what I can't deliver,' quipped Sheinberg to the Publisher, keen to emphasize his blue-sky honesty. To Sheinberg's staff, though, it seemed that the American was close to Maxwell, more like a colleague than a pure broker. But Sheinberg, privy to so much, knew only what suited his secretive client. The Chinese walls throughout Maxwell House were so thick that only Kevin and a handful of accountants and investment advisers in his private office were permitted to transcend the deliberate compartmentalization. Inevitably, the secrecy bred loneliness.

Maxwell's loneliness was aggravated by the absence of Andrea Martin, his small, demure personal assistant whose unexpected promotion from receptionist had been won after she spoke impressive French during a trip to Paris. For nearly four years until May 1990, the blonde Martin had uncomplainingly worked arduous hours, travelled extraordinary distances and loyally kept those secrets which Maxwell divulged. At the end of the working day, when he retired to his bedroom in the penthouse, Martin would enter, kick off her shoes and sit on the sofa while her boss ordered refreshments from Douglas Harrod, his entertainment manager: 'Let's have never ending champagne, Douglas, and smoked salmon and caviar.' The tall, benign, well-dressed butler, whom Maxwell had gleefully poached from Rupert Murdoch, would oblige with an obedient smile. After supervising the delivery of his master's order, he would close the heavy double doors. Maxwell, he realized, was 'besotted by Andrea'. Harrod was less clear what Andrea Martin 'could see in someone like Robert Maxwell except a high salary'. But he had noticed a special relationship of 'endearments and those sort of things'. However, those days had sadly passed. In the aftermath,

Andrea Martin always insisted that their relationship had been strictly professional.

A few months earlier, Maxwell had summoned John Pole, his head of security. A former detective chief superintendent employed for thirty years at Scotland Yard, where he had earned sixteen commendations, Pole had become accustomed, like all Maxwell's staff, to responding unquestioningly to the summons day and night, regardless of the inconvenience. 'We need to talk,' growled Maxwell as he replaced the telephone receiver. Minutes later Pole was sitting erect and attentive opposite his employer. 'I'm concerned about Andrea Martin's loyalty,' sighed Maxwell. Pole had noticed the millionaire's infatuation with the young woman. 'She knows a lot of confidential information and I fear she's having an affair with Nick Davies. She has promised me that it's over, but I don't trust him and she might be telling him more than is healthy.'

Davies was the snappy foreign editor of the *Daily Mirror*, a journalist generally disliked by his colleagues, who had given him the sobriquet 'Sneaky'. Maxwell suspected Davies's loyalty, but was uncharacteristically unsure how best to neutralize an employee who had invaded the heart of his private territory. He then uttered the phrase which preceded his most intimate instructions to Pole: 'I need to know if this person is being loyal to me.' It was Maxwell's euphemism for instructing that he wanted Andrea Martin's telephone tapped.

Maxwell had long enjoyed the use of listening devices or bugs. His black briefcase contained a concealed tape recorder operated by a turn of the lock, and a bug had been inserted into a table lamp in his home. During the 1984 negotiations with the Mirror Group's trade unions, he had used crude tape recorders to monitor his adversaries' negotiating position. In later years, another former police officer in his employ was regularly to bring him cassettes of taped telephone conversations among his own executives. Sitting in his apartment at the end of the day, the congenital eavesdropper would race through the tapes listening for clues to disloyalty, weaknesses or hidden mistakes. In an atmosphere reminiscent of Stalin's Kremlin, Pole had supervised in 1988 the concealment of two microphones in Maxwell's own office – activated by a switch under his desk – and one in the conference room in the Mirror building. A microphone was also secreted in Kevin's office in Maxwell House.

This followed the disappearance of the banker's draft worth £4.7 million (see p. 10). Telephone taps on the suspect revealed nothing. The draft had never been cashed.

Maxwell's ruse was to invite guests to remain in Kevin's room or the conference room while he excused himself briefly to tend another chore. Lumbering along to his own office, he would unlock the cupboard behind his desk and activate the recording machines, which Pole had rendered foolproof to accommodate his 'banana fingers'. Having eavesdropped on the conversations to glean his competitors' secrets, he would return at the appropriate moment to exploit his advantage. The subterfuge had won him undeserved acclaim as an outstanding negotiator. Pole's tap on Andrea Martin's telephone produced different results.

At the end of the week, Pole returned with a tape: 'You'd better listen to this, Mr Maxwell.' For twenty minutes Maxwell sat motionless as the recognizable voices of Andrea and Davies giggled over their previous night's romps in a car. When Davies mentioned details of Andrea's underwear, Maxwell flinched. Pole noticed his hurt: 'Heartbroken, even shattered.' The woman with whom he was in love had lied. Despite her promise that her affair with Davies had ceased, it was in full flow. Emotionally, Maxwell was vulnerable. Estranged from his family, he had lost the one person upon whom he felt he could rely. He had paid for her loyalty with an annual contract worth £36,000, a considerable sum for a secretary, but after that betrayal there was no alternative but her dismissal, which followed in July 1990. Douglas Harrod noticed the result. 'Maxwell went down in the dumps. He was a very unhappy man.'

Ever since, there had been no one with whom Maxwell could relax at the end of the day. Besides that emotional deprivation, he was also losing control of his private office. Having failed to replace Peter Jay, his self-styled chief of staff in the years 1986–9, he no longer employed anyone as competent to arrange his papers and organize his diary. As his moods and sympathies oscillated violently, secretaries and personal assistants in his private office changed with damaging regularity. Gradually, despite his roared demands for efficiency, his private office was becoming chaotic.

By contrast, the management of his tenth-floor penthouse was immaculate. Normally waking at 6.30 after fitful sleep, Maxwell would find his staff ready to fulfil his every whim, especially the most unreasonable. Deprived of his family's company and support, he had thrown himself into a routine which had moved from hectic into frenetic. Increasingly cancelling invitations at the last moment, he would collapse into bed in the early evening to be served dinner while channel-hopping on television or watching a video.

Martin Cheeseman, his chef, had been recommended four years before by Harrod. 'He's worked in Downing Street,' boasted the butler. 'But can he cook?' retorted Maxwell. He had proved to be a devoted servant. 'I knew my customer and gave him what he wanted,' explained Cheeseman, a thirty-seven-year-old south-east Londoner who served 'mostly salmon, roast chicken and avocados'. Sufficient food was always prepared for Maxwell's night-time feasts, especially melons filled with berries and cornflakes. Improbably Cheeseman insisted, 'I only fed him healthy food. He didn't pig out. He was that shape when I arrived.' Their relationship flourished because Maxwell tended to treat his servants like directors and his directors like servants. He had warmed to the young man's unassuming conversation, inviting him to accompany him on longer journeys so that he could avoid eating unwelcome dishes.

Alongside Cheeseman were Juliet and Elsa, the Filipina maids. Their predecessor had been fired after accusations of stealing television sets, clothes, food and cases of wine. In any event, Maxwell had not prosecuted. But the maids were obliged to tolerate an unfortunate development in his personal habits: his obesity had spawned filthiness. Not only were his soiled clothes and half-eaten food thrown on the floors, but the lavatory after use was abandoned unflushed and the bed linen was occasionally oddly coloured. 'We're short of face towels,' Terry Gilmour, a chief steward, once told the Publisher's wife Betty. Puzzled, she reminded him that twenty-four Valentino flannels had been delivered just weeks earlier. 'Mr Maxwell's using them instead of toilet paper,' explained Gilmour expressionlessly, 'and discards them on the floor.' To save the staff the indignity, Betty Maxwell arranged for the towels to be brought in sealed plastic bags to the family home in Oxford, for washing. All these members of Maxwell's personal staff shared one quality: their ignorance of his business activities. Although his bedroom was occasionally turned into an office with documents piled beneath a computer screen, none of those in such close proximity would have understood his orders to move money and shares.

Similar ignorance infected Sir John Quinton, chairman of Barclays Bank, who lunched with Maxwell on 7 November, the day after the Berlitz share certificates had been hidden in the safe. Britain's biggest bank had lent Maxwell's private companies over £200 million, and Quinton, who deluded himself that he could understand London's more maverick entrepreneurs, was easily persuaded by his host of the health of MCC's finances. As Quinton drove back into the City after lunch, the Publisher climbed the metal staircase to the roof of Maxwell House, walked across the astroturf and boarded his helicopter for Farnborough airport.

An unmistakable sense of relief always passed through Maxwell's mass as Captain Dick Cowley, his pilot since 1986, pulled the joystick and the Aérospatiale 355 rose above London, passing directly over the glinting scales of justice on the dome of the Old Bailey. Cowley enjoyed being used by Maxwell as a £250 per hour taxi and would laugh about the gigantic insurance premium paid to cover landing the helicopter on the roof. Maxwell always refused to travel to the airport by car. If the weather was bad, he preferred to wait, meanwhile keeping his aircrew waiting on the tarmac for his arrival. Cowley savoured memories of flying Maxwell through snowstorms to Oxford, peering into the white gloom for recognizable landmarks, and the enjoyment of intimate conversations during those flights. He even tolerated midnight calls, hearing his employer's lament about Andrea's departure. Cowley was respected because he was employed to perform one task which Maxwell could not undertake: 'I stayed and put up with all his nonsense because he paid me well.'

The flight from Holborn to Farnborough lasted fifteen minutes. As they flew that November afternoon, Maxwell could reflect on his growing disenchantment with the technicalities of finance. The excitement had long disappeared; indeed, in recent months his usual exhausting long hours running the empire had become positively unpleasant. Those financial chores he was pleased to delegate to Kevin, who, despite their past quarrels and the estrangement when Kevin decided to marry Pandora Warnford-Davis, he could now trust more than any other person. Father and son were working jointly to overcome their temporary difficulties. As the helicopter whirred down to the airport the strain of the past days was dissolving. Kevin could look after the business problems while his father embarked upon what he enjoyed most – powerbroking among the world's leaders.

No sooner had he been deposited alongside his new $24 million Gulfstream 4 executive jet, codenamed VR-BOB (Very Rich Bob), than Maxwell was bustling up the steps shedding the last of his tribulations. Captain Brian Hull, the pilot, welcomed his passenger, aware that 'he always became happy after he boarded. He saw me as home.' Minutes later, they were flying at 500 m.p.h. towards Israel, a three-and-a-half-hour journey costing £14,000 in each direction.

Few things gave Maxwell more pleasure than his new Gulfstream, capable of flying the Atlantic without refuelling (unlike his Gulf-stream 2, which he nevertheless retained in event of emergencies). For hours he had discussed the G4's interior design with Captain Hull. In the end, he had settled upon a light-cream carpet, six seats covered in light-brown leather and six in cream cloth. The brown suede walls offset the gold fittings. Flying at 35,000 feet, the passen-ger relished the pampering he received from Carina Hall, the stew-ardess, and Simon Grigg, his valet. At the merest intimation that his finger might flick, he could be assured of instant service. The food in the plane's kitchen – cheddar cheese, smoked salmon, caviar and chicken – had been sent ahead by Martin Cheeseman. Krug and pink champagne were in the fridge. Thoughtfully, Hull always provided a selection of new video films – his employer especially liked adventure stories such as *The Hunt for Red October*. Some-times, Maxwell would read biographies or work through a case of papers. Music was rarely played. Facing him on this occasion was the empty place where Andrea had sat in the past, her feet often resting on his seat, tucked under one of his massive thighs. Beyond was where the divan could be set up for him to sleep. Captain Hull had noticed on flights across the Atlantic that some-times both Maxwell and Andrea slept on it – quite innocently, he stressed.

The new Gulfstream was more than a toy. It was a testament to Maxwell's importance and wealth. The telephone was fixed next to his seat. One night he telephoned Roy Greenslade, then the editor of the *Daily Mirror*. 'Where am I?' he boomed.

'I don't know, Bob. Israel? Russia . . . ?'

'I'm above you!' Greenslade looked up at the ceiling. 'I left

Montreal this morning. I was in New York this afternoon. Now I'm going to Hungary. Not bad for a pensioner, eh?'

Constant travel was Maxwell's way of escaping from reality. Over the following twelve months, the Gulfstream would fly 800 hours, more than double an average pilot's duties. Other than New York, no other destination was more welcoming than Jerusalem's small airport surrounded by the Judaean hills.

Ever since Gerald Ronson, the British businessman, had taken the Publisher on Maxwell's own private jet to Israel in 1985 to reintroduce him to his origins, the erstwhile Orthodox Jew had abandoned his repeated, vociferous denial of his religion, which had even prompted him in the 1950s to read the Sunday lesson at an Anglican church in Esher. Considering the anti-semitism still lingering among Britons after the war, that denial had seemed a natural ploy for an ambitious foreigner, dishonest about so much else. But with his recent achievement of financial security and the decline in overt anti-semitism, Maxwell had grown closer to London's Jewish community.

Tears had welled in Maxwell's eyes on that first trip with Ronson. 'Thanks for bringing me here,' he repeated as they toured the country, visiting the major powerbrokers, including Yitzhak Shamir, the prime minister. 'I want to do things and be helpful,' Maxwell told Shamir as they posed for the photographer accompanying him. 'I'm going to be a big investor.' Ronson smiled at the prospect of collecting millions for charity. 'I want to be buried here,' Maxwell confided that night over dinner in the King David Hotel.

Thereafter on Friday nights, Maxwell occasionally travelled to Ronson's home in north-west London to eat the Sabbath dinner or celebrate Jewish holidays. Gail Ronson, Maxwell acknowledged, cooked like his mother, especially chopped liver. He also appeared at Jewish charity functions, mixing with Trevor Chinn, Cyril Stein and Lord Young, the politician, who had invited Maxwell to his daughter's wedding. His presence in that community had been welcomed, although some feared that his financing of a Holocaust conference in 1989 signalled an attempted take-over. After all, his urge to dominate was indiscriminate.

The interest in his Jewish background had been encouraged by his wife Betty. Together in Israel they had met Chanan Taub, a childhood friend from Solotvino, Maxwell's impoverished birth-place on Czechoslovakia's eastern border with Russia and Romania. 'Poor, hungry and unmemorable' was the Publisher's emotional recollection of the muddy pathways, ramshackle, overcrowded dwellings and suffocating destitution there. Sixty years earlier, he reflected, he had shared a solitary pair of shoes with a sister. In 1939 Taub had swum illegally from a ship ashore to Palestine as a penniless Zionist – unlike Maxwell, who had escaped from his homeland, on the eve of Nazi Germany's invasion, to make his way overland through Hungary and the Balkans to Palestine and then by sea to Britain as a member of the Free Czech Army. When they met again nearly fifty years later, Taub had become one of Israel's richest diamond dealers. Yet the contrast between the two former Orthodox Jews was striking. While Maxwell boasted of wealth he did not possess, Taub concealed his enormous bank balance beneath dishevelled clothes and a twenty-six-year-old, dented and dirty Chevrolet. Ever since their first reunion, Taub had been mesmerized by Maxwell's extraordinary transformation from the thin, small boy with pious ringlets swinging along his cheeks who uniquely arrived at Zionist classes in their village clutching a book and stuttering Yiddish phrases. Now Maxwell was *ein Mensch*, possessed of riches, power, influence and a large family.

Their childhood reminiscences helped to fill a void in Maxwell's life. Israel further calmed his turbulent emotions, enabling the refu-gee to put down roots of a kind. In particular, he would become transformed when he entered the presidential suite of Jerusalem's King David Hotel. Throwing open his windows, he would gaze at the old city of Jerusalem, mentioned so long ago in his itinerant father's daily prayers at home in Ruthenia. The serenity evoked by the sunlight glinting from the Dome of the Rock above the Wailing Wall, that sacred shrine for Jews through two millennia, seemed to testify to the historic endurance of the Jews. Even he, the bulldozer, would tremble with emotion as the spectacle reawakened memories of his Orthodox childhood, the history of the diaspora, and stirred the survivor's guilt for escaping the gas chambers.

That evening, 7 November, Maxwell dined with Ariel and Lily Sharon, the former military commander, minister and leading right-wing member of the Israeli parliament. To Sharon, as to so many other Israelis, Maxwell was 'a friend – a Jew who had finally come home'. Their conversation concentrated upon politics, especially the question of Israel's relations with the Arabs. The visitor glowed with pride that his opinions should be taken seriously.

Maxwell's schedule the following day confirmed his importance in the country. After breakfast with Ehoud Olmert, the health minister and a friend with whom he shared a passion for football, he spent half an hour with Yitzhak Shamir, the prime minister. Their regular meetings were welcomed by the diminutive former terrorist. Maxwell had not only committed himself to substantial investments in Israeli industry, newspapers and football, but he had established a direct link between Shamir and Mikhail Gorbachev, the Soviet leader. The benefit to Israel had been considerable. Through Maxwell's efforts, 300,000 Soviet Jews had been allowed to emigrate to Israel. He had also flown dozens of Soviet children afflicted by Chernobyl's 1986 radioactive blast to Israel for treatment. In 1990, he had stood among the guests of honour at a solemn reunion of 1,000 Czech Jews, blessed by the presence of Václav Havel, the Czech president, and senior Israeli politicians.

That morning, at Shamir's request, Maxwell had telephoned Gorbachev's direct number in the Kremlin from the prime minister's office. Speaking in halting Russian, he had passed on Shamir's greetings and his request that the Soviet leader should remove an obstacle in Soviet–Israeli relations. The warmth of the conversation reconvinced Shamir of Maxwell's importance. Emerging into the sunlight, the Publisher returned to a hectic schedule of meetings with his employees and advisers, interrupted only by lunch with David Levy, the junior foreign minister, and dinner with Yitzhak Modai, the finance minister. That night, as he lay in his room reflecting upon his importance, his financial troubles in London appeared thankfully remote. In one of those characteristic moments of rashness, he pondered first whether to buy El Al, Israel's beleaguered national airline, or the Israeli Discount Bank, and even about bidding $11 billion for Paramount film studios.

After a short nap, at 4 a.m. on 9 November Maxwell flew to Frankfurt. There he lunched with George Shultz, the former US secretary of state whose memoirs Macmillan had published at enormous financial loss and whose company Maxwell often sought. He also met Ulrike Pöhl, the wife of the German central banker, a woman upon whom Maxwell was able to unburden his emotions and whose company he eagerly sought.

By nightfall, Maxwell had returned to London for dinner with Shimon Peres, the Israeli foreign minister. The two men, with a common ancestry in Eastern Europe, had deepened their bond when, with Peres's approval, Alisa Eshed, his vivacious personal assistant for twenty-two years, had been appointed Maxwell's co-ordinator and representative in Israel. These were the close relationships to which Maxwell had long aspired in Britain. But other than the occasional meeting with Margaret Thatcher, the prime minister, an occasional lunch with Norman Lamont, or conversations with other government ministers at charity parties, Maxwell could satisfy his frustrated political ambitions only by meeting leaders of the Labour Party.

Overcoming their antipathy, both Neil Kinnock and Roy Hattersley, Labour's leader and deputy leader, accepted Maxwell's invitations to meetings and meals in order to secure the continuing support for their beleaguered party of the Mirror Group's newspapers – the *Daily Mirror*, the *Sunday Mirror* and the *People*. In Maxwell's dining room, the entertainment manager, Douglas Harrod, would overhear both of them seriously seeking his advice and on one occasion listening to his request for a peerage. 'It's normal for a newspaper owner,' Maxwell urged, expecting a positive response. Both visitors had smiled benignly, without committing themselves.

The delivery of the proofs of that night's *Daily Mirror* interrupted the dinner with Peres. It was a familiar ritual, enjoyed by Maxwell as a means of demonstrating his influence. To emphasize to any doubters his unquestioned authority, he would push a button on the telephone to hear the editor's attentive voice on the intercom. After he had barked an order and pushed the button again to cut off any possible response, his eyes would shine. His irrepressible pride was expressed in this telephone terrorism, harassing employees regardless of the time by insisting on their constant availability to his summons. To Peres, like so many others who saw the ritual with the proofs, his host seemed truly potent. But Maxwell's life in his glossy apartment had in fact become a torment.

His forty-six-year marriage to Betty had effectively terminated long before. Ever since their first wedding anniversary after a whirlwind romance in wartime Paris, he had sporadically tired of the older French woman, but her devotion and his loneliness had always compelled his return. Her patience during his long absences and the regular arrival of new children had compensated for his irritation with her cold, unhumorous, unJewish demeanour. While most voiced warm respect for Betty, chiming that she was the sane, modest, reasonable and honest side of the unlikely duo, marvelling at her forbearance as her husband changed from being a muscular, brave, handsome charmer into an obese tyrant, he believed that their wartime romance should have been brought to an end after their first passion. Their markedly disparate backgrounds were not suited for an enduring relationship. Unlike Robert Maxwell, with his impoverished Jewish childhood, Betty Maxwell had been born into the tranquil, even dull, Protestant comfort of a large house in the French countryside, supported by the wealth of a silk manufacturer.

Not surprisingly, the small, plain woman with the rasping French accent had enjoyed the partying and jet-setting around the world's most exclusive hotels and beaches, paid for by her husband. She had even tolerated appalling rows caused by his inexplicable emotional outbursts whenever his financial pressures seemed overwhelming. For years she had concealed her repeated humiliation in private by uttering public declarations of passion and loyalty. 'Our love for each other', she had told *She* magazine in 1987, 'is not in doubt, it is the rock and rudder of my life.' Few doubted her. Yet seven years later, in her autobiography, she would accuse her late husband of taking 'sadistic pleasure' in behaving during their long marriage in a 'harsh, cruel, uncompromising, dictatorial, exceedingly selfish and inconsiderate fashion'. During his life her concealment of this truth had been near perfect. Annually, she had chosen and collected within a new leather-bound scrapbook all the newspaper cuttings and letters reporting her husband's activities, presenting the volume to him on his birthday.

So by 1987 a woman described by an Oxford don as 'sharp as a knife. All brain,' could be in no doubt about the myriad accusations of fraud, deceit and dishonesty which he had attracted. Yet, rejecting the accumulated evidence and as an additional gift that year, she presented her husband as testimony to his 'boundless energy and originality' with a green volume listing the 2,418 bundles of documents used by one of Britain's most litigious individuals in his lawsuits between 1945 and 1983. Prefaced by a quotation from Abraham Lincoln, Maxwell's self-styled 'personal archivist' recalled how his 'opponents dragged out every skeleton they could find from every cupboard imaginable . . . The British press and the British establishment have a nasty habit of never letting sleeping dogs lie and their attacks have to be nailed every time.' In particular, she recalled the 'seemingly unending bleak, sombre days' of the 'infamous DTI inspectors' disgraceful attacks on your reputation' and how their lives were ruined by 'iniquitous' High Court judges and 'Trotskyites' in the Labour Party's 'grotesque kangaroo court'. There were years, Betty recalled, when the number of loyal friends 'could be counted on the fingers of one hand' and when 'Every morning, the slim thread holding the Damocles sword seemed to have frayed a little more.' That loyalty had been rewarded by her appointment as a director of Headington Hill Investments, a controlling company linking the London & Bishopsgate companies (among other constellations) to Maxwell's worldwide empire and to the Liechtenstein trusts. But Headington was separate and deliberately unconnected to the Robert Maxwell Group and its subsidiaries. (See company plan after notes.) Blessed, according to Betty's own account, with high intelligence, some would think that she could not be ignorant of the developing financial crisis. Yet, for Maxwell, whether she was aware or not was irrelevant.

For twenty-five years, he had proposed separation from Betty. During the early 1950s he had fallen in love with Anne Dove, his secretary. Her lightheartedness, efficiency and typically English attractiveness, in contrast to Betty's plodding worthiness, had resulted in a long, passionate affair. The relationship's termination when Dove exiled herself to the Indian Himalayas had led to an uneasy reconciliation with Betty, which, after his fraud as a book wholesaler had been exposed in 1954, was interrupted by ferocious rows, complete with renewed demands for separation.

In the 1960s, he had enjoyed the company of Jean Baddeley, another devoted secretary. Pleasant looking and efficient, Baddeley had dotingly remained with Maxwell throughout the dark years after the DTI inspectors' 1971 condemnation and had organized his office after his resurrection in the 1980s. 'My love for him', she would explain, 'was based on huge respect and deep affection for someone who was very important to me.' But when her looks declined and her imperious, jealous manner earned her the nick-name 'Queen Bitch', Maxwell shuffled her to a side office.

By 1990, the pressure of his continuing deceit had made the demands of marriage intolerable. Effectively, he had separated from Betty. On her visits to London, she would sleep either in a hotel or with friends. Other than his occasional return on a Friday night to Headington Hill Hall, the Oxford mansion he had leased in 1959 from the council for a fixed £2,000 per annum and used as an office and family home, he barely lived under the same roof as his wife. Typically, on Saturday, 10 November, after sleeping one night in his own bedroom in Oxford, he summoned Captain Cowley to fly him back to Holborn.

For the following day, Maxwell had invited Professor Fedor Burlatsky, a well-connected Russian historian, and his wife Kira Vladina, a journalist, to lunch. To impress the couple, he sent his maroon Rolls-Royce to collect them from the Waldorf. The gesture was more rewarding than he could have anticipated.

As usual, he kept his guests waiting. His eventual appearance was dramatic: 'If only I'd known it was you waiting for me, I wouldn't have taken such a long time getting here.' Maxwell was staring at Kira Vladina, a shapely forty-seven-year-old blonde. For her part, already awed by the display of wealth, Vladina was struck by the giant figure which was apparently filling an enormous living room.

Over lunch, Maxwell could hardly take his eyes off the woman. At the end of the meal, they agreed to continue their conversation, because she wished to interview him for a Moscow newspaper. Professor Burlatsky departed, Maxwell cancelled his other appoint-ments and Vladina, accustomed to her small, sparsely furnished apartment in Moscow, relaxed in the company of the noticeably admiring billionaire. Their conversation soon switched from Max-well's customary bombast and inventions about his wartime heroism – 'I escaped from Czechoslovakia on a raft at dawn with German bullets flying over me,' he claimed, forgetting that he had simply boarded a train in peacetime – to an intimate outpouring of his misery, his loneliness and his forlorn search for affection. 'I love the dawn,' he murmured in Russian, correctly guessing that his listener would be impressed by sensitivity.

'You have everything in life,' said Kira.

'Not love,' replied Maxwell.

'But everyone loves you.'

There was a long pause. 'I don't believe that. It's my money they love.' Maxwell paused again and moved closer to the Slav, so different from the women he usually met. 'I absolutely adored my mother. With all my heart. And that's why I always dreamt of loving and being loved in return.'

'Are you happily married?'

'Well, she's French. You know how the French are. What they love more than anything is money. I never sensed any of the warmth or affection I got from my mother in my own family and which I gave to the world around me.'

Kira moved closer, responding to and even sharing Maxwell's emotion. The man was 'sad and lonely', she realized, 'even within his family'. Yet she was unable to change anything.

Maxwell continued talking about Betty: 'She's so calculating. A calculating Frenchwoman, putting up a good front, but she gives me no love. Not the love I got from my mother.'

Naturally, Kira knew nothing of the tempestuous rows which took place between Maxwell and Betty. Instead she noticed only the Publisher's vulnerability: 'His big, piercing, fatal wound'. It was already nightfall. Kira felt an intimacy towards a man who was 'overweight, old and plain'. He spoke of his love for Russia and the culture which was his own. 'I sympathize,' she whispered. 'I understand.' Letting his imagination run wild, Maxwell had become infatuated with the woman.

Some time later that evening, he spoke of his children. 'They're very good at spending the money I earn. They're not like me. They don't work hard and take risks.' Maxwell was clearly bothered by his seven surviving children. His favourite, Michael, he confessed, had died in 1968 after being kept alive for seven years on a support system following a motor accident. His new favourite was his son Ian, conceived in 1955 when Maxwell had been mistakenly told by a doctor that he was dying of cancer. 'I adore him. He's a bit like me.' Pause. 'But not in work. And I love my youngest daughter, Ghislaine. The rest are a cold lot. Like their mother; and they want to live off what others earn.'

Kira returned late to her hotel and her husband. Maxwell's last words had been memorable: 'Kira, I would so like to be in your suit of clothes or, even better, your skin.' He had been, she thought, so tender, so trusting. The whole intimate experience had been 'a fantasy which took hold of our hearts'.

Alone once again in his penthouse, Maxwell might have reconsidered his description of his children. He unashamedly doted upon Ghislaine, his youngest daughter, naming his luxury yacht after her and financing her unprofitable corporate-gifts business, though he would not tolerate the presence of her boyfriends, whom he suspected were hoping to benefit from a piece of the action. His relationship with Ghislaine was becoming increasingly intense, some would say indulgent. He no longer had much interest in his twin daughters, Isabel and Christine, born in 1950. Of Anne, his daughter born in 1948, he had quipped to colleagues, 'What have Anne and Pope John Paul in common? Both are ugly and both are failed actors!' His eldest son Philip, born in 1947, a donnish, decent man, disliked his father, and the sentiment was reciprocated. When he married in South America, his father refused to attend the ceremony. Some suspected that Maxwell had always resented the death of his elder son Michael and the survival of Philip.

Maxwell often spoke to Ian, a joint managing director of MCC and a director of over eighty private companies, but he permitted him few responsibilities, despite his annual income of £262,000 plus practically unlimited expenses. Ian, it was agreed by most, was a charming, easygoing playboy, sought by many young, attractive women, whom he tended to address as 'princess'. But there was also an arrogance. On one occasion, Ian had told Bob Cole, Maxwell's spokesman, to collect a suit from his London flat. Cole arrived to find the chaotic evidence of the previous night's revelry. Scattered on the bedroom floor lay several used condoms. Ian clearly expected his Filipina maid to clear *everything*. A similarly casual attitude affected Ian's responsibilities to work. Educated at Marlborough College and at Balliol College, Oxford, he understood the legal requirements expected of directors of companies but adopted his father's cavalier attitude towards those laws, smoothing things over with a modicum of charm.

Robert Maxwell, however, noting that Ian lacked an astute appreciation of finance, engaged in the real conversations with Kevin. As the empire's finances became perilous, it was Kevin whom he increasingly trusted. But there was little intimacy, and frequently, as in the past, he ignored his son's advice, not least when Kevin urged that they renegotiate all their loans with the banks. 'They'll eat us alive,' snapped Maxwell each time he raised the issue. All those bankers, lawyers and other professionals visiting the Publisher were appalled by the father's treatment of his son. 'Shut up, you don't know what you're talking about!' Maxwell would yell. The eyewitnesses to those humiliating outbursts, admirers of Kevin's talent, would gaze stupefied as his father 'treated him like dirt'. None was more surprised than Bill Harry, Macmillan's tax adviser. At a celebratory party on board the *Lady Ghislaine* in July 1989, Harry was explaining the tax implications of the company's recent merger with McGraw-Hill when Kevin asked a question. His father exploded: 'Don't ever interrupt a tax expert!' A chastened Kevin fell silent, while the others present stared at their shoes.

Yet at 7 a.m. most days during 1990, Robert Maxwell was ensconced alone in his office with Kevin, taking the place of his son's early-morning German lessons. Dignified with the label 'prayer meetings', their encounters allowed them to plot and plan their agenda.

So much in Kevin's life had changed in the last months. In 1988, his father had dispatched him to New York to manage Macmillan and their new American empire. There, to Robert Maxwell's irritation, he had been joined by Pandora Warnford-Davis, his tall, thin, toothy, aggressive, thirty-year-old wife, whom he had met at Oxford and whose assertions of independence both before and since their wedding in 1984 had not endeared her to Robert. 'What shall I call you?' she had coldly asked Dick Cowley, the helicopter pilot, on first meeting. 'You can call me Captain,' he replied. Robert Maxwell was never able to establish that advantage over a woman he regarded as spoilt and foolish. For his staff, the defining moment of Pandora's attitude towards her father-in-law had occurred one day when the Gulfstream was parked on the tarmac at Le Bourget airport outside Paris. Maxwell was fuming because Kevin and his wife were late for take-off. 'Fuck them! Let's go!' he shouted eventually, sending Terry Gilmour, the chief steward, to deposit their passports at immigration. At that moment the couple arrived, only to be tongue-lashed by a furious Maxwell. To his astonishment, Pandora then turned on him and snarled, 'Who the fuck do you think you are?' Silenced, Maxwell stared out of the window until touch-down in London. The relationship worsened as the financial crisis grew, with the helicopter being frequently dispatched to collect Kevin from Hailey, his Oxfordshire country home near Wallingford. Unintimidated, Pandora once mockingly threatened to 'use a gun [on her father-in-law] if you disturb our life again'. Her outbursts won only temporary respite. Like most bullies, Maxwell retreated when challenged but soon resumed his egotistical behaviour, demanding total obedience to his needs.

By the autumn of 1990, Kevin had abandoned his New York residence and was commuting from London on the 9.30 a.m. Concorde to New York, cramming up to twenty-one meetings into one day before sleeping on the overnight British Airways 747 flight home, with a helicopter hop to Maxwell House at 6.30 in the morning. During that year, his use of conventional airlines within Europe had declined. Under increasing pressure, he flew on chartered jets, accompanied by Carolyn Barwell, his lively assistant – to Zurich for lunch, to Hamburg for dinner, or on one occasion overnight to see his father in Istanbul, returning the following day to London. He had also more or less abandoned watching his own Oxford United football club on Saturdays or playing with his children, Tilly, Teddy and Chloe. His regular cultural outings organized by Pandora – to the theatre, Covent Garden or the Festival Hall, followed by dinner in London's fashionable restaurants – also tended increasingly to be cancelled, prompting frequent absences from their chaotic home in Jubilee Place, Chelsea. Despite Pandora's shrill complaints about the working hours her father-in-law required from Kevin, she enjoyed the perks of Maxwell's fortune. Even her family shared the benefits. John Warnford-Davis, her father employed by Maxwell, used the helicopter to avoid the traffic to Newmarket, while her brother Darryll, employed at brokers Astaire and Partners, regularly approached Kevin with 'business propositions' in return for monitoring and buying MCC shares.

Initially, Kevin had not complained about the pressure. No other man of his age in London could helicopter from the city centre to land alongside Concorde, receiving special dispensation from customs and passport control. Like his father, he revelled in the exercise of power, seeking acceptance from the establishment as befitted an old boy of Marlborough College and a graduate of

Balliol College, Oxford. He even used a barber at the Savoy, a custom Robert Maxwell had adopted more than forty years earlier. He had not complained when his summer holidays in 1990 had been forsaken. While his friends were relaxing in expensive resorts, his August days had been filled by endless meetings with bankers, lawyers, accountants, analysts and staff. His most frequent visitors were Colin Emson, the managing director of Robert Fraser, a merchant bank chaired by Lord Rippon, an independent director of MCC; Neil Taberner, a senior partner of Coopers, the empire's accountants; Scott Marden and Andrew Capitman of Bankers Trust; Michael von Clemm of Merrill Lynch, a friend anxious to win some of the business; Sir Michael Richardson of Smith New Court, MCC's stockbrokers, and reputedly close to the prime minister; and Thomas Christofferson of Morgan Stanley. These men were unified by more than their financial profession and their proximity to the Maxwells. Individually, each was contributing to the Maxwells' appearance of probity and financial security.

As another group of visitors, his employees, members of the inner sanctum, the heart of the operation, were probably more important. By the end of September 1990, to help him to cope with the financial crisis, they were being summoned by Kevin to daily meetings. All were men and women of unquestioning obedience and unremarkable technical competence, closely associated with the empire's finances. The overriding criteria for their employment were their loyalty and their readiness to become beholden to their employer in return for their over-generous salaries. Among them were Deborah Maxwell, a thirty-three-year-old dark-haired lawyer who was not related to her employer, although outsiders sometimes mistakenly believed there was a connection; Mark Tanzer, a 'poor man's Peter Jay'; Robert Bunn, forty-two years old, an accountant and RMG's finance director, of whom Maxwell irreverently joked, 'I could order him to rob the Midland Bank!'; Basil Brookes, the acting finance director recruited from Coopers; and Albert Fuller, the head of the treasury.

As the crisis deepened, Kevin included in those meetings Michael Stoney, an ambitious accountant, and Jean-Pierre Anselmini, a forty-eight-year-old Frenchman and former director of Crédit Lyonnais, who in 1988 had helped to organize the $3 billion Jumbo Loan to the Maxwells and had been flattered by the subsequent

invitation to join MCC as deputy chairman. Although blessed in
Maxwell's propaganda as 'brilliant', Anselmini was the fullest
embodiment of his state-owned bank's naivety. 'The bank which
could never say "no"' had lent Maxwell $1.3 billion, its accumu-
lated bad debts now totalling over £20 billion. For the Frenchman,
wilfully ignorant of Maxwell's past, his new employer was 'a fairy
tale everyone needed to believe in', especially because he proclaimed
himself a socialist while offering an entrée into the giddy world of
the media. 'I wanted to believe in Maxwell's success,' Anselmini
later confessed. He was hypnotized by Maxwell's 'star quality, and
I loved the Maxwell family'. That same warmth was reflected by
Sam Pisar, Maxwell's French lawyer and business representative
engaged in deals in Russia and Israel and had become a close confi-
dante: 'We needed myths and heroes in those dark times.'

One of the recent casualties of that trusted group was Ron
Woods, a director of MCC whom Maxwell had inherited as a tax
consultant (just as he had inherited the deputy managing director
Richard Baker) on his spectacular relaunch into business in 1980
when he bought the British Printing Corporation. The forty-seven-
year-old from the Rhondda Valley fell under Maxwell's spell and
came to regard him with a mixture of awe and fear as a 'hero and
father-figure'. To his delight, Woods had discovered that his new
employer was hyper-sensitive about taxation and wished him to
deploy his skill to minimize the tax liabilities on the empire's purchases, take-overs and disposals. Little pleased Woods more than
to work on his computer to produce an innovative tax scheme.
The empire, he knew, was 'tax-driven' and he more than anyone
understood its complexity. According to a senior company auditor,
'Only Woods could explain why it was so complex.' The challenge,
Woods would attest, was 'very exciting'. It was also legal and ethi-
cal. There was no need to resort to the criminal evasion of taxes.
Maxwell's empire was ultimately owned in Liechtenstein, so few
taxes were unavoidable and they could be neutralized if, by careful
anticipation, MCC and the 400 private companies accumulated the
appropriate debts and losses. When he bought Macmillan, $1.8
billion of the $2.6 billion purchase price was charged to Macmillan
itself so that the interest charges could be offset against the profits,
thereby avoiding all taxation. Indeed, Maxwell's only serious liability was advance corporation tax (ACT) on dividends. 'I don't want

to pay taxes,' he had told Bill Harry, his American tax adviser, 'but I don't want to go to prison either.' This was a reference to the fate of Leona Helmsley, recently jailed in New York for tax evasion, a poignant moment for Maxwell, who regularly occupied the presidential suite in her Manhattan hotel.

Although with hindsight Woods would regret his own simplicity, he had never suspected his employer, even though he personally negotiated with the two lawyers responsible for the Liechtenstein trusts: Dr Werner Rechsteiner in Zurich and Dr Walter Keicher in Vaduz, the principality's capital. With awe, Woods retold Maxwell's fanciful story of how, dressed in a British army uniform, he had met Keicher's father in Zurich all those years before and had had the savvy to lay the foundations of his empire. The Liechtenstein Anstalts, the impenetrable trusts, Woods knew, did not contain any cash, only shares. Maxwell's claim in 1988 at the time of the launch of his authorized biography that they boasted funds of £1 billion, a figure calculated by Woods himself, referred only to Maxwell's shareholding in his own companies, including MCC, not to his cash. With Woods's compartmentalized knowledge, those shares were always used as collateral to raise private loans, liable to be sold by the lending banks if the Publisher defaulted.

Maxwell had trusted Woods to override the rigid compartmentalization between his private and public companies, moving from one to the other. Although during 1990 the tax expert, seeing through the maze of figures, had realized that the private companies were 'short of cash' and that Maxwell was making an effort 'to prevent MCC's share-price fall' by purchasing his own shares through Liechtenstein, he remained faithfully silent. His loyalty was all the more remarkable given that their relationship had been fractured ever since Maxwell had used one of his private companies (Hollis) to buy AGB, a research company, in the summer of 1988. Woods's protest to Maxwell, who was at the time sailing on his yacht, was rebuffed with the words, 'It's not your business to question my judgment. Just obey your orders.' To break the impasse, Kevin had driven to Woods's home on a Saturday morning and, after going through the figures, had understood his criticism. Both men had telephoned Maxwell to protest. But their appeal was in vain. That deal, recalled Woods, was the first sign of Maxwell's bad judgment. The Macmillan deal in October 1988 was the second.

In the midst of the Macmillan saga, Woods had cautioned Maxwell about the price. 'Don't worry,' smiled the Publisher, touching Woods on the knee, 'I won't offer more than $80 a share.' Shortly afterwards, he paid $90.25, nearly $1 billion more than the company was worth, just to secure a place in history. Woods was appalled and invoked the innovation of which he was proudest – a computer programme capable of predicting Maxwell's profits. On the eve of that final bid, he had unfolded over his employer's desk a spread-sheet forecasting the consequence of the Macmillan purchase. 'You'll be liable for surplus ACT,' he said, referring to heavy exposure to taxation. 'That's going to hit profits. And that's going to hit MCC's share price.'

For a moment, there was silence. None of the usual telephone calls interrupted Maxwell. 'Very interesting,' he murmured at last. 'Has anyone else seen this?'

'No,' replied Woods, understanding the reason for the question. 'If MCC's share price falls, it will affect the private-side companies' – many of whose loans were secured against MCC shares.

Again there was silence. Woods added, 'I'm predicting a five per cent to eleven per cent growth rate – at best.'

Maxwell folded the paper: 'I'll get twenty per cent.' Woods was dismissed from the room.

Days later, Maxwell borrowed a further £170 million from Lloyds Bank to part-finance his purchase of the Official Airline Guides. For Woods, it boded another tax nightmare, with more harmful consequences for MCC's share price.

Ever since then, Woods's fears had grown as he observed Maxwell's efforts to prop up MCC's profits. In October 1990 he offered Kevin an unorthodox solution. If MCC's share price fell further, said Woods with an air of self-congratulation, the family would be able cheaply to buy (through the Mirror Group, still privately owned by Maxwell) the remaining 40 per cent of MCC shares owned by the public. 'That's an interesting idea,' answered Kevin, recognizing Woods's naivety about the state of the family's finances. 'I hadn't thought of that.' To his relief, the real crisis had not yet penetrated even into the inner sanctum.

Woods's misgivings had been interpreted by Maxwell as evidence of disloyalty, the cardinal sin in the dictator's eyes. Maxwell's displeasure was aggravated when a secretary in Woods's department was suspected of leaking to the satirical magazine *Private Eye* stories of a sexual affair between herself and Maxwell.

'Sack her,' ordered Maxwell, doubly outraged by the association with the magazine he had successfully sued for defamation. Woods refused. 'She's innocent,' he insisted. But he was proved wrong. The secretary had forged letters and had invented the relationship. Woods was deemed to be a traitor. 'Kick him out of his room,' instructed Maxwell. Woods was removed from his plush office and dispatched to the equivalent of a dungeon, a shabby room in an outbuilding without a secretary. He hinted that he would resign his directorships, but Maxwell gambled correctly that his tax expert, like so many employees, would bear the embarrassment to avoid losing his high salary.

Of all those people in autumn 1990, few were as trusted by Robert and Kevin Maxwell as Larry Trachtenberg, an excitable, thirty-seven-year-old Californian international relations graduate who until 1985 had sought a PhD at the London School of Economics. During his period at the LSE, Trachtenberg had been renowned as the legman, the gofer amiably operating a photocopying machine late into the night to please a tutor, until he abandoned his studies to earn his fortune. In 1987, his babbling self-salesmanship had beguiled both Robert and Kevin Maxwell into believing him to be a talented investor and, keen to become rich, he had wilfully lent himself as the Maxwells' tool. The American's misfortune was his ignorance about the rules governing behaviour in the City. Untrained in finance, he casually assumed an expertise he lacked.

Almost every day, after the 7 a.m. 'prayer meeting' with his father, Kevin awaited Trachtenberg in his office. Together they agreed the implementation of Robert Maxwell's orders: principally to use the £700 million plus in the pension funds to finance the empire's difficulties. In Maxwell's opinion, it was a stroke of genius to delegate to an underling under his own and Kevin's supervision the negotiations being undertaken with banks over the use of the pension funds. By removing himself from personal contact, Maxwell could always deny any knowledge of any wrongdoing and maintain his worldwide profile as one of the globe's media moguls. Concealing reality was, he knew, vital for survival.

Maxwell had begun using pension fund money as a temporary

palliative in 1986. In that year he borrowed £1.5 million from MCC's pension fund. In 1987 he borrowed £9 million. Both sums were repaid. His alleged legal authorization flowed from the 'Powers of Investment' clause in the fund's deed of trust. But the clause stipulated that the trustees could only 'lend money on such security as the Trustees think fit to any person except an Employer'. Accordingly, Maxwell was breaking the terms of the trust from 1986 onwards. Only the Publisher understood the irony of the presence in his wooden bookcase of a book called 'Creative Accounting' by Ian Griffiths. Chapter 4 was entitled, 'How to pilfer the pension fund'.

In 1988, two of Maxwell's financial ambitions coalesced. He wanted common management for the nine pension funds under his control – Mirror Group Pension Scheme, Maxwell Communication Staff Pension Plan, Maxwell Communication Works Pension Plan and six private pension schemes – and he aspired to own a bank. Both ambitions would allow him to authorize investments of other people's funds for his own personal benefit. He prided himself on being a shrewd investor, in currencies and gilts as well as shares. In 1986, he boasted that he had earned £76 million by buying and then breaking up the Philip Hill Investment Trust, an operation which had earned him genuine acclaim from cynical City observers. His genius was that he had not paid a penny. Instead he issued 112.6 million MCC shares worth £306 million. He then sold off most of the Trust's assets and used the cash to finance a buying spree in North America. Among the purchasers of the shares owned by the Trust was his own staff pension fund.

On Maxwell's instructions, the pension fund bought from Philip Hill 12.4 million shares in Beechams, the pharmaceutical company. Three months later, just before a take-over bid for Beechams was announced, he ordered that the same shares be sold to MCC. When the news of the bid broke, the share price soared. Then, in March 1987, just before the end of the company's financial year, MCC sold the same shares back to the pension fund and pocketed £17.4 million in profit. That ploy allowed Maxwell days later to boast that MCC had earned 'record profits'. Only after his death would he be accused of receiving insider knowledge about Beechams, enabling him to manipulate the ownership of the shares and steal from the pension funds.

Over those ensuing years, Maxwell's personal investments in banks – Ansbacher, Guinness Peat, Singer and Friedlander, the Midland and Robert Fraser – reflected his ambition to earn a fortune by controlling other people's money. In his dream, he was emulating Lord Stevens, another newspaper baron and in Maxwell's opinion 'a spectacular success,' who with Lord Rippon had transformed Invesco MIM into a £2 billion investment management fund. Hence in 1988 Maxwell established a new framework for the management of the pension funds. He had few qualms about his use of the funds. Soon after buying the *Mirror* in 1984, he had told Ken Angell, a former Mirror Group employee, 'I own the pension fund.' Angell, knowing that pension funds are vested in trustees on behalf of their beneficiaries, was surprised, but, when challenged, Maxwell logically explained his assertion. Since he personally owned the Mirror Group, and the pension fund effectively came under his control, he 'owned' the pension fund. To his delight, the funds were always in surplus.

The instrument for Maxwell's control of the pension funds was BIM's manager Trevor Cook, born in Northumberland in 1949, who had obtained a first-class degree in mathematics from Newcastle University. Appointed on 2 October 1985 as manager of the Mirror Group Pension Scheme, the inoffensive Cook was a pension fund administrator, not an accountant. Maxwell's grounds for the selection were easily established: Cook willingly complied with his employer's demands in return for a handsome salary. Having engineered an unusually close relationship, the Publisher insisted that he be notified in advance of all Cook's movements. 'Maxwell regarded his time as one hundred times more valuable than anyone else's – so he wanted to talk at his convenience,' recalled Cook, who made himself available to his employer's telephone calls at all hours, knowing how much he relished disturbing his minions. Cook had proved himself malleable and easily impressed by Maxwell's investment prowess, convinced that he 'was a safe pair of hands'. Having asserted his 'ownership' of the pension funds, Maxwell directed the investments to suit his requirements. To Cook it appeared that the Publisher's investments were astute and profitable, even if unconventional.

In March 1988, Maxwell had pooled four pension funds – benefiting at the peak 23,400 employees and worth over £700 million

– into one Common Investment Fund (CIF). The management of CIF was entrusted to another Maxwell creation, Bishopsgate Investment Management (BIM), a non-profit-making organization. Both inventions had been established under the 1986 Financial Services Act with the permission of the Investment Management Regulatory Organization (IMRO), the government-appointed regulator. Given Maxwell's history, John Morgan, IMRO's director, should have been cautious. On his original written application, Maxwell had written that BIM was owned by the Pergamon Foundation Stiftung, a charitable body based in Liechtenstein. After reading the application, an IMRO official asked Cook for the Liechtenstein accounts. Cook asked Ron Woods, who in turn asked Maxwell. 'Impossible!' screamed Maxwell. 'They can't have them!'

'They won't authorize BIM without the accounts,' pleaded Woods. But Maxwell was implacable – for good reason. The Foundation had no staff and no premises and produced no accounts to prove that it controlled any money. It was a legal fiction managed by his Swiss lawyers, who were paid to refuse answers to any questions. Maxwell was chairman of the trustees and, in his opinion, beyond mortal scrutiny. 'There are no Liechtenstein accounts,' Cook wrote to IMRO. Surprisingly, there was no reaction.

Maxwell's escape from the potential trap had been effortless. Since the law required that BIM be owned by a registered charitable trust with proper accounts, he just invented one. The figment of his imagination was called the Maxwell Charitable Trust, its creation partly supervised by Deborah Maxwell, his legal adviser. Under the proposed structure, the Trust would control BIM, although neither actually employed any staff. The Trust was effectively just Robert Maxwell, without any trustees appointed by the pension funds, though including one trustee, David Corsan, a retired Coopers auditor who was also an IMRO director. BIM's manager Trevor Cook and his staff were employed by Headington Holdings, a subsidiary of Headington Hill Investments. That extraordinary structure was ignored by the government's regulator after the initial application was withdrawn, and on 6 April 1988 BIM received formal approval to manage the pension funds of over 20,000 employees from offices at 4/12 Dorrington Street, near Maxwell House. Cook was appointed the compliance officer, formally responsible for BIM's obedience to the laws and for the company's liaison with the regulatory authority.

Under BIM's articles, Robert, Kevin and Ian Maxwell, the leading
directors, wielded only limited powers, but inevitably those rules
were ignored by Robert Maxwell, albeit unchallenged by Ron
Woods, Trevor Cook, Robert Bunn (until his resignation in 1990)
and the other directors. Unknown to them, in a legal ruse to protect
himself in the event of any future inquiry, Maxwell had falsified the
board minutes to appoint himself the sole arbiter of the company's
management. In the event, he decided on investments – sales and
purchases – without reference to anyone else. His action mirrored
MCC board minutes of November 1981 which permitted him to
act as a 'committee of MCC's board of directors', bestowing upon
himself uncontrolled powers over the public company, including
the right to be the sole signatory of cheques for unlimited amounts.
Naturally, these changes in the running of BIM were kept a close
secret. They existed only as a legal safeguard if trouble arose.

Maxwell quickly established a pattern of management of the
pension funds. At BIM's monthly meetings, religiously attended by
Robert and Kevin and occasionally by Ian, the directors reviewed
and approved BIM's portfolio of investments. Cook and his deputy,
Jeffrey Highfield, merely took care to monitor the minutes,
acknowledging that the right to buy and sell shares belonged to the
directors. Every month, they circulated a schedule of BIM's portfolio of shares. So none of the Maxwells could ever be in any real
doubt whether particular shares belonged to the pension funds or
to their private companies.

In September 1988, Maxwell decided to establish tighter control
over the pension investments. His excuse was the discovery of a
fraud of £7,000 in the payment of pensions to former employees.
A subsequent report by accountants concluded that the pensions
administration was a 'shambles'. Summoning Cook and Highfield,
he announced that authority for the management of BIM and the
CIF investments was to be vested in Robert Bunn, the accountant
employed by his private companies. 'Bunn will handle all relations
with the brokers and investment houses,' he said. 'We are involved
in a large number of take-overs and mergers. Bunn has better
expertise. Bunn will have all the powers. Your responsibility will
be solely BIM's administration.' At the end of their employer's
ten-minute speech, neither man protested.

But within weeks Highfield was complaining to Cook: 'Bunn isn't

telling me about the actual investments.' Cook remained silent, unwilling to question Maxwell's edict that 'We are ruled by IMRO, and
we must not reveal price-sensitive information.' Highfield was puzzled.
Cook had already accepted another limitation upon himself. Three
months earlier, in July 1988, Maxwell had decided that BIM and the
pension funds would enter into a special and unusual relationship
with yet another private Maxwell company, London & Bishopsgate
Investments. LBI was the preliminary vehicle for Maxwell's
ambitions to control a bank. Not surprisingly, Cook did not understand the importance LBI would assume. 'Go and talk to the LBI
people,' urged Maxwell soothingly, 'and satisfy yourself of their competence.' Cook had obliged and did not object to the relationship.

The creation of LBI was the direct consequence of Maxwell's
introduction to Larry Trachtenberg and another American, Andrew
Smith, renowned as 'a smooth New York computer jock'. Model-
ling himself on the Wall Street brokers in Tom Wolfe's novel, *Bon-
fire of the Vanities*, Smith was a fast-talking, self-confident smoothie
wearing braces over heavily starched shirts. His appearance and
manner shrieked a dealer determined to make his fortune. In 1989,
Smith, introduced to Maxwell by his father, a German banker,
had professed that his hero was Michael Milken, the American
arbitrageur and junk-bond specialist who by 1990 was on course
for imprisonment.

Trachtenberg and Smith had met at the London School of Economics in 1985, both of them eager to join the rich in that booming
era. Their initial ploy had been to exploit the exploding market for
information and sell newsletters of financial and political analysis
to banks, industrialists and investors. The information had been
compiled by LSE students based on published sources. That easy
money fed the two men's ambitions. Technology was their answer.
By 1987 when they met Maxwell, they had invented a computer
system which, in theory, monitored all the international economies
and markets to identify perfect investment opportunities before any
mere mortals could do so. Calling themselves Global Analysis
Systems (GAS), they were presented to Maxwell, an unrestrained
admirer of technology, not as mere analysts but as investment managers. All they required was other people's money to earn millions.

Entranced by their gimmick, Maxwell felt that they lacked grav-
itas. They needed the respectability that could be provided by

employing in their firm an established personality in the financial community. That role, he believed, could be best performed by Lord Donoughue, a socialist academic who in the 1970s had served as a policy adviser to Harold Wilson before self-interest prompted him to switch ideologies in the 1980s to capitalism. In 1988, Bernard Donoughue, aged fifty-four, was employed as a director at Kleinwort Benson, the merchant bank, where he was responsible for research. Maxwell, the frustrated Labour politician, was keen to recruit any of Wilson's team, and Donoughue leapt at the giant salary offered. He would be paid £180,000 per annum, plus £36,000 annual contribution towards his pension and an annual Christmas bonus of £200,000. In addition to that total of £436,000, Maxwell would provide a home in Westminster, close to parliament. An added attraction to LBI's new, full-time executive vice-chairman (under Maxwell himself) was his belief that £300 million of Maxwell's money was 'sloshing about' in various merchant banks waiting to be invested.

Donoughue's income matched those of his two colleagues and co-directors. Trachtenberg's initial annual salary in 1988 had been £80,000 but his income was boosted in the following year by a performance bonus of £125,000. Soon after its payment, Maxwell's auditors realized that the bonus for all three directors had been paid on what were called 'erroneous figures', but it proved impossible for Kevin to overcome Donoughue's stubborn objections and recover the money. That largesse, the loss of hundreds of thousands of pounds by sheer dilatoriness or negligence, contradicted the cultivated image of Maxwell as a ruthless cost-cutter and was a measure of the true state of the empire's finances. Accordingly, in 1989, Trachtenberg's income was consolidated at an annual salary of £185,000 plus £18,500 towards his pension, and Smith was paid £150,000 without any pension contribution. Trachtenberg was assured of a Christmas bonus of £125,000, Smith one of £200,000.

The trio, Trachtenberg, Smith and Donoughue, were formally embraced within Maxwell's empire as directors of LBI – London & Bishopsgate Investments – with Robert and Kevin Maxwell. (Headington Hill Investments, the controlling company of all Maxwell's private companies, bought a 60 per cent stake in GAS, which was then renamed London & Bishopsgate International Investment Inc. – LBII.) It was no coincidence that 'London & Bishopsgate' featured in the names of a growing number of Maxwell's private companies. Among the twelve Bishopsgate companies was London & Bishopsgate Traders, London & Bishopsgate Holdings, London & Bishopsgate Group, London & Bishopsgate International NV and London & Bishopsgate International Management. All performed very different functions but, as Maxwell intended, the similarity of the names was liable to confuse outsiders. Adding to the confusion, some of the different London & Bishopsgate companies operated from the same premises and with the same staff.

Having established LBI as his new 'investment bank', with IMRO approval, Maxwell sought customers to establish his credibility for financial management. In spring 1988, he bought 25 per cent of First Tokyo Trust, a Scottish investment trust founded in 1980 which controlled £70 million of Japanese shares owned by institutions and private investors. Although Maxwell posed as a buyer in the name of London & Bishopsgate Holdings, a third of the money he used belonged to the pension funds.

Initially, Maxwell's investment (codenamed 'Setting Sun') did not alarm Alan McInroy, the sober Scottish chairman of the First Tokyo Trust, who thought Donoughue 'charming and competent'. Over the following two years, if any man other than the Maxwells could understand what was happening within First Tokyo, it was Donoughue. Donoughue presented himself, Larry Trachtenberg and Andrew Smith as investment geniuses. Their proposal to McInroy was to improve First Tokyo's unspectacular performance. Instead of simply investing in Japanese shares, said Donoughue, the Trust should sign a contract to use LBI's computer programme 'Japan 60 GAS' to anticipate the Japanese market's performance and beat other investors.

Initially, McInroy was irked by Donoughue's ambitions and opposed the plan, because it contradicted the Trust's sober purpose, and anyway the transfer of the Trust's powers to LBI would be expensive. But McInroy was soon outmanoeuvred. Exploiting his svelte patter and his political background, Donoughue had toured the institutions, winning their support for his idea. His management of the Trust was confirmed on 9 January 1989 when he joined First Tokyo's board with two other Maxwell employees, George Willet, a taciturn merchant banker, and Robert Bunn. Just at the moment when Maxwell's need for money – to buy MCC shares, to pump

money into MCC by purchasing assets, and to pay for his accumu-
lated losses since the stock market crash in 1987 – became pressing,
McInroy had effectively allowed his control over the board's six
directors to dissolve, except *in extremis* by use of his casting vote.
'I had no choice,' he would explain. 'The institutions supported
Donoughue and Maxwell.'

Soon after, the Tokyo market fell sharply and Andrew Smith
offered Maxwell a solution. It was called stock lending, a perfectly
legitimate strategy invented in New York. Financial institutions and
investors often required shares for a short period – overnight or a
few days – to comply with securities laws or to cover speculative
positions. Rather than buying the shares and incurring substantial
costs, the investors borrowed them for a fee. In turn, to protect the
registered shareholder from loss or theft, the borrower provided
securities or cash worth more than the shares. Undertaken in this
way, stock lending was risk-free.

It was in its pure form that, on 27 January 1989, Trachtenberg and
Smith suggested to McInroy that First Tokyo could generate extra
income at no risk by stock lending the shares in its reduced £60 million fund. Overcoming his initial reservations, McInroy agreed to a
six-month trial. Unfortunately, however, he failed to ask a number
of pertinent questions about the transactions, and most of all he failed
to examine the contract between First Tokyo and LBI. He merely
demanded that Morgan Stanley, the Trust's bank which held the
share certificates in its safe in London, should accept all the risk.
Trachtenberg and Donoughue were told to obtain an undertaking
to that effect from Morgan Stanley, whose vice-president Thomas
Christofferson duly gave it. Trachtenberg and Donoughue then
assured McInroy that the bank had agreed to be the guarantor,
though the First Tokyo chairman appears never to have asked for
written evidence. 'That wasn't my responsibility,' he later explained.

Inevitably there was confusion about responsibility for the man-
agement of First Tokyo's £60 million – confusion which was very
much Robert Maxwell's intention. First Tokyo had a contract with
London & Bishopsgate International Investment Management, who
were to manage the fund in accordance with the wishes of First
Tokyo's board of directors. LBIIM was owned by London &
Bishopsgate Holdings, which in turn was owned by Headington
Hill Investments, Maxwell's private company ultimately owned by

the Liechtenstein foundation. But it was the entirely distinct LBI which was undertaking the stock lending. This confusion was ignored by McInroy, not least because during the first year the profits seemed to exceed expectations.

McInroy's legal advisers seem also not to have appreciated the deft self-protection of LBIIM's contract with First Tokyo. While one clause at the top of the agreement permitted stock lending, another, much later clause allowed LBIIM to stock lend 'in house' for a 'fair price'. Astutely, Maxwell and his cohorts had covered themselves in the event of future recriminations.

Unknown to McInroy, soon after the stock lending was approved Maxwell allowed Trachtenberg to use First Tokyo's shares in an unauthorized manner. First Tokyo's stock was being lent, not in an orthodox way on the open market, but to Maxwell privately, that is to London & Bishopsgate Holdings. And the collateral for the prime Japanese stock was not cash but MCC shares. To the Maxwells, the beauty of the operation was that First Tokyo's shares were never sold, so preserving the myth that the fund was inviolate and untouched. The only risk was to First Tokyo's innocent investors. The evidence suggests that by February 1990 Lord Donoughue ought to have suspected the unannounced use of those shares. In September of that year, Kevin would offer some of those First Tokyo shares to Julie Maitland of Crédit Suisse as collateral for the £50 million private loan.

By November 1990, as Maxwell vainly searched for relief from the recession and from the rising interest rates on his total debt of $3.5 billion, First Tokyo's £60 million was only a small part of his requirements. For more than a year, he had also been stock lending pension fund shares using the technique proposed by Trachtenberg and Smith. During summer 1989, on the Maxwells' instructions, Trachtenberg had negotiated the use of pension fund shares to raise cash from John Di Rocco, head of Lehman Brothers' International securities lending department. To conceal the scheme, the contract signed by Kevin on BIM's behalf was made complicated. Lehmans would be given shares from BIM's portfolio, and in exchange would give Treasury bills to Maxwell. Maxwell would immediately sell the bills back to Lehmans, who would pay him in cash. The end result would be that Maxwell had cash and Lehmans had the security of the pension fund shares. In theory, the pension funds would retrieve their shares after buying back the Treasury bills. In the meantime, the impression was preserved that the pension funds still owned the shares unencumbered.

There was one major obstacle to overcome to obtain that cash. On each share certificate, the owner was registered as BIM. To use those pension fund shares, Maxwell needed to invent a cover story to explain his entry into such an unusual transaction.

The reason provided by Trachtenberg to Di Rocco was that BIM needed cash so that it could reinvest the money in shares which would produce higher returns than its existing portfolio, while simultaneously retaining the investment benefit of the shares it pledged. To Maxwell's delight, Di Rocco accepted the business. Whether the banker realized by specific inquiries that BIM was the manager of pension fund assets would remain uncertain and be subsequently contested. But he and his superiors did realize that the arrangement was 'purely a funding exercise', and their suspicions ought to have been aroused because the circumstances were so unusual. It was unusual in two ways: first, the bank was to pay the cash into Maxwell's private accounts; and second, neither Trachtenberg nor Andrew Smith was a director of BIM. Indeed, Trachtenberg said he represented LBIIM, which was acting as BIM's agent.

There was one final hurdle. Before the pension fund shares could be used for stock lending, Trachtenberg required Trevor Cook's consent. At the end of October 1989, after reading LBI's terms for stock lending, Cook, BIM's manager, signed an agreement. But that agreement – between BIM and LBI – was different from the contract with Lehmans signed by Kevin on LBI's behalf, which was not for stock lending but for a loan.

To Cook, everything appeared normal. Working in an open-plan office in Dorrington Street with files marked 'Stock lending accounts', he and his deputy Jeff Highfield received monthly accounts from LBI recording the value of the stock lending: Cook in turn would bill LBI for the agreed 1.75 per cent fee. Cook's willingness to be helpful made the Maxwells' task much easier. He never asked to see the contracts.

Throughout 1989, with Cook's agreement, Maxwell had also been personally borrowing increasing amounts of money from BIM, rising from £5 million to £22.5 million. To extinguish the debt, Maxwell 'sold' to BIM privately owned shares, but publicly he did not reveal the change of ownership. 'We'll always give the pension funds first refusal to earn profits from our share deals,' Maxwell had told Cook. To the manager, the offer appeared generous. Apparently he remained unsuspicious even when Maxwell's £22.5 million borrowing during 1989 cost the pension funds £510,000.

Having established Cook's willingness to accept directives, Maxwell summoned him in January 1990. 'I have decided it would be in BIM's interest to buy more MCC shares,' he said. 'The price is certain to rise.' Cook agreed, without questioning Maxwell's misplaced confidence. BIM would pay £63.2 million for MCC shares owned by Maxwell personally. Cook not only agreed to the 'offer' but did not demand that the shares be registered in BIM's name. Instead, the shares remained registered as Maxwell's property, and he borrowed another £26 million of the pension funds' money to finance MCC. Cook would subsequently explain, 'I didn't realize the ownership could be abused.'

That March, Maxwell called in Cook twice more. The price of MCC shares was falling despite his prediction two months earlier and he wanted to push it back up. 'I think it would be beneficial for BIM to buy more MCC shares,' he said. Two deals were concluded, which were to lose the pension funds £7.4 million. On the 20th, BIM purchased a call option on 10 million MCC shares through Sheinberg at Goldman Sachs. Days before the end of the financial year, BIM paid £20 million for the shares, £2.4 million more than their worth, to boost MCC's price. On 29 March, BIM sold 7.9 million MCC shares through Goldmans. In the second deal, BIM bought a call option from Goldmans on a further 10 million MCC shares for £18.9 million. One month later, the deal was booked to BIT (Bishopsgate Investment Trust, the nominee company used by Maxwell to retain pension fund shares and cash). The option, exercised on 29 June, cost BIM £5 million.

On 31 March 1990, the end of the financial year, Maxwell's debt to the pension fund was still £13.5 million, so to remove it from the annual accounts he repaid it. The following day, he withdrew the money again. Thereafter his use of pension fund money rocketed. By 29 June, he had taken £105 million from BIM. To settle that debt, he told Cook that he was 'selling' to the pension funds his private stake in Invesco MIM and 5.4 million shares in Scitex, an Israeli high-tech company producing imaging systems for the publishing industry. Maxwell had bought 9.59 million Scitex shares (after rights issue) in December 1988 for $39 million or £24 million. Their value would rise to $220 million. The shares Maxwell offered Cook represented three-quarters of his stake in the company and would be worth £102 million.

Cook accepted this 'offer' too. He listed the Scitex and Invesco shares as part of BIM's management of pension funds and removed Maxwell's private £105 million debt from the accounts. But he failed to register the shares officially in Israel as owned by the pension fund. This, he explained, was 'because I had signed a personal agreement with Robert Maxwell that he was holding the shares on BIM's behalf'. Even worse, he did not secure possession of the share certificates.

Maxwell's complete control over BIM and the pension funds was, to his and Kevin's increasing irritation, not duplicated at LBI, where a crisis had arisen among the directors. The cause was Mark Tapley, recruited as the new managing director in January 1990. Clean-cut, honest and ambitious to make his fortune in London's rollicking financial markets, Tapley had been employed in the 1970s at J.P. Morgan and had been lured to LBI from Lehmans by Smith and Lord Donoughue on a generous salary for a three-year contract plus bonuses.

Within days of his arrival, Tapley had become alarmed by LBI's administrative chaos, for which he blamed Larry Trachtenberg. He was also unhappy with Andrew Smith's exaggerated claims about past performance and who, moreover, appeared to be trading in shares in what Tapley considered an unacceptable manner. 'That's a conflict of interest,' he cautioned Smith. Soon afterwards, Smith returned to New York to establish LBI Inc. with £10 million capital provided by Maxwell, continuing his collaboration with Trachtenberg and Donoughue, although the latter referred to the American as 'Adolf Smith'. 'We must get rid of Trachtenberg,' Tapley told Donoughue. 'We must get him out of LBI.' But Donoughue did not respond. By then, he had become Kevin's confidant and no week passed without his name featuring in the Maxwell son's diary.

On 1 April 1990, glancing at LBI's 1989 accounts, Tapley noticed the high fees LBI was earning from the stock-lending programme. 'Where are these fees coming from?' he asked Trachtenberg. The American only replied, 'It's all done through Morgan Stanley with their guarantee.' Tapley's curiosity was not satisfied. Searching through the records of the stock lending, he came across the name of Thomas Christofferson, of Morgan Stanley. Christofferson was grateful to Kevin for placing LBI's custodian business with his bank. It was an easy source of income. Until November 1991, Christofferson would, on demand from either Kevin or Trachtenberg, innocently sign letters and release share certificates which diverted the shares belonging to First Tokyo and others.

Although Tapley noticed that Trachtenberg was telephoning Morgan Stanley and ordering them to pledge First Tokyo's shares to other banks as formal stock lending, reading LBI's print-outs he was puzzled that they failed to identify the shares loaned. Instead, Trachtenberg's oral instructions to Morgan Stanley were recorded on the computer only as 'shares held on order of . . . bank'. Tapley demanded to know what was the authority for stock lending First Tokyo's shares. 'We're doing it on Maxwell's orders,' stated Trachtenberg. He then added disingenuously: 'We don't know to whom the stock is being lent.'

Tapley's initial concern had been that Trachtenberg was carelessly omitting to keep a record of his instructions to Morgan Stanley. By April 1990, he realized it was worse than that. His source was Jonathan Ford, a former Coopers accountant recruited by Maxwell to work in LBI. 'I've been in the investment business for twenty years,' said Tapley, 'and I've never earned so much from stock lending. How do you do it?'

'Because it comes from the Mirror Group,' replied Ford with startling honesty.

Tapley gasped, 'This is another conflict of interest. It will be forbidden by IMRO.'

Tapley appealed to Kevin. It was an unwelcome approach and Kevin repeatedly cancelled the appointment. When they finally met, Kevin agreed, 'We must close that stock-lending operation down.' But he made it clear that Tapley was no longer welcome in his office – he was disrupting the Maxwells' operation. Of course the stock lending would not stop, but Kevin agreed with his father that it might be dangerous to dismiss the manager in breach of his contract. Better to keep him inside the tent and quiet. For his part, Tapley did not welcome the prospect of litigation with the Maxwells if he himself sought to break his contract, nor would he relish the loss of his high income in the middle of a recession.

Come July 1990, Tapley was still concerned by LBI's stock lending of First Tokyo shares. 'Why are you bothered?' asked Trachtenberg. 'It's nothing to do with you!' By then, Stuart Carson, LBI's new compliance officer, responsible in the new self-regulatory era for ensuring fulfilment of statutory requirements, had consulted IMRO. The regulatory agency confirmed that IMRO rules did not forbid the conflict of interest prompted by stock lending. 'It isn't forbidden,' reported Carson.

Two palliatives were proposed. Jean-Pierre Anselmini, MCC's French deputy chairman, was that same July temporarily appointed an LBI director. Tapley's initial relief disappeared when Anselmini began to postpone important meetings. 'You're intransigent,' he told Tapley in stilted English, 'making the management more difficult by distressingly insisting upon standards against Smith.' Tapley's appeals to Donoughue were also rebuffed. Urging self-restraint, the peer told him, 'We must try and keep this together. We're a good team.' Donoughue was supported by George Willet: 'Don't go to IMRO. Stop making distinctions between moral and legal issues.' Tapley was persuaded to keep quiet by three men whose motives he found unclear. Tapley accorded Donoughue the nickname 'Manuel', the character in the television sitcom *Fawlty Towers* famous for his repeated claim, 'I know nothing.'

At the end of the day on 3 August 1990, after many cancelled meetings, Tapley was finally admitted once more into Kevin's office. 'The stock lending must stop,' agreed Robert Maxwell. Satisfied that he had got what he wanted, Tapley distributed a memorandum describing a newly reorganized LBI which would exclude Smith and Trachtenberg. Two hours later, Kevin telephoned, his voice betraying deep anger: 'That memo must be withdrawn. It's premature.' During that short interval, Kevin had understood the implications for the empire's survival of Trachtenberg's removal.

In the course of successive meetings in late October and November, Tapley was convinced by Kevin and Donoughue that LBI would be reorganized. 'We'll get rid of the Max Factor,' both pledged, referring to the negative influence of Robert Maxwell. Tapley was relieved. But in reality he had been sidelined. The Maxwells' priority was to silence their critic while they sought cash from any source to sustain their increasing debts. In September Kevin had committed himself to his father's scheme of arrangement. Searching through BIM's monthly schedule of shares owned by the pension funds, he had noticed the name Euris, a French investment fund. Euris, he knew, did not issue share certificates. Instead, the only proof of ownership were the records held by the company's secretary. Transfer of ownership was settled by a simple letter notifying a sale.

On 3 September 1990, Kevin wrote, as a director of BIM, to Euris's company secretary instructing that 2.2 million shares worth £32 million had been 'transferred' from BIM to Pergamon Holdings, a transfer which contravened the trust deed. (The board minutes were signed by Kevin, Ian and Robert Maxwell, with Anselmini as a witness. BIM's articles required two signatures for a transfer.) On the same day, Kevin pledged the shares to BNP, the French bank, as collateral for a private loan. He then kept silent about the transfer. Trevor Cook, BIM's manager, was not told, and Euris remained listed on BIM's schedule as a pension fund share. By any measure, it was unauthorized, but it was a mere curtain-raiser to the increasingly drastic measures undertaken by Kevin to raise cash during October.

His targets were two fund managers of pension fund shares. In October 1990, he asked the managers of Capel Cure Myers and Invesco MIM for the temporary return of shares owned by the pension funds for stock lending. On 8 October, Capel Cure, on Kevin's instructions, sent shares worth £40 million for stock lending to Lehmans. Capel Cure's covering letter explicitly informed the bank that the shares were owned by the Mirror Group Pension Scheme. The reason for their action, some suggest, was that an assistant director at Capel Cure appreciated that the pension fund shares were to be used as collateral for a loan rather than for stock lending and sought to protect his position.

The following day, 9 October 1990, Kevin and Cook, acting as BIM directors, instructed Invesco to send its pension fund portfolio worth £30 million to Lehmans. The letter, signed by Kevin on behalf of the Mirror Group Pension Scheme, assured Invesco that the shares would be used for normal stock lending and returned 'within 30 days'. Lawrence Guest, a Mirror Group director and one of the fund's trustees, was not told about the 'stock lending'. He would only discover in November 1991. Initially, there was no reason for the other fund managers to suspect that Kevin's instruction was not straightforward, but the arrangement did disturb Tim Daily, Invesco's expert in stock lending. Daily, twenty-seven years old, was an ambitious, working-class trader born in Watford with just six O levels who unashamedly wanted 'to taste the good things in life'. Hired in April 1990 to expand Invesco's stock-lending business, he had recently been appointed the chairman of the International Stock Lending Association, the industry's spokesman in dealing with both the media and the Bank of England. Among his targets for Invesco's new stock-lending business were the Maxwell pension funds.

The news that Maxwell was intending to use a rival for stock lending was passed to Daily that same day, 9 October, in a panic telephone call from Peter Smith, his subordinate. Daily, in Naples, Florida attending a stock-lending conference, was chastened by the report. 'It all sounds a little bit fishy,' Smith told Daily, 'and not quite as cut and dry as it seems.' On hearing the news, he added, he had telephoned a friend at Lehmans and had been told that the portfolio was to be used not for stock lending but 'purely as collateral for a loan'. Smith added that, to his surprise, Trachtenberg had also telephoned asking him not to speak to Lehmans. Daily decided to approach Mark Haas, the bearded and ambitious Lehmans securities executive responsible for negotiating the transaction with Kevin and Trachtenberg, who was also attending the conference in Florida.

Minutes later, Daily found Haas watching a game of pool. 'Are you taking away our client for stock lending?'

'No,' replied Haas. 'We're doing a Treasury repo. Not stock lending. Maxwell is having trouble raising cash' and was using pension fund assets. Haas knew that MCC, under pressure to repay debts, had asked Lehmans for a $15 million loan for one month. His superiors, after reading MCC's accounts, had vetoed the idea out of fear of Maxwell's 'potential for manipulation [of] profits' and because MCC's accounts revealed assets of minus $2.2 billion because of the debts. Moreover, at Lehmans, the very nature of the transaction – whereby shares 'borrowed' by Kevin were exchanged for the final total of $83.9 million in cash and paid to Maxwell's private company – enabled the bankers to understand precisely the unusual use that was being made of pension fund assets.

Haas did not reveal those details that day in Florida, but enough had been said to prompt Daily's comment: 'I don't like the sound of it. It's a bit dodgy.'

'We haven't had this conversation,' replied Haas. 'I know my half. You know your half. Together we know too much.' Haas would deny this version of the conversation.

Daily ignored this advice and reported the conversation to Bob Southgate, his superior in London. Southgate's reaction was, 'It's all very sensitive,' referring not to Maxwell's financial predicament, but to the fact that Maxwell owned a 20 per cent stake in Invesco MIM and was a friend of the fund's chairman, Lord Stevens (moreover its president was Lord Rippon, a director of MCC). After a number of huddled conversations, Invesco's managers agreed to accept Maxwell's assurances.

In the event, the pension fund shares were exchanged with Lehmans for Treasury bills which were then cashed. The money was paid not to the pension funds but to LBI and then to Headington Hill Investments, Maxwell's private company. The bankers' apparent lack of concern that Maxwell might have been using pension fund shares to raise cash was reflected in their confused records. Haas was dealing with LBI, Maxwell's private investment company, which allegedly was representing BIM, the pension fund managers. Yet in Lehmans' records the depositor of the shares was recorded as 'LBIIM', a different entity, suggesting unusual carelessness by the bank.

Trevor Cook, meanwhile, was not only ignorant of the deal negotiated by Trachtenberg and Kevin with Lehmans, but when on 16 October Daily arrived at a Maxwell office in Shoe Lane to meet him and Trachtenberg, he remained unaware of the Invesco trader's conversation with Haas. Daily had invited himself to present his expertise in stock lending. Towards the end of the meeting, Trachtenberg explained to Daily that LBI was paying 1.75 per cent for stock-lending fees. Although Daily realized that the figure was higher than normal, he said nothing. Cook also stayed silent: he knew that LBI's fees might be high but he 'had no point of reference'. Any doubts were offset by Donoughue's presence within LBI. 'I trusted Donoughue and he knew that we were stock lending the pension fund assets. I assumed it was all right,' recalled Cook.

'That was a load of rubbish,' Daily said to his colleagues as they descended in the lift.

'Don't say anything here,' replied one of the other occupants. 'The lift's probably bugged.'

Cramped into a small office on their return, Daily told his superiors, 'It's all wrong.' The response was equivocal. To refuse to comply with their client's request was out of the question, not least because Maxwell was a shareholder and a friend of Lord Stevens. So, on 19 October, after several telephone calls asking, 'Is it all ready?', Trachtenberg arrived in Invesco's entrance hall and personally took the share certificates from Daily, signing a receipt. On one issue Trachtenberg was insistent: the transfer was temporary. The certificates were to be returned in thirty days.

To regularize the arrangement, Kevin and Robert Maxwell signed a contract. Kevin (on behalf of BIM) and his father (on behalf of the Robert Maxwell Group) agreed that RMG could borrow BIM's stock. Although dated 1 October 1990, it appears to have been formulated at the end of 1990 to cover the Capel Cure and Invesco transactions. It allowed both Kevin and Trachtenberg to reinforce the claim they were making to Cook that pension fund assets were involved in stock lending. But Cook, although he was BIM's manager, was not suspicious. After he had received a letter from Lehmans stating that the shares and Treasury bills 'were held for your account', he assumed that the pension funds were covered by genuine collateral of between 125 and 150 per cent. But he never actually saw any share certificates, nor did he ask to see anything. 'I just got lists and letters,' Cook later reflected ruefully, 'from Trachtenberg on behalf of LBI.' Everything, he believed, was held by the banks. He did not ask to see the Treasury bills nor did he realize that they had been cashed. 'I should have checked the share certificates but I didn't suspect anything. I was fooled.'

The deception was intentional. On returning to his office after meeting Daily, Trachtenberg had sent a revealing memo to Kevin about their arrangement: 'I assured them [Tim Daily and colleagues] that LBI's involvement was in a strictly advisory capacity, and that our [LBI's] involvement in no way involved LBI utilizing stock in security transactions on its own behalf.' The problem, he realized, was how to orchestrate 'a clean transfer' of the pension funds' shares from BIM to the banks, concealing their true ownership. Kevin's reply was not preserved.

At the end of this period of frantic activity, Kevin agreed over the weekend of 3 November to play poker with some friends in the City and host a firework party at Hailey, his home near Wallingford. It was a brief interlude before he secured the £50 million loan from Julie Maitland at Crédit Suisse and obtained the Berlitz share certificates.

THREE

Hunting for Cash

– 19 November 1990 ·

On Monday, 19 November, Kevin flew to New York on the evening Concorde. As usual he stayed at the Carlyle, the choice of many international tycoons as Manhattan's most discreet yet sumptuous hotel. After shuttling between seventeen meetings with Macmillan executives and bankers the following day, he slept overnight on a British Airways Jumbo back to London. He had every reason to feel satisfied. Everyone he had met had appeared reassured by his self-confident manner, his deep-voiced, decisive tone and his air of efficiency. None would have guessed that the polite, well-dressed Englishman was concealing near-bankruptcy. Punctually at 6.30 a.m. the Jumbo glided on to Heathrow's runway, and Kevin separated himself from his fellow passengers to be whisked through the special customs facilities, before being helicoptered by Captain Cowley to Maxwell House in Holborn to begin the day meeting Larry Trachtenberg. The pace was unremitting.

Robert Maxwell was at that moment flying to Los Angeles. Since 12 November, the Chairman had been travelling across America in what he called a roadshow to launch the Central and Eastern European Fund, a banking venture concocted with Merrill Lynch to entice financial institutions into investing $250 million on the basis of his expertise in the former communist countries. To Maxwell, short of money yet eager to exert the influence of a billionaire, the Fund was a last effort to grasp large amounts of other people's money to be used for his own benefit. Over several days, he met bankers, pension fund managers and corporation presidents in an attempt to persuade them to earmark funds. For those like Katherine Pelley, one of the banking aides in his retinue, the roadshow was becoming a harassing adventure. Regularly late to meetings and delivering lacklustre speeches, Maxwell was proving to be a 'nightmare', a liability rather than an asset to his own ambitions. The burden of his deception was sapping his self-confident assertions of his financial prowess. Dispirited, he returned to London for an MCC board meeting, which was to be held at 5 p.m. on 23 November.

Regardless of his perceived troubles and bad press, Robert Maxwell believed that he could still count upon the support and sympathy of the six non-family directors who, though acknowledging that he was a difficult man, believed in his genius. Besides the executive directors Jean-Pierre Anselmini, Ron Woods, Richard Baker and Basil Brookes, the young acting finance director recruited from Coopers in 1986, there were two older non-executive directors: Lord Rippon, the former Conservative minister who had negotiated Britain's entry into the European Union, and Peter Laister, a former managing director of Thorn EMI with a fair reputation in the City.

For all of them, the DTI inspectors' damning judgment in 1971 that Maxwell could not be 'relied on to exercise proper stewardship of a publicly quoted company' was 'history'. All of them had witnessed the 'City process' and tended to feel contempt, even 'disgust', for the slickers' 'behaviour around the carcass'. Maxwell impressed them on several levels: as a polyglot at the centre of an extraordinary network of relations with world leaders; as a newspaper tycoon who had broken the trade unions; and as a superman able to revive dying companies. Accordingly they were prepared to allow the Chairman near-dictatorial powers.

Of course, these men were well rewarded, especially Rippon. As chairman of Brassey's, the military publishers owned by Maxwell, he was paid $100,000 per annum, and he drew generous expenses. On one occasion, Maxwell simply wrote a cheque for £10,000 at his request. For his part, Maxwell admired Rippon's transformation of Invesco MIM, but it was Rippon's bank, the Robert Fraser Group, which gave him the greatest help. Through Robert Fraser, Maxwell had pumped into MCC and Pergamon Holdings some of the money taken from the pension funds, and had completed three property deals to pump profits into MCC which later investigation would reveal to be dubious. In 1989, no less than 33 per cent of MCC's profits were 'one-off' transactions with Robert Fraser recorded just before the announcement of the interim profits. In

1990, 43 per cent of the Group profits were one-offs with companies incorporated in Liechtenstein and the Isle of Man or with BIM and Robert Fraser. But although he could count upon Lord Rippon, Maxwell knew that there were tensions with the other directors. Anselmini, the proud French banker, did not appreciate the way the Publisher ignored his title as deputy chairman, and failed to consult him. A newspaper revelation that Maxwell, to boost MCC's share price, had gambled on a put option with Goldman Sachs had alarmed him. 'You're not the regulator' was Maxwell's response, surprised that the Frenchman should choose to protest now, since the Publisher had bought a similar option from Goldman Sachs of 10 million MCC shares in March 1990 and another from BIT for £18.9 million.

'I don't understand,' sighed Anselmini. 'You do not do what you say or say what you do.' Maxwell had nevertheless abruptly promised not to repeat the ploy.

When eight MCC directors met on 23 November (without Ian Maxwell), Robert Maxwell anticipated some disagreement but, given that around the table were gathered well-paid subordinates whose devotion and above all loyalty had hitherto been unconditional, he expected them to exercise a degree of reticence. All of them had, after all, witnessed how MCC's profits had been maintained only by his skilful property deals and currency speculation – transactions which had attracted the critics' scorn and, more recently, some suspicion, but they had provided the company's only respite from commercial decline. Two items dominated their agenda that day: finalizing the interim accounts, and agreeing the interim dividend.

As always, Maxwell's priority was to maximize the profits. Only high earnings would support MCC's share price. Kevin naturally sided with his father, a stance also adopted by the company's auditors present at the meeting. Both Neil Taberner (for MCC) and Peter Walsh (for RMG), the faithful and all-too-unquestioning accountants from Coopers, were content to be used by the Chairman to fulfil his puff which featured prominently in the partnership's annual report: 'Coopers always gives an immediate response and always provides what I want within my deadline.' In earlier years, Reg Mogg, MCC's previous finance director, had with Taberner's help legally transformed the debt-laden company's accounts so that they boasted profits. Not the least of his successes was persuading Taberner in 1990 that the value of MCC's 'intangibles' (its goodwill and publishing rights) was £2.2 billion. Coopers were not only generous in their valuations but were allowing MCC to retain an 'intangible' on its balance sheet even after the sale of a subsidiary. One year later, other accountants valued the 'intangibles' at £300 million.

Ron Woods, the tax expert and MCC director, had already seen the in-house accountants' preliminary treatment. Nearly all the proposed profits had been earned from foreign exchange speculation. Unlike the non-accountants, he noticed that the auditor had bowed to Maxwell's pressure in allowing the foreign exchange profits to be placed above the line to boost overall profits, while camouflaging losses in the 'transition account – reserves'. Taberner knew precisely what Maxwell expected from his accountant.

That creative treatment provoked no dissent. Instead, a row erupted over the proposed dividend. Maxwell wanted shareholders – of which he was by far the largest – to receive £44.5 million in cash. One consequence of Coopers' treatment of MCC's accounts, certified as 'fair and true' for the shareholders and Inland Revenue, was the concealment of the company's net liabilities. Analysts would later discover that in 1989 the company's real liabilities had been £684 million, in 1990 they had risen to £859.2 million and during 1991 they would zoom to £950.2 million. But the reality of those debts was not apparent in the published accounts. Anselmini, knowing the company's precarious state, condemned the notion of a pay-out. He was supported by Richard Baker, the rough managing director. Although Baker's office walls were covered with Pirelli calendars of semi-nude girls and although visitors had to endure his crude jokes, it was his integrity which had secured Maxwell's original 'war chest' in 1988 to finance the Big One, the acquisition of Macmillan. Bankers trusted Baker, and ten banks had pledged £200 million each, an event celebrated with a champagne party on board the Lady Ghislaine. But in the years since then Baker's loyalties had frayed. Now, for the first time, he opposed Maxwell's demand for an increased dividend. The company's finances, he argued, were too perilous. A lot of the published profits, he knew, were illusory and there was simply no cash to pay for a dividend. To Maxwell's fury, he was supported by Woods.

After a thirty-minute explosion of emotion, Anselmini gave way, having been assured that Maxwell would take his dividend in shares. But in the vote Baker and Woods remained opposed, though they were outvoted by the other six directors. Over the following three days, Baker and Basil Brookes, the thirty-four-year-old finance director appointed at the board meeting on 23 November, argued for a compromise statement that 'a satisfactory outcome for the year is dependent upon the disposals'. Much of the empire would need to be sold to raise money to repay the loans – a self-defeating strategy. Both men visited Kevin at home. Baker's persistence had infuriated the Maxwells and, despite his loyal service, he was instantly excommunicated. He had little option but to take early retirement, allowing Kevin to inherit his powers. Robert Maxwell was delighted. Baker had been too straight. Whenever the Maxwell private companies had bought or sold something from MCC to boost profits, Baker had argued MCC's case too strongly. A cash dividend would now be paid; and the accounts, without a caution, were approved. Anselmini did not protest. The empire took another lurch towards doom.

With that issue settled, at 9.30 a.m. on 26 November Maxwell flew by helicopter to Farnborough to board the Gulfstream for Vienna. As he gazed at the print-out of the day's programme, his sense of his own importance was appreciably enhanced. He noted that Charlotte Thornton, his pretty new secretary ('A diluted successor to Andrea Martin,' commented Woods), had listed the telephone numbers, much as if he were a head of state, of the two Mercedes which would meet him at Vienna airport. He would be driven to the Imperial Hotel, the capital's best, to dispense a succession of newspaper interviews before handing over a cheque for £15,000 to the director of the national library at a ceremony attended by Franz Vranitsky, the Austrian prime minister. Altogether, his profile would be raised in that small, former Nazi state.

The highlight of the visit was that evening's dinner arranged by Ulrike Pöhl, the wife of Germany's central banker. A private room had been reserved at the Steirer Eck, one of Vienna's best restaurants, to entertain the Austrian prime minister and his wife. Although Betty was listed among the guests, Maxwell had not bothered to invite her. At the end of an enjoyable meal – it was especially agreeable for Maxwell, who had taken the opportunity to lecture the prime minister about the confidences shared with him by the world's leaders – he pushed his plate back and announced, 'Well, I've got to get to America.' The admiring gaze of his hosts was like a tonic, dispelling any doubts: the Austrian politician could not claim to have an executive jet at his beck and call.

At ten o'clock that night, Maxwell boarded the Gulfstream. The divan bed was already prepared. An adventure movie was in the video machine. A bottle of Perrier and one of Dom Pérignon 1982 were ready to be opened, and because Maxwell enjoyed a second dinner the fridge was filled with food prepared by Martin Cheeseman. Clearance was given to Captain Hull to take off. After refuelling at Luton, the Gulfstream headed for Atlanta, Georgia, a ten-hour flight. As usual on the transatlantic flight, Maxwell swallowed a sleeping tablet and slumped into deep unconsciousness.

Awaiting him were endless meetings across the USA, in Florida, Illinois, Washington, New York and Minneapolis, to persuade more bankers and pension fund managers to invest in his Central and Eastern European Fund. Getting control of their money had become important to his survival, but to his irritation Merrill Lynch was failing to deliver eager investors. A telephone call to Kevin reconfirmed their precarious financial position. Supporting MCC's share price was proving expensive: the £50 million loan from Crédit Suisse had been spent, as had the $84 million raised through Lehmans. Maxwell's needs seemed limitless. He ignored any suggestion that his strategy was flawed, that he was spending too much to save the company and losing any chance of survival.

FOUR

Misery

– December 1990

The financial crisis was made worse by his loneliness. On 2 December, Maxwell awoke in the Halekuani Hotel in Hawaii. Anyone else welcomed at the airport by the presentation of garlands around his neck would have gazed at the blue Pacific and at the soft yellow sand and have marvelled at life in that paradise. Maxwell could contemplate only his imminent eight-hour flight to Tokyo, where he was to spend three days peddling his Fund to expressionless Japanese bankers and fund managers. No one cared how he felt. One message from London caused particular anxiety.

John Cowling had just arrived in Dorrington Street to carry out the audit of the 1990 accounts for BIM and the pension funds. A partner in Coopers since 1988, Cowling was accompanied by John Mellet and Clare Gardner. Since their completion of the 1989 accounts, much had changed and it was Maxwell's fervent hope that those developments would remain concealed. But it was not long since he had praised Coopers for 'always [providing] what I want within my deadline', and the omens seemed favourable that he would receive the familiar service.

A tremor at the end of November when two IMRO officials had paid their first visit to BIM's office had fortunately proved short lived. Although it was flagged as a 'routine visit', Cook reportedly was 'in a bit of a flap'. Robert and Kevin Maxwell had beckoned him to the Chairman's office at 4.30 p.m. on 21 November to offer reassurance. 'There's no need for any concern. Get Stuart Carson in to help,' Maxwell had advised. LBI's compliance officer was a lawyer recruited from Lautro, another government regulatory agency. Maxwell hoped that the inspectors could be steered in the right direction if they demanded sight of the pension funds' share certificates. In the event, the Maxwells' nonchalance infected Cook and he managed to greet the IMRO officers in an unconcerned manner. Just as the Maxwells anticipated, the bureaucrats proved to be incompetent. The two inspectors – described by both Highfield and Cook as 'young and inexperienced' – had stayed for one day. Their only recommendation was that BIM needed to improve its documentation. 'A bit of an anti-climax,' concluded Highfield.

Cowling's visit, Maxwell feared, would be worse. There were good reasons for his concern. Since the last accounts, dated 30 June 1989 and covering the previous eighteen-month period, his private companies' debt to BIM, despite the recent settlement, had risen to £40 million. Moreover, to any practised accountant, the pension funds' involvement in Maxwell's share sales on the eve of the financial year's end would have suggested questionable window-dressing. Yet Cook's fear that Cowling would complain about the delay in repaying the debt proved unfounded: he had underestimated Maxwell's relationship with the partners at Coopers, whose tolerance, understanding and willingness to take the Publisher's assurances on trust were a great comfort to him.

Taken together, Maxwell's 400 companies were by far Coopers' biggest clients, producing annual fees of £5 million. Although he occasionally feigned innocence about taxation, Maxwell possessed an astute understanding of accounts and accountants. Twenty-five years earlier, he had tyrannized John Biggs, the stuttering, alcoholic auditor of Pergamon, into approving his fictitious accounts and concealing the fraudulent management of his first public company. Such tactics were no longer appropriate. Instead, he resorted to a charm offensive, smothering with eyewash John Cowling, Neil Taberner, Stephen Wootten and Peter Walsh, all Coopers accountants responsible for different branches of the empire.

John Walsh had been auditing Maxwell's companies since 1970 and prided himself as 'one of the trusted old faces'. In 1991 Walsh explained in a self-congratulatory memo to his colleagues that Coopers' close relationship with Maxwell was unusual since, though he had 'used almost every lawyer, every broker and every merchant bank in London, he has been totally loyal to Coopers . . . because we stood by him in the 1970s when everyone else avoided him (National Westminster Bank is in a similar position)'.

Recognizing the importance of Maxwell's accounts, Coopers had even established an office in nearby Plumtree Court from where they had easy and continuous access to the Maxwell finance departments. The accountants adopted a trusting approach towards the Maxwell empire – believing that it was the directors' responsibility to compile the accounts and indicate any problems. 'An auditor', Walsh would fondly repeat, 'is not like a ferret pointed at a rabbit warren just to see how many rabbits come out.' Walsh would also defend the absence of any discussions between the Coopers auditors working for the empire's different segments. Maxwell's canny compartmentalization between MCC, RMG, BIM and many other companies was willingly self-imposed by Coopers upon themselves. 'I never spoke to Neil Taberner,' Walsh would admit. That self-denying ordinance was vital to the auditors' subsequent claims that they had not known of the huge inter-company loans between Maxwell's public and private companies, including BIM. 'Auditors are not given crystal balls,' argued Walsh, in support of his professions of ignorance. Responsibility for the accuracy of the accounts, the Coopers men endlessly repeated, rests with a company's directors, and that was a responsibility which the Chairman was pleased to accept.

To aid him in that task, he looked out for those weak but ambitious Coopers employees who could be recruited to work directly for him. The presence within the empire of young men like Basil Brookes and Jonathan Ford, and retired senior auditors like David Corsan (who had previously audited the whole Maxwell empire), tempted by higher salaries, made that disingenuous eyewash easier to dispense inside the auditors' headquarters. The beneficial result was that, consistently in previous years, the value of MCC's assets and its profits had been wildly inflated. Maxwell's £49 million losses after the 1987 crash were relegated to an obscure footnote; suspicious currency speculation featured as trading profits; while the valuation of 'intangibles' at £2.2 billion was eight times higher than their true value. Coopers' annual blessing of Maxwell's fabrications had allowed his regular boast about 'record profits' to pump up both MCC's share price and his own self-esteem.

Pinpointing the chaos in BIM's accounts should have been an uncomplicated task for Cowling. In 1989, an auditors' report had mentioned that Maxwell appeared to control BIM – 'a high-risk company easily influenced by senior management' – and criticized the supervisory systems as 'poor'. An internal Coopers memorandum about the pension funds' investments highlighted the risks of stock lending and the funds' growing stake in MCC, prompting the auditor's comment that Maxwell's management of the fund as his personal vehicle free of any independent, basic controls was 'risky'. One year later, matters were made worse by the apparent confusion of information sent to Cook by Larry Trachtenberg. Although BIM's investments, income and payments to pensioners had been systematically recorded, Cook complained to Cowling that he was 'confused about the income from stock lending. We're going backwards and forwards, and we're getting contradictory information.' He claimed to be puzzled because LBI had not submitted proper accounts to BIM. 'Nothing they give us makes any sense,' Cook told Cowling. 'It's all late, incomplete or wrong.' Since Cowling was also LBI's auditor, it seemed that he was ideally placed to unravel the confusion.

Cowling could be forgiven for thinking that Cook was foolish. After all, Cook had received regular statements from Trachtenberg but admitted not to have calculated BIM's actual income. Moreover, he claimed to be baffled about the interest accruing to BIM because, to avoid handing over cash, Trachtenberg had told him that he was also investing the interest payments. In the event, Cowling did not criticize either Cook or Trachtenberg.

Imposing not so much a Chinese wall as a concrete one around himself, Cowling had not discussed his task with his Coopers colleagues working on other Maxwell companies' accounts. Nevertheless, within days he noticed that pension fund money had 'disappeared' because the systems, controls and records of BIM and LBI were chaotic. He also discovered that important details about the stock lending were 'unknown'.

When Maxwell returned to London in the early hours of 7 December, he could only hope that Cowling could be placated if he unearthed any discrepancies. His major concern was that Cowling would ask to see the actual share certificates rather than photocopies. Since many of them were held by the banks, that would pose a tricky problem. Maxwell's first conversations with Kevin seemed encouraging. To comply with the law governing the formal submission of annual accounts, Cowling had agreed to sign BIM's accounts immediately, although his work could only be completed over the following weeks.

Relieved by that outcome, in the run-up to the Christmas holidays Maxwell closeted himself with lawyers. Despite the millions spent in legal fees over the years, he had won few victories in the courts, yet his threats of litigation often served his purpose, silencing enemies and deterring creditors. Not surprisingly, his massive expenditure on lawyers galvanized most of the profession to offer him their services unconditionally. But, contrary to his practice with accountants and bankers, he made no effort to retain the services of the large, prestigious partnerships mushrooming around the City. Instead he sought individuals who could be relied upon to devote themselves – personally and professionally – more than whole-heartedly to his cause.

In-house he relied upon Oscar Beuselinck to manage his writs for defamation against the growing number of critics. Although the seventy-one-year-old solicitor had represented *Private Eye* against Maxwell in 1986, he had agreed to work for the Publisher at a salary twice as large as he had expected.

The second in-house lawyer was Debbie Maxwell. Preoccupied by the need to defend several writs against Maxwell for payment of millions of pounds in unpaid fees and damages for broken contracts, she had become renowned for asking her employer, 'How shall I describe this: half full or half empty?' At 10 a.m. on Sunday, 9 December, she was sat discussing a more serious problem with him. Increasingly her name was being used as MCC's compliance officer, and in three memoranda she had warned the Chairman that his secret purchase of MCC shares broke company law, infringed stock exchange regulations and damaged the interests of the pension funds. Unable to persuade him to cease these transgressions, Debbie Maxwell resigned her compliance duties and was subsequently criticized for not revealing her knowledge to the statutory authorities – the police, IMRO, the Department of Trade and Industry or the stock exchange.

Over lunch that day, Maxwell consulted David Maislish, a thirty-nine-year-old solicitor managing his own small firm. Its slender resources made it eminently suitable for his purposes, for regardless of any other professional or domestic obligations, Maislish was always ready to jump to his bidding. His direct competitors were

Dick Russell and David Vogel of Titmuss Sainer and Webb, a medium-sized firm of solicitors linked to Charles Clore, the property developer. An even closer connection was that Vogel had become godfather to one of Kevin's daughters, and Russell was married to Mandy, Pandora's sister. Summoned to Maxwell's office to give advice, the brother-in-law and godfather would rush round from their nearby offices knowing full well that the Publisher had already decided his course of action but wanted assurance that his chosen ploy would escape prosecution. Listening to the most litigious man in the kingdom enjoying the sound of his own voice, the trio of lawyers would console themselves with the reflection that they billed by the hour – and that their income was phenomenal.

In the very nature of Maxwell's way of business, it was essential to prove that his course of action had been taken only after consultation with and approval by a lawyer. The law, he believed, was nothing less than a weapon – the more lethal the better. The 'comfort' letters provided by Maislish and Vogel were Maxwell's first line of defence against any criticism, and they usually sufficed. In London, lawyers were still blessed with the aura of professionals, apparently bound by a Hippocratic oath to serve the interests of justice rather than Mammon. Throughout the capital, Maislish, on Maxwell's behalf, had won an unenviable reputation for pulling every legitimate trick in the book to delay and defeat unwelcome writs.

Maislish knew that, should he fail his paymaster, others would be eager replacements – not least Philip Morgenstern, a senior partner at Nicholson Graham and Jones and a confidant of both Kevin and Robert. Unlike Maislish, Morgenstern was something of a sleuth, always hovering quietly in his master's footsteps, undertaking the more private work, arousing suspicion even eulogizing the Chairman's qualities in 1995. Like Maislish, although he evinced only circumspect emotional commitment to Maxwell, Morgenstern's dedication seemed passionate. Maxwell's was an account which none of those lawyers wanted to lose.

But all the lawyers recognized that Maxwell's memory and energy were waning. As his affairs grew more complicated, the interlocking and overlapping corporations he had constructed to confuse outsiders were proving difficult even for him to untangle. It was a condition which his vanity would deny as he restlessly drove himself to protect his achievements and sustain his ambitions.

By Tuesday, 11 December, Maxwell's formidable spirit had risen to the level required if he was to match an exhausting climax of constant meetings. Employees and representatives were flying into London from Moscow, Berlin, Frankfurt, Sofia, Tel Aviv, New York and Hong Kong to bring news of deals, ventures and problems. While the underlings were transported from Heathrow by helicopter to be housed in hotels at his expense, Maxwell was seated in his office, planning new banks in Russia and Bulgaria, media purchases in Israel and Germany, and the development of market research in the Far East. His adrenalin was racing as he burst into the dining room that lunchtime to confront his newspaper editors and senior executives.

As Joseph Pereira, his quiet Portuguese valet, served another unmemorable dish, Maxwell's dissatisfaction with the *Daily Mirror* engulfed the room. His target was Roy Greenslade, the newspaper's editor. Greenslade's sin was to have refrained from printing Maxwell's offer of a scoop – that six ministers would resign in protest against Margaret Thatcher's refusal to stand down after her failure to pass the threshold vote in the Conservative leadership election on 20 November. 'Just print it!' Maxwell had shouted. 'I am your publisher!' But since there had been no corroboration (the prime minister had resigned two days later), Greenslade had refused, and in Maxwell's opinion had shown himself to be untrustworthy. During that lunch, the insubordinate editor seemed unrepentant, and Maxwell appealed for support to Charles 'Gorbals' Wilson, the former editor of *The Times*. Wilson, a small, pugnacious Scot, had gratefully accepted the Captain's shilling to become the editor of the Mirror Group's *Sporting Life* after his removal by Rupert Murdoch. It was a road to somewhere for a man who was going nowhere. Naturally, experience had long taught Wilson to satisfy his employer's whims, even with tongue in cheek: 'I would have said it sounds like a flier to me, Bob.'

'What?' exclaimed Maxwell. 'A flier. It was a scoop. The scoop of the decade.'

Like most editorial lunches, this one ended on a baffled note. Maxwell astonished his employees by blowing his nose into a napkin, but he had failed to cajole anyone into castigating Greenslade. Even so, the editor would agree to depart shortly afterwards.

Maxwell's real business followed lunch. Waiting in Kevin's office were Michael Moore and Andrew Capitman of Bankers Trust.

Capitman had more reason than ever to be grateful to Maxwell. Recently, he had flown at his client's expense to visit him on his yacht in Istanbul and had eaten pounds of the best caviar while exchanging a few sentences which could have been spoken quite safely on a telephone. Despite the largesse, Capitman had become convinced that Maxwell's finances were worse than precarious. Although the *Sunday Times* was about to list Maxwell among Britain's richest men worth £1.2 billion, Capitman suspected the truth. But that, he felt, 'wasn't our problem'. Although Bankers Trust was in business to lend money, the loans were always syndicated to other banks, thus avoiding any risk.

'We need a short-term loan,' said Maxwell, looking at Moore, a brusque, unrefined Cockney and the bank's technician. 'The security is the Mirror Group.' Both bankers expressed their readiness to oblige. The bank would earn by cross-selling the loan for a small profit to other banks. How the money was repaid was not their problem but Maxwell's – and the other banks'.

After the bankers had left, Maxwell and Kevin agreed to hold back on this transaction. Loans against the Mirror Group would contaminate any future plans to float it on the stock exchange. The two hoped that the profits from the newspaper's sale would pay off all the debts incurred by using the pension funds. The sale was already codenamed 'Project Andy Capp'. The lawyers to be involved would be chosen after a beauty parade later that week, and Maxwell would chair the first meeting with bankers on 14 December.

That night, Maxwell decided to show himself around London. At 7.15 he appeared at Tobacco Dock for the *Sunday Times* Christmas party. His invitation from Andrew Neil, the editor, followed several conversations and a lunch during which they had discussed Neil's possible employment by Maxwell. As he shuffled through the crowd towards his host that evening, his face betrayed the satisfaction he derived from being universally recognized. He was a man who loved attention and sought the spotlight. Publicity was his oxygen, and if he was too long absent from the limelight he began to feel suffocated.

From Tobacco Dock, Maxwell was driven to Jeffrey Archer's penthouse apartment on the Thames embankment. Having powdered his face in the lift in front of the novelist's son, he entered the party expecting to be greeted like royalty. Unlike other guests, including most members of the Cabinet, who stayed for at least an hour, Maxwell exited after just ten minutes. His entry had not been sufficiently applauded and he had not quickly enough become the centre of attention. Worst of all, the sight of people enjoying themselves had been depressing. Over the next days, he failed to appear at successive parties to which he had accepted invitations, not least those of employees, including LBI's at Les Ambassadeurs club. Instead, he remained in his penthouse each evening drinking heavily, a habit which had developed with startling speed.

He even missed his own party. Traditionally, Maxwell had hosted a Christmas dinner and dance for senior executives at Oxford. One hundred had been invited on Saturday, 15 December, but despite all the enthusiasm for dispensing hospitality he had shown in previous years, he now felt drained, having exhausted himself that afternoon in meetings with Israelis, Mongolians and Italians. The prospect of smiling at those with their noses in his trough was too much. At the last moment, Betty whispered to the guests, 'Bob's sick,' and the seating arrangements were changed. 'I bet he's up there in his room,' quipped Ernest Burrington, the Mirror Group's new managing director. 'He's in a huff with his family.' Maxwell was in fact consuming his second bottle of champagne. In the hall at the end of a high-spirited evening, most agreed the party had gone better in the absence of the host.

Everyone, Maxwell told himself, was oblivious to his depression, even his children. Over the following days, his sons and daughters celebrated Ghislaine's birthday, partied at Joe's Café in Draycott Avenue and split off to various festivities. There was no plan for the family to gather for a Christmas meal. Maxwell was alone and estranged. Even his youngest son's Christmas card, a tasteless photograph of anonymous racing horses, was signed with an unemotional message: 'Bob, many thanks for all your help and kindness – Kevin and Pandora.' The parents had not bothered to list his four grandchildren. Needless to say, there was no hint of love. The awareness of fractured relationships was painful.

At 7 a.m. on Friday, 21 December, he was seated in his kitchen, switching between the morning television breakfast shows and drinking coffee from a large mug while George Wheeler, his hairdresser for the past twenty-one years, was applying L'Oréal No. 7 to dye his hair black. 'Have you checked all the roots?' asked Maxwell as he grabbed for a telephone. 'Don't worry,' laughed Wheeler, well aware of his client's obsession with banishing the slightest hint of age. 'A phobia about grey hair' was the hairdresser's explanation. 'Even if he saw a grey eyebrow, he would go berserk.'

His time was ebbing and his failure to own a share of Britain's growing television industry had come to seem a depressing indictment of his career. Poor finances had compelled the premature sale of a 13.8 per cent stake in Central Television, losing him over £20 million in extra profits, and had prevented him bidding for the licence for Britain's first satellite channel. Murdoch had now cleaned up on that gravy train. All Maxwell owned in the world of broadcast television was an unprofitable stake in French television and 51 per cent of MTV in Europe, the pop station. MTV was an inspired investment, but it was still losing money. Everything was losing money, and there seemed no respite.

As Wheeler waited for the dye to dry, he hoped that he would be spared a repetition of a previous calamity when the Publisher's hair had turned the wrong colour. Fraught hours had been spent washing the hair back to its natural grey and reapplying the dye. The sight of Maxwell's vast, naked girth quivering in underpants had amused some eyewitnesses among his personal staff. 'How can anyone fear that man?' thought his valet. Once dressed, Maxwell had resumed his hectoring.

'Have a good Christmas,' Maxwell joked to the hairdresser. Ever since Wheeler had complained of not being given a seasonal tip, he had been listed to receive a bottle of Scotch and another of gin. Now an ordeal lay before his employer, his hair freshly blackened. At lunchtime there were Christmas drinks for staff on the tenth floor. Maxwell made a brief appearance, oppressed by the evident happiness of others. The prospect of the holidays was awful.

His delight would have been to rest and recover on the *Lady Ghislaine*, anchored and awaiting his arrival in the sunshine of the US Virgin Islands. Sleek and towering five decks high, the 155-foot, 430-ton yacht had been designed by Jon Bannenberg for the brother of Adnan Kashoggi, the Saudi arms dealer. The Arab had commissioned a gin palace with maximum internal luxury and volume for pottering around off the South of France rather than a craft suitable for crossing the Atlantic. Visitors to the *Lady Ghislaine* could only be awed by the sumptuous, white-carpeted state room; the comfortable dining room, the bathrooms with gold-plated fittings, the elaborate kitchen and the sheer scale of private luxury. Maxwell regarded the craft as a most precious possession, one which he was unwilling to share. Yet fearing loneliness, he had impulsively agreed that Betty should join him. The opportunity would be used to complete a chore.

That summer, when relations had collapsed beyond recall, Betty had delivered in writing her terms for a final separation. Her husband was to provide sufficient money to complete her house in Fraytet, in the Dordogne, France, to buy a *pied-à-terre* in London, to meet her removal expenses, to pay her debts and to transfer a capital sum which would provide her with 'an adequate income' for life. Her final request was that they spend eight days together, alone, to discuss the 'separation in a civilized manner, as two people who have loved each other very much and spent forty-six years together'. They had barely spoken or met since July, yet, lonely and exhausted as Maxwell now was, Betty was better than nothing. He had instructed her to fly to St Thomas.

Maxwell arrived on the islands in the Gulfstream on Christmas Eve. He had not bothered to consider that the aircraft's crew would be separated from their families over the holiday. That inconvenience was part of the deal, although it would contribute to Captain Hull's eventual divorce. After all, Maxwell was also missing the wedding of Isabel, his daughter, in San Francisco. 'It's her second,' he had snapped. The news awaiting him at the airport from the *Lady Ghislaine*'s captain, Stephen Taylor, was infuriating. While the yacht was being manoeuvred into the harbour, a wind had swept the craft on to an uncharted sandbank, damaging her rudder. Hull was dispatched to Miami to fetch an engineer, while the Publisher went on board. But the expert's verdict was miserable. Without a spare, the *Lady Ghislaine* could not sail. 'Maxwell's upset,' Hull told his co-pilot with studied understatement.

Stuck motionless on a sandbank watching videos with Betty would not have amused Maxwell at the best of times. He was renowned for having once, in a fit of contemptuous pique, ordered his chauffeur to drive off from a London hotel, abandoning his wife, although she could be seen in the entrance hall. On Boxing Day, he fled from the imprisonment and flew to New York, leaving

Betty to open Christmas presents, still wrapped, with the crew. Captain Taylor was fired shortly afterwards.

Maxwell's depression did not lift in New York, which was disagreeably cold and still attuned to seasonal cheer. Worse, however he looked at the accounts, he could not see an easy escape into profit. The remedy, he decided, was to sell more of the empire and seek temporary relief by raising further loans to buy MCC shares. His telephone call to Kevin at Hailey was calculated to interrupt his son's holiday. While the father remained in New York, his son would organize the finances.

On 28 December, after spending the morning with Trachtenberg discussing the finances, Kevin lunched with Basil Brookes, Albert Fuller and Robert Bunn at Chez Gerard in Chancery Lane. Their discussion about the group's finances was for once uninterrupted by telephone calls since Kevin had left his portable in the car. Even so, with so little candour, their conversation produced no result. Three days later, before leaving the office to celebrate the New Year, Kevin and Bunn signed transfers for two more Berlitz share certificates. Both were handed to Lehmans, in exchange for $29.7 million. The Maxwells' total debt to Lehmans had soared to $113.6 million.

FIVE

Fantasies

– January 1991

The holiday mood had been forgotten when Robert Maxwell met his son in his penthouse at seven o'clock on Sunday morning, 6 January 1991. Over the previous two weeks, Kevin seemed to Andrew Capitman, the banker, to have matured from gofer into joint manager. In his conversations with bankers, he was giving the impression that his was a major corporation suffering only transitory problems. But the secret purchase of MCC shares to stabilize the price was proving unsuccessful, and newspapers were speculating that an American-led coalition would at any moment launch an attack against Iraq in the Persian Gulf to free Kuwait from occupation, triggering chaos in the world's financial markets. These were the worst conditions, undermining Maxwell's hopes of recovery.

Among those who sensed Maxwell's increasing problems was John Halloran, the manager of BPCC, the former printing division of Maxwell's empire, who had bought the company in a management buy-out in January 1989. Ever since, Halloran had been pressing for payment of £97 million owed by BIM to the BPCC pension fund. Maxwell had resisted, but the sum was to be paid in July 1991. In the meantime, anxious to get more cash, Maxwell had persuaded Cook that it would be better eventually to pay BPCC in money because share prices would be falling. So BIM began selling shares. As the proceeds arrived, they were deposited on Maxwell's orders in the account of RMG, his private company. From there they were used to repay his private debts. Halloran, with excellent sources in Maxwell House, detected the crisis and reminded the Publisher that he expected prompt payment with interest in the summer.

The financial crisis was no longer a secret. Jean-Pierre Anselmini recognized the critical sign: bankers were telephoning daily and Kevin was often avoiding their calls. Yet, like so many others, he believed that the Maxwells' fortune in Liechtenstein could cover the debts. After considerable negotiating effort, Anselmini proudly presented Maxwell with a plan to repurchase MCC's debt at a 25 per cent discount from certain European banks. 'Can't do it,' said Maxwell. The profitable deal could not be completed because there was no money. Anselmini, like Ron Woods months earlier, was still too gullible to understand. Maxwell instead wanted another deal. Proffering a document written by Robert Bunn explaining all the outstanding loans of the private companies, he asked: 'Can you arrange to get these restructured? Just as you did for MCC?'

Bunn's report suggested that those private companies had debts of £1 billion against assets of £2 billion. Naturally, Maxwell did not confide that some of the assets belonged to the pension funds. Even so, Anselmini reported shortly afterwards: 'It's impossible.' Maxwell's disappointment was only too plain. 'I don't have a magic wand,' added Anselmini. The mood in the City was deteriorating. A wave of financial scandals, the deepening world recession and the threat of a gigantic leap in oil prices because of the Gulf war had made bankers naturally wary. Now Anselmini's telephone calls to the banking village had sparked suspicion. Bankers began contemplating Maxwell's stricken finances and noted a crop of adverse newspaper reports. The burden to find a solution was firmly placed upon Kevin.

That month, Kevin began negotiating the extension of loans for MCC and the private companies with dozens of the banks. His negotiations with Julie Maitland persuaded her to write a new strategy paper about MCC (following one composed the previous July). Once again the bank, which had accepted £100 million in collateral for private loans, failed to take account of the fact that the shares were registered in the name of BIM. Some would claim that the omission was proof of negligence. The bank would plead ignorance, insisting that it had no duty to investigate.

Robert Maxwell's palliative for the problems was to board the Gulfstream. On Sunday, 12 January he flew for dinner to Munich, departing early the following morning for New York to embark on a renewed effort to sell his Central European Fund on the West

Coast. By the 20th his absence from London had fractured his relationship with reality. Instead of seeking solutions to MCC's indebtedness, he flew to Bulgaria and then Croatia with Rudi Perpich, the former governor of Minnesota, to negotiate investing millions of dollars in those countries' newspapers and television services. His hopes of profits were distant dreams. In London, the reality was increasing turmoil within the Maxwell empire caused by fears that the auditors' finalization of BIM's accounts might instigate a new dispute among LBI's directors.

The trouble had started when Mark Tapley, LBI's managing director, had returned to work on 2 January to find Larry Trachtenberg sitting in the office. 'I don't know what your role is in this firm,' Tapley said angrily to the fat American, 'but you're meant to be out.' Trachtenberg shrugged; despite Kevin's promise to halt the stock lending, he had not been removed.

Unknown to Tapley, Maxwell had received a report from John Pole, the head of security, about Trachtenberg's strange activities. During a routine search for a missing cassette tape of Trachtenberg's telephoned market dealings, Pole discovered that the American was being threatened by a BIM employee. After some negotiations, a woman deposited the tape at the Mirror headquarters' reception. Maxwell had clearly decided to ignore the incident, for Trachtenberg had celebrated his fortieth birthday hosting an expensive party at Mossiman's, the Knightsbridge restaurant.

Trachtenberg was clearly secure within the Maxwell citadel. That very day, 2 January, he had typed a memorandum to the Maxwells setting out his value to them, now that it was time to calculate the 1990 bonus. Not only had he arranged transactions totalling $725 million in the previous year, but, he added in chilling prose, 'If one were to include stock loans which were ultimately used in cash generation exercises, the total would easily surpass $1 billion.' There it was, a stark admission of the misuse of the funds. Not surprisingly, his bald statement of facts encouraged Maxwell to increase Trachtenberg's salary to £200,000 and to add a 10 per cent contribution towards his pension, a performance bonus of £100,000, a car and a rent-free house estimated to cost the London & Bishopsgate Group £78,000 every year.

These favours had not gone through without internal opposition. Gillie Bryson, an accountant, had noted to Kevin that Trachtenberg's income had risen 154 per cent in two years and that he was 'earning more than many of the top Chief Executives of the top FT-SE 100 companies', despite the loss by London & Bishopsgate Holdings (LBH) of 'a great deal of money'. Although Bryson complained, 'I am at a loss to understand what possible justification there would be for any bonus to be paid,' the Maxwells understood Trachtenberg's value very well. Keen to capitalize on that sentiment, Trachtenberg's latest proposal was that he exchange his shares in LBH, estimated by himself to be worth £250,000, for his house, which was valued £599,000. Although LBH was actually worthless, the Maxwells had agreed to consider his proposition.

Trachtenberg's inviolability encouraged Tapley's anxiety to resign, but he was persuaded by Anselmini, Willet and especially Bernard 'Manuel' Donoughue 'not to rock the boat'. Pointing to the letters from lawyers and accountants approving the stock-lending scheme, Donoughue urged, 'We're going to arrange a buy-out of LBI so we can keep it for ourselves.' Tapley was becalmed. By then, Trachtenberg was concealing the use of the pension fund shares while John Cowling completed BIM's accounts.

On 5 February, Cowling asked Cook for a detailed explanation of the stock lending. He was answered with a statement of ignorance. Cook replied, 'I don't know much about the arrangements except that I have an agreement with LBI.' In his files was a letter from Trachtenberg sent in early January assuring him that all BIM's assets were safe. Attached to that letter was a note from the American acknowledging receipt at LBI of another batch of shares owned by BIM. Unknown to Cook, on that very day Trachtenberg had sent those same shares to Crédit Suisse to raise more money.

Cowling's questions raised doubts in Cook's mind. Three days later, on 8 February, he met Maxwell and asked for assurances about the stock lending. Since the beginning in December 1988, over £200 million of pension fund shares had been passed over on Maxwell's orders to Trachtenberg. 'Everything's fine,' said BIM's chairman, not revealing that at 3 p.m. that day Kevin would telephone Julie Maitland to ask for a further $3 million loan guaranteed as he knew by pension fund shares.

Cook's sanguine response to this reassurance did not immediately placate Cowling. By mid-February, the auditor had become puzzled by Trachtenberg's vague replies, especially after he had provided two different lists of the pension fund shares held by LBI. There were other good reasons for Cowling's unease. He had not seen any written authorization for the stock lending from BIM's directors; and there was a letter from Mark Haas of Lehmans confirming that the pension fund's shares handed over by Invesco were held as 'collateral for *loans* in connection with the stock-lending agreement'. (Haas would subsequently claim that either Trachtenberg or Cook had composed the letter.)

In an attempt to clarify his confusion, on 13 February Cowling listened to a telephone conversation between Cook and Trachtenberg. 'Can you put the whole position in writing because it seems you're doing collateral swaps which aren't authorized?' asked Cook. Trachtenberg's replies clearly contradicted his earlier explanations. Talking about Lehmans, he actually mentioned 'collateral swap', a term which should have alarmed Cowling.

Although Trachtenberg did accurately say, 'There was no stock-lending position with Lehmans on 5 April 1990,' he confused the auditor by saying of the later agreement, 'The Treasury bills are held as collateral for the stock' for BIM's account. Subsequently Cowling received a similar assurance from Mark Haas, who stated in a letter that the BIM shares were held as collateral under the stock-lending agreement. In fact, Haas knew this was not conventional stock lending, only pure borrowing against collateral.

By then, other matters should also have aroused the auditor's suspicions: Maxwell had 'invested' £5 million of BIM's money in the Robert Fraser Group, the private bank chaired by Lord Rippon; BIM had 'deposited' £69.7 million in cash with LBI; a Maxwell private company had 'borrowed' £37.6 million cash from the pension funds; and BIM's stake in MCC had doubled from 13 to 25 million shares.

There was one simple chore which Cowling should have undertaken to complete his audit. The original certificates for all the shares managed by BIM ought to have been seen and ticked off the inventory. Cowling's problem was that the certificates were scattered in more than one dozen places and in several countries. Instead of demanding sight of each certificate from Trachtenberg, he was content to be shown photocopies or to listen to the American's oral explanation that the missing certificates would be produced in the future. 'Don't worry, it's all part of the normal stock-lending arrangements,' gabbled Trachtenberg, and the auditor was persuaded.

To prove the point, Cowling was shown certificates for 1 million shares in Banco Commercial Portugues. Although owned by BIM, Maxwell had already pledged the shares against a loan. Among other certificates promised was one for 12 million MCC shares 'lent' by BIM to LBI. Trachtenberg had pledged those shares with Goldman Sachs and, to cover that discrepancy, he offered a polite letter to Cowling simply stating that LBI 'held' the share certificate.

Cowling would return to Cook towards the middle of February: 'I've received all the information I need from LBI. Everything's fine.' Since Cook was not an accountant but an administrator, he gladly accepted Cowling's assurances. 'It's miraculous,' thought Highfield. 'They say there's no problem any more.' He reasoned that after all LBI was staffed by men – Tapley, Donoughue, Ford, Carson and Trachtenberg – of higher qualifications than himself.

Cowling's only caveat was that he would send a letter to BIM listing the serious problems to be solved. There were, he would write, 'control deficiencies and weaknesses' in BIM and confusion because share certificates were kept in 'various locations'. He noted a catalogue of errors in BIM's accounting system and stated that 'LBI's systems had collapsed.' His conclusion was that there was need for a substantive review, 'due to lack of basic controls'. But he did certify that the pension funds possessed £792 million, adding that the interest earned from lending money to Maxwell was £0.5 million and that 'this should please the pension fund'. The audit was completed. Maxwell's special arrangements remained concealed.

Robert Maxwell greeted the news of Cowling's self-deception by immersing himself among the famous and rich to discuss the world's problems. Constant travel was not only a distraction from what he still believed were temporary difficulties but immunized him from reality. He flew to Davos in Switzerland to address the World Economic Leaders. After a dinner at the Fluela Hotel, where he reassured the chairman of Crédit Suisse of his empire's well-being, he basked in the limelight of constant receptions and meals, happily anticipating his own lecture on 'Acquiring Media in Eastern Europe'. Naturally, when he delivered the lecture, Maxwell did not confess that his own efforts in Berlin, Sofia, Prague, Zagreb and Moscow were proving expensively unprofitable. Instead he boasted about his close relationships with presidents and ministers across the continent, especially with Mikhail Gorbachev. That relationship, cemented in Minneapolis, Minnesota in June 1990 during their joint consecration of the $100 million Gorbachev Maxwell Institute, had propelled Maxwell's self-esteem to new heights. Although he had unfortunately forgotten to contribute his promised $50 million towards the institute, founded with the lofty intention of uniting the world's scientists, the pictures and soundbites of Gorbachev praising Maxwell and warmly shaking his hand had been profitably flashed by satellite around the globe.

That impression of influence was the reason for the request by Yitzhak Shamir, Israel's prime minister, for Maxwell to visit Jerusalem on 12 February. Shamir needed Maxwell's help in passing a message to Gorbachev about the danger posed by Iraq should the war with Kuwait spread to Israel. The proximity to power and his importance in Israel, where every minister made himself available, gave Maxwell special pleasure. At the end of twenty-four hours of meetings in Jerusalem he flew on to Zagreb to meet Rudi Perpich, in order to finalize preparations for Maxwell's hoped-for television and newspaper empire in Croatia. Perpich, hired as Croatia's lobbyist after his defeat in the Minnesota elections, knew how to impress Maxwell. Lunch had been arranged with President Tudjman to celebrate the signing of letters of intent, an encounter which took place on former President Tito's Mediterranean island, in the breathtaking villa compound. Perpich watched Maxwell's spirits rise as he savoured the treatment normally accorded to heads of state. By the second day, Perpich was impressed to find that the visitor had, within his first twenty-four hours on the island, learnt sufficient Croatian to speak with the president without an interpreter. On their return flight to London, for Perpich's benefit Maxwell reflected at length upon his own glory, ignoring the cost of flying 6,000 miles to earn nothing. At £3,500 per hour, the Gulfstream's journey cost over £90,000 – £50,000 for the flight plus £42,815 for insurance in a war zone.

Maxwell's distance from reality struck Rupert Murdoch, who had at last fulfilled a long-standing and much postponed visit on 11 February. 'We are two big publishers,' Maxwell had boomed on the telephone, 'and we should talk.' Murdoch's secretary had taken the precaution of warning Maxwell that her employer could not be kept waiting and that he had precisely forty minutes before the next appointment. Their recent but rare encounters, thought Murdoch as he ascended to the ninth floor of Maxwell House, had invariably been characterized by Maxwell's bombast and Murdoch's teasing response. Ever since he had outwitted Maxwell in 1969 to win the *News of the World*, Murdoch's capacity to irritate him had grown.

At ten minutes past four, five minutes into their meeting, Murdoch's impatience with Maxwell was turning into contempt. With few pauses for breath, Maxwell was boasting about his worldwide diplomacy, especially his intimate relations with the Kremlin and with the leaders of Israel. His self-indulgence had bemused and then silenced his visitor. At the end of forty minutes, Murdoch asked: 'Is there anything else we need to talk about?'

'No,' replied Maxwell with a satisfied grin. In his opinion, he had proved his importance to his rival.

As Murdoch descended to the street, he exclaimed, 'What was all that about? He's ludicrous.'

Even for Maxwell, the glow was brief. Five days later, at seven o'clock on the morning of 16 February, he was once more sitting in his kitchen, switching television channels while George Wheeler applied L'Oréal to his hair. The Gulf war, one month after the first Allied attacks, dominated the airwaves, especially on Murdoch's Sky channel. Once again, Maxwell was morose. The previous evening, after landing by helicopter on the roof, he had deliberately stayed away from the cocktail party to mark Richard Baker's retirement as managing director of MCC: disloyalty was unforgivable. He would also ignore the invitation to Andrew Lloyd Webber's Berkshire estate that evening to celebrate the composer's wedding. He struck that idea out of his mind. Betty could go alone. Maxwell's thoughts were on his journey the following day to Istanbul to meet the president of Turkey. The $40,000 flight would allow him to speak to the president about the country's participation in the Gulf war for one hour before returning home for dinner with President Zhelev of Bulgaria.

Maxwell's interest in Bulgaria, that irrelevant and impoverished Balkan people's republic, was irrational. Although he confided to Sir John Morgan, a former British ambassador who had joined his staff, that he felt sentimental about the country which had helped him during his escape from the Nazis in 1940, his investments in a school for business management, a newspaper, a television station, a hotel chain and a bank were costing millions without any chance of profits. Ognian Doynov, his Bulgarian adviser and a disgraced former member of the Politburo who had replaced Morgan, appeared to some to be encouraging Maxwell's waste of money. Paid £110,000 annually plus a motor car and free company flat, Doynov could not, however, be blamed for Maxwell's waning interest in his expensive fantasy. 'The Bulgarians', noted Brian Cole, Maxwell's fixer in that country, 'did not trust Maxwell. They just wanted his money.' Among those travelling to Sofia as part of the team to invest MCC's money was Helen Liddell, a future Labour member of parliament, employed as director of personnel and public affairs at the *Scottish Daily Record*, part of Mirror Group Newspapers. Maxwell, with Liddell in attendance, paid out millions but received little more than a royal welcome in return.

Maxwell's reveries about international stardom were disturbed by Kevin, who was about to fly with Anselmini to Zurich on a mission to reassure the bankers that new anxieties about the empire were groundless. Kevin's solution was radical. More of the empire needed to be sold, he urged, despite the poor prices they might earn. The recent sale of their shares in TF1, the French television station, had prompted, a temporary rise in MCC's share price – the market had not realized that some of the shares were in fact owned by the Maxwell pension funds. More sales were needed. His father agreed and added another ploy: 'We'll have to buy more shares.' By 19 February, Maxwell officially owned 68.1 per cent of MCC, an increase of about 5 per cent over three months. A genuine market for the shares had practically ceased to exist.

Among those scenting a profit from the dismantlement of the empire was Robert Pirie, the Rothschild Inc. banker blamed by many for his part in the crisis after he had advised on the $2.6 billion purchase of Macmillan. Although Maxwell had insisted in the glory hours of winning the battle that he would never sell any Macmillan asset, the American publisher's break-up was inevitable. He had begun selling Macmillan assets in December 1989, although the $131 million he received in a public offering for 44 per cent of Berlitz had been a disappointment. This remedy in any case bore a sting: each sale after the Berlitz disposal would attract tax, reducing the proceeds.

On a recent Saturday morning, Pirie had drunk coffee with Maxwell in London. 'A client wants to buy Pergamon Press,' he smiled, asking the Publisher whether he would sell.

'Yes,' said Maxwell, agreeing that Rothschilds could investigate Pergamon's accounts on behalf of their client. But before the bank completed their investigation Maxwell told the banker that he was out of the running. The sale of Maxwell's jewel, the foundation of his fortune, was already under way – codenamed 'Project Tokyo' – convincing the dispirited founder of the empire that it was time to contemplate retirement. The purchaser was Elsevier, a Dutch competitor of Pergamon.

The arguments seemed incontrovertible. MCC was suffering from the 'Max Factor': his own presence was devaluing his company's value. Recent resignations had compounded his troubles, and window-dressing was no longer a sufficient cure. Only his retirement would improve the image and the share price.

Kevin's proposed successor as MCC chairman was Peter Walker, the Conservative member of parliament and former cabinet minister who had earned his millions in the 1960s with Jim Slater. Their controversial partnership had introduced a new era of unit trust investments in Britain, only to culminate in disaster and scandal long after Walker had departed. Walker, however, had secured his fortune and went on to become a successful politician.

The idea of recruiting Walker had first been mooted by Sir Michael Richardson, MCC's new stockbroker and the chairman of Smith New Court, which also employed Walker. Richardson, who had willingly accepted MCC as a new client after Maxwell had dismissed Laing & Cruickshank for failing to puff his shares, had first dealt with Maxwell twenty-five years before, when he had floated Pergamon shares on the stock exchange. In the decade after the Pergamon scandal in 1969, he had enjoyed only occasional contact with his erstwhile client, but that changed during the 1980s with Maxwell's resurrection. During those boom years Richardson had established himself in the City's higher echelons, reputedly becoming close to Margaret Thatcher, and switching to N.M. Rothschild, the bankers, where he earned a fortune. Like so many in the Square Mile, he wanted to believe, when MCC became a client in 1989, that Maxwell was 'squeaky-clean'. Sensitive, obliging and knighted for his polished performance in the City, Richardson would plead gullibility in the face of Maxwell's self-salesmanship, coupled with his promise of enormous fees. In recognition of that special relationship, Richardson had given the speech of thanks in 1988 at Maxwell's grandiose sixty-fifth birthday party for 500 of the great and the good in Oxford – it was 'the party of the decade', Richardson had declared extravagantly, before claiming that their relationship with Bob had 'enriched' all his guests' lives.

Peter Walker's introduction to the Maxwells was undertaken by Richardson, whose admiration for the politician, as for Maxwell, was unconditional: 'He's as tough as they come.' The result had been an invitation for Kevin to dine, on 21 November 1990, at Walker's home in Cowley Street, Westminster. That evening, Kevin had propositioned the politician to become MCC's chairman. The notion appealed to Kevin because, as he observed his father's increasingly erratic performance, he had, with his mother's encouragement, developed the desire to run the whole show himself. Walker was seriously interested. The two men had found they had enough in common: lean, mean, ambitious, self-admiring and brutally self-interested.

Three months later, at nine o'clock on 12 February 1991, Richardson and Walker visited Robert Maxwell to discuss the terms for what Sir Michael called 'an ideal solution'. The outline was blessed by Maxwell and, over lunch two days later, Kevin and Walker settled more details. To Kevin, one of the empire's problems seemed to have been resolved. Walker would be paid £100,000 per year and would, in addition, benefit from the executives' 'incentive' scheme. He was promised, over the following three years, 605,380 MCC shares in three instalments, and he would receive them free. At that date the shares were worth £1,350,000.

Kevin's thirty-second birthday fell on 20 February. As a treat, he chartered a Falcon jet and invited three other couples to fly at 7.30 in the morning from Heathrow to Venice for lunch, staying overnight at the Pensione Accademia. The cost could be charged to the company because he would briefly attend a board meeting of Panini, a sticker manufacturer which his father had bought in an expansionary fit and which was losing money.

While his son took a break, Robert Maxwell flew to the American southern states, to relaunch his Central European Fund. Within two days he had tired of the seven-day programme, which was costing

£140,000 and flew instead to Miami to inspect the *Lady Ghislaine* after her repairs. Once there, he decided that the new captain was unsuitable. Summoned to the bridge, the American seafarer was fired for dereliction of duty: he and the first officer had been absent from the boat shortly after Maxwell arrived.

Adding to the army of those dismissed caused Maxwell no concern. Once he had tired of people, their departure was convenient. No one, he believed, other than himself, was entitled to any security of employment, an opinion which he probably did not discuss over lunch with Norman Lamont at 11 Downing Street on 27 February – a meeting which the new chancellor of the exchequer could not subsequently find in his diary.

SIX

Vanity

– March 1991

A night-time telephone call from New York on 5 March 1991 pushed Maxwell further into his indulgent fantasy, sending him off on an adventure that would dangerously compound his plight. The caller was Sidney Gruson, a director of Rothschild Inc. and formerly a renowned journalist and editor of the *New York Times*. Ever since the Macmillan deal, which had netted Rothschilds $17 million in fees (albeit extracted from MCC only after substantial pressure), Gruson had known that Maxwell was 'fishing for an American newspaper'. At one time, Gruson had started negotiations with the Reverend Sun Myung Moon (founder of the Unification Church, or Moonies) to buy the *Washington Times* and had flown to London. Going straight to Maxwell's office from Heathrow, he was greeted by the Publisher's then personal assistant Andrea Martin: 'I'm afraid Mr Maxwell cannot see you.'

'That's not important,' replied Gruson. 'All I want is a men's room.'

When he emerged, relieved but anticipating either a long wait or a swift return to New York, he found Maxwell in his socks anxiously searching for him. That was Maxwell's charm – so different from Kevin, characterized by Gruson as 'an unmitigated shit without his father's flair'. Plans were completed for the two men to fly to South Korea, the Reverend Moon's homeland, but the proposed deal collapsed.

Next Gruson had suggested a bid for the *National Enquirer*, a sensation-seeking tabloid. A team of Maxwell's 'experts' toured the newspaper's Florida offices and discussed the project at length, only for Maxwell to baulk at the price – in retrospect a missed opportunity, for the profits were enormous. Gruson's next proposal, the purchase of the *New York Daily News*, was different. One of three tabloids in New York, the *News* in its heyday was the nation's largest daily with a circulation of 2 million. But in March 1991 its staff had been on strike for nearly five months. Although published and sold throughout the dispute by non-unionists, its circulation had collapsed to 300,000 and its advertising revenue had practically disappeared, aggravating its accumulated losses since 1980 of $250 million.

The Tribune company of Chicago, owners of the *Daily News*, had adopted abrasive tactics which had in Chicago successfully broken the unions' power. But in New York politicians and even the police, guided by self-interest, had supported the strikers. 'Stay strong,' Governor Mario Cuomo urged strikers, who had been burning delivery trucks and intimidating non-strikers. 'You're fighting for all of us.' The problem had been made worse by the naivety of the Tribune company, whose senior executives in Chicago could not understand the ruthless competitiveness of New York's Jews and mobsters and ignored the reality that New York City was not a suitable location for printing newspapers. Unable to cope with the violence and the daily losses of $700,000, the company's management had threatened that unless the strike ended by 14 March the newspaper would be closed permanently. Closure, however, would cost an estimated $100 million in redundancy pay-offs to the workers.

The *Daily News* was suffering an illness which Maxwell believed he could cure: overmanning by a rebellious and corrupt labour force, crippling restrictive practices, uncontrolled expenditure, antiquated print machinery and weak management. Over the previous years, he had stayed in contact with Jim Hoge, the *News*'s erudite and handsome publisher and president, who counted Henry Kissinger among his friends and owned a fashionable Manhattan address. From time to time, Maxwell or Sidney Gruson would discreetly telephone Hoge to ask if the paper was for sale. Politely Hoge would decline their offer.

That changed when the Tribune company issued its ultimatum to the unions and started to look for buyers. Maxwell declared his interest, but told Hoge that he refused to become involved in a competition. His participation would depend upon other bidders leaving the arena. 'He played it according to Hoyle, the whole way,' remarked Hoge, comparing Maxwell to the bridge master. On 5 March, Gruson gave Maxwell the all-clear. The Tribune company had offered to pay Maxwell $60 million if he took over the liability within ten days. On the same day, Hoge told George McDonald, coordinator of the nine trade unions involved, to telephone Maxwell in London. McDonald, a generous-minded Democrat stalwart, knew that his call was crucial. Without any competing bidders, the newspaper's existence depended upon Maxwell's decision. Even McDonald, a seasoned fighter, was nervous when he made that night-time call. Maxwell's position was potentially powerful and the unionist's weak. But McDonald's fears soon dissolved. 'Do you think it's worth my while to come?' was Maxwell's surprisingly meek response.

'We'll give you concessions,' answered McDonald. Ten minutes later he felt he had achieved more with Maxwell than he had in two years with the Tribune group. Maxwell, he sensed, was hooked. 'You know,' he later reflected in his strong New York accent, 'owning the *Daily News* is like a visiting card for sheikhs, kings and queens. It opens the door for people and I guessed he wanted it that bad. He could taste it.'

Bestriding an apparently irreconcilable dispute was honey to Maxwell. Not since he had defeated the Mirror Group's unionists during the 1980s had such an opportunity arisen, and it was in the same city where Rupert Murdoch had lost a fortune before abandoning his attempt to modernize another tabloid, the *Post*. Nevertheless, a more rational man, confronting such massive and unresolved problems as Maxwell was, might have shied away from new time-consuming tasks at that stage. Maxwell, however, saw the *Daily News* not as a distraction from his other problems but as a solution to them.

Fresh from plotting his new empire in Eastern Europe (he had flown for a night to Berlin), he began discussing with Ian McIntosh, of the British bank Samuel Montagu, the sale of 49 per cent of Mirror Group Newspapers, insisting that he should receive £500 million in cash. He desperately needed money and hoped that he might raise a better price selling shares in New York. Unfortunately, however, despite his acquisition of Macmillan, he was unknown to American investors. This weakness was mentioned by Charlie

McVeigh of Salomon Brothers, chosen after a beauty parade as the project's New York brokers for the flotation. McVeigh, a 'handsome goy', employed as much for his charm as for his talent, was accompanied by Nancy Peretzman, a stylishly dressed, tough investment banker who had caught Maxwell's eye when she thwarted his bid in 1986 to buy the magazine *Scientific American*. Together they had stressed the Publisher's need to overcome his anonymity in Wall Street. Over twenty-four hours, Maxwell calculated that buying the *Daily News* could solve several problems.

After an emergency session with George Wheeler – Maxwell had spotted a single grey root – he boarded the Gulfstream at six o'clock on Wednesday, 6 March at Farnborough to fly to Whiteplains, New York. His headquarters would be the Waldorf Astoria in Park Avenue rather than the Helmsley Palace on Madison Avenue. During his last visit to the Helmsley there had been a row. His special telephone fittings in the three floors of the presidential suite had been removed by the US Secret Service when the rooms had been occupied by President Bush, and they had not been replaced. Maxwell had exploded, refused to pay his bill and vowed never to return.

As he arrived at the Waldorf more flamboyant than ever, no one could have guessed his financial predicament. Even Maxwell had probably forgotten it somewhere across the Atlantic. To those whom he met over the following three weeks he was 'Mr $4.4 billion', a conjured estimate of his wealth. The combination of money and power attracted Americans, most importantly Charles Brombach, the Tribune's president. Charming Brombach, who had so misjudged New York's unions, was not a problem for Maxwell. In a pattern which he had repeated on hundreds of previous occasions, he pulled out a copy of his own biography written by Joe Haines, the idolizing *Daily Mirror* columnist, from the piles which were always stored on his Gulfstream, on his yacht and even in his hotel suite, and presented it as his visiting card, just as he presented the same volume to the heads of every nation which he visited. Unlike the heads of state, the Chicago Brahmin actually read the hagiography and was convinced by its portrait of 'a great family man, a brilliant entrepreneur and a brave soldier who could bring the unions to heel'. Brombach understood the difference between his own company and Maxwell's. 'We were looking at a fifty-year investment. He was sixty-seven years old and wanted to enjoy a piece of his lifetime's ambition.' It would be another vanity purchase.

The public announcement of Maxwell's interest preceded his arrival in New York. 'I'm negotiating to save the newspaper,' he boomed soon after touch-down. Although there were only nine days left in which to finalize a deal, he threatened that the unions had just five, until 11 March, to capitulate to his demands. The following morning he met McDonald on the tenth floor of Macmillan's Manhattan offices. The union leader had already said, 'Maxwell will not be granted "management rights" but we will of course consider any demands he makes.' The hint of concessions, albeit limited (the unions were determined to deny the aspiring proprietor the absolute power of hiring and firing), had been music to Maxwell, who had demanded that 800 of the 2,300 employees be dismissed but had rashly conceded, 'I'm not asking for "management rights".'

At the meeting, McDonald noticed another sign of weakness when Maxwell announced, 'I want the paper.' True to form, their conversation was marked by the tycoon's particular charm and cordiality, precisely what McDonald had been warned about by a British trade union leader: 'He's a scoundrel. Get everything down on paper. He charms the birds off the trees and then shoots them.' McDonald knew that he had a deal if all nine unions on the paper gave a few concessions for the redundancies which the Tribune company was funding.

The negotiations followed Maxwell's favoured pattern. Each union was given its own office so that he could shuttle between the fiefs, playing upon old rivalries. This kind of theatre gave him the opportunity to shine – as a printer, a publisher and a professional. 'I know newspapers and trade unions better than anyone else,' he told Robert Pirie, once again advising on behalf of Rothschild Inc. 'Leave the negotiations to me.' The banker watched Maxwell and Charlie Wilson, quickly flown from London, moving from office to office in a punishing schedule saying 'yes and no often to things they didn't understand'.

'I bet Murdoch couldn't beat this,' smirked Maxwell to Hoge for the umpteenth time.

'These are the concessions you need from the unions to make

profits,' warned Hoge. But Maxwell ignored the advice. 'He doesn't analyse,' grimaced Hoge. 'He wants the newspaper.'

Maxwell wanted the publicity just as much. Television camera crews and journalists were encouraged to camp in the Macmillan building to await appearances and pronouncements. 'The progress made was terrific,' proclaimed a grinning McDonald after the first day. The crisis hit at the weekend when, inevitably, Maxwell reneged on his earlier promises. He said after all that he wanted the 'management rights' which the unions had adamantly refused to concede. It was a good moment for Maxwell to play his ace. 'I'm going back to London now,' he told the startled negotiators on Saturday evening, 9 March. As he passed through the waiting journalists his parting judgment was intentionally ominous: 'I'm not so optimistic.' He added, 'When I pass a belt, I can't resist hitting below it.' This was vintage Maxwell, exhibiting the qualities which a decade earlier had humbled Britain's print unions.

Yet his return to London on Saturday night was not really an example of astute tactics. Rather, it was under the orders of Kevin. Maxwell was obliged, said his son, to attend Betty's seventieth birthday party. For weeks his diary had included the engagement, embellished with an instruction in capitals to 'KEEP FREE'. He had already missed the family dinner that evening in Oxford.

One hundred and fifty guests had been invited to 'Betty Maxwell's Special Birthday' in the Dorchester Hotel's Orchid Room. Included among the throng were the Duke of Bedford and Lords Forte, Sieff, Stevens, Weidenfeld and Young. Other well-known City celebrities were Eric Sheinberg, Richard Branson and Sirs Kit McMahon, Alastair Morton, Frank Roberts and Michael Richardson. Among the more controversial guests were Jean Baddeley, Sir Edward du Cann, Lady Duncan-Sandys, Vivien Duffield, Joe Haines, Lady Porter and Gerald Ronson. The most expensive guest was Boris Pankin, then the Soviet ambassador in Prague. His account for staying overnight at the hotel, paid by MCC, would amount to £2,011.

The family had attempted to inject humour into the celebration, although others would remark on the gauche taste. Each of the ten tables was named after one of the houses inhabited by the Maxwells in London, Oxford and France, and not forgetting the *Lady Ghislaine*. The main course was Lamb Meynard (Betty's maiden name) served with Légumes du Maurier (Maxwell's adopted name when he met Betty). The wines, costing £95 per bottle, were *grand cru*. The £250,000 dinner, to be paid for by MCC, was certain to be memorable – but not in the manner Betty's children had intended.

Arriving late, Maxwell appeared distinctly uncomfortable. As he mingled with his guests, he made little effort to pretend he was enjoying the occasion. His presents to Betty – jewellery and an elegantly bound book describing their life – had been arranged without his knowledge by someone else. After picking at his food, constantly glancing at his watch and ignoring his wife, Maxwell rose. While his guests were still eating, Maxwell began uttering a short speech about his negotiations in New York, practically forgetting his wife. 'I've now got to leave for New York,' he ended, already walking towards the door, abandoning his guests and family with their forks in mid-air and their mouths open in astonishment. With barely a farewell, he walked through the exit. He would neither wait for the dance nor see the midnight trumpet fanfare with the champagne toast. His wife could cut her birthday cake without him. She could make her own speech without him. He did not care that she was upset. Betty was his doormat. And she would sleep the night in the hotel – she was not welcome in his penthouse.

Outside, in Park Lane, Maxwell fumed, not about the wretched affair he had left behind but about his temporary chauffeur. He needed to reach the Battersea heliport before it closed and had no confidence in the man. Cursing, he abandoned the hapless chauffeur on the pavement, heaved himself into the driving seat and sped furiously towards the river. Within the hour he was flying back to New York. The thought that he could have flown on Concorde the following morning and so not have missed anything did not occur to him.

During that seven-hour flight he could muse on his new adventure. Owning the newspaper would be compensation for other recently failed ambitions. He had considered buying Paramount Pictures, and one year before had even bid for Sears Tower in Chicago. After a weekend's negotiation, it had become clear that his sole interest was in securing a name-change for one of the world's tallest buildings. 'If I buy this,' he had said, 'it must be a condition that it will be renamed Maxwell Towers.' Shortage of money had eventually curtailed the negotiations. But this time he would succeed. Here was a deal made in heaven: he would acquire a newspaper, and not only for nothing – he would actually be paid for assuming the ownership. He knew he would still be losing $1 million every week thereafter but the prize, the fame and $60 million in cash was too great to ignore. He needed that money badly even if he would soon need to pay it to the print workers.

During his absence, Charlie Wilson had continued the negotiations, alleviating fears that Maxwell might back out. 'They're rewriting what we don't like,' McDonald reported to his colleagues. Maxwell's bluff had been called when the union leader had telephoned London: 'Come back. We're still talking.'

Maxwell's eagerness disturbed Hoge. 'You're giving too much away,' he warned. 'You're throwing away money on overtime. If you don't fight hard now, you'll lose.'

Maxwell was uninterested. 'Yes, yes,' he smirked condescendingly. 'Don't worry. I know my business.' He would renegotiate later, he reckoned. Getting the newspaper was all that mattered.

By then, gauging precisely how to impress New York, Maxwell had ordered the *Lady Ghislaine* to speed from Miami and moor on the marina by New York's 34th Street, not far from the United Nations building. Ranked as he was by *Forbes* magazine as Britain's sixth richest citizen personally worth £1.2 billion, his yacht – like his Oxford mansion – confirmed that Maxwell 'lived like a king with kings'. In this floating headquarters, Maxwell dreamt of entertaining the emperors of America's media: men like Steve Ross, Larry Tisch and Ochs Sulzberger. In the event his first guest on board was Jim Hoge, the *News*'s publisher and president. 'I am going to buy your newspaper,' boomed Maxwell standing in stockinged feet to protect the thick-pile white carpet. 'A whore's rug,' mused Hoge, who was nevertheless, like even the most hard-boiled New Yorkers, impressed by the vessel. 'Maxwell's walk-out didn't work,' he later observed. The Publisher would do anything to get the paper. The unions knew that he wouldn't walk away.

On Monday morning, 11 March, the day of his self-imposed deadline, Maxwell sat across the negotiating table from Steve Ratner of Lazards, who had vouched to the Tribune company for his probity after consulting Bob Pirie of Rothschilds. In the Publisher's absence they had been negotiating the Tribune's payment to him. Pirie's demands, made amid paroxysms of emotion, had bounced off Ratner's array of cold calculations. 'We want $70 million,' burbled Pirie. 'No way. $65 million is final,' replied Ratner, knowing full well that the Tribune would indeed pay the extra $5 million to clinch a sale. Maxwell agreed to extend the deadline. Two days later, despite his passionate rhetoric, Pirie surrendered. Maxwell always demanded sycophants as advisers, and Pirie, keen to remain on the gravy train, failed to restrain his client's own excitement. Ratner and the Tribune executives smiled at Pirie's failure to get the last $5 million. Fed by his regular walks through the Macmillan lobby, surrounded by eager journalists and waving television cameras, Maxwell became infected by his own prominence and gradually lost the freedom to say the deal was off. The deal with the Tribune was only half the battle. Next, he needed to conclude the employment contracts with the trade unions.

At 11 p.m. on the 13th as Maxwell sat exhausted on the *Lady Ghislaine* drinking, unusually for him, vodka and orange, McDonald rang. 'If we don't sign tonight,' he said, 'it's all off.'

'Come down,' said Maxwell, visibly not at his best when McDonald walked shoeless into the state room. For once the Publisher showed no appetite for attempting a last squeeze of the lemon. Thirty minutes later he clinched a deal which supposedly saved $72 million a year on costs. But he lost on critical issues. It was, McDonald would admit, 'not the best he could have won. Maxwell could have got more concessions. We weren't hurt as much as we might have been.'

Ratner was less diplomatic: 'He was so arrogant and unreceptive to advice. He could have got a much better deal if he had driven harder. He lost tens of millions.'

'We're in danger of soon making a profit,' Maxwell said with a smile as he approached waiting newsmen in the lobby of the *Daily News* building on 42nd Street. His red bowtie glowed incongruously below the plebeian blue *Daily News* baseball cap, artfully jammed on to his head. In classic Maxwell-speak, he announced a deal which was 'historical and unprecedented'. Watching from the side as Maxwell basked in the publicity, Hoge understood the new owner's motives as he stood amid cheering and weeping *News* employees. Maxwell then led the jubilant, ever growing throng towards the printing presses. The headline was already set. 'Roll 'Em!' screamed his newest acquisition. As, with a great fanfare, he pressed the button to print 1 million copies, the headline was changed to 'Cap'n Bob bites the Big Apple'. They were genuinely dancing in 42nd Street that night – on the pavements, in the road itself and on the delivery trucks. 'Let's see if Murdoch can beat this,' shouted Maxwell, enraptured by the enthusiasm.

With the cheers still ringing, he was next led along Third Avenue by Pirie to Mr Fu's, the 'best Chinese restaurant in town'. As he sat down to spicy fish, John Lindsay, a former city mayor, led the applause for the man who had saved the *News*.

By daybreak, Maxwell was the news. 'Brit saves Daily News', blared a rival's headline as the Great Saviour allowed himself to be sucked into a rapacious publicity machine. Every television and radio station beamed his voice across the city as he declared his love for New York, just as on earlier occasions he had expressed his love for Holland, Canada, Russia and Israel. Over the following six months, he pledged, he would remain as a 'hands-on' publisher. Maxwell, the star, was surrounded by genuine admirers. It was a glorious moment for him.

The previous night, John Campi, the newspaper's energetic publicity director, had told Maxwell, 'I want you at nine a.m. at the *News* stand outside 42nd Street. I'll collect you from the boat. If you don't turn up for this, the press will never show up again.' With unusual punctuality, the Publisher arrived, donned a *News* hat once again and played to the hundreds who appeared. 'Go, Maxwell!' they yelled as autograph hunters thrust newspapers under his nose and women begged to get near the city's latest hero. 'I've been with celebrities all my life,' thought Campi, 'but this is *big*. He's the biggest ticket.'

New Yorkers are not easily impressed, yet few remained unswayed by the Briton's style. Living on board the *Lady Ghislaine*, Maxwell was repeatedly featured on television news programmes in whatever pose he desired: the mega-tycoon, interrupted by phone calls, receiving a parade of shoeless guests in the splendid state room bedecked with photographs of himself greeting world leaders. As the city bosses paid their respects, he was not averse to comparisons with Randolph Hearst. His presence was felt, and nowhere was it bigger than on his own newspaper's front page, where – in all seriousness – he declared himself to be 'a peacemaker'.

Once back inside the *News* building, the returning strikers discovered that the joviality was strictly confined to the streets outside. *Lex Maxwelliana* now ruled. Telephone operators were cursed for failing to man the switchboard twenty-four hours a day. Others were cursed for failing to leave their posts and greet their new employer. Among the first to be fired were 130 security men, spluttering bewilderment about who would protect the middle management from the ire of the returning strikers. Little did they realize that the managers were the next in line to be fired. The peacemaker's presence was abruptly imposed: 'When I call, I require instant service.' Somewhere from beyond a voice counselled, 'When Maxwell shouts "jump", just ask, "how high?"'

'Bob, you've lost the very people who can help you,' sighed Hoge, who had decided weeks earlier to resign. His employer was oblivious to all but one mantra: 'I bet Murdoch couldn't have done this.' To underline his challenge, Charlie Wilson was ordered to launch a new newspaper in New York, the *Racing Times*, to compete with Murdoch's *Racing Form*. The gambler was going for broke.

Meetings, orders, summonses and declarations poured forth from a man whose task was herculean. Restoring a newspaper's morale, motivation and style required the energy and leadership which were Maxwell's forte. This was a rerun of the *Daily Mirror* in 1984, a challenge which only Maxwell was either sufficiently courageous or foolhardy to undertake. With time and money, he was sure of success. Juggling had always eventually proved profitable.

In the first days the omens were not good. Important writers were still deserting; advertising revenue remained poor; and the value of the Tribune's shares zoomed up by $1 billion just for having paid Maxwell $65 million to get rid of the problem newspaper.

Only gradually would Maxwell realize that this was not Britain: that his ban on overtime would need to be revoked; that the replacement for the managers would need to be ex-union men; that the newspaper's distribution was controlled by the Mob; and that, unless he remained in New York, his revolution would dissipate. All that was ignored. For his real desire, as the representative of a new constituency, was recognition.

Throughout the negotiations, Maxwell had known that Hoge was due at the end of that week to attend the celebrated Gridiron dinner at the Capital Hilton in Washington. The hosts were the nation's top satirists and their guests were the president, senators, judges, bankers and the Great and Good of America. Maxwell wanted to attend that dinner. Indeed, some in the Tribune camp believed that his haste in signing the agreement with the unions was to qualify for the invitation. This he duly did.

The occasion required tails. Having just risked millions which he did not have, Maxwell naturally showed no hesitation in requiring Bob Cole, his spokesman, to be dispatched by Concorde from London with his best suit. Cole would be given a $200 tip. 'Buy something for your wife,' said Maxwell with underwhelming generosity.

Having enjoyed the most expensive meal of his life, he revelled in the attention. Never had he featured more in newspapers. He stayed in Washington overnight. The following day, Hoge was invited to a private lunch for about twenty-five at which President Bush was guest of honour alongside Generals Schwarzkopf and Powell, leaders of the victorious US forces in the Gulf war. Maxwell, understanding only too well the power of association and endorsement from American presidents, ensured not only that he was invited but that he was seated next to the president. During that meal, Bush's face gradually fell as he glumly sat through a monologue about Maxwell's triumphant peacemaking between Gorbachev, Shamir, Thatcher and other leaders. 'Oh my God,' Bush groaned to an aide as he departed. 'Absolutely terrific!' cried Maxwell to John Campi on his return to New York.

The extravaganza showed the symptoms of the Last Hurrah. For the next week, Maxwell remained in New York to manage the *News*. To recover the circulation and demonstrate his skills as the master of promotion, he rented a clipper moored in the Hudson River and invited past advertisers to a grand party serenaded by a band named New York Pops. In response to his own advertisement, 'We're Back – Buy Us', the circulation soared from 300,000 to 700,000, a hopeful sign but still too low a figure to produce profits.

The only interruption to the euphoria was a report from Kevin. Oblivious of the celebrations on 42nd Street, several banks were pressing for more collateral or repayment of debts. Kevin had summoned Basil Brookes, the young finance director of MCC: 'The private side needs a £75 million loan.' Brookes, although it was obvious to him that the banks were squeezing, agreed to the temporary transfer. There seemed no reason to refuse. Neil Taberner, the

Coopers partner, had raised no problems over the 1991 audit, and the finances appeared sound. By way of further reassurance, Kevin added, 'We've agreed the terms to sell Pergamon.' The £446 million paid by Elsevier, the Dutch publisher and competitor, was a good price, and the rationale for the sale was convincing. Scientists in the future would not read magazines, but would obtain their data through computers. Pergamon and its books, explained Kevin, represented an adventure past its prime, overtaken by electronic publishing, and MCC was retaining those rights. Brookes agreed, but after reflecting that MCC would lose the prodigious cash flow generated by Pergamon he insisted, 'We will have to issue a press release warning that MCC's profits will be down.' Kevin paused. Profit forecasts were among the icons which his father held sacrosanct. Anything other than ecstatic predictions were inconceivable. But according to stock exchange rules Brookes was right. Kevin telephoned New York. 'No. Absolutely not,' shouted Maxwell. The last contact with reality had clearly been lost in the midst of New York's adulation. But there was no alternative, Kevin decided. Only one method of persuasion could succeed: a personal conversation.

On Sunday, 17 March, Brookes flew with Kevin by Concorde to New York and by helicopter onward to the *Lady Ghislaine*. There they found long black limousines stretched along the 34th Street quay. Inside each car sat strikingly large men with dark glasses waiting for the trade union leaders who were aboard the yacht negotiating with the owner. Maxwell emerged on to dry land and, for fifteen minutes, Brookes and Kevin walked along the sunlit seafront haggling with him. Finally he gave way. 'Write out a draft and let me see it,' he growled, and returned to his yacht. Without even being offered a drink, the two visitors flew back to London. 'I could have done all that on the phone,' thought Brookes. It would have saved £10,000.

On his return, Brookes spent three days on the telephone arguing with Maxwell about the circular. 'He wants to water it down,' he complained, though he eventually agreed to words 'which I could live with'. The good news was that Elsevier's payment would soon be deposited in the bank to reduce MCC's debts.

In New York, Maxwell was still enjoying the glory, the fame and the banter associated with reviving the newspaper. Even Murdoch's

Sunday Times in London, a veteran critic, published a glowing profile of his achievements. Yet, by the end of the week, no permanent manager had yet been appointed. At the last moment, Jim Hoge agreed to remain for ninety days. Considering the past acrimony between him and the unions, it was an ill-considered choice. That was ignored by Maxwell. The *Daily News* deal had provided a brief diversion from his financial problems.

The $65 million from the Tribune company had been deposited in a private NatWest account in New York and $14.4 million was immediately transferred to TIB Corporation, a company controlled by Ellis Freedman, on Maxwell's behalf. The remainder was diverted to Pergamon Holdings, his private company, and used to pay private debts. Only $16,000 remained in the *Daily News* account managed by Marshall Genger, the financial controller. Genger was not troubled, because he saw another $23 million passing through the newspaper's account. He wrongly believed that the money stemmed from the Tribune payments. In fact, Maxwell was laundering the proceeds of further loans of pension fund shares before passing the money to banks in New York which were pressing for repayment of private debts.

Intoxicated by the publicity, Maxwell remained in New York, believing that his fortunes in London would reflect his dazzling American performance. Even in a career as frantic as his, the frenzied succession of announcements made in his absence as he unfolded his latest strategy was unprecedented. The most unexpected was the first of his proclamations.

On 24 March, he announced that he was resigning as chairman of MCC and would hand over the task to a 'senior City figure' to whom his two sons would be answerable. The decision was presented as a mark of his determination to pass on the inheritance while he expanded his newspaper interests, managing the Mirror Group, whose flotation was at last imminent, and saving the *Daily News*.

The news of Peter Walker's agreement to lead the controversial company was greeted with wonder. Among the most bewildered were MCC's other directors. Anselmini, the company's deputy chairman, first heard of it after a query from the *Financial Times*. His bewilderment was shared by Peter Laister, one of the non-executive directors: 'I was totally surprised.' Walker's appointment was nevertheless welcomed. Despite his colourful past, he had become the epitome of respectability. To the delight of MCC directors like Basil Brookes, he wanted the business to be run 'more conventionally'. The minutes of past board meetings generally revealed the directors discussing only finance and rarely the actual business of the group. 'I want proper, regular reporting,' said Walker, 'and more information published in the accounts.' Brookes agreed and noted the meteoric rise in MCC's share price from 150p to 223p. The *Sunday Telegraph*'s puff about Maxwell suited his requirements: 'One of Britain's most successful businessmen in the past decade . . . one of the most outstanding performers of the year'.

Kevin began to appear less beleaguered. On 25 March, he hosted a small meeting with Crédit Suisse bankers in his office. Among those invited was Julie Maitland. In previous weeks, Kevin had again been wooing Maitland and her boss Paul McDonnell, describing the finances of his organization and encouraging their belief that they were trusted, core bankers to the group. The benefit had been Crédit Suisse's agreement four days earlier to continue the loans. To underline their relationship, during that afternoon meeting Kevin revealed Pergamon's sale. 'It's consistent', he emphasized, 'with our commitment to sell off assets to reduce our debts.' To allay any other fears, he continued, 'We can still rely on £1 billion of our unpledged private wealth.' His serious and intelligent tone reassured the bankers. 'We can provide security for everything.' Kevin was simply repeating his assurances of July 1990: that the Maxwell family 'had long owned a very significant portfolio of equities'. Maitland, who had over the previous months compiled another assessment of the Maxwells' organization and assets based on Kevin's information, was not surprised by his latest assertion. Naturally Kevin did not reveal that he included pension fund money and Macmillan's Berlitz shares in that gigantic sum. But then, fortunately for the Maxwells, the bankers had made no effort to scrutinize his claims. On the contrary, Maitland and McDonnell were anxious to believe him. By then, the Maxwells owed the bank over £100 million, and they needed reassurance. In fact, Kevin's performance was superb – not only in the colourful presentation of his family's wealth but in his concealment of a crisis at the First Tokyo Trust which, if leaked to the public, would have irretrievably fractured the empire.

At the end of 1990, under Donoughue's management, the value of First Tokyo's shares had fallen by 8 per cent. Under its articles, the investors had the automatic right when that level was breached to vote whether to close down the Trust. Alan McInroy, the chairman, asked John Woolant, a broker at Rowe and Pitman, to examine the Trust's past activities. In the course of what he believed would be a routine examination, Woolant discovered First Tokyo's stock-lending agreement with LBI. He was more than perplexed. Further investigation revealed that First Tokyo was earning so much from stock lending that the Inland Revenue would certainly withdraw its valuable 'investment trust' status and class it as an ordinary 'trading' organization. 'You won't be allowed to undo this,' McInroy was told. There could be no appeal. Blaming Donoughue and Trachtenberg for that unforeseen calamity, McInroy asked Barry Walker, a tall, aggressive City solicitor at Ashurst Morris Crisp, to investigate. Walker arranged a conference with Andrew Thornhill, a barrister specializing in taxation. They would meet at the Temple at 3 p.m. on 22 February 1991.

The previous afternoon, in a telephone call to Mark Tapley, Woolant had expressed surprise that no one from LBI would be present at the conference. 'Both Lord Donoughue and Larry Trachtenberg are unavailable,' he said. 'Could you come?' Tapley was irritated. After all, he was trying to resign as LBI's managing director and was unwilling to be identified with First Tokyo's affairs, over which he had no control. Nevertheless, he agreed.

The conference in Thornhill's chilly room soon ground to a halt. 'I know nothing about the details and dates of LBI's management of First Tokyo,' said Tapley. He telephoned the office and insisted that LBI's only employee present, Jonathan Ford, should appear. The young accountant was soon nonchalantly answering the lawyers' apparently mundane questions. 'And to whom is LBI stock lending precisely?' asked Thornhill.

'To London & Bishopsgate Holdings,' replied Ford.

'And who owns that?' asked the lawyer.

'Ultimately, I suppose, the Maxwells,' answered Ford.

An awkward pause was interrupted by Thornhill's crystal accent, 'I see.'

'The cat's well and truly out of the bag,' Tapley thought to himself, looking at the expressions of the others. 'He's spilled the beans. The die is cast.' He departed the barrister's chambers fearing an 'imminent explosion'. The lawyers, however, remained silent. They would fully understand the implications only after reviewing their notes.

One month later, on 19 March, McInroy was telephoned by Barry Walker. His news was grave. Contrary to LBI's assurances, First Tokyo's stock was being lent to associates of LBI, a clear conflict of interest and possibly worse. Even more grave, said the lawyer, Morgan Stanley no longer had custody of the share certificates. 'My reaction could be described as shock, horror,' recalled McInroy. 'From our point of view this was dishonest. They'd given us false reports.' Also culpable were Coopers: 'They never investigated the stock-lending programme.'

McInroy contacted Tapley, who in turn told Kevin of the discoveries. Within hours, the Maxwells ordered Tapley in writing not to speak to McInroy. Tapley asked Stuart Carson to consult IMRO. 'There's no reason to go to IMRO,' replied the compliance officer. 'I've already got a letter from IMRO that there are no rules on stock lending.'

Anxious to protect himself, Donoughue told Robert Maxwell, 'I'm going to Clifford Chance for independent advice.' James Barlow, the Clifford Chance solicitor, was ready to provide a comfort letter tailored to Donoughue's instructions because it was his belief that Carson was technically correct: stock lending was permitted and there was no need to consult IMRO. Later, asked about the morally uncertain nature of his advice, Barlow would explain to Tapley that he had not been aware of the unusual form of stock lending taking place, nor had he realized that LBI was dealing with RMG.

The news was passed on to Maxwell in New York. Sitting in Kevin's office, Donoughue listened to the conference call, noting how his young employer seemed unfazed. The agreement between First Tokyo and London & Bishopsgate International, the Chairman reiterated, contained a clause specifically allowing the Maxwells to invest at their discretion in their own companies. 'No problem,' was his optimistic verdict.

At 3.30 p.m. on 26 March, Kevin chaired a meeting with McInroy, Walker and the LBI directors, having satisfied himself

beforehand that he could hold the line. Donoughue and Trachtenberg were reliable; George Willet would remain silent; but the
potentially dangerous exception was Tapley. Kevin hoped that Donoughue, recalled from his holidays in France, would keep that lid
down. Indeed, Donoughue persuaded Tapley to hold back and went
on to criticize Barry Walker's report. Bolstered by the advice from
Clifford Chance, Donoughue strongly denied that there was a conflict of interest. 'Donoughue's defending Maxwell's position,' McInroy realized. 'I'm dealing with a man who's defending himself in
the best way he can.'

With the legalities apparently settled, Kevin placed the blame for
the misunderstanding. 'It was Trachtenberg's fault,' he said apologetically. Trachtenberg had lied to everyone and would be dismissed, he alleged. Although satisfied with the explanation,
McInroy was uncertain whether Donoughue and Kevin were culpable. It was bizarre. Trachtenberg seemed perfectly likeable; it was
Donoughue who came over as an opportunist. And Andrew Smith
was disagreeably arrogant.

'We must get our money back immediately,' said McInroy. Then
he threatened to sack London & Bishopsgate before saying, 'I'll
have you investigated.' Kevin's face betrayed a flicker: McInroy had
scored a hit.

The issues of culpability were no longer relevant. Putting aside
McInroy's own possible liability, Kevin feared that any row would
damage the future flotation of the Mirror Group. 'I'm sure we can
settle this amicably,' he said soothingly. 'Dad's still in New York.
Let's agree to meet as soon as he returns.' McInroy, an uncombative
man, nodded. Kevin shot off to other meetings, first with the American executives of Macmillan and then for lunch with the new editor
of the *Kenya Times*, another recent acquisition. The editor's visit
to London was typical of the Publisher's phenomenal waste of
money: he had been waiting for a week at the Intercontinental
Hotel to see his new employer. No one seemed concerned about
the mounting costs.

After sleeping across the Atlantic, Maxwell arrived back in
London the next morning, Wednesday, 27 March – his promise to
remain in New York to care for the *Daily News* long forgotten. His
schedule was frantic. Having immersed himself in the excitement of
Gulf war diplomacy, he planned to fly that night to Israel. In

between he would closet himself with Kevin for a report about a sensitive operation.

The sale of Pergamon and the news of Peter Walker's appointment had pushed MCC's share price up to 223p. Some spoke of Maxwell's salvation. If the £446 million from Elsevier was repaid to the banks, MCC's remaining debt would be $1,200 million. With the prospect of falling interest rates and an advantageous exchange rate between sterling and the dollar thanks to the ending of the Gulf war, the current interest payments were manageable. Moreover, Maxwell's remaining companies, Macmillan, Berlitz, Molecular Design, the Official Airline Guides and Panini, seemed to optimists like Anselmini to be 'outstanding world-beaters'.

The rise in the value of MCC shares, doubly welcome in the volatile and falling market, also augured well for the flotation of the Mirror Group. Yet even to Basil Brookes, simultaneously an insider and an outsider, it seemed too fortuitous to be purely coincidental. 'Is there something I should know about who is buying the shares?' he asked Kevin.

'I don't know who it is,' Kevin replied politely, 'except I know it's not us. So I'm very happy.'

Of course the truth was different. Through his private companies and Liechtenstein trusts, Robert Maxwell had begun spending £400 million to buy MCC shares – an extraordinary attempt to manipulate the market using money taken from MCC itself and the pension funds. One chunk, bought through Goldman Sachs by Ellis Freedman, his New York lawyer, would cost $58 million.

As MCC's share price rose, Trevor Cook had urged that the pension funds' investment in MCC shares should be reduced. 'It's an opportune moment,' he told Maxwell, 'to sell some of BIM's stake.' The Maxwells had no option but to concur. Cook was therefore pleased when Robert Maxwell agreed to sell 25 million MCC shares. He was even more pleased when the initial price was renegotiated upwards by Kevin. To Cook it seemed to be a normal sale negotiated by Kevin through Goldman Sachs in New York. Kevin's plan would only become apparent the following month.

For Robert Maxwell, the clock was ticking towards yet another flight to Israel. The retiring Chairman had agreed to be photographed with Peter Walker before flying from Heathrow. As an additional boost to his self-esteem, he would be accompanied by

Peter Boyer, a writer from *Vanity Fair*, the celebrated New York magazine. Recognition in America had finally arrived. Although the arrangements for Boyer to profile Maxwell had been confirmed, the star had played a cat-and-mouse game with the journalist. At one moment, Boyer was talking to Maxwell on board the *Lady Ghislaine* in New York, and the next moment – asked to wait outside the bedroom – he discovered that his subject had jumped ship and disappeared. Pursuing him to London, Boyer succeeded in extracting an invitation from Maxwell 'to fly with me to Israel'. When the journalist duly arrived at the airport, he was unceremoniously dumped.

Perhaps the pace had become too frantic even for Maxwell. Reality had outpaced his image. During that flight, Sam Pisar, his French lawyer and an Auschwitz survivor who had become a confidant and business adviser, noticed a creeping metamorphosis as his client unconsciously distanced himself from the world around him. Maxwell's behaviour was becoming erratic, but by the time he stood with Pisar on the balcony of Jerusalem's King David's Hotel, clutching a glass of champagne, he had mellowed. Pisar attributed the change to Maxwell's rediscovery of his origins, but he was puzzled by his refusal to pray in a synagogue or observe the Sabbath. He saw only part of the truth. In reality, Maxwell was calmed by Israel's uncritical acceptance of him, allowing him alternately to meditate upon or exclude his troubles. Others said that Maxwell's restless life was taking a toll. The constant jet travel, ceaseless meetings and escalating deceit were having a deteriorating effect upon an ageing man. Those who witnessed him dozing off in meetings and even while telephoning concluded with hindsight that he was manifesting early symptoms of senility.

After a few hours' sleep in the King David Hotel and breakfast with Yaakov Neeman, the country's pre-eminent lawyer who looked after his interests, Maxwell drove to the prime minister's office and then hosted a celebration for the launch of *Vremya*, a Russian-language newspaper for the 400,000 immigrants whose recent arrival in Israel owed much to his negotiations with Gorbachev. Glad-handing his guests, a beaming Publisher assumed his rightful position at the centre of attention.

That night, he boarded the Gulfstream for New York to continue his management of the *Daily News*. He would stay in the presidential suite at the Waldorf Astoria. The gimmick of using the *Lady Ghislaine* was abandoned. He embarked upon establishing himself as a power broker in the city.

New York always stimulated Maxwell. Gazing at the unique skyline he reflected that there was every hope for better fortunes ahead. A favourite and unproven tale for the stream of interviewers passing through his suite was that in 1940, despite the rare offer of a visa, he had chosen Britain rather than America as the land in which to build his future. Unspoken was his suspicion that, had he sought to earn his fortune in New York, he would have disappeared among the hundreds of similar types struggling to earn reputations and millions. Instead, as a unique Englishman, he was now accorded special treatment by Americans. On the agenda was the launch of *Racing Times* at the Rockefeller Center, dinners with the famous such as Seagram's chairman Edgar Bronfman at his penthouse on Fifth Avenue, and the opportunity for endless pontification in newspapers and television about his ambitions. The hyperactivity fired his vanity, silenced his critics and stimulated – or so he hoped – financial relief. The next step was the flotation of Mirror Group Newspapers (MGN).

SEVEN

Flotation

– April 1991

Ron Woods had started working on the MGN flotation in autumn 1990, driven by Maxwell's expectation that the newspaper would be valued at around £1.2 billion. The Publisher instructed that 26 per cent of the company should be floated to raise, with Mirror Group's existing debts, £330 million. But that expectation had eroded as the weeks passed. The purveyors of the bad news were Sir Michael Richardson, his trusted broker, and Samuel Montagu, the second-league merchant bankers.

Samuel Montagu were not Maxwell's first choice to mastermind the flotation, but when other banks had rejected his approach he remembered Samuel Montagu's work on raising the billions for his Macmillan bid and reasoned that he could rely upon the bankers' docility in return for approximately £4 million fees. Samuel Montagu were delighted to be appointed. 'We find him to be straight,' sang the senior bankers Andrew Galloway and Ian McIntosh in unison. The 'air of doubt' sparked by the old DTI report of 1971 had long been dispelled. It suited the bankers to assume that what currently prevailed 'was a climate where nothing dodgy was going on' – although McIntosh had worked with Maxwell twenty years earlier and could be in no doubt about his business methods. 'He's now prepared to take advice,' claimed McIntosh, who understandably found the fees very attractive.

The bankers accepted that Peter Walsh and Ian Steer of Coopers would present the accounts for the flotation. Until recently Maxwell had resisted close scrutiny of those accounts until the sweetheart deals set up by the myriad of inter-company contracts within his private empire had been disentangled and concealed. One problem which particularly concerned him was a £535 million private debt secured against the Mirror Group. The accountants agreed to work with Ron Woods to find a way of removing that albatross.

The bankers could also be satisfied that Linklaters and Paines, one of the City's most respected firms of solicitors, had agreed to take Maxwell's fees to undertake the statutory compliance work – the production of reports assuring the public that the contents of the prospectus were accurate. They were also comforted by the presence of Sir Michael Richardson as stockbroker for the flotation. 'Richardson knew Maxwell better than any of us,' recalled a Samuel Montagu banker, 'and he was involved in everything and every meeting. He was frequently in and out of Maxwell's office and never queried anything.' Richardson's defence would be eloquent: 'My job was to sell the shares. Nothing else enters a broker's life.'

The only remaining chore was to appoint non-executive directors, the independent guardians of the public interest. The hurdle to overcome was the automatic unwillingness of respectable City figures to be associated with Maxwell – alias the 'Max Factor'. Their disinclination suited the Chairman who was determined to accept only his own nominees.

One candidate was telephoned by Maxwell himself. Sir Robert Clark, former chairman of the merchant bank Hill Samuel, was one of Maxwell's earliest City supporters and friends. They had met in the autumn of 1968 when Maxwell bid for the *News of the World*. The acrimonious battle which had followed with Rupert Murdoch, the rival bidder, had shocked Clark: with City support, the Australian had ridden roughshod over the rules, comprehensively out-smarting Maxwell. In 1980, Clark had helped Maxwell buy the British Printing Corporation (BPC), observing how Maxwell had persuaded Peter Dodds, a manager of National Westminster Bank, to lend the aspiring owner £90 million. 'That was very impressive,' remembered Clark. Ever since, Maxwell had regularly telephoned him, although Hill Samuel were never used for Maxwell's string of take-over bids.

Maxwell's invitation to Clark to join the new Mirror board was 'out of the blue', the banker would later suggest. Clark would say he had taken 'the prudent course of speaking to the bankers, lawyers and accountants'. He prided himself on being an experienced City operator but in reality he was effortlessly seduced by Maxwell flattery: 'You were in at the beginning and so you'd better be in at the end.'

'This one's okay,' boasted Ian McIntosh to Clark. 'It's protected from Maxwell whatever he does.' He continued: 'This is a well-managed company with a huge cash flow and huge profits, and Maxwell will have no role.' Even the reassuring term 'ring-fence' fell from McIntosh's lips, although he would later strenuously deny parenting the notion.

Like so many so-called professionals knighted for the wrong reasons, Clark required no reassurance about Maxwell's new probity. Any doubts had been drowned by the extraordinary celebrations for the Maxwells' fortieth wedding anniversary in 1985. Among the 500 guests who attended the gala at Headington Hill Hall were Sir Robert Armstrong, the cabinet secretary, Harold Wilson, Lord Rothermere, Lord Sieff, an array of senior bankers including Sir Kit McMahon and even the television presenter Robin Day. Since then, there had been the even more glittering party in 1988 for 500, including many senior politicians, to celebrate Maxwell's sixty-fifth birthday. Additional respectability was bestowed by the eleven peers closely associated with Maxwell: Lords Spens, Silkin, Rippon, Havers, Williams, Donoughue, Stevens, Mishcon, Elwyn-Jones, Bramall and Cudlipp. Like Clark, all of these men represented the gullible British establishment, willingly seduced by an unusual personality who had fabricated a sob-story about the DTI inspectors framing an innocent man in a Star Chamber trial. Many even swallowed his fantasy that the English courts had nullified the DTI reports.

So Clark joined Maxwell's bandwagon, alongside his second nominee as a non-executive director, Alan Clements, the quiet, undistinguished former finance director of ICI whose presence on the board, the Publisher accurately predicted, would be imperceptible. To sugar the pill, Maxwell had offered Clements a consultancy with LBI at £30,000 per annum. After accepting, Clements was asked instead to be a non-executive vice-chairman of the Central European Fund, his nascent investment bank. He would be paid £20,000 per annum and his name would be featured on the glossy brochure dispatched to all prospective investors.

The introduction of Clark and Clements to the Mirror Group was inauspicious. Neither of the new directors sought to meet either

Ernest Burrington, the company's managing director, or Lawrence Guest, the finance director. Maxwell's derogatory asides about Guest left no one under any illusions about the Chairman's contempt for him. On the night Maxwell had bought the Mirror in 1984, he had summoned a board meeting at 2 a.m. Guest, roused from his sleep, had first croaked, 'Is this a hoax?' When reassured that Maxwell was on the telephone, he had refused to drive to London in the middle of the night. But threatened with an unpleasant alternative – 'I never joke. Your job's at risk if you don't oblige' – he had capitulated. Ever since, he had obsequiously obeyed Maxwell, though playing only a limited, technical part in the newspaper's management. But even Guest's good-natured weakness was too independent for Maxwell. Guest, he said, should be replaced by Michael Stoney, a young, ambitious accountant employed in his private companies. Stoney, in Maxwell's opinion, was more intelligent and more presentable for the flotation than the chain-smoking Guest, but also more amenable, more sympathetic to the Chairman's whims. Unusually, that desire was thwarted. 'It wouldn't look good at the moment,' Maxwell was told by the bankers.

With extraordinary speed, the prospectus offering the Mirror Group for sale was finalized during late-night sessions in Maxwell House attended by a group of thirty bankers, accountants, lawyers and executives. During one memorable night, which required that a branch of the Midland Bank remain open, £304 million of Maxwell's debt in the company was removed by an ingenious piece of financial engineering for which Ron Woods claimed the credit. In a complicated manoeuvre, no less than £683 million was dispatched in a circle to pay dividends and buy the Mirror Group's titles, producing tax-free profits which helped to solve his employer's problem.

Yet none of those participating in that charade voiced any reservations that the same genius might have been misused, not by Woods but by his master, to conceal other activities. John Walsh of Coopers had grounds to be suspicious as he prepared the flotation, yet the auditor's task, he believed, was 'not to ask questions' but to work on the accounts prepared by Maxwell's staff. Although he realized that the Mirror Group's pension scheme 'looks too good' and knew that pension fund money had been deposited in the past in Maxwell's private companies, he resisted making any inquiries which would have shown that in April £96 million of the Mirror

Group's pension funds were loaned to Maxwell. Over the years he had seen cash pass around the whole Maxwell group, including the pension funds, and he was unconcerned. Robert Maxwell, he believed, was the proprietor of the whole group and could exercise his jurisdiction over every aspect, including the pension funds.

Even after he noticed that the lawyers' references in the prospectus about the pensions had 'very clearly' been written under 'the control of Mr Maxwell', Walsh did not deem it correct to query the information supplied to the lawyers by his colleague, John Cowling, the auditor of BIM. The concrete compartmentalization erected by Maxwell within his own empire was faithfully adopted by the Coopers partners who were auditing the different parts. All Cowling admitted to his colleague was, 'I have a number of observations because the prospectus doesn't get behind the facts.' But since Walsh believed his own favoured homily, that 'auditors are not given crystal balls to guess where money might come from', he accepted Cowling's 1990 audit at face value.

That attitude was not questioned by Samuel Montagu, the bankers. Neither McIntosh nor Galloway had contemplated a special investigation of Maxwell – 'just the normal requirements' – but the bankers did caution that inter-company trading would be outlawed without the board's express permission. In a bravura performance, Maxwell gave his undertaking and convinced the bankers that he was taking the process seriously.

On the frequent occasions when Maxwell was not present, he relied upon George Willet, the LBI director and former merchant banker, to report any hiccups. With Willet's help, the customary six-month process of flotation was squeezed into six weeks. 'Everyone was leaning over backwards to accommodate Maxwell's requirements,' observed Burrington, a former editor of the *People* who had been a Mirror employee for forty years and had in 1991 been appointed MGN's managing director. He had never witnessed a flotation before and was moved to remark that 'Expediency was the priority.'

By the end of those six weeks, all were agreed – especially about one issue. For all Maxwell's intemperate telephone calls, the company could not be sold for £1 billion: the bankers would not risk offering it for even £500 million. 'Our biggest problem, Bob,' said one of the more courageous of the team on the telephone to New

York, 'is you.' Maxwell was effectively silenced. Desperate for the money, he was paralysed, unable to negotiate. To his disappointment, because he would be personally assuming a proportion of the £500 million of debt previously secured against the private company, he would receive only £230 million for 49 per cent rather than his original hope of £330 million for 26 per cent.

Reluctantly, Maxwell returned to London from New York on Saturday, 6 April. George Wheeler was his first visitor the following morning. As the chemicals dried on his hair, the Publisher indulged in a few bursts of telephone terrorism. 'I need you here immediately,' he snarled at an underling disturbed from his weekend relaxation, replacing the receiver before there was any chance to protest. As always the unfortunate victim would be left stranded and ignored in the outer office for some hours before being allowed to return home. Then, glancing at his watch, Maxwell telephoned Alexander Yakovlev in Paris. Later that day President Gorbachev's aide would be flying to London, to be housed at the Savoy at Maxwell's expense. Everything, the Russian was assured, was in order. By noon, relieved that he had made his presence felt across the capital, Maxwell began a series of meetings to prepare for the week's big media event, the launch of the Mirror Group's prospectus – the subject already of intense media speculation.

At 8 a.m. every day, the Samuel Montagu team was due to meet in Maxwell's office to discuss the progress towards flotation. From all of those professionals, Maxwell believed that he had successfully concealed the crucial detail that his strategy was dictated by his financial crisis and the state of the pension funds. That was not a self-delusion. As for the Mirror Group's own pension fund, Maxwell and Kevin had certainly managed to divert the attention of the so-called professionals. In preparing the flotation prospectus, the 'long form' report (the professionals' testimony about the company's financial probity) and the evidence that MGN and the remaining private empire had been totally separated, the Coopers team of accountants could theoretically demand complete access to every record and share certificate. Maxwell knew that, if the accountants were diligent, the flotation would be torpedoed, and much worse would follow.

Since Maxwell's acquisition of the Mirror Group in 1984, the pension fund's value had grown to £431 million, including an accumulated £150 million surplus. Despite its wealth, Maxwell had staunchly resisted the demands of the Association of Mirror Pensioners that their benefits should be increased. As their complaints became more specific, especially about the fund's actual investments in foreign and Maxwell's own companies, and as the threat of legal action increased, Maxwell appointed Ian Pittaway, a solicitor specializing in pensions, to defend his management. Pittaway, like Philip Morgenstern, another partner in the firm Nicholson Graham and Jones, satisfied Maxwell's expectations. Rather than personally investigating the complaints, he relied solely upon information supplied by Cook and Brian Chapman, one of the Mirror Group trustees, and aggressively delayed sending relevant replies and adamantly refused to divulge information to which the pensioners believed they were entitled. His obstructive tactics, as required by his client, admirably served Maxwell's purpose. In self-congratulation Pittaway would say, 'I have no regrets about the advice I gave or my actions.'

Unannounced, Maxwell had appointed Kevin and Ian to the board of the Mirror Group pension fund trustees, leaving just one trade union representative. On 16 April, Kevin resigned as director of the pension trust, apparently to avoid a conflict of interest with his directorship of BIM. The remaining pension trustees, other than the Maxwells, were unfamiliar with BIM's activities and its relationship with LBI. Even Lawrence Guest, MGN's finance director and a trustee, was unaware of the stock lending. Indeed, Guest could not recall reading in BIM's regular statements to the trustees that the pension fund owned shares in Scitex and Teva, two Israeli companies. The Scitex shares would be transferred to BIM by Maxwell to settle a debt, while the Publisher's $30 million investment in 1989 in Teva, a pharmaceutical company, had been funded entirely by the pension funds. Like Guest, the Israelis believed that both investments were owned by Maxwell personally rather than by BIM. Making sure that no one's interest was aroused in the pension fund's affairs helped to avoid a proper audit, which would expose how Maxwell had by then, through the phoney stock-lending operations, diverted £114 million of pension fund stock from BIM to the private companies. In that high-risk strategy, the continuation of Maxwell's deception depended upon his approach to Peter Walsh, the accommodating Coopers auditor responsible for the flotation. His gambit was strengthened by his assiduous nurturing of their relationship over many years.

'Nothing has changed in the pension funds since your audit earlier this year,' Maxwell told Walsh, a soft-spoken accountant projecting the image of an English gentleman. 'We're in a hurry. Can we not base the prospectus on the [BIM] accounts you completed just weeks ago?' Maxwell's trick carried a risk. John Cowling, the Coopers auditor responsible, might have objected. His recent accounts reported on the financial year ending 1 April 1990, and in the intervening year, he might have thought, much could have changed. If Cowling had been marginally more perceptive, he might have spotted a strategy familiar to the victims of Maxwell's previous swindles. Instead, he succumbed to the familiar charm offensive. 'The pension funds' financial year ends in March,' soothed Maxwell, 'but Mirror Group's ends in December. It would make sense to bring both the pension fund and company accounts into line in December 1991.' Not only to Cowling but also to the bankers, the Chairman's proposition sounded entirely reasonable. It *did* make sense that all the groups should be brought into line. Guest, the chairman of the accounts committee, did not oppose his employer. Walsh too proved amenable and agreed to delay the 1991 audit.

So, instead of descending upon Cook and the pension fund offices, demanding to see the actual pension fund share certificates in Maxwell House, in the banks and in the fund managers' offices, Cowling completed the vital 'long form' on the basis of the 1990 accounts, merely asking Cook to fill in some gaps relating to the stock lending. Without access to LBI's accounts, Cook was dependent on Trachtenberg's assurances. 'I've physically checked the collateral at regular intervals,' Trachtenberg had told him repeatedly, and as usual Cook believed him. Eventually the auditors Walsh and Steer reported that, relying upon Cowling's audit, they were satisfied that there were no discrepancies in the pension funds. 'They did not even show me their completed, formal report,' Cook would complain.

The bankers did not query Coopers' decision. Galloway was not suspicious: 'It didn't interest me frankly. I accepted what Coopers told me.' The bankers were not even alerted by the pension funds' unusual and confused ultimate ownership by the Maxwell Charitable Trust, while the employees of BIM, the trustee for the funds, were paid by Headington Investments owned by a Liechtenstein trust. Galloway was unconcerned by his inability to undertake any investigation in the tax haven. Similarly, no comments were made about the pension funds' unorthodox investments. Maxwell had successfully cajoled the professional advisers to dance to his tune, and could rely on their shortcomings to ensure that they failed to spot his repetition of the pre-1969 trick by which he had perpetrated the Pergamon fraud.

During that Sunday afternoon, 7 April, his first full day in Britain for five weeks, Maxwell reviewed with Kevin, Michael Richardson and the bankers the preparations for the flotation. All listened to Tony Carlisle, who was masterminding the critical marketing and media campaign, and approved his proposals. There would be mass advertising on television, in the newspapers and on hoardings, interviews with key journalists, and a press launch. 'Good, right, fine,' huffed Maxwell, and pushed everyone out of his office.

The Publisher then pressed a telephone button. From another door, David Burnside, the aggressive Ulster publicist employed by British Airways, entered with his friend David Montgomery, a journalist. Having fired Roy Greenslade, Maxwell was considering employing Montgomery as editor of the *Daily Mirror*. After the introductions, Burnside departed, returning to a flat owned by Lord King, the chairman of British Airways. He and King sat drinking for an hour, and then both invited themselves to Maxwell's flat to continue drinking and talking. Maxwell, it appeared, was unenthusiastic about Montgomery.

At the end of that Sunday, late at night, Mark Tapley arrived, answering Maxwell's order that he should complete the housekeeping essential for a successful flotation. At weekends, Tapley had noticed, Maxwell was always easier, even nicer, than he was during the week. The Publisher seemed relaxed as the trim figure approached across the room. This employee's protests, Maxwell realized, about the mismanagement of LBI and the unauthorized use of First Tokyo's shares could, if publicized, cause fatal damage. Naturally, Maxwell did not reveal his perception of his own weakness. By then, he had arranged for Dick Russell of solicitor Titmuss Sainer to provide the necessary documents proving that no misdemeanour had occurred at LBI. Indeed, the lawyer had at one session sat at Maxwell's right hand, dictating their duties to LBI's directors.

After pleasantries had been exchanged with Tapley, Maxwell repeated the sermon: 'Your duty is to LBI's shareholders.' From his desk, he drew out a letter written to Tapley by Cowling, who 'advised' that the stock lending undertaken by First Tokyo was not a problem. Tapley agreed to remain silent, allowing Maxwell 'satisfactorily to settle the problem'.

Two days later, Tapley sent Alan McInroy an apology for the stock-lending programme, blaming Trachtenberg for providing wrong information. His letter also mentioned that both Cowling and Stuart Carson had 'carried out spot-checks' to reassure themselves that First Tokyo's shares were safe and that the 'collateral was in excess of the stock'. McInroy accepted the assurance, unaware that neither man had personally checked the certificates. The Scotsman was preparing himself for a showdown in London on 11 April, immediately before taking a holiday.

In anticipation of that confrontation, Lord Donoughue sought that afternoon to distance himself from the disaster. In a letter to Maxwell, he protested that Trachtenberg had not only failed to keep proper records but had also undertaken a form of stock lending beyond the agreement between LBI and First Tokyo. There was, he added, a 'reasonable prosecution case against LBI'. Maxwell was neither impressed nor concerned. He had Donoughue's measure. The man appeared more interested in his salary than in principle. Of greater concern to Maxwell was McInroy.

At 2.30 p.m. on the 11th, McInroy landed on the roof of Maxwell House. Under strict instructions from Maxwell, the Publisher's staff had provided the helicopter from Heathrow and had whisked the Scotsman ahead of dozens of other visitors waiting in the anteroom – 'I was kept waiting for minus two seconds' – to the ninth-floor office, where Donoughue and George Willet were already waiting. Kevin, skiing in Tignes in the French Alps, had decided at the last moment not to return and had cancelled a private jet. Maxwell was unusually affable. His fears that LBI would be publicly dismissed from First Tokyo were quickly encouraged by McInroy: 'You realize that it will be difficult for us to keep you as managers.' No telephone calls or other interruptions were allowed as Maxwell repeated that the stock lending was legal although perhaps unfortunate. 'I'm sure we can settle this quietly,' he smiled. 'After all, it wouldn't look too good for you if this came out.' After a pause, he added, 'We might need to take action against you. You're responsible for gross mismanagement.' The threat might have been less effective if the contents of Maxwell's desk had been emptied out. Inside one drawer, underneath a brochure of corporate gifts offered by Ghislaine's sorry enterprise, were dozens of photographs of naked girls and a packet of suppositories. Instead McInroy, having agreed to search for a solution, was flown by Maxwell's helicopter to the Denham golf club to start his holiday.

Later that evening, John Pole, the security chief, was summoned. The past days' events had intensified Maxwell's paranoia. Unknown enemies were targeting him, he believed, unauthorized microphones had been inserted inside his own offices and his visitors were, like himself, carrying briefcases with concealed transmitters. 'I want you to sweep the ninth and tenth floors,' Maxwell told the former policeman. 'Do it in the next half-hour.'

'I need three hours!' exclaimed Pole, believing that Maxwell the exhibitionist had warmed to the idea of the security chief, burdened with microphones, aerials and electronic gadgets, sweeping the offices in front of the staff. Exasperated, Pole announced his solution two days later: 'I'm going to alarm the two floors, Mr Maxwell. We'll have cables everywhere connected to a permanent spectrum analyser and radio receiver to trace any transmissions from bugs. A permanent alarm system.' Maxwell enthusiastically approved the £30,000 scheme. The system would be installed by a former army communications officer, under Pole's supervision. No unauthorized bug would ever be found.

One cause of Maxwell's sudden paranoia was the Mirror Group launch. All the preparations were passing smoothly, but he lived in fear of a leak about his financial deceits. Until Wednesday, 17 April, the daily pattern was uninterrupted. After dozens of interviews and presentations to analysts he believed that he had evaded the potentially bad publicity. He had scoffed about the dismissal of Roy Greenslade, the *Daily Mirror*'s editor, and about the 19 per cent decline in the newspaper's circulation; he had laughed off the criticism that his own repeated appearance in the newspaper, both in favourable articles and in large photographs, suggested that it was a self-promotion sheet; and he justified his repeated interference in the newspaper's editorial content by acclaiming his own expertise in domestic politics and foreign (especially Soviet) affairs. Still unknown was his bewildering insistence to Greenslade that the fighting in the Gulf would be over 'in two days' (it continued for many weeks); or his dismissal as 'unimportant' of the Soviet invasion of Lithuania: 'Do you realize that Gorbachev wouldn't do anything without ringing me first?' More than other newspaper proprietors, Maxwell expected his editors to curtsy to his vanity and his power; and he expected everyone else to respect his apparent intimacy with the world's leaders.

After all, in his diary was an invitation to 10 Downing Street; and he had on 10 April personally hosted a tête-à-tête in his flat between Alexander Yakovlev, Gorbachev's aide, Henry Kissinger and Robin Leigh-Pemberton, the governor of the Bank of England. After that conversation, he had hosted a dinner for Kissinger, Neil Kinnock, James Callaghan, Paddy Ashdown and Soviet diplomats. Anyone still doubting that he was a world player needed only to witness the delegations and ministers from every East European country coming through his door; or to hear the telephone calls to his office from Shamir in Israel, Genscher in Bonn, Mitterrand in Paris and respected power brokers in Washington and New York. Even as he flew across the Atlantic on Friday, 12 April to spend the weekend caring for the *Daily News*, he was maximizing his influence among the handful who directed the world's affairs. On his return to London to launch the flotation, his self-esteem was once more bubbling fiercely.

That such a world-renowned person should be ridiculed to his face seemed inconceivable, especially in London. But that was Maxwell's fate at the press conference to launch the Mirror Group's flotation just after 11.30 on 17 April. Despite exhaustive rehearsals, a drinks party for his guests and last-minute rearrangements of the seating plan, Maxwell seemed irrepressible as he sat complete with huge red bowtie in the crowded Rotunda in the Mirror headquarters facing the bankers, brokers and journalists whom he had fooled. Yet within minutes his mood had soured. How, he was asked by a young reporter, could he square his statements in the Mirror Group's prospectus with the DTI inspectors' conclusions in 1971 damning his fitness to manage a public company?

Maxwell could not disguise his pain and embarrassment. 'My record since then as chairman of many British companies will, I hope, even satisfy even you, sir.' The reply was naturally misleading.

He was the manager of just one public company. Despite the master salesman's best efforts, the atmosphere remained sullen. 'No, you can't ask another question,' he snapped at the bold reporter, one of the few in the capital who remained unimpressed by the waves of propaganda disseminated by the Publisher. The launch was ruined as the conference limped to an early conclusion. Maxwell's advisers were perplexed. 'A cheap shot,' moaned one, seeing his colleague 'sick as a parrot'. 'I thought that was all forgotten,' lamented Galloway, the banker who had suggested that the new Mirror Group would be immune to Maxwell's interference or dishonesty. In the vestibule afterwards, the Publisher himself complained, 'The bitchiness of British journalists continues' – forgetting that, on the floors above, his own journalists were writing stories intended to cause others embarrassment and misery. 'This country hates success,' he sniped, ignoring the unpalatable fact that the sale of the Mirror Group shares had been forced upon him by his own failures.

'It's ring-fenced,' insisted the Samuel Montagu bankers to every potential shareowner over the following days. Their claim confirmed that the professionals did not think that the DTI inspectors' detailed description of Maxwell's frauds in 1969 were any longer relevant, and they were apparently unaware that in 1954 the Official Receiver had accused Maxwell of stealing £133,000 while managing the insolvent Simpkin Marshall, a publishing wholesaler.

Yet their client was vulnerable, more than they imagined. The open scepticism voiced by Derek Terrington, a City analyst who issued a circular acronymically entitled 'Can't Recommend A Purchase' – CRAP – which condemned the shares as overpriced, provoked a succession of complaints and threats culminating in what was as near to an admission of defeat as Maxwell ever uttered: 'It's the last straw.'

That night, Maxwell was invited to dinner in the private dining room of Mark's Club in Mayfair by Andrew Lloyd Webber and his wife Madeleine. Increasingly, he had been cancelling invitations at the last moment even from the most prestigious hosts. On that night, however, the pattern was broken. Lloyd Webber owned the publishers of a critical biography, *Maxwell the Outsider*. Extensive and expensive litigation between Maxwell and his host remained unresolved, despite a letter drafted by Peter Jay and signed by

Maxwell warning the composer in October 1989 that 'hostile' photographers were offering certain pictures 'exclusively to the *Mirror*'. The letter carried Maxwell's implied but unstated threat that the newspaper might publish twelve photographs of the composer dancing with young girls in nightclubs. Maxwell, it was clear, was also using bugs and detective reports in his relentless pursuit of the litigation. Lloyd Webber's fear of embarrassment was aggravated by Maxwell's additional ploy of buying 14 per cent of his Really Useful Group from a disgruntled executive solely to block the composer's plan to privatize his company. The attempts by Robert Kretowicz of Salomon Brothers to mediate between his two clients had proved unsuccessful. Lloyd Webber, sensitive to any adverse criticism and keen to be admired, arrived anxious to settle the litigation.

During the meal, Maxwell's cheerful conversation degenerated into innuendoes and threats. 'I want £100,000 and an apology,' he demanded. 'And there are more photos.' The composer shuddered. Fearful of Maxwell's wrath, Lloyd Webber departed contemplating capitulation, unaware that his opponent's threats were prompted as much as anything by his own fears that his enemies, real and imagined, were about to discover the truth about himself. But at the end of the following day Lloyd Webber's proposed retreat had been blocked by advisers and friends. 'Don't give in to that bully,' urged a cabinet minister.

Maxwell's mood was darkening. Over the next few days, as he toured the City and flew to Scotland attending lunches and dinners in a bid to persuade fund managers to buy Mirror Group shares, he lambasted those who dared pose awkward questions. At the press conference in Glasgow on 22 April arranged by Helen Liddell, Maxwell's temper snapped. 'I'm not putting up with this any more!' he roared, to Michael Richardson's embarrassment. Anxious to escape the pressure, he flew to America, pleading an invitation to dinner at the White House. Abandoned was a dinner the following evening at Claridge's with ten fund managers. Their goodwill was essential to the whole venture, yet Maxwell insisted that he could speak with them via a satellite link from the *Daily News* office in New York. It was the disaster bankers and brokers trying to sell Mirror Group shares had feared. Instead of pouring charm and reassurance over the fund managers, Maxwell's patience evaporated

– 'What do you know about printing?' he asked rudely – just before the satellite link likewise evaporated.

The possibility of doomsday was again resurfacing. The price of MCC shares was slipping following a *Financial Times* report that 'Maxwell warns on MCC results'. In his statement, Maxwell had blamed the slow progress of disposals in the recession, but the City gossip had told another, more accurate story. Bankers, worried about their money, were renegotiating the terms. Their inducement was to give the Maxwells a few extra millions to get their huge loans secured against valuable assets. Their latest manoeuvre was completed on 24 April in the Rotunda where Kevin watched a signing ceremony by Lloyds Bank after the renegotiation of an existing £150 million loan to RMG.

Brian Brown, the robust corporate manager at Lloyds responsible for daily relations with the Maxwells, was under orders to reduce sharply the bank's loans to the group from a high of £490 million. Although good fees had been earned in the past – £4 million in 1988 alone – there was concern about the bank's exposure at the beginning of the year, when the debt was already down to £350 million. A new target of £200 million had been set, placing pressure upon Maxwell to sell off more assets and repay the loans, a policy common to all four of London's major banks. Brown and his colleagues had been particularly 'scathing' about a NatWest circular in February urging support for a £350 million loan for the Mirror Group. NatWest was criticized by Lloyds for 'asking for an act of faith in Maxwell' and for 'not doing him any favours' by their unobjective analysis of his business. Brown had been ordered to reduce the bank's loans even more following the resignations of MCC executives: he had seen Maxwell's unpredictability for himself. So at the end of the signing ceremony Brown asked Kevin to spell out his plans. As if he had swallowed the drug Prozac, the banker relaxed. Basing himself on Kevin's surefooted reply, he subsequently reported to his superiors, 'we do not feel any anxiety'. Kevin had effectively promised to 'sell off virtually anything' to reduce the debts. 'Nothing was a sacred cow,' noted the banker approvingly.

For his father, it was the moment to take a bold initiative. That night, he flew from New York to Zurich to catch a helicopter to Vaduz, the capital of Liechtenstein. His pretext was meetings with the principality's prime minister and ruling monarch with inspections of the Art Gallery and the castle. Instead, he closeted himself first with the managers of the Bank of Liechtenstein in order to secure a £25 million loan, and then with Dr Werner Rechsteiner, the lawyer caring for his secret trusts.

Not trusting the telephone, Maxwell needed to brief Rechsteiner personally on Kevin's plan to take another £55 million from the pension funds. Having done so, Maxwell flew at 6.45 the following morning, Thursday, 25 April, back to London and then on to Washington. The White House was hosting a dinner for news correspondents, and John Campi, the *Daily News* publicity director, had arranged a table for senior staff. 'It's going to be a great opportunity to meet everyone,' urged Campi, a well-meaning, enthusiastic New Yorker. 'The president will be there, a lot of music, dancing and table-hopping. You'll meet everyone.' Maxwell could not be held back. He had always done well with American presidents, he felt. In May 1989, in Los Angeles he had sat on President Reagan's table at a dinner for the Winston Churchill Travelling Fellowship alongside Walter Annenberg and the Duke of Edinburgh. His host that evening, John Loeb, had arranged for Maxwell to be 'specially recognized' in the course of the evening. Crossing the Atlantic for the ninth time that year, Maxwell expected and received similar treatment. 'He was all over the place,' observed Campi, who also organized a reception hosted by Maxwell at the Washington Hilton late that night. Campi's 'hottest ticket in town' stayed for another dinner the following night in New York with the mayor and other celebrities, before euphorically boarding the Gulfstream to return home to England.

The mirage continued in London. On his first evening, he met with John Major, who had become prime minister five months earlier, and the following day he lunched with Hans-Dietrich Genscher, the German foreign minister, to perpetuate his self-appointed role in the settling of international issues between the statesmen. During all that power-hopping, he disguised any concern he might have felt that Kevin was flying to Edinburgh for another showdown with McInroy and the First Tokyo board. Internally, Maxwell believed, the problem had been contained. Tapley's dangerous offer of resignation had been rejected. 'I won't accept it. Help me sort out this First Tokyo mess first,' Maxwell had countered, reinforcing the impression that his family were Trachtenberg's innocent victim.

The next day, 30 April, at 4 p.m., Kevin, Donoughue and George Willet arrived at Coopers' offices in Queen Street in Edinburgh. Facing them were their three fellow First Tokyo directors, who had decided to vote for London & Bishopsgate's dismissal as managers of the fund. McInroy no longer trusted Kevin: 'I realized that he was lying.' On the table was a letter signed by Kevin, Donoughue and Stuart Carson, the compliance officer, claiming that the report submitted by Ashurst the solicitors contained 'inaccuracies and consequent wrong conclusions'.

'We need a commercial agreement but without any public disclosure,' insisted Kevin, speaking with his customary intensity but with unusual passion as he fought to prevent the dismissal. 'Dick Russell of Titmuss Sainer says that's not required.' Unmentioned was the current three-week campaign to sell the Mirror Group's shares.

Towards 9 p.m., McInroy, weary of the protracted discussion, called for a vote on London & Bishopsgate's dismissal. McInroy and his two Scottish-based fellow directors would inevitably vote for the resolution. Whether there would be a hung vote depended upon Willet and Donoughue. Would either have the courage to vote against their paymaster? 'We're all in this mess together,' said Donoughue, looking embarrassed. 'Oh no, we're not,' thought McInroy. 'You're in a mess. Not me. You've failed. It's the moment for people to stand up and be counted.' In the event, Willet voted for openness, against Maxwell and for LBI's dismissal. Donoughue procrastinated and then abstained. McInroy was not surprised: 'It's a fairly natural position for him to take. He's protecting himself from Maxwell's anger and caring about his income.'

Asking for an adjournment, Kevin telephoned his father. He returned with an offer to buy First Tokyo for a premium price, on condition that there was no publicity. Although McInroy was reluctant to allow Maxwell to escape all criticism, he knew that he himself could be accused by shareholders of negligence for failing to seek proper advice about the management agreement with LBI. 'Your sole and most important duty,' urged Barry Walker, his lawyer, the following day, 'is to protect the shareholders' interests. They are paramount. You must remain silent about everything else.' Justice and openness were to be forsaken. Reading the board minutes written by Carson a few days later, McInroy was taken aback: the criticisms of Maxwell had been toned down. 'This is a propaganda document,' he thought, 'written by a committee.' His prime suspect was only too obvious. Soon afterwards, he received a call from Robert Maxwell. 'You've falsified the minutes of the last meeting,' thundered the transgressor, resorting to his favoured tactic of attack in defence.

EIGHT

A Suicide Pill

– *May 1991*

On the advice of Charlie McVeigh, the 'handsome goy' from Salomon Brothers who was organizing the European roadshow to sell the Mirror Group, Maxwell flew on 2 May to Paris to address fifty fund managers at the Bristol Hotel. Exuding charm – it was a skill which revived whenever he left Britain – Maxwell humoured his audience in French, inviting them to accept that the Mirror Group was a secure investment. More than ever he needed banks to buy the shares and then trade actively to push up their price. McVeigh was delighted. 'He flittered around like a butterfly,' recalled Michael Richardson ruefully, unable to arouse the same enthusiasm in London, 'and Maxwell saw wonderful colours in the American's wings. McVeigh simply pitched it all too high.'

From Paris, Maxwell flew to Toronto, New Haven, New York and Boston. Speeches at breakfasts, lunches, dinners interspersed by meetings with 'limited groups' and 'one-on-ones' had been carefully slotted into a high-speed timetable by McVeigh and his colleague Nancy Peretzman. To emphasize Salomon's regard for their new client, Maxwell was invited for dinner at the Fifth Avenue apartment of John Gutfreund, the legendary emperor of Salomon Brothers, who was keen to assure his fellow gambler of respect and support. The bankers were pleased by few of the reports that reached them but one was worse than others. In a roomful of bankers in Manhattan, with one woman present, the subject of rape had arisen. 'When rape is inevitable,' Maxwell had laughed, 'the best policy is to lie back and enjoy it.' In that politically correct environment, his flippancy was greeted by nervous silence.

Impervious to the reactions to his own behaviour but convinced of his inevitable success, Maxwell flew overnight on 7 May to

Zurich for more presentations, and then on to Bulgaria to sign an agreement for his new European Bank. Over a jovial dinner with Dimitar Popov, the prime minister, Maxwell was assured that the government would license his new bank in Sofia. 'It will be the beginning of a new era,' exclaimed Maxwell. 'From here I will direct investments across the whole of Eastern Europe.' After toasts and warm handshakes, he was driven to the airport for the flight back to Britain, promising to transfer $20 million as an initial deposit. Brian Cole, his Bulgarian specialist, was left behind to conclude the details. The following day, Cole discovered that the Bulgarians would not honour their oral assurances. Maxwell had deluded himself about his hosts' intentions.

As Maxwell was driven back from Heathrow at midnight in his red Rolls-Royce – it was too late for helicopter flights – he pondered over the disappointing sale of Mirror Group shares. Orders were not exactly pouring in. 'We've got difficulties,' Richardson had sighed. Few major British institutions or investors were prepared to buy the shares. Unusually, the refusal by Prudential and Mercury Asset Management had been leaked to the media. The odds against the outstanding salesman persuading the world's bankers to believe in him were lengthening. Critical newspaper comment in London was prompted by the adverse gossip percolating through the banking village about his embarrassing failure to launch the Middle and Central European Fund. No one was prepared to entrust money to him. Anxiously, Maxwell argued that the shares should be sold on better terms. The bankers refused.

The solution, the Publisher then decided, was to contrive a story that British fund managers were scrambling for shares in New York. Publicists would be directed to work overtime to generate comment in British newspapers about over-subscription. 'Even a one-eyed Albanian can work out there is going to be a premium to the issue price,' boasted Maxwell the following day, promising a hefty profit for his admirers and himself. By the end of that week, the crisis appeared to be resolved. Charlie McVeigh of Salomons, always enthusiastic, claimed to have sold more than his allocation in America. In the event, Salomons had bought shares on their own account which supported the price, later admitting losses of £5 million on the flotation. Some would suspect that Maxwell had guaranteed to buy any surplus shares privately.

Of all his achievements, Maxwell was proudest of receiving the Military Cross from Field Marshal Montgomery for his bravery in France in 1944. Similarly, he boasted in 1981, when Betty celebrated the award of a DPhil degree at Oxford, that his children – *(back row)* Anne, Ghislaine, Isabel, Kevin, *(bottom row)* Christine, Ian and Philip – were also Oxford graduates.

Maxwell's publishing fortune was built upon his relationship with the leaders of the Soviet Union – from Khrushchev in 1958 *(above)* to Gorbachev in 1991 *(below)*.

The basis of Maxwell's influence in the Soviet Union was the services he provided to the KGB. Zaloman Litvin *(above)*, a Soviet intelligence officer, successfully sought Maxwell's assistance in 1968, and that relationship continued under successive KGB chairmen until Maxwell met Vladimir Kryuchkov *(below)* in 1991. Soviet intelligence was unaware that in 1948 Desmond Bristow *(right)*, an MI6 officer, had with other officers agreed to finance Maxwell's publishing business as a cover to spy on the Soviets.

(Above) Critics were unwelcome on the board of the Maxwell Communication Corporation in 1990. From the left, Brian Gilbert, Ian and Kevin Maxwell, David Shaffer, Reg Mogg, Richard Baker, Ron Woods and Jean-Pierre Anselmini. *(Below)* Lord Rippon *(centre)* and Peter Laister were non-executive directors, while Peter Walker *(left)* resigned from the board in July 1991, taking over £500,000.

The Mirror Group flotation in May 1991 was Maxwell's unsuccessful ploy to raise enough money to pay off escalating debts. *(Above)* From right, Andrew Galloway of Samuel Montagu, Lawrence Guest, MGN's financial director, Michael Stoney, Sir Michael Richardson of brokers Smith New Court, Ian McIntosh of Samuel Montagu, Ian Maxwell, Victor Horwood and Ernest Burrington, the managing director of MGN. After Maxwell's death, Burrington and Guest were criticised for misjudgements, but *(below)* Charlie Wilson, Sir Robert Clark, Alan Clements and Horwood remained as directors despite their failure to oppose Maxwell during his lifetime.

Despite their nine children and the appearance of happiness, Maxwell's marriage to Betty was fraught from the outset.

His friendships with other women included *(right)* Jean Baddeley, a personal assistant for nearly thirty years, posing with a bar of gold; and *(below)* Andrea Martin, a personal assistant until 1990, with whom he was besotted. *(Above)* In 1991, Maxwell confessed his unhappiness and loneliness to Kira Vladina, a Russian journalist.

Maxwell in the good times: playing chess in his penthouse with
Kevin's son Teddy; and introducing the Prince and Princess of
Wales to some of his achievements.

Just before 2.30 p.m. on 17 May, Maxwell arrived at Smith New Court to watch the trade in the shares begin. Richardson had arranged a flotation party, but Maxwell refused the champagne, accepting only a cup of coffee. Standing behind the dealers' screens he gazed as the shares were launched at 125p. His face twitched as the price faltered and then began to fall a few pence. Sellers outnumbered buyers. Burrington watched as Maxwell 'stormed off in anger'. Richardson was embarrassed: 'He was surprised. He didn't believe there would be sellers. I don't think he understood the Max Factor. He had the ability to blank that out of his mind.'

The broker was supremely naive. Maxwell's real anger was against himself: his gamble had failed. The sale of his stake in the Mirror Group had not only denied him assets to use as collateral but more importantly denied him unimpeded access to the newspapers' enormous cash flow. Worse still, with only a 51 per cent stake left in the Group, his private earnings would be sharply reduced. The private side was collapsing into a fatal condition: negative cash flow. Effectively, he had swallowed a suicide pill: the question was whether he could find an antidote which could quickly neutralize its effect.

Maxwell now bore a grudge against Richardson. Some would say that he was furious. The following evening, on Saturday, 18 May, he hosted a dinner and dance in Oxford to celebrate the flotation. Traditionally, every institution involved in those money-making exercises hosts a lavish celebration to toast itself and discreetly seek more work. On this occasion, Maxwell had volunteered to host a combined affair. In the past he had given many generous champagne parties, but none had been funded by stolen money.

Tension permeated the party even before the meal began. Looking at the seating arrangements, astute guests spotted that Richardson had been relegated from Maxwell's table. Instead, McVeigh was seated beside the host. The slight was inflamed in Maxwell's speech of thanks. After effusively congratulating Salomons, he intentionally omitted any mention of Richardson. Eyes swivelled to witness Richardson's embarrassment as he quietly complained to Betty: 'I'm absolutely amazed that he could praise McVeigh and make no mention of me.' Eyes switched back to the main table. Kevin was whispering in his father's ear. 'Oh, I do apologize,' said Maxwell over the tannoy after he had lumbered back to the microphone, 'I unintentionally omitted my thanks to Sir Michael Richardson for all his help. Thank you, Michael.'

Embarrassments were common with Maxwell and were so easily forgotten. Although most of the guests dancing in the marquee that night imagined that Maxwell's immediate problems had been overcome, the host knew better. But, outsider though he was, he was no less a survivor. Battles, even as he approached his sixty-eighth birthday, had always seemed quite manageable. MCC, after a few more disposals, would probably be safe under Peter Walker and Kevin. Meanwhile, he would indulge in his expanding news-paper empire, especially in New York, where the *Daily News*'s losses were already reduced to about $30 million a year and were expected to be zero by Christmas.

America was his salvation. The next day, he ignored Andrew Neil's invitation to a lunch party in Onslow Gardens and, after briefing Richard Fenhalls of Ansbacher Bank on the negotiations to purchase First Tokyo, flew with Ghislaine by Concorde to New York. Maxwell loathed the aircraft, especially if he could not fly at the very front. The other seats did not provide sufficient space, and he missed the pampering from his personal stewardess. But the Gulfstream was being serviced.

Maxwell's relationship with Ghislaine had become noticeably close. Lacking any other female escort, he had come to dote upon his youngest daughter, encouraging her to adopt his worst charac-teristics of arrogance and rudeness, tempered by an ability to charm when required. Ghislaine evidently enjoyed her father's wealth and power, marginally retaining her independence by staying at the Lowell Hotel rather than with her father at the Waldorf.

New York offered both Maxwells so much. That evening, 20 May, Robert attended a dinner for the 'Rich and Famous', clearly a gathering of like-minded individuals, and the following night he would meet Henry Kissinger for drinks before dining with former secretary of state General Alexander Haig and then breakfasting with Larry Tisch, another media mogul. Ownership of the *Daily News* had proven to be an invaluable passport.

In the middle of all this he had a conversation with Eric Sheinberg, the Goldman Sachs broker. The subject was the sale of 25 million MCC shares owned by the pension funds, which would divert £55 million into Maxwell's private account. Before his father had left

London, Kevin had spelt out their financial predicament to him in a confidential memorandum headed 'Goldman Sachs Status': 'On 28 May we are scheduled to repay . . . £123m.' After listing four payments which might require 'Eric' to extend a loan for two weeks, he continued: '£55m of the above is self-financing, as you know.' Kevin was referring to the illegal MCC share deal.

For some time, Trevor Cook had urged that the pension funds should sell part of their immense stake in MCC. Finally his wish had been satisfied. At 11 a.m. on 26 April Kevin, on behalf of BIM, had sold 25 million MCC shares in two equal amounts to Goldman Sachs at £2.20, producing after tax £54.9 million for the pension funds.

According to Kevin's arrangement with Eric Sheinberg, the deal would be transacted through New York with settlement on 28 May. To protect the Maxwells from exposure, Sheinberg printed on his slip special instructions for the confirmation: 'Do not mail – memo only'. There was to be no mention of the deal on the file. A 'with-holding' was 'in effect'.

As prearranged, three share certificates were delivered in London to Adam Mathews of Goldman Sachs. One certificate for 12.5 million shares showed the owner to be the Maxwell Works Pension Fund, while the other two certificates for 12.5 million shares stated the owner to be the Mirror Group Pension Trust. Goldmans were instructed by Cook to pay the whole £54.9 million to MGPT. At that stage Kevin, wreathed in smiles because the sale had generated a price rise on the market, intervened.

Cook was told by Kevin that the £54.9 million was to be deposited in a bank earning interest. He did not question the orders and faithfully recorded in BIM's accounts a £54.9 million cash deposit with the Bishopsgate Investment Trust (BIT), Maxwell's nominee company. Unseen by Cook, a second part of the plan now unfolded.

Sheinberg had agreed to buy the shares on behalf of Goldman Sachs only because Maxwell had provided a customer who would in turn buy the shares from the bank – namely, two Liechtenstein trusts, Servex and Yakosa Finanzierung, controlled by Maxwell through Dr Werner Rechsteiner. However, the payment for those shares, as Kevin had indicated, was 'self-financing'. Sheinberg was told that the two trusts would pay for the shares with the very money Cook had deposited with BIT. In other words, Goldman Sachs would send £54.9 million to BIT and, a few hours later, receive almost £55.3 million back from BIT, the surplus to cover payment for commission and stamp duty. By the end of the day, Maxwell would gain control over 25 million shares to be used to raise more loans.

In four letters signed on 27 May, Kevin told Larry Woods at Goldman Sachs how the millions were to be channelled through different NatWest accounts at the Lothbury branch in the City, delegating the supervision of the details to John Gould, BIT's accountant. The brokers understood precisely how the money would travel in a circle. In a recorded telephone conversation between two Goldman Sachs employees on 31 May, the settlement day, one stated: 'We can't get the purchase money *from* BIT until we pay the money for the sale *to* BIT.'

Legally, Kevin held no authority to divert that money to BIT. His letters to Woods were signed as a 'pension fund trustee', but he had recently resigned his trusteeship to avoid a conflict of interest with his directorship of BIM. He could only accomplish that ruse because Trevor Cook had agreed to his suggestion that the money should be deposited in BIT's account. 'I wanted the money in BIM's account,' recalled Cook. 'Kevin countermanded my orders and I didn't protest because Coopers approved the use of nominees.' The pension funds had lost another £55 million.

Cook's compliance with the Maxwells' desires was already profound, especially in their joint rebuttal of renewed complaints by Tony Boram of the pensioners' group, published in the *Daily Mail*, on 18 May, that only one of the pension fund's twenty investments, worth £160 million, was in a top UK company. Of the remainder, 40 per cent were in foreign companies or in MCC and the Mirror Group.

Boram's publicized grievance prompted an early-morning telephone tirade from Maxwell himself. Shaken but undeterred, Boram hoped that, with the Mirror Group a public company, the trustees and the new audit committee supervising the pension fund's assets would join in his protest. But neither Lawrence Guest, the chairman of the audit committee, nor non-executive directors Alan Clements and Sir Robert Clark felt moved to summon or attend meetings to consider the complaints. On the contrary, they remained inactive, while Maxwell easily persuaded Cook to counter-attack Boram.

That co-operation was welcomed by the Chairman. MCC's share price was slipping again, prompting telephone calls and visits from bankers anxious about the Maxwells' ability to provide more collateral or repay their debts. Maxwell's solution was to begin secretly transferring £130 million of MCC's money raised from the sale of Pergamon to his private accounts to repay the banks.

Among the army of visitors was Mike Moore, the Cockney from Bankers Trust. Moore's concern, indeed his job, was to ensure that Bankers Trust did not suffer any losses on loans worth £50 million or more. In recent days, his superiors had concluded that MCC's health was deteriorating, and, in a perceptive memorandum, noted that there was 'certainly the possibility that MCC could go into bankruptcy' before 1995. Kevin was at his most persuasive with Moore. 'MCC', he admitted, 'has temporary difficulties.' His suggested solution was to rely upon the family's £1 billion in Liechtenstein. So polished was his performance that he persuaded Moore to conclude an unusual agreement: the security of MCC's debts should be borne by Maxwell's private fortune. Two days later, on 24 May, Moore submitted a memorandum to his superiors. 'The balance sheet of RMG itself', he wrote, 'is strong, with a fixed-asset base of $2 billion and net worth of $1 billion.' Bankers Trust, he recommended, should loan $100 million to RMG.

By then, Kevin, Pandora and their children had flown in a chartered plane to France, expecting to spend the bank holiday week in Betty Maxwell's new country house in Fraytet, near Montagnac sur Lède – bought by his father as part of his formal separation from his wife. But it was a broken holiday. At 7 a.m., on Tuesday, 28 May, Kevin was flying by helicopter from Heathrow to Holborn for another emergency meeting about First Tokyo.

'My offer is generous,' Maxwell told Richard Fenhalls, his banker, 'because my management has fouled up. It's an administrative cock-up. It's all the fault of Larry Trachtenberg and he's out. I've suspended him. Trachtenberg will be fired after we've settled the compensation. Everything is being investigated by David Vogel [the solicitor from Titmuss Sainer].' Kevin listened to his father's account without comment. His face, remembered Fenhalls, was inscrutable. 'This is the position my idiot son has got me into,' screamed Maxwell, as Kevin sat placidly near by. Fenhalls' deputy

John Shaw, who was also present, wondered whether Robert Maxwell was not after all a genuine victim. His anger seemed heartfelt rather than theatrical.

One hour later, Kevin was flying in the Gulfstream to Edinburgh to save his father from further embarrassment. Alan McInroy was demanding full reimbursement of the £60 million. Kevin assured the Scotsman that his father had negotiated a £55.7 million loan from the Swiss Bank. The collateral, he said, would be the shares from the fund. Unspoken was the truth – that all First Tokyo's shares had already been pledged by the Maxwells for other loans. Securing the £55.7 million loan *without* the First Tokyo shares would require the genius of a magician. But that was the Maxwells' secret. Having secured McInroy's innocent agreement, Kevin returned to London and summoned Basil Brookes. 'The private side needs to borrow £75 million for five weeks,' he told him earnestly. Without asking the reason or requiring any security, Brookes agreed. Kevin at once boarded another private jet and flew back to south-west France to resume his holiday.

In London, his father was sitting in his penthouse kitchen watching the television news as George Wheeler once again applied L'Oréal Crescendo to his hair. He had been plugging more holes. That afternoon, he had mortgaged 13 million Mirror Group shares to Samuel Montagu in return for more cash. Of course, his fellow MGN directors knew nothing of that transaction. They shared Sir Robert Clark's opinion that Maxwell was 'behaving like the voice of reason'. Clark was satisfied that the Mirror Group remained 'very profitable', although he had still not introduced himself to either Burrington or Guest, the senior non-family executives in the company. Had Clark contacted Guest, he would have discovered that Maxwell had persuaded the Mirror Group's finance director to allow him to continue his private use of MGN funds – a blatant breach of the undertakings in the prospectus. Guest had been assured by Maxwell that the transactions were 'in order'; as he later said, 'I never thought anything would go wrong.' Such unconditional support allowed Maxwell, with considerable relief, to anticipate dinner that evening with Republican Senator Howard Baker in Harry's Bar, Mayfair, before flying in the morning to Washington for another infusion of adulation.

NINE

Two Honeymoons

– *June 1991*

Wearing the sash of a Grand Marshal, at 9.30 a.m. on a warm Sunday morning in Manhattan, Robert Maxwell stood beaming alongside Mayor David Dinkins, Governor Mario Cuomo and an army of dignitaries on a platform watching thousands march past for the Salute Israel Parade. Hovering behind, John Campi, his public relations executive, witnessed the arousal of his employer's self-importance. 'He's a big ticket,' preened Campi. Maxwell's announced retirement from MCC had raised his spirits as if demobilized from military service.

In London, Kevin, the heir designate, was taking the decisions and adopting the trappings of his father's lifestyle. Later that week, on 6 June, he would use the helicopter to fly to Glyndebourne and, the following day, fly in a chartered jet to Paris with Pandora for a weekend, staying at the Ritz. Like his father, Kevin believed that the worst of their problems had been overcome, although much of his time was still spent in successive meetings with the intimate circle around LBI: Larry Trachtenberg, Lord Donoughue and Jon Ford.

Those discussions had not been disclosed by Kevin to Peter Walker in the course of their frequent meetings in the previous month nor when they ate dinner at Bibendum, the fashionable Fulham restaurant, on 3 June. Kevin also did not reveal to Walker that during those early days of June his father was grappling to find deals which would improve MCC's paltry annual profits. Manipulating the company's profits was an annual undertaking by Robert Maxwell. In previous years, he had contrived to 'sell profitably' property, subsidiaries, shares or currency just as the financial year was ending, confirmation of his prowess as a speculator.

Pumping money *into* his company to shore up the share price was Maxwell's favoured ploy during the Pergamon fraud in 1969. Since the 1987 stock-market crash, when his losses had been tucked away in a footnote, his frenetic dealings in MCC shares, gilts, other stock and currency had slid into substantial deficit. For the 1991 accounts, his task was especially arduous. The deficit would be concealed and MCC's annual profits boosted. His gambits were presented for approval to Neil Taberner of Coopers.

Maxwell claimed that he had earned £80.7 million ($146 million) while speculating over £1 billion in foreign exchange. By any reckoning it was evidence of his outstanding abilities. Taberner had no reason to doubt the authenticity of these figures, yet they were bogus. Four statements recording his profits, apparently dispatched by Jon Lopatin of Goldman Sachs, had in fact been forged by Maxwell and presented to Albert Fuller, who was responsible for MCC's treasury. Since Maxwell had not earned those profits, his problem was to find £80 million to pump into the company. One source was the cash MCC had received from the sale of Pergamon. Dipping into the £446 million received from Elsevier, Maxwell described the transfer of money as an 'inter-company loan'. Fortunately for him, the finance director Basil Brookes neither objected to the mounting internal loans from MCC to Maxwell nor queried the Publisher's claims to have achieved enormous profits by speculation. 'I was just given the figures by Albert Fuller,' explained Brookes. Yet there were grounds for suspicion. Just two months earlier in April, Maxwell had told Brookes that his earnings from foreign exchange speculation were £40 million. Brookes' belief that Maxwell had doubled his profits in that brief period was based on information from the treasurer. 'I relied on Fuller and what the Maxwells told me,' said Brookes.

Maxwell's second source of phoney income for the annual accounts were two property 'sales'. The first was the sale of 74 Worship Street, off the City Road, a property owned by MCC, to Corry, a Liechtenstein trust, for £59.7 million. The second was the disposal of his interest in the Arche, President Mitterrand's vast modernistic office complex in Paris, to Hesto, another Liechtenstein trust, for £15.6 million. Both Liechtenstein trusts were controlled by the Maxwells. Naturally, the board was required by law to be satisfied that there was no relationship or a conflict of interest between the trusts and MCC which might cause MCC to lose money – and there were good reasons for suspicion. MCC's directors knew that in the past Maxwell had used Corry and Hesto for property transactions with MCC; more pertinently, they knew that Corry's 'headquarters' had the same address as the Robert Maxwell Foundation.

Six months earlier, on 29 January, the relationship between Maxwell and the Liechtenstein trust Corry had been explicitly described by David Vogel of Titmuss Sainer. In a letter to Basil Brookes, the solicitor had stated, 'Neither the Maxwell Foundation nor any director of Maxwell Communication Corporation plc is interested in 30 per cent or more of the voting power of Corry Stiftung or is able to control a majority of the directors of Corry Stiftung.' But in June, when Maxwell decided on the property transaction to boost MCC's profits, Vogel sent a letter to Brookes, in which he reported that Corry had bought the 74 Worship Street property and 'confirmed' that there was no relationship whatsoever between Maxwell and the Liechtenstein trust. No one queried a further oddity: that the transactions also involved two companies incorporated in the British Virgin Islands which were clients of Robert Fraser, the bank.

The evidence for that change in ownership was a letter written by Edmund Frick, a Liechtenstein lawyer, on behalf of Corry. Dated 12 June, it stated, 'Dear Mr Vogel . . . we confirm herewith that there is no connection between Corry Stiftung and MCC or any of its subsidiaries, associated companies, its substantial shareholders or directors.' Again, Brookes did not question Vogel about the contradiction or probe the Maxwells about what looked like an outright conflict of interest. Instead, he silently accepted the lawyer's comfort letter.

Combined with four other property deals he contrived during those weeks, Maxwell injected a total of £126.2 million into MCC, no less than 87 per cent of the profits. Only £49 million of that was immediately payable, saving Maxwell the need to find all the money to boost MCC's profits.

Those inter-company deals were presented by Kevin to Neil Taberner of Coopers. On 12 June, after some negotiation, Taberner agreed to certify that MCC had earned £145 million in pre-tax profits. Although that represented an unfortunate 16 per cent fall from the previous year, Kevin was relieved. If the property 'sales' and all the other non-recurring items had been disallowed, MCC could have announced at best just £17.3 million profits and the share price would have collapsed. Over the previous years, analysts would subsequently decide, Coopers had consistently allowed MCC to overstate its pre-tax profits: by 60 per cent in 1989 (£75 million rather than £192 million); by 58 per cent in 1990 (£71.1 million rather than £172.3 million); and by 88 per cent in 1991. At the July board meeting, Neil Taberner also did not attempt to dissuade the directors from approving the payment of £95.9 million in dividends, although the trading profits, even on the most favourable interpretation, were £49.7 million. To the public, MCC was presented as a company worth £3.6 billion with debts of £1.8 billion – an apparently good bill of health.

Later that same afternoon, soon after Taberner left, Kevin was closeted with Trachtenberg. The American was ordered to arrange with Mark Haas the following day to borrow $42 million from Lehmans in the name of London & Bishopsgate Group, another of the private companies. The collateral would be 45 million Mirror Group shares owned by the pension funds. The Maxwells would use $27 million to reduce further their loan from Lloyds Bank, while £12.8 million would be channelled to RMG to buy MCC shares.

Although Maxwell absented himself from those negotiations, he knew the outcome as he flew in the Gulfstream to celebrate his sixty-eighth birthday in New York on 10 June. John Campi had arranged a special event. After standing on another platform in a ticker-tape salute to the Gulf heroes, this time alongside General Colin Powell, his employer would be the guest of honour at a party codenamed 'Operation Welcome Home'. Campi had spent money with abandon for a man whom he had grown to adore. 'I wanna cake bigger than the man himself,' he ordered, renting the tall ship *Peking* at the South Street Seaport and inviting 200 guests to 'the most incredible party I've ever attended'. The music, the food, the entertainers and the gigantic fireworks display awed even Maxwell, by then practically immune to the flamboyance prompted by his own celebrity. Beaming at his guests, he barely reflected that among the many people missing from the army of well-wishers were his family. The birthday boy's celebrations ended abruptly at 11 p.m. Thirty minutes later, he was on board the Gulfstream flying back

to London to meet Richard Fenhalls, the Ansbacher banker negotiating the purchase of First Tokyo. A crisis had arisen.

At the outset, Fenhalls had believed that he was negotiating a
simple take-over. After all, a letter from Coopers (addressed to
Ansbacher, London & Bishopsgate Holdings and Morgan Stanley)
had certified that all the First Tokyo stock was held free of encumbrances. By 11 June, Fenhalls realized that the 'administrative
cock-up' was more complicated than this. John Shaw, his deputy,
reported a series of unsettling conversations. 'Can I see the stock-
lending records?' he asked Stuart Carson, LBI's compliance officer.

'I can't find any,' Carson had replied, before adding disconcert-
ingly, 'I've only just arrived, and taken over from Trachtenberg.
It's a shambles.'

'Have you got any records?' John Shaw asked Jon Ford, LBI's
new finance director.

'It's all in the safe,' replied Ford, believing that to be true.

'I'll come back tomorrow then.'

'No problem.'

The following day, Ford 'swore blind' that there were records
but he could not produce any. Unhappy with that explanation,
Shaw concluded that the former Coopers accountant was a 'lapdog
who did what he was told'. Even Thomas Christofferson, the banker
at Morgan Stanley, the custodians of the shares, seemed to be
unaware who had borrowed the stock. The bank had sent them to
Ford and knew nothing more. In the banker's view, matters were
'out of control'.

'Did you know about the stock lending?' Shaw asked Lord
Donoughue.

'I don't know anything about it,' replied Donoughue.

'But you were the vice-chairman of London & Bishopsgate!'
hissed Shaw at a man who, he later said, had 'three whistles in his
mouth and he didn't blow any of them'.

The Ansbacher team looked at the last published LBI accounts
of 1989. 'You didn't mention stock lending,' Shaw challenged John
Cowling, the Coopers auditor. It was a 'disgrace', he felt, that the
risks being taken had been concealed by LBI.

'Disclosure of stock lending is not required by law,' replied Cowling. Technically, the accountant was correct. The whole truth was
not required by law to be revealed.

Over lunch on 11 June, Fenhalls and Shaw discussed the deal with Robert Maxwell. Their worries were in the process of being allayed when Maxwell abruptly summoned Trachtenberg. Shaw did not hide his surprise: he thought Trachtenberg had been dismissed in February. 'Oh,' said Maxwell, 'Trachtenberg has only come back to start a Polish investment trust.' Sitting nearby, Kevin, whom the two Ansbacher bankers considered inventive, articulate and convincing, sought to speak. 'Shut up!' Maxwell shouted. 'If I want you to contribute to this discussion, I'll ask you.' Kevin crumpled.

Experience had taught Robert Maxwell precisely how to extricate himself from embarrassment. 'Your man has got problems,' he told Barry Walker, the lawyer for First Tokyo. McInroy's problems were trivial compared to Robert Maxwell's, but he was comparatively inexperienced in brinkmanship. To win a speedy settlement, he agreed that the offer document issued by Maxwell should 'say as little as possible'. It would 'just satisfy the legal requirements and be acceptable to Bob Maxwell'. This silence was based on advice from Barry Walker: 'Your duty is to the shareholders. Not to IMRO or the stock exchange' – nor, the lawyer implied, to the public at large. The public interest was in those circumstances ignored. 'First Tokyo's assets', warned Walker, 'could be frozen or worse if this gets to court.'

By then Kevin had negotiated with Carol Barrazone, a thirty-three-year-old executive at Swiss Bank, a loan of £55.7 million to pay for First Tokyo. The security for the loan was the First Tokyo portfolio. 'We're not going to take any risk on this,' reported Barrazone. 'None of the shares are to be sold by Maxwell,' she stipulated, entrusting Allen and Overy, the solicitors, with the task of certifying that the agreement was watertight.

Content that they had at last blocked a potentially disastrous leak, the Maxwell family prepared to fly to Jackson, Wyoming for Ian's marriage to Laura Plumb, an attractive twenty-eight-year-old television producer from Chicago. Kevin's elder brother had met the tall, blonde American at a party in London and was thrilled that his father had approved the marriage. While Ian, Kevin and Pandora flew by Concorde to New York and then by private Lear jet to Wyoming, at a cost of £22,000, Maxwell flew with Martin Cheeseman, his chef, in the Gulfstream, at a cost of £60,000. The Maxwells had rented a house with a spectacular view over the

Teton mountains; here Cheeseman would organize the food for the family.

The ceremony, held in Jackson's austere, log-built Sacred Heart Chapel at 4 p.m. on Saturday, 15 June, was, the Maxwell family agreed, perfect. For the father, his second eldest son bore certain similarities to himself as a young man – not least a sense of fun. Sadly though, despite earning over £300,000 per year, he did not understand finance or hard work. After the sermon, which focused on Christian–Jewish relations, Maxwell greeted the priest with the words, 'You are the first priest I have ever heard who has moved me. You are a good man and I am pleased to shake your hand.'

Early the following morning, the two brothers and their wives flew by Lear jet and Concorde back to London, at a cost this time of nearly £30,000. Ian and his bride continued on to the Adriatic port of Dubrovnik, where they were to board the *Lady Ghislaine* for their two-week honeymoon. On the same day, Maxwell told Cheeseman: 'I'm going to take you somewhere you've never been before. Prepare a great picnic.' Packing the customary cold chicken, cheeses, salmon and salads, Cheeseman drove behind his employer, Betty, Ghislaine and two secretaries into the Yellowstone National Park. There they ate the meal by a river. Recalled Betty, 'That day is one of my last really happy memories of Bob, joking, relaxed and good company.' Cheeseman agreed: 'Everyone was so happy.'

Maxwell was still in a buoyant mood when the Gulfstream landed at Burbank airport in Los Angeles, for a meeting with Joe Jacobs, a chemical engineer who employed 15,000 people across the world. Maxwell's detour was to secure the support of the American self-made millionaire for his appointment as chairman of the Brooklyn Polytechnic University in New York. The new owner of the *Daily News* understood that his status in the city would be enhanced by affiliation to the institution.

Maxwell's relationship with the Brooklyn Poly stretched back to 1985 when the board had bestowed upon him an honorary doctorate of science. In 1987, he became a member of the board of trustees. Now he wanted to inherit the chairmanship of the board from Jacobs. The American was willing to help, although he was already bemused by the ceaseless changes in the Publisher's schedule. Not only had the dates of his arrival in California been repeatedly altered, but Maxwell's staff had insisted that he required one whole floor of the Pasadena Huntington Hotel. In addition, his office had requested that private direct telephones and fax lines be installed in his suite. In the event the reservation was cancelled, and Maxwell was reluctant to pay the $2,000 bill – 'It took us a lot of effort to get that money,' sighed Jacobs later. For at the last moment Maxwell had suggested that they meet for lunch on his Gulfstream at Burbank airport.

Jacobs was suitably impressed: 'I'd never seen such a beautiful plane before.' That performance was only the curtain-raiser. In the air-conditioned cabin, Martin Cheeseman served vintage champagne, Beluga caviar and a succession of rare delicacies flown from London. Jacobs was being wooed in Maxwell's finest tradition. First came the Haines hagiography and then the promise that Macmillan would publish Jacobs's own memoirs, *Anatomy of an Entrepreneur*. Jacobs's vanity stoked the romance. At the end of two hours, the two men shook hands on the deal. 'I'll give $10 million to the Poly,' laughed Maxwell, 'if you contribute $6 million.'

'Done!' exclaimed Jacobs, unaware that Maxwell did not honestly possess a single $10 bill.

'We'll tie up the ends in New York,' boomed Maxwell, ushering his visitor off the plane. The Gulfstream took off, flying the Publisher eastwards across the continent.

In high good humour, Maxwell landed in Manhattan on 17 June. His purpose there was to meet Peter Walker and persuade his successor of MCC's success in America. Macmillan's nine senior executives had been alerted to provide briefings and lunch before Walker flew on to Chicago. Since the chairman-designate had not still spoken with MCC's directors in London, Maxwell believed that he had little to fear from the American visit. Walker's introduction to the empire was a jovial affair until the two Britons met Bill Harry, Macmillan's taxation expert. As Maxwell explained the intricacies of 'sheltering profits from tax', Walker's eyes fastened on the retiring Chairman. The tycoon was putting forward the absurd suggestion that interest payments made by Macmillan to MCC were 'real' profits rather than mere book-keeping. Harry spotted Walker's grimace: 'Maxwell was puffing the profits and Walker saw right through that.' Embarrassed, Maxwell left the room: 'I'll leave you two to it.'

Others in Macmillan were bewildered by Maxwell's decision to bring in Walker. 'How can Bob let someone get between himself and Kevin?' asked David Shaffer, the president. 'I can't believe Bob will let Walker in.' The rise in MCC's share value, however, was extremely welcome. As for Walker himself, despite the 'heavy entertaining' he left America realizing that MCC was troubled. The company's profits were uncertain. He was beginning to have second thoughts about his decision to join.

Left behind in New York, Maxwell had returned to the *Daily News* to be greeted with complaints about his long absence. Costly absenteeism, thefts and Mob control of the circulation had continued. The newspaper's finances remained precarious. Circulation had not reached the promised 1 million and the annual revenues were $100 million less than Maxwell had expected. No new manager had been appointed, leaving George McDonald, the trade union leader, to deal with the same old disliked and distrusted Tribune managers. Jim Hoge had resigned, and Jim Willse, the editor, was either incapable of managing the newspaper or had been denied authority by Maxwell to negotiate. 'Listen,' McDonald said, 'we've got problems. You need to stay here.'

'I'm going to fix this,' Maxwell answered grittily, grabbing the telephone and pushing buttons to call the presidents of the nine unions in his newspaper building. Each call was received by an answering machine. On to each tape, Maxwell uttered the same threat: 'If you don't arrive in my office within fifteen minutes, your employment will be terminated.' Not one union representative arrived. Maxwell had already lost control. 'The mice are playing while the cat's away,' grunted McDonald wearily.

Maxwell next summoned Hoge to his Waldorf suite. The former publisher had agreed to inspect and report on all Maxwell's newspapers around the world. His two-week tour through Britain, Germany, Hungary, Israel and Turkey was summarized in a two-page survey. 'I was expecting a one-hundred-page report!' Maxwell exploded.

'You never read even one page,' countered Hoge. 'I'll summarize it. Britain is excellent. The rest is disastrous. You'll never make profits in any of them. I'm telling you to get out.'

'It's terrible here,' moaned Maxwell, calming himself. 'There's thefts and fraud. They're stealing one hundred thousand copies a day.'

'I warned you,' said Hoge, realizing that his role now was to provide a shoulder for the tycoon. 'You negotiated too much away.'

For a moment, Hoge saw a forlorn tycoon. Every fibre of his being, all his experience, commanded Maxwell to take control and turn his newspaper into profit. But he was hamstrung. The crisis in London had higher priority than the problems in New York. Once more he feared that the First Tokyo deal might explode.

Barry Walker, the Ashurst lawyer representing First Tokyo, was insisting that the prospectus would have to mention stock lending. Maxwell had refused, although David Vogel had managed to whittle down the relevant clause into little more than an inanity.

Back in London, Maxwell hosted a lunchtime meeting of the First Tokyo protagonists on 19 June. Once more, he withheld his agreement to the clause. Walker, driven by his famous testosterone, encouraged his client to issue an aggressive ultimatum. 'I'll give you until 8 a.m. tomorrow to agree to these clauses,' said McInroy, on a flying visit from Edinburgh, 'or it's all off.'

Minutes before the deadline the following morning, Maxwell's bluff collapsed. No bargaining power remained. 'Right,' he told McInroy. 'But just keep quiet about it all.' It was Maxwell's good fortune that McInroy had been given the same instructions by Walker. 'When the prospectus is published in a few days,' he advised, 'don't say anything to the press. Just stay silent.' Believing that the whole settlement would otherwise collapse, endangering his shareholders, McInroy would obey. No bankers or lawyers in the City seemed to understand the prospectus. At Samuel Montagu, Andrew Galloway and Ian McIntosh did not read the document which hinted so tantalizingly at Maxwell's wrongdoing. As instructed, McInroy refused to answer the few journalists' questions and was surprised when a well-informed (though harmless) article appeared in the *Daily Mail*. 'I was told to keep quiet by the lawyers,' McInroy would later admit. 'We didn't put out a flag and say, "Here are crooks."'

The irony, that Ashurst's offices were in the same building as IMRO's, was lost on everyone. If Walker had taken the lift up two floors of Broadwalk House, he could have warned the regulators about his discovery of Maxwell's dishonesty. Instead, the lawyer felt obliged to remain silent.

Maxwell was relieved. London's lawyers operated under a code by which other interests prevailed over truth and justice. Bankers were equally amoral, but, increasingly, feeling provoked by the growing rumours and newspaper speculation about the Publisher's declining fortunes, they were turning from servants into masters. A crop of critical newspaper reports was particularly noted at Lehmans. Maxwell's debts to the bank now totalled $160 million, and Graham Hancock, a credit analyst, had become curious about the source of the Maxwells' shares.

In the course of a meeting on 20 June between Trachtenberg, representing LBI, and five Lehmans officials, Hancock asked, 'Why is BIM involved in these deals?'

'For yield enhancement,' replied Trachtenberg in the jargon which he hoped disguised the truth. He had no opportunity to consult Kevin, who at that moment was hosting a party of bankers from the NatWest and Midland in a box at Ascot. He could only hope that his waffle would suffice. His success was limited.

After Trachtenberg had departed, Hancock examined BIM's accounts. It was, he noted, a trustee for pension funds. By any measure, it was a startling revelation. BIM was not managing ordinary funds, but pension funds, yet he did not directly challenge Trachtenberg about the private use of the pension fund money. With £113 million at stake it was deemed more prudent to avoid unpleasant disclosures. To cover themselves, Lehmans asked Robert and Kevin Maxwell to sign three letters formally assuring the bankers that they owned the pension fund shares.

Maxwell's natural inclination was to procrastinate, but his ploy was abruptly halted by the bank's ultimatum: the letters were to be signed by 5 p.m. on 26 June. Failure to obey would lead to a 'review'. Fearing that the bank would betray their secret or cancel the loans, Robert and Kevin signed the assurances that they were entitled to pledge pension fund shares.

By then, however, the bankers' anxieties had deepened. The MCC and Mirror Group shares provided as collateral were no longer sufficient. The bank wanted better collateral. In anticipation of that demand, Kevin had written to the law firm, Herzog Neeman and Fox in Tel Aviv. His father had first summoned the firm's senior partner, Yaakov Neeman, to breakfast in his apartment in summer 1987. Then at the pinnacle of his ambitions, Maxwell had told the orthodox Jew, renowned as Israel's foremost lawyer and boasting impeccable relations with the nation's rulers, about his childhood, life and achievements. 'I've done well in England,' he told his visitor, 'and now because of the Holocaust I want to invest in Israel.' Neeman returned home and searched for projects, on the understanding that he would receive a 2 per cent 'success fee' on the profits whenever an investment was sold. Among the investments Neeman proposed were Scitex, pioneers of computer imaging, and Teva, a manufacturer of pharmaceuticals.

Amid great fanfare in May 1989, Maxwell had purchased just over 50 million shares in Teva for $30 million – unknown to the admiring Israeli government and public, however, the shares had been bought with pension fund money, and BIM was registered on the certificates as the owner. Ian became BIM's representative as a director on Teva's board. In February 1991, the certificates were deposited in Neeman's safe. Three months later, on 27 May, Kevin received photocopies of the three certificates, which confirmed the holding – by then reduced to 49 million shares worth $74 million – as owned by the pension funds. The photocopies – for approximately 25.1 million, 22.8 million and 1.1 million shares – were passed by Kevin to Cook with a handwritten message in capital letters, 'TREVOR FOR YOUR FILES'.

Unknown to Cook, during June Kevin negotiated a loan with Lehmans for which the collateral was 22.8 million Teva shares worth £18 million. That quantity of shares was represented by one of the three share certificates held in Neeman's safe. Accordingly, Kevin wrote to Michael Fox, Neeman's partner, asking that the originals of two certificates for 25.1 million and 22.8 million shares be forwarded to London with signed stock transfer forms.

As Kevin was completing those housekeeping chores, his father had swept grubby financial dealings from his mind and re-entered the mirage in which he played a figure of global importance. At lunchtime on 23 June, after months of preparation, he flew to Moscow. The arrangements and his itinerary had been finalized by Colonel Vyacheslav Sorokin of the KGB, a veteran of Soviet espionage in France and Vietnam. In recent years, Sorokin had been tasked to recruit Maxwell back into the fold as an agent of influence. Sorokin was working under the direct orders of Vladimir Kryuchkov, the KGB chief.

Maxwell had met Kryuchkov on previous visits. Their first conversation in the Lubyanka, the KGB headquarters, had been scheduled for forty-five minutes, but Maxwell's charm and his fluent Hungarian persuaded the Russian to extend their meeting to two and a half hours. 'He was sincere and wished us well,' recalled Kryuchkov, an unusually eager intelligence chief. 'He was a friend of the USSR.' In their several subsequent meetings, Kryuchkov reminded Maxwell that, to repay the debt he owed the country, he should explain Russia's policies to other statesmen. In the KGB's newly sanitized parlance, Maxwell was an 'unusual foreign relation' who could be relied upon to share information to which he enjoyed privileged access. 'We would try and exploit him and vice versa. It would be mutually profitable,' attested Leonid Shebashin, then the suspicious chief of the KGB's foreign intelligence branch.

Sorokin had been told that in the KGB's opinion Maxwell was 'a very important man, like an aristocrat, and loyal to Russia. He would be useful as a source of information and as an agent of influence. He was to be cultivated and helped.' Sorokin's interest was fuelled by Maxwell's admission that 'I feel a little bit Russian.' Accordingly, ever since 1986 Sorokin and his colleagues had extended a standing offer to solve any personal problems Maxwell might encounter in Russia. By the summer of 1991, the Publisher had cultivated many relationships around the Kremlin, not least with Gorbachev himself. The president had been the protégé of Yuri Andropov, a previous KGB chairman, so he relied upon the intelligence service's judgment of Maxwell. Hence, it was through the KGB's good offices that the highlight of Maxwell's visit to Moscow – a new honeymoon – was to be a private meeting with Gorbachev in the Kremlin. Kryuchkov would be present at those Kremlin discussions, continuing a relationship between the KGB and Maxwell stretching back to Berlin in 1946.

As an officer in the British Control Commission responsible for supervising German newspapers and publishers in 1945, Maxwell had occasionally encountered Soviet officers in Berlin. It was natural for Maxwell, born in Carpo-Ruthenia, which had been incorporated into the Soviet Union in 1945, to feel some interest in those who shared a common heritage rather than in his fellow British officers. At some stage during that period, Maxwell established a relationship with an unnamed Soviet intelligence officer who would reappear in Maxwell's life twenty years later when he welcomed the Publisher to Moscow.

Several British officers would complain in later years that Maxwell's behaviour in Berlin had been reprehensible. They had criticized his involvement in black marketeering, they had noted that he had been active in business in London while still employed as an army officer in Berlin, and they carped about his commandeering of army trucks to transport scientific publications owned by the German publisher Springer Verlag from the Soviet zone first to West Berlin and then to London, where they laid the foundations of his publishing empire. But none suspected that Maxwell had established any contact with Soviet intelligence. Yet there is no doubt that, before he finally left Berlin in 1947, Maxwell had formally agreed to co-operate with the KGB.

His relationship with the KGB was so well hidden that in 1948 his publishing business in London was launched with the direct financial assistance of the British intelligence service, MI6. The architect of that recruitment and subsidy was Count Frederick 'Fanny the Fixer' Vanden Heuvel, a successful MI6 officer in wartime Switzerland whom Maxwell had met in Berlin. In 1948, Vanden Heuvel, based in MI6's headquarters in Broadway Buildings, was pondering the practicalities of collecting scientific intelligence, an operation which had been perilously neglected before the war. His musings were encouraged by Charles Hambro, a merchant banker who had also served as a wartime intelligence officer.

The two had embarked on their venture at a meeting of senior representatives of the British scientific establishment held in November 1946 at the Cabinet Office. Hambro wanted to help Butterworths, the respected publishers, to enter the field dominated at the time by Springer, which Maxwell represented in London. It was agreed at the meeting to create Butterworth Scientific Publications. But by 1948 Butterworths was failing, while Maxwell, representing Springer, was flourishing. With East–West tension increasing and the Soviets known to be building an atomic weapon, the importance of scientific intelligence had increased. One front for espionage was a publishing company, and Vanden Heuvel believed that a suitable vehicle could be a new company formed by a merger between Butterworths and Maxwell.

Vanden Heuvel summoned a meeting of MI6 officers in Broadway to consider his proposition. Included were Desmond Bristow, Tim Milne and Stephen McKenzie. 'Maxwell', explained Vanden Heuvel, 'was born a gypsy and won the Military Cross during the war. He did odd jobs for us in Berlin, and I think it would be valuable to bring him onside now.' He added, 'We need someone who can recruit scientists. We need a co-operative.' During the brief discussion, it was agreed that Maxwell would not be an agent or paid regularly, but would be available to pass on information. After an hour, the intelligence officers agreed to provide Maxwell with £3,000 to finance a new publishing venture under his own control. Under that cover, Maxwell's services would be used on MI6's behalf to contact and recruit scientists in the new communist countries. Over the following years, Bristow reported, 'He did produce quite a lot of results.'

By 1950, Maxwell's relationship with Springer had sharply deteriorated, after the Germans had uncovered his systematic dishonesty and theft. But by then he had created Pergamon, his own company, to publish scientific journals, and it was in that guise that he arrived in Moscow in 1954, his first visit.

Accompanying Maxwell was Anne Dove, his secretary and sometime mistress, who had been a secretary during the war in British intelligence. Theirs was a pathfinding foray across the Iron Curtain, entering East Berlin from the West on foot during a snowstorm to catch a plane to Moscow. Maxwell wanted to negotiate the right to translate and publish Soviet scientific journals and books in the West alongside his German and British publications. After weeks of patient waiting, playing chess and drinking vodka, he eventually persuaded the KGB to approve his venture. Yuri Gradov, the lawyer at Mezhdunarodnaya Kniga, the Soviet copyright agency, was told that the KGB had approved Maxwell's venture: 'I was ordered to conclude a deal at any price.' Indeed, the price paid by Maxwell was astonishingly low. To Gradov's surprise, the Briton was allowed to meet Russia's most important scientists and to sleep in room 107 at Moscow's National Hotel, which had been occupied in 1917 by Lenin. 'Only an important person would get that room,' concluded Gradov. Maxwell's new representative in Moscow was Victor Louis, soon to become famous as a KGB journalist in the West. It became apparent that Maxwell's relationship with the Soviets in post-war Berlin had borne results: that success aroused suspicions in one part of London.

After her return to Britain, Dove was discreetly invited by the Security Service, MI5, for an interview in the War Office. 'They wanted me to vouch for his loyalty,' said Dove, who unhesitatingly gave that guarantee. Maxwell meanwhile was confiding to section DP4 of MI6 his reflections about Russia, a country at that time barred to foreigners except under the most stringent controls. So, bizarrely, in the mid-1950s Maxwell was trusted by MI6 and the KGB, but suspected by MI5. Regardless of those contradictions, his relationship with the intelligence services had assisted his bid for fame and fortune. By 1964, his publication of Soviet scientific journals had helped to transform Pergamon into a multi-million-pound public international company of great benefit to the West.

Maxwell's relationship with the KGB took a new twist in 1968. By then, he had been a Labour member of parliament for four years, but his ambitions had been blighted by his impulsive, often boorish behaviour. Reconciled to his unpopularity and seeking to earn an ever greater fortune, he continued his promotion of Pergamon and, on 28 May 1968, was travelling by train from Moscow to Kiev. During that visit, he was approached by Zaloman Litvin, a Jewish officer in Soviet military intelligence. Litvin had been an 'illegal' agent in Los Angeles in 1940, pursuing the secrets of America's atomic research. Twenty-eight years later, he had been asked by the KGB to contact Maxwell and invite him to fulfil his promise in Berlin in 1946 to assist the Soviet Union. Speaking fluent English, Litvin made his approach in a Kiev hotel. Showing neither surprise nor emotion, Maxwell agreed to Litvin's suggestion of another meeting in Moscow.

On 3 June, meeting Litvin in the capital, Maxwell was taken to meet Yuri Andropov. The KGB chairman spoke of the turbulent times in Europe, the Middle East and Vietnam. A nuclear holocaust was prevented only by the policy of détente and the superpowers' agreement since 1945 delineating their spheres of influence. Soviet Russia 'owned' Czechoslovakia but the liberalization of the so-called Prague Spring under Alexander Dubček threatened Soviet control. Andropov anticipated Soviet intervention to crush the opposition, and he hoped Maxwell would use his influence in the

House of Commons to urge a restrained response in the West. Maxwell agreed.

On 26 August, amid unforgettable scenes of turmoil and emotion, the Red Army crushed the Czech bid for independence. British MPs interrupted their holidays to attend an extraordinary sitting of the House of Commons. On the Labour benches, Maxwell rose and, giving his best parliamentary performance, urged the continuation of détente. At the end of that solemn debate, the House uncommonly seemed to take note of his argument, and the Labour government's ensuing protest to Moscow was muted. Maxwell had served Andropov's wishes to perfection.

One year later, Maxwell's empire crashed in the midst of the take-over bid by Leasco, the American company led by Saul Steinberg. Accountants had discovered that Pergamon's accounts were fraudulent, and Maxwell was branded by the Take-over Panel as a liar. Defeated in the 1970 general election and ousted from control of Pergamon, he was condemned to the wilderness. But in 1974, having recaptured control of his company, he returned to Moscow. Ambitious to rebuild Pergamon, he agreed with the KGB and with General Secretary Leonid Brezhnev to publish biographies of Soviet and other communist leaders in the West. He would be paid by the KGB for undertaking to publish 50,000 copies of the books, though understandably the KGB's subsidy would never feature in Pergamon's accounts. Maxwell in fact deceived the KGB about the number of copies in the World Leaders series that he actually printed, but he did satisfy the dictators' vanity. Nicolae Ceausescu, the Rumanian president, was praised by him for his 'constant tireless activity for the good of the country'; Gustáv Husák, the Czech autocrat, who had succeeded Dubček, was dubbed 'this impressive man'; while Todor Zhivkov, the Bulgarian tyrant, was credited with building 'a prosperous and happy nation'.

Four years later, Maxwell met Brezhnev for a personal conversation in the Kremlin; their photograph appeared in *Pravda* and the Publisher was accorded a 'state visit' to his birthplace, a border zone normally forbidden to foreigners. For a businessman, Maxwell had indisputably established a privileged position in the communist state.

That historical background did much to enhance Maxwell's status in Moscow when his Gulfstream landed at Sheremetevo airport at 7 p.m. on Sunday, 23 June 1991. Among the other passengers was Senator Howard Baker, his lobbyist. As they emerged into the warm summer's night, the waiting Kremlin officials could not fail to be impressed by the man, his personal jet and his entourage of subordinates. Appropriately, Maxwell would stay at the October Hotel, reserved for the country's most important visitors.

Maxwell's prestige in the Soviet Union had risen sharply ever since his appearance alongside Gorbachev in Minneapolis in June 1990 to launch the $100 million Gorbachev Maxwell Institute. Gorbachev had been groomed by the KGB to become the Communist Party's architect of change, intent on removing unnecessary controls, encouraging innovation and introducing limited capitalist ideas. But, like all the members of the communist hierarchy, Gorbachev was ignorant about capitalism and sought friendly advice. Maxwell, in turn anxious to cultivate Gorbachev and to step into the shoes of Armand Hammer, the American tycoon whose fortune had been built on his relationship with Lenin after the Revolution in 1917, offered to fulfil that role. But there was an important difference between the two entrepreneurs. While Hammer brought real business to Russia, Maxwell brought only promises. Nevertheless Gorbachev, unaware that the Briton's donation to their Institute had never been received, had a high opinion of him, despite the souring collapse of *Moscow News*, a Maxwell-financed pathfinder of *perestroika* edited by Yegor Yakovlev, a friend of Gorbachev. That unpleasantness was forgotten amid Maxwell's new promises: a business and cultural magazine, a television station, a school for business management, and a 'Heritage' agreement with Gorbachev's wife Raisa and the Cultural Foundation. To the communists grappling with the Soviet Union's perilous finances and its adoption of limited capitalism, Maxwell personified a hope for salvation.

Throughout the following day, 24 June, Maxwell shuttled between the Soviet leaders, uttering more promises, negotiating deals to expand his media empire and lecturing on the Soviet Union's future.

After his final meeting with Yevgeny Primakov, a future intelligence chief, Maxwell met Kira Vladina, the forty-seven-year-old blonde Soviet journalist whom he had first met in November 1990. Since that intimate evening together, Maxwell had telephoned her from hotel bedrooms across the world, grasping for a reassuring, friendly voice. In Moscow, his adrenalin was surging. The pressure of the past weeks combined with his eager anticipation of the following day's meeting with Gorbachev required her presence: 'I have to be feeling right for this thing and if you don't come I won't feel good at all.' Kira rushed to the hotel to meet Maxwell at a moment of unusual vulnerability. Although surrounded by his retinue, including Jean-Pierre Anselmini and Senator Baker, Vladina was 'so struck that he was a thoroughly lonely man'.

During their passionate hours together, Maxwell unburdened himself with the familiar flood of confessions. 'I'm so lonely,' he told the Russian, revealing morbid depression. 'The people around me only want my money – even my children and especially my wife.' Attracted by this plea for genuine love, Vladina felt herself moving spiritually closer as Maxwell continued: 'Ever since childhood, I've been traumatized by love. I was crazy about my mother. I loved her to utter distraction and I wanted the same from my wife and family. But I didn't get it.'

'But why did you marry her?' exclaimed Vladina. 'Why did you choose your wife?'

'I didn't choose her. She chose me!' Maxwell went on: 'She could shut her eyes to a lot of things. She was good at pretending that black was white and vice versa. But everything was for her profit. She loves money.' For the relatively impoverished Russian, Maxwell's next confession was bizarre: 'I wouldn't mind if I lost all my money. I'd be just as happy and I'd start again. In any case, my family won't inherit anything. The only ones who deserve anything are my youngest, Ghislaine and Kevin. I adore both of them. Kevin is so much like me and Ghislaine is a friend.' As his dependency upon Kevin increased, the father had switched his affection from Ian to the son who was orchestrating the empire's survival.

By dawn, Vladina knew that Maxwell needed a soulmate. 'He had so many enemies,' she later lamented. 'His ability to earn money was only surpassed by his ability to make enemies.' But she herself was a friend, and eagerly accepted his invitation to join him on the *Lady Ghislaine* later that summer. 'I was something like his dream come true. That's why he was so uninhibited, so lucid. I was simply a product of his imagination.' But Vladina would be in America when, weeks later, Maxwell expected her arrival on his yacht.

At 9.30 in the morning, Maxwell was driven through the Kremlin gates. After his first introductory meeting with Alexander Yakovlev, the president's adviser, he was escorted through vast rooms to the panelled conference chamber where Soviet leaders have traditionally welcomed fellow heads of state. Minutes later, Gorbachev appeared. After the characteristic Russian bear-hug, Maxwell was also greeted by Kryuchkov, the KGB chairman. Kryuchkov's presence was confirmation that the Briton's admission to the Kremlin had been arranged by the KGB.

Nothing stimulated Maxwell more than sitting opposite a member of that select club of world leaders, including George Bush, Margaret Thatcher, John Major, François Mitterrand, Helmut Kohl and Gorbachev. Such a meeting not only fed his self-importance but provided an opening immediately afterwards. Then he could telephone other members of that club with the words, 'I've just seen Chairman Gorbachev and my impression is . . .'

The agreed purpose of their encounter was to discuss how Maxwell could assist the modernization of the beleaguered Soviet economy. If at that moment a select number of bankers in New York, Tokyo, Zurich, London and Paris had heard the Publisher advising the Soviet leader, their laughter would have drowned the conversation. Yet Maxwell was promising a new 'mountain of gold': he spoke airily of a business school, of equipping scientific institutions with computers and of setting up joint ventures to provide 'online' technology via satellite. One idea in particular interested Kryuchkov: an English newspaper, to be edited and printed in London but controlled by the KGB. Finally, Maxwell proposed that Russia conclude a contract to buy tea and coffee from Kenya.

Gorbachev was naturally puzzled by Maxwell's involvement with Kenyan coffee. The Soviet president was unaware that in the late 1940s his guest had earned his fortune bartering across the world, pork for cement and silk for timber. Even during a recent visit to Mongolia, Maxwell had agreed with the local leaders to buy locally produced vodka and cashmere. Having signed a contract, Maxwell inquired on his return to London about the price he had paid for the cashmere. 'I've been had!' he shouted and refused to honour the agreement with its overly generous price.

Naive about the workings of capitalism, Gorbachev concealed his ignorance about Maxwell's new interest in coffee, and responded enthusiastically to his praise for the new economic policy and to his promise to teach Russians how to become business managers. As they progressed down the shopping list, Kryuchkov was instructed to liaise with the tycoon. After an hour, Gorbachev rose. 'Both of us', he said with evident seriousness, 'have important work to attend to.' Being treated as an equal by such a figure not surprisingly appealed to his visitor. After another warm hug, Gorbachev departed with Kryuchkov. On his return to the Lubyanka, the KGB chairman delegated future liaison with Maxwell to General Leonid Shebashin, the English-speaking head of foreign intelligence. 'Appoint one of our officers in London to keep in touch with Maxwell,' the chairman ordered. Here was further evidence that Maxwell, unlike other international businessmen, was seen as a KGB asset. 'He was special,' agreed Shebashin, who would read a KGB report on Maxwell's first meeting with his Russian contact in London on 10 July.

Maxwell left the Kremlin without any illusions. Money invested in Russia would be lost for ever; and in any case he had no money. In fact, it was he who needed money. That would be the purpose of his next call.

For months, Maxwell had been negotiating to trade the Soviet Union's international loans and borrowings, worth trillions of dollars – both the money owed by Third World countries to Russia and the money owed by Russia to the West. He proposed to earn commission by recovering portions of those debts, which would be settled at a discount. Considering the enormous sums involved, he calculated that even moderate success would earn enough to relieve his own predicament. His approach was to Boris Pugo, the finance minister. Harping on his ability to influence Russia's fortunes by brokering on its behalf with Western political leaders, by the end of the day Maxwell sensed success. Pugo, a serious and intelligent technocrat, had accepted the offer and would promptly establish a representative's office in Zurich.

On that high note, Maxwell flew back to London via Berlin. Viewed from inside the Gulfstream, surrounded by fawning acolytes, his own empire appeared secure. Indeed, Rodolfo Bogni of the Swiss Bank Corporation had invited him to address his executive committee in London on 1 July about 'his success, how he made his decisions and what created the vision by which those decisions were driven'. The Publisher would regale the twelve bankers with a tale about deploying his skills to build an empire. Much to his own amusement, he would not reveal to his hosts how he planned to misuse the £55.7 million advanced by those bankers to buy First Tokyo. But deception was ingrained in his subconscious. Even if he understood his own nature and recognized the irony, he was, despite his frequent visits to Germany, certainly unaware of the apt verse by the German humorist Christian Morgenstern:

> And thus, in his considered view,
> What did not suit – could not be true.

Among the first messages handed to him once he was back inside Maxwell House was a written report from Ghislaine. His imperious daughter, despite being his favourite child, had been reduced to tears by an outburst of his temper shortly before his departure to Moscow. On his behalf, she had attended a dinner in New York honouring the Nazi-hunting Simon Wiesenthal Centre, and it was her report by telephone which had provoked the tirade. 'I am very sorry that my description of the dinner this morning was inadequate and made you angry,' she had written. 'I should have expressed at the start of our conversation that I was merely presenting you with a preliminary report of the evening and that a full written report was to follow . . . Please forgive me.' Ghislaine then recounted the laudatory messages: 'Rabbi Hier expressed great admiration for you; Sammy Belzberg said he was sorry you were not at the dinner but how thrilled he was to have me sitting next to him . . . Ace Greenberg passed on his regards . . . Alice Williams of NBC News said she was disappointed that you were not at the dinner. . . . I was honoured to be present and to be able to represent you. Thank you. Attached is my program from now till I return. I will call you again tomorrow to receive your precise instructions for the Kennedy wedding.' The respectful tone clearly satisfied Maxwell.

A second file contained a fax from Ian aboard the *Lady Ghislaine*, off Piraeus in Greece. With his two-week honeymoon at an end, his son asked for the Gulfstream to be sent to Athens to collect him and his bride. Alternatively, he asked for permission to charter a private jet, at a cost of £26,000. After a few seconds' contemplation, Maxwell tore the fax in half. 'Send the following,' he instructed the secretary: ' "Two seats reserved on Olympic Airways".' After a pause, he growled: 'The honeymoon's over.'

On board the yacht, a poker-faced Gus Rankin, her new captain, handed the abrupt message to his passenger. The previous two weeks had been a pleasurable trip, marred only by one unhappy incident when Laura, tearful and chain-smoking, had confided a momentary unhappiness to a stewardess in the aft of the yacht. As Ian read his father's fax, his anguish was evident. 'Will you help me?' asked the thirty-five-year-old. Rankin felt oddly sympathetic. Knowing that the owner's son feared the chaos of Athens airport, he duly obliged, watching the couple board the scheduled flight before returning to the yacht. His orders were to await Maxwell's imminent arrival for a long holiday.

TEN

Buying Silence

– July 1991

His double, even triple life was eroding Maxwell's stamina. Sleep was becoming difficult. Instead of solid rest, he managed only naps, rising during the night, scavenging through the kitchen cupboards for food, eating whole cornfed chickens, bowls of cornflakes and large cheeses, scattering the debris around the floors for the staff to clear the following morning. The lack of sleep, the constant travel and the persistent tension induced a seemingly permanent cold. His remedy was copious amounts of Night Nurse and paracetamol purchased by Bob Cole, his spokesman, at Boots opposite his London headquarters.

His sexual appetite was relieved by summoning secretaries to his office, often during the afternoon. Douglas Harrod, his entertainment manager, supervised the girls' entrance and ensured that, until Maxwell unlocked the doors, 'RM is not to be disturbed.' The girls chosen by Maxwell – 'young blonde and busty ones', according to Carol Bragoli, an older secretary – were always rewarded. 'I understood that gifts, usually jewellery, were given to them afterwards. A sort of "thank you" present,' observed Harrod. Bragoli heard from some of the girls that her employer would open a bag of gold coins to encourage those who were slow to overcome their shyness. Or he would offer the girl a car from the company's fleet.

His loneliness aggravated the sense of turbulence. Lying to bankers, brokers and other businessmen was second nature to him, but his deceit had never encompassed so many of his close associates, including fellow directors. Their loyalty had been retained by high salaries and by his personality, which stimulated their professional excitement. Although none was allowed to feel too indispensable, and potential resignees were threatened with the certainty of expensive litigation for breach of contract, even the loyalists were becoming disillusioned.

During their recent trip to Moscow, Anselmini had told Maxwell that he intended to resign. 'You're excluding me from everything,' he complained. 'You don't need me any more. I'm just part of the landscape. I've been constructively dismissed.' Maxwell remained silent as the Frenchman concluded, 'I have only one life to live, so we must bring our arrangement to an end.' Maxwell made no effort to persuade him to reconsider. Unspoken was Anselmini's appreciation of his own self-interest. The Publisher's financial plight could not help the ambitious Frenchman's career, and he knew more than most about his activities. 'We'll settle the terms on our return,' agreed Maxwell, knowing that Anselmini would expect a generous pay-off to persuade him to remain discreet (although he could not expect the £1 million paid to Brian Gilbert, another director who had resigned some months earlier). But Anselmini's was not the only imminent departure.

Debbie Maxwell, the dark-haired in-house lawyer, unrelated to the family, also wished to escape. In recent months, she had become embroiled in completing and submitting detailed questionnaires relating to the empire's compliance with statutory regulations. Aware of Maxwell's financial problems and suspecting transgressions, she had protested in October 1990 to Alan Stephens, Maxwell's trusted company secretary, about her description as a 'compliance officer'. In December she had relinquished some of those duties while electing to remain silent. By July 1991, she had become seriously concerned. Maxwell had publicly admitted to owning 70 per cent of MCC's stock, but she knew that secretly he had bought more. 'We'll have to declare the extra deals to the stock exchange,' she told him. 'No we won't,' he retorted.

Anxious to avoid personal liability, she agreed with Maxwell a discreet and profitable alternative – she would resign from full-time employment. There was even a drinks party on the tenth floor to wish her well. But the following morning Debbie Maxwell returned to work as a full-time consultant, retaining her office, her responsibilities and her access to the Maxwells. The transition proved very profitable. After receiving severance compensation of £50,000, and a £75,000 increase in her salary – sufficient to pay off her £40,000 mortgage – she earned a high salary without legal anxieties. To the benefit of the Maxwells, her continuing silence was secured.

A third resignation had been submitted by Ron Woods, the tax expert. Although unaware of the full reality of the Maxwells' activities, Woods realized that the empire was mired in difficulties. His solution was to seek immediate resignation from the boards of the private companies, so limiting his legal responsibilities, while remaining a director of MCC. Initially Maxwell did not oppose that strategy. There was an advantage, he calculated, in changing some personnel to deepen the compartmentalization between the conspirators and the ignorant. Generous payments on termination combined with non-disclosure clauses ensured that the departing never revealed their knowledge or their complicity.

Having detached himself somewhat, Woods was therefore appreciative when Kevin telephoned on 2 July with an invitation to attend Wimbledon as a guest of Hill Samuel two days later. Woods accepted, knowing that he would have been unable to accept for the day after, 5 July, when the MCC board was scheduled to meet and approve the company's annual report and accounts.

But Kevin's invitation to Woods had not been issued out of generosity. In their effort to win rapid approval of the accounts, the Maxwells required his absence. The tax expert knew about Corry, the Liechtenstein trust. If he were present, he might raise a question about a conflict of interest in the phoney property sales. In fact, he would claim, 'Nothing clicked. I didn't realize the significance of the board meeting. I never knew what was coming up. That was quite normal.' The two Maxwells could just as reliably count on his convenient and in the circumstances strange naivety when he eventually read the proposed agenda and saw a reference to the two Liechtenstein Anstalts buying property from MCC. Puzzled, he telephoned Rechsteiner. 'Have you ever heard of Hesto?' he asked.

'No,' replied the lawyer, faithful as ever to Maxwell.

'Oh good,' sighed Woods, relieved to find that his suspicions of a special Maxwell deal had proved unfounded.

So with Woods's certain absence on 4 July, Robert Maxwell told his secretary the evening before to advance the board meeting by one day. 'Mr Maxwell must leave Britain on urgent business,' she informed the other four non-family directors. Just thirty minutes were assigned to the formality at 5 p.m. in the tenth-floor dining

room. None of those summoned believed the meeting to be crucial.
All had accepted Maxwell's habit of not circulating a detailed
agenda, and all knew that he would arrive with the minutes already
completed and signed. Such were the terms of working for Maxwell.
Nevertheless, in case of hiccups, separate breakfast meetings were
arranged with Anselmini and Geoffrey Rippon for the following
morning. To the Publisher's satisfaction, neither director raised any
queries. 'If the directors were gullible, then so were the lawyers and
accountants,' insisted Laister.

The property profits were listed as £49 million. There was a letter
to Basil Brookes from David Vogel of Titmuss Sainer guaranteeing
that 'the board were not aware of any connection' between the
Maxwells and the two Liechtenstein trusts. As Laister later claimed,
'I relied upon Titmuss to tell us if anything was wrong.' Everything
had been approved by Neil Taberner, including Maxwell's fraudulent foreign exchange profits totalling £80.7 million.

On schedule, MCC's directors met on 4 July. Brookes watched
Robert and Kevin deny with 'deadpan, poker faces' any connection
between themselves, the Liechtenstein trusts and the three companies involved in the property deals. He would claim not to have
noticed that Hesto, Corry and Maxwell's own Liechtenstein trusts
had identical addresses, while Laister 'didn't question anything'.
Lord Rippon was absent, although Robert Fraser, his bank-cum-
property company, had an interest in the Liechtenstein sales. The
meeting was completed in less than the half-hour allotted. The misleading accounts had been endorsed. To the non-family directors,
the meeting seemed to have been uneventful. Robert and Kevin
Maxwell had expected little else. There was naturally no mention
of Robert Maxwell leaving London the next day, the reason given
for advancing the meeting. There was no seepage and no suspicion.
When Ron Woods heard the following day of the board meeting,
his passive nature remained undisturbed.

Across London, only one man was angry, or so he later suggested.
Peter Walker, the chairman-designate, was fuming because the draft
accounts had been delivered only that morning with a letter from
Maxwell informing him that the board meeting would be held at
5 p.m. because of the Publisher's need to fly abroad afterwards.
Brookes had intended to dispatch the accounts to Walker the night
before, but Maxwell had insisted on a delay. He had already decided

that Walker's imminent arrival was too dangerous. Their precarious finances made digestion of the outsider difficult to contemplate. Some drastic action was required, because Walker's presence could only complicate their hope for survival.

For his part, Walker understood the position perfectly well: Maxwell had not wanted his presence at the meeting. By now, after several meetings with Kevin, he had seen the disadvantages of continuing the relationship. Moreover, several serious players in London had queried his decision to his face. One solution he had proposed to Kevin was to split up MCC, creating Macmillan as a separate interest. The Maxwells had agreed to consider the so-called demerger of all MCC's American companies, but Walker doubted their commitment, especially after he had studied the accounts in New York. Now the late delivery of the 1991 accounts was a perfect excuse for withdrawal. After consulting Sir Michael Richardson, Walker faxed to Kevin a stinging rebuke: 'There is no way I can see [the accounts] before your meeting and therefore please make sure that it is minuted that I have neither seen nor therefore taken part in the approval of the Report and Accounts.'

In the contrived anger which so suited his purpose, Walker then listed two items which caused him 'shock': that no decisions had been taken about the other new directors which Maxwell had agreed to appoint; and that a 'crucial' meeting of directors for 18 July had not been arranged. Walker had asked Alan Stephens ten days earlier to summon that meeting, but Stephens had refused. Walker wrote that he was 'staggered' by Stephens' explanation, which was that Robert Maxwell had not given his permission. 'The present chairman', he said acidly, 'does not decide what happens after July 15.' He concluded, 'As you can imagine, I do wonder what the hell is going on in this company.' The politician's anger prompted a predictable reaction.

Before the board meeting, Kevin consulted his father and dictated a swift reply, one which was hardly calculated to placate Walker. Robert Maxwell, he wrote, 'is not only the current Chairman and Chief Executive Officer which I am sure you have not overlooked, he is also the founder and our family have over 70 per cent of equity of the company.' Kevin then added fuel to the argument. His father, wrote Kevin, had told Walker that the job offered was not that of 'executive chairman' and there would have to be a 'division between me as the new CEO [chief executive officer] and yourself as the new Chairman'.

After the board meeting, Robert Maxwell added his own scorn. The politician, he complained in a hand-delivered letter, was 'impatient', adding that while he would be 'welcomed . . . as a team player' he was not joining as an executive. 'If there has been a misunderstanding between us over the division of labour between yourself and Kevin then I am sorry and we had better forget the whole thing.'

That night Michael Richardson, who had arranged the union, telephoned Maxwell to mediate. 'Peter agrees to keep his office in Smith New Court,' purred Richardson. It appeared that Walker was backing off from his insistence that he manage MCC. But Maxwell did not welcome mediation. He wanted a divorce. The politician, he believed, was feigning as much as he was himself. After all, in just two weeks Walker would be chairman and these upsets would probably become worse. But, to maintain the pretence, Maxwell wrote to Richardson to say that Walker's bid to become executive director would create a 'twin-headed hydra' and would be 'a recipe for disaster'. He looked forward, he concluded, to a discreet solution.

Maxwell's edict stung Kevin. His plans for taking over and rebuilding the company would crumble without Walker. What was more, the prospect of keeping their problems under wraps seemed to be endangered.

At lunchtime on 5 July, while Pandora was flying over London in Maxwell's helicopter with her son Teddy and two of his friends as a birthday treat, Basil Brookes glanced at MCC's bank statements. With all the pressure of finalizing the annual accounts, he had left that chore undone for several weeks. It took some moments for him fully to understand what he was reading. To his horror, he saw from the statement that MCC's current account was £200 million in debt. The first call for an explanation was the treasurer's office. Racing to the eighth floor, he asked Jane Roberts, the twenty-nine-year-old recently appointed RMG's treasurer, for a print-out of the 'inter-company accounts', to show the amount owed between Maxwell's public and private companies. He anticipated, he later explained, seeing 'nil or the £75 million Kevin borrowed after March'. Instead, he saw that Maxwell had drawn £180 million, and a further £20 million had trickled out unseen. At that point, Brookes did not think of comparing his usual print-outs with the latest copy revealing the vast debt. Whereas Roberts gave Kevin statements marked 'INCO KM', the statements given to Brookes carried the reference 'INCO 91/92'.

Brookes immediately telephoned Maxwell for an appointment. That afternoon, Maxwell's schedule was as frenetic as ever. Consultations about world events with the Russian and American ambassadors were interspersed with unusually long meetings with Anselmini to stem the effects of resignations, and with John Halloran about the £97 million owed to BPCC's pension fund. Halloran's persistence was connected with advice he had received from his solicitors, Ashurst Morris Crisp – well briefed on Maxwell's activities at First Tokyo. After Halloran's departure, Maxwell would normally have sought to delay Brookes's entry, but the secretary reported that 'Basil Brush' was more excited than usual.

So at the end of day, Brookes was admitted to Maxwell's office. Both Robert and Kevin were waiting. 'Don't worry,' began Maxwell with a smile, at once affecting bonhomie, 'it's a short-term cash problem. We're trying to sell our Scitex shares, and then all will be settled.'

Kevin nodded. Brookes was unaware that the Maxwells owned only one-quarter of the Scitex stake; the remainder belonged to the pension funds. Nor did Robert Maxwell reveal that on that very day he had signed a letter to NatWest, drafted by Fuller, arranging the transfer of a further £75 million from MCC to RMG, his private company. Instead, Brookes's suspicions melted away. He had no reason, he believed, to distrust the Maxwells. For their part, the father and son believed that the fuse, although lit, would be extinguished. After all, Brookes appeared to be an amenable employee.

Two days later, on Sunday, 7 July, the morning after hearing Placido Domingo sing in *Tosca* at Covent Garden in the company of Jean Baddeley, his trusted secretary and old friend, and his sister Sylvia Rosen, Maxwell awoke in Oxford. He went out into the sunlight to swim in the pool, and there waited for Kevin. The time had come for some unpleasant decisions.

As the Filipina maid prepared chicken for lunch, Carol Bragoli, a secretary, brought the message that Michael Richardson had refused to take Robert Maxwell's call. 'It's not convenient,' the

broker had said. 'I'm having a lunch party for twelve. I'll call back.'
But on a list of incoming calls were messages that Eric Sheinberg
had telephoned along with several bankers. Everything would wait,
said Maxwell driving himself, while he spoke to Kevin, who had
just arrived. 'Walker cannot have the job,' he said to his son. 'The
demerger is ridiculous. We could never get it through the SEC
[Securities and Exchange Commission in New York] for a start.'
Kevin's bewilderment was made greater by his father's clear refusal
to consider altering his policy of using the pension funds for
borrowing money. There was no possibility of adopting another
strategy. From a distance, Bragoli watched the two men start to
shout at each other. 'Kevin was rubbing his eyes, then holding his
head and looking angry and very distressed,' noticed Bragoli. Then,
barely holding back the tears, Kevin rushed angrily away just as
the maid was bringing his lunch. His car could be heard roaring
from the house as he drove back to London.

Snatching a list of messages from his secretary, Maxwell went to
his room to watch tennis on television, while stabbing at the telephone. His first call, to Richardson, confirmed that a consensus had
developed. 'Peter feels', intoned Richardson, 'that it's not going to
work out. He'd have difficulty running the operation in America.'
Delighted that Walker had found a publicly acceptable excuse,
Maxwell replied, 'Good. We'll sort out the terms.' Replacing the
receiver, he called Sheinberg in France. After a conversation about
buying MCC shares, Maxwell summoned the helicopter to return
to London. 'Get in fast,' the pilot told Bragoli. 'Once he's inside,
he won't get out. He'll leave you here.' In Holborn, Kevin was
waiting nervously on the tenth floor having unquestioningly
accepted the Chairman's verdict.

The consequences were noticeable the following morning. Peter
Walker's new office on the ninth floor was given to Robert Bunn,
the finance director of RMG. The accountant had become ever
closer to Kevin, working long hours and over the weekends. In
return, he was rewarded with a flat in the Barbican. Like the
Jehovah Witnesses, the Maxwells cared for their most trusted
employees; 'You are part of our family – we'll care for you.' Bunn
accepted their offer and his marriage collapsed.

For the Maxwells, the emotions of that Sunday had been forgotten by that Monday morning. The NatWest Bank rejected Robert

Maxwell's latest request for a £150 million loan from their 'back pocket' – as he called it – prompting Kevin to complain about 'Dad's considerable surprise'. Even his father's personal appeal to John Melbourn, a chief executive, had failed. Without the lifeline, the debt crisis appeared insoluble, even overwhelming. Millions were needed immediately to pay for MCC shares, to repay loans, for interest payments, for losses on gambles in the markets, to pump into MCC to sustain the phoney profits and for their expensive lifestyle.

Since Brookes would now be constantly monitoring MCC's bank accounts and since their need for cash was urgent, the remedy for their plight, the two Maxwells agreed, was to exploit their status and trust by supposedly buying foreign exchange and playing on the markets. Using MCC's reputation but not the company's money, they would initiate fifty-four transactions, buying dollars for sterling from a succession of banks. But after taking delivery of the dollars, they would not immediately deliver the pounds. Together they gambled that by 'cross-firing' they could earn from the fluctuating exchange rate, from the interest payments of the dollars deposited in their account and from interest-free loans. Over the following days, the banks innocently accepted Kevin's excuses that 'an office snafu' was delaying the transfer of the sterling. There was no precedent for the bankers to believe anything else.

On the Tuesday morning, Basil Brookes noticed that MCC's debts had increased by the £75 million transferred to RMG. 'What the hell is going on?' he cried, rocking with amazement. Bursting into Kevin's office, he demanded an explanation. The newly appointed chief executive adopted a poker face: 'I'm instructed not to speak to you about this. Go and talk to Dad.' Brookes was taken aback. Kevin was normally so helpful. Why, all of a sudden, was he being so difficult?

Eventually, Maxwell agreed to meet Brookes. 'They're forex [foreign exchange] deals,' he said shortly. 'You don't need to know the details. Just trust me.'

'But I'm the finance director.'

'You'll have to trust me.'

Brookes was devastated. Maxwell was demanding total loyalty and total silence but offering no explanations. For Brookes to succumb to temptation and confide in anyone would breach that understanding, endangering his position and salary. There was no one, he lamented, whom he could trust.

The pressure was taking its toll on Maxwell too. Those close to him witnessed the effect. At 2 p.m. on that day, Bill Harry and Ron Woods were sitting in the Publisher's apartment pointing at figures on the spread-sheet laid out on the table. 'Walker's idea of a demerger', said the American, 'cannot be successful. The taxation will be punitive.' Woods agreed that demerging the American business would be a financial disaster. In mid-sentence, Woods looked up. Maxwell was sound asleep. The two employees shrugged and sat in silence. After fifteen minutes, Maxwell jolted awake. 'Right, we'll go ahead with it,' he said. The two accountants glanced at each other and, without another word, departed, unaware that the tycoon had already decided not to proceed with the idea, but to allow Kevin – now unquestionably in control – an opportunity to play with the notion.

Suddenly the banks' demands for money were remorseless and unending. No fewer than thirty-three public banks and twenty-nine private banks had lent funds. Kevin was no longer managing a business; instead he spent his time wooing banks and offering collateral. Despite the pressure, his performance was always faultless. Sitting in his office, speaking by telephone to dozens of bankers daily – most often to David Leal-Bennett of NatWest – he masterminded the offer of collateral to the 'suits' in the financial institutions. His promises were brilliantly delivered: 'These shares are available to the family, so I can offer them as collateral.' The impression he created calmed those bankers anxious for reassurance that their money would be returned. Liechtenstein and the private side represented the reservoir available to satisfy their needs. Among the more concerned callers was Brian Brown of Lloyds. 'The results', he said, referring to MCC's announcement, 'are disappointing.'

'Don't worry,' replied Kevin, 'we intend to sell the Scitex shares. It'll reduce the private side's debt by $220 million.'

Brown was barely placated. 'If you don't repay your loans, Kevin,' he warned with unusual vehemence, 'it will be catastrophic.'

Kevin only smiled. 'I had no idea,' Brown would later confess, 'that any money was owed to the pension funds.'

After replacing the receiver following these calls, Kevin shouted a series of two-second orders to subordinates before returning to the telephone. Among his countless orders on 8 July was to repeat that Michael Fox, the Israeli lawyer, should send the two Teva share certificates for 47.9 million shares from Israel. On their arrival, Kevin signed a transfer form as BIM's director, while Alan Stephens signed as BIM's company secretary, transferring a certificate for 22.8 million shares from the pension fund to Lehman Brothers as collateral for a £18 million loan. The certificate would be delivered to the bank on Trachtenberg's orders with an accompanying letter written on LBI notepaper implying that the shares were controlled by the Maxwells privately. The second certificate Kevin placed in his safe along with the third (for 1.1 million shares) when it was handed over by Neeman a few days later. So more pension fund shares had been appropriated for the Maxwells' private use. Meanwhile, from another telephone, his father was arranging that 7 million Mirror Group shares, owned personally, should be transferred to Goldman Sachs as collateral for further loans. That pledge, Maxwell knew, breached the rules of the flotation, which required him to retain 51 per cent of the company's shares.

At 9 a.m. on Thursday, 11 July, Richardson seated himself in Maxwell's office to settle an agreement for Walker's divorce. Reassured to find that Maxwell was 'at his most charming', he returned three hours later with the chairman-designate himself. Their unspoken agenda was to agree a public explanation for Walker's departure. Within forty minutes they had settled upon the excuse that the proposal to demerge MCC, separating its US from its British interests, would allow Walker to say, 'It would be absurd for me, with a limited knowledge of American publishing and no intention of living in the United States, to preside over this new company.' He was also prepared to state that the demerger had been discussed and encouraged by the board. However, he may have been misled; this discussion was not recorded in the minutes nor recalled by some of the other directors. Walker refused, however, to sign a total confidentiality agreement, though he conceded that there could be an informal understanding.

Walker would receive generous compensation: £100,000, of which £30,000 would be tax free, and the opportunity to buy his new Mercedes and the fax machine installed at his home for just £1. He would be allowed also to keep or sell one-third of the shares promised as part of the incentive scheme: he would thus receive

201,793 MCC shares worth £400,000 absolutely free for just twelve weeks' service. The divorce and settlement, due to be announced on 15 July, was later signed on Walker's behalf by Sir Michael Richardson.

At the last moment, Maxwell changed the agreement. 'You can only have the shares if you remain a director until the annual general meeting in September. I want you sitting with us.' Walker agreed. 'The press release will say that you will continue to participate in the demerger programme.' Walker again agreed, knowing that Maxwell had no intention of implementing that condition. Clearly, Maxwell hoped that the promise of £400,000 would persuade Walker not to reveal his dissatisfaction with the Maxwells and the company's finances. But just as his appointment had boosted MCC's share price, his unexpected departure irreversibly fractured the empire's tarnished image. Effectively, the politician's silence was bought.

That night, Maxwell flew to New York. Charlie McVeigh had arranged, in a bid to win the demerger business, that Maxwell should lunch with John Gutfreund at Salomons. But, behind the window-dressing, Maxwell's real business was to advise Andrew Smith, managing LBII, to withhold his demand for a promised further £1 million investment; to discuss with Ellis Freedman the details for secretly buying more MCC and Mirror Group shares; and, most of all, to meet Mike Tomasieski, the trade union leader at the *Daily News* printing plant in Brooklyn to discuss the mounting thefts by the Mafia.

Dissatisfied with the results of those meetings, Maxwell returned to London at midnight on 15 July, to find MCC in the throes of a crisis prompted by the announcement of Walker's resignation. MCC's shares had fallen 6p to 190p and were weakened further by an article in that day's *Independent* alleging that Walker had written a damning report which concluded that MCC, rather than earning £145 million profits, had lost £8 million in the previous financial year. Walker himself meanwhile remained silent, refusing to deny writing a report and unwilling to utter any substantive public comment, thereby ensuring still more severe press comment. The report, if written, has never been seen. 'Coming apart,' judged *The Economist*, while Lex in the *Financial Times*, the most perceptive commentator on the troubles, wrote, 'It is one of the depressing features of the Maxwell empire that every time its rickety features seem finally to have been patched together it gives another lurch.'

In the wash of that adverse coverage, Kevin feared that a presentation he was due to make to ninety-two bankers at the end of that week would be a disaster. Nervously, he appealed to Walker to attend the meeting and calm the waves aroused by his unexpected resignation. Walker refused, unprepared to compromise himself by testifying that MCC's finances were sound.

Over the next forty-eight hours, the two men argued about the exact terms of Walker's resignation letter. Adamantly, the politician resisted giving any hostage to fortune. The hefty compensation was to buy his silence, not his endorsement of the business. Eventually his statement, drafted on Kevin's word processor in Maxwell House, was signed and faxed by Walker from the office of John Selwyn Gummer, the minister of agriculture, in the House of Commons. Addressed to the ninety-two representatives of banks, it limply explained Walker's absence from the meeting on the ground that he would be driving to Wales that day for a weekend engagement and would be saying nothing. Walker assured the bankers, however, that to his knowledge there was no internal financial report of the kind described by the media. Even so, the bankers' suspicions were not allayed.

Both Robert and Kevin were furious. Walker was pocketing over £550,000 for his discretion; it was money they did not even possess. The other MCC directors were simply puzzled. 'I just assumed he'd fallen out with Bob,' explained Laister, unconcerned that he had received no explanation from the Maxwells. Only in retrospect were he and Brookes unhappy about Walker's statement and payments. Brookes complained about 'the effect of Walker's statement on the market' and Laister was equally irate: 'Peter Walker had spent months going over the company's affairs and said nothing.'

Maxwell detonated a counterblast to the bad publicity by summoning Ray Snoddy of the *Financial Times* on 16 July. The Publisher's personal staff rated Snoddy as one of the few people their employer was happy to meet; at any rate Maxwell always ordered the best food for the journalist. At the end of an hour, Snoddy departed to report in a decidedly factual manner about the planned demerger 'to enhance shareholder value', the endorsement of that policy by Peter Walker, the Chairman's intention to retire and Kevin's plea 'to get back to being a publisher and not just a debt manager'.

Maxwell was not displeased by the article. To Kevin's relief none of the ninety-two bankers who gathered in the Rotunda at 10 a.m. on the 19th to listen to his presentation voiced hostile criticism or even appeared unconvinced by his explanations. Supported by David Shaffer, Macmillan's New York president, Kevin predicted a rosy future for the company. His professionalism and his understanding of corporate finance were equal to those of any member of his audience. Although some were puzzled by the speed of Walker's appointment and departure, no banker contradicted Kevin's version, recorded on video: 'Peter Walker is not rejecting the company but acting in the best interests of MCC.' The family, complained Kevin, were the victims of 'extremely ill-informed, vindictive press reports'. Unmentioned was the fall in MCC's share price and its detrimental effect on the value of the collateral for their loans. Kevin's reassuring voice promised that the debts would be 'offset by the sale of Scitex shares'. That sale would, he added, have 'no significant impact on RMG', the private company. MCC's future profits, he promised, would 'rise to £230 million'. Not one banker challenged that dream.

Kevin's final performance that day was at an MCC board meeting to discuss the resignation of Walker and record the formal resignation of Anselmini. There was every reason for Kevin and his father to expect an uneasy ride. Woods had been tricked by Maxwell into missing the previous board meeting; Brookes had discovered that £275 million had been borrowed from MCC without authorization; MCC owed creditors, according to its latest accounts, £580 million; Robert Maxwell had revoked his decision to retire as chairman (although Kevin remained chief executive); and the share price, in the wake of media criticism, was again falling. Yet not a word of criticism was mouthed by the MCC directors. Maxwell did not even bother to mention to the board that he was meeting bankers from Goldman Sachs and Bankers Trust to discuss the demerger codenamed 'Project Monaco'. It was, after all, just for form. Sheinberg was promised that Goldman Sachs could handle the demerger; Bankers Trust wanted to be hired too to check that the valuation which Goldman Sachs recommended was accurate. Since together the two firms had lent Maxwell about $125 million, it was best to allow them to play, entertain them to good dinners, and encourage their fantasy of earning fat fees.

The Chairman's plight was worse than it seemed. Unknown to most of the directors, MCC's debts were much higher than the accounts revealed. Just before the board meeting, Maxwell had signed a cheque for £180 million drawn on RMG (the cheque was written by John Gould, Robert Bunn's assistant) and told Basil Brookes of the payment to MCC. Maxwell, needless to say, was aware that RMG had no money at all – he never intended that the cheque should be cashed. His strategy's success depended upon the amenability of MCC's finance director. His judgment proved correct. Brookes knew that the cheque would not be deposited in a bank account but nevertheless listed it in MCC's quarterly accounts as 'cash in hand'. An MCC letter confirming 'receipt' of the money was sent to Crédit Lyonnais by Kevin. Since at that moment there was a mere £367,562 in the bank's account, Maxwell's phoney cheque for £180 million substantially reduced the company's real debt of £761 million, easing the company's plight.

Kevin left the office that night, pleased that he and his father had escaped further embarrassment, to celebrate with friends Pandora's thirty-third birthday outside Oxford at Le Manoir aux Quat' Saisons, one of the country's most expensive restaurants. He was also celebrating his appointment as MCC's chief executive, a position which his mother had strenuously urged him to assume. Thankfully, the other directors appeared to trust him. Peter Laister had been heard to say, 'Kevin's well regarded and liked.' There was every chance of recovery. No one would have guessed, as Kevin paid the restaurant bill of nearly £500, that the money was, as usual, paid out of the millions 'borrowed' from the pension funds.

His father that evening had been obliged, much against his will, to accompany Betty to a dinner for 125 people organized by the World Wildlife Fund in honour of the Duke of Edinburgh's seventieth birthday. Sitting at the table of Hans Rausing, a publicity-shy Swede who ranked as Britain's richest resident (worth an estimated £5 billion), Maxwell might have dreamt of changing places. Afterwards it was too late to fly back to Holborn, so he waited impatiently for dawn at Headington Hill Hall. He detested spending the night under the same roof as Betty, but even worse was driving to London. Early on Saturday morning, Maxwell flew to his Holborn home. Downstairs, the duty secretary sat in trepidation. Weekends for the staff were occasionally like a carnival, but she feared

that her employer would as usual get bored after watching the
football match on television and start to behave foolishly. All the
secretaries were accustomed to his telephone terrorism over the
weekend, but her predecessor's experience had been particularly
traumatic.

'Ever been to New York?' Maxwell had asked one day.

'No,' she replied.

'We're off then.' An hour later she was flying in the Gulfstream
towards the Atlantic. 'Got your hat?' laughed the Publisher.

'I don't wear one,' she replied meekly.

'You've got to have a hat in New York,' he scoffed. Within
twenty-four hours, the scoffs had changed to snarls: 'No hat? Go
back to London. Now!' The woman returned shaken.

But, on that Saturday, Maxwell was disinclined to stage such a
prank. Bill Kay, a *Sunday Times* journalist, was waiting to interview
him on the 'turning points' in his career. He had met the tycoon
often over the years, but he was startled by his appearance: 'Very
tired, overweight and depressed. Not his usual display of ebullience
for journalists.' Unknown to Kay, who would write an uncritical
article, Maxwell had been warned that his juggling acts on the
foreign exchange markets would be brought to an abrupt halt the
following morning.

Senior representatives of Barclays, Lloyds and the Midland banks
passed, one after the other, through Kevin's office on the Monday
morning, formally declaring themselves unamused by his antics.
David Leal-Bennett of NatWest alone did not personally complain.
Kevin had been paying special attention to him and had entertained
the company's most important banker with his children two days
earlier at the Royal Tournament. Pressing the flesh and providing
hospitality always succeeded, it seemed, in softening a banker's
judgment. But the visitors' politeness that morning barely concealed
their anxieties. The gossip in the City was that Maxwell was badly
pressed. All those owed money still assumed that the debts could
be paid from the private funds, and Kevin did nothing to dispel
that illusion. Later that day, René Müller of Crédit Suisse sent
him a valuation of the portfolio pledged as collateral for the debts
incurred by RMG, the private company. Although it included shares
from First Tokyo's portfolio, partly owned by the pension funds,
Kevin kept his silence.

That Monday afternoon, the completion of the First Tokyo purchase was celebrated with champagne in Robert Maxwell's office. Kevin opened the bottle. 'Well done,' he said to John Shaw of Ansbachers. 'Dad will sort out the fees.' Shaw was well satisfied. The First Tokyo shareholders had received all their money. Kevin and Robert Maxwell were also relieved. No suspicions had surfaced. Abiding by Barry Walker's advice, McInroy had refused to reveal the background of the saga to inquiring journalists.

Julie Maitland at Crédit Suisse might have had more reason than others to be suspicious, because she had accepted shares from First Tokyo's portfolio as collateral. When Kevin volunteered the explanation that 'back-office snafus' (an increasingly favoured phrase) were to blame for the take-over, she seemed satisfied, although in an internal memorandum she wrote, 'it does raise important questions regarding the control systems operating with London & Bishopsgate and as a result steps have been taken to invoke more rigorous controls in our forex dealings with them.'

Not every banker held off. Alfred Hüber of the Swiss Volksbank called on Kevin that week. His head office, he announced, had decided to terminate the bank's relationship with the Maxwells. 'They complain', said the Swiss, 'of your companies' complexity, lack of transparency and ever changing strategy.' Kevin showed no emotion and wished the banker farewell. Hüber did not reveal that his bank had decided to keep all the securities pledged by Maxwell as a guarantee against losing money. Among them were the Berlitz shares which Kevin had said were owned by the Maxwells privately through RMG. The Swiss bankers already suspected that he had lied. As a precaution they had checked the Berlitz share register and had found no reference to RMG as a shareholder. Although they would later explain, astonishingly, 'We thought a page of the register was missing,' the bank had resolved to sell the shares to recoup their loan.

By 23 July, the Maxwells' borrowing from MCC had reached £276 million. Their appetite was insatiable. Two days later, their plunder peaked at £305 million. The last £19 million had been spent secretly buying more MCC shares. The pressure on the Maxwells to repay the debts was matched only by their inability to borrow any more money legitimately.

Robert Bunn understood better than most the reason behind that chaos. Over the previous weeks, RMG's insecure finance director had observed with mounting alarm that the company's debts were inexorably mounting, and Kevin gave no hint of a respite. The flotation of the Mirror Group had sharply reduced RMG's income while the company's expenditure was rising. Nervously, Bunn looked around for an ally to whom he could confess his concern. There was none within the empire and he feared the consequences of disloyalty if he betrayed any secrets to outsiders. His only hope, he gradually came to believe, lay in John Walsh and Stephen Wootten, the Coopers auditors finalizing RMG's 1990 accounts. A board meeting was due on Tuesday, 23 July, to finalize and approve those accounts, and Bunn decided to use that opportunity – when the auditors were present – to raise a potentially earth-shattering question: whether RMG was bankrupt. He knew that, if the answer were positive, the Maxwell empire would collapse; and for the directors to trade while knowing that RMG was insolvent was unlawful.

Over the weekend before the meeting, Bunn had telephoned Wootten, a young and unimpressive accountant, and suggested that the auditor might review a schedule he had prepared showing RMG's assets and liabilities. When they met, Bunn looked 'under enormous stress'.

The schedule showed assets worth £1.59 billion and liabilities of £845 million. But Bunn's single sheet of paper, carefully checked by Kevin, had serious omissions: $100 million was owed to London & Bishopsgate Group (LBG), £85 million was owed to BIM, £276 million was owed to MCC, £97 million was owed to BPCC's pension fund and over £100 million was owed to three banks. His projections for July showed a cash surplus of £26 million. In fact the overdraft would increase by £49 million, a flaw which was repeated in future projections. In total, the concealed debts amounted to more than £600 million, and there was no provision for the £100 million which RMG would need to pay for BIM's Scitex shares.

On the assets side, there were also mistakes. The MCC shares valued at £350 million were already pledged against loans and the value of those shares was inflated. The New York *Daily News*, taken over for nothing two months earlier, was valued at £120 million. And RMG was listed as owning all the Scitex shares worth

£120 million while its stake was really worth £30 million. Knowing of those mistakes but apparently too nervous to disclose them all, Bunn nevertheless urged upon the auditors the dramatic truth that RMG was insolvent. Wootten's response after two hours' conversation was to remain uncommitted, although he had good reason for concern.

In preparing the 1990 RMG accounts, Wootten had discovered that they had been poorly presented by Bunn's department, with important gaps in the inter-company accounts and irreconcilable disputes between Maxwell and his accountants concerning transactions of enormous sums of money. Although forewarned, the auditor had 'not focused' on RMG's payments to BIM of £4.6 million. That those millions might be part of the £37 million interest payments within the group apparently did not cross his mind. The auditor knew that Maxwell treated all the money 'very much as his own possessions', and he was not minded to challenge that assumption despite the involvement of the pension funds. Accordingly, after Wootten had consulted Walsh, his superior, the two auditors agreed to do very little. Neither considered consulting either Cowling, BIM's auditor, or Taberner, MCC's auditor, for information about any undisclosed inter-company debts. Their sole interest was RMG's external debts, not those to other Maxwell companies, and for that they relied solely upon the erroneous figures presented by Bunn.

By Monday, the two auditors had hardly reacted to Bunn's concern. They reflected Coopers' wisdom that their 'first requirement is to continue to be at the beck and call of RM, his sons and staff, appear when wanted and provide whatever is requested'. In Walsh's opinion that meant that if Maxwell shouted 'jump' he would obey, and the auditor was certain that his esteemed client did not want an opinion from him declaring that RMG was insolvent. The responsibility lay upon RMG's directors, he believed, to warn the auditors of any impecuniosity or of massive undisclosed debts. The auditor avoided such a disconcerting discovery by refraining from probing RMG's accounts during 1991, sticking rigidly to the legal requirements. Walsh consoled himself with the reflection that there was 'no reason to believe that suddenly out of the blue there would be enormous debts due to MCC' or to BIM from the Robert Maxwell Group.

Walsh had naturally not come to that conclusion without consulting Kevin, who volunteered his own solution to RMG's problems. 'We're prepared to sell everything,' confided Kevin, 'including our stake in MCC. In an emergency, we'll even sell our stake in the Mirror Group.' Walsh was not minded even to question such an alarmist scenario, since Kevin admitted that RMG could not meet its liabilities. 'But we can count on the support of the banks to continue trading,' said Kevin. That, announced the auditor, was sufficient to satisfy the criteria of solvency. Bunn was not told of that conversation. Instead, he awaited RMG's board meeting in the hope that the professionals would provide his escape from a nightmare.

At the last moment, on Tuesday morning, Derek Reynolds, the insolvency expert at solicitors Titmuss Sainer, was summoned to attend and formally explain the position of the directors if their company traded while insolvent. No other lawyer had ever previously been requested to attend a Maxwell board meeting for such a purpose. The lawyer joined Walsh and Wootten in Maxwell House to wait with Kevin, Ian, Ron Woods, Michael Stoney and Bunn for the arrival of Robert Maxwell. To Bunn it still seemed that a showdown might occur. When the Chairman failed to turn up, Reynolds began reciting the law. Suddenly, Maxwell burst in, pushed Stoney out of a chair and sat down; he was, Walsh noticed 'very obviously bored'. Directors, said the lawyer, 'once they know or ought to know that their company is insolvent and cannot avoid the prospect of liquidation, must immediately take every step to minimize the loss to creditors. If they fail, then each of them could become personally liable.' When Reynolds finished, he left, and the Chairman asked Walsh to define formally the requirements that had to be met if RMG was to be classed as 'a going concern'.

'A company must be able to pay its debts,' intoned Walsh, adopting a markedly passive role. After Kevin had run through the financial schedule, Bunn – 'looking very unhappy', Walsh noticed – expressed his conviction that the company was insolvent and should cease business. His caution was overridden by the auditors. 'With the banks' support, RMG can meet its obligations,' said Walsh. 'There's no problem.' Bunn looked at the one man who might have prevented the inevitable catastrophe. The auditor had relied upon legal jargon to satisfy his paymasters. Quick to spot the reprieve, the Chairman rose, declared that there was no need to continue, and departed. Later that day, both he and Kevin signed the accounts, which included a declaration that since December 1990 'nothing had happened to materially change the condition of the company'. Bunn did not protest.

Exhausted, Robert Maxwell flew on Wednesday, 24 July to Palma, Majorca to sail on the *Lady Ghislaine*, intending to remain on his yacht until the end of August. He was welcomed at the airport by Gus Rankin, the new captain, whom he had met only briefly on his appointment in May 1991.

A tall, overweight, British-born seafarer, Rankin had been employed on barges on the River Thames before moving to Arkansas with his wife in the 1970s. After becoming an American citizen, he alternated between captaining yachts and working in shipyards. John Hemple, the desperate manager of MAMI, the Maxwell subsidiary which controlled the yacht and the jets, had telephoned to Pocahontas to offer him the *Lady Ghislaine*'s captaincy, and had then ordered him to arrive in London the following day. 'That'll cost you a lot of money,' Rankin replied. 'You're hired,' said Hemple, 'on condition that you immediately take over the yacht in Dubrovnik.' It was on his return to London from Yugoslavia that Rankin met Maxwell. 'Remember,' warned the Publisher, 'whatever anyone else in my family says, I'm the one who makes the decisions.' Over the following six months, Rankin discovered that his telephone calls to Maxwell from the yacht, unlike those of almost anyone else, were immediately connected. The *Lady Ghislaine* was Maxwell's private refuge, denied to anyone unless he approved – and he approved only with reluctance.

Rankin's crew of ten men and three women stewardesses were the usual mixed crowd found on such craft. Grahame Shorrocks, the first officer, had served on the yacht with his stewardess girlfriend Lisa Kordalski for nearly two years. Leonard Graham, the second engineer, had served for more than a year. Others had served for shorter periods, but the turnover was no different from that of other yachts, not least because there was little pressure of work. Maxwell's presence was infrequent, and charters were rare.

Maxwell arrived in Palma in good spirits, accompanied by his trusted chef Martin Cheeseman and Simon Grigg, his valet. Sailing on the £23 million yacht in the sunshine, drinking pink champagne and eating lobster imposed a convenient distance between himself and grubby London. As Rankin steamed slowly around the island and across to Minorca, the Publisher spent the days working, using his two satcom telephone links, occasionally rushing to the bridge himself to collect an incoming fax. But his search for privacy rarely drove him to use the scrambler device fitted to the telephones. Although he prided himself on its installation and glowed at the sight of twenty listed telephone numbers around the world with similar systems, he found its use too complicated. The Publisher's frequent boasts about technology concealed his own inability to master even its more simple applications. In the evenings, he stayed on board to watch a video or read, or went ashore for dinner.

The neighbouring berth in Palma was reserved for the yacht *My Gail*, built in the same shipyard as the *Lady Ghislaine* and owned by Gerald Ronson. In fact Ronson had negotiated on Maxwell's behalf both the purchase of the *Lady Ghislaine* and acquisition of the berth in Palma. On this occasion, the Publisher hoped that his friend would join him for the holiday, but Ronson was wary of repeating an earlier two-yacht trip to Turkey. On one occasion, when Ronson had invited Maxwell on board for a dinner party for sixteen guests, the Publisher had spent the entire evening rising from the table to make business telephone calls across the world on Ronson's satcom – an expensive imposition upon his host's hospitality. Even when he was sitting down, he was bad company – constantly boasting that the *Lady Ghislaine* was faster than *My Gail*, which also did not please Ronson.

So Maxwell was alone on his yacht. Kevin's regular telephone calls from London were invariably prefaced with a question to Rankin: 'What mood is the old man in?' His son's news would rarely improve Maxwell's humour. In separate inquiries to Trevor Cook and Larry Trachtenberg, Bob Southgate of Invesco MIM and Henry Boucher of Capel Cure had asked for the return of the portfolios of pension fund shares 'borrowed' for stock lending with Lehmans in October 1990. Both fund managers had become concerned by the rumours of Maxwell's financial predicament.

Both were stalled by Cook and Trachtenberg, but Boucher stubbornly called Mark Haas at Lehmans. To his surprise, Haas replied that there was no arrangement for the portfolio's return. Boucher summoned a meeting with Cook and Trachtenberg to establish the truth. Cook 'just let Larry speak, explaining the success of stock lending. Henry seemed uncertain about what was going on.' On 30 July, Boucher issued Haas with a demand: 'I expect the return of the pension fund portfolio.' Haas did not reply. The bankers could no longer deny any knowledge of the shares' true owners. Instead they were relying upon the Liechtenstein billion to pay off the debts.

Both Boucher's telephone call and the adverse newspaper articles after Walker's resignation – 'Doubts grow over Maxwell' reported the *Sunday Times* – increased concern in the upper echelons of Lehmans about Maxwell's predicament. His loans had stabilized at $152 million, and the repayment of $42 million was overdue. Kevin was under pressure, because the bank refused to accept more MCC shares as further collateral. 'We want other shares if the loans continue,' he was told. In Kevin's eyes, these were the 'yo-yo days' when banks faltered about loaning money.

'Don't worry, the loans will be repaid soon,' he replied. The money, he explained, would come from the sale of the shares in Scitex, the Israeli hi-tech imaging company. By then, Maxwell's stake in Scitex had been split. While RMG owned 1.7 million shares, BIM owned 5.4 million (2.4 million Scitex shares had been sold privately in July, leaving 7.1 million). On 4 July, Maxwell had agreed with Cook that the private and pension fund interests would be sold together to get a better price, and the proceeds would be divided. In a formal contract on that day, which Maxwell as usual read very carefully, Cook sold BIM's Scitex shares to RMG with a critical proviso – that the shares would continue to belong to the pension funds until settlement day, 4 August, or until the appropriate share of the proceeds was paid into BIM's account. In the meantime, Cook's accountant entered a notional transfer of £100 million on the Call Deposit Account (CDA) between BIM and RMG. Thereafter, although Maxwell failed to transfer the funds on 4 August, both he and Kevin spoke to their bankers as if all the Scitex shares were privately owned – a claim facilitated beause the registered owner was RMG.

Kevin's second source of money was as usual the pension funds. He was gratified to find that Cook was still co-operative and apparently unsuspicious. Some days earlier, two IMRO officials had called at LBI's offices to investigate First Tokyo. Mark Tapley, having decided to resign, was on holiday. Lord Donoughue, who had talked about resignation but still wanted to negotiate his departure terms, refrained from telling the IMRO regulators about the unauthorized stock lending. It was not that type of visit. Neither the IMRO officials nor Maxwell's employees were inquisitive or talkative. Yet a probe into the circumstances of just one development – the recent termination of LBI's management agreement with BIM – would have unravelled Maxwell's whole swindle.

On 10 July, Trevor Cook had been told by Kevin, 'LBI cannot manage money properly.' Cook was not surprised by this since LBI had failed to find any clients as investment managers, and First Tokyo was to be dissolved. He was apparently similarly unsurprised that Trachtenberg and Ford, with Carson's knowledge, were to continue their stock-lending activities in Maxwell House under a new guise – the Middle and Central European Fund, Maxwell's failed attempt to launch an investment bank. During the month, LBI had sold its entire portfolio of shares for £60.1 million but Cook was untroubled by Maxwell's direction that the money should be deposited in the account of RMG, a private company. 'We'll act as your agent,' said Maxwell. With Cook apparently unaware of any problems, the IMRO officials departed without comment, disinclined to probe the tangled arrangements.

Among the Chairman's other diversions which remained undiscovered was his use of the £97 million due to be paid later that month to John Halloran for the BPCC pension fund. At successive meetings with Maxwell, Halloran had demanded his cash quickly. The Chairman had agreed, without mentioning that he had already spent the money, which Cook had obligingly deposited with RMG. In an act of grand theatre, Maxwell told Cook, 'The money for Halloran will be transferred from RMG', and then disappeared to Palma. Just before leaving for his own holidays, Cook passed that message to Jeff Highfield. As his deputy sought Maxwell's help to organize the transfer from RMG, he was greeted by silence. But Highfield did not become alarmed. 'Just more chaos,' he muttered to himself.

Unfortunately for the Maxwells, Basil Brookes was less sanguine. Over the previous three weeks, he had struggled to find a solution to MCC's gigantic secret loans. For most of that period, the finance director had been successfully intimidated into silence by Maxwell, though he was desperate to discuss the problem with the other directors. Finally, unable any longer to cope with the pressure alone, he had telephoned Richard Baker, the former deputy managing director. Too terrified to risk being seen by Maxwell's spies, the two men had sat in a car in a rugby club car park near High Wycombe. Baker's advice was unequivocal: 'Go and see Kevin and, if he refuses to help, go to a lawyer.'

'I can't tell you anything more,' said Kevin, when challenged by Brookes.

'I'm going to have to resign,' countered the finance director.

'I'm sorry about that, but there's nothing more I can say.'

Brookes consulted Roddy McKeen and Geraldine Proudler of the Holborn solicitors Lovell White Durrant. The problem was not easily solved, said the lawyers. There was a conflict in the law between a director's obligations under the Companies Acts and the requirement of the Financial Services Act that directors must not disclose price-sensitive information. 'You cannot resign, because of your legal obligations,' the lawyers added. 'Instead, confide your problems to the other directors at a formal board meeting.' That advice pleased Brookes: he wanted to recover MCC's money rather than blow the whistle.

On 29 July, Brookes summoned up his courage and told Kevin, 'We must have a board meeting about these debts. And here's my letter of resignation.'

Kevin was startled. Until that moment he had not taken Brookes's threat seriously. With Peter Walker's walk-out and Anselmini's request to depart, he could not risk any more resignations. 'Just wait,' he said. 'We'll have a board meeting on 1 August.'

Unknown to Brookes, across in the Mirror building, Lawrence Guest, the Mirror Group's finance director, on the eve of his own holiday was facing similar problems. Maxwell had never concealed his dislike of Guest, convinced that he was not bright and irked by his non-stop worrying. Fortunately, he reflected, he was weak. Unfortunately he was also fundamentally decent and honest.

As his various sources of money began to fade, Maxwell had spied one unmilked cow – the Mirror Group. Within weeks of the heralded public flotation, which supposedly protected the company's finances by a ring-fence, the Publisher had effortlessly breached the barrier. Exuding unusual charm at the first board meeting after the flotation he had spoken about 'a lot of business and effort to be undertaken' and the impossibility of summoning board meetings 'every five minutes'. He continued, 'I would like you to approve the formation of an executive committee.' Its purpose, he explained, would be to take quick decisions, which could later be referred to the full board for approval. 'I of course will be its chairman, with Ian as another member.' Although some directors disagreed, the minutes recorded a unanimous vote, giving Maxwell exclusive powers. He had fabricated those minutes, but, even so, the full board would meet only twice more before 5 November. Yet no one protested. As Maxwell had anticipated, key decisions would be approved by the executive committee – namely, as before, by himself.

His second breach of the ring-fence was the appointment of Michael Stoney as deputy manager, above Lawrence Guest. The self-confident accountant, who had been employed by Maxwell's private companies, had been registered as a director when the newspaper group was floated. But he was considered 'valuable' by the Maxwells. 'You're to live in each other's pockets,' beamed Maxwell to Guest – whom he correctly predicted would suffer demotion without protest.

To emphasize his control over the Mirror Group's funds, Maxwell instructed Stoney not to move his office into the newspaper's building. Everything would be tightly controlled at the centre. With the weak finance director cut out of the loop, the Publisher transferred £38 million from the Mirror Group's bank account to his private company to pay off another two clamouring bankers, including Goldman Sachs in settlement of a purchase of MCC shares. In Mirror Group's internal accounts, the vanished millions were entered as 'deposits' with American banks and BIM.

Guest queried the movement of that money and was told, 'Michael Stoney is placing the company's money on short-term deposit'. Although puzzled that he had not been consulted, he did not ask to see the receipts and duly departed for his holidays. His pliability was welcome to the Maxwells.

To take stock of all these developments, Kevin and Ian flew on 28 July to their father in Palma, carrying $20,000 in cash to cover the *Lady Ghislaine*'s expenses. As the yacht cruised across the blue Mediterranean, the three Maxwells discussed their commercial plight. Aware of the monumental problems they were facing and unable to conceive a plan for survival, they opted for patience and procrastination. After lunch, the two sons swam, skimmed across the calm sea on jet-skis for an hour and then flew back to London. There seemed no sign of panic or even concern.

At eleven o'clock the following evening, Rankin stood on the quayside by the moored yacht holding a taxi. As the minutes ticked by, Captain Hull, seated a short drive away in the Gulfstream, became increasingly nervous. Maxwell was due to fly to Israel and Palma airport closed at 11.30 p.m. But brinkmanship was a sport Maxwell enjoyed. At 11.17, he dashed ashore and jumped into the taxi, excited as a schoolboy as it roared through the port's narrow streets and reached the airport just before the deadline. Two hours later, he landed in Jerusalem.

MCC was paying £40,000 for Maxwell to be filmed later that day at Yad Vashem, the stunning memorial in Jerusalem to the 6 million victims of the Holocaust. He would be interviewed in the recently completed valley of the Destroyed Communities, an extra-ordinary, haunting maze of galleys carved deep into the rock, recalling on granite stone the towns and villages where Jewish settle-ments across Europe had been obliterated. The finished film was due to be shown at a ceremony nine weeks later in New York at which Maxwell was to receive an award.

As the Publisher ate breakfast in his suite at the King David Hotel with the film's director, discussing his role in the forthcoming emotional drama, Larry Trachtenberg was in Kevin's office, hand-ing over share transfer forms and letters for his signature, pledging more pension fund shares to banks.

That afternoon, as the temperature dropped to the low 90s, Max-well, dressed in a light suit and accompanied by a film crew, walked through the eerie, artificial valley, past hundreds of names rep-resenting the Holocaust victims in Hungary, the Soviet Union, Hol-land and Poland, until he reached the stone carving listing the destroyed communities in Czechoslovakia. There at the very bottom was Solotvino, his birthplace, an impoverished community of 3,000 Jews in the Carpathian mountains where, according to legend, there was no money even for a cemetery: the inhabitants either emigrated or their corpses were eaten off the gallows by birds.

Standing by the carved name, Maxwell began describing to the camera his childhood of 'hunger, misery, no shoes and nothing memorable'. He spoke of his discovery after the war of his family's fate – nearly all had perished – and of his anger that the Allied leaders had refused to bomb the railway line to Auschwitz. 'I cannot imagine what my family thought as they stood in the gas chambers and realized they had been tricked . . .' Tears spontaneously welled up in his eyes and he began to shake uncontrollably. Touching the stone, he felt near to his family. Then he took a handkerchief and stumbled away from the camera, dwarfed by the towering granite obelisks. Crowding through his memory was the image of his mother – 'a woman who was so proud of me', he had recently told a gathering of graduate American students, 'who believed in me and told me that I would one day be famous.'

His tears were not only for his mother but also for himself. At that same American ceremony, where he had received an honorary doctorate, he had also pontificated on morality: 'My mother taught me the difference between good and evil.' After a dramatic pause he added, 'She also told me that confidence, like virginity, can only be lost once.' His mother's lessons had clearly been ignored. Worse still, he had no one to turn to. His only friend was dead, remembered by no more than the village's name carved on stone. He wished desperately he was still a child. How he missed his mother's love.

As he dried his tears in the air-conditioned limousine back to the hotel, he wondered where he should spend the night. He had planned to fly to New York to supervise the *Daily News*, but that seemed pointless. Then he thought of flying to London, but that would only bring trouble. Instead he returned to the *Lady Ghislaine*.

ELEVEN

Showdown

– August 1991

Just five minutes before MCC's board of directors were due to gather on Thursday, 1 August 1991, Maxwell cancelled the meeting. His absence, he calculated, would delay a confrontation with the directors. Calling from the *Lady Ghislaine* he told Basil Brookes, 'I'm abroad on urgent business and I want to be present. Postpone the meeting until tomorrow morning.' Unaware that Maxwell was on the yacht in Palma, Brookes at first accepted the excuse without demur, not realizing that the two Maxwells were agreed on a policy of procrastination.

In another telephone call, Maxwell urged Kevin to reduce their borrowings from MCC. By then, the family's debt to the company had fallen to £218 million. The source of the money paid into MCC's account was loans (raised by pledging more pension fund shares to banks) and foreign exchange deposited through the cross-firing. But the bankers' irritation about the delay in paying for those foreign currencies intensified the pressures upon Kevin to raise more money – especially in relation to $200 million which had been due to be paid the previous day to four banks and Elsevier – and there had been neither cash nor credit available at any of the sixty-two banks the Maxwells used. Fearing public embarrassment, Kevin had telephoned David Leal-Bennett at NatWest on 31 July asking for an 'urgent facility' for RMG. Against the $200 million which the Maxwells owed, he said, they expected three payments totalling $130 million on foreign exchange deals to arrive in their accounts during that night from New York. Leal-Bennett, a soft-spoken, weak-looking corporate banker, needed authorization because Kevin's request exceeded the £32 million limit. Consultations had gone to the most senior level in the bank. Although Robert Maxwell was an old customer, his value had recently deteriorated and Leal-Bennett was under instructions to monitor and record the Maxwell accounts every day in a black book. That had proved difficult because there were so many Maxwell accounts in so many different currencies. Eventually, Kevin's request had been approved, but on condition that he provided collateral. Within one hour, Jane Roberts had sent an envelope to NatWest's headquarters at Lothbury containing certificates for 20 million Mirror Group and 3 million Scitex shares. The stock transfer certificates for the Scitex shares were signed on behalf of RMG by Kevin and Robert Bunn. Since RMG owned only 1.7 million Scitex shares, Kevin knew that he was also using shares belonging to the pension funds. Once Leal-Bennett physically possessed the share certificates and had approved the release of $200 million, he went home.

The following morning, 1 August, Leal-Bennett got a nasty shock. The $130 million had not arrived overnight as Kevin had promised. Consequently, his clerks told him, the Maxwells' overdraft was £78 million – £55 million over the limit. Baffled and concerned, Leal-Bennett and his superior Bob Brown rushed to Kevin's office. There the bankers found Kevin, lacking his usual confident demeanour, declaring that he was 'not fully aware of the position'. Reluctantly, Leal-Bennett returned to his own office in Lothbury, only to find a further nasty shock. His clerks had erred. The real overdraft was £144 million – £112 million over the limit. Kevin's assurances that money was coming into the Maxwell accounts had proved to be untrue. 'This is an extremely serious matter,' commented Leal-Bennett, troubled by the appearance of 'considerable confusion in the Maxwell organization' but unable to believe that Kevin had broken his promise. Brown would be more graphic. 'It was horrific,' he would later say. 'This was a *Guinness Book of Records* excess overdraft position. In my thirty-six years I had never experienced anything like this before. I guess it was any banker's nightmare scenario.' But the two bankers resolutely decided 'not to panic'.

In his own office, Kevin had other problems to consider. Anxiously he had been searching for more shares because Lehmans, who were owed $152 million, had that afternoon rejected MCC shares as collateral. 'Give me three days to provide new collateral,' replied Kevin. His first delivery (on 13 August) was of pension fund shares worth £7 million, accompanied by a letter signed by himself and Cook.

In presenting these new shares, Kevin clearly suggested that they were drawn from the Maxwell private fortune. Yet both bankers and lawyers at Lehmans had become suspicious of that explanation. There was niggling evidence of an unresolved confusion. Trachtenberg was offering shares for stock lending on behalf of BIM, yet he was employed by LBI, which was using the shares to raise loans. To the bankers, the relationship between the two companies was unclear. An alternative explanation is that the confusion had always been understood, but now the danger was realized. At any rate, to protect the bank its lawyers drafted a letter for Trachtenberg to sign. It stated that BIM, on behalf of the pension funds, was willing to provide the collateral for the private loans and that BIM and LBI were associated companies. Lehmans' attitude was surprising because even cursory scrutiny of the two companies' purposes revealed the truth. In reality, the bankers feared the consequences of rejecting the pension fund shares: unrecoverable loans. Like Maxwell himself, the bankers believed, or at least hoped, that the tycoon's financial pressures were temporary.

On the yacht, Maxwell had resolved that further delay was his best tactic. Early the following morning, Friday, 2 August, he again postponed his return to London. 'Tell them that I'll be back at 5 p.m.,' he told Kevin. At lunchtime, he decided to sail to Sardinia for the weekend. His directors, he judged, were still his pawns, responsive to his *diktat*. But he was gravely mistaken. Brookes, realizing Maxwell's agenda, had become furious about the first cancellation and instigated the first serious boardroom revolt Maxwell had ever faced.

The young finance director resolved to reveal MCC's debt problem to Anselmini. Brookes's disclosures were not totally unexpected by the Frenchman. Over the past months, he had been aware of the loans being negotiated by Maxwell's private companies. But, whenever he had mentioned the money borrowed from MCC, the Publisher had retorted, 'This is all my money.' Maxwell believed he could rely upon the Frenchman's loyalty. In turn Anselmini, the representative of Crédit Lyonnais's $1.3 billion loan to MCC, was slave to his own initial misjudgment. Until lunchtime on Friday, 2 August, Anselmini had bowed to Maxwell as the Chairman and the largest shareholder, despite his growing misgivings about Maxwell's habit of turning over his papers whenever he entered the office. Anselmini's loyalty began to evaporate when he heard from Brookes of the extent of the Publisher's debts. His self-interest required a survival plan.

Anselmini telephoned Ron Woods. 'MCC's problems', he told him, 'are far worse than you realize. MCC is in default on forex deals and is owed much more money by Maxwell than we realized.'

'I didn't know it was that serious,' replied Woods.

Anselmini's next call was to David Shaffer, the president of Macmillan in New York. 'I'm shocked by the scale of the problem!' exclaimed the American.

By then, Brookes had also outlined the unauthorized plunder of MCC's cash to Peter Laister, the non-executive director, who found it 'very odd'. As a result, when Maxwell cancelled the second meeting that day, Laister exploded. 'You've got to see Kevin,' he insisted to the finance director.

The arrival in his office of three directors – Anselmini, Brookes and Woods – at 2.30 gave Kevin a considerable jolt. A delegation was an unprecedented sight. To reduce the odds, he insisted that Woods should leave. 'We've accepted his resignation,' he explained. Woods meekly left vowing not to abandon his responsibilities. But the tax expert's departure did not alter the sterility of the ensuing conversation. 'I'm not telephoning Dad,' insisted Kevin protectively. 'He'll be back next week.' In the midst of his procrastination, Laister walked unannounced into his office. 'This is all unacceptable, Kevin,' barked the older man. 'There must be a board meeting by next Tuesday at the latest.'

'All right,' agreed Kevin coolly.

After the three directors had departed, Kevin telephoned his father. He then summoned Woods. 'I want your resignation immediately.'

'I refuse,' answered the normally taciturn Welshman. 'I'll resign from everything except MCC.'

'We want you off everything,' insisted Kevin.

The tax adviser became stubborn. 'I have my responsibilities. I'm not resigning and I've got to go home to a party for my parents-in-law.'

'Take the helicopter home,' offered Kevin, becoming conciliatory.

On Saturday morning, Maxwell was breakfasting on the deck of his yacht as it steamed towards Sardinia. The glittering sunshine and the deep-blue sea obliterated the problems accumulating in Holborn. Rankin telephoned him from the bridge: 'Captain Hull wonders whether you would like the Gulfstream to fly low over the boat on its way to Sardinia?' 'Good idea,' replied Maxwell. One hour later, Hull flew the jet 200 feet above the *Lady Ghislaine*. 'Terrific!' yelped Maxwell. 'Tell him to do it again!'

At lunchtime, as Maxwell sat eating smoked salmon, lobster and fresh berries and drinking Krug champagne, he pondered his strategy. Exhausted and fed up, he felt drawn to the Mediterranean. But, after speaking to Kevin, he realized there was little alternative but to return to London the following day.

Early on Sunday morning, 4 August, Maxwell flew back to London. *En route* he telephoned Woods at home in Berkshire. 'I need to see you immediately to discuss the demerger.' Woods was dismayed, but before he could convey his reluctance Maxwell announced that his helicopter would shortly be landing in Woods's garden.

Once in London, Woods waited two hours before being admitted to the Publisher's cavernous office. The demerger, it was quickly apparent, was simply a ruse to lure him to London. Maxwell wanted to gauge the opposition: 'What's the problem?'

'We must have a board meeting to discuss the loans.'

'Of course we will,' replied Maxwell in a comforting voice before dismissing Woods for his return journey by helicopter. 'Don't talk to any other directors,' he warned as the Welshman departed. Standing between their adjoining offices, the Maxwells understood only too well the unfortunate consequences of a cast-iron conspiracy between the other directors.

The next visitor to the office was Leal-Bennett. The banker had spent the day in the Holborn office trying to unravel the whereabouts of NatWest's unsanctioned £150 million loan to RMG. His conversation with Kevin the previous day had been particularly unsatisfactory. 'What's gone wrong?' asked the insipid banker. Kevin mumbled an incoherent reply. 'You've got to come clean,' urged Leal-Bennett. 'This is extremely serious. Lay your cards on the table so we can work together and find a solution.' His appeal had been ignored.

So, in his quest to find the answer, the banker had come to Maxwell House to ask the accountants from Coopers working in the building about 'Maxwell's liquidity problem'. It was during that visit that Leal-Bennett encountered Basil Brookes. 'Why has MCC a cash problem?' asked Leal-Bennett.

'Only because Mr Maxwell takes money out for himself,' replied Brookes, pausing briefly before breaking his loyalty. 'You've no idea how bad things are here. The private side owes MCC about £190 million.'

The banker blinked and stared. 'I never knew about that. And we've got another problem. There's a £150 million debt from the Maxwells for forex transactions. I'm trying to compile a list of their deals.' Leal-Bennett had found yet another three unpaid forex deals worth $105 million, which increased the Maxwells' debts to NatWest. The two men gazed forlornly at each other. So much was unspoken and so much was unknown. Both were victims of the same manipulator. Suddenly, Brookes was overcome once again by his need to confide: 'I just don't know what's happening.'

'I'm also puzzled,' admitted Leal-Bennett. 'Mr Maxwell told me that MCC had received money from Goldman Sachs and Morgan Stanley on successful currency speculation. Do you know about that?'

Brookes shook his head. 'I had nothing to do with that. This is typical of my problems,' complained the finance director confessing to his own powerlessness. 'I'm worried because the problems are not in MCC but in the private side.' After further silence, Brookes added, 'I've even taken my own legal advice.'

Leal-Bennett blinked again. That was astounding. 'I'd better report this,' he thought, packing his briefcase. 'I can't keep this to myself.'

When the banker had left, Brookes walked into Albert Fuller's office. The treasurer had unexpectedly taken a long holiday. But, irritatingly, he had locked his cupboards, thereby denying Brookes access to the records of MCC's currency activities. Yet, for all his anger, Brookes remained unsuspicious.

Leal-Bennett in the meantime had walked into the Chairman's office. 'If I don't get a loan,' threatened Maxwell, 'I might have to go to the Bank of England.' The implication was that Maxwell's insolvency would wipe out the security of NatWest's loans to the empire.

'If you do that,' answered Leal-Bennett, knowing that Maxwell was requesting a massive sum, 'could you tell someone more senior than me at the bank?' His life experience had not prepared the banker for this scenario: a client had borrowed £112 million more than was authorized and was suggesting that the cure was for the bank actually to increase the loans! Leal-Bennett departed uncomfortably aware of Maxwell's plight but unsure if his threat was mere bravado. There was another possibility. Maxwell had known Robin Leigh-Pemberton, the governor of the Bank of England, since the early 1970s when Leigh-Pemberton had been first a director and then chairman of the National Westminster Bank, so perhaps he was threatening to embarrass NatWest's new managers. But Leal-Bennett hardly considered those personality problems as he contemplated the possibility of MCC becoming insolvent. NatWest risked losing a mammoth amount. Back in his Lothbury office, his superiors decided after hearing his report that their best course was to start renegotiating the terms of the loans promptly. In consolation, they blessed their possession of the Scitex shares. The following morning they would request another 790,000 shares from RMG, unaware that the real owner was BIM. The transfer forms would be signed by Kevin and his father. Kevin had also promised to deliver 100 million Mirror Group shares.

That Sunday night, ignoring Maxwell's strictures, Woods telephoned Brookes. The Publisher's unpredictability and his assertion of authority had disoriented the dissidents, sowing confusion. 'My meeting was a non-event,' Woods confided, worried even so that he should be breaking Maxwell's orders not to discuss the company's problems. Brookes did not reply. The two directors were beginning to resemble trussed chickens, awaiting an unknown fate.

Maxwell awoke on Monday, 5 August determined to exploit the directors' confusion by deferring the board meeting once more and isolating his critics. After a 7 a.m. conversation with Kevin, he admitted Woods to his office. The quiet Welshman was delivering his letter of resignation from all the private companies. 'This is no good,' scoffed Maxwell. 'You've mentioned the loans and your "concern to protect MCC". Rewrite the letter!' Woods complied but refused to resign from MCC. 'Fine' grunted Maxwell, 'but I don't want you speaking to any other directors about this.' He was now sure Woods's wholehearted loyalty was purely historical.

It was certainly that. At 11 a.m., Brookes, Anselmini and Woods met in what seemed to them a conspiratorial fashion. 'He's using MCC's money for the private companies,' protested Brookes, scrutinizing the other men's pained faces. All three desperately wanted to avoid a confrontation. Maxwell's financial problems, they reasoned, were clearly acute but his mooted meeting with the Bank of England (reported by Brookes) implied his own search for help. 'Let's give him time to solve his problems,' suggested Anselmini. Later urged by Laister not to resign because 'MCC has a problem,' they meekly obeyed. 'We followed Laister. We didn't know what else to do.'

At 11 a.m. the following day, the four directors – Woods, Anselmini, Brookes and Laister – met again. Rippon, the highest paid, was again absent. Overnight, the mood of each of the four men had changed dramatically. Each separately had felt a shiver of self-doubt at the realization of his own complicity in allowing Maxwell to continue to exercise the near unlimited authority he had enjoyed since 1981. For the first time, the directors acknowledged their own culpability in ignoring the Chairman's conflicts of interest, as he served both his public and his private companies. By ignoring the warning signs, they had allowed him to withhold information. Yet none would be honest enough to admit that their motivation might have been cowardice or greed.

'I think we've been deceived,' suggested Brookes. 'After all, Maxwell hasn't told us he intended to sell MCC's remaining interest in Berlitz; nor about his foreign exchange deals; nor about his borrowings from MCC.' The others looked glum. 'That was all reckless at best,' Brookes continued, speculating that Maxwell had secretly bought MCC shares and used MCC money to bolster the private companies. 'Now Kevin's having meetings with bankers which might not be in MCC's interest. It's all a conflict of interest between MCC and the private companies and it's continuing.' His audience could barely nod, paralysed by their inability to invent a remedy. 'I've given them my resignation but they haven't replied yet,' announced Brookes.

'But he told me he hadn't received any protests!' exclaimed Anselmini. 'And even I have written I want to leave.'

'So have I,' added Woods.

For the first time, they suspected that Maxwell's private billion-pound fortune had disappeared. And they knew that MCC could collapse if his private companies were bankrupt. The four hoped to discuss those issues with him at a finance committee meeting to be held at noon. Their only consolation was the news that, overnight, Maxwell's debt to MCC had continued to fall, this time by another £21 million to £151 million. 'That's still too high,' said Laister. Then a secretary telephoned. 'Mr Maxwell', she announced, 'says the finance committee meeting is postponed until 2 p.m.' At 2 p.m., the meeting was cancelled again.

'That's it!' fumed Laister. 'We need some legal advice. We'll meet again at 4 p.m.'

Lawyers had already played a substantial role in Maxwell's more recent fate. Both Titmuss Sainer and Nicholson Graham had provided him with comfort letters and reassurances which he had used to sanctify controversial property deals designed to boost MCC profits. The same lawyers, together with Oscar Beuselinck, Lord Mishcon and Jonathan Crystal QC, had all been regularly summoned to advise on his quest to silence his critics by issuing writs and doom-laden threats.

Even lawyers not in his pay had assisted him. Lovell White had recommended silence to Basil Brookes in July rather than expose Maxwell's unauthorized plunder of MCC's funds. Barry Walker of Ashurst had also ended up by helping Maxwell's interests by advising his opponents (in Walker's case, the directors of First Tokyo) not to speak to journalists. One beneficial result of Walker's advice was to silence Alan McInroy, who on 1 August had noticed that Maxwell was selling shares from the First Tokyo portfolio, which by then had been pledged to the Swiss Bank Corporation as collateral for a £55.7 million loan to buy the Trust.

So there was ample precedent when the lawyers' imposition of silence was repeated to Laister by Vanni Trieves, a senior partner at MacFarlanes, that afternoon, 6 August. 'Your prime responsibility', counselled Trieves, 'is to recover the money owed to MCC. Don't make any public statement which could endanger the private companies or risk the repayment of the loans to MCC.'

'Who can we tell?'

'Nobody. You must exercise absolute caution. Find out what's happening and keep clear records of what everyone says.'

Laister returned to discover that Maxwell had just cancelled the rearranged finance committee meeting due to be held at 5 p.m. Unwilling to tolerate more procrastination, he barged into the Chairman's office: 'Bob, we must meet immediately. This situation cannot continue for another minute.'

'It's not necessary,' said Maxwell, looking tired and drawn.

'It is, Bob. It's for the good of the company and to protect the shareholders' interests.'

The two men glared at each other. The unusual tension was broken by Maxwell. 'All right,' he sighed. 'In one hour.' The delay was necessary to allow Kevin time to wriggle out of two other problems – the debris of July's forex gambles.

Nine days earlier, in another of his many uncompleted forex deals, Kevin had bought $32 million from the Bank of Nova Scotia for sterling. The bank had delivered the dollars and awaited payment with increasing impatience. Maxwell was a valued client who had borrowed £68.5 million in March and had successfully negotiated another loan on the promise that £40 million would be repaid from the proceeds of the sale of Scitex shares. That relationship crumbled on 31 July. 'This is the fourth delayed forex deal,' threatened George Marlatte, a red-faced vice-president of the bank. 'You've got thirty minutes to pay up.'

'Just hang on,' replied Kevin. 'There's been a snafu. I'll get someone at the NatWest to contact you with an assurance you'll be paid.' He then added with unusual tact, 'I think it's best if I cancel the fishing trip to Norway you invited me to. It's not a good time to go fishing.'

When the delegation of three bankers met Kevin on 6 August, Kevin appeared contrite. All the loan would be repaid, he promised: 'For a start, you'll get the money from our sale of 1.9 million Scitex shares.' That completely separate sale had been completed on 8 July and the proceeds had been already paid out to other banks, but Kevin pretended to the three Bank of Nova Scotia representatives that the money was due in mid-August. That deception – what he would call 'a fateful decision not to tell the truth' – was compounded by others. 'RMG owns all the Scitex shares,' Kevin reassured the bankers, referring to the 7.1 million shares which were the collateral for a £40 million loan. 'And totally free of any encumbrances.' The truth was the opposite. All the Scitex shares were pledged. Additionally, Kevin falsely assured his visitors that neither MCC nor RMG was suffering a liquidity crisis.

Having spun more tales, Kevin gradually reduced the bankers' suspicions, leaving them relieved that they would receive repayment of at least £30 million from the imminent sale of the 7.1 million Scitex shares. Fortunately for Kevin, they were still so trusting that they had failed to demand possession of the actual share certificates. The notion that Kevin could be less than truthful did not occur to the Canadian bankers. 'Please accept $100,000 as compensation for your extra efforts,' offered Kevin. 'Thanks,' replied his audience. It would never arrive. Nevertheless, they still refused Kevin's plea to make a further loan. 'We're too concerned for that,' said Marlatte.

Kevin next met Mike Moore, a senior corporate banker of Bankers Trust. Moore wanted reassurance about the repayment of a £50 million loan. 'Don't worry,' urged Kevin. 'We are selling 7.1 million Scitex shares and we'll be able to repay your loan.'

This was all part of what would subsequently be described as Kevin's 'dodging and diving', a piece of theatre which continued at 6 p.m. on the same day when Laister, Anselmini, Woods and Brookes sat opposite the three Maxwells. Ian Maxwell, who had deliberately shied away from involvement over the previous week although he was a managing director of MCC, had been ordered to attend to support his family. Robert Maxwell appeared ragged, clearly past his prime. For those, like Woods, who had known him well, the 'filial love remained even if he said things which were untrue'. Laister shared that sympathy. He did not suspect any evil; he simply wanted a cure. The rows, he believed, were caused by Maxwell's cavalier behaviour rather than by any criminal conspiracy. He decided that the solution was for the directors to issue threats and to hear some answers.

'This has got to stop,' said Brookes. 'All this money has disappeared. We need a schedule of repayments.'

'You'll get one,' replied Kevin, breaking the Maxwells' silence. 'It's all a short-term problem. All the loans will be repaid and new procedures instituted to prevent further abuses. In the last few hours, we've reduced the debt to £138 million. After we've sold our Scitex shares next month, we'll be able to repay MCC another

£80 million.' He spoke so convincingly that Brookes thought, 'Kevin has crossed to our side of the argument.' He effectively promised that MCC would no longer be used as the family's private bank. Brookes did not realize that the majority of the Scitex shares belonged to the pension fund or that the Bank of Nova Scotia, Bankers Trust and several others had also been promised the proceeds.

But the apparent reconciliation was at once exploded by Maxwell, his face turning purple. 'Stop taking notes!' he screamed at Anselmini. 'I want these conspiratorial discussions to cease. If there are any problems, please come to me rather than speaking among each other [sic].' An outburst of verbal brutality was imminent. For Brookes, the atmosphere had become 'extremely hostile'. He would later be seen white-faced and close to tears in his office. For Laister, the hour's meeting was 'appalling and surprising'. Even so, as he wrote a memorandum of the meeting afterwards in Woods's office, he remarked, 'All things considered, that was reasonably successful.' All agreed that none would resign until the debt problem was solved. 'Our strength', continued Laister in his bluff, reassuring manner, 'is that together we can outvote the Maxwells.' By the end of the day, the four seemed more relaxed, although suspicions remained. 'I didn't know who to trust,' sighed Woods.

Upstairs, Maxwell sat in fury. Anselmini, who knew so much, was clearly the ring-leader of the cabal. Pole was summoned. 'I need to know Anselmini's loyalties.' Pole naturally understood. That night, a diversion was installed on Anselmini's telephone: it led to a recording machine.

Maxwell's next thought was to win a majority on the board. A start was the removal of Woods. The next morning, he summoned the tax adviser: 'I'd like you to resign from MCC.'

'I won't,' replied Woods.

'You're behaving like a cabal. I won't tolerate that.'

Two hours later, the Publisher called Woods again: 'Will you resign?'

'No,' insisted Woods. 'Only when everything is settled.'

Disturbed by the apparent solidarity among the directors, Maxwell ordered Kevin to persuade Woods to resign. During their meeting, Bob Keene of the Midland Bank arrived to finalize the details of a $30 million loan. Unknown to Woods, Kevin had submitted his name to the bank as one of the directors responsible for that arrangement. Yet Kevin still demanded his resignation.

That afternoon, 7 August, after Kevin had smilingly bid farewell to Keene, David Leal-Bennett arrived for lunch, more disturbed than ever. Believing that £200 million was missing from the group – a gross under-estimate – the banker concluded that NatWest had become 'a lender of last resort', meaning that without the loans the Maxwell empire would crash. Still puzzled about the background, he once again 'implored Kevin to come clean'. Instead, Kevin coldly referred his visitor 'to the Chairman' for an explanation. But the chief executive did assuage the banker's fears about the debt. 'We expect to sell the Scitex shares within seven weeks,' said Kevin, 'which should release £120 million for the private side. That should settle some of our debts.' Leal-Bennett was reassured. A strict monitoring regime, he told Kevin, would be imposed on all the group's financial transactions, for which the bank would levy a fee of £1.1 million. Kevin looked shocked and then excused himself. A new crisis had arisen with Goldman Sachs in New York.

The Chairman had pledged 40 million Mirror Group shares to Goldmans for a $35 million loan – the same shares that Kevin had offered NatWest. Goldmans already held MCC shares as collateral against private loans of $60 million and £106 million. Now John Lopatin was threatening to sell those shares if Maxwell did not pay for his foreign exchange purchases. 'Don't worry,' urged Kevin – and the American wanted to accept that reassurance. The bank had been exposed as breaching British laws by failing to declare its MCC stake four months earlier, and its excuse was thin: there was a confusion between its status as a bank in New York and as a broker in London. The bank found itself accused of supporting Maxwell's share price. Nevertheless, by the end of the thirty-minute transatlantic conference call, the bankers left Kevin in no doubt that their goodwill could not be taken for granted. He had every reason to believe them.

The next visitor was Richard Pelly, the intelligent and efficient corporate finance director of Barclays Bank. Pelly wanted an explanation for Kevin's failure to pay £35 million for his purchase on 17 July of $47 million – another of the uncompleted forex deals. Pelly was furious about 'the breakdown in confidence'. To his relief, the Chairman was also present. 'It was a major mistake,' soothed

Maxwell in an unusually sincere voice, 'which I realize has had a serious impact on our relationship with Barclays. We'll get Albert Fuller to supply a full explanation when he returns from his holiday.' Pelly's suspicions were further reduced by Kevin's assurances: 'Our finances are stable. The private side owes MCC £75 million which we'll repay by selling Scitex.'

'Fine,' said Pelly, 'but we need more information about your private finances.'

'Coopers have just signed off RMG's accounts,' replied Kevin defensively. 'You've got enough information.'

'I think Richard Stone of Coopers should come in,' said Pelly, referring to the accountants' insolvency expert.

'We don't need the undertakers,' interrupted Maxwell. 'But Kevin could do with some help. Perhaps one of your bankers.'

Pelly agreed to consider the idea. Kevin, he conceded, was overloaded. On his return to his office, the banker would embark on a detailed report to the Maxwells suggesting how they could improve their business. It would be ignored.

Late that afternoon, exhausted, Kevin helicoptered to Luton to catch a chartered jet to the island of Zakinthos in the Ionian Sea. Four days of his week's holiday on the *Lady Ghislaine* had already been lost and his father had evinced neither gratitude nor understanding. Indeed, despite Kevin's unconditional devotion to the business, his father had behaved in his characteristically abominable fashion. Throughout the previous weekend, the Publisher had refused to approve Kevin's and Pandora's use of the yacht for a week's holiday. Before returning to London, he had ordered Captain Rankin not to reveal whether he intended to leave the boat. 'What sort of mood's the old man in?' Kevin had asked on one of his repeated calls to discover whether the boat was available. Even when Maxwell flew out of Sardinia, Rankin was instructed not to tell anyone about his departure. 'Keep them guessing,' was the Publisher's last edict as Rankin set sail to Corfu to meet Kevin.

Forty-eight hours later, as the *Lady Ghislaine* anchored in Greek waters, Pandora and her friends Charles and Jane Morgan were still in the dark as Maxwell's deliberate harassment continued.

'Can we fly the G4 from Heathrow?' asked Pandora, since that was the most convenient airport.

'Go to Luton,' grunted her father-in-law. 'The plane's there.'

Minutes after the families, including five children, had boarded the Gulfstream, the pilot received a telephone call from Maxwell: 'I'll need the plane. Kick them off.'

'Where and when do you want to fly, Mr Maxwell?'

'To New York, tonight.'

'Don't worry, I can do both,' chuckled the pilot, anxious to help his fretting passengers.

Their eventual embarkation on the yacht had been preceded by another telephone instruction from Maxwell, this time to Rankin: 'Don't let them make the crew work for them. I don't want them to abuse the hospitality.' Nevertheless, by midnight on 7 August, when Kevin arrived, they had enjoyed the sun, the ski-jets, the water-skiing and plenty of good food during the four-day cruise from Corfu.

When Kevin awoke in the yacht's sunlit bedroom and ordered breakfast, which was to be eaten overlooking the sea, the four directors, unknown to the Maxwells, had been sitting since 9 a.m. with Vani Trieves in MacFarlanes' offices in the City. 'You're in a dangerous position,' advised the lawyer. 'You could be held liable for breaches of the Companies Acts which require you to protect the shareholders' interests. You must urgently get all the facts, but don't talk to anyone, including the auditors. Talking to others could mean leaks and endanger MCC's chance of retrieving its money from Maxwell's private companies.' Before leaving they agreed to codename their strategy 'Cricket'.

The four returned to Holborn. Maxwell was in New York, having flown overnight after listening to the tapes of Anselmini's telephone conversations. Reassuringly, the suspected conspiracy did not appear to exist. The Publisher's diary that day, the 8th, listed eighteen separate meetings, starting at 7.30 a.m. with Charlie Wilson, the newspaper executive whom Maxwell rightly assessed he could trust, although his editorship of the *Racing Times* in New York had miserably failed to sabotage Rupert Murdoch's newspaper. Engrossed in these disconcerting meetings, Maxwell evaded a telephone call from Laister in London.

Laister instead approached Ian Maxwell. 'We need assurances, Ian.'

'I don't know anything about this,' replied the director of MCC, 'and I cannot pass on any messages or letters.'

'I'm wasting my time,' thought Laister, who next tried telephoning Kevin on the yacht.

'How are things?' sang Kevin cheerily.

'We've consulted our lawyers,' said Laister, staring out at London's grey skyline while imagining the blue sky over Kevin. 'We need to have a very precise breakdown of all your financial transactions to check that they were all properly authorized and there were no conflicts of interest.' The satcom telephone starkly conveyed Kevin's terror: for the Maxwells to comply with Laister's demand would be self-destructive. Every hope of survival would collapse. Kevin exploded in an unexpected and unprecedented outburst. 'Don't do anything until I return!' he screamed. 'You're going behind my back!'

'Calm down, Kevin,' urged Laister. 'We had no alternative.'

At the end of the conversation, Kevin called Brookes. 'How dare you go to lawyers!' he shouted. 'I'm not coming back. You've obviously got no confidence in me.'

'We do, Kevin,' replied Brookes. 'We just need to organize things better.' Kevin was too cool to allow his holiday to be ruined. Both he and his father believed that their emotional appeals to the directors had stemmed the challenge. For the moment, that judgment was correct.

To reassure themselves, the four directors had invited Coopers to give a presentation proving the value of the 'intangibles' cited at £2.2 billion in the accounts. At the end of ninety minutes, Laister was 'satisfied by the auditor's confidence' and believed that MCC's problems were 'temporary'. Taking the lead, he sought a solution which would avoid an embarrassing showdown yet enable him to fulfil his statutory duties. At 5.30 that afternoon, the directors returned to MacFarlanes to draft a letter to Maxwell outlining a quiet compromise designed to protect the minority shareholders and reduce the debt.

Unseen by them, at that very moment Trachtenberg was borrowing another $69 million from Lehman Brothers, in US Treasury bills, and pledging to buy a further $10.4 million on 13 September. As collateral he was offering shares in Berlitz, MCC and the Mirror Group, as well as approximately eighty pension fund investments and the remaining shares from the First Tokyo portfolio which had been pledged to the Swiss Bank Corporation.

The money was needed to repay Maxwell's debts to Goldman Sachs and other banks, and to reduce further his private debt to MCC to £130 million.

On 9 August, Maxwell awoke in the presidential suite at the Waldorf in New York to find a letter from Laister and Lord Rippon – stirred by Laister to take action against his generous employer – demanding assurances within seven days about his past activities, most sensitively about inter-company loans and foreign exchange speculation. The three executive directors (Woods, Brookes and Anselmini), they concluded, 'have now expressed uncertainty about their continuing role as Directors'. That, Laister announced, 'is an open-ended threat'. There was little alternative, Maxwell appreciated, but to defuse the challenge. In a telephone call to Laister, he roused his famed charm: 'Peter, believe me, this is all a short-term problem.'

Laister relaxed. 'I wanted to believe he was telling me the truth,' he later explained.

Both Kevin and Robert Maxwell returned to London over the weekend of 10 August. Robert landed in the middle of the night at Luton, while Kevin, having pondered quotations of £26,000 to charter a jet from Athens, flew British Airways. 'I can't justify this sort of expenditure,' he said to a bemused Captain Rankin, who wondered why his employer should bother to justify any expenditure to him. On Maxwell's orders, the *Lady Ghislaine* was to remain at Piraeus. 'I'll be out any day now to continue my holiday,' he told Rankin.

Only one overriding issue prevented Maxwell's flight back to his yacht: how to juggle more loans and raise more cash. Newspaper reports added to the pressure. The *Financial Times* had reported on 15 August that Goldman Sachs held stakes in MCC and Mirror Group worth £143 million as collateral for loans, 'prompting suggestions that his private finances are under pressure'. That report ignited a chain reaction. Bob Southgate of Invesco MIM, who ten months earlier had not acted upon Tim Daily's warnings about LBI's stock lending, became nervous about Kevin Maxwell's failure to honour his pledge since October 1990 and return the pension fund portfolio. He telephoned Trachtenberg asking for its return. Trachtenberg offered assurances but did not reveal that the portfolio, pledged with Lehmans, was effectively irretrievable. Meanwhile, John Di Rocco at

Lehmans refused to provide another £10 million loan, telling Kevin, 'We no longer will accept MCC stock for more than 10 per cent of the collateral.' Kevin believed that his only recourse to satisfy the banker was to pledge more pension fund shares.

Other bankers, to the Maxwells' concern, were also rejecting MCC shares. 'We are limiting the amount of MCC shares as collateral,' Julie Maitland at Crédit Suisse told Kevin. 'Either replace the remaining MCC shares with other stock or repay the debt.' To forestall that disaster, Trachtenberg had secured from Capel Cure another package of pension fund shares in seventeen companies and asked Jane Roberts from the treasury department to deliver the envelope to Maitland personally.

But by then Maitland had more reason to be suspicious. The bank had received £29.1 million worth of shares from the First Tokyo portfolio, yet their history was readily discoverable: the Maxwells' purchase of First Tokyo had been financed by a loan from Swiss Bank secured by those same shares. But Maitland accepted Bunn's reassurance that she was mistaken, despite her own lawyers' query about Maxwell's ownership. In fact, by 15 August, the Maxwells had already sold, contrary to their agreement with the Swiss Bank, shares from the First Tokyo portfolio worth £16 million. The pace of the familiar pattern, Maxwell realized, would increase.

The Chairman's control over all the pension fund shares depended on BIM manager Trevor Cook, who at that moment was holidaying in France. The Gulfstream was dispatched to collect him, and he was met on 15 August on the ninth floor by Maxwell, Kevin and Trachtenberg. 'I want you to hand over all the pension fund share certificates to Trachtenberg for safe keeping,' said Maxwell.

'Larry', added Kevin, 'will give you signed confirmation that the shares belong to BIM and will keep them in his safe.'

Cook nodded, without querying the new arrangement or consulting BIM's other directors or the pension fund trustees. 'I relied upon Trachtenberg,' he said later, 'and had no impression of danger.' He was equally 'unconcerned' by Trachtenberg's statement that the shares owned by First Tokyo had been 'liquidated'. The pension fund manager simply filed a letter from Trachtenberg stating that £36 million belonging to the pension funds 'has been placed on deposit with RMG generating profits of £1.5 million for BIM'.

He also filed a letter from Kevin in which he reassuringly mentioned that the collateral for BIM's shares 'has a current value greater than the value of the stock'. As Cook later admitted, 'I didn't think of the possible misuse of share certificates. I was fooled.' Others would conclude that Cook had been appointed by Maxwell only because he could so easily be fooled.

The price of Cook's negligence materialized that same day. Within minutes of receiving the certificates, Trachtenberg forwarded them to Crédit Suisse, enclosing a letter to René Müller on RMG notepaper, pledging the shares as collateral for Maxwell's private loans. Maitland ought not have been in any doubt about the real owner of the shares. BIM was clearly identified on the certificates as the owner.

That evening, Cook was flown back to France in the Gulfstream to resume his holiday. He departed unaware that Jeff Highfield, his deputy, had noticed that LBI had not paid the interest on the stock lending for the past three months. Highfield called Bunn and was referred to Michael Stoney.

'Sorry,' said Stoney, 'I've only just taken over. I need to find my way around.' Amicably, it was agreed that LBI would pay interest on the outstanding debt. (Highfield was unaware that by then LBI, on Maxwell's orders, had been absorbed into the Middle and Central European Fund.)

Highfield also telephoned Jonathan Ford, LBI's finance director, to say he had not received the July account. 'Sorry, it's the summer holidays,' he was told. Highfield's concerns were subsequently brushed aside by Cook: 'Don't worry. They're always late.' Cook's pliancy made life much easier for Maxwell.

Working feverishly, by the end of that day Kevin had also assembled a package intended to reassure MCC's directors. First, to allay Laister's concerns about the legality of the family's debts to MCC, he obtained a comfort letter from his lawyer Philip Morgenstern, validating these loans.

Secondly, he wrote to Rippon: 'I have put together with Basil an agreed bundle . . . of new procedures' to avoid unauthorized loans and speculation. Brookes would dispute any participation in any discussions. Kevin also stated: 'the private side has disposal assets equalling 3 or 4 times the inter-company balances'. Indeed, he had given Brookes a list of unpledged assets apparently showing that 'the private side has £600 million in the Headington Investment Group', which was the successor holding company to Pergamon. Although the list was dated 14 May, three months earlier, Kevin wrote reassuringly, 'It hasn't changed since then.' The truth was the opposite. The assets were all pledged. Kevin concluded his memo to Rippon with the injunction, 'Please remind all concerned that a house divided is a house destroyed.' That much was true.

While Kevin rushed on 15 August to catch the evening Concorde for New York for fourteen appointments the next morning starting at 6.15 a.m. (and he was to return the following night to France for the weekend with his mother), his father spent the weekend in Salzburg with Hans-Dietrich Genscher, the German foreign minister. Maxwell departed in good humour just as dramatic events began to unfold in Moscow. A coup, organized by the KGB and some Soviet army officers, had been launched against Mikhail Gorbachev. Maxwell relied upon the Russian, more than any other politician, to give him credibility and some hope for a financial lifeline trading in Russia's international debts. The following Monday morning, putting aside his own problems, he appeared on radio and television pontificating about his fears for Gorbachev – 'It's a *coup d'état*. We must prevent civil war' – and later telephoned John Major, James Baker, the American secretary of state, and Genscher, urging support for the detained Soviet leader. By the evening, political worries were replaced by his own problems.

Bankers were ringing constantly while he agreed with Kevin a package designed to achieve reconciliation with the irate MCC directors. One chore was unavoidable. Laister had demanded an assurance that Maxwell was not borrowing cash from MCC to buy MCC shares – an unlawful act. Uttering one more lie presented no problem. 'I confirm', scrawled Maxwell in a handwritten note, 'that the borrowings by Headington Investments from MCC have not been used in any way which would mean that MCC had in any way contravened the Company Act.' After signing the note, the father pushed it towards his son. Unhesitatingly, Kevin also signed the undertaking that they had not used MCC's money to buy MCC shares. Thankfully, Philip Morgenstern had provided advice that MCC, as a subsidiary of HIL, could loan its parent money – but only with the approval of the independent directors. 'We're pushing the law to its limits,' thought Kevin. After reading the promise Lord Rippon, the only director present, said: 'Thank you, Bob.'

'And I'm very grateful', said Maxwell with real sincerity, 'that none of this unfortunate business has leaked.' Kevin nodded his agreement.

Maxwell momentarily considered abandoning his plans to fly to Athens to meet the *Lady Ghislaine* but, by now quite exhausted, calculated that his absence might advance a solution. His judgment proved correct. In a more relaxed atmosphere, at 11 a.m. on 21 August Rippon, Laister, Brookes and Anselmini were seated in Kevin Maxwell's office being assured that the family could repay the entirety of the debt, apparently already reduced to £113 million, by 30 September. 'Dad has agreed to a number of changes,' Kevin announced. To sanitize the whole operation, he said, 'I'm going to resign from all the private companies.' He also promised that the Maxwells would no longer undertake any inter-company business. To persuade the directors of that commitment, he agreed that the treasury department should be split from the private companies. New procedures would prevent repetition of past abuses. Once the last £100 million had been repaid to MCC, the public company would be secure.

The four directors departed, relieved that the Maxwells were at last co-operating. Kevin's promise that the debt to MCC would disappear by September 'fits in with their explanation that it's a short-term problem', Laister told Derek Hayes at MacFarlanes just before leaving for his holidays. 'All at the moment seems to be progressing satisfactorily. We're getting all the information we need and new procedures. Everything's back on the rails.'

The Maxwells' strategy had been perfectly executed, but their appetite for money remained insatiable – and impossible for others to ignore. The very next day, as Brookes set off on holiday, the father and son, constituting themselves the board of MCC, borrowed £15 million from Lloyds Bank. But other bankers in London, suspecting the worst, were already scurrying for legal cover. James Scrymgeour-Wedderburn of Invesco MIM had asked Maxwell to answer his concern about BIM's stock lending for the Mirror Group Pension Trust. 'We confirm', wrote Robert and Ian Maxwell, 'that we are aware of and concur with the stock-lending operation being carried out by Bishopsgate on our behalf. We are aware that this is not being carried out as classic domestic stock lending and we are satisfied that this is an activity which can be carried out on behalf of the pension scheme.' They promised untruthfully that the stock would be returned by 9 September. 'We confirm', they added, 'that this letter has been approved by the board.'

Placating Scrymgeour-Wedderburn with a comfort letter was easier than mollifying Lehmans. The bankers were tiring of BIM, which had become a troublesome customer. During that week, Mark Haas had been persuaded by Trachtenberg to take 7 million MCC shares at collateral, only for his superior to go ballistic: the danger signs were glaringly obvious. Loans were not being repaid and packets of shares were being offered, withdrawn and swapped in a blizzard of phone calls, letters and faxes. MCC, Lehmans, realized, was veering towards bankruptcy. Nevertheless, the bank accepted £4.6 million worth of pension fund shares.

Some just discovered the truth and kept quiet. During that same day, 27 August, Henry Boucher of Capel Cure met Trachtenberg and in the course of their conversation established that Capel Cure's pension fund portfolio was not being used for conventional stock lending. Having urged the shares' return, he did nothing more.

At NatWest, Bob Brown was fast realizing that 'I'm learning as I go along.' All his 'novel and common' conversations with both Maxwells drew him towards one conclusion: their crisis was 'severe'. Yet the bank, like the other three major British banks, was paralysed, able to do no more than hope that their loans would be gradually repaid. Through personal relations with the Maxwells, all those British bankers had been beguiled into believing the sincerity of their promises, and any doubts were drowned by the flood of media images recording the Publisher's diplomacy on the international stage. Being reminded of their client's trusted position among the Great and the Good neutralized the bankers' growing scepticism.

That bank holiday weekend, although Robert and Kevin Maxwell suspected that their empire was bankrupt, they made no attempt to save money. With the *Lady Ghislaine* still on standby in Piraeus, Maxwell flew on Saturday, 24 August to Fraytet, Betty Maxwell's new home, to celebrate Ian's wedding. Kevin flew there in another private jet, his chauffeur having driven an Espace the 800-mile journey to France before flying back to London – an amusing extravagance.

Betty Maxwell was shocked by her estranged husband's appearance. 'All of a sudden he looked very old; he was gasping for air and sweating profusely.' They embraced at the airport. Maxwell's weight had increased, and a doctor among those invited diagnosed – albeit only visually – that he was suffering an excess of carbon dioxide in the blood. The tycoon could tolerate only twenty-four hours of his wife's and family's company. They were all, he believed, freeloaders. The following day, 25 August, he flew to New York.

Denied access to MCC's cash, he searched like an addict for new supplies. His hunt was partially satisfied. On his instructions, Macmillan's accountants had unwittingly paid $2.6 million of his debts, relieving a couple of pressure points ($400,000 to Bankers Trust and $2.2 million to the Chemical Bank) unaware that their Chairman had alighted upon another vulnerable source of funds to alleviate his private ills.

In his absence, another fuse was lit in London. On 29 August, *Daily Mirror* executives were celebrating awards to sportsmen at the Savoy Hotel. In the mêlée after lunch, Lawrence Guest, the Group's finance director, pulled Ernie Burrington, the managing director, to one side. 'I've got some problems,' he said. 'There's some money missing – about £38 million – which I can't understand. They're loans which I didn't agree. And, just as worrying, Maxwell has appointed Michael Stoney as deputy manager above me.'

Burrington was confused. Although he was the managing director, he was hardly involved in the company's financial activities. So he could not quite understand Guest's predicament nor see how Stoney, a private-side accountant, could be appointed above him. The two men gazed at each other. Burrington, a small, rotund former journalist, and Guest, a thin, chain-smoking accountant, were both too honest, too naive about Maxwell and too compliant to notice the web in which they were caught. Although neither man was a patsy, they were unsuspicious. 'I trusted Maxwell,' admitted Burrington later. After all, the City's support for the Mirror Group's flotation confirmed their own conviction that the sinner had been redeemed. Burrington, like others, 'wanted to believe that Maxwell was honest'.

Guest had seen Maxwell four weeks earlier for thirty minutes in his ninth-floor office. 'Where's this money gone?' he had asked. To Maxwell's amusement, Guest had earlier sought support from Ian Maxwell and Trachtenberg, not realizing that his son was the pianist in the whorehouse while Trachtenberg also had some involvement. 'Don't you worry,' boomed the Publisher, 'I've deposited it with American banks. It's no problem.' He expected his charm to sweep Guest's suspicions aside.

But the uncertainty continued to niggle at Guest. That money had gone and he, the finance director, did not even know how much interest it was earning. 'I'll do something,' murmured Burrington at the Savoy celebration.

'I've deposited the money with Goldmans in New York,' explained Maxwell on Friday, 30 August, 'to improve our credit rating.' He had flown back from New York overnight to extinguish more fires. 'Oh, I see,' said Burrington, and departed more puzzled than before.

TWELVE

'Borrowing from Peter to Pay Paul'

– September 1991

Minutes after Basil Brookes returned from his holidays on Monday, 9 September 1991, he began searching for MCC's latest financial statements. He obtained the information from Albert Fuller, the treasurer. The Maxwells' debt to the company, Brookes was relieved to find, had fallen. But what really surprised him was the discovery that, since 3 September, Robert Maxwell had been plundering Macmillan's bank accounts for cash. Knowing that the Publisher had flown five days earlier to New York, Brookes went straight to Kevin's office. 'What's going on?' he demanded excitedly.

'It's all Bob's fault,' protested Kevin. 'I had no idea.'

'I can't stay here if Bob continues like this,' cried Brookes.

'I'll sort it out,' said Kevin. Brookes felt that the son was someone upon whom he could rely. 'He's intelligent, honest and diligent,' he thought. 'He's like me, a victim of his father's anarchy.'

Kevin passed on Brookes's threat to his father, back again at the Helmsley Palace in New York. The Chairman had every reason to feel anxious. The vultures were circling. The Swiss Bank Corporation was demanding the shares owned by the First Tokyo Trust because Maxwell had not repaid the £55.7 million loan; worse, Lehmans had sold pension fund shares worth £84 million after Trachtenberg had admitted on 6 September that the family would default on repayment of a loan. Daily, in unscripted rotation, Maxwell's lawyers, accountants and office managers were mouthing increasingly less credible reasons for delays in delivering share certificates and repaying loans. Plugging the holes had become a constant preoccupation. And now a new threat had materialized.

A *Panorama* team from BBC Television was researching a programme about Maxwell. He feared that it might expose the truth about the First Tokyo deal and his plunder of the pension funds. His investigators had still not reported but he feared leaks from his directors. He rang Brookes from New York: 'I gather you think one of us should leave.' Brookes was silent. 'I think I should retire,' challenged Maxwell, placing the burden upon the small finance director.

Brookes became obsequious: 'Oh no, that's not necessary.'

Unwilling to believe that Brookes's deference was genuine, Maxwell switched to John Pole, his security chief, one of the few whom he trusted.

The former Scotland Yard chief superintendent prided himself on his loyalty, discretion and professionalism. 'Report only to me,' Maxwell had ordered, and Pole saw no reason to question the Chairman's instruction. So far that year he had bugged at least four of Maxwell's confidants. In early September, he once again heard the invitation: 'I need to know if this person is being loyal to me.' This time the target was Brookes. Pole obeyed without hesitation.

The first tape was ready when Maxwell returned to London the following day. In several conversations, Brookes spoke only of the size of the financial package he would demand as the price of his silence after he had resigned. Further tapes, delivered by Pole every night during that week, bore repetitions of the same preoccupation. The negotiations were, Brookes complained, delaying his departure. There was no mention of the real crisis. So the tapes satisfied Maxwell. He would drag out the discussions while he settled with Anselmini.

The negotiations with the Frenchman were almost concluded. They had been a sensitive undertaking because in the background lurked the unspoken danger that Anselmini would reveal Maxwell's activities to Crédit Lyonnais, the French bank which was owed $1.3 billion by MCC. To guarantee his silence the terms were both generous and false. 'Because you have chosen to be re-elected to the board,' Maxwell's letter of 12 September stated, 'the monetary calculation of your settlement is undisturbed at the agreed sum of £420,000 plus 30 days holiday pay.'

Anselmini's original resignation letter had been dated the

following day, 13 September, and it was to have taken effect on the 27th. Within twenty-four hours of his return, Maxwell was urging him to delay his announcement and his departure until after the company's annual general meeting. Understanding that Maxwell wanted to minimize the number of earthquakes threatening to fragment his empire, Anselmini had crossed out 27 September and inserted 3 October. The shareholders were not informed of those manoeuvres or that Anselmini had been promised generous compensation. One man aware of the dangers besetting MCC was parachuting out without pain. Brookes wanted the same, but Maxwell required a delay. To allow Brookes's departure so soon after Anselmini's would generate additional alarm.

Exhausted once again, Maxwell slept overnight on the Gulfstream, returning to London on Tuesday, 10 September. Even the fine food the crew had bought in a Manhattan delicatessen remained untouched. 'Just a glass of Perrier and my pills,' he ordered, wanting to blot out everything and sleep. Waiting in his office as he helicoptered to London was John Halloran, ready to repeat his demand on behalf of the BPCC pension fund.

Months earlier, Trevor Cook had handed over £97 million to Trachtenberg, appointed by Maxwell as the 'transfer officer' of the 'BPCC Portfolio'. So far as Cook was concerned, 'It was out of my hands.' The money was also out of Maxwell's hands, used for other purposes. Yet Halloran departed a very satisfied man. Behind, he left unseen mayhem.

Trachtenberg had been ordered to buy shares to create a portfolio. But after spending £15 million, he was ordered to stop. The costs of buying a portfolio and the risks of the market falling were too high. So Halloran was given those shares and £82 million cash. In order to raise the £97 million for him, Maxwell had indulged in further deception. The first £60 million had been taken straight from MCC's bank account, the proceeds of a firesale of a Macmillan subsidiary called Directories and the Pergamon Medical Journals. His second source was the pension funds, by then firmly subject to Kevin's control. The method employed was, in the usual disarming, self-confident tone, once again to summon Cook. By then Cook had good grounds to harbour suspicions but, consistent with his past attitude, he would later admit, 'I never quite knew what was going on.'

'RMG has at the moment', said Maxwell, 'not enough cash to settle the BPCC transfer, so I'll need the £55 million for a bit longer.' He was referring to the proceeds from the sale in May of 25 million MCC shares belonging to the Mirror Group pension fund. Cook had never hesitated to allow the Chairman the use of that money. With other BIM deposits, Maxwell wanted to continue borrowing £100 million of money belonging to the pension funds.

'Oh, that's what you're worried about,' said Maxwell. Pushing a button, he spoke on the telephone's speaker to Trachtenberg, an indispensable employee because of his unquestioning loyalty. In return for that fidelity, Maxwell had agreed that Trachtenberg should be paid a discretionary annual bonus of £350,000, but for his part Trachtenberg was pressing that he be allowed to offset that bonus against his house (owned by Maxwell), then revalued at £495,000. Maxwell was agreeable, because he could count upon Trachtenberg's response. After describing Cook's anxiety, he told him, 'Get more collateral from Morgan Stanley. Just make sure that Trevor is covered.' Turning to Cook, Maxwell continued, 'We will pledge Berlitz shares which are owned by RMG.' Although Cook had reason to doubt that the Chairman owned any Berlitz shares, he did not question his assertion. Nor did he check the Berlitz share register. The manager once again succumbed to Maxwell's requests, but not before adding, 'I'll need collateral for BIM's cash deposits with RMG.'

Later, sitting in Maxwell's office with Kevin and Trachtenberg present, Cook was given by the Chairman himself a copy of a statement from Andrea Low at Morgan Stanley declaring that unnamed shares worth $100 million were held to BIM's account and could not be moved without Cook's approval. 'This is RMG's stock,' said Maxwell, smothering any doubts the gullible Cook might harbour. To reassure him, Trachtenberg, newly appointed a director of BIM, sent a letter stating, 'The value in account still covers the pension fund cash.' Cook would confess, 'He had all these hats and rabbits and I was fooled. I was naive about financial matters.'

Maxwell was delighted by Cook's confusion. The pension fund manager had not noticed that, though Maxwell was borrowing £100 million from the pension funds, the security he had provided was worth only $100 million. 'I didn't see the difference between the pound and dollar signs,' explained Cook when the discrepancy was subsequently discovered.

At Maxwell's direction, Andrea Low sent Cook a letter stating that the Berlitz and MCC shares were held on trust for BIM (pledged by Maxwell in the name of LBI). But, unknown to Cook, the bank had likewise not investigated Maxwell's claims of ownership to Berlitz.

After Cook had left, Lawrence Guest entered Maxwell's office. The sight of the Mirror Group's finance director at once irritated and amused Maxwell. John Pole, already tasked with checking Guest's loyalties, had reported that he was talking about his concerns only to Burrington.

'Yerse?' bellowed Maxwell with flittering enjoyment.

'The money hasn't come back yet, Mr Maxwell,' stuttered Guest, referring to the £38 million missing from Mirror Group's accounts.

'Don't you worry, Lawrence,' roared Maxwell. 'You're getting tired. You really need a holiday. Take three weeks immediately. Everything will be sorted out by the time you return.'

Guest departed, nervous and uncertain of his responsibilities in the wake of Michael Stoney's appointment. On Burrington's recommendation, he next sent a memorandum to Stoney. Guest was comforted by the reply. The money, wrote Stoney, was deposited in American banks to improve the Mirror Group's credit rating as a company with surplus funds. 'I've spoken to Bob. The money is coming back within one week. You've nothing to worry about. But please don't shake the tree. You must be loyal to the company.'

Guest consulted Burrington about the assurances. 'We're not disloyal,' grumbled Burrington. 'I'm the King's servant, but God's first.' At that moment, Maxwell was still God and Stoney was among His son's elite disciples. 'I think', continued Burrington, 'we should consult the other [Mirror Group] directors.' But their choice, as Maxwell had intended, was limited. Joe Haines, the former spokesman for Harold Wilson, was totally loyal to Maxwell. Having denounced Maxwell as a 'crook' just hours before the bidder's purchase of the newspaper in 1984, he quickly swallowed his judgment, took the Captain's shilling and ever since had acted as a swooning poodle. Charlie Wilson, recently editor of The Times, was a new disciple of their paymaster. Lord Williams was a third acolyte. Burrington had noticed that, on occasions when a sensitive matter was to be discussed by the board, the former Charles Williams rose saying, 'You'll have to excuse me, chairman. I must go to the Lords.' All three, he feared, were unreliable and would disclose their confidences to Maxwell, aggravating matters. Their only possible allies were Alan Clements and Sir Robert Clark, the non-executive directors, the independent policemen on the board. The idea of consulting these two men appealed to Guest despite their failure to meet the company's two senior officers. 'I thought it a bit odd that they didn't even come in for a cup of tea,' complained Burrington.

Knowing that Sir Robert Clark was abroad, Guest telephoned Alan Clements. Ever since his appointment as a director, Clements had banked his £30,000 per annum salary, even though, Burrington complained, 'We've got great difficulties getting Clements to board meetings.' Despite also being a trustee, he was less than diligent in supervising the administration of the pension fund, to the extent that he missed most committee meetings. Consistent with his approach, even the audit committee, formed under Clements's chairmanship, rarely met. Letters to Clements from Tony Boram, of the Association of Mirror Pensioners, appealing for help in the campaign against Maxwell, were never acknowledged. Throughout September, Guest, who had decided that it was inopportune to take a holiday, received a regular reply from Clements's office: 'He's on holiday.' In fact he was caring for his sick wife.

Lacking outside help, neither Burrington nor Guest dared mention their concerns when the Mirror Group board of directors met on 12 September. They remained silent. Stoney, who had conferred with Maxwell privately two hours before, reflected the cynical satisfaction of the tycoon himself.

Some plugs were easier to fill than others. Among the hardest to placate was Lord Donoughue. The executive vice-chairman of LBI had offered his resignation in July but had remained to negotiate his severance payments, while continuing to earn his annual salary of £180,000 and the £36,000 annual contribution towards his pension. In normal circumstances, there could be little justification for his receiving any money after he had volunteered to depart. But, as both he and Maxwell well understood, his silence was worth some consideration.

At 9 a.m. on 11 September, the fifty-seven-year-old peer arrived to negotiate. The rumours in recent weeks had disturbed him. It was, he decided, the moment to drop his insistence on including in the severance package ownership of the elegant house in Bloomfield Terrace, SW1, which he occupied practically rent free. Even Maxwell, the epitome of gluttony, could not stomach such greed. 'I'll agree to £200,000,' he said. 'No more.' Donoughue was not satisfied. After hesitating, Maxwell agreed to pay an extra £30,000 tax free. Most importantly, another £50,000 would be paid in return for Donoughue's promise never to talk or write about Maxwell and his business affairs. Given that Donoughue had remained silent for two years about Maxwell's secret use of First Tokyo's investments and had not interfered with LBI's 'stock lending' programme of the pension funds' shares, the beleagured Chairman had good reason to believe that he could rely upon the man who pompously signed their agreement 'Donoughue of Ashton'.

Having bought Donoughue's silence, Maxwell walked across into the Mirror building for MCC's twenty-eighth annual general meeting in the Rotunda. It would, he had agreed with Michael Richardson earlier that morning, 'not be the easiest of meetings'. Indeed, in the abnormal circumstances then prevailing it would require a virtuoso performance. Few of the one hundred people present failed to notice Maxwell's strained appearance. Even his multi-coloured tie was stained: no one had either cared or dared to warn him. Many had read the front-page criticism in the *Wall Street Journal* of 10 September headed 'Bloated Empire', which highlighted the problems of prodigious debts, unrealistically high valuations of the so-called intangibles, suspect profits and questionable accounts.

Attending his first and last meeting as an MCC director, Peter Walker appeared uncomfortable, but he refrained from bridging the gulf between his knowledge and the ignorance of the few shareholders inquiring about the company's debts. In the face of the innocent but doomed shareholders, Walker – like all the other directors, Anselmini, Brookes, Woods, Laister and Rippon – did not contradict Maxwell's injunction: 'Take the criticisms with a pinch of salt. Your company's future is secure.' Like Anselmini, Walker would be well rewarded for his appearance.

To buy Walker's goodwill, Maxwell had agreed in the severance deal brokered by Michael Richardson in July that he could take his full entitlement of 201,793 shares free. Although the price had fallen to 169p, Walker still pocketed an outright profit of over £341,000 minus commission so long as he attended the annual general meeting. The only advantage Maxwell grasped from the deal was that on Walker's behalf Richardson bought the shares through the stock exchange rather than from the unissued 10 million still available to the company. Richardson then sold the shares back to the company. In that minor manipulation, Maxwell feebly attempted to persuade the market of activity in his shares.

Walker's presence at the meeting reassured some of the shareholders. With Maxwell's spirits rising as he robustly countered the allegations of disarray, even doubters like Brookes admired his resilience – encapsulated most memorably in a trade unionist's vintage quip: 'You could shoot bullets at Maxwell and they would just bounce off his broad armour-plated bum.'

At the traditional lunch for VIPs in his apartment on the tenth floor, Maxwell spoke confidently about overcoming 'our temporary problems'. The glossy annual report with a grainy black and white photograph of himself boasted of MCC's 'strong management' and its 'strategy for a demerger'. Many of the insiders eating good food and drinking fine wine wanted to be convinced by the Publisher's good tidings because it was more convenient and profitable to live in hope. After all, it seemed that the Maxwells' £305 million debt had been sharply reduced since July – proof of the Chairman's private fortune – and that the new procedures would prevent MCC's money going back into the private companies.

Spotting David Leal-Bennett and Bob Brown of NatWest, Maxwell walked towards them. 'You saved us last August,' said the Chairman, 'but we'll need some more help.' Brown smiled. The bank had no intention of increasing its loans. On the contrary, it wanted its money returned as fast as possible.

At the end of the day, exhausted, Maxwell was back on the same floor to spend the night alone in his apartment. After inhaling over a bowl of boiling water to rid himself of a persistent cold, he lay on his bed watching a video, drinking heavily and gorging on a vast but plain dinner prepared as usual by Cheeseman. Drifting back and forth within the darkening world which he had created, he had lost his grasp on the imperatives required for his survival. There was no moral framework for his activities or utterances. His world was surreal, immoral and restless. Just before midnight, the first editions of the newspapers were left in his living room. During the night he awoke, and arose from his bed to see how the meeting had been reported. To his dismay, there was hardly any mention of it beyond carping repeats of the criticisms made when the report had been published in July about his peculiar accounts, low dividends, dismal reading and difficult outlook. 'The words "strategy" and "Maxwell" should never be used in the same sentence,' one journalist had written when the report was published, and the jackals had not changed their tune.

The repercussions began early the following morning, the 12th. Mark Haas of Lehmans summoned Trachtenberg for what both realized in retrospect was a crisis meeting. The bank had embarked upon an 'exit strategy', said the bearded American, without revealing that a corporate decision had been taken that both 'Larry's and Kevin's reliability had decreased'. The Maxwells' debt to the bank, emphasized Haas, would have to be reduced from $155 million (interest had accrued) to $100 million – immediately. If the Publisher were unable to produce the money, the collateral would be sold. Trachtenberg scurried back to Holborn. The collateral consisted of pension fund shares. The implications were distasteful. Kevin meanwhile was immersed in one of those relentless machine-gun days: every thirty minutes, a different finance meeting with a different group of bankers or employees.

Trachtenberg was admitted to Kevin's office at the first opportunity. 'I'll write to Haas,' said Kevin. In a letter dictated immediately, he promised to reduce the debt to $25 million within two weeks and asked the banker not to sell the Teva and Scitex shares pledged as collateral. To induce Haas's co-operation, Kevin promised that Lehmans could earn the underwriting fees when the family shortly sold the Teva shares. Kevin's letter did not quite satisfy the bank. He mentioned that the Maxwells were 'considering' using Lehmans to sell Teva. Although Haas often boasted that Lehmans was 'customer-oriented', he knew that the priority was to earn fees and profits. If the Maxwells wanted to retain the bank's goodwill, he said, and expected a new $10.4 million loan to BIM, then Lehmans required something enforceable and profitable in return. That same day, Kevin sent a second letter to Haas which 'confirmed' Lehmans as the lead underwriter for the Teva sale. Kevin's motives were not purely commercial. The Teva shares and the majority of the Scitex shares were owned by the pension funds, and their immediate sale would shine an unwelcome light on his activities. His ploy worked only to a limited degree.

Kevin's request had added to the bankers' suspicions: they became more interested in the ownership of the shares they were intending to sell. Trachtenberg was the target of the initial queries. Why, he was asked by Gerald Tamburro, was a pension fund trust involved in collateralized loans? After hearing Trachtenberg's reply, Tamburro quipped to a colleague, 'I'm sort of suspect [sic] to take physical shares from this guy. Right now there might be a lien against them.' Yet, despite the pension funds' ownership, the bank felt entitled to sell the shares, and their knowledge began to seep out into the wider world.

At Barclays Bank, Richard Pelly, the corporate finance director, realizing that the Maxwells were in the midst of a crisis, wrote to Kevin that, while the bank wanted to reduce its loans, it did not 'want to sit on the sidelines until you reach the precipice'. In particular, Pelly was concerned that in making their repayments the Maxwells were ignoring his advice and were favouring NatWest against Barclays by 'borrowing from Peter to pay Paul'. Unannounced, the group had been placed on a 'watch list', but that did little to ameliorate Pelly's frustrations.

At Lloyds Bank, Brian Brown, responsible for the Maxwell account, sent a memorandum to his superiors: 'September is a torrid month for the Robert Maxwell Group and Kevin Maxwell is counting the days until the receipt of the Scitex monies in October. The cash position is tight and there is nothing to spare.' NatWest executives were equally aware of the Maxwells' plight and told Kevin, 'we've reached the limit of our support and we don't want to see any more surprises.' For the bankers and Kevin, the sale of the Scitex shares was akin to seeing the cavalry on the horizon. But Kevin frankly conceded that 'everything is up for sale'. Although that pleased the bankers anxious to recoup their money, Kevin realized the utter folly of selling off profitable parts. 'I'm fed up with all this,' he confided to a few bankers. 'I'm not getting more than the book value and the loans don't get paid off.' The demerger, he forlornly dreamt, might lift the pressure.

While Kevin and Pandora flew on 16 September by a chartered Lear jet to Paris for the evening to hear a performance of *La*

Symphonie fantastique by Berlioz at the Conservatoire National, Maxwell sat closeted with George Carman QC, the pricey doyen of the defamation bar, and Oscar Bueselinck, his in-house lawyer, demanding that they obtain injunctions to prevent the broadcast of the proposed *Panorama* programme. 'They've been looking for dirt about me everywhere,' he complained. 'Ex-employees, people in the City, and they're in touch with the pensioners' association.' The information, reaching him from several sources, suggested that the *Panorama* team had been successful. To the lawyers' bewilderment, their paymaster appeared most concerned about the journalists' probing into the pensioners' complaints. 'There's little chance of a judge issuing an injunction,' advised Carman. 'Try a softer approach.'

The upshot was a rambling letter from Maxwell to Mark Thompson, the editor of *Panorama*, which appealed for fairness, offered assistance and an interview, threatened doom in the courts and sought to impose the Publisher's editorial control over the programme. Peculiarly, Maxwell also voiced his 'personal concern at the anxiety and damage that you may cause to the pensioners of Mirror Group and their families'. But, unknown to him, *Panorama* had abandoned its investigation of Tony Boram's complaints and had failed to persuade Alan McInroy to break his vow of silence and reveal the background to the First Tokyo deal.

Thompson's non-committal reply infuriated Maxwell, but further threats and appeals to the BBC's director-general were even less satisfactory. On the eve of his return to New York on 18 September, Maxwell was still left asking Thompson, 'whether this programme is to be transmitted on Monday next'. He had discovered unfortunate limitations to his power.

From the plane, Maxwell telephoned Trevor Cook. Ever since Boram's complaint in May, Cook had shown no sympathy towards the 'indelicate' former *Daily Mirror* journalist. In his slanted opinion, Boram was getting more than a fair pension because it had been raised when he took premature retirement. He was, Cook complained, 'greedy', and the other Mirror Group pensioners were also getting 'a very good deal – even better than the employees'. To Maxwell's momentary relief, Cook's assurance that he was co-operating with Ian Pittaway, the solicitor at Nicholson Graham and Jones, to resist the pensioners' demands sounded genuine. 'It's better to work with Maxwell than challenge him,' Cook had suggested to Boram. He was clearly not helping *Panorama*. But Maxwell's fear of exposure remained intense throughout the seven-hour flight. Gripped by deep paranoia, he imagined that his enemies were plotting against him, just as he was against them.

Those sentiments were concealed from Joe Jacobs, who had arranged Maxwell's chairmanship of the Brooklyn Polytechnic and had offered to establish a Maxwell Foundation in anticipation of his $10 million gift. Weeks earlier, Jacobs had enjoyed a champagne lunch with Maxwell in his Helmsley suite. 'My problem', the Publisher had explained, 'is that I can't decide whether to take the money from Macmillan, the Liechtenstein trusts or MCC.' Jacobs nodded in awe, precisely as intended. Reaching for a telephone, Maxwell pushed some buttons. 'Joe Flom,' he commanded, knowing that Jacobs would be impressed by his host talking to America's star corporate lawyer. 'Joe,' boomed Maxwell, 'I'm sitting here with Joe Jacobs. I want you to handle the paperwork. I'm giving $10 million and Joe's giving $6 million and the accountants will soon be contacting you.' Jacobs was awed: 'I was completely taken in. He was so imperious. The trappings were so impressive. It was impossible to believe that he wasn't a great man.'

'We must have a celebratory dinner for your chairmanship,' offered Jacobs.

'I'll get Mayor Dinkins to come.'

'You'll never pull that off.'

'I'll bet you a dollar,' smiled Maxwell.

And now, on this latest trip to New York, Maxwell was sitting next to Mayor Dinkins in front of 200 guests at the Lotus Club, to celebrate his $10 million donation and his appointment as the Poly's chairman. The current newsletter lauded their new chairman: his 'story as a self-made man is indeed an inspiring one', consistent with 'the American dream'. Maxwell, the star, was at his most boisterous, and he gave a well-received speech. 'Thank God,' thought Jacobs, cringing at the memory of a previous Maxwell tirade against the Japanese. The only glitch was the new chairman's dislike of the food. 'I want an omelette,' he ordered, pushing aside the well-cooked veal. The cheers were still resounding as he stepped into his stretch-limo to be driven downtown. His performance, perfected over forty-five years, had become impeccable – but it was only so to new audiences. Unsurprisingly, the cheque for $10 million would not arrive.

At seven the following morning, 21 September, John Pole telephoned Maxwell in the Helmsley Palace: the taps had not revealed anyone from inside speaking to the *Panorama* team. Basil Brookes, he reported, was still talking exclusively about his exit package, and Anselmini, when speaking English, appeared to be saying nothing derogatory about Maxwell. But, unknown to the Chairman, his suspicions had been well founded. On 6 September, Anselmini had told Brian Brown of Lloyds over lunch 'to protect your loans, especially to the private side'. Brown was grateful for that indiscretion. For Maxwell, Anselmini's behaviour was precisely the disloyalty he feared.

That same morning, while continuing to telephone London in a bid to prevent the *Panorama* programme, Maxwell dictated an editorial for the *Sunday Mirror* condemning BBC executives, alias 'the three monkeys', as 'jackals' for 'the needless anxiety which the programme may cause to pensioners in our group', who 'are better treated than they would have been by their former employers'. The size of his lie could be judged by the ferocity of the counter-attack.

As he changed into black tie that evening, his anger gradually subsided. He was hosting dinner for Boris Pankin, the new Soviet foreign minister, Senator Howard Baker, Hans-Dietrich Genscher, Ambassador Tom Pickering, Senator Abraham Ribicoff, Larry Tisch, the head of the CBS television network, Ambassador Yuri Vorontsov, the Soviet ambassador at the United Nations, and William Webster, the former director of the FBI and the CIA. Loftily they discussed the world's fate. His own fate was easily obliterated in that forum.

Reality returned at 4.30 on Monday afternoon. Sitting in his suite, Maxwell listened to the *Panorama* programme played down the telephone line. Simultaneously, Bob Cole faxed pages of transcript, typed live as the programme unfolded. The opening statements were as bad as he had anticipated. The programme, announced the reporter Nisha Pillai, 'raises grave questions about the way Mr Maxwell sometimes does business'. The next sequence suggested the worst. Maxwell, alleged the reporter, had personally organized a bogus spot-the-ball game: 'It was Mr Maxwell himself who decided to run a dishonest game and cheat his readers.' It was a staggering accusation, clearly based on accurate information supplied by a disgruntled employee. Although what followed was by comparison mild, Maxwell was livid. There was no mention of the pension funds, but a ragbag of pundits assembled by the BBC had poured scorn on his accounts and on his veracity.

That night he read the faxed headlines of the *Sun* and the *Guardian* screaming, 'TV claims hit Maxwell share price', 'Maxwell to sue BBC' and 'Maxwell tricked Mirror readers out of £1m'. 'Issue the writs!' he shouted at Beuselinck. But his threats only prompted the BBC to re-endorse the allegations. 'It's a criminal libel,' Maxwell told George Carman, asking him to fire the biggest guns. 'I don't want this dragged out,' he continued prophetically, 'I can't wait two years, by which time I will either be dead or retired.'

Having dispatched his driver to Mr Fu's to collect dinner, he telephoned Burrington. 'Ernie, why are people always trying to destroy me?'

'You're a big man,' replied Burrington with unhelpful naivety, not realizing how tragically he misjudged his employer. 'You can fight back.'

'What can we do to stop it?'

'We can't. Just give intelligent answers.' Burrington replaced the receiver, pondering upon Maxwell's sudden sensitivity to public criticism. As he turned away, he bumped into Ian. 'What a load of bollocks,' fumed Maxwell's son, referring to the spot-the-ball allegation. 'How dare they suggest that my father would want to deny people the right to win money.' The Publisher, Ian appeared to be suggesting, would not involve himself in small swindles.

During the break from his catnap, Maxwell heard that MCC shares had fallen only to 167p and the Mirror Group's to 89p. His secret purchases of MCC shares had stemmed the decline. And fortunately the bile being spewed out in Britain had not crossed the Atlantic. Thanks to Campi, his profile in New York remained high and positive. Over the next two days he would appear at the Harmonie Club for a celebration of His Life, to be filmed for a broadcast about leadership, and receive the Shalom Peace Award from the Jewish National Fund. Dr Henry Kissinger, his host that morning at a 'stag breakfast' at the River Club in honour of Dr Mahathir bin Mohamad, prime minister of Malaysia, had greeted

'Bob' effusively. Bearing the brunt of the crisis was a task delegated to Kevin, for whom the week was collapsing into a nightmare of frenzied juggling as bankers scurried about demanding repayment.

The NatWest bankers Bob Brown and David Leal-Bennett had set the tone by warning him on 19 September that the bank had 'reached the limit of our support and we would not wish to see any surprises going forward' in the run-up to the agreed repayment of £25 million at the end of the month. The money, suggested the bank, should if necessary be taken from MCC's £83 million sale of the Macmillan subsidiary Directories. 'My father doesn't agree to that,' Kevin had told Leal-Bennett.

The same calm performance which deflected the banker had been applied by Kevin to Stephen Wootten, the Coopers auditor, during their discussion the previous day about RMG's debts. '$280 million will soon be available to the private side,' cooed Kevin, 'from the sale of Scitex.' Unquestioningly, Wootten noted down his client's good news and would later report to his superiors, 'Kevin seemed quite bullish and quite confident about the repayment of the loans. I certainly got the impression he was more relaxed than he has been in recent months.' Others in London were neither so sanguine nor so easily fooled.

Capel Cure on 25 September asked for the return of a share certificate from the pension fund portfolio already sold by Lehmans. Trachtenberg's rapid solution was to buy the appropriate shares in the market, present the certificate to Capel Cure and pretend there was no problem. To pay for the shares, he telephoned Gerald Tamburro at Lehmans for a loan. The reaction was cold. 'The *Panorama* documentary and the newspaper articles', grumbled the banker, 'sort of raises some eyebrows up and down the line.' A handful of informed financial journalists were using the programme as a launching-pad for a general attack. They appeared to know more than the bankers. 'It's a pension fund deal,' said Trachtenberg, trying to distance BIM from MCC's plight.

'I'm just gonna be as blunt as I can with you: why would the pension fund be doing this?'

Trachtenberg's reply was long and unconvincing and eventually faded out. Julie Maitland had telephoned. Crédit Suisse, she told Trachtenberg, wanted to terminate its rolling £50 million loan, first granted a year before. The administration costs, she explained, were

too high. 'Your constant changes of collateral cause us expense.'
Since 5 September, the bank had sold the shares from First Tokyo
to repay Maxwell's debts. By then, most of First Tokyo's portfolio
had been pledged to other banks and was being sold to recover
unpaid debts. But, as the value of MCC and Mirror Group shares
fell, Crédit Suisse had required new collateral for the existing
debts.

Ever since the *Panorama* programme, Kevin and Trachtenberg
had been telephoning the bank hourly, urging that Crédit Suisse
take collateral for further loans. By now, however, the bankers
realized precisely the source and nature of the shares offered by
Maxwell. Trachtenberg had offered shares held by Invesco MIM,
Capel Cure, Thornton Securities and Lazards, all pension fund trustees. Richard Khawam, a junior, was told, 'Say okay, Richard, but
stress we prefer not to take investment trusts!' Among the shares
delivered to Maitland as new collateral was a certificate for 1.1
million Teva shares owned by BIM. For their own reasons, the
bankers would not step off the rollercoaster.

That afternoon, 26 September, Bank of America, the legal custodian of some pension fund share certificates, in compliance with
Trachtenberg's instructions delivered an envelope of share certificates to Crédit Suisse. The package arrived with a letter from the
bank identifying the owners as 'Thornton/Mirror Group Pension
Trust' and a transfer form, signed by Kevin and Trevor Cook.
René Müller signed for the delivery. Upstairs, Maitland received
the package and the Bank of America letter. The share certificates,
which identified BIM as the registered owner, and not RMG, were
sent to the bank's Securities Department.

Soon after, there was consternation among the staff at Bank of
America. Although Kevin had said that the shares were 'for stock
lending', Crédit Suisse were not conventional lenders and the transfer form had not been completed with their name. Aware of the
City gossip about Maxwell's dire finances, the Bank of America
employees rushed to absolve themselves of legal responsibility.
Anthony Pedley, in charge of the certificates' physical custody, telephoned Müller asking for the return of the transfer form. To his
surprise, Müller refused. Three other Bank of America officials telephoned. Each time, Müller refused to return the form. 'We don't
want to remain responsible for the shares!' exclaimed Pedley.

'Nor do *we* want responsibility,' replied Müller, an attitude that would subsequently be endorsed by a British judge.

'Well, we're not going to remain responsible!' shouted Pedley.

'But someone has to. They belong to a pension fund.'

Pedley then asked: 'What is the stock for?'

'For a collateral swap,' replied Müller, suggesting that the shares were for loans and not for stock lending.

The troubled executives at Bank of America complained to Kevin. 'No problem,' replied Kevin. The following day, 27 September, the bank received a comfort letter, signed by Kevin and Ian as directors of BIM, stating that Bank of America were relieved of all responsibility for the securities.

As a finale to those two days' manipulation, Kevin and Trachtenberg directed Morgan Stanley to transfer 2 million Berlitz shares to Banque Paribas in New York as security for another loan. Even Kevin must have gulped at his own audacity. For he and his father had just instructed John Bender, Macmillan's lawyer, to complete the formal negotiations for the sale of Berlitz to Fukutake of Japan, owners since 1989 of a 20 per cent stake. At $27 per share compared to a market price of $19, thought Bender, it was a good deal. The lawyer was unaware that most of the Berlitz shares had been pledged to three other banks and to Trevor Cook.

In his suite at the Helmsley Palace, Maxwell sensed that his options were narrowing. For some hours during that week, he had sat closeted with Ellis Freedman, his lawyer for forty years, and Shelly Aboff, a forty-four-year-old crony who had been employed by Maxwell seventeen years earlier. Because of his unfortunate personality, Aboff had recently been transferred from Macmillan's headquarters to another MCC subsidiary, the Thomas Cook travel company in Connecticut. Both he and Freedman were similar types to those who had carried Maxwell through his last crisis in 1969: admirers who never questioned their paymaster.

As their discussion unfolded, Maxwell composed a twofold strategy. First, more money would be poured on the flames. As Mirror Group's and MCC's prices again dipped, he channelled $7.84 million from London & Bishopsgate to Aboff and instructed his acolyte to buy shares through Astaire and Partners, the London brokers who employed Darryl Warnford-Davis, Pandora's brother. Secondly Maxwell sought to lay the foundations of a new empire. In the

1969 crisis, his saviour had been a small and apparently innocuous American holding company, Pergamon Press Inc., which, to Saul Steinberg's surprise, exercised a stranglehold over Pergamon in Britain. Maxwell's legal ploy obliged the American to sell back Pergamon for a pittance.

Maxwell's new ruse, conceived in 1990, was called the 'exodus transaction'. A new legal vehicle, Pergamon Holdings (US) Inc. or Ph(US)Inc., would control his Liechtenstein interests from the USA. On 27 September 1991, seated in the Macmillan headquarters with Ellis Freedman and Ron Woods, specially flown from London, he invited Bill Harry, Macmillan's tax specialist, to join a discussion. 'The *Daily News* is in my name, isn't it?' Maxwell asked Harry.

'No, Mr Maxwell.'

'Who owns it?'

'AGB, as you said.' Harry was referring to the loss-making research company which Maxwell had bought privately in 1988 and which was used as a vehicle for inter-company deals.

'No!' exclaimed Maxwell. 'My orders were to put it in my name. I have always thought it was. Those were my orders.' Unexpectedly, the tension rose. Woods and Harry became suspicious. 'Put it in my name.'

'Bob, you can't do that,' said the two tax advisers. 'You can't reverse what has happened. It's owned by AGB.'

'I don't remember agreeing to that.'

'But you asked and I told you!' snapped Harry.

'Prepare papers which prove that I did buy it personally.'

'That's impossible,' retorted Harry, uncomfortable that Maxwell should be seeking his participation in a dishonest act.

The room fell silent. All gazed at Maxwell, slumped sullen, spiritless and sick. Without another word, he dismissed the three men. Unknown to his employees, he had that morning, 27 September, summoned to his hotel Dr Paul Gilbert, a general doctor at the Mount Sinai hospital, who had been recommended by Henry Kissinger. 'I can't get rid of this cold,' grumbled Maxwell, pointing to his runny nose and sore throat. 'And I've got pains in my chest.'

Gilbert performed the normal rituals: 'You'd better have an X-ray.'

At 10.30 a.m. the following day, Maxwell arrived at the cramped, poorly furnished Fifth Avenue consulting rooms of Dr Alfred

Rosenbaum, a radiologist also recommended by Kissinger. Maxwell waited patiently to be X-rayed, while complaining, 'I'm short of breath. I've got pains across my chest. They're getting worse.' Rosenbaum suspected pneumonia or a blood clot near the heart, but the X-ray revealed no dilation of the organ. While the two discussed their common background in pre-war Czechoslovakia, Maxwell admitted that the pain could have arisen from anxiety. 'It would take a whole day to conduct a thalium test on your heart and photograph the arteries,' said Rosenbaum, who could only confirm that Maxwell was not suffering from a chest disease. 'You probably need a rest,' he advised, noting that his patient was 'a walking case for an imminent heart attack'.

In anticipation of Maxwell's return to London, Captain Hull had stocked the Gulfstream with smoked salmon, cheeses and caviar, bought from the Manhattan delicatessen. 'Welcome on board, Mr Maxwell,' smiled Hull as his debilitated employer puffed up the steps on Saturday, 28 September. As he settled in his leather arm-chair Maxwell relaxed. 'He always felt he'd arrived home when he sat in the plane,' recalled Hull. After a few glasses of champagne, the Publisher undressed and slept on the divan until shortly before arriving in Luton. As usual, his valet Nigel Crow had prepared his clothes. Having dressed and drunk a cup of coffee, he could see, as the G4 landed, the helicopter waiting. In his absence in New York, he had failed to attend a number of important meetings intended to improve his businesses, including a day's seminar about inefficiencies in printing his newspapers. Instead of concern about his empire, he feared the critical articles which would appear in that Sunday's newspapers. Under the headline, 'Cap'n Bob at Bay', the Sunday Times described the tycoon's 'troubled times' but attested that 'the ebullient tycoon is not in the least downhearted'. That opinion was later supported by Robert Pirie, the Rothschild banker: 'I haven't seen any sign that Bob is in financial trouble and I don't believe he is.'

That night as Maxwell sat in his kitchen allowing George Wheeler to spread L'Oréal No. 7 over his hair and to colour his eyebrows, he read the transcript prepared by John Pole of Lawrence Guest's recent telephone conversations. The evidence of Guest's continued fumbling was reassuring.

Increasingly nervous, Guest had just flapped rather than confront

Maxwell and demand a meeting of the Mirror Group's accounts committee. Still unable to contact Clark or Clements, he was relying upon Burrington for help. The managing director, hardly more agile than his colleague, later explained that he 'didn't realize that Maxwell's finances were going down. No one told me.' Neither Burrington nor Guest, any more than the other directors of Mirror Group Newspapers, apparently believed what appeared in newspapers. Nevertheless, four days earlier Burrington had confided in Michael Jones of Samuel Montagu. The merchant bank, responsible for floating the Mirror Group, was the only independent insider which he trusted to 'tell about my concerns'.

Burrington had met Jones to protest about Maxwell's latest ploy for extracting extra cash, going through a charade of leasing the Mirror building to one of his private companies and increasing the rent. 'I'm against this,' Burrington told Jones. Realizing that his complaint had been overheard by Michael Stoney, he smiled to the banker, 'I've got the concert tickets you wanted. Come with me.' Burrington's offer was an excuse to continue the conversation out of Stoney's earshot. 'Maxwell is taking money from the Mirror without approval,' Burrington continued. Jones said nothing as the managing director mumbled on about unapproved deposit accounts. 'We just don't understand what Maxwell is doing with the money. I feel like throwing it all in.' Unknown to Burrington, earlier that week Kevin had pushed aside a suggestion by Cook and Cowling that interim work commence on the BIM accounts and had similarly rejected an audit of the individual pension schemes.

Back at Samuel Montagu's headquarters, Andrew Galloway was 'horrified' by Jones's report that Burrington did not understand his own company's finances. Burrington even apparently believed Maxwell's explanation that the missing money was on deposit with Goldman Sachs 'to win a good credit rating in America', although he had not asked to see the bank statements. 'That's all ridiculous rubbish!' exclaimed Galloway, who then telephoned Guest for a full report, but heard only 'vagaries'. By the end of the conversation, the banker was incredulous. Guest was 'panicking'. The finance director did not understand that in a public company he enjoyed enhanced powers, which he was failing to exercise. On the other hand, the bankers were reluctant to interfere. 'It's not our job,' they consoled each other. 'It's up to the directors.'

Nevertheless, Galloway telephoned Maxwell in New York. 'It's all being sorted out,' he was told 'in an unforthcoming manner'. Galloway pondered asking Clark to intervene, but soon dropped the notion, suspecting that the non-executive director was too close to Maxwell and might easily be misled by a lie. Nor could he appeal to Charles Williams, who was also a Maxwell toady. Since Charlie Wilson and Joe Haines were similarly tainted, Galloway tried to contact Clements, the other independent director. The board's external policeman, he hoped, could push Guest into action. Guest, it appeared to the bankers, was 'mysteriously' unwilling to challenge Maxwell. But Galloway's hunt for Clements initially proved no more successful than Guest's.

On Monday morning, 30 September, Maxwell knew that numerous executives were begging for an appointment. Among them were lowly accounts officials puzzled that there was no money to pay for the Mirror Group's paper supplies, or for printing machinery in Israel, or for the lawyers. The financial crisis was hitting the Publisher's daily operation just as his self-imposed deadline loomed: he had to wipe out his private debt to MCC within twenty-four hours.

While Maxwell sat with Sir Michael Richardson, Kevin was again juggling loans to secure the company's finances for another day. To secure one old debt (the loan of US Treasury bills to LBI), Kevin had already assigned 1.4 million Berlitz shares to Lehmans, but there was now little left to plunder. Instead of facing the problem, Kevin began refusing to take difficult telephone calls. 'Tell him I'm in a meeting,' he snapped that morning when Stephen Foster of Swiss Volksbank telephoned. The call was diverted to Trachtenberg.

'Where are the securities for our loan?' asked Foster anxiously, referring to £25 million advanced days earlier. 'Morgan Stanley say they don't have them.'

'Oh God!' exclaimed Trachtenberg with commendable conviction, spotting some fortuitous confusion at the bank. 'Morgan Stanley are terrible. We'll have to change banks. Your securities are definitely there.'

Foster was relieved. He did not realize that Trachtenberg was lying and that the shares, mostly First Tokyo's portfolio, had been sold. But when new shares were suddenly produced, taken from the pension funds to replace those missing, Foster asked: 'Who is the owner?'

'I am writing to confirm', faxed Kevin Maxwell in reply, 'that RMG is the beneficial owner.' No eyewitness recalls Kevin betraying any nerves as he dictated that false claim of ownership.

Even so, Foster summoned Trachtenberg and Cook to answer a question: 'We do not and cannot understand the exact responsibilities of each individual and the relationship between the different companies among the Maxwell companies.' Their explanations might have been unsatisfactory to a sceptic but the bank nevertheless agreed to release the loan.

Although the conspiracy of silence and of collaboration was joined by many bankers in the course of that day in London, some were still touting for business from the carcass. That evening, Kevin and Pandora were invited by Charlie McVeigh of Salomon Brothers to *Lucia di Lammermoor* at Covent Garden. McVeigh would continue to pursue his quarry, even visiting Kevin on Sunday morning in his Chelsea home. In common with all the bankers, he recognized that Kevin was now running the empire. His father, it appeared, was barely involved. For Robert Maxwell had become convinced that he was the target of numerous enemies – both known and unknown.

THIRTEEN

Whirlwind

– October 1991

Balancing precariously on the balustrade of a balcony overlooking the English Channel at Brighton just before lunch on 2 October 1991, Robert Maxwell uttered a warning: 'They're trying to get at Neil through me.' Maxwell was speaking to Alistair Campbell, the *Daily Mirror*'s young political editor. The two were waiting for Neil Kinnock, the Labour leader, to arrive for the lunch traditionally given by the newspaper at Labour Party conferences. 'The whole world's against me,' the Publisher continued. 'People are out to destroy me.' His paranoia startled the journalist, who feared that his employer risked toppling backwards down to the pavement below. But Maxwell revealed little of his fears during the meal. Instead, he pontificated about world leaders, passing Solomonic judgment on individuals and reporting his conversations in the citadels of power. His audience, eager to retain the *Daily Mirror*'s allegiance to Labour, did not deign to contradict him. Nor did they mention the reports of their host's financial plight. In truth, they hardly contributed to a conversation. Their silent attention was the only requirement.

Maxwell's presence in Brighton aroused little comment among the stalwarts. Ever since he had bought the *Daily Mirror* in 1984, he had enjoyed hosting the functions the newspaper held for the party's powerful and faithful. It was compensation, even revenge, for his own humiliating rejection in the two parliamentary elections of 1974. But such was the man that the newspaper group had not won him even limited influence.

Back in his hotel suite, Maxwell's agitation resurfaced. Jabbing constantly at his telephone, he was furious to find that all Kevin's lines were engaged. That very morning, as Maxwell had flown in the helicopter to Brighton, Lehmans had sold £29 million worth of pension fund shares from the Capel Cure portfolio to recover a debt. The pittance which remained – £225,000 – was returned to LBI as surplus to its requirements.

To repay another debt, the Maxwells agreed to sell the pension funds' 1 million shares in Banco Commercial Portugues, which were already pledged to Lehmans. 'I want the full price,' Kevin had told Bernie Leaver, a managing director of Lehmans, the previous day. 'I'm not taking any discount.' Leaver sensed that 'the guy is obviously struggling for money'. Whereas previously Kevin and his father had succeeded in staving off new threats every week, they were now pouring in daily, even hourly.

Kevin's attempt to restore credibility within MCC appeared to have stemmed some pressure. On 1 October, he had assured Peter Laister about the family's borrowing from MCC. 'The debt has been reduced to zero,' he said, referring to the promised target set in August.

Laister was unconvinced: 'But Basil says it was £96 million this morning.'

'That's true,' replied Kevin, realizing that he had been caught out, 'but it'll be down to £60 million during the week.' The atmosphere had become tense again. So much was at risk for the Maxwells and so much depended upon Kevin's cool nerve. Fortunately for Kevin, Laister trusted the young man (at that time there was no reason not to, reasoned Laister with hindsight) and believed that he was trying to be helpful, acting as an intermediary between the directors and his father. For the moment Laister was prepared to allow this breach of the procedures they had agreed on 21 August, but he gave warning: 'The truth will come out in the audit, Kevin, and that's that.'

Spying a chink, Kevin quickly sought to exploit Laister's sympathy, and at 6.55 p.m. on the same day telephoned Lord Rippon, 'to give assurances that everything was in order with regard to inter-company borrowings'. Lord Rippon, the experienced lawyer and politician, simultaneously noted their conversation. 'Everything has been approved by the other independent director [that is, Laister], and also Brookes and Woods.' Kevin was clearly pleased by the success of his manoeuvre.

Before coming to Brighton, Maxwell had met George Willet, the

LBI director who had voted against his employer on First Tokyo. Gently Willet had submitted his resignation. The 'Treacherous Trachtenberg', complained Willet, was intolerable. In a hurry to leave, Willet handed in his pass, bid goodbye to Carol Bragoli, his secretary, and departed. Soon after, Maxwell frantically summoned Bragoli. Passing through the Publisher's outer offices, the small secretary noticed that 'all the girls looked worried'. Concern was clearly reflected on her own face as she entered Maxwell's sanctuary. Both Robert and Kevin were standing at the far end. 'You don't need to be afraid,' said Maxwell in a tone of syrupy menace. 'Just tell me the truth. What has happened to Willet's papers?'

'I bagged them up as secure waste, Mr Maxwell.'

'They should have been shredded.'

'But there were three cabinet loads.'

'You can go now,' ordered Maxwell. Minutes later, both he and his son had rushed to the basement to find two bags, still sealed by security tags. That night, he would sift through the sacks, thankfully finding no evidence that Willet had leaked the truth to outsiders. Back in her office, Bragoli reflected to a colleague that they worked in 'a madhouse or a circus. Every time the lion master is about to put his head into the lion's mouth, he calls in the clowns. It's so frustrating.'

Returning from the basement, Maxwell was told that Eric Sheinberg of Goldman Sachs was waiting on the telephone. The bank classed by its competitors as enjoying a 'unique' relationship with Maxwell was anxious to shed its by then disadvantageous links. Sheinberg's message was abrupt. It was an ultimatum about two margin loans of £25 million and $35 million due for settlement seven days after 27 March. Ever since, Maxwell had delayed paying. 'Bob, we'll give you until 11 October,' said Eric. 'It'll be very uncomfortable if you don't pay. There'll be no more time.' The bank would use the MCC shares against which all the loans were pledged. A very loud alarm bell was now ringing. Few banks like lending money to people who actually need it, and Goldmans were pursuing their own interests. 'Trust me, Eric,' urged Maxwell. 'We'll sort it out.' At least he had prevented Trevor Cook from bringing Tony Boram to discuss their disagreements about the amount paid to Mirror Group pensioners and the fund's investments. Thanks to the solicitor Ian Pittaway, a seventeen-page letter, under draft since

July, was nearing completion. The contents, suitably unrevealing, would buy time. For these pages of obfuscation, the solicitor would charge nearly £50,000.

In between his efforts to contact Kevin on the afternoon of 2 October, Maxwell was repeatedly telephoning Ernest Burrington as the managing director drove to Brighton. His car telephone did not respond. Furious with him for protesting to the banker Michael Jones (Michael Stoney had duly reported the exchange), Maxwell decided to frighten the Mirror Group executive. As Burrington walked into his bedroom at the Metropole, the telephone was ringing.

'Come down,' ordered Maxwell.

'I haven't even unpacked yet,' cried Burrington, before realizing that the Publisher had already replaced his receiver.

'Ernie, I thought you were a friend,' growled Maxwell as Burrington entered his suite. Moving on to the balcony and perching himself once more on the balustrade, he continued, 'Stoney says you're making trouble. Are you trying to blow us out of the water?'

'This is ridiculous,' choked Burrington.

'And I'm having too much trouble from Guest. He's no good.'

'You're not giving us information.'

'Your job is to run Mirror Newspapers profitably. Nothing more. Corporate finance is not your concern.'

Surprised by Maxwell's abrupt manner, Burrington feared (as Campbell had done earlier that day) that the Publisher might slip backwards into space. 'We're a public company now, Bob. We can't go on like this. I'd better resign, Bob. It's all too much bother.'

'Okay,' replied Maxwell equably. 'No hard feelings. But you're to cancel the meeting tomorrow about the lease [of the Mirror building]. Everything will be discussed at the next board meeting.'

During the remainder of the afternoon, Maxwell presented himself only intermittently as the Labour Party statesman. Near by, Douglas Harrod, his entertainment manager, was supervising the arrangements for the Publisher's own dinner later that evening. Harrod had brought from London two pounds of Russian caviar and bottles of Dom Pérignon 1982 and Château Latour 1966. The hotel would be allowed to provide the smoked salmon and saddle of lamb. 'Cancel the dinner,' Maxwell told Harrod without explanation when at 7.30 p.m. he finally appeared, one hour late, at his own party. While he lumbered through the room, speaking at length with Sir Robin Day, the television presenter, Burrington and Guest were anxiously searching for either Clark or Clements. 'We were looking everywhere so we could tell them about the problems,' lamented Burrington later. But, though both men had accepted the invitation, neither had arrived. Instead Burrington and Guest met Vic Horwood, another Mirror Group director, based in Scotland. After hearing of their concern, Horwood advised them not to contact either of the independent directors. 'You'll stir up a hornets' nest,' he warned. Maxwell was benefiting from the atmosphere of fear he had created.

Oblivious of that search, Maxwell was finally persuaded by Harrod at 8.15 that if he did not leave immediately it would be too late for the helicopter, waiting at the nearby football stadium, to land in London. 'I had a lot of trouble getting him out,' frowned Harrod.

As usual, Maxwell slept badly that night. Summoning the maid early the next morning to prepare his breakfast, he was drained just by the thought of the day's events. At the office, he saw Kevin first. Robert Maxwell's appointments diary was filled by meetings with lawyers to discuss his action against the BBC, termination of employment contracts and an impending court action against him to pay a bill. Kevin's diary was positively sparse, reflecting his desire to see no one. His meeting the previous day with Michael Richardson to settle Peter Walker's final demands for payment had proved difficult. 'There's a final £110,000,' Richardson had written, referring to the purchase and sale of MCC shares, 'and I undertook to make all the necessary arrangements between your father and Peter Walker.' The broker, with better sources than most, could see Maxwell's impending doom and feared the resulting loss of earnings. Walker's claim was met by the Publisher drawing a cheque on a private company rather than MCC.

Across the bridge in the Mirror building, Lawrence Guest, 'fed up' that no one would answer his questions, dictated a protest for Maxwell and Stoney. 'I have been increasingly concerned with regard to the lack of information,' he dictated, before demanding information enabling him 'to keep a proper financial record'. Satisfied with his missive, Guest finally decided to contact Ian McIntosh, the Samuel Montagu director. 'Money's disappearing and I don't know where,' he confessed.

'I'll get on to it straightaway,' said the banker, puzzled by Guest's vagueness.

Having unloaded his burden, a beaming Guest arrived the following day at Nuffield Priory, in Surrey. 'McIntosh says he'll see Maxwell today,' he whispered to Burrington. The two were attending a conference of MGN executives to discuss a three-year strategic plan. But the projections, graphs and market research were abjectly dumped just minutes after Maxwell's helicopter landed close to the building. Entering the conference room, he grasped a handful of papers and snarled, 'You're all ninnies. You don't know what you're talking about.' The disruption was complete. The temple was being destroyed by its founder. His irrational behaviour was inexplicable to the eyewitnesses, unaware of the terminal pressures – both medical and financial – bearing down upon their employer. Having vented his spleen, Maxwell rose and walked from the room. His bewildered audience gathered on the veranda, gazing at the hulk heaving himself back in to his helicopter. Guest smiled at Burrington: 'He's going back to London and McIntosh is waiting for him.'

'Great.'

'It'll be interesting.'

Awaiting Maxwell in London with McIntosh were Michael Richardson and Neil Taberner of Coopers. The three had been summoned to discuss the impact of the *Panorama* programme. After an hour, interrupted by telephone calls, they concluded what had been a desultory meeting. As he walked out, McIntosh approached Maxwell: 'There's apparently a question about some deposits, Bob.'

Maxwell was unfazed. 'No problem,' he told the banker, once more giving an immaculate performance. McIntosh was satisfied and never bothered to telephone his report to Guest. Another potentially defining moment had been allowed to pass.

The following day, an agitated Stoney walked into Guest's office. 'Everything is okay. There are no problems,' he said, automatically repeating the phrases which Maxwell had dictated for the memorandum he now proffered. 'It's all explained here. All the money is earning extremely favourable rates of interest. But it's very

damaging that you've spoken to McIntosh and the other bankers.'
Although he could not understand all of Stoney's explanations,
Guest was placated by the promise that the money would be
returned by the following Monday.

That afternoon, 4 October, John Featley, Maxwell's Cockney
chauffeur, realized something was amiss. For the first time in three
years, he was driving both Maxwells to the NatWest Tower in
Broad Street. It was the latest of the bank headquarters the Publisher
and his son were visiting – 'flying around like headless chickens',
scoffed Featley. The chauffeur had driven them to Goldman Sachs,
the Swiss Bank, Crédit Lyonnais and Guinness Mahon. 'Even I was
surprised because normally they were the people who got the Big
Phone Call from the man himself telling them, "I want to see you
and I want to see you now."' During all these journeys, Maxwell
was sombre, but after each meeting he emerged pleased with his
performance, apparently convinced that he had bought more time
with his repeated assurances: 'As you know, I've been in the City
a long time, and whatever my problems, I've never defaulted. We've
got temporary problems, but with patience and understanding we'll
be able to get through.'

At 3.15, as father and son rose up to the thirty-ninth floor of the
NatWest Tower, they must have reflected upon the untidy reversal
of fortune. Yet neither man's demeanour betrayed their plans as
the lift's doors sprang open. None of the waiting 'suits' could have
guessed that earlier that morning the pension funds had lost still
more money. After further prompting by Mark Haas at Lehmans,
Kevin had agreed to sell the shares in Banco Commercial Portugues
at a 20 per cent discount rather than the 'full price' he had
demanded days earlier. 'He's a distressed seller,' sighed Haas, who
would gratefully receive $15 million for Lehmans' benefit through
an RMG account in New York, neatly arranged by Trachtenberg.
(The shares were sold for $14.9 million to a friend of Kevin's.)

The meeting at NatWest was more than a charade. At the outset,
Roger Byatt, the bank's general manager, fired a warning shot.
'Your companies' survival is as of today questionable.' The bankers
voiced their concern about the £265 million debt to NatWest and
went on to discuss an unpleasant surprise they had just suffered.
Over the previous two days, MCC cheques worth £8.5 million had
arrived at the bank to cover payment of the declared dividend to

shareholders. (The company had announced dividends worth £51.4 million, most of which theoretically went to Maxwell himself. The ruse cost the company £6.3 million in tax.) The limit on Maxwell's loans had been exceeded, but the bankers knew that a failure to honour the cheques would destroy the group, because payment of the dividends had become a legal obligation. 'This is very serious,' continued Byatt. 'Equally serious is the non-arrival of $15 million, the money you promised from the sale of Banco Commercial Portugues.'

'Oh, a stupid lawyer made a mistake,' lied Robert Maxwell. 'He transferred it to the wrong account. You'll get it soon.'

'You promised us $40 million,' said Byatt. 'Until now, we've received nothing.'

Maxwell looked at the banker and began uttering expressions of regret and proffering assurances that 'this unfortunate situation will be rectified'. Once again, the imminent sale of the Scitex shares was mentioned as a source of relief. NatWest would get £117 million of the proceeds. In the meantime, Maxwell and Kevin agreed to reschedule their loans against better security. 'I'll always see NatWest out,' said Maxwell. 'You've been my bankers for forty years and I wouldn't let you down.'

'Fine,' said one of the bankers, 'but we need repayment of $40 million soon. Let us know your plans on Monday.'

As the two Maxwells began to leave, Leal-Bennett asked Kevin, 'Why are the pension funds buying MCC's commercial paper [short-term loans]?' The banker had been surprised to discover the identity of the regular purchaser of MCC's loan notes. Why, he wondered, would anyone, least of all a pension fund, want to invest in a practically insolvent company?

'Oh,' replied Kevin, 'that has nothing to do with us. It's the independent trustees who make the decisions.'

The bankers never asked for the identities of BIM's so-called independent trustees.

With evident relief, father and son stepped into Broad Street. The only good news was that it was a Friday. The world's banks were closed for two days. Among so many unrevealed details, neither had mentioned to the bankers that MCC was under pressure to pay taxes of £14 million. As he drove the two men away, Featley noticed that Maxwell was 'all smiles. Happy as Larry. It was like someone had given him an enhancement drug.' Such was the Maxwells' accomplished performance.

Another empty weekend stretched in front of the Publisher. Despite the thousands whom he employed and the hundreds of people whom he knew, he was alone in his sumptuous apartment. Glancing at the pile of latest videos while hopping between television channels, Maxwell was stuffing food into his mouth at an unusual rate: comfort food for an unhappy man. In a drawer were unopened letters from the wife he had grown to dislike; somewhere in the building was a secretary who could be summoned at a moment's notice, but the energy to do so was lacking; and in Moscow was a woman he could trust, but she was too far away. It was a miserable prospect.

That evening, Maxwell telephoned Pole: 'I want Guest's material early tomorrow.' In the background, the security officer could hear blaring music, the sound of a forlorn man filling the void with noise. During the night, Pole transcribed Guest's desperate words: 'It's all going up.' At 6 a.m. on Saturday morning, he roused his employer and handed over the paper. 'Did you write this yourself?' mumbled Maxwell.

'No one else saw it.'

The evidence was stark. Stoney's attempt, on Maxwell's orders, to reassure Guest that everything was under control had utterly failed.

Maxwell rose on Monday morning more troubled than ever. Overnight he had decided to seize more millions from the Mirror Group, the only source of immediate cash, in order to repay Crédit Lyonnais. The repayment, he hoped, would quell the nasty rumours humming in the banking village. His hope was unfulfilled. The MCC share price had slipped to 145p, a 78p drop in six months. Quietly, as Sheinberg had warned, Goldman Sachs was selling MCC shares. The 11 October deadline had passed and Maxwell still owed over £140 million. Failure to repay loans was, for the banker, a capital offence. The mood at Goldmans was unsentimental: 'Maxwell isn't special to us. We should do what we feel we have to do.' By 25 October, 25 million shares would be unloaded. 'We had gotten rid of everything we were holding,' boasted a Goldmans executive inaccurately. 'We're not a bank but brokers,' said another. 'We want our money.' What remained was approximately £80 million loaned to Maxwell, secured by a further 26 million MCC shares and 40 million Mirror Group shares. The American bank was merely following the lead of other banks owed money by the Maxwells: quietly selling collateral to recover its loans.

The same sentiment – nervousness about the security of their loans – was echoed by Crédit Suisse, another loyal bank. Julie Maitland visited Kevin the following day. 'Please be assured,' he said, 'MCC is trading profitably and we're selling private assets to reduce our debts.' Although she seemed relieved, Maitland never-theless declined his request for an additional £25 million loan. But she accepted 1.1 million Teva shares as additional collateral.

Among the other bankers queueing at Kevin's door was Stephen Foster of Swiss Volksbank. 'The £25 million loan will have to be repaid,' said the banker.

'I can provide excellent security,' said Kevin. The banker relented. So Kevin went to his father's safe and withdrew five Berlitz certificates for 2.5 million shares and other shares belonging to the pension funds. In the whirlwind of his constant shuffling, the certificates had just been redeemed from other banks.

'I'll need proof of your ownership,' Foster had stipulated.

'No problem,' replied Kevin, dispatching a letter signed by Trachtenberg 'confirming' that the pension funds had sold the shares to RMG, the Maxwells' private company.

One banker with a most pressing claim was Rodolfo Bogni, of the Swiss Bank Corporation: the £55.7 million borrowed to purchase First Tokyo had not been repaid. Bogni was puzzled by Kevin's failure to forward First Tokyo's share certificates, the agreed collateral. In previous weeks, Trachtenberg and others had presented apparently plausible excuses for the delays: legal, administrative and accounting. The excuse now changed. 'I think we'll just repay the whole sum,' Kevin suggested amicably. That suited Bogni, unaware that his shares were gradually being sold by Crédit Suisse and Lehmans. Anyway, he liked Kevin, so he remained a believer.

While Bogni was being reassured by Kevin, Trachtenberg was oozing balm to a worried fund manager at Capel Cure. The manager had spotted on his screen the sale on 2 October by Lehmans of shares in a company called Ewart. 'Larry, are those not the same shares owned by Capel Cure for the pension trusts?'

'Well, I don't think so,' contradicted Trachtenberg. 'They are sitting in my hand, right here. I've got them in my hand, with a blank stock-transfer form.'

Another telephone call produced some panic. Speaking in his deadpan drawl, Mark Haas of Lehmans asked whether the money paid against the collateral was being used 'for further financing of other entities'.

Trachtenberg paused, 'Um, er, um,' he replied in a strangulated voice, fearing that the misuse of BIM's funds had been discovered.

As Haas listened to the incoherent and stumbling reply, he was unaware that his innocent question, prompted by a lawyer's require-ment for an innocuous board resolution, was producing paroxysms of fear in Holborn. But eventually Trachtenberg recovered, and was soon gratefully replacing the receiver.

Down on the seventh floor, Robert Bunn, RMG's finance direc-tor, was finding the pressure intolerable. Nervous at the best of times, he was now having to cope with a weeping assistant, Jane Roberts. RMG's attractive twenty-nine-year-old treasurer had been thrilled eight weeks earlier to be promoted to the post which gave her £36,000 per annum and a car – a fivefold increase since she had joined the group in 1986. But the treasurer's role, she pleaded with Bunn, 'is not what I had expected. It's very stressful.' Roberts's telephone was constantly ringing with brokers demanding money or bankers demanding more collateral for RMG's loans. Every morning, carrying a new spread-sheet, she met Kevin and Bunn to discuss whether to expect 'shortfall of collateral' that day. To pla-cate her honest, ordered but untrained mind, Roberts also presented her own innovation – an 'outstanding payments' list. Neither Kevin nor Bunn passed any comment. 'I don't want to be involved,' she told Bunn. 'I want to step back.' Over lunch, Bunn had urged the woman to wait until the new year when 'everything will have settled down'. She agreed, and returned to her desk and to her repetitive routine. On the instructions of either Kevin, Bunn or Trachtenberg, she completed stock transfer forms, received share certificates from either Bunn or Kevin, and, after getting their signatures on the transfer forms, organized a courier to deliver the package worth millions of pounds to the banks. It was an unpleasant, daily chore she undertook – while the Chairman once again disappeared.

By then, Robert Maxwell was again in Suite 5311 at the Helmsley Palace in New York with Nigel Crow, his valet, enjoying his status as a billionaire world statesman, waiting to join the beauty parade of the rich and famous. The occasion on 7 October was a dinner with Elie Wiesel, the chronicler of the Holocaust, and many other stars including the King and Queen of Spain. Although he planned to have Ghislaine accompany him, Betty had appeared and had been allowed to use a room in the suite. It would say much about Betty that, despite spending a whole week so close to her husband at this critical stage of his life, she would claim to be ignorant of the empire's plight. Even if Robert Maxwell was not confiding to her details of his problems, his telephone conversations with Kevin about suspicious creditors and rebellious directors in London must have been understood by a woman awarded a PhD, proud of her intellect and with forty-seven years' experience of the tycoon.

Any lingering doubts about Maxwell's condition did not survive his appearance on Thursday, 10 October. At 6 p.m. he was chauffeured with Betty and Ghislaine to the United Nations headquarters to celebrate the launch of the *European* newspaper in America, one year after its launch in Britain. Sweating profusely, his eyes watering and able to speak only in stuttered phrases, Maxwell stood beside Javier Pérez de Cuéllar, the UN's secretary-general, to host the party – complete with a string orchestra. Even in normal circumstances, the cost and effort of promoting an unknown newspaper in that region would have been formidable. But for a bankrupt to undertake that adventure was sheer folly. Since its launch, the newspaper had lost £18 million, and with monthly losses of £900,000 its latest wages cheques were about to be dishonoured by the Midland Bank. That evening, as he ordered Peréz de Cúellar to 'Turn the paper round' so that photographers could snap an ideal promotion shot, Maxwell appeared nervous and uncertain. 'Meet the editor,' he said to the secretary-general as Ian Watson stepped forward. Very briefly, Peréz de Cúellar's hand was outstretched, but his head was turned towards the exit. It was one of those occasions.

Maxwell's misery was to return to the Helmsley Palace that night after dinner at the Pierre Hotel with Hans-Dietrich Genscher and Dick Cheney, the US secretary of defense. Nigel Crow, his butler, had flown to London for his annual holiday. In his absence, conditions in the suite had deteriorated. Nothing had been washed. Papers, plates and clothes were strewn over the furniture and across the floors. By the time Betty left for London, she would be unable to find even a kettle to make her husband a final cup of coffee: 'I have a last vision of him on the settee that day, full of his cold, looking miserable and angry.' Clearly, she was beyond caring for him or capable of clearing up herself.

In London, Jean-Pierre Anselmini had hosted a farewell drinks party. Most of London's bankers arrived, not out of mere politeness but more to test the atmosphere. Among their number was John Leftley, the double-chinned senior manager of the Bank of Nova Scotia. Leftley had always liked the Maxwells but had been shaken by the fracture in their relationship caused by the summer foreign exchange problems. There was only one issue still remaining with the family, the repayment of a £30 million loan secured against the Scitex shares due to be sold any day. As Leftley talked to other bankers, he sensed growing panic. One after another, his competitors whispered about their eager anticipation of the Scitex sale. Like his own bank, all of those carefully coiffured men expected some benefit from the proceeds. Alarmingly, his own bank still did not possess the share certificates which guaranteed their loan. Leftley rushed off to report his shocking discovery. The following morning he would stake his bank's claim. The race to grab the empire's assets was intensifying.

Elsewhere in the building, Kevin was reporting to his father that Basil Brookes had been persuaded that their debt to MCC had fallen. 'It's zero,' Kevin had said smilingly to the finance director, who 'guessed' it might in fact be £60 million but did not protest.

The diminishing challenge from his directors encouraged Maxwell, after reading Pole's telephone-tap reports, to telephone Guest at 7 p.m. on Sunday evening, the 13th. 'Bob here.'

'Oh hello, Bob,' replied Guest cheerily, thinking it was a friend from his local sailing club.

'I hear you're not happy,' said Maxwell, and Guest's heart sank as he belatedly recognized the voice. 'We'd better meet. I'm flying back tonight.'

At noon on 15 October, after Maxwell had spent an hour in his office discussing his defamation action against the BBC with a roomful of lawyers, Guest entered for what he believed would be a private conversation. Instead he found Stoney and Burrington already seated. 'Well, what's wrong?' asked the Publisher.

'There's money still missing, Mr Maxwell.'

'All the money has been returned,' replied Maxwell, stealing Guest's thunder, 'and I've now reinvested it in gilts. You'll get the contract notes for the gilt deals soon. The money will be back within two weeks.'

Since interest rates at the time were volatile, Guest reasoned that it could be a shrewd investment. Yet when he saw Burrington later that morning he complained again, 'I'm not getting the information I need.'

Back in his office, Guest typed an unusual memorandum to himself on his portable computer. 'I am now convinced', he wrote, 'that MGN resources have been used to support other parts of the group. But I have no proof. I think I have frightened the chairman, but my main concern must be to get the money back.' The following morning, Guest's secretary retyped the memorandum into her own computer and printed two copies, one for herself and one for Guest to take home. Guest's fellow directors remained unaware of the finance director's suspicions.

Guest's apparent unworldliness was indeed worrying the Maxwells. Survival had been possible until then because the silence of the directors – of MCC, of the Mirror Group and of LBI – had effectively been bought. Anselmini was on the verge of leaving without a murmur, properly enriched. Donoughue's departure payments would be finalized the following day. Walker likewise was saying nothing. But Guest simply could not be bought off. The finance director kept telephoning, unwilling to accept Kevin's explanations.

That afternoon, Kevin approached Burrington: 'What's the problem with Guest? Is he for us?'

'He's not disloyal.'

'Why is he asking about the gilts? Don't you know that my father is one of the best gilt players in the world? We've all got to be on the same side, fighting for the same thing!'

Burrington was nonplussed. Four months earlier he had blindly signed a transfer proffered by Kevin which had removed £11 million from the Mirror Group. 'It's for a currency transaction,' Kevin had said. 'Dad's in Moscow. If we're quick we can make some money for this company.' Although Kevin was not a director of the Mirror Group, Burrington complied because the young man seemed to be regarded by everyone as in charge when Robert Maxwell was away. So £11 million had flowed into Maxwell's private account before

Burrington could have second thoughts. His life's experience in the Mirror Group, a paternalistic company, had not prepared him for such blatant lies. 'I saw smoke but no fire,' Burrington remarked later. Similarly, he 'wanted to believe' that Maxwell's investment in gilts was beneficial. 'There was no reason to believe the contrary.' He assured Kevin of their total loyalty.

Sitting in his kitchen that evening, with Sky News on the television screen, while Wheeler worked the L'Oréal dye into his hair, Maxwell, his complexion unusually sallow, was clasping a bottle of port. His client, the hairdresser noticed, was 'in a pretty bad way', and, to his surprise, within thirty minutes the whole bottle had been consumed. Unknown to him, his client's secret drinking had caused irreparable sclerosis of the liver. 'You know, Mr Maxwell,' Wheeler volunteered tactlessly, 'against your advice I've sold all my MCC shares.' There was no response. Maxwell was speaking alternately to Kevin and Ian on two telephones. Kevin was in Switzerland, at the end of a day trip around Geneva and Zurich persuading bankers that the family's well-publicized problems were only temporary. His report only intensified the depression evident in his father's voice.

In another desperate attempt to prevent MCC's share price from falling, Shelly Aboff had bought that day, on Maxwell's orders, 2.6 million MCC shares through Townsley & Co., a small London broker. Ironically, Kevin had just circulated a letter to MCC's directors warning them against dealing in MCC shares 'whilst the demerger proposal is being developed'. Although Aboff had ordered the shares on behalf of Edgeport, a private company, the £4 million cheque was drawn on London & Bishopsgate International Investment Inc., one of Maxwell's private companies. But the effect of the transaction on the market was negligible. Another £4 million had been wasted.

Over the previous twenty years, Wheeler had seen Maxwell experiencing both peaks and troughs – losing his seat in parliament and suffering business triumphs and disasters – but never previously, he later reflected, had he seen him 'so down'. The hairdresser himself felt 'upset'. 'There's something radically wrong here,' he thought as he sat waiting for the dye to dry.

'Do you know, Mr Wheeler,' said Maxwell as his visitor was about to leave, 'you're my oldest friend?'

'Mr Maxwell,' laughed the hairdresser spontaneously, 'you mean, I'm your only friend!'

'I think you're right,' replied Maxwell starkly, disappearing into his bedroom.

That night he should have attended a dinner for Fleet Street's proprietors at Spencer House, hosted by Conrad Black, the majority shareholder of the Telegraph group. In previous years, Maxwell would have flown from anywhere in the world to assert his status among his peers. But he had already telephoned his personal apologies to the host. Unflattering gossip about late payments and the fall in his share price could only please that crowd of smirking cynics. Instead, he went to bed, ordering his dinner to be delivered on a tray. He was anticipating the materialization of a new source of money.

On 9 October, 7.1 million Scitex shares had been offered for sale in New York. Fortunately for Maxwell, the lawyers at Lehmans had not queried his claim to own the whole block personally. Having successfully concealed in the prospectus that three-quarters were owned by the pension funds, he was looking forward to RMG receiving a cheque for $239 million (£139.7 million) by the 18th. Of course that was the dream. The reality was that all the money was already pledged to NatWest and to the Bank of Nova Scotia, and Bob Brown of NatWest was taking no chances. Hand-carrying the share certificates to New York, the banker clung to the pieces of paper whose loss would cost him his career. At night, he had even kept the certificates in his bedroom and, on one occasion, hid them under his duvet. Dozens of bankers, Brown knew, were hunting for an opportunity to seize an unencumbered Maxwell asset to pay off a loan. Brown could relax only when he personally witnessed Lehmans transfer the millions into a secure NatWest account.

The following morning, Maxwell gave to Bob Cole for distribution the draft press release announcing the Scitex sale, boasting a profit of £116 million. The announcement, he hoped, would stop some rot. Noticing that the draft was typed on RMG notepaper, Cole asked, 'Should this not be on BIM notepaper, Mr Maxwell?'

'Get it out, Mister,' snarled Maxwell. 'You're my postman, not my fucking censor!'

On leaving Maxwell's office, Cole bumped into Anselmini, still lurking on the ninth floor. His pay-off cheque, signed by Maxwell, was for £30,000 less than the agreed amount. The Frenchman understood the signs, since a porcelain dish, his gift to the Maxwells, had been removed from the tenth-floor apartment, but he was determined to secure his money. 'Is anything the matter?' he asked on seeing Cole's face. The spokesman showed him the press release. 'He can't say this,' Anselmini murmured and walked into Maxwell's office. Minutes later Anselmini emerged: 'Mr Maxwell said it must go.' Across the road in BIM's offices, Trevor Cook, the pension fund's administrator, was awaiting his share of the Scitex proceeds. 'Maxwell's difficult to get hold of,' he complained to his deputy.

Not surprisingly, London's least sceptical bankers paused on learning that Maxwell had personally raised the enormous sum of $239 million. Added to the news that he had sold three Macmillan businesses for $214.5 million in the previous three weeks, it appeared that he might well possess sufficient funds to repay the next tranche of MCC's Jumbo Loan – $750 million due in October 1993. Over the past months Kevin had emphasized to his bankers his desire not to 'relive the experience' of 1990, when he had organized the repayment of the first tranche. It had been, he told every banker, 'awful'. The care he seemed to be taking to amass the money well in advance had impressed the bankers, unaware that £100 million from the Scitex proceeds was owed to BIM. But encouraged by that repayment, NatWest reluctantly agreed to another loan for a pressing creditor, the Ansbacher bank. 'Things are very tight,' Kevin told a sympathetic Leal-Bennett.

One of the more sceptical bankers, unimpressed by these announcements, was sitting in Kevin's office at 8.30 on Wednesday morning, 16 October. This was Mike Moore of Bankers Trust, the Cockney-accented corporate finance manager. Normally excited by dealing with the Maxwells, his biggest customer, the banker knew that Robert Maxwell had recently met some of his colleagues in New York to discuss various sales – a good revenue-earner for the bank. But he was preoccupied by other matters.

Bankers Trust had lent £50 million to RMG some years earlier. Moore's concern was that the loan was secured on RMG's assets and he knew that the rumours about RMG's debts were true. A survey by his colleague Scott Marden had confirmed that the empire faced possible extinction. The bank could lose £50 million, an ugly prospect for Moore's supervisor, Ralph McDonald, the head of corporate finance. 'You're dead if we don't get it back,' Moore had been warned in the indelicate language favoured by macho bankers.

'We need our money back, now,' said Moore to Kevin, without making any pretence of friendship.

'That'll be difficult,' replied Kevin with considerable understatement, noting that Moore's attitude reflected a banker determined to jump a step ahead of his rivals. 'We might be able to repay you from the Scitex proceeds,' he continued, concealing the fact that all that money had long disappeared and that he had also promised the same money to the Swiss Volksbank to settle an unpaid loan, 'or we'll do something else.'

'Okay,' said Moore, sceptical about receiving Scitex money. 'But we need to move fast.'

Returning to his office, Moore sent a memorandum to his superiors offering a 'musical-chairs scenario'. 'If we go into MGN,' he proposed, 'our fate is in our hands.' Moore would justify that idea as 'helping Kev to solve his problems'. It was a solution which Robert and Kevin Maxwell accepted as an escape plan. Bankers Trust would loan £50 million to the Mirror Group and that money would be processed to repay the RMG loan. Since MGN had limited debts and huge assets, Bankers Trust's millions would be well secured. Moore was naturally not too curious about why the Mirror, flush with cash, would want to borrow £50 million. His only interest was to complete the transaction and reassure McDonald that the money would not be lost. The legal problems were also not Moore's concern. They were the responsibility of those charged with bestowing legal respectability upon the loan.

As part of that transaction, Bankers Trust recorded that the Maxwells were repaying their £50 million loan from the proceeds of the Scitex sale. At the same time, an internal Bankers Trust memorandum stated that $38.7 million of the loan to the Mirror Group would be used for a *Daily News* property development, ignoring the fact that the development had been abandoned months earlier and that there was no legal relationship between the *News* and the Mirror Group. 'Of course,' said a Bankers Trust lawyer, 'we'll need proof that the loan had been sanctioned by the Mirror Group board.' Another condition of the loan was that the recipient 'is not a

Maxwell Affiliate'. The transfer was undertaken using a 'Debenture Deed' completed in an earlier application for a loan with another bank.

Naturally, Maxwell had no intention of revealing his plans to anyone, least of all his fellow directors. Laying claim to powers which he had surreptitiously inserted into the minutes of the Mirror Group's first board meeting, and which therefore had no legal validity, that he alone could 'constitute a board', he arranged with Alan Stephens, the faithful and long-serving company secretary of nearly all Maxwell's 400 companies, to authenticate the minutes of seventeen Mirror Group board meetings attended by only himself and Michael Stoney. In identical fashion, the minutes recorded that the loan had been approved on 21 October after 'careful discussion'. In fact, on that day, Maxwell would be in New York. After the seventeen 'meetings', Stoney presented to Moore the comfort certificates signed by Maxwell.

Responsibility for routing the money was assigned to Kevin, although he was not a Mirror Group director. With Stoney's help, he introduced the £50 million into a giddy circle which passed through the New York *Daily News*.

On 18 October, Robert Maxwell telephoned Larry Bloom, the newspaper's chief financial officer, from London. 'Over the following days,' he purred, '$86 million will come into the *News*'s Chase Manhattan account. You are to promptly retransfer that money according to our instructions.' The $86 million equalled £50 million.

Bloom noted the instructions. By then, the newspaper's circulation and advertising revenue had substantially increased, but finding the money for daily payments of newsprint was a constant strain, which imperilled the recovery. Hoping that some of the $86 million would remain in the newspaper's account, Bloom briefed his deputy Marshall Genger and left New York for business elsewhere.

Genger, aged forty, had become used to Maxwell's brief and often startling telephonic barks, each of them terminated without a farewell by the cutting of the line. 'Take orders only from me,' the Publisher had instructed him. 'Even if Kevin gives an instruction, you're to confirm it with me.' Those tactics prevented Genger ever posing a question and suggested that the father lacked confidence in his son. But, for him, the Maxwells were 'the toast of the world controlling an empire worth billions', so he saw no reason to question his employer 5,000 miles away.

On Monday, 21 October, the £50 million was advanced by Bankers Trust to the Mirror Group in London, but of course the money was not paid into the newspaper's normal account. Instead, Moore deposited it in a special Lehmans account in London, from where it passed, in a transfer supervised by Michael Stoney, to Lehmans in New York; from there it passed into a Chase Manhattan account of the *Daily News*. Anxiously, Moore awaited the repayment. At first, the operation appeared to be going according to plan, but Maxwell had departed for New York amid newspaper reports of new financial difficulties. As the day developed, Moore became alarmed.

Early in the morning New York time, Kevin, having just returned on a private jet from a weekend with his mother in France, telephoned Marshall Genger since Bloom had already left New York.

'$239 million will arrive in the Chase account today,' he said. 'It's the proceeds of the Scitex sale,' he untruthfully claimed. '$86 million is to be transferred to Bankers Trust.' Two hours later only $56 million had arrived at Chase. 'There's been an administrative error,' Kevin told Genger, having meanwhile decided to transfer $30 million of Bankers Trust's money to Goldman Sachs in an attempt to pacify that increasingly irate institution. 'Transfer the $56 million to Bankers Trust.' Genger obeyed.

The following morning, Moore sounding upset, telephoned Genger: 'Where's the rest of the money?'

Genger was baffled: 'Who are you? I've never heard of you.'

Genger then telephoned Kevin: 'Who's Moore?' he asked, unused to bankers from London demanding money. Kevin did not reply, but promised that the remaining money would be arriving that day.

Unseen and unheard by Genger, Kevin was, as usual, frantically keeping bankers at bay while shovelling what little money was available into widening holes. Among the few admitted into his office were David Leal-Bennett of NatWest and Brian Pearce of the Midland Bank. The two men were probably unaware of Edmund Burke's aphorism, 'For evil to succeed, all that is necessary is for good men to do nothing.' The two bankers wanted to renegotiate their loans. Among the many callers who were told 'Kevin is in a meeting' was Mike Moore, already many jumps ahead of Kevin's visitors.

Moore was nevertheless frustrated. 'What's gone wrong?' he asked Genger repeatedly.

'Ask Mr Kevin Maxwell,' replied Genger. 'But what's it all about?'

'We're winding down a currency deal,' explained Moore.

In London, Kevin was struggling to produce enough money to satisfy Bankers Trust. Over the next four days, Genger watched as $113 million was paid into the account and the same amount paid out – a sum bafflingly unrelated to Kevin's original instruction. All the money came from the Mirror Group. By 24 October, Bankers Trust, having received its £50 million from MCC, had been paid £43,904 interest on its loan to the Mirror Group. Genger only discovered the truth about the movement of funds some weeks later: 'I felt soiled about being used like that.'

That Friday, Robert Bunn was busily telephoning a currency dealer at Citibank. 'Kevin Maxwell asked me to give you a ring. You may have heard that we have now completed the sale of Scitex shares . . . So we've got a lot of dollars in the States. So Kevin wanted to convert 40 million of those into pounds for value on Monday.' Bunn of course knew that the proceeds had already been transferred to London, converted into pounds by NatWest and distributed to Maxwell's creditors, but he nevertheless continued giving the false impression. Once again Marshall Genger at the *Daily News* was unknowingly used.

The Citibank dealer was forty-eight-year-old Graham Bell, who had risen since he joined the bank at age of seventeen from the very lowest rung to become a well-paid, conscientious relations manager. Instead of going on holiday to Arizona with his sick wife, he had agreed to stay and work at the bank. When Bunn's offer arrived, Bell was reluctant to accept. In March, Citibank had decided to cease all its business with the group because Robert Maxwell was 'regarded as disruptive'. But this particular forex transaction, preceded by a personal conversation with Kevin, appeared conventional and safe. 'Deal, deal, deal,' shouted Bell, after receiving his superior's approval. 'Make money, make money.'

On the basis of a letter signed by Kevin and Bunn, Citibank on 21 October transferred £23 million to the Midland Bank in London and awaited the $40 million from the *Daily News* account in New York. The money never arrived. By then Robert Maxwell had flown across the Atlantic.

Maxwell's return to New York on Sunday, 20 October was intended to consolidate his patronage of the Brooklyn Polytechnic and deny easy access to those MCC and Mirror Group directors who were voicing suspicion. He also used the opportunity, after the sale of a Macmillan subsidiary, to divert £14 million from the company for his personal use. By then he had taken £41 million from Macmillan, leaving the American publisher struggling to find enough cash to pay the weekly wages. The latest theft coincided with what he perceived as the gravest attack on his honour.

That Sunday, Faber & Faber, reputable London publishers, had launched *The Samson Option*, a book by the prize-winning American investigative journalist Seymour Hersh. The book claimed to contain 'stunning disclosures' about the politics and deployment of Israel's secret nuclear weapon.

Israel's 'bomb in the basement' had long been a subject of conjecture but the 'final' proof of its existence had been offered in 1986 by Mordechai Vanunu, an Israeli technician who, while employed in the Dimona nuclear facility, had illegally taken photographs. Those photographs had been offered for sale to Maxwell and the *Sunday Mirror*. After the offer had been rejected, they were bought by the *Sunday Times*. In the days before publication, Vanunu was in London, courtesy of the newspaper. But, unknown to the journalists, Vanunu's presence had been revealed to the Israeli government. In a deft entrapment operation using an attractive female agent, the Israeli secret service Mossad had lured the unsuspecting technician to Rome, where he was drugged, kidnapped and shipped to Israel. Charged with espionage, he was sentenced to eighteen years' imprisonment.

In his book, Hersh alleged that Vanunu's address in London had been betrayed to Mossad on Maxwell's orders by Nick Davies, the *Daily Mirror*'s foreign editor and Andrea Martin's boyfriend. Maxwell, according to Hersh, was known to be a Mossad source. Hersh also accused Davies of involvement as an arms dealer on behalf of the Israeli government. His source was Ari Ben-Menasche, an Israeli who had been introduced to Maxwell in April 1989 by Davies. Ben-Menasche claimed that Davies had travelled to Ohio to buy arms for Iran, suggesting that Maxwell was also involved in that operation on Israel's behalf. Since Ben-Menasche had, earlier, falsely claimed to be a former Mossad officer, Hersh's allegations were sharply devalued.

In his Helmsley suite, Maxwell exploded in anger. All his financial problems were forgotten as, in his wrath, he trashed his hotel suite and devastated its furnishings. In calls to London, he denounced the claims as 'ludicrous, a total invention', and supported Davies: 'He is innocent of whatever the allegations are.' Hersh's exposé was greeted by a writ for defamation.

Initially, no newspaper dared to publish the accusation, but two days later, spurred on by Maxwell's critics, two members of parliament repeated them in the House of Commons. Now protected by parliamentary privilege, every newspaper gleefully reprinted the story of Maxwell's alleged relationship with Mossad. 'Mirrorgate' was born, and even Hersh's lacklustre press conference and his discredited source – Ari Ben-Menasche – were glossed over by newspapers eager for ammunition to attack the ogre.

Maxwell's protestations of innocence were ignored as the attack switched to Davies, accused of gun running. Davies's denial – 'I swear I've never been to Ohio in my life' – prominently supported by Maxwell and the *Daily Mirror*, was countered by the *Sun*'s headline: 'YOU LIAR'. Davies, the flash journalist distrusted by Maxwell when the Publisher had been in the grip of his passion for Andrea Martin, was shown to be a charlatan. A photograph proved that he had visited an arms dealer in Ohio. Despite apologizing for his 'lapse of memory', Davies was fired and the *Mirror*'s reputation sank. The target was now exclusively Maxwell.

Invigorated by his 'scoop' about the tycoon, albeit still unproven, Hersh added fuel to the flames. An anguished Maxwell heard reports of the journalist's brazen accusation that he had, on Israel's behalf, laundered money and dealt in weapons. The Publisher's anger was for once justified. He was not a Mossad agent, but an overt and close supporter of the Israeli government. He had never dealt in arms and not a scintilla of evidence to prove money laundering for Israel would ever be produced. But there were few sympathizers. He had perpetrated too many calumnies himself for others not to delight in his discomfiture. He lost no time in consulting George Carman and other lawyers in London, while discussing his plight in New York with Yaakov Neeman. The Israeli lawyer's promise to obtain some official rebuttal from his government provided only limited relief. Neeman had in fact flown to New York for another purpose, namely to secure his 2 per cent commission on the profits of the Scitex sale, which he had agreed with Maxwell when he gave the original advice for the investment in 1988. After Maxwell agreed to pay the $4.8 million 'success fee', which he did not possess, Neeman departed. By the time the former *Daily News* president Jim Hoge walked into the Helmsley suite he encountered 'a man who looked bull-whipped'.

'We're losing a fortune at the *News*,' moaned Maxwell. 'The Mob's to blame.' The Mafia in the print unions were haemorrhaging the company. The circulation was at 720,000, fatally allowing advertisers to demand refunds because the newspaper was failing to meet guaranteed targets. Maxwell's request to one executive to massage the circulation figures upwards had been refused. Hoge was not surprised to hear the Publisher's complaints but was taken aback to find that, for the first time, he actually listened, refusing all telephone calls during his hour in the room. 'I warned you,' said the American during an uninterrupted ten-minute homily. 'You can't run this operation jetting in and out.'

'Come back and help me,' pleaded Maxwell, before lapsing into a rare silence, staring out across the city.

'I'm afraid there's nothing I can do,' replied Hoge, rising to leave.

'Goodbye,' said Maxwell quietly. Unusually, there was no hearty handshake, no belly laugh.

Cooped up in the suite, ordering spicy fish to be brought from Mr Fu's, Maxwell hugged the telephone in search of salvation. At least he saw the absurdity of attending as co-chairman and benefactor a Time-Warner dinner and dance at the Pierre Hotel to mark the tenth anniversary of the Committee to Protect Journalists. Drained of any charity towards that ilk, he cancelled. He felt increasingly vulnerable stepping into the unwelcoming Manhattan streets.

The news from Kevin in London was bad, and worsening by the hour. Fifty-five bankers were telephoning for reassurance about their loans or payments for the delivery of foreign currency. Typical of the visitors was Brian Brown of Lloyds for what he regarded as 'a difficult meeting', although the Maxwells' debt was down to

£166 million. After hearing Kevin's request for a '£10 to £20 million loan', the banker was blunt: 'We are at the top of our limits, Kevin. We don't want any more requests for loans. They're not welcome.'

Among the few requiring personal attention was Crédit Lyonnais. On 22 October, Kevin had flown by private jet for dinner with Pandora and his mother in the Dordogne. Since his mother had encouraged Kevin's ambition to undertake greater responsibilities in the business, it is inconceivable that he did not reveal some of his problems over dinner. Possibly for that reason, Betty Maxwell had by then transported some of the family archives from Oxford and had ensured that she had received over £3 million from his father in their separation settlement, so it is likely that Kevin revealed his predicament. However, he certainly served an undiluted farrago of falsehoods over breakfast the following morning in Paris with Jean Cedella of Crédit Lyonnais, assuring the French banker that he was 'on target' to repay the next tranche of the Jumbo Loan. Cedella was understandably relieved. His bank was owed $1.3 billion, and, while politely declining Kevin's request for another loan, accepted the reassurance that 'our difficulties are temporary'.

In repeating the same line to successive bankers on his return to London later that morning, it appeared to Kevin that Julie Maitland at Crédit Suisse was the most easy to satisfy. In a new strategy report written on 14 October, she had misdescribed BIM, LBI and LBG as 'subsidiaries' of RMG (in fact they were owned by Headington Hill Investments). Her confusion was beneficial because it allowed the bank to sell more pension fund shares to settle the Maxwells' private debts.

Maitland's bank should no longer have been under any illusion about the identity of the shares' owners. A letter to Crédit Suisse from Matthew St Paul of Morgan Stanley confirmed that the latest delivery of shares came from 'LBI a/c AGB Pension Trustee Limited and a/c Mirror Group Pension Trustee'. Nevertheless, Crédit Suisse having obtained Kevin's signature to an undertaking drafted by their lawyers that RMG was the lawful owner of those shares, £12.8 million was paid the same day into a private Maxwell account.

Maitland and her superiors explained that they had been satisfied by Kevin's undertaking. 'I never checked the ownership of the shares,' Maitland herself would claim, asserting that she had been

After Larry Trachtenberg *(above)* was employed by Maxwell in 1988 as an investment expert, he was joined by Lord Donoughue *(top right)*. On Maxwell's orders, their company, London & Bishopgate International, received from Trevor Cook *(top left)*, the pension funds manager, share certificates worth over £200 million which Maxwell contrived to use to raise cash for himself. John Pole *(left)*, Maxwell's chief of security, bugged many internal telephones, but never those of the directors of LBI.

Among the dozens of bankers who were critical to the Maxwell's survival during the last year, few were more valued than Julie Maitland of Credit Suisse and David Leal-Bennett of NatWest. The bankers' regular contacts among Maxwell's staff included Robert Bunn *(back row, third from left)* Albert Fuller *(front row, fifth from right)*, Basil Brookes *(front row, fourth from right)* and Jane Roberts *(front row, third from right)*. With Kevin *(standing next to Bunn)*, the finance team played football against a NatWest team on Oxford United's ground, owned by the Maxwells.

On 19 September 1991, Maxwell was appointed chairman of New York's Polytechnic in return for his offer of a $10 million bequest negotiated with the outgoing chairman Joe Jacobs *(far right)*. Nine days later, on Dr Henry Kissinger's advice, Maxwell consulted Dr Alfred Rosenbaum about chest pains. Rosenbaum *(left)* concluded that his patient was a 'walking case for a heart attack'.

Captain David Whiteman *(centre)* flew Maxwell on his last trip to Gibraltar and recalled, 'He seemed in a very good mood.' But Sergio Rodriguez *(left)*, who served Maxwell his last dinner in the Hotel Mencey in Santa Cruz, reported that the guest appeared 'preoccupied'. *(Main picture)* Maxwell, at the stern of his yacht the *Lady Ghislaine*, from where he probably fell into the Atlantic on 5 November 1991.

Gus Rankin captained the *Lady Ghislaine* on her last voyage and photographed Maxwell's cabin shortly after the Spanish police began to investigate the owner's disappearance.

The first autopsy conducted by Dr Carlos Lopez de Lamela *(left)* in the Canaries declared the Maxwell had died of a heart attack. Both Lamela's methods and his conclusion were criticised by Dr Iain West of Guy's Hospital *(above)* after a second autopsy in Jerusalem. But even West could not give a definitive cause of death. Kevin and Ian Maxwell announcing their father's death on 5 November 1991. Both were charged with conspiracy to commit fraud on 18 June 1992. Their trial started three years later.

Maxwell's burial on the Mount of Olives was arranged by his Israeli lawyer, Yaakov Neeman. His grave is regularly surrounded by broken glass, thrown deliberately from the road above. The stone was placed upon the grave by the author.

(Below) Maxwell's 'state' funeral in Jerusalem compounded the mystery of his life. 'Now the circle closes,' said Betty Maxwell emotionally. 'He has returned to his roots.' But soon she too was to write of his wrongdoings.

A *Daily Mirror* photographer was able in December 1991 to record Kevin's newfound poverty as he, his wife Pandora and his children left their Chelsea home and gloomily boarded a bus. Soon after, Kevin regularly flew club class to Moscow, Vienna and New York establishing a new lucrative business.

fooled by Kevin. But the army of other bankers from Sumitomo, Lloyds, Salomons, Bank of Nova Scotia, Citibank and Swiss Bank calling on Kevin were no less willing to be beguiled by his firm, intelligent and sensitive response to their anxieties. To continue outperforming most mortals, Kevin managed at 4 p.m. on 24 October to stand with Robert Bunn in Barclays' headquarters in Royal Mint Court to witness a signing ceremony for the rescheduling of the empire's loans. None of those preening, dark-suited bankers from Barclays, Lloyds and Sumitomo, convinced of their own astuteness, revealed a flicker of doubt that Kevin's talk of 'private holdings', 'Liechtenstein', 'temporary liquidity problems' and 'asset disposals' might disguise a financial quagmire. In retrospect, they and Maxwell's broker Sir Michael Richardson would claim that 'Bob was squeaky-clean on the surface to his British advisers; the frauds were only with American bankers.' But privately, at the time, those bankers knew that the Maxwells were on the verge of bankruptcy. After all, NatWest had been obliged to pay an account of £420,000 to Titmuss Sainer because RMG had no money. Yet, while none of those bankers had probed close enough into *all* their client's accounts, they were scrambling to protect their money by rearranging the terms of their loans.

In New York, Robert Maxwell, still fuming about the Mossad allegations and the *Panorama* programme, found some relief in pulling off another coup. Robert Katz, one of Goldmans senior lawyers, had been badgering for repayment of the bank's loans. Ten days earlier, Katz and Ken Brody, a Goldmans banker, had given Maxwell a deadline to repay the money by 11 October. The date had passed and further reminders had been answered by Maxwell's unfulfillable promise that the debt would be repaid from the Scitex sale. By 22 October, Goldmans were on the verge of selling their collateral, MCC shares.

That morning, Maxwell telephoned Katz: 'I'm in New York, I want to come and see you.'

'I'm not interested in any meetings,' replied Katz. 'Our only interest is being paid. There's nothing more to discuss.'

Twenty minutes later, Katz was called by the bank's security desk in the Broadway entrance: 'Mr Robert Maxwell is in the lobby to see you.' In characteristic style, the Publisher was barging his way uninvited into the bank. By the time he had reached the twelfth-floor conference room, Katz had summoned three colleagues. Maxwell arrived accompanied by Ellis Freedman, his lawyer.

'How much money is involved?' asked Maxwell nonchalantly, hoping that his offer – 'You'll be paid by December' – would convince his audience. Instead, Brody, weary of Maxwell's promises and of all the associated problems, offered a fable and the atmosphere began to improve. 'It's about a condemned man,' he began, clearly enjoying the moment. 'It's on the eve of his execution and he says to the Sultan, "If you don't execute me, I'll teach your dog to talk." Now everyone knew what the guy was thinking: the dog's lessons would take one year and in that time the dog could die and the Sultan could die and if not, who knows, by the end of the year the dog might learn to talk.' The tension broke. Everyone laughed, Maxwell the loudest. The banker's message was clear: there had been a lot of talk and it was now time to talk about payment.

'I'll make an offer,' said Maxwell exuding unusual charm for that time. 'I'll pay you £5 million a week.' He added some other conditions. The bankers, still laughing, lost something of their urge to be harsh and made a counter-offer. 'Done!' shouted Maxwell, still laughing as he walked into the lift. The repayments were to start in one week. Another breathing space had been grasped. Now he needed to address another gambit. Aware that Burrington and Guest opposed the extension of the Mirror Group lease on its Holborn headquarters at a cost of an extra £80 million, he planned to hold the necessary board meeting in their absence. 'Why don't you take a holiday?' he had asked Guest once again before leaving London. 'You look tired.' Grateful for his employer's considerateness, Guest booked a golfing weekend in Spain, departing 24 October. By then Maxwell had flown to New York, so Burrington assumed that the lease decision had been postponed: 'I knew Maxwell was in America so I didn't think there could be a board meeting.'

Shortly after noon on 24 October, Guest returned to his home outside London just before leaving for Heathrow. He had completed some last-minute shopping. The message light on his telephone recording machine was blinking. 'There is to be a board meeting at 12.30,' announced the secretary. He rang Holborn, but having failed to obtain an explanation and in any case unable to reach London within fifteen minutes, he departed for Heathrow,

WHIRLWIND 269

unaware that Maxwell was 'chairing' a board meeting by telephone. Similarly Burrington was beguiled. 'It didn't dawn on me that Maxwell could chair a board meeting in London if he was in New York,' he explained. Obligingly, enough of the Mirror Group directors, including Charlie Wilson and Joe Haines, did attend the meeting and agreed to the Publisher's proposal to extend the lease, reversing their earlier policy of moving from central London to save money.

Moments later, with the minutes signed, Maxwell, as a director of MCC and the owner of the site, 'agreed' that MCC would 'borrow' a further £80 million on the strength of the new agreement with the Mirror Group. When Burrington and Guest heard of his coup, neither publicly protested. Both were still relying upon Clark and Clements to approach Maxwell, though neither director had yet obliged. In fact, Andrew Galloway of Samuel Montagu had finally reached Alan Clements and explained the problem of the missing millions. 'Will you investigate it?' asked the banker. Clements appeared to nod, but nothing happened. 'I assumed he was getting on with it,' said Galloway, but he felt sufficiently uneasy to note down a reminder to telephone Clements the following week.

Threats from employees in London barely encroached upon Maxwell's consciousness any more. Events in Holborn seemed irrelevant to his daily existence in Manhattan. Years before, he had become accustomed to defying hostility in London. The hatred directed towards him could always be explained as jealousy, chauvinism, the resentment of the British establishment, or anti-semitism. But those sentiments did not explain the new antagonism in New York. The bankers now threatening him were rich, powerful Jews boasting foreign names: Friedman, Sheinberg, Rubin, Krueger, Gutfreund and Lopatin. None fitted the stereotype of his historic persecutors. Yet their incessant demands for money had fractured his relationships with them. He sensed that his voice was no longer welcomed, that his telephone calls now represented an irksome problem rather than lucrative business. The countless New York voices demanding repayment merged with the BBC, Hersh and other critics into an all-encompassing menace. 'There's a serious threat to my life,' Maxwell told Julian Kroll, one of the world's leading private detectives, in his Manhattan headquarters on Third Avenue. There was no reason for Kroll to believe that Maxwell was other than serious.

Maxwell's belief that his life was threatened had grown as his troubles increased. In 1988, Ernest Burrington had been approached by Alex Manson, a self-proclaimed former Mossad officer, who suggested there was a plot afoot either to sabotage Maxwell's business or to murder him. Burrington had agreed to pay Manson £10,000 for expenses and a report. In return he received a file detailing an exchange of arms for hostages held in Iran mentioning Paul Halloran, a *Private Eye* journalist, a British arms dealer living in Texas and some Americans with alleged 'intelligence connections'. The Israeli also suggested that Halloran was seeking to establish the truth of Maxwell's Liechtenstein connection. Although it was irrelevant to his plight, Maxwell took the file from Burrington and acknowledged self-importantly that 'CIA interests are out to destroy me,' adding 'It's not wide of the mark.'

By the end of the two hours with Kroll, Maxwell seemed relieved. His outpourings, akin to a confession, had drawn his venom. Calmly, he returned to the Helmsley Palace to await a dinner at the New York Hilton celebrating his receipt of the 1991 Remembrance Awards from the Yad Vashem Society.

On the evening of the dinner, Sunday, 27 October, the emotions returned. Watching the video of his tearful performance in Jerusalem's Valley of the Destroyed Communities and listening to accounts of the Jews' suffering awakened his feelings of vulnerability. Within that vast figure, hidden behind that harsh, bullying exterior, was unconfessed trepidation and loneliness. Like its predecessors, his speech of thanks that evening was unmemorable, but the sentiments were plain: the grief for his mother; the guilt of the survivor who for years had denied his heritage and parentage; and his allegiance to the last group who respected him. 'I am deeply grateful for this award,' he told his large audience with evident sincerity.

'I'm going to find the yacht and bake this cold out,' Maxwell told John Campi the following day. An invitation to lunch in Washington with the vice-president Dan Quayle and the Republican Senatorial Inner Circle was abandoned.

Through the night of 28 October, Maxwell slept in his Gulfstream for what would be the nineteenth return crossing that year and his last journey across the Atlantic. Forty-three years earlier he had flown to New York for the first time. In those pre-jet days, transatlantic travel was so unusual and America so exciting compared to Britain's gloomy austerity that he had, ever since, occasionally toyed with the notion of emigrating. But the proposition was easily resisted. Being a big fish in a small pond was preferable, and the English had been so easily misled and so willing to forgive. Had he left Britain, he might not have been nominated Man of the Year by the American–Israel Chamber of Commerce: he was due to return to collect the award in New York in two weeks.

Whether he would be able to show his face in the City of London was uncertain. Compared with his crash in 1969, the stakes this time were so much bigger. Somehow everything had spiralled out of his control. The amounts of money were gigantic; every bank in the world was involved; and this time he had failed to arrange an escape plan. There was money slopping around, but not enough. Twenty-two years before he had had so much more energy, and he had weighed thirteen not twenty-two stones. He would and could still fight, but the opportunities were slipping away. Even his sobriquet, the Bouncing Czech, seemed inappropriate to his worn-out condition. And worst of all, there was no one to turn to. No friends at all.

Maxwell's return to London on Tuesday, 29 October was certainly unpleasant for him. John Featley, his Cockney chauffeur, noticed that he was suffering 'the worst case of cold I'd ever seen in the three years I was there'. The symptoms were unmistakable: 'He couldn't breathe. He couldn't talk properly. He had a sore throat. If he'd been a horse, you'd have put him down.' In the previous weeks, Featley had been running his employer around the City to call at banks. On this occasion, Maxwell remained in his tower – staring at the low price of MCC's stock on the trading screen – as his creditors intoned their litany of demands. Crédit Suisse and Lehmans were selling shares held as collateral for loans. The shares belonged to the pension funds. Capel Cure wanted the return of the pension fund portfolio lent for thirty days more than one year earlier. Line managers from NatWest, Lloyds and Barclays Bank all wanted reassurance of repayments to reduce his outstanding debts.

Kevin had been fighting off Graham Bell of Citibank, who was persistently demanding his $40 million for the forex deal, initially by avoiding the dealer's calls and then, in a meeting, voicing his apology and 'utter surprise'. Kevin added, 'I'll look into this straightaway and report back.' One hour later, he was explaining,

'Lehmans snafued and deposited the money into a Chase account.'
Bell found it all very vague because Kevin could not explain where
the Scitex money was located, but his doubts were quashed by
Kevin's 'look of astonishment'. Now Robert Maxwell heard that
Kevin had been summoned to Citibank headquarters to be confronted by two senior bankers. He awaited news of his latest escape
plan. Thankfully there was no call from representatives of Invesco
MIM, proving the value of Maxwell's personal relationship with
its chairman Lord Stevens.

By contrast, Mark Haas of Lehmans had taken the first step
towards plunging the empire into the abyss. His bank, convinced
that the group was about to default, sent their demand for repayment of loans worth £93.8 million by the following day, accompanying it with an official international recall notice which
promised embarrassing exposure.

Rudi Bogni of Swiss Bank, anxious for his £55.7 million, spoke
darkly of his 'public duties' which required him to inform the 'authorities' of suspected breaches of the law. The most ominous ultimatum was from New York. Steve Friedman and Bob Rubin of
Goldman Sachs announced their decision to 'pull the plug'. Any
more sales of collateral held by Goldmans, Maxwell realized, could
not be concealed as easily as before.

The message had been passed to Sheinberg. Eyewitnesses noticed
that no trace of emotion passed across his face on hearing the news.
Termination seemed the right business decision. Maxwell was no
longer an interesting proposition. Sheinberg booked Concorde to
fly to London. His dry request cleared his office as he telephoned
the Chairman: 'Unless you repay £25 million by tomorrow, we're
going to sell collateral.' Maxwell understood the threat. More MCC
shares would be dumped on the market, triggering another fall in
price. From across the City, he also heard that Citibank was on the
verge of selling MCC shares to raise money for an unpaid foreign
exchange transaction worth $40 million.

The outflow of pension fund share certificates was apparently
unnoticed by Trevor Cook, who signed an internal memorandum
to Ron Woods, assuring Maxwell's taxation adviser that, after consulting Kevin Maxwell and contrary to Boram's concerns, the pension funds were sound. Cook's gullibility was essential to the success
of Maxwell's last desperate act – using the remaining Berlitz shares

held by Morgan Stanley to raise money. The ruse was doubly perilous because at that moment the Macmillan directors in New York were finalizing the sale of those very shares to Fukutake of Japan. If they were to win the release of the shares from Morgan Stanley, they needed Cook's agreement. Six weeks earlier, Cook had accepted the Berlitz shares as collateral for a loan to RMG after Maxwell had persuaded him that the shares were privately owned by the family. BIM's interest in the shares had been officially notified to Morgan Stanley. To remove that legal constraint, Cook was asked to Kevin's office. Although he would subsequently say that he did not realize that a formal meeting was taking place, Cook was recorded as agreeing to transfer the shares from Morgan Stanley. 'I didn't know what properly constituted a board meeting,' explained Cook. 'Since Berlitz didn't belong to the pension fund, I could not refuse whatever the Maxwells requested as long as BIM had sufficient collateral.' That assurance, said Cook, had been provided by Trachtenberg.

Having cleared the legal hurdle, Trachtenberg sent Matthew St Paul of Morgan Stanley a letter on BIM notepaper reporting that, following a resolution by Kevin, Trachtenberg and Cook, the banker was to transfer 2.3 million Berlitz shares worth $62 million to Shelly Aboff, Maxwell's long-time New York crony. A second letter from Kevin authorized the transfer of the shares to 'Aboff's personal account'. In the meantime, Aboff used headed notepaper which listed him as a BIT director. On one of those sheets, he wrote to the brokers instructing that they 'immediately transfer' 200,000 Berlitz shares to his private company. The remainder were held for Kevin Maxwell himself.

In his own office, Kevin believed that he had found a clever way to plug some of the holes. Macmillan in New York had contracted to sell Que, a computer publishing division, for $160 million. The money could be expected to be in MCC's account by 18 November. In anticipation of that cash, he summoned David Vogel, his solicitor from Titmuss Sainer and godfather to one of his daughters, who arrived with David Fairfield.

'Citibank', he told the solicitors, 'are still after their money.' The lawyers were already aware of the unpaid forex deal. 'Lehmans snafued,' Kevin told the lawyers, blaming the bank for paying the Scitex money into a wrong account. The solution, said Kevin, would be to pay Citibank from the proceeds of Que. There was an unusual silence. 'Can RMG use MCC's money?' asked Vogel. 'Absolutely,' replied Kevin. 'MCC owes RMG £80 million.'

The two solicitors were puzzled. Only two months earlier, Kevin had told them that RMG's debt to MCC had been reduced from £300 million to £125 million. Now Kevin was suggesting that it had swung by a further £200 million. Neither however dared challenge their paymaster. Fairfield, a small, timid man, did not contradict a 'very authoritative and well-respected' client. Nevertheless, Vogel again asked, 'Can the Que proceeds be used by RMG? You would need the MCC board's approval.'

'I'll see to that,' replied Kevin curtly. His cool, self-assured efficiency silenced his lawyers, who had earned enormous fees from his business and had been unquestioning Keepers of the Flame.

'You'd better double-check that debt,' Vogel ordered after they left Maxwell House. 'I'm sure RMG owed MCC money, not the other way round.'

'My notes show Kevin saying', replied Fairfield, 'that MCC owes RMG money.' Puzzled, Vogel sent several letters to Kevin advising on the problems of RMG using MCC's money. They were never acknowledged. For the moment, the lawyer's loyalty extinguished his instinct for trouble, while Kevin could only hope that somehow he would find a way to extricate the $160 million from MCC's account.

So far that day, 29 October, none of Maxwell's employees had challenged his stewardship of the publicly owned companies or of their pension funds. But the telephone taps on Lawrence Guest as well as a conversation with Sir Robert Clark, who warned that there could be some discomfiting moments at that afternoon's Mirror Group board meeting, only the third since the company's public flotation, convinced the Publisher that such challenges were imminent.

The mood within the Mirror building was fraught. The accusations that Maxwell was a Mossad agent who had betrayed Vanunu remained unanswered. The abrupt dismissal of Nick Davies for lying had destabilized the editorial team. The Mirror Group share price had fallen to 80p (a 36 per cent fall since the flotation five months before) and MCC's sat uneasily at 149p. At the editor's lunch that day, Maxwell had spoken ceaselessly about the 'outrageous stories peddled by Hersh and Allason'. (Rupert Allason was one of the MPs who had raised the matter in the House of Commons.) Only Ian among his nine employees present might have perceived a hint of the financial earthquake which loomed, but his face remained expressionless.

Ian, a Mirror Group director, was also silent about Guest's earlier complaints that £38 million had been deposited in gilts without the board's approval. One month after the finance director had revealed his concern to the bankers at Samuel Montagu, no one had seen proof of Maxwell's investment and no remedy for this state of affairs had been suggested. Despite Galloway's telephone calls, Alan Clements had not approached Maxwell, but had confined himself to recommending that the matter be considered by the audit committee. 'That's no use,' Burrington had fumed. 'Joe Haines is Maxwell's poodle. He'll pass everything back. All the others are the same.' Burrington despaired of mounting a challenge. His only hope lay in the meeting Guest had at last succeeded in arranging with Clements.

Over lunch that day, 29 October, at the Terrazza-Est off Fleet Street, Guest told the non-executive director about his concerns: 'I don't really know what's going on in the company.' Clements agreed that he and Clark would approach Maxwell at that afternoon's board meeting.

Neither Guest nor Burrington had sufficient courage to pose their own challenge when the directors assembled at 3 p.m. Instead, after an inconsequential meeting, both watched as Maxwell stood talking to Clements. Clark strolled up. Together the three walked across the mock-Renaissance hall into Maxwell's office. 'There are concerns about some unauthorized investments, Bob,' said Clark half apologetically.

'It's all a mistake,' replied Maxwell. 'I'm going away for a few days to get rid of this cold. I'll explain everything when I return. We'll meet on Tuesday.'

Clark agreed: 'Bob, we want to convene an audit committee to investigate.'

Briskly, Maxwell replied, 'Go ahead straightaway.' His brazen performance satisfied both men. Clements and Clark left the Mirror building without any suspicions. 'I'd fall into the same trap again if it ever re-arose,' confessed Clark.

Up in his penthouse that evening, the Publisher gathered his energy, charm and iron will to survive, before embarking upon a succession of telephone calls to his creditors. Among those dozens of calls, one typically reflected his predicament. At 8 p.m., he telephoned Joe Gregory of Lehmans in New York about their demand for £93.8 million: 'We have a short-term liquidity problem. We cannot repay that sum immediately.' Instead he offered more collateral of shares.

Gregory, a thirty-nine-year-old bearded dynamo, supervised 400 staff and $110 billion worth of equities. In his mega-world, Maxwell was a small player, albeit with the neat cachet that he was the new owner of the *Daily News*. In fact, Gregory only became aware of this Lehmans client after the Publisher had bought the newspaper. So, in what Gregory would call 'a difficult conversation', he listened with increasing sympathy to the lament. 'The publicity will cause difficulties,' said Maxwell emolliently, concealing his desperation.

'We won't declare a default if you transfer more shares like the BCP,' said Gregory, referring to the Portuguese bank. 'And we want $15 million in cash.' His leniency surprised his staff. On Maxwell's instructions, the following morning, 30 October, Trachtenberg offered £68 million worth of shares in the Telegraph group, a Lazard trust and Invesco MIM. During the late morning, as New York awoke, Gregory accepted the shares with a letter from Kevin authorizing the bank to sell BIM's securities 'free from all charge'. Hours later, the New Yorker abruptly reversed his decision and declined the offer. The shares were not transferable and the origin of Maxwell's securities had become suspect, although that did not prevent the bank selling the Capel Cure shares owned by the pension funds. Trevor Cook was told about the sale by his own staff at BIM. 'I'll investigate,' he said. 'That bank's incompetent.' He turned to Kevin for an explanation. 'It's a mistake,' snapped Kevin.

Even as he spoke, his father was shaken by a new message. Gregory's promise not to issue the default notice had not been passed to London. A Lehmans official, Maxwell heard, was waiting in the entrance hall with the fatal envelope, a threat to the empire's very existence.

In a polite letter faxed to Gregory during the afternoon, the Chairman expressed his 'surprise', given their earlier conversation:

'I cannot accept the validity of these notices ... we are trying to arrange an orderly disposal of the necessary securities and we do not understand why you are acting so precipitously. I am trying to reach you now to discuss this and trust that we can reach an amicable solution.'

But amicable solutions were fast disappearing. The dam, Kevin discovered, was breaching.

Throughout that day, Leal-Bennett had refused to honour three RMG cheques for £6.5 million. 'Unless I get the money by 4.50 this afternoon,' Leal-Bennett told Kevin, 'I shall refer them.' The signal to the outside world that MCC's cheques had 'bounced', the banker knew, would be catastrophic.

'I've got $11.5 million coming into the account from America,' urged Kevin. For once Leal-Bennett was unwilling to be reassured by a mere promise. He gave Kevin a new deadline of 6.30 p.m. to deposit the dollars in London. At the end of the day the money had not arrived. Kevin's bluff had been called. Humiliated, he withdrew the cheques. 'You're manipulating the system,' Leal-Bennett told him, having heard that Barclays Bank had also refused to honour a cheque for £1 million. Kevin did not reply. Henceforth, warned the banker, each cheque issued by Maxwell would require special scrutiny.

To cover the worsening financial crisis and raise cash, pension fund shares were being desperately flung in every direction. Each delivery was accompanied by a warning.

A batch of twenty-nine new securities held by Lazards delivered by Bank of America to Julie Maitland at Crédit Suisse was identified as belonging to Mirror Group Pension Trust. Despite Kevin's written assurance of ownership, Maitland was for the first time openly concerned. The bankers were alarmed by Cook's denial that he had seen letters signed by Kevin and Trachtenberg taking responsibility for BIM's shares. 'Either Trevor does not realize what's going on,' memoed a banker, 'or the whole thing is planned to confuse us and he didn't know; or he planned the whole thing so that we would be caught off-guard each time.' The bank's bewilderment was eased by Maitland's request for yet another comfort letter. 'No problem,' said Kevin, promising that it would be delivered the following day.

Soon after, Kevin wrote to Maitland confirming that RMG

owned twenty-five different securities formerly managed by Invesco MIM on behalf of BIM. Crédit Suisse, holding the shares as collateral for a loan, sold them and received £12 million.

Outside Maxwell's office, Trevor Cook was waiting. 'I'm going to RM to get the Scitex money,' he had told Jeff Highfield, his deputy. But his 4 p.m. appointment was delayed, and Cook was made to wait in the hall for an hour. On entering, he was 'surprised' by Maxwell's pale appearance. 'I'm too ill to speak about it now. I'm going away. I'll see you when I come back.' Obediently, Cook departed.

One floor below, Kevin had performed, as best he could, a similar task of defusing the suspicions of Laister, Brookes and Woods. Their arguments were irrefutable. Despite the agreement of 21 August to adhere to precise procedures, no board minutes had been circulated and the pure inter-company debt was £81.5 million instead of zero. 'There were no other directors around for us to consult,' explained Kevin. 'It'll be down to nil by the end of the year. And there are no other liabilities.' Both Brookes and Woods, accountants at the very heart of the Maxwell empire, accepted that statement of intent. But they were less convinced by Kevin's explanation for why his father had taken, without any authority, £14 million from Macmillan. Brushing aside the idea that there might be a problem – 'Dad did that in New York' – Kevin produced papers to 'prove' that 'the private side will provide all the necessary cash'.

Brookes was blunt: 'You've breached the agreements.' Kevin's face did not flinch. Instead he glanced at a pile of papers, transactions requiring Brookes's and Laister's approval.

That morning, Graham Bell of Citibank had called, demanding a cheque for $40 million, and refused to leave Bunn's office – an embarrassing experience. Over the previous days, five other banks had also been demanding repayment of £60 million for foreign exchange ordered by Kevin for RMG. Those six debts had been entered by Jane Roberts, RMG's treasurer, on the inter-company accounts between MCC and RMG. In anticipation of his meeting that evening with Brookes and Laister, Kevin had the previous day summoned Roberts, asking her to bring the current spread-sheet showing the inter-company debts, codenamed INCO 91/92. 'I want you', ordered Kevin, 'to delete the six former payments from INCO

91/92. Give Basil a sheet without those payments.' Although Roberts found his instruction 'strange', she obeyed. The sheet given to Brookes was codenamed 'INCO BASL', while a third sheet, shown to Kevin but including the payments, was codenamed 'INCO KM'.

By the time Brookes arrived at the meeting with Kevin that evening, unaware that his spread-sheet was inaccurate, he had marked the paper with eleven asterisks representing queries from the Macmillan treasury in New York. The atmosphere was clearly strained. Laister was about to leave on holiday, while Brookes wanted to finalize his resignation. 'Are you happy with these?' asked Laister, whose signature would verify the accounts. Brookes mentioned the eleven transactions which required further proof and replied 'Yes,' thinking, 'I've done the best I can.' Together, the two directors, accepting Kevin's assurances, signed papers approving his phoney accounts. Laister would never complain about that mistake. Indeed, none of his fellow executive directors would ever criticize Brookes. To their minds, he had, despite his small stature, single-handedly initiated the challenge to Robert Maxwell.

Minutes later in the same office, Kevin addressed Brookes and Ron Woods. 'It will be difficult if both of you resign together.' While Woods had no intention of resigning, Brookes planned to leave that week, although his severance deal had not been completed. The two men listened to Kevin in silence. He was concerned about more than appearances.

'He's worried sick by all the resignations,' said Laister as they walked out. 'He hasn't got any replacements.'

That evening Robert Maxwell telephoned Laister, who at that moment was driving his car around Hyde Park Corner: 'Can you return to the office?'

'What about, Bob?'

'I want Kevin as finance director,' said Maxwell.

'That's not on, Bob. It's a straight conflict of interest and the City won't have it.'

'You always give me good advice, Peter. I suppose I'll have to agree. Would you agree to be MCC's deputy chairman?'

'I don't think so. I've had enough aggravation as it is.'

'Well, ring me in the morning and let me know.'

'I'll be on a boat to France.'

'Ring me from the boat.'

By then, Maxwell had already decided to leave London early the following morning. Living in the penthouse being subjected to unrelenting pressure was proving intolerable. Dispirited, exhausted and alone, he yearned to escape. He had intended to fly to Israel for a weekend of business meetings and consultations with ministers, but suddenly the prospect appalled him. Even in Israel where he was so popular, the pressure would be unbearable. Instead, he wanted to be alone. Bob Cole, his long-suffering and faithful press officer, already knew of his new plan. In the early evening, Maxwell had embraced him. 'You're well on your way to being a good press officer,' he joked. 'But you will never be good for me. You still try to help the press. I want someone who will hinder the press.'

At 9 p.m., he told a secretary to telephone the *Lady Ghislaine* in Gibraltar and announce his arrival the next morning. He personally telephoned Captain David Whiteman, the pilot on duty: 'Get the Gulfstream ready for early tomorrow morning. We're going to Gibraltar.' The *Lady Ghislaine* was docked under the Rock, about to start a three-week crossing of the Atlantic because Maxwell wanted her to be berthed at the 34th Street marina in New York for Christmas Day. Given that most owners would prefer to be sailing in the sunny Caribbean rather than stuck in freezing Manhattan, the crew malevolently assumed that the Publisher needed to be near a hospital. None considered that perhaps he had found a woman friend whom he hoped to impress. In his last conversation with Captain Rankin earlier that day, Maxwell had been told that the weather forecast for an Atlantic crossing was perfect. 'I'll be leaving tomorrow morning,' said Rankin. Maxwell had not demurred.

The news of Maxwell's imminent arrival was brought to Rankin by a stewardess that evening while he enjoyed his 'last curry' in the town's centre: 'Mr Maxwell's coming at 9.30 a.m. and quote "This is no joke."' Rankin hurried back to the boat. At 11.06 he telephoned an MCC secretary in London, waking her. 'Do you know anything about Maxwell coming to Gibraltar?'

'No,' she replied.

Rankin rang Maxwell's flat. There was no answer. In desperation, he telephoned MAMI, the Gulfstream operations manager in Farnborough. 'It's true,' replied Chris Weller. 'The Gulfstream has already been moved from Farnborough to Luton for the early departure.'

Passing through the ninth-floor reception, meanwhile, Maxwell saw Featley, his chauffeur, leaning on a desk. 'Still here, John?' he asked. 'What are you doing?'

'Looking at the share price. It don't look too healthy.'

'Oh,' mumbled Maxwell with a weak smile, walking on. Then he turned. 'John, come here for a word. How's that football team of yours doing?'

'Oh fine, Mr Maxwell. Do you want me to give you a hand with all the stuff into the helicopter tomorrow morning?'

'If we want you, we'll call,' the Publisher said, stepping into the lift to travel to the tenth floor.

At 6.30 in the morning Rankin telephoned Maxwell. So many 'imminent arrivals' had been cancelled that he was still sceptical: 'I'm just confirming the instructions.'

'I'm coming. Do you need anything?' asked Maxwell.

'We've got no special food and the boat's ready for a storm crossing. The portholes are covered; everything's stowed. We're not ready.' Rankin feared Maxwell's explosion if denied his comforts.

'Don't worry,' urged Maxwell. 'So be it. I'll fit in around you. I've got to get rid of my cold.'

Rankin was not surprised by that remark. Maxwell, he knew, had been complaining about a cold since the summer. 'Are you bringing your butler?' he asked.

'No.'

'We don't have a chief stewardess. She's on leave.'

'Don't worry. We'll do our best. I'll fit in,' he repeated.

There was nothing unusual, Rankin believed, in Maxwell's decision to travel alone. During his summer cruise in Palma, neither a butler nor a secretary had sailed on the yacht.

'Where could we go?' asked Maxwell.

'Well, I'm heading towards Madeira for the crossing. It's 600 miles.'

'Fine, I'll fit in. Whenever you're ready, I'll be ready.'

Moments later, Maxwell walked up the iron stairs to the helicopter pad on the roof. Captain Dick Cowley, the pilot, was waiting. During the fifteen-minute flight across the darkened capital, Maxwell told his companion that he was heading for some sun.

'I'd go to Tenerife in the Canaries,' advised Cowley as Luton airport came into view.

Maxwell was travelling with less baggage than usual. Four document cases and one suitcase containing clothes were loaded. He was carrying two bundles of papers wrapped in pink ribbon: the lawyers' papers for his two defamation actions against Hersh and the BBC. As soon as the Gulfstream took off on its two-and-a-half-hour flight, he relaxed. 'He seems his normal self,' Captain Whiteman remarked to his co-pilot. In the cabin, Emma Cumming, the stewardess, served coffee and a light breakfast, also noting that her employer was in a good mood. Before they reached the crown colony, she had accepted his invitation to go on board the *Lady Ghislaine* in the port. Showing off his beloved yacht was a gesture Maxwell adored.

Rankin was waiting for him at Gibraltar's airport with two cars. Noting that the tycoon was in an unusually 'jovial' mood, he led the way to the harbour. After showing Emma around the yacht, Maxwell said to her, 'Tell Captain Whiteman to fly to Madeira. There's nothing for you to do here.'

Soon afterwards, having committed himself to the two-day journey to the Portuguese islands, Rankin swung the compass to check his bearings and, in good weather, set sail. 'I'm just here for the ride,' the owner told him and settled down to a routine he would enjoy over the next forty-six hours. Listening to music and reading documents, he appeared to the crew to be less busy than usual and trying to relax. The telephone calls were certainly fewer than on previous trips.

By then, Maxwell's disappearance from London was no longer a secret. Initially, his secretary Charlotte Thornton had obeyed his instructions not to reveal his whereabouts. Early that morning, Basil Brookes had arrived to offer his resignation, only to be told, 'Mr Maxwell is not in the country.' His first instinct was to telephone New York. 'Is he there?' Brookes asked David Shaffer, the president of Macmillan. 'No one will tell me where he is.'

Ernie Burrington, the veteran journalist, was better at extracting information. 'He's done a runner,' he told Guest.

Shortly afterwards, Ian Maxwell telephoned him. 'What's your man Lawrence Guest up to? After yesterday's board meeting he gave Clements an envelope. What's it all about?'

Burrington was able to explain. 'Clements had lost his Mirror Group prospectus and just wanted a copy.' Paranoia had infected another Maxwell.

As the *Lady Ghislaine* headed south-west towards the equator, Goldman Sachs fulfilled their threat, selling 2.2 million MCC shares. 'We gave him a warning,' said Sheinberg. To allow time for reflection, the American told Kevin that formal notification of the sale would be delayed for two days, the maximum allowed under the rules. Viewed from any aspect, it was the final threat in a bid to obtain repayment of some of the loan. 'We wanted to save the pain and hoped we could slip it out when no one noticed,' explained one banker, not realizing that the vault was empty. On the other hand, there was good reason for the bank's caution. Goldman Sachs held another 24.2 million MCC shares. To announce the sale brazenly would drive the price down, a self-inflicted wound.

To Kevin's horror, a Lehmans official was in the foyer of Maxwell House waiting to serve a default notice on BIM despite his father's conversation with Gregory the day before. Haas, it seemed, was aggressively seeking the bank's pint of blood. He had read Trachtenberg a list of BIM shares which were to be sold. Trachtenberg had said 'hold' only in relation to Teva before going to Kevin's office to reveal the news. The empire's survival was balanced on a knife edge.

On Kevin's instructions, Larry Trachtenberg had again telephoned Haas at 9.50 a.m.: 'I've just spoken to Kevin. He's pretty upset about his notice, 'cause even if we don't accept it, the fact that it's issued puts the entire group in default across the board, and his comment to me was that he doesn't think it is Lehmans' intention to bring down the entire group.'

'Certainly not,' replied Haas.

'This goes against the spirit of the conversation Robert Maxwell had with Joe Gregory.'

'We'll try and get New York,' replied the banker, without offering to withdraw the ultimate sanction and adding a further threat to sell MCC shares held as collateral.

Shortly after noon, as the *Lady Ghislaine* sailed from Gibraltar, Kevin was being urged by Haas, 'Your father should ring Joe Gregory. Joe can't get through to the boat.' In the meantime, asked the banker, knowing that their conversation was automatically being taped, 'Do you have the authority to approve the sale of the shares?'

'I'm a director and authorized to act for all the companies,' replied Kevin, including BIM in the list of his directorships. 'You always had the right to sell,' he added. The pension funds were on the verge of losing more shares, worth a total of $77 million.

That morning, Kevin was also visited by lawyers acting on behalf of Swiss Bank. The Fraud Squad, he was told by Rudi Bogni, would have to be informed of serious discrepancies in the failure to repay £55.7 million. 'A file is being compiled to present to the police. It will be delivered on 5 November unless we receive our money.'

In between, Kevin was also told that Citibank were selling MCC shares and that Lehmans would sell their Berlitz shares. Individually, each of the many bankers believed that he or she was astutely jumping to the front of the queue for repayment. Only Kevin, alone in his office, saw the whole picture, although those in the inner sanctum like Larry Trachtenberg understood the group's dire predicament. Yet when Basil Brookes entered, Kevin showed not a trace of concern. He was ice cool. 'I want to resign,' said Brookes.

'Please be patient,' Kevin replied. 'Talk to Dad. I'll ask him to telephone you.'

In Dorrington Street, Cook was at that moment listening to a manager of Capel Cure. 'There's something odd going on at Lehmans,' grumbled the BIM manager. 'We would seem to be getting offers of stock from traders, and we know we've got an interest in these shares.' After a pause, he cried, 'Shit, oh bugger it, I don't know what the hell's going on!'

FOURTEEN

Death

– 2 November 1991

In warm sunshine on Saturday, 2 November 1991, Maxwell was standing prominently on the *Lady Ghislaine*'s deck as the yacht inched her way into Funchal harbour, Madeira. To the handful of eyewitnesses, he seemed in a good mood. Evidently intent on enjoying himself while Captain Rankin completed the tedious harbour authority paperwork, the Publisher walked down the gangplank, stumbling slightly, and stepped into a taxi. With Mark Atkins, the rugby-playing second mate and former policeman acting as his bodyguard, he drove into the town. After unsuccessfully searching for a guidebook on Madeira, he bought some newspapers, visited the famous Reid's Hotel and, after drinking a beer at a bar, returned to the yacht.

Passing through waiting journalists, who were hoping for a quote about the continuing Mossad row in London, Maxwell told Rankin: 'I want to swim.' With the harbour master's permission, the captain swung the boat towards Desertas, a neighbouring island. Forty minutes later, he 'dropped the hook'. A nude Maxwell lowered himself down the steps into the water and squeezed his torso into a white lifebelt. After a few minutes' paddling he complained, 'It's too cold,' heaved his way up the steps to the crewman holding a towel and lay in the sun. The crew member pointed at an English newspaper published the previous day. Seeing his photograph on the front page, Maxwell groaned, 'Oh, more lies in the press.'

Pondering his fate, he decided that he needed to discuss everything with his sons. 'Tell Captain Whiteman to return to London and collect Kevin and Ian,' he instructed Rankin on the yacht's telephone. His next telephone call was to Kevin. Ten minutes later, Rankin called the pilot again: 'Cancel that trip to London.' Kevin had warned that his absence from London, even for a matter of hours, would be too dangerous.

Throughout that afternoon, the *Lady Ghislaine* rode at anchor in the bay. At dusk, Rankin steered back into Funchal harbour, 'an unpleasant place because of the heavy swell'.

That evening, after dining on the yacht, Maxwell went ashore again with Atkins as his bodyguard. Thirty minutes later, Atkins returned: 'He wants some money for the casino.' Rankin handed over $3,000 from the safe and Maxwell disappeared into the Ta-Madeira casino. After playing roulette for half an hour, he emerged having won a small amount and returned to the yacht to sleep for the night. Up on the bridge, Rankin assumed that, according to plan, Maxwell would return to London the following morning and the *Lady Ghislaine* would start her transatlantic crossing.

In London, Kevin had by nightfall manoeuvred the next way to obtain more money in order to avoid his nightmare, 'a meltdown'. Goldman Sachs were already selling MCC shares, while he sought to delay other banks by promising assets owned by the pension funds and MCC. Lehmans had, for the moment, stepped back from issuing the default notice after Kevin had signed a letter authorizing the bank to sell 22.8 million Teva shares as 'the absolute and beneficial owner ... and I authorize you to do all that you deem necessary for the purpose of acquiring such ownership'. Haas seemed placated by that perfection of the bank's legal rights. But now Citibank were persistently demanding repayment of $36.5 million for the phoney foreign exchange deal agreed by Bunn or threatening to sell without further notice MCC shares held as collateral. (Unsuccessfully, Kevin had sought to silence their demands with a small repayment of $3.5 million of the original $40 million.) Kevin had decided to divert the money from the imminent sale of Que, the world's largest computer book publisher owned by Macmillan. At a Macmillan board meeting on 25 October, Kevin and Ian had agreed to sell the company for $160 million and had authorized Shaffer to sign the agreement. (Que had previously been valued by MCC at $190 million.)

Late on Friday, 1 November, Kevin undertook the next step. In a short telephone conversation with John Bender, Macmillan's lawyer in New York, he ordered the American to sign a contract on Macmillan's behalf to transfer $36.5 million from the Que sale to a special new account at Citibank itself rather than into Macmillan's normal NatWest account.

Concerned, Bender telephoned David Fairfield at Titmuss Sainer (it was midnight in London) to ask whether under the arrangements between MCC and the private companies he could sign the transfer. 'We have spoken to Kevin Maxwell and can see no reason why you should not sign,' Fairfield later told Bender. The lawyer complied and Citibank waited for the money to arrive. Contrary to the procedures agreed in August with MCC's directors and reaffirmed just two days earlier, Kevin kept that agreement secret. But one bank had ceased harassing him, for the moment. To cover himself, however, he asked Philip Morgenstern, the solicitor, for a legal opinion about the transfer, since David Vogel had advised that it was not permitted. Morgenstern's reply appeared to answer Kevin's questions positively. But within the pages of legal gobbledygook, the lawyer told Kevin that MCC's money could not be used to pay off private debts. Kevin was not accustomed to act on unwelcome advice and was set on using the Que proceeds.

On Sunday morning, 3 November, Maxwell as usual awoke early. After breakfast in Funchal port, he watched Captain Rankin refuelling the yacht for the non-stop voyage to Bermuda. 'Is there an airport between here and Bermuda?' he asked casually. 'I'd just like to spend a few more days on the boat to get rid of this cold.'

'There're no airports,' replied Rankin. 'Nothing except ocean.'

'How long to Bermuda?'

'Nine days.'

'I can't stay away that long. If I want to stay on board, where else could we sail?'

'We could either go up to the Azores or down to the Canary Islands. If we go to the Canaries, we would be there tomorrow and the weather's good.'

'Right, that's it then.'

Rankin completed the chores and telephoned Captain Whiteman, the pilot: 'A change of plan. We're going to Tenerife. Be there by the morning.' In mid-afternoon, as the *Lady Ghislaine* set sail, Maxwell sat in the upper lounge, uninterrupted by any telephone calls or faxes, reading a book, listening to classical music and occasionally watching a video chosen from a new selection: *Hannah and Her Sisters*, *The Spy Who Loved Me* and Clint Eastwood's *The*

Gauntlet. For the first time, the page proofs of the following day's *Daily Mirror* were not faxed nor was Maxwell dispatching rewritten editorials. To the crew's bemusement, he was even complimenting them on their efforts. In a short conversation with Rankin, he condemned the *Panorama* and Hersh attacks as 'All lies'.

From the bridge, Rankin telephoned Maxwell: 'Captain Whiteman wonders whether you would like him to fly a couple of low passes over us on his journey to Tenerife?'

'Good idea!' exclaimed Maxwell. Another pilot had performed a similar stunt during his summer holidays, and it was good fun. Everyone seemed to enjoy the sight. One hour later, Whiteman's co-pilot, in radio contact with Rankin, announced his imminent arrival. 'He's coming on the left-hand side,' pronounced Maxwell, moving across the deck. Flying low over the yacht, Whiteman could clearly see the Publisher waving. After completing a second pass, the Gulfstream flew for another twenty-five minutes to land on the Spanish island, sixty miles off the north-west African coast.

On board that evening, Maxwell ate dinner and, as on the previous two nights, slept without complaining to the crew. But in the early hours of Monday, 4 November he again decided to change his plans. That evening he was due to give the keynote speech to the Anglo-Israeli Association in London, an invitation and an honour he had welcomed. Britain's Jews would be celebrating both the seventy-fourth anniversary of the Balfour Declaration, the keystone of Israel's existence, and the unprecedented discussions between Israel and the Palestinians due to be held in Spain. In other circumstances, Maxwell would have been proud to let the spotlight shine upon him, but his return to London, he knew, would be greeted with a rush of the very problems which he was trying to avoid.

Maxwell's next call, at 9.50 a.m., was to Kevin. The news was grim. Among the first messages his son had received that morning was that Lehmans were rejecting the shares offered as collateral by Maxwell the previous week, despite a letter from Trachtenberg which guaranteed, 'we are the absolute owners of all the securities free from all charges'. Worse, Trevor Cook had prevented the formal transfer of 'Lazard' shares, a package owned by the pension funds, to another bank. And the Maxwells' plan to use Telegraph shares as collateral had failed because they were subject to restrictions. Kevin added, 'Haas is complaining that they haven't received the $15 million you promised them.'

The implications were so obvious that few words needed to pass between father and son. Their safes were now practically bare. 'Lehmans are threatening to issue a default notice at the end of the day if we don't repay the loan,' Robert Maxwell was told. But still the tribulations did not end. Basil Brookes insisted on resigning. 'He wants to talk to you,' said Kevin.

'Put him on,' grunted Maxwell. Minutes later, Brookes telephoned. 'Please be patient,' urged the Publisher. 'I'll be back soon and we can settle everything.' Brookes seemed placated, temporarily at least. Neither father nor son, however, could claim to have produced any solutions.

By now, at 10.25 a.m., the *Lady Ghislaine* had sailed into Dársena Pesquera, a port two miles north of Santa Cruz, the attractive capital of Tenerife, where the Gulfstream was waiting to fly Maxwell home. Captain Whiteman and Emma, the stewardess, arrived at the quayside by taxi. The Publisher was leaning over the rail. He beckoned to them: 'Come up for some coffee.' The pilot found him in 'a fairly good mood' as he inquired about any future plans. 'I'll be leaving tomorrow,' said Maxwell, 'probably to London, but perhaps to Jerusalem or New York. Let's leave it flexible.'

Robert Keating, the yacht's chef, had just returned after an unsuccessful search for lobsters, and Maxwell was impatient to swim. 'Why can't we leave?'

'I'm waiting for the mate to change some money into pesetas,' said Rankin.

'You should have told me,' laughed Maxwell, pulling out a big roll of escudos. 'My winnings from the other night.'

While Rankin sailed south, searching for a suitable bathing spot, Maxwell telephoned Pisar. 'I've got a terrible cold,' he said. 'Could you give my speech to the Anglo-Israel Society?'

'I can't. I did it last year.'

'Can you write one for me, for Ian to deliver?'

For Pisar, the author of many books and speeches, it was an easy chore. 'Okay, Bob, I'll do that for you.' Pisar also mentioned that

President Mitterrand was proposing to award Maxwell the *Légion d'honneur*.

'Will the president award it himself?'

'I don't see why not,' replied Pisar, aware of his client's pride.

Replacing the receiver, Maxwell then rang Ian: 'I'm not coming back tonight. I still haven't got rid of my cold. Make my speech for me. Sam Pisar will help you write it.'

After a ninety-minute journey, at 12.50 Rankin anchored in Poris de Abona, a secluded but ugly spot with limited swell. Taken nearer to the shore by a tender, Maxwell descended into the sea and paddled in the water wearing the lifebelt. On his return, he went up to the wheelhouse. 'You're running the boat very well,' he told the captain. 'I'm very pleased. The crew, the food, are excellent. It's never been better.' Rankin, normally taciturn, was both gratified and surprised. Then the tycoon added, 'I've decided to stay one more night and fly home tomorrow. If it's calm, I'd prefer to sleep at sea. It's better than in port. Tomorrow you can leave for New York. And tell the chef, I shall be eating on shore tonight.' The two men then settled that Keating would return with Maxwell to London to learn from Martin Cheeseman the type of cooking which Maxwell enjoyed.

During the afternoon, Rankin passed on the latest plan to MAMI, Maxwell's flight managers at Farnborough. 'I'm going to cruise during the night and end up tomorrow morning at Los Cristianos on the south of the island. The Gulfstream should relocate there to take Mr Maxwell back to London.'

Meanwhile Maxwell spoke again to Pisar. The Frenchman mentioned that the speech would include a current joke deprecating Yasser Arafat, the PLO leader, and praising Yitzhak Shamir, the Israeli prime minister. Maxwell laughed and they agreed to speak again later that evening.

Other calls were less amusing. Bankers from the Banque Paribas and Crédit Lyonnais complained that loans had not been repaid, and Michael Richardson reported on MCC's falling share price. He and Maxwell arranged to meet the following day after the Publisher's return. In the midst of those calls, at 3.30 London time, Maxwell telephoned Ernie Burrington, who was finishing a late lunch in the Mirror Group executive dining room. 'Anything wrong?' asked Maxwell.

'Just the old money problems,' replied the managing director.

'I'm so sorry to have disturbed you,' sighed Maxwell, leaving Burrington eternally puzzled.

At 6.10 p.m., just as Rankin was sailing back to Santa Cruz, Lehmans sent Kevin a letter issuing a formal notice of default (on the Treasury bills) which was to expire at the end of business on 5 November, the following day. Another fax from Lehmans warned that the bank intended to seize 1.4 million Berlitz shares, although Kevin's urgent plea to Joe Gregory to hold back seemed momentarily to have delayed the fatal move. The next day was also the deadline for the announcement of Goldman Sachs' sale of MCC shares and the threat by Swiss Bank to complain formally to the Fraud Squad about the loss of £55.7 million. The ticking timebomb was uncomfortably audible, yet Kevin had concluded another of his unfulfillable foreign exchange deals, this time taking £20 million from Salomon Brothers in exchange for non-existent $35 million. In isolation, the threats would seem retrospectively final and fatal, yet the emergency that day was only slightly more severe than so many other crises over the previous weeks.

As Maxwell stepped ashore in Dársena Pesquera at 8.15 p.m., Ian was apologizing to the dinner-suited guests in London that his father was too unwell to attend: 'If ever there was a night my father would have wished to be here, this was it.' The speech he delivered was a hawkish attack on President Bush's decision to freeze loans to Israel: 'We Jews of the Diaspora and of Israel are willing to go into hock ourselves . . . No one can understand the world today and no one can understand Israel and the Jewish people unless they can appreciate how close Hitler came to wiping us out.'

Squashed into a Toyota Camry, Maxwell was at that moment being driven to the Hotel Mencey, the best in Santa Cruz. Wearing a beige blazer, check trousers and a blue baseball cap, he walked into the elegant, turn-of-the-century hotel perched on the hilltop. While the taxi driver warned the hotel's reception of the visitor's wealth, he was escorted along the high marble veranda to a corner table set for six in the empty restaurant. When he asked for a beer, Sergio Rodriguez, the waiter, brought two 'because he was so big'. On Rodriguez's recommendation, Maxwell ordered a green salad followed by hake with clams in parsley and mushroom sauce. While he waited, he ate an asparagus mousse dip and jabbed agitatedly on his non-functioning portable radio telephone linked to the *Lady Ghislaine*. After puffing on a Havana cigar, an unusual habit by this time, he paid his £24 bill and bid farewell. Rodriguez soon ran after him carrying his jacket. Maxwell, he thought, 'seemed preoccupied'.

Squeezing back into the waiting taxi, Maxwell remarked that the meal had been 'very good' and ordered the driver to take him to a coffee bar. After sitting outside the El Olimpio for fifteen minutes drinking a cappuccino, he asked if there were any flamenco shows. Since the nearest was twenty miles away, he abandoned the idea and returned to the harbour at 9.45. There, needing an extra 1,000 pesetas to tip the driver, amid laughter he borrowed a note from a crewman who had been guarding the boat. It was the last debt he would incur. It would not be repaid.

Throughout the hours the *Lady Ghislaine* had been moored in the harbour, Rankin had not mounted any special watch or guard. As usual, the entrance to the yacht up the gangway was monitored by the crew, but no precautions were taken on the waterside. Throughout the trip, Maxwell had never mentioned to Rankin that he feared for his life.

At 10 p.m., the captain gave the order to cast off. In his opinion, no one could have crept on to the boat unseen while she was tied up during the two hours in Santa Cruz. 'It was under proper watch,' he would claim. Considering the dearth of artificial light around the port and the lack of people on the quay in November, his certainty would be questioned by some, but not convincingly.

As he emerged from the harbour into the darkness, Rankin began plotting that night's course. After calculating that he needed to arrive at Los Cristianos ten hours later, he decided to head towards the north of Gran Canaria and then turn south. Travelling at a steady 14 knots, he would arrive on time. No one else, even Maxwell, knew the course they would sail during those hours.

The Publisher had gone directly to his bedroom. He made one telephone call that night. It was to Derek Haynes in Manchester. Five weeks earlier, Haynes had acrimoniously resigned at Maxwell's request as the managing director of the Mirror Group in the north. After thirty years' service, rising from a schoolboy apprentice, he had himself tired of Maxwell's increasingly irrational behaviour. 'He's gone mentally,' he complained as their disagreements grew more bitter. The demand for his departure had been unexpected, but it was no different from many others. 'Maxwell just tired of people,' he explained. At first he thought that the telephone call that night was a joke. But, once he recognized Maxwell's voice, Haynes bluntly refused to take the call. He was still furious about his treatment. He would remain forever baffled by the unexpected call, Maxwell's last.

On the boat, Maxwell changed into his nightgown. When Lisa Kordalski, the stewardess, entered to inquire if he had any other requirements, he simply asked for his bathroom door, which led into his study, to be locked. Kordalski would leave through the main door of the bedroom leading into the central stairway. As usual, since the cabin door would otherwise slide open, Maxwell turned the lock from the inside after she left.

Rankin was on the bridge when the satellite telephone rang at 10.40. 'Ian,' he told Maxwell as he connected the call. After hearing his son's report on the dinner, the father confirmed that he would return to London the following day. 'See you tomorrow,' ended Ian.

'You bet,' replied Maxwell, the last words he is known to have spoken to his family.

'No more calls,' ordered Maxwell. Ten minutes later, the telephone rang again. Rabbi Feivish Vogel of the Lubavitch wanted to discuss the recovery of Jewish archives from the Lenin Library in Moscow.

'Mr Maxwell is not taking any calls,' said Rankin.

'Oh please,' urged the rabbi, 'I'm calling from Moscow. It's so difficult to get through and it's urgent.' Rankin relented and buzzed Maxwell.

'Okay,' said Maxwell. 'But absolutely no more.'

Rankin stayed on the bridge until midnight. Nothing in Maxwell's voice or routine alerted him that anything was other than normal. Control of the *Lady Ghislaine*, cruising five miles off the coast of Gran Canaria, was handed over to Grahame Shorrocks, the mate, while Rankin went to sleep in his cabin adjoining the bridge. His only possible exit from his cabin was through the bridge and past the two members of the duty crew. His last order was succinct: 'Call me if any craft shows up on the radar within five miles.' He would remain undisturbed throughout the night. The radar never revealed that any craft approached within five miles of the *Lady Ghislaine*. Rankin would later insist that the security cameras were active throughout the night, although that was disputed.

Knowing Maxwell's habits, the crew habitually left food both in his room and in the kitchen refrigerator for him to eat during the night. He certainly ate two bananas in his cabin, leaving the skins on unopened Sunday newspapers.

As he lay amid the splendours of his yacht, Maxwell's torment was irrepressible. Financial ruin appeared inevitable. The tidal wave of social scorn that must ensue would be intolerable. His loneliness would be exacerbated. Unlike Gerald Ronson, who would actually be jailed, Maxwell could not expect any family support during his tribulations. At the age of sixty-eight, he would become immersed in yet another solitary fight for survival.

Battles were nothing new in his life. There was no fear of the mystery that might lie ahead of him. Anyone who had fought on the front line from the Normandy beaches to Germany, facing constant danger and death for months on end from the enemy's snipers and shells, was unlikely to suffer fear. And he had overcome much worse. The humiliation after the insolvency in 1954 of the publishing warehouse Simpkin Marshall, the excoriation heaped upon him in 1971 by the DTI inspectors after the Pergamon disaster and his triple defeat in the parliamentary elections of 1970 and 1974 had all been survived. He had fought back to be fêted by kings, queens, presidents and prime ministers. Despite all his enemies, he had, like Lazarus, risen from the dead. Having cheated Hitler and the Holocaust, he could survive, fight and win again.

The turmoil which he anticipated the following day prevented him from sleeping, and his Halcion tablets, a favourite for some time, had had no effect. At 4.25 in the morning of what was now Tuesday, 5 November, he unlocked his cabin door, traversed the staircase area, slid open a glass door and walked on to the rear deck. Leonard Graham, the second engineer, having escaped the heat of the engine room, was leaning against the rail, gazing out to sea. Turning around, he saw the yacht's owner dressed in a V-neck nightgown. After exchanging pleasantries, Maxwell complained: 'The temperature in my room is too hot. Could you adjust the air conditioning?' The engineer immediately returned to the engine room. Although the security cameras were on, that encounter was not seen by Mark Atkins in charge in the wheelhouse: that aft deck was not covered by the cameras.

Twenty minutes later, at 4.45, Maxwell called the wheelhouse. 'The temperature is now too cold. Turn the air conditioning off.' Atkins passed on the order. It was the first time during the voyage that Maxwell had complained about the temperature on the yacht. Indeed, he had rarely mentioned the temperature on previous trips.

Some time during the next hour and a half, the final ninety minutes before dawn, Maxwell again left his cabin and walked to the end of the lower deck, his favourite spot, not least because a telephone was fixed to the rail. As he stood watching the lights of Las Palmas twinkling in the near distance, he felt unwell. His unsteadiness in recent days, aggravated by lack of sleep, the pressure of financial ruin and exhaustion from constant travel suddenly became much worse. Grossly overweight, with only one functioning lung, sclerosis of the liver and a constricted artery leading to an enlarged heart, not to mention the effect of all the various drugs he ingested, he was anyway in appalling health.

Propelled either by a light heart attack or by unexpected dizziness, he stumbled against the rail, which was particularly low where he was standing, and toppled forward. Stretching out his left hand, he sought to steady himself. As a right-handed man, he lacked the strength to halt his fall. Determined to survive, he grabbed the rail and hung there, twisting, his twenty-two stone held by no more than his feeble left arm. Within seconds, muscles in his body ripped in three places, causing internal bleeding. In excruciating pain, he fell barely ten feet into the sea: in circumstances which could result in neither further injury nor immediate drowning. His cries could not be heard from the wheelhouse nor could the commotion be seen in the darkness. All eyes up there were looking forward, blind to events below and behind. At some stage, to improve his buoyancy, he discarded his nightgown. In his last moments, he inhaled some water, marking his lungs with froth. Whether he died from exhaustion or from an immediate heart attack as he bobbed, breathless and in pain, on the surface of the dark sea could never be established. But, for certain, he had not chosen a slow, lingering, unpredictable way to die. His natural impatience would have excluded anything so time-consuming.

At 6.30 a.m., dawn, Rankin was back in the wheelhouse as the

Lady Ghislaine headed towards Los Cristianos. At 9.45, he guided the yacht to anchor in the waters just off the unlovely seaside resort. While waiting for Maxwell to leave the ship, he telephoned a shipping agent in Santa Cruz to organize refuelling.

In London, Kevin was sitting with a journalist from the *Financial Times*. After diligent research at Companies House, she had produced the first scheme of the Maxwells' many-tentacled empire and, after calculating the debts of the 400 companies, concluded that the family's debts amounted to a staggering £2.2 billion. Kevin did not deny her conclusions but naturally denied the inference: 'For the first time in years it's not much of a strain on us all.' The article would be published the following morning under conditions which neither had anticipated.

At 10.30 a.m., Robert Pirie, the Rothschilds banker, called the *Lady Ghislaine* hoping to put a client's proposition to Maxwell. 'He's still asleep,' said Rankin. 'Is it important enough to disturb him?'

'No,' replied Pirie.

At 11 a.m., John Bender, the Macmillan lawyer, called. It was 6 a.m. in New York but Bender, disturbed by his orders to deposit the Que money in a special account, wanted to challenge Maxwell.

'He's asleep. Is it important?'

'Yes,' replied Bender. 'Imperative.'

Rankin buzzed Maxwell's bedroom. There was no reply. Calmly, he began buzzing telephones in other rooms where the Publisher could have been sitting. No reply. 'That was the first inkling that something wasn't right,' he would later explain. He had not telephoned the stewardesses to inquire whether they had seen their employer that morning.

His next call was to Robert Keating, the chef. Rankin suggested that they go together to Maxwell's cabin. The captain's unconvincing explanation for this plan was that Keating was trained in heart resuscitation and he suspected that Maxwell had suffered a heart attack. The two men tried the study door into the cabin's bathroom. It was locked. Walking around to the main door in the rear, they knocked, then banged; hearing no reply, they tried to open it. It was, claimed Rankin, also locked. Using a pass key, he slid it open. 'I was expecting to find Maxwell lying unconscious on his bed or on the deck. I was surprised. He wasn't there.' It was 11.15.

'Where is he?' wondered Rankin. 'He's trying to evade us some-where on the boat. I haven't put the calls through to the right place.' The whole crew hunted through the yacht, from top to bottom, side to side. Then they repeated the exercise, three times. 'We were even opening drawers, we were so confused,' admitted Rankin.

Perplexed, a crew member called out, 'Look, there's somebody swimming near the shore!'

Searching through binoculars, Rankin saw a black-haired man. 'He's gone for a swim!' he shouted, apparently forgetting that during the trip Maxwell had swum only inside a lifebelt. 'Get the boat to bring him back.' Through the binoculars, he watched the swimmer emerge from the sea on to the beach: 'I could tell it wasn't Maxwell.'

At 11.45, it was, Rankin recalled, 'beginning to sink in' that Maxwell was not on the boat. But no crew member had seen him go over the side. Rankin went to the wheelhouse to call Gomera Radio, the local SOS station, by radio. No one spoke English. Rankin called John Hamilton, a shipping agent in Santa Cruz: 'This is serious, please call the authorities in Los Cristianos on my behalf and explain what's happened.' Grahame Shorrocks, the first officer, set off at 11.50 by tender to ask the harbour master to raise the alarm.

At 12.02, Rankin telephoned MAMI in Farnborough. The call was taken cheerfully by Brian Hull, the pilot. 'How are things?'

'We're not doing very well,' replied Rankin. 'We've lost Mr Maxwell.'

'Don't worry, Gus,' said Hull supportively. 'He's probably nipped into town and not told anybody.'

'But we're still at sea, Brian.' There was silence. 'Who should I tell, Brian?' asked Rankin.

'You'd better phone Kevin,' advised Hull, understanding only too well why Rankin was subdued. He'd just lost the boss. Kevin would be more concerned than Mrs Maxwell, thought Hull. 'Roll out the G2,' ordered the pilot, realizing that another plane would be needed in the emergency.

At 12.10, Rankin sent his first SOS on the satcom to the emergency station in Norway – the co-ordinating site, he wrongly believed, for the area. It was now one hour after Maxwell had been found to be missing. The response was not encouraging. 'I'm sorry,

I can't help you,' replied the Norwegian operator. Rankin, without any experience in such an emergency, was flummoxed. Quite simply, he did not know what to do. He paused. 'Don't hang up,' interrupted an American voice. It was an eavesdropping satcom operator in New York. 'I'll connect you to the New York coast-guard.' At 12.20, having telexed his alert to the New York coast-guard, the captain read a message on the Imersat communications system reporting that Maxwell was missing. By then, he had calcu-lated on his chart the position of the yacht at 5 a.m., the last time Maxwell was known to have been on board: 27 degrees 39' north, 15 degrees 39' 15" west, course 286 true.

Having tied up the boat alongside a quay, he called Captain Whiteman, the pilot, at the Los Cristianos airport: 'I can't tell you on the telephone what's happened. Just come down here as fast as possible.' When Whiteman saw him shortly afterwards and heard the news, he thought that Rankin 'looked shaken', but the captain 'had no explanation of what had happened to Mr Maxwell'.

Rankin braced himself to call Kevin. 'This is very important,' he told the secretary in a call which strangely enough would not be registered on the satcom list of charges. In the preceding minutes, Kevin had bid farewell to the journalist. His well-rehearsed self-portrayal of financial probity, he knew, would need to be repeated throughout the day. Elsewhere in the building, Sir Michael Richard-son was discussing with a group of financial advisers MCC's forth-coming half-yearly results, which for the first time would reveal a loss. The calamitous effect on the share price, Kevin knew, did not require much imagination.

But the most imminent dangers were the announcement of Gold-man Sachs' sale of MCC shares and whether the Swiss Bank would fulfil their threat to complain formally to the Fraud Squad. Those thoughts were interrupted by Rankin's call.

'I'm sorry to tell you that your father's gone overboard during the night. We've looked everywhere. We just can't find him. I've alerted all the emergency services.'

There was a pause. 'Call me back in ten minutes,' said Kevin, rapidly shedding his customary cool.

'He's flabbergasted,' thought Rankin, who believed himself to be 'in a situation of disbelief'. At 12.40, he called again. In the meantime, Kevin had summoned Ian to his office. The two brothers listened in shocked silence as Rankin repeated his earlier report. There was little more he needed to say. The captain had lost their father.

'I don't care how much it costs for rescue planes,' said Kevin, 'just find the body.' Rankin passed the message on to Madrid control.

After telephoning members of their family, Ian Maxwell summoned Ernie Burrington: 'Dad's missing, lost overboard.' Burrington looked at both sons. Neither was tearful. Both behaved, thought the managing director, as if they had prepared themselves for that moment.

'We must keep this quiet,' ordered Kevin instinctively.

'We can't,' sighed Burrington. 'Our people will read it in tonight's *Evening Standard* and tomorrow's *Sun*. We'll look stupid.'

'It's an accident,' said Ian.

'Yes, an accident,' agreed Kevin.

'I know you're under stress, but it's not proven. We can't speculate.'

'Ernie, you must take charge of the press—PR side of this,' said Kevin.

'I would if I had nothing else to do. Give it to Charlie Wilson. He's doing nothing.' Accordingly, the former editor of *The Times* was appointed spokesman for the Maxwell family, a task to which he was ideally suited.

Exterior reality drowned Kevin's emotions. When his father's disappearance became known, he realized, the share prices would spiral down. Desperately, he sought Sir Michael Richardson, who had left the building and disappeared for a lunch appointment. Next he searched for Ian McIntosh, but the Samuel Montagu director had also vanished into a City hostelry. He settled on Clive Chalk, a junior colleague of McIntosh, and urged him to come to Holborn immediately.

If at that moment, 2 p.m. in London, an hour ahead of Tenerife time, Kevin had glanced at the stock exchange screen, he would have noticed a short statement ribboning across: it was the announcement that Goldman Sachs' holding in MCC had been reduced. MCC's share price was drifting down to 130p. Across the City's trading rooms, those cognoscenti following Maxwell's fortunes understood precisely the implications. Telephones were lifted and more MCC shares offered for sale. Kevin authorized a press release about the sale.

At 2 p.m., a Goldmans executive watching the screen gasped. MCC's price was tanking: 'Everyone's selling!' Clive Chalk was at that moment in Kevin's office telephoning the stock exchange's Quotation Committee. 'Maxwell is missing at sea,' said the banker, trusting that the conversation would remain confidential, unaware that Captain Rankin's alert was being simultaneously flashed around the Atlantic. 'MCC and Mirror Group shares should be suspended.' The circumstances made the request highly unusual. The official asked for time to consider. By 2.20, when Richardson was walking into the distraught atmosphere of Kevin's office, the news of Maxwell's disappearance had leaked, although the reports spoke of the *Lady Ghislaine* sinking. Richardson, who had known both Maxwells as young children, found the 'boys' white-faced. 'Dad's missing,' Kevin told him.

If anyone beyond the three Maxwells ought to have suspected the precarious state of the empire, it was Richardson, the salesman of Maxwell's shares, yet he would plead ignorance. 'He was squeaky-clean with me,' Richardson would repeat with growing fondness. 'There'll be a false market if trading continues,' he warned an official at the stock exchange. Even Richardson's stature was insufficient to overcome institutional reticence immediately. Bureaucrats have many things other than facts and arguments to consider, principally their own position before taking an initiative. Richardson's intervention was treated with great caution. Turning to look back at the sons, the banker felt genuine pity. There was so much to say, but nothing that seemed appropriate.

Outside, across the City, the financial village was ablaze with rumours. Telephones were ringing as those seeking profits, fearing losses or wanting to report the news sought confirmation or staked a position. Few found themselves in a stranger situation than Goldman Sachs. For some weeks, Eric Sheinberg had been running a bear raid on behalf of clients against MCC's shares, earning good profits as the price fell; and since 31 October Goldmans had been selling the shares on their own account to recoup the unpaid loans.

That lunchtime, Sheinberg was as usual watching the screen. No trace of emotion showed in his face as MCC's price fell, although he did not appreciate one unprofitable irony. As the bank sold their own MCC shares, they were simultaneously compelled as an MCC market-maker to buy shares, and they were buying in faster than they could reduce their price. When a telephone message was passed to him reporting that his client was missing, Sheinberg's expression remained unaltered. Adhering to his own dictum, 'When things don't go well, don't panic,' he remained cool but concerned – mostly for his bank's huge remaining stakes in MCC and Mirror Group, and for his own reputation. Nevertheless, he was among the first who were spotted passing speedily that afternoon through the entrance hall of Maxwell House up to Kevin's office.

When Sheinberg arrived, Ian's tears were evident, while Kevin seemed cool, even desiccated: the chief executive within him rather than the mourner had already decided that salvation depended upon retaining total self-control. Having spoken to his mother and arranged for her and his brother Philip, fluent in Spanish, to fly to Tenerife, Kevin allowed himself little time for grief, for he knew the position of the Sword of Damocles. His only respite came at 2.58 when the shares were suspended.

Around Gran Canaria, the search for Maxwell had been under way since 1.10 p.m. London time, two hours after the first distress message had been transmitted by the Spanish authorities. It would be another ninety minutes before two helicopters were dispatched. In the meantime, Rankin, accompanied by Whiteman, had been summoned to the harbour master's office to sign a form declaring that he had requested assistance. The harbour master himself had done nothing to satisfy the plea. Rankin then drove to the local police station, situated in the basement of a hideous concrete tower block. In retrospect, even he spotted the irony. In the tatty, brash awfulness of Los Cristianos, the cheap haven for sunseekers, he was surrounded at the police station by cheats queueing on the eve of their return home to register 'thefts' for insurance claims.

While Rankin was ashore, Betty Maxwell called the yacht for information; and at 3.20 the first newspaper called. The *New York Post* was checking a report that the *Lady Ghislaine* had been lost at sea. The crew had already been told to refer all messages to Charles Wilson in London.

At 5.25 p.m., after a fisherman had reported sighting a body, a Spanish rescue plane roared over the *Lady Ghislaine* and thirty minutes later buzzed confirmation on the radio. The position was given as about twenty-eight miles off the coast of Gran Canaria, and about a hundred miles east of Tenerife. The co-ordinates were 27 degrees 46.6 north, 16 degrees 0.6 west. Assuming Maxwell had gone overboard around 5 a.m., his body had drifted about fifteen miles. Since it was unusual for a body not to have been swept away for ever by currents in that area, it was later assumed that Maxwell might have survived for some time, treading water before dying.

At 6.46, a Superpuma helicopter hovered over the recognizable corpse. 'It was naked, stiff and floating face up, not face down which is normal,' reported the pilot. Fat and gasses, in unusually large quantities, had kept Maxwell afloat and face up. Guided by a searchlight, the crew struggled to winch the twenty-two stone corpse on to their craft. Rankin passed on the news simultaneously to Kevin's office. The son, chairing an emergency MCC board meeting, broke down in tears.

Outside the Mirror building, an army of excited journalists with cameras and glaring television lights had gathered for comment. Bracing himself for his first public performance, guided by Wilson, Kevin led his elder brother out to utter the first of many public statements over the coming five weeks: 'Love him or hate him he touched the lives of many millions of people.'

At that moment, the body was being transported by helicopter in the darkness to Gando military airport on Gran Canaria. Wearing black, Betty and Philip Maxwell landed at the same airbase at 8.30 p.m. and, accompanied by the deputy judge, walked across the tarmac to identify the body, which had been moved to the Salón de Juntas, a room in the airport building reserved for important meetings. The mortal remains of Betty's husband, whom she had met forty-seven years earlier, as a poor, handsome, idealistic and courageous soldier, lay on the helicopter's stretcher on a table. At 9 p.m. the mother and son walked towards the corpse covered by an orange sheet of heavy plastic.

There was silence in the room as the plastic was lifted and Betty nodded. No tears showed as she murmured, 'He's a colossus lying there, as he'd been in life.' Eyewitnesses say that she was 'composed, calm and dignified'. Tears fell from Philip. Betty was questioned by Dr Carlos Lopez de Lamela, director of the local forensic institute where the autopsy would be conducted. Asked whether Maxwell could have committed suicide, she replied, 'It is absolutely out of the question.' Lamela asked about his medical history and the drugs which he took. Betty revealed that her husband had been taking drugs to counter his pulmonary oedema. Other medicines were mentioned. Twenty minutes had passed. 'As far I'm concerned, we're done,' announced Lamela.

The formalities completed, a local judge ordered the helicopter to deliver the body of Robert Maxwell to the morgue in Las Palmas. After speaking to her two sons in London, Betty flew to Los Cristianos and at midnight boarded the *Lady Ghislaine* accompanied by two *Daily Mirror* journalists. Minutes later, Gus Rankin and members of the crew returned after questioning, accompanied by the police. Although Maxwell's cabin had been sealed by the authorities, the crew were allowed to roam elsewhere on the yacht. To their surprise, the widow was not grieving. There were no tears. 'What do you think happened?' asked Betty in a businesslike voice.

'I can only imagine suicide,' replied Rankin, apparently surprised by the question from a woman he had not previously met.

'Impossible. He'd never do that,' declared Betty imperiously.

Solving the mystery of Maxwell's death depended upon the police investigation. But, by the time Betty boarded the yacht, any hope of finding forensic evidence was fast disappearing. Unaware of Robert Maxwell's controversial life, the police were negligently unsuspicious. Tests were not conducted on the rails, decks or walls. Worse still, despite the earlier order that no one was to enter Maxwell's bedroom, the police agreed that Betty could sleep there. The seals were removed and the stewardesses allowed to clear up the mess of the owner's last night and the untidiness caused by the search in the previous thirteen hours. If any clues to his disappearance were to be found on the cabin's carpets or furniture, they were swept aside for ever as the two girls cleaned the room – noting that his nightgown was not among the discarded clothes. That night, Betty Maxwell slept for the first time in years in her husband's bed.

FIFTEEN

Deception

– 6 November 1991

Kevin Maxwell awoke on Wednesday, 6 November 1991 to discover that his father's death had provided a strange and unexpected breathing space. The flood of tributes and condolences abruptly silenced the media's clamour for blood. In the metropolis where Maxwell had sought to impose his writ, the deceased was given the universal attention he had spend his lifetime seeking.

Momentarily, Robert Maxwell's death preoccupied people in many parts of the world. Broadcasts in every language announced his passing and recited his achievements. As with the assassination of John Kennedy and the resignation of Margaret Thatcher, many would never forget where and how they heard the news. Tributes flowed from world leaders praising his character, his wide-ranging interests and his humanitarian activities. Douglas Hurd, the British foreign secretary, declared that his death 'robbed Britain of one of our most colourful and energetic figures'. According to the prime minister John Major, 'He was a great character who will be missed.' Neil Kinnock recorded, 'I valued his personal friendship.' Presidents Mitterrand, Bush and Yeltsin, Gorbachev's successor, all added eulogies.

Within Kevin's own organization, Richard Stott, the squat editor of the *Daily Mirror*, outperformed his habitual obsequiousness towards the family by transforming his newspaper into a panegyric, adopting Maxwell's own assessment that he had been the 'man who saved the *Mirror*'. Unusually the tabloid sensation-seekers were emotional about their proprietor's death. Eyes were even moist as they chronicled the life of their erstwhile bully. No eulogy would be more craven than that of Joe Haines, a director of the Mirror Group. Under the headline, 'Turbulent Colossus', he painted a picture of a courageous hero whom he 'ended up loving or at least standing in awe of.' However, not all voices were so compassionate that day. Kevin would naturally ignore the *Independent*'s judgment that his father had been a 'liar, a cheat and a bully [who] did more than any other individual to pervert the British law of libel', and he would also disregard the opinion of *The Times* that he was 'an egoist and a monstrously improbable socialist'.

Others, including Seymour Hersh, were already hinting that this had not been a natural death but was 'directly linked' to Maxwell's Mossad-controlled participation in gun-running, money-laundering and worse. 'There is a lot more involved in this story than has come out,' alleged Matthew Evans, Hersh's publisher, suggesting suicide but hinting at murder.

Kevin's meetings started early that day. In fact, they had continued for much of the previous night. For the first time, there was no reason to be frightened of his father or to act under duress. He was now his own man, answerable to no one, responsible for his own actions. Here was the defining moment of his own morality and his own complicity. Free of Maxwell's domination, he might immediately have confessed to an unease about his father's methods or doubts about the finances. But that was not the nature of the thirty-two-year-old. Emphatically, he rejected that option. Instead, generating new energy, he chose to continue as before. Kevin Maxwell irreversibly crossed the Rubicon with never a backward glance.

The breathing space provided by the media did not embrace the familiar army of visitors. To those dozens of bankers, brokers and executives passing on the conveyor belt through Kevin's office on the night of his father's death, the new emperor was a man not to be berated but pitied. All had witnessed Robert Maxwell humiliating his son, ordering him to 'Shut up', castigating him for voicing opinions and cowing him into nervous silence. Surely his son, so viciously maligned by the ogre, would transform the companies, free them from the autocracy he had inherited.

The sympathy for Kevin during his father's lifetime hardened into greater trust after the death. His frill-free intelligence and cool mastery of finance attracted admirers and inspired confidence among the majority of his peers. Those who had perceived his involvement in any uncertainties preferred to place the blame upon his father. Accordingly, Kevin's visitors, prefacing their discussions with expressions of condolence, suppressed any suspicions of the son's deliberate wrongdoing. His self-nomination to succeed his father as chairman of MCC would be accepted. Ian would inherit the chairmanship of the Mirror Group. The family's stranglehold would be preserved. Indeed, some even wanted to jump on to the ship before the first dawn broke.

Just hours after the Publisher's corpse had been heaved on to the helicopter, Scott Marden, writing as the managing director of Wertheim Schroder, the merchant bank in New York, suggested that he join MCC as Kevin's deputy and help turn the company around. Marden, married to Kevin's former secretary Sarah Nurse, had been previously employed by Bankers Trust. His self-promotion was as breathtaking as his opportunism and reflected the types to whom Kevin was attracted. 'Aside from you,' wrote Marden, 'there isn't any other person I know of who has the combination of investment banking skills . . . ability to deal with banks or reputation which I have.' After quick negotiations, Marden would send Kevin a draft contract which included an annual salary of $500,000, a 20 per cent cash bonus and the receipt of 1 million MCC shares per year. The American's dream was unrealized, yet he and Kevin clearly believed that the gravy train still operated, an opinion not shared by all those eager to see the new chairman hours after his father's disappearance was announced.

To the familiar army of bankers and brokers whose clamour for the repayment of loans had dominated the previous weeks, Robert Maxwell's death looked suspiciously like suicide. His reason, they guessed, was the possible collapse of the empire. Eschewing any sensitivity, these professionals thought up ruses to secure their millions ahead of the pack. Some had chanced their approach in the first hours of Kevin's grief. On the evening of 5 November, Richard Pelly of Barclays Bank had rushed to see the new chairman to retrieve a loan of $30 million. The banker was rewarded with an unorthodox and probably illegal method of repayment which suggested that, for the bereaved son, even that night had been business as usual. Kevin proposed that RMG transfer £27 million of the debt owed to Barclays to the pension funds. 'I'll sell the pension funds the private side's property portfolio worth £80 million,' continued Kevin, 'and that will be the security for the bank. And I'll use that £80 million to repay other debts.' Soon after daybreak, Pelly told Kevin that his superiors rejected the idea.

Briefly, Kevin had also closeted himself that night with David Vogel, his solicitor. A nearby television was blaring – everyone was waiting for the next news broadcast. Sitting alongside was Larry Trachtenberg. The American was reciting an awesome list of the empire's problems – rattling off banks, debts and default notices. Then, as Kevin wandered out of the room, Trachtenberg added one of the solutions: 'RMG is owed substantial sums by MCC.' The lawyer understood that the money, to be transferred after the sale of Que publishing, would alleviate the pressure.

At seven on the morning of 6 November the solicitor was back in Kevin's office. 'The creditors are knocking at the door,' said Kevin. Among his list of unremovable problems was the Swiss Bank. 'Comfort equals half the Que proceeds,' he said, deciding to offer the bank $80 million of MCC's money.

Among the next to enter Kevin's office were Lawrence Guest and Ernie Burrington. Overcoming their previous timidity, the two Mirror Group executives, with Ian sitting silently nearby, voiced unease. 'When are we getting the £38 million back?' asked Guest.

'The money is in gilts,' bluffed Kevin, 'but now we've lost our expertise in gilt trading we'll close our positions next Monday and get the money back.' Guest has not yet seen the contract notes but, hearing the promise uttered so emphatically, he accepted Kevin's word. Unknown to the finance director, the problem was much worse. Since 29 May, the three Maxwells and Michael Stoney had signed twenty-six cheques transferring £121 million from the Mirror Group to BIM and American banks to settle private debts.

Among the later callers, each given ten minutes, was the familiar cast of consorts and creditors: Julie Maitland of Crédit Suisse, Mike Moore of Bankers Trust, Ian McIntosh of Samuel Montagu, David Leal-Bennett of NatWest, and whole gangs from the Swiss Bank Corporation and the Sumitomo Bank. None was more active than the smooth Sir Michael Richardson, scurrying back and forth, 'to help the boys', while in contrast, Eric Sheinberg of Goldman Sachs, among the most pressing of the visitors, replied brusquely to Kevin's request for more time: 'It's got beyond the stage of promises.' In humiliating circumstances, Kevin agreed to the request that he personally sign the receipt for the Lehmans default notice. He hoped that he could tap the remaining goodwill in London to stem the renewed threat.

'Some foreign banks are threatening to default on loans to the private side,' Kevin told Leal-Bennett later that morning. The fall in MCC's share price would destroy the collateral. 'Everything is up for sale, including the boat,' continued Kevin, before asking one more favour. 'Could you look after my mother's day-to-day bills? There's a problem with her account at Coutts.'

The banker agreed. 'Kevin will need a window,' Leal-Bennett noted, the jargon referring to his client's requirement for time.

Kevin found time for Basil Brookes and Trevor Cook, and for Ray Snoddy from the *Financial Times*. The friendly journalist could, he hoped, be relied upon to spread reassurance. An internal memorandum by Brian Brown of Lloyds summarized the opinion of the more gullible visitors. 'Kevin', he wrote, 'appears to be well on top of the situation. If there are any problems, the most likely cause will be a bank or banks running for the hills.' Like all the visiting bankers, Brown knew that the empire was on the brink of collapse but hoped it would survive.

Peter Laister felt no less benign. After driving through the night from France, he arrived in time for the MCC board meeting at 11 a.m. Like all the other loyal executives, he sympathized with Maxwell's family and wanted to help rebuild the company. 'I felt sorry for Kevin and Ian,' he recalled. 'After all the ups and downs with Bob, I thought we had to help his sons.' Although the majority of the board seemed to want Laister as chairman, they bowed to Kevin's insistence that the non-executive would be his deputy. Basil Brookes agreed to defer his resignation, reflecting an unspoken relief among the directors, who now expected to enjoy greater freedom to restore the business.

To all these visitors, Kevin seemed a model of virtue and calm. No one, absolutely not one of those professionals, voiced any recognition that they were addressing the architect of the manipulations still so cunningly concealed. Taking advantage of that sympathy, Kevin continued with his strategy, hoping to win extra time – though to what end was unclear. 'He must have foreseen something credible to save the empire,' reasoned Jean-Pierre Anselmini, 'considering that he was on the verge of destroying his career to win an extra month.' Even Anselmini, an eyewitness of the private companies' financial mayhem and a handsomely paid escapee, had been deluded about the extent of the manipulation over the previous twelve months. 'They're all fools,' Kevin smiled to himself.

Kevin's contempt flowed through every meeting and telephone conversation that morning. To George Marlatte, a vice-president of the Bank of Nova Scotia, Kevin spoke of a 'pool of £400 million still free to be pledged by the private side'. He added, 'I'm thirty-two years old, and I hope we can still have a long relationship with the bank.' He would play the age card several times during that period. Connected to four Lehmans bankers listening alongside three lawyers in a conference call between London and New York, Kevin agreed that BIM should repurchase the Teva shares, although towards the end he cursed Gregory for his mealy-mouthed apologies. 'This is all bullshit,' he shouted into the intercom. 'I want as much time as you can give me. How much time can you give me?'

'Until tomorrow,' offered Gregory, gazing at the bank of screens dealing in the $110 billion worth of securities he controlled. 'You gotta show us the colour of your money.'

To Rudi Bogni of the Swiss Bank, whose threat to approach the 'authorities' was still dangling, once more demanding his £55.7 million, Kevin blamed the sale of First Tokyo's shares on 'a security dealer's oversight' and promised that 'the position would be made good'. Kevin offered alternative shares as collateral without revealing that most were already pledged, and then offered 'half the Que proceeds'.

When the Macmillan lawyer John Bender telephoned from New York, he received renewed instructions to pay the proceeds of the Que sale into the special Citibank account, to pay off a private debt, the very issue about which he had fatefully telephoned Robert Maxwell on the *Lady Ghislaine*. Now, he was simultaneously told to sign an agreement to sell Macmillan's 56 per cent interest in Berlitz to Fukutake, the Japanese company. Kevin's voice, Bender noted in retrospect, sounded 'normal'. There was no hint that, as Kevin knew, the majority of those same Berlitz shares had been pledged to banks.

Nor did Kevin grow flustered when David Shaffer, the president of Macmillan, telephoned with alarming news from New York. Lehmans had filed an interest in 10 per cent of Berlitz with the New York stock exchange. 'How do you think they acquired that big stake?' asked Shaffer. 'There's been no trade in that stock.'

'I don't know,' replied Kevin in a flat, unemotional voice. 'I'll have someone investigate.'

Later in London, Laister asked Kevin for a similar explanation. 'I don't know anything about it,' he was told.

Laister departed satisfied: 'It didn't dawn on me that Kevin was lying.'

In Tenerife, Betty Maxwell had made some progress arranging her husband's funeral. Two years earlier Maxwell had told Yaakov Neeman, his small, balding Israeli lawyer, that he wanted to be buried on the Mount of Olives, the holiest of Israel's cemeteries in Jerusalem where Jews were first interred 3,000 years before. 'I want to be near my parents,' he later told Betty. He was referring to the stone obelisk in the Yad Vashem memorial engraved with the name of his village, Solotvino. The tragedy of the Holocaust had by then completely permeated his life. 'I cannot ever forget it. I can't forgive it,' he murmured of his parents' murder. 'I was my mother's favourite.' Within that tormented tyrant was a small boy wanting to return home.

Until the early hours of Wednesday morning, nothing had been arranged to implement Maxwell's wish. As a Christian, Betty naturally was ignorant of the requirements. But that night Ian Maxwell had telephoned Neeman, seeking help. 'Under Orthodox law, the body must be here before Shabbat,' the lawyer explained. There were less than sixty hours in which to complete the formalities in Tenerife and fly the body to Israel before sundown on Friday. Since the local pathologists had spoken of keeping the corpse until their tests were completed three weeks later, that undertaking would be herculean.

While the family marshalled their lawyers and advisers to dragoon the Spanish authorities into compliance, Neeman contacted Chananya Chachor, the cemetery's administrator. There was, said Chachor, no problem for Maxwell's burial on the Mount of Olives. Every Jew was entitled to that privilege. However, securing a prominent position required negotiation. A certain Italian who had reserved a good plot might be prepared to change sites. With that settled, Neeman began calling in every political debt to produce a memorable funeral. It would be a pleasure to succeed.

At noon in Tenerife, three pathologists began their initial autopsy, called an 'opening of the cavities'. Dr Carlos Lopez de Lamela, Dr María Ramos and Dr Luisa García Cohen were working in a grubby and badly ventilated room adjoining the cemetery which, by any standards, was a disgrace to modern forensic medicine. Worse, they lacked not only important instruments needed to dissect the corpse but the means to perform critical chemical tests on the organs. Lamela, a young, reluctant pathologist, cursed that his concentration was being disrupted by the chatter of dozens of journalists just yards away, on the other side of the breeze-block wall.

As they proceeded, the three pathologists recorded finding only a little water in the respiratory tracts leading to the lungs, a graze on his forehead and a fissure behind the ear. They also took samples from the brain, lung, kidney, pancreas, stomach and blood on which tests could be carried out in Madrid. Those tests would not only establish the presence of toxic substances and provide evidence of Maxwell's medical history but would measure the minuscule traces of algae which would have entered the bloodstream through the lungs and would determine how long Maxwell had spent in the water and whether he had drowned. As a routine procedure, scrapings were taken from beneath the nails to discover any fragments which would disclose whether Maxwell had clutched at an object or a person as he fell.

After three and a half hours, the pathologists reported to the investigating judge Luis Gutiérrez that their work was completed. 'I found no sea water in the lungs,' reported Lamela, 'no signs of murder or violence. I believed the cause of death was heart failure.' With the destruction of any evidence that might have been found on the yacht, Judge Gutiérrez seemed uninterested in pursuing the contradictions and gaps in Lamela's autopsy. Instead, he volunteered to a local radio station that there was 'no evidence of criminality. We are treating it as a simple accident.' Suicide was clearly ruled out because there were no clues to suggest how Maxwell could have killed himself, and Lamela had been 'assured that Mr Maxwell was a good swimmer'. Despite the exaggeration, there was no doubt that Maxwell could have stayed afloat in the prevailing calm water for a considerable time.

Death, reasoned Lamela and the two other pathologists, could not have been by drowning because there was no water in the respiratory tract. Other pathologists, confirming the imperfection of their science, would dispute that the absence of water could exclude drowning as a cause of death. 'The initial forensic report suggests a natural death before Mr Maxwell fell into the sea,' Gutiérrez told Betty Maxwell, who by then was clutching a Bible. When she emerged from his office, the widow said that she believed that death had been due to natural causes. Other doctors in Spain spoke of a 'cardiac' or 'cardiovascular attack'.

That evening, Ghislaine tearfully arrived in Tenerife carrying £15,000 in cash for Rankin. 'Can I have the money?' he asked, but she ignored his request. Her pilot, Brian Hull, had been instructed by Kevin to retrieve from the yacht six personal bags – one more than he had brought – filled with Maxwell's papers and medicines, and deliver them all to Maxwell House by noon the following day. 'It was a frantic race,' recalled Hull, who took off from the Canaries at 6 a.m. to be met by the helicopter at Farnborough. The only documentary evidence of Maxwell's state of mind in the hours before his death had thus been deliberately appropriated.

Throughout that night in London, Ian McIntosh, Clive Chalk and other Samuel Montagu bankers worked with Dick Russell, Kevin's brother-in-law, and David Vogel, the solicitor from Titmuss Sainer, to draft a press release stating that MCC's net debt was £1.4 billion, nearly three times more than the debt stated in the annual report, and pledging the bank's support for the company.

In between, Russell and Vogel sat in Kevin's office listening to the new chairman's scenario for saving the empire. The most potent threat, they all agreed, came from the Swiss Bank's warning of a default announcement the following morning. The bankers were repeating their refusal to wait for half the Que proceeds in ten days. 'Previous deadlines have not been met,' warned Charles Covell from Basle, but Kevin gambled correctly that he could out-bluff the banker by the tantalizing promise of money without public aggravation.

By dawn on 7 November, confirmation of the size of MCC's debts had spread through the City. Many investors had seized the opportunity to earn fast profits by going short – selling MCC shares which they did not own in the expectation that the share price would drop. But even they were surprised when, with the suspension lifted, trading resumed at 8.30 and the price plunged from

121p to 74p. Nervous bankers mentioned for the first time the advantage of checking Robert Maxwell's private finances.

As MCC's price fell, the Mirror Group's shares rose from 77p to 106p. Investors were betting on the disappearance of the Max Factor and the protection of the 'ring-fence'. The term, common among bankers lending money, had been reintroduced by Kevin after his father's death. 'Don't worry about the Mirror Group's finances,' he soothed, 'It's all ring-fenced from any dangers.' That reassurance fuelled the share price to rise to over 130p, while MCC's rattled fragilely.

News of the plunging price had not gravely disturbed MCC's directors. At 7.20 a.m. on Thursday, 7 November, Kevin struck both Peter Laister and Lord Rippon as honest and amenable. The two non-executive directors presented a list of demands designed to rectify past ills. If Kevin approved, MCC would transform itself from a dictatorship into a properly regulated corporation. Ten minutes later, at the company's board meeting, the new chairman accepted proposals whose implementation would ensure strict control of MCC's future financial relationship with the family's private companies. Laister and the other directors relaxed. Some more sales, Laister suggested, unaware of RMG's insolvency, would relieve the pressure. They would publicly announce the sale of Macmillan's Berlitz stake to Fukutake for £149 million, a deal which Shaffer had negotiated under Kevin's supervision. The meeting disbanded in quiet satisfaction for everyone except Kevin.

The fall in MCC's share price had fatally undermined the collateral for many of the private loans secured on MCC shares formerly owned by Maxwell. The result was, Kevin conceded in his conversations with Robert Bunn, that RMG was 'in technical default', a conclusion which plunged the finance director into nervous despair.

During that day, Kevin had received repeated calls reminding him of three unavoidable payments due from MCC the following day. He needed to find $2.2 million to pay the wages of Macmillan's staff, $3.1 million for a bank transaction and $25.3 million due in interest for Crédit Lyonnais. His only hope was the self-proclaimed 'lender of last resort', the NatWest bank.

Three hours later, David Leal-Bennett and his superior, David Ingham, the deputy general manager of NatWest's corporate finance, were shown into the penthouse at Maxwell House. After a fifteen-minute wait, Kevin arrived clutching a share certificate. 'I found this in Bob's safe,' he told the bankers with an air of surprise. 'It's one of his better investments in Israel.' The certificate, Kevin explained, was for 25.1 million Teva shares worth $35 million. Teva was the pharmaceutical company. 'Would you lend me $30 million against this stock?' He continued, 'Lehmans want smaller exposure on a very complex transaction involving London & Bishopsgate, BIT and the pension funds.' In retrospect, there was no doubt that Kevin had mentioned the Teva shares in the same breath as 'pension funds'. But the bankers, who were under 'incredible pressure', also insisted that they had made no connection between the pension funds and BIM during Kevin's thirty-second explanation of the issue – even thought BIM had maintained a separate NatWest bank account since 1988. All they knew, they would claim, was that Lehmans had aggressively reduced the Maxwell debts from $160 million to about $60 million by selling collateral and were now threatening to sell another stake of 22.8 million Teva shares, a name the NatWest bankers heard for the first time.

Both Ingham and Leal-Bennett knew better than most the plight of the Maxwell fortunes: they were owed £205 million by RMG. But the recent collapse of Asil Nadir's Polly Peck empire amid allegations of fraud unsettled the nervous bankers. Kevin's plea was rejected.

Later that afternoon, as Lehmans aggressively threatened to sell their MCC, Mirror Group and Teva shares, Kevin telephoned Ingham. 'I'm desperate,' he said. 'I need $27 million immediately for MCC. Will you take the 25 million Teva shares worth $35 million?'

'Who owns them?' asked the banker.

'RMG,' replied Kevin. 'It's only temporary. As you know, I'm expecting $160 million from the sale of Que.' Kevin did not mention that he had already pledged the $160 million to Citibank and for that matter to other banks too.

After consulting John Melbourn, the chief executive responsible for corporate risk, Ingham relented. But since NatWest had never loaned money to MCC, only to RMG, Ingham insisted that the loan to MCC should be routed through the private company. In his opinion it was not a bridging loan, nor was there any under-standing about when the Teva shares would be returned.

'Take these share certificates and transfer forms immediately to NatWest,' ordered Kevin. The stock transfer forms had been signed by Robert and Kevin Maxwell but left undated. First they trans-ferred the ownership of the Teva shares from BIM to RMG, and second they transferred it from RMG to anyone – the transferee had been left blank. One week later, the bankers would claim surprise at finding that Robert Maxwell was one of the signatories.

Fortunately for Kevin, Leal-Bennett did not immediately query, when he saw the Teva certificate, why the shares' registered owner was BIM. He would subsequently affirm his belief that BIM was just 'another Maxwell company' and that he was 'not aware' of its relationship to the pension funds. That innocence would be strenu-ously challenged by Kevin. Since August, both Leal-Bennett and Bob Brown had asked Kevin why the pension funds were trading in MCC's commercial paper or short-term loans. The bankers' unease had been reflected in an internal memorandum on 30 Sep-tember which warned Brown that the pension funds were the only purchaser of MCC's debts and 'this pig on pork flavour is not attractive'. Opposed to Leal-Bennett's enthusiasm, Brown had sought to halt those purchases, but his position had been weakened following an internal row sparked by his criticism of the bank for allowing RMG's debt to rise again after the Scitex sale. Even on 5 November, NatWest was allowing the pension funds to buy MCC's commercial paper. Yet Brown and Leal-Bennett would claim not to know that BIM *was* the pension funds' manager.

That self-proclaimed ignorance was unconvincing. In a secret deal between Robert Maxwell and NatWest on 4 November 1988, the Chairman had negotiated a £200 million short-term loan secured against specific shares provided by himself. In what became known as the Cordmead arrangement, the £200 million was routed by NatWest through Cordmead, a subsidiary of BIM, to MCC. In a classic 'warehousing' operation with the clear purpose of relieving Maxwell's cash shortage, the bankers had taken the risk knowing that BIM was the manager of pension funds.

Nevertheless, caught up in what Leal-Bennett called the 'frantic' pace of 7 November 1991, the NatWest bankers asked only for proof that Kevin, on behalf of RMG, was entitled to hand over the

Teva shares. Once satisfied, they did not mention BIM's responsibility for the pension funds.

Between meetings with other bankers, Kevin was shuffling the dwindling pile of shares to raise new loans for pressing creditors. The only light relief amid that frenzy was provided by the error of a Swiss bank clerk, who wrongly transferred £20 million to a private Maxwell account.

The day's critical discussion began at 2.15 p.m. in Kevin's office. Robert Bunn, Michael Stoney, Albert Fuller and Larry Trachtenberg were meeting alone to discuss the empire's finances. Each man, in his individual, compartmentalized role, had been directed over previous months by Robert and Kevin Maxwell to move shares, foreign exchange and companies in an attempt to disguise the crumbling of the empire. For months, Bunn had been convinced that RMG was insolvent and had feared legal retribution if the correct procedures were not followed. That afternoon, Bunn nervously returned to the subject. 'We must have a formal board meeting to consider our solvency,' urged RMG's finance director, recalling his failed attempt in July. Kevin was understandably reluctant to draw attention to RMG's plight when MCC was practically overwhelmed by pressure. 'Let me think about it,' he replied.

None of the four highly paid employees emerged from the meeting to disclose their activities and fears to the world. Unanimously, they had pledged themselves to continue their task for the brothers. One clue to their mood lay in the slogans Trachtenberg inscribed in his notebook. 'Don't Over React [sic]', he urged himself, and 'Resolve to hang on'. Later that morning, he scribbled a note of the meeting: 'Lehmans – getting them off our back; SVB [Swiss Volksbank] – keep away and off our back; Close fund ASAP.' Which 'fund' was unclear. Perhaps acting on his self-admonition, Trachtenberg was spreading a dark, gallows humour. 'A sweepstake,' he announced in Kevin's office, pushing his notebook forward. The inner circle was asked to bet on the following day's price of MCC shares. Kevin's estimate – like all the participants, he benefited from an insider's knowledge – was among the lowest: just £1.

In Tenerife, the spotlight had fallen on Isabel Oliva, an investigating magistrate who had inherited the supervision of the Maxwell case. An attractive woman aged thirty-one, Oliva gave the firm impression to some British journalists on the island that she was more interested in her sex life than in the death of Robert Maxwell. With limited experience of criminal investigations and no idea of the background to the case, she would confess to Rankin, 'We have hundreds of tourists dying here every year. This man's death is nothing special.' She was propelled towards that judgment by the pathologists' report and by the crew expressing their complete bafflement about Maxwell's fate. Among the many critical mysteries she failed to solve was whether the door to Maxwell's cabin had been locked as Rankin claimed.

As an eyewitness, Rankin's reliability was crucial to Oliva's investigation. An honest man, the captain was nevertheless of limited education, inexperienced in luxury seafaring and never previously involved in an emergency. Although his languid demeanour gave the impression of calm reason, he admitted that he was nervous after Maxwell's disappearance. Thereafter, on several issues, his memory had become vague. For example, why would the captain, after failing to rouse Maxwell in his cabin for the telephone call, not initially ask the stewardesses to look for the owner? Rankin's unprecedented decision to descend personally from the wheelhouse with another crew member, expecting the worst, suggested some forewarning of a disaster or Rankin's blurred recollection of the events. In the same category of imponderables was his assertion that Maxwell's cabin door was locked.

Investigation of his controversial version of events, which fuelled the suspicion that Maxwell had been murdered, depended upon Judge Oliva's investigation. She in turn was being encouraged by Julio Claverie, a local lawyer appointed by Betty, to complete the formalities in haste so that the body could be flown to Israel. The lawyer relied upon the report of Judge Gutiérrez that Maxwell's death was natural and unsuspicious.

By this time, the *Lady Ghislaine* was anchored in Santa Cruz. During the night, to escape onlookers, she had sailed from Los Cristianos to the north of the island. At daybreak, a posse of journalists had chased her up the moonscape coast to resume their vigil in the surreal setting of a quayside off the African coast. To the Maxwells' consternation, Judge Oliva requested that the crew, reported by Campbell Livingstone, the British vice-consul in Tenerife, to be 'shocked and depressed', resubmit themselves for questioning.

Oliva had decided to reinvestigate one critical question: was he pushed or did he fall? If it was murder and he was pushed or thrown into the sea, then, since the boat was sailing on an unscheduled, unpredetermined course, only members of the crew could be responsible. No second boat was known to have encountered the *Lady Ghislaine* during that night. So far, no member of the crew had been identified as a murder suspect. Oliva's murder inquiry was hampered by the scientific evidence provided by the pathologists, who had ruled out both suicide and foul play. There were no unexplained bruises, pinpricks, lacerations or fractured bones to suggest a violent death. Similarly, there was no evidence that he had been pushed into the water either alive or dead. After several hours pondering the lack of evidence and her interviews with the crew, Oliva ruled out murder and decided that the only issue was whether the cause of Maxwell's death was accidental or natural.

Judge Gutiérrez had originally announced that Maxwell had been dead before he fell into the water, on the grounds that the autopsy had found that he had suffered a heart attack and did not drown. The mystery was whether he fell over the 1.5-metre solid rail around the decks, over the low metal rail at the rear, or under (or over) the very low, steel cord strung between chrome barriers on the aft, lower deck, a place where Maxwell often stood. The investigators decided that he could easily have toppled over the rails or slid over or under the aft cord.

If Maxwell had fallen, there were two options. Either he had suffered a heart attack on board the boat and had toppled into the sea; or he had accidentally fallen alive into the water and had suffered a heart attack while swimming. The pathologists could not say which option was more likely. Few in Britain had much confidence in the ability of Judge Oliva and the Spanish police to establish the truth.

Forty-eight hours had passed since Maxwell's death. The shock had been digested and the reports from Tenerife were receiving closer scrutiny. British pathologists pointed out that the cause of death entered on the death certificate, 'respiratory cardiac arrest', was 'meaningless'. It was a mode of death, not the cause. Signs such as myocardial infarct or coronary thrombosis would be required to indicate a heart attack, but no such signs has been mentioned.

Having deliberately praised the local authorities for their co-operation in order to ensure the swift completion of formalities, allowing the corpse to be flown to Israel, the Maxwell family now cast doubt on the Spanish pathologists' conclusions about the cause of death. After several exchanges between the sons in London and Betty, Philip and Ghislaine in Tenerife, the family claimed that the heart attack could have occurred after Maxwell had fallen into the water and that therefore his death had been an accident. Pressed to reply to those questions Isabel Oliva confirmed that the time and cause of death were still unknown: 'As far as I'm concerned, the investigations carry on.' To fuel the mystery, one of Maxwell's private doctors, Dr Joseph Joseph, suggested that the death was 'suspicious'. Dr Joseph's judgment from Wimpole Street in London succeeded in multiplying the widespread speculation and the doubts about the conflicting medical and expert evidence. By the end of that day, the confusion produced two contradictory results. Judge Oliva declared herself satisfied that Maxwell's death was unsuspicious and released the corpse for burial. But the British insurers, liable to pay £21 million if Maxwell had died accidentally, revealed dissatisfaction with the Spanish autopsy and arranged for another examination to be conducted in Jerusalem.

By then, Neeman had secured a superb burial plot at the summit of the Mount of Olives cemetery. The administrator Chananya Chachor was paid $5,000, and both men were satisfied with the deal. Neeman's telephone calls to the offices of the president, prime minister and other leading politicians confirmed that Maxwell's parting from the world would be marked as an important event. His client would be proud of his lawyer. 'We must show how we value Jews who return to Israel' was the message which passed around Jerusalem's corridors of power. There was now a countdown, as efforts were renewed to extricate the body from the authorities in Tenerife in time for it to reach Israel before the Sabbath.

To satisfy international law, the corpse required embalming, both for the journey and because decomposition had already begun. While an undertaker completed that task, a 200-kilo mahogany coffin, including viewing window, was transported to the airport. Late at night, loaders sought to manoeuvre it into the Gulfstream. But, whichever angle was chosen, the coffin proved too big. A Challenger, chartered in Switzerland, was summoned to Los Rodeos.

After dinner, Betty Maxwell, Philip and Ghislaine had a last look around the vessel and prepared to depart. 'I'm in charge of the yacht now,' Ghislaine told Rankin, nevertheless grateful for the captain's concealment from her father of the night during the summer when she had commandeered the yacht at Piraeus for a disco party with friends. 'You'll take your orders from me. I'll tell you where you'll go. I'm thinking of charters in the Caribbean.'

'I won't be going anywhere unless I get that money,' Rankin replied, referring to the £15,000 Ghislaine had brought from London. Reluctantly, she handed over £5,000, retaining £10,000. Rankin smiled. He knew that Kevin would be giving the orders. Betty Maxwell bade the captain farewell, apparently suspicious that he harboured unrevealed details about the death. Throughout her stay on the island, no one had seen her shed a tear. Robert Maxwell's portrayal in Moscow of a harsh Betty had been shown to be accurate.

At 3 a.m., one hour after the deadline, Maxwell's coffin was loaded on to the Challenger and the rush to clear formalities was completed. The undertaker insisted on bidding the tearless widow farewell. Her husband's death, he assured her with professional certainty, was not painful. But she seemed unemotional, he later reflected. Perhaps she instinctively realized that undertakers irresistibly mouth inanities, which in this case were completely inaccurate. Then, with a powerful jolt, the plane sped off from the runway. Clearance had been given for the flight into Israeli airspace, and for the landing in Jerusalem. No special permission was required. 'I was born Jewish and I shall die Jewish,' Maxwell had said in 1986, but few had believed him.

Six hours after Maxwell's body had been flown from the Canary Islands, Kevin and Carolyn Barwell, his personal assistant, were sitting in Concorde *en route* to New York. Later that day, 8 November, Kevin would hold court at Macmillan's headquarters on Third Avenue and at the *Daily News*. Publicly his message was 'business as usual', reinforced by a pose at the newsstand on Second Avenue, close to the *Daily News* headquarters. Although he looked uncomfortable re-enacting his father's gimmick, everyone appreciated the gesture and expressed their sympathies. Outside the *Daily News* building, the flag flew at half-mast. Inside, everyone assumed that the newspaper's future was safe in Kevin's hands.

Privately, Kevin was seeking loans from the bankers among the procession of those offering condolences. To Robert Katz and Ken Brody of Goldman Sachs, Kevin promised to resuscitate his father's proposal of weekly repayments of £5 million. 'That would be helpful,' said the bankers. 'It should start tomorrow.' Since that was clearly impossible, Kevin added that the course of the full repayment would come from the Que proceeds. 'Isn't Que owned by the public companies?' asked Katz.

'Yes,' replied Kevin confidently, 'but that's no problem. The public side owes the private side money.'

Ralph McDonald and Andrew Capitman of Bankers Trust were among those proffered the *Daily News* as collateral. 'We'll consider it,' they replied, knowing it would be rejected and grateful to have secured through their deft handiwork £50 million ahead of the other banks. No offers of other loans had materialized by the time Kevin met Shelly Aboff, his father's crony, for what must have been one of the more unusual schemes finalized in Manhattan during that day.

Shortly before his father's death, Kevin had ordered the return of 2.3 million Berlitz shares which he had transferred to Advest, Aboff's company. Aboff did not quite obey the instructions. Money, raised against some of the 2.3 million shares, had been deposited in an account of Pergamon Holdings (US) Inc. or Ph(US)Inc., Maxwell's private company. From that account, Kevin directed a succession of payments. First, he paid for his father's burial plot in Jerusalem and an additional $50,000 in advance for prayers to be said three times a day over the following two years. He then dispatched two deposits of £100,000 to two British solicitors, experts in defending those accused of fraud, and a further deposit to a firm of accountants specializing in the defence of fraud. Since his sister Christine had just lost her house in a fire in California, her brother advanced a sum from Ph(US)Inc.'s account to buy a new house and a BMW convertible. His sister Isabel would also receive money from the account to finance her film research, while both Kevin and Aboff used the Ph(US)Inc. account to reduce their mortgages.

Whether Kevin, as he climbed with his secretary into the helicopter to return to Kennedy airport, realized that the truth would come out eventually is debatable, but undoubtedly he hoped that the delays would help him control the impending disaster. So far as he was concerned, one piece of housekeeping had been completed.

In his absence, Ian had completed another item of housekeeping – securing the $30 million loan from NatWest using the Teva shares. That morning, David Leal-Bennett had nervously telephoned Bunn. 'Is RMG the owner of the Teva shares?' asked the banker.

'Yes,' replied Bunn, who had been a director of BIM when the Teva shares were originally purchased. Evidently relieved, the banker requested that, on legal advice, new board meetings should be held to effect the transfer. 'It was frantic,' recalled Leal-Bennett.

Thereupon Leal-Bennett sent a memorandum addressed to Kevin confirming their agreement pledging the Teva shares and the diversion from MCC of some of the Que proceeds to RMG to reduce the overdraft. In Kevin's absence, Ian signed the memorandum, adding 'Agreed'. In quick succession, he then chaired a BIM board meeting with Trachtenberg to transfer the Teva shares to RMG to secure the loan and chaired a board meeting of RMG to transfer the same shares to NatWest. Minutes of both meetings were signed by Ian. Kevin was recorded as 'present' at RMG's meeting, although he was in New York. It would be said that he attended by telephone. The other BIM directors listed as agreeing to the transfer were Trachtenberg and Cook. 'I was unaware that I attended that meeting,' Cook would later say. For his part, Bob Brown could only spit, 'I had no reason to doubt Kevin's honesty.'

Eight days later, Kevin and Trachtenberg signed new stock forms transferring the shares from BIM to RMG and then to the bank. Accompanying those bits of paper was a formal memorandum from BIM which included among the dense, small print the company's claim to undisputed ownership of the Teva shares. NatWest's lawyers did not spot that landmine for some time.

London was still grey when Kevin returned from New York on the overnight Jumbo on 9 November and was flown by helicopter to Holborn. Soon after descending the metal staircase, he was chairing a formal RMG board meeting. Bunn had succeeded in persuading John Walsh and Stephen Wootten to give formal advice once again on whether the company was a 'going concern'. Once again, too, a lawyer had been summoned from Titmuss Sainer, this time Dick Russell, the senior partner. All the evidence pointed to RMG's insolvency, yet Russell, the faithful brother-in-law, continued to accept the assurances from Bunn and Kevin that 'MCC owed RMG £70 million'. The auditors passed no comment about that assumption, despite the evidence presented at the meeting.

Around the table Bunn stuck out, 'looking extremely ill and dreadful', according to Walsh. The company's liabilities, said Bunn, exceeded its assets. 'RMG should cease trading.' Everyone's eyes fastened upon Kevin. 'There is no doubt', he said, 'that the company cannot meet its liabilities without the banks' help.' With that, he looked at the two auditors. Once again, the auditors neither questioned the directors nor probed RMG's list of assets – which still included Teva and the proceeds of Scitex – nor examined its external debts. Both would insist that their only task was to give advice, not to investigate whether the directors were honest in their listing of the company's assets and debts.

So once again the two professionals advised the directors that, so long as they enjoyed the banks' support, RMG was a going concern. That opinion was endorsed by Russell. Four years later, the auditors would deny acting as 'tailor's dummies' and without 'moral' scruple. Their task was not, they testified, 'to look at the meat between the sandwich' but to rely purely upon the information they received from the directors. At the time, the auditors had plainly satisfied Kevin's wishes and had not prompted Bunn's resignation. Yet both directors knew that they had secretly pledged the Teva shares owned by the pension funds to finance RMG's existence – an act which subsequently would be alleged to be criminal.

By then, Maxwell's body had been transferred to the forensic institute in Tel Aviv. During Saturday night, Dr Iain West, one of Britain's senior pathologists, retained by the insurance companies, rushed to complete another autopsy by early Sunday morning. The handicaps were formidable. Maxwell's heart was in Spain and the remaining organs had been too damaged by Dr Lamela and formaldehyde to permit an effective investigation. The evidence necessary to prove that the cause of death was either drowning or a heart attack did not exist. The torn muscles and internal bleeding proved a sudden, painful jerk just before falling into the sea. West, to his frustration, would be unable to provide a certain cause of death, yet there was understandable pressure for a verdict. 'Considering the circumstances, most likely suicide,' he would later say, 'or possibly an accident.' Maxwell's 'financial circumstances' strongly influenced the pathologist's opinion.

Not far from the stymied pathologist, a toiling Palestinian grave-digger was confirming on his portable telephone his latest instructions: the grave should be wider and longer than normal. At that moment, after a morning with his closest confidants – Stoney, Trachtenberg and Fuller – Kevin was flying in the Gulfstream jet to Jerusalem to join his family at the King David Hotel.

To those passing through the Maxwells' suites during the evening, the atmosphere resembled a colourful scene from a Fellini film rather than the solemn preparations for a funeral. Instead of grief and tears, there was laughter, concern about dress and appearances, telephones constantly ringing, and shrill voices demanding room service. The rooms, filled with flowers, fruit and food, were a magnet for journalists, photographers, well-wishers and sympathizers.

The party spirit was rekindled the following morning, 10 November, as four women of the Maxwell family fussed about their dresses and hairstyle while Kevin began a round of business meetings in the only country where the sentiment towards him was untarnished goodwill. Over breakfast, on the day of his father's funeral, Kevin asked Yaakov Neeman to arrange a private $24 million loan. 'The security', said Kevin, 'will be the 49 million Teva shares.' The lawyer did not realize that those shares were owned by the pension funds or that they were already pledged to several banks. Kevin did not mention his niggling fear: that Lehmans would sell 22.8 million Teva shares held as collateral unless a loan was repaid. To avoid that unpalatable predicament, Kevin fired off instructions which Neeman's partner Michael Fox would later reflect had sparked 'fever-pitch' activity.

As Kevin discussed the empire's future, his father's dissected cadaver was moved to Israel's Hall of the Nation and placed upon a plinth. There, covered by a shroud, lay the remains of the man who in life had claimed ownership of £250 million worth of Israeli assets, which included a leading newspaper and industrial investments, and who, most important of all, had possessed the private telephone number of President Gorbachev, with which he had helped to hasten the emigration of Soviet Jews to Israel.

Neeman had organized the funeral and acted as catalyst, but it was sentiment that galvanized the nation's statesmen into attending.

Israel's leaders wanted to show their countrymen and Jews through-out the world their appreciation for the contribution of the Dias-pora Jews. Above all, they were chuffed that an apparently authentic Englishman should choose to be buried away from home.

Among those flying to Israel at their own expense were Lord Coggan, a former Archbishop of Canterbury, John Campi, the *Daily News* public relations executive, Jean Leveque, the president of Crédit Lyonnais, Sir Michael Richardson, Gerald Kaufman MP, and a clutch of the insalubrious characters who had always faith-fully answered Maxwell's call. They joined, at 2.30 p.m., the 400 mourners filing by the body and, over the next hour, paying their respects to the family, who stood in a half-circle.

Neeman could reflect that Maxwell would have been delighted by the spectacle. Unlike in England, he was remembered in Israel for his successes and his ability to overcome his failures. 'Robert Maxwell was a folk hero in Israel. A Holocaust survivor who made good,' said one mourner. Israel, he continued, 'is the only solution for the Jews. Maxwell's return was the symbol to Diaspora Jews to return to your own people.' Those sentiments would have puzzled the British, who had accepted Maxwell's declarations of patriotism – 'I am British by choice' – at face value. But, for those in Jerusalem, there was no mystery: Maxwell had been rejected by the British because, despite his best efforts, he remained a Jew. Only in Israel did he find acceptance and peace.

The first to speak was President Chaim Herzog, who had met Maxwell just once. (Betty Maxwell was wrong to state that Herzog was 'Bob's friend of many years'.) After starting in Hebrew, Herzog realized that none of the family could understand, and switched to English. His tribute was resounding: 'He scaled the heights. Kings and barons besieged his doorstep. He was a figure of almost mytho-logical stature. An actor of the world stage, bestriding the globe, as Shakespeare says, like a colossus.' Britons would be bemused by Herzog's praise. Searching for a hidden connection, many would conclude that Maxwell was being rewarded for his services to Mossad. Few could understand that the connection was simply the Publisher's uncompromised relationship with his fellow countrymen.

Herzog was followed by Maxwell's eldest son Philip, who was unable to disguise his emotions: 'Dear Dad . . . soldier, publisher and patriot. Warrior and globe-trotter. Father of nine children and grandfather of eight. We love you, we need you, we miss you . . . May you rest in peace.' Forgotten was Maxwell's unconcealed dislike for his eldest son, a dislike that had been richly reciprocated.

Sam Pisar, the French lawyer, said Kaddish, the Jewish prayer; and then the mourners moved outside. There Rabbi Shear-Yashuv Cohen of Haifa, who, according to the laws of the Cohens, cannot enter a building containing a dead body in case of impurity, gave the final blessing: 'Robert Maxwell started his life as an Orthodox Jew and has now travelled the full circle and returns to his origins.' United by a common bond – the survival of two millennia of persecution – Cohen praised the brother who, having overcome prejudice and malice, had come home. The outsider had become an insider.

It was approaching sunset when the cavalcade drove through closed roads, passing the Damascus Gate, towards the Mount of Olives, which overlooked the Garden of Gethsemane. On the site most coveted by Jews, where it is said those buried will be the first to hear the call of the Messiah on the Day of Judgment, the mourners collected. Cynics would add, 'Trust Cap'n Bob. Making sure that he would be first in the line.'

A pink light from the horizon reflected on the Dome of the Rock as the Jewish ceremony began, mingled with Moslem laments from the Old City. Not so long before, Maxwell, looking out over the cemetery from the royal suite in the King David Hotel, had been playing his power games. How he would have enjoyed seeing all the nation's most powerful – the president, the prime minister Yitzhak Shamir, cabinet ministers Ariel Sharon, Moshe Arens, Ehud Olmert and Shimon Peres – gathered as if it were a state funeral. It was an honour which would provoke mockery in Britain – hence Maxwell's rejection of that country, signalled by his final wish to be buried elsewhere.

Ehoud Olmert, who months earlier had sat with Maxwell in Holborn watching the soccer World Cup, delivered the graveside farewell: 'He once said to me, "After all, I have not done so badly for a young Jewish boy from the *shtetl*."' Looking down at the grave, Olmert continued, 'Indeed, Bob Maxwell, you have not done badly at all. May your soul rest in peace in this ancient ground which finally became yours.' The sentiment was echoed by his widow: 'Now the circle closes. He has returned to his roots.'

Piloting the Gulfstream 4 from Jerusalem to London that night, Captain David Whiteman was surprised by the light-hearted atmosphere in the cabin behind. Betty and her children seemed to have abandoned all pretence of mourning. 'It was champagne, chocolates and laughter,' Captain Whiteman recalled. 'No tears.' The malevolent might have speculated that the Maxwell family were relieved to be rid of the tyrant and eagerly anticipated inheriting the fortune he had amassed. For, despite his loudly proclaimed assertion that the wealth accumulated in Liechtenstein would go to charity rather than his family, it was rightly suspected that they would not be forgotten. Seven Liechtenstein trusts were, contrary to Maxwell's lifetime boasts, assigned to each of his children. Ghislaine, his favourite daughter, enjoyed a trust which already paid her a handsome monthly income through the Bank Leumi in New York. Those celebrating on the Gulfstream were content to believe that, under Kevin's stewardship of the family empire, they would receive more benefits than they had in their father's lifetime.

The following day, 11 November, reading the glowing newspaper reports of the funeral and especially of himself in the *Sunday Times* as he flew in the Gulfstream to Zurich, Kevin was determined to exploit the goodwill when he met Swiss bankers. During the seventy-five-minute flight, he must have wondered how much longer his juggling could continue. The two public companies were in breach of dozens of undertakings. He had used the pension funds as collateral and there were few assets left to offer. Berlitz had been sold to Fukutake, but the shares were held by the banks. Yet his plight was ignored when he spoke with Captain Hull about the fate of the private jets. 'The G4 will have to go. We have to show the shareholders that we're saving costs. However, I'd like to use the G2. How much is it worth?'

'$4 million, Mr Maxwell,' replied Hull.

'Okay. Put it up for sale at $6 million.' At that price, there would be no buyer and it could be retained in the pretence that its sale was imminent.

Awaiting Kevin at Zurich airport with a banking colleague was Rolf Beeler of Swiss Volksbank, anxiously seeking repayment of $36.5 million. After the pleasantries and condolences, the banker mentioned his requirement. The money had been owed since

October. The Swiss bank had released the money as a foreign exchange deal on Kevin's promise that £20 million had been deposited in a Chase Manhattan account in New York. In fact, there was no money in New York. The Swiss banker did not receive his money; instead he was offered an immaculate performance. Confidently employing the calm language and mannerisms which he knew appealed to bankers, Kevin assured Beeler that everything would be effortlessly resolved over the next few days. 'It's been an unfortunate error,' apologized Kevin, explaining a chain of unforeseen circumstances in New York which persuaded the banker of Kevin's good faith. But any chance of further questions was prevented by Captain Hull's shout: 'If we don't leave now, we won't be allowed to land in London.'

'Sorry,' said Kevin, beginning to walk. 'But don't worry, you'll get the money tomorrow. On my return I'll make over to you 2.4 million Berlitz shares as collateral.'

'Who owns them?' inquired Beeler trying to keep up.

'The family,' answered Kevin, rushing through the exit. How could the banker, watching the Maxwell jet taxi down the runway, know that those same shares had already been sold to the Japanese by Macmillan, the true owners? Satisfied by his performance, Kevin returned to London. In Paris, the government was arranging a memorial service for his father to be attended by the president; in London, Lord Goodman responded to the widow's request for a service of thanksgiving at Westminster Abbey by proposing the same in St Paul's Cathedral; while in New York the print unions had announced that they would pay for trees of remembrance to be planted in Israel. At Maxwell House, the staff were preparing a dinner party for Kevin in his father's dining room. 'The King is dead. Long live the King!' – or so Kevin might have thought, unaware that the following morning the first disturbing fissure would appear on the empire's surface.

At 7.30 a.m. on 12 November, Kevin was in his office with Trachtenberg, Bunn and Stoney. Each knew that something was amiss. The news had leaked that Maxwell's private empire had borrowed £758 million from over thirty banks and that the collateral was insufficient. Insiders suspected that the source was a City adviser. Only outsiders speculated about the reasons for the steep fall in MCC's share price. All the bankers understood the consequence: as MCC's share price fell, the private companies faced a squeeze. The sole question was whether the crisis was terminal, since MCC was apparently not insolvent and three American banks – Lehmans, Goldman Sachs and Citibank – had agreed with British banks not to sell any more MCC shares, in order that the Maxwells should have time to regain stability. But the agreement had already been broken. Citibank, to Kevin's fury, had sold 3 million shares. 'He's very upset about that,' commented Charles Covell, the sharp vice-president entrusted with the responsibility of debt collection.

To remove the uncertainty about RMG's debts, later that morning some of the leading banks appointed Richard Stone, a corporate rescue specialist at Coopers, to investigate the finances of the 400 private companies. By the time Stone had arranged to visit Maxwell House, Kevin had already obtained signatures from Trachtenberg and Ian Maxwell to transfer Berlitz shares to Swiss Volksbank and Crédit Suisse. 'Sign here,' he said, pushing forward the minutes of the board meeting.

To release those Berlitz shares, Kevin needed to provide new collateral for the Maxwells' debt to the pension funds. One solution was instead to repay the debt from proceeds of the sale of Que, the Macmillan subsidiary. 'I can irrevocably assign $77 million of the proceeds for family use,' Kevin told Cook. Beguiled by that promise, and without seeing evidence of any approval by MCC's other directors, Cook signed a letter on BIM's behalf (with Trachtenberg as co-signatory) to Matthew St Paul at Morgan Stanley, sanctioning the transfer of the Berlitz shares from BIM to RMG. Cook believed himself to be protecting the pension funds, although in reality he was exchanging shares held as collateral for promises. 'I was fooled,' he explained in retrospect.

But Cook was showing less than his usual pliability, and this was now worrying Kevin. That morning, Cook had queried his suggestion that BIM's financial year be delayed again – 'because of all the confusion' – beyond December 1991. Eventually, Kevin reasoned, someone would discover the pension fund discrepancies. The solution, he believed, was to lay a trail which was to be used to show his concern. Since Robert Bunn had been voicing the same fear since the RMG board meeting, Kevin agreed to the finance director's request to summon a meeting with Jeff Highfield, BIM's finance controller, Jonathan Ford of LBI and John Gould, who worked for both RMG and LBI. It occurred later that morning. 'We know there is a problem,' began Bunn. 'Kevin has asked me to investigate the exposure of BIM to the private companies.' In a concerned voice, Bunn listed the daunting agenda. There was the still uncertain source of the money which had funded the transfer of £97 million to BPCC's pension fund demanded by John Halloran; a transfer of Mirror Group shares as collateral to Crédit Suisse; and the 'lost' proceeds of the Scitex sale. 'We need to know the facts and take appropriate action,' said Bunn to the puzzled Highfield, who had never previously heard of these Maxwell liabilities to the pension funds.

Back in his office, Highfield totted up the sums. If Bunn's startling disclosures were correct, the total owed by the Maxwell family to BIM approached £200 million. 'This is shocking!' he exclaimed, although he was still convinced by Trachtenberg's assurances that the pension funds were protected by the collateral held by LBI in shares and cash. Nevertheless, he opted for a precautionary move: 'I think we need an inventory of all the share certificates in all the safes in the offices.' John Gould, an uncreative gofer, was asked to undertake that chore because he enjoyed access to Kevin's safe.

Soon after lunch, as the first Macmillan executives were arriving at their New York headquarters, Peter Laister burst into Kevin's office. 'What's all this about?' he cried, waving a fax. Kevin's agreement with Citibank to deposit $36.5 million earned from the Que sale into a private account had been reported by Shaffer.

'This is terrible,' stuttered Kevin in apparent surprise. 'There's been some misunderstanding. A mistake. We'll sort it out.'

'I'm going to stop this!' shouted Laister, for the first time suspecting that there was more to the overall problem than he had hitherto understood. 'You know you shouldn't have done that, Kevin.'

'It's a mistake.'

'I'm telling Basil exactly what we'll now do,' seethed Laister.

'Stop the payment to Citibank,' Basil Brookes instructed the Macmillan accounts department in New York and went home for the night.

That night, Kevin met David Vogel, the loyal solicitor. The new chairman's problems had escalated. Not only Citibank but also the Swiss Bank were moving beyond any point where he could charm

them into compliance. 'I need advice,' Kevin asked, 'whether Macmillan's agreement to deposit the Que proceeds with Citibank is
binding.' Then he added, 'Even if it was not considered by the MCC
or Macmillan board.' The lawyer sat silently making notes, but a
worm of doubt about his client's sincerity and his own position
had made its first wriggling appearance.

Consciously, Kevin had adopted a twin strategy: to blame everything on to his father while simultaneously adopting Maxwell's
practice of brazening out any criticism. In the meantime, he would
continue as the innocent involved in a rescue mission. A visit to
John Melbourn, the chief executive of corporate risk at NatWest,
proved pleasantly inconsequential because the banker believed
everything he said and in return promised continued support. Kevin
would write to Melbourn, 'words cannot express our gratitude to
you personally and to your colleagues for the tremendous support
we have received under these exceptionally trying circumstances
. . . We are committed to the survival of Bob's legacy . . . Bob would
have been immensely proud of the bank.' Accompanied by Melbourn, Kevin then visited Eddie George, the rotund deputy governor
of the Bank of England. By any reckoning, George, the supervisor
of the City's financial institutions, ought to have demanded proper
explanations for the growing confusion. Instead, he appeared satisfied by Kevin's patter, which included a reference to Robin Leigh-
Pemberton, the governor, who as the former chairman of the
National Westminster Bank had known his father for twenty years;
and by an inconclusive discussion about whether the Bank would
support a further loan from NatWest to RMG of £250 million.

Buoyed by the simple fact that George had not censured him,
Kevin continued in the same vein after he had flown by Concorde
with Pandora the following day for an eight-hour stay in New York.
Touring banks, he assured his creditors that, although the problems
were not slight, he was working towards a solution. The family's
debt to MCC, he said, was down to £60 million. In truth, the
private debt to MCC across the whole group had zoomed to £230
million. The bankers' reaction was sympathy mixed with threats.

At the end of the day, after Kevin had given a self-serving television interview to CBS, he and Pandora spent thirty minutes at the
reception hosted by the American–Israel Chamber of Commerce.
Had he lived, Robert Maxwell was to have received its Man of

the Year Award. In an unfaltering performance, his son thanked everyone for their kindness, reminisced about his father's qualities and his affection for both Israel and New York, and briskly stepped into a limousine to return to Kennedy airport.

When Kevin stepped off the helicopter on to the roof of Maxwell House the following morning, 14 November, he knew that there was no hope of raising any further loans in New York, London or anywhere. He was also aware that there was only limited time before the truth began to emerge. Richard Stone's assessment of the private debts on behalf of Coopers would inevitably reveal more than was comfortable despite the slow flow of information. But a message from David Vogel, his solicitor, suggested that over the previous day Stone had unearthed more truth than Kevin had antici-pated. Vogel had finally understood that Kevin's assurance sixteen days earlier – 'MCC owes RMG £80 million' – was patently wrong. The opposite was the truth. It was RMG which owed £230 million to MCC. Relations with his advisers would become sticky, Kevin realized, although thankfully he could rely on their loyal discretion. If he was to brazen things out, he would have to stay unwaveringly on course, controlling any damage by limited disclosures.

Seemingly contrite for once, at an MCC board meeting that after-noon he admitted that the Que deal had been wrong. 'Bob gave the order,' he explained.

'But you issued the instruction,' countered Laister.

'Those were Bob's instructions,' repeated Kevin. 'In any case, the private companies will compensate MCC. The debt is now down to £60 million.' His repetition of the erroneous claim was not con-tradicted by Basil Brookes, who was apparently still unable to estab-lish the truth. Instead, the finance director and his colleagues accepted Kevin's assurances and discussed the rebuilding of MCC. Kevin's façade was immaculate. 'Trevor Cook is preparing a report on the pension funds,' he said matter-of-factly, prompting neither comment nor suspicion, although Laister was puzzled about the inordinate time Kevin spent with the private-side group. None of the directors realized that Kevin had presented to John Melbourn and other NatWest bankers that day an astonishing proposal: that MCC could no longer survive and should be liquidated. His prime concern was to save the private empire's investment in the Mirror Group and the *Daily News*.

But during that same visit to Melbourn he had lied, and his brother-in-law Dick Russell, the solicitor who was present, was discomforted, not least by his own predicament. Kevin had told the banker that RMG's liabilities to the Mirror Group and to BIM were £100 million. Yet Russell had heard earlier that the hole was £400 million. Back in his office, the lawyer dictated a stern warning to his client reflecting his anger about the duplicity and the threat to the pension funds: 'There must be serious questions as to whether the trustees of the various schemes (which I know include yourself) have properly discharged their duties.'

Kevin, after insisting that he had concealed nothing from his lawyer or the bankers and that 'a lesser figure than £400 million' would be involved, wrote, 'I think it would be inappropriate and damaging to provide information piecemeal . . . My duty to make such disclosures has to be balanced against my duty not to provide the institutions with incomplete information which may lead them to take steps prejudicial to the companies . . . I am conscious that I must comply with the law and I intend not only to comply with the letter of the law, but also its spirit.' There was, not surprisingly, a final sting in Kevin's letter: 'I rely on you to advise me in this regard, as I have done in the past.'

Despite those pious declarations, soon after dictating that letter Kevin ignored both the letter and the spirit of the law by firing off a succession of faxes to Michael Fox in Tel Aviv about the Teva loans, messages which confused the normally calm lawyer. Kevin's plan was to repurchase the 22.8 million Teva shares held by Lehmans with a loan from an Israeli bank. Six days earlier he had contemplated borrowing $24 million against the 49 million Teva shares, but the collateral required by the banks was rising beyond his ability to comply. Now he urgently needed $12 million to buy back Lehmans' certificate, and he was offering the same Teva certificate as collateral. It was worse than complicated: it was messy. His message to Fox urged utmost speed, 'to close [the loan] as quickly as possible'. He added, 'Please confirm that no announcement need be made' – an understandable request considering the shares' ownership, which became more ambiguous on 15 November.

At 8.25 a.m., Trachtenberg discussed with Piers La Marchant, the Lehmans lawyer in London, the final details of the 'contract for sale' allowing BIM to repurchase the Teva shares. The two men had frequently spoken since the crisis erupted at the end of October, but two elements were never disputed: that BIM was the true owner of the Teva shares and that they were negotiating a package for the group to repurchase the Teva and Berlitz shares. 'We've got a lot of irons in the fire,' Trachtenberg told La Marchant, adding prophetically, 'but we need a bit more time.' Later that morning, La Marchant arrived at Maxwell House and watched Kevin and Trachtenberg sign the contract on BIM's behalf. After he had left, the two men signed a new transfer required by NatWest regarding the 25.1 million Teva shares as collateral for the loan. On that occasion, they signed away the pension fund shares on behalf of RMG. Returning to his office, Trachtenberg found a note from Jeff Highfield, the BIM administrator, inquiring about the location of various certificates for BIM's securities, including Teva. He decided not to reply.

Upstairs, Kevin was telephoning Philip Morgenstern, asking the solicitor to provide a formal letter stating that BIM owned the Teva shares. 'BIM needs to borrow some money to cover some commitments in Israel,' Kevin told the solicitor misleadingly. The lawyer did not query why a pension fund would urgently need to raise a loan. Instead, he resolved to check quietly how the shares had been transferred from BIM. Kevin, however, was satisfied that the lawyer would follow his instructions and, by the end of the day, he had directed Fox to pledge the 22.8 million Teva shares worth $24 million in return for the $12 million loan from the Israel Discount Bank. 'We want $48 million,' Trachtenberg told Fox during one telephone conversation that day, unaware of the constantly changing circumstances.

'But where's the other certificate [for 25.1 million shares]?' asked the lawyer, increasingly mystified by the unorthodox events. Trachtenberg did not reveal that it had been pledged to NatWest.

'Despite our herculean efforts,' Fox faxed Kevin on Friday afternoon, 'it has proved impossible to carry out the financing today.' With the Sabbath and the closing of his office the following day, Fox promised to continue the arrangements on Sunday.

In Dorrington Street, Cook and Highfield were becoming increasingly uneasy. Adding up for the first time RMG's debts to BIM, Cook arrived at an unexpectedly large amount: no less than £296 million. 'This is amazing!' Cook told Highfield, revealing the quality of his management. 'We'd better do something.' After a pause to reflect, he announced, 'I'll send Kevin a memo.' Cook's message was unusual in its firmness. 'There are points arising out of my review', he wrote, 'which require urgent clarification.' Simultaneously, Highfield asked Trachtenberg again for the location of various share certificates owned by BIM which he had over the previous year handed over for stock lending.

On Monday, 18 November the dam crumbled a little but was holding – just. Kevin awoke to discover that MCC's shares had opened at 46p, down 17p from Friday, and falling to a mere 5 per cent of the price they had reached in their heyday in 1987, when his father has boasted that he was building a £3–£5 billion international corporation. In the stock market, the rumours were unkind and Richard Stone of Coopers was complaining about 'a lack of information'.

The facts did not disturb Kevin's performance. At 8.10 a.m., he seated himself in a BBC radio car in Fetter Lane to tell John Humphrys live on the *Today* programme, 'We're confident that MCC's results will be well received.' In a firm voice, he assured his interviewer, 'The public companies' finances are robust,' and denounced as misleading the claim that Robert Maxwell had 'robbed Peter to pay Paul'. The questioner, alluding to reckless inter-company trading, did not quote the source of his accurate question. However, the sensitive ear might have detected a constriction in Kevin's voice when he was asked whether he could assure investors in MCC that their money was safe. 'Absolutely,' gulped Kevin.

That morning Ian sang from the same song sheet when the BIM directors, including Cook and Trachtenberg, met for a formal board meeting. 'We haven't received a reply from Larry about the location of various BIM share certificates,' said Cook, 'and we need to resolve RMG's debt.'

'How much are the pension funds owed?' asked Ian.

'£296 million,' replied the manager.

'Well, that's no problem,' replied Ian, 'RMG has at least £500 million free.' Ian's assertion was inaccurate. Ever since the last 'going-concern meeting' on 9 November, he had known that RMG was insolvent, but he did not share that knowledge with Cook. The authority for his assertion was a review of RMG's assets produced by Bankers Trust. The bankers, however, had been unaware of the true ownership of many shares used by RMG to raise loans.

The pressure was mounting upon Kevin. One lifeline had been abruptly snapped. Over the weekend, nearly $160 million had been deposited in MCC's account from the sale of Que. Unfortunately, NatWest managers had decided to seize all the money and wipe out MCC's overdraft. Kevin's hope of taking £55.7 million to pay the Swiss Bank for the First Tokyo shares and $77 million to pay BIM had also evaporated. Subsequently he would claim to have asked for the return of the Teva shares from NatWest, but all the bankers denied that Kevin had ever expected the certificate to be returned. The proceeds of Que were being offered everywhere. When Robert Katz of Goldmans telephoned that afternoon complaining that the £5 million payments had not started, Kevin feigned utter surprise: 'I can't imagine what's happened. Something's gone terribly wrong, I'll look into it.' Two days later, he would still assure Katz, 'The MCC directors have authorized the payment of the Que proceeds to the private side.'

Telling stories to fringe bankers to buy time had become second nature, but those closer to home could no longer be totally deceived. Kevin had decided that he had no alternative but to admit formally to BIM's directors that RMG could not after all immediately repay its debts to the pension fund. 'We're looking for a major investor,' Kevin told Cook.

'That's right,' agreed Ian, 'and our priority will be to repay BIM.'

'Where are the Teva share certificates?' asked Cook.

'Neeman's got them in Israel,' replied Kevin. Neither his face nor his voice betrayed him.

'Oh, good,' said Cook, collecting his papers. 'Clearly,' he thought, 'I've been mistaken.' The certificates were not, as he had imagined, in Kevin's safe, but Cook was too obsequious to challenge a Maxwell.

Shortly afterwards, in a nearby office, Trachtenberg was presented by Stuart Carson, LBI's compliance officer, with a list of BIM's shares. Nearly all those shares had been sold and the money taken, but theoretically LBI had provided collateral to repay the pension funds. 'Just insert the collateral,' instructed Carson. Trachtenberg was finding the chore unusually difficult to complete, especially since his attention was distracted by an unfortunate discovery. A tape recording of an incriminating conversation existed, but so far his attempts to arrange its seizure had proved fruitless.

The conversation, recorded on 4 November, featured Trachtenberg instructing a foreign exchange dealer employed by Robert Maxwell Group Trading to offer $35 million to Salomons in New York in exchange for £20 million in London. In normal times, Trachtenberg's order would have been unexceptional but, since July, Adrian Black, RMGT's manager, had watched the group's forex lines dwindle from fifteen to one as banks perceived that a 'forex line with the Maxwell group was the equivalent of a loan'. That truth re-emerged on 6 November when Salomons called Black in anger, complaining that the $35 million had not been received. Alarmed, Black dialled Trachtenberg fifty times that day until he finally got through, only to be told, 'Kevin is dealing with this personally. Your assistance is no longer required.' Five days later, Black was told that RMGT was to close down. During the following week, still concerned by the continuing failure to pay Salomons, he listened to the tape. His dealer had clearly not committed any errors but in the background he could hear Kevin's voice. Desperately looking for money, Kevin was urging Trachtenberg to find a bank willing to deal.

On 17 November, Black telephoned Trachtenberg: 'I've just listened to the tape of the Salomons deal.' The American at once became irate. 'He was very, very alarmed,' Black would say, 'which was completely out of character.'

'I don't understand why you're so worried,' declared Black.

'Because it incriminates me,' retorted Trachtenberg.

As a precaution that night, Black took the tape home 'to keep in a safe place'.

The next morning, the 18th, Trachtenberg contracted John Pole. Soon after, the chief of security arrived in Black's office with an assistant. 'I'm here on Kevin Maxwell's and Larry Trachtenberg's orders,' said Pole. 'I want the tape. I'm not leaving until you hand it over. And nor are you.' Black felt threatened. For thirty minutes the three men sat in the room until Black found an excuse to walk into the corridor. A security guard, standing by the lift, momentarily glanced the other way, allowing the heavy dealer to escape. Outside in Holborn, Black called his office on his mobile telephone. The security guards, he heard, were 'ripping his office apart, searching for the tape'. Black telephoned Trachtenberg. 'If the tape isn't on my desk by 6.30 tonight,' warned Trachtenberg, 'I can't be responsible for what happens.'

That evening, Black met Trachtenberg in a restaurant and handed over the tape. 'Larry sat there smiling, tapping the package,' Black would recall, conjuring up an image of Al Capone. Black, the two agreed, would leave the following day with a severance payment in return for signing an agreement promising his silence. When he got back to his office in Maxwell House, Trachtenberg was relieved. Throwing the tape into a drawer and pondered his next problem: another telephone call from Lehmans.

In the neighbouring Mirror building, in an office adjacent to Lawrence Guest's, bags of documents were being systematically shredded. Secretaries, accompanied by Maxwell's private treasury staff, were delivering incriminating evidence for permanent destruction. Unseen elsewhere, embarrassing computer records were being expunged by operators pressing a button marked 'DELETE'. One systems analyst, however, thought long and hard about Kevin's order to destroy his father's computer records. In the end Lisa Payne decide to half obey: she deleted the working version but retained the back-up. Alone in his room, listening to the mechanical whine of the shredding machine seeping through the partition, Guest doodled another memorandum to himself on his computer, with dots between the words: 'Fraud . . . LBI . . . Serious Fraud Squad . . . destroy evidence . . . £36.5 million . . . Oak Room . . .'

On his way to consult Kevin that morning, 18 November, Peter Laister had been puzzling over the collapse of MCC's share price. 'I just don't understand,' he told the other MCC directors; they were considering a stock-exchange inquiry whether they were aware of any price-sensitive information unknown to the market. 'Perhaps we need new financial advisers?' he asked. To his surprise, Kevin appeared unconcerned by the threat. Other matters were preoccupying him.

That evening, as Kevin digested a report to a BIM board meeting from Philip Morgenstern about the legal ramifications of the Maxwells' £296 million debt to the pension funds, he took a telephone call from David Shaffer, the Macmillan president in New York. 'We've received notice of a second 13D filing of Berlitz shares,' said the American. 'Lehmans claim that they own another 1.9 million shares from a defaulted loan.'

'They can't be ours,' soothed Kevin, although he had known that the bank was proposing the sale. Indeed, he had himself pledged the shares to Lehmans in three stages over the previous twelve months.

'They must be ours, Kevin!' exclaimed Shaffer. 'No one else has such a large holding.'

'I'll look into it,' promised Kevin, replacing the receiver.

Dissatisfied, Shaffer called Bob Hodes, the eminent New York lawyer who had acted against Robert Maxwell during the 1969 fiasco but had been retained by his adversary in 1989. 'I need information,' explained Shaffer.

Hodes called Philip Morgenstern, the first time they had ever spoken. 'I need information,' said the quietly spoken New York lawyer. 'The complete file.'

'I'll send you what I have,' promised Morgenstern.

That night, Basil Brookes was summoned from home back to Maxwell House by Kevin. The new chairman was sitting in his office with two Citibank representatives, furious because his promise to deposit the Que proceeds in their bank had not materialized.

'Can you tell these two gentlemen why we didn't transfer the Que money?' Kevin asked Brookes.

'Because it wasn't authorized,' replied the finance director, who was surprised to find himself thereupon quickly ushered out of the meeting.

'Sorry about this,' said Kevin plaintively to his visitors. 'This is not the way it should be done.'

'We want our money,' said Charles Covell, the Citibank vice-president, who had believed the promises Kevin had uttered over the previous twelve days.

'The independent directors are questioning my authority,' moaned Kevin, mourning his inability to reimpose Robert Maxwell's tyranny. 'But the truth is', he continued, 'that MCC owes RMG money.' The bankers noted that reassurance. They had no reason to doubt its authenticity. 'Kevin looks upset,' Covell thought, though he nonetheless announced that his bank would sue. The banker's threat was the least of Kevin's problems.

At 9.45 the following morning, 19 November, as Lord Mishcon, the lawyer whose advice had enabled Robert Maxwell to use the defamation laws to suppress the truth about his client's activities, walked sedately out of Kevin's office, Laister marched in. 'What the hell is this?' he thundered, waving a fax from Shaffer about the Berlitz shares.

'I know nothing about it,' said Kevin, caught on the hop. 'It's not what you think it is. It was all done by my father.' He had retreated to his second, dramatic line of defence: from pleading ignorance to conceding that his father might have been dishonest.

'We'll have to follow this through, Kevin,' warned Laister, somewhat intimidated by a performance which he later warranted 'should have won an Oscar'.

'Of course,' replied Kevin, seemingly unworried.

As a precaution, Kevin telephoned Hodes in New York: 'I'm absolutely shocked about what Bob did with the Berlitz shares.'

Hodes, still trusting Kevin and unsurprised by the revelation of his father's fraud, uttered some reassurance: 'Lehmans' title on Berlitz is uncertain. It's robber's due. We've got to see whether a thief like Bob can get good title.'

'Good idea,' replied Kevin, apparently heartened. He was suggesting that the problem was probably confined to just 9 per cent of the stake in Berlitz.

At noon, Kevin chaired a meeting of six MCC directors. In what his audience later realized was a show of bravado, he admitted that Lehmans' Berlitz shares belonged to Macmillan. 'My father improperly pledged them about one year ago.'

'What about the rest?' asked Shaffer on an open telephone line from New York. The mood soured at once.

'This is fucking disloyalty!' screamed Kevin down the intercom. 'You've gone behind my back.'

'Come off it, Kevin,' soothed Laister. 'David's only doing his job.'

Regaining his self-control, Kevin once more sought to portray himself as the victim of someone else's wrongdoing. 'I'll ask Basil Brookes to look for the shares. Basil,' he said, in his normal efficient way, 'I'd like you to take command and search for the missing Berlitz share certificate. We must find it.'

Brookes nodded, believing that MCC's survival depended upon

the sale of Berlitz to Fukutake. 'Kevin was very clever at that meeting,' he later reflected. 'He put the burden on me to find the missing shares, but he knew they had been pledged.' Brookes, an affable accountant, had been bewitched: 'We wanted to believe him.'

Sustained by this credulity, Kevin then promised, 'The family will reimburse MCC for the $32.3 million to buy back the shares from Lehmans. The money will come from the sale of private assets in Israel.' No one asked Kevin to identify those assets or pointed out that the most valuable investments actually belonged to the pension funds. Ron Woods, the tax expert, reflected that there had been 'concern at the meeting but no notion of a loss'. Despite all the dramas over the preceding days, Kevin was still trusted as he conjured up a new 'source' of money to save the empire: 'I'm dealing with rich Israelis who will fund the shortfall.' The notion of selling the 'private' assets in Israel had not surprisingly been allowed to evaporate. Finding that 'white knight' had been delegated to Yaakov Neeman, who had travelled to London to spread reassurance about the loan. The lawyer confirmed to Laister that a fax would be sent from Israel before noon the following day, 20 November. The Bank Hapoalim, he said, had agreed to loan the private companies $32.3 million, allowing the Berlitz shares to be repurchased from Lehmans and the sale to Fukutake to be completed. Even that was optimistic. Now that Gould had opened Maxwell's safe, Kevin knew his problems would multiply. Of the twenty-one Berlitz certificates for 10.5 million shares which Ghislaine had brought back from New York one year earlier, only two certificates for a total of 1 million shares had been found. Certificates for the remaining 9.5 million shares were missing.

The following morning, the arrival of the Israeli money was mysteriously 'delayed'. Unknown to Neeman, the Teva shares which the bank had accepted as collateral for the loan had proved difficult to extricate from Lehmans (who wanted cash in return); moreover, Kevin had pledged the second certificate to NatWest.

Undaunted by that conundrum, Kevin asked NatWest for a 'bridging loan for a few hours' until the Bank Hapoalim had released the funds. But that was blocked. 'No more loans,' asserted David Leal-Bennett. That draconian decision was delivered about the time that Kevin signed a 'letter of representation' for Richard Stone which did not reveal the relationship between the pension funds, BIM and their ownership of Teva shares: 'I didn't give the pension funds or BIM any thought,' Stone would say.

Soon after, Kevin, Ian and Trachtenberg were hearing from Trevor Cook at a BIM board meeting about a new calculation of the pension funds's exposure to RMG. 'It's even worse than I reported yesterday,' said Cook squinting with discomfort. 'I make it £454.7 million.' Then he added, 'I can't determine the fate of the Teva shares.' No one else said a word. In Tel Aviv, Michael Fox was still waiting for the Teva share certificate as Kevin walked up to the roof to catch the helicopter for Heathrow and a flight by Concorde. That evening in New York, faltering in his act as a master of the universe, he telephoned Robert Pirie, the banker. 'I'm feeling very low,' he said. 'Can we meet for dinner?' Pirie booked at the Lutece. He could later recall only that Kevin had lamented his lost father, a sentiment heard by no one else who encountered Robert Maxwell's son during that month. Certainly there was little comfort to be offered to Pirie and he played no part in selling off the empire whose construction he had facilitated.

The following morning in London, John Gould handed Highfield a handwritten list of the share certificates he had found in Robert Maxwell's safe. 'There's only photocopies of the Teva certificates,' he noted.

Referring to the last audit of pension fund shares conducted by John Cowling of Coopers on 5 April 1990, Highfield saw that the accountant had certified that the Teva shares were in BIM's possession. Puzzled, Highfield recalled Kevin's assertion four days earlier that the actual certificate was held by Neeman in Tel Aviv. 'A strange audit,' mused Highfield. Shortly after Kevin returned to London on 20 November, Cook again asked, 'Where are the Teva certificates now?'

'Neeman's got them,' replied Kevin, who had just received a fax from Michael Fox in Neeman's office confirming that he had arranged a loan and asking, 'I therefore need to know which [Teva] shares are to be used [as collateral] and where we can obtain the certificate?' It was a simple question which might have baffled the great Houdini.

SIXTEEN

Meltdown

– 21 November 1991

Overnight, Cook and Highfield became first suspicious and then alarmed. As a precaution, early on Thursday, 21 November, Highfield dispatched a fax to Michael Fox: 'Can you confirm whether you still hold the Teva share certificates? How many do you hold today?'

In Tel Aviv, Fox found the inquiry 'extremely odd'. Since he had sent the certificates to Kevin on 8 July, he assumed that Highfield knew the answer to his own question. After a confirmatory search in his office safe, his prompt reply was, 'None.' Highfield read the abrupt reply several times. And then he reeled in bewilderment.

'Can you advise when and how the Teva certificates left your safe-keeping?' Highfield scrawled in a handwritten fax.

One hour later, Highfield rushed into his superior's office, shouting at Cook, 'What the hell's going on? Fox has just told me that Lehmans have 22 million of our Teva shares!'

Cook telephoned Trachtenberg. 'Where are the Teva share certificates?' he asked.

'Maxwell had them on the boat,' answered Trachtenberg, who had signed the transfer form for one certificate of 25.1 million Teva shares to NatWest on 8 November and was constantly negotiating with Lehmans about the second certificate for 22.8 million shares.

Both Cook and Highfield then rushed across the street to Maxwell House. 'Look at this,' urged Cook, thrusting the Israeli lawyers' latest fax at Kevin. The typewritten words were unmistakable: 'We no longer hold Teva share certificates.'

'Neeman's made a mistake,' confided Kevin, telling a different story from that offered by his fellow director.

Soon after Highfield returned to his office he became more

bewildered, first by a report compiled by Bankers Trust of RMG's assets, which stated, 'LBIIM bought 8 per cent of Teva in 1984 at a cost of $30 million,' and secondly by a Coopers report on the pension funds' share holdings. Reading down the list, Highfield noticed that Coopers had listed as 'private' shares which he identified as pension fund assets. Among those 'private' shares were Teva. 'Look at this,' he said to the BIM manager.

Cook glanced at the list and then at the minute book of BIM's meetings. The entry for 7 November recorded the transfer of 25.1 million Teva shares to RMG. 'I wasn't at that meeting!' he yelled as he rushed towards Kevin's office.

'I know all about it,' replied Kevin coolly. 'New capital is coming from outside investors and we'll restore the capital to BIM.'

Mollified, Cook returned to his office. 'Kevin knows all about it,' he told Highfield. 'But something's funny,' he added with belated insight. 'And I still haven't got the Scitex money.'

The manager decided to consult a lawyer. Ian Pittaway, Maxwell's representative against the pensioners, seemed the ideal choice to advise on BIM's best course. 'The Maxwells have been using pension fund money,' Cook told him, 'and they can't pay it back.'

'What's your priority?' asked Pittaway. 'Whose interests are you trying to preserve?'

'The pensioners.'

'Is Kevin telling the truth when he says that he can get new capital to restore BIM?'

'I have to believe there's a chance,' said Cook, on the basis of Kevin's frequent assurances.

'If you believe there's a chance, will the police and IMRO enhance the chance of that happening?' Cook understood the drift. 'We mustn't blow the whistle otherwise we'll never get the money back,' advised the lawyer. Cook nodded, always amenable to suggestions. Understanding his need for self-protection, Cook sent a memorandum to Trachtenberg, Kevin and Ian. 'I was somewhat astonished', he wrote, 'about the loan of Teva shares to RMG.' Highfield had also sent a query to Trachtenberg, but would receive no reply.

The worst secrets were still being kept from Richard Stone of Coopers. 'Kevin appeared honest,' said the accountant later, 'and gave us all the information we required.' Stone's willingness to accept Kevin's explanations was more remarkable because his colleagues were auditors to the private companies and because, present at one of his conversations with Kevin, were Michael Moore and others from Bankers Trust, who knew how the Maxwells had used the Mirror Group to support a private £50 million loan.

Other bankers, including Julie Maitland, watched nervously as the value of the Maxwells' collateral fell. 'I need £17 million in shares or £11 million cash,' Maitland had demanded daily ever since 8 November. To silence her, Kevin offered 1 million Berlitz shares. She readily accepted. The last two certificates were taken from the safe and delivered by an electronic messenger to Crédit Suisse's headquarters in the City. Kevin had pledged 4 million Berlitz shares over the past seven days.

To stave off further requests, Kevin was trying to raise loans to buy back the pension shares. Piers La Marchant at Lehmans was among his particular targets. The lawyer agreed to hand back the pension fund shares in exchange for cash – a solution which only accentuated Kevin's anxieties as he flew to Paris on 21 November to meet more bankers demanding money and forestall another breach in the defences.

In his absence, Lawrence Guest met James Scrymgeour-Wedderburn, a director of Invesco MIM, the managers of a pension fund portfolio, for a regular quarterly meeting to review the portfolio's performance. Shares worth £750,000, Scrymgeour-Wedderburn told Guest, 'are missing, probably due to an administrative error'. Guest 'passed the information on to Cook'. There, momentarily, it remained. Guest was more concerned by Kevin's continuing failure to return the £38 million.

Over the weekend, dozens of Coopers accountants were burrowing through the citadel in Maxwell House, slowly stripping away the layers of deceit delicately put in place by Robert Maxwell to conceal his frauds. The newspapers reported unease, but no one yet imagined the explosive truth: that Kevin needed more than $1 billion to save RMG, the heart of the empire, at a time when all the bankers whom he and his father had so assiduously cultivated were declining to offer more loans. Instead, those same dark-suited men who for years had presented themselves as Kevin's friends now entered his office with a single purpose. 'You owe us $167,000,' said Charlie McVeigh of Salomon Brothers, referring to an unpaid fee, 'and we want to be paid now.' After an uncomfortable attempt to stall, Kevin summoned Brookes. 'Can you draw a cheque immediately?' he asked, clearly embarrassed.

Even more embarrassing was the personal call made by Richard Pelly and a colleague of Barclays Bank. 'We're not extending the $30 million,' said Pelly, pointing at yet another of Kevin's orders for foreign exchange which had been delivered but not paid. 'We want our money now. We're not leaving until we get it.' The banker, true to his threat, remained firmly seated. Once more, Brookes was summoned and bidden to scurry around the building in order to deliver a valid payment. 'I'm having problems with NatWest,' Brookes whispered to Kevin. That bank was holding all the money deposited in the Maxwells' accounts. A telephone call failed to release $30 million. Money in another account was produced and Pelly finally departed.

During those hours of Kevin's absence, on 21 November, three reports about the pension funds landed on Jeff Highfield's desk. One report by Bankers Trust listed 13 million shares in various companies pledged by the family (in the name of RMG) to Crédit Suisse. Peculiarly, all the shares were owned by the pension funds. A second report, by Lehmans, listed the shares pledged to them by the Maxwells as collateral. Again, the list featured shares owned by BIM. Together, they confirmed the extraordinary assertions in the Coopers report which, after detailed examination, revealed that the auditors had failed to itemize specific debts owed to BIM by RMG worth £232 million – an astonishing omission. Glancing down the list of shares, Highfield noticed the repetition of a familiar error. Teva and Euris shares were shown as privately owned (by RMG). 'These belong to the pension fund,' he muttered to himself.

Euris, the French company, was particularly puzzling. Highfield had written to the company's secretary on 4 October asking for confirmation that BIM was registered as a shareholder, but had received no reply. On 22 November, he faxed a handwritten note urging a response: 'La matière est toujours très urgente!!' On the same day, Odile Muracciole, the secretary, replied that the shares had been transferred on the orders of Kevin Maxwell more than one year earlier to Pergamon Holdings, a private family company.

Simultaneously, a reconfirming fax arrived for Cook from Neeman: 'We no longer hold any share certificates of Teva.' Cook had also just heard from Kevin that the £104 million due to BIM from the Scitex sale was 'missing'. 'I know this is a problem,' said Kevin, with impressive understatement.

White-faced and trembling, Cook stumbled into a meeting in Ian Maxwell's office. Waiting for him were Guest and Burrington. '£100 million is missing from the pension fund,' he stuttered, 'and there might be more.' But his outburst sparked little reaction. 'I don't think Ian realized how serious it was,' recalled Guest. 'He relied upon his little brother.' Even Guest himself, still anxious about the missing gilts, was untroubled. He did not connect his problems with the pension funds. 'I don't think the Mirror Group directors should have known what was happening,' he later reasoned, though he was a pension fund trustee. 'It was not their responsibility.'

'At that stage, I became worried,' remembered Cook. Over the weekend, he dictated a letter to the directors of MCC which opened with a memorable understatement: 'I have become aware of certain transactions . . . with the rest of the group.' Cook had still not realized the truth about the so-called stock lending.

New rumours were now swirling around the City of London. None was more concerned than the bankers at Crédit Suisse. That morning, Julie Maitland had received a letter from the Bank of America warning that the securities she had received in September and October were trust property, owned by the pension funds. Richard Khawam of Crédit Suisse telephoned Trachtenberg and asked for an explanation. 'All the allegations are inaccurate!' laughed Trachtenberg. 'Coopers have done an independent investigation and we're clean, and NatWest are completely happy.' The auditors' investigation was indeed independent, but the result was not 'clean'. Yet Trachtenberg even supplied Khawam with a letter stating that the 1 million Berlitz shares pledged to Crédit Suisse were owned privately by the Maxwells.

That weekend Kevin adopted his father's ploy: 'When in a hole, shout loud to drown out the criticism.' Summoning the City editors from three quality Sunday newspapers, Kevin pumped propaganda to previously unquestioning puff merchants whose gullibility over the years had been so profitably exploited. His first hurdle was to explain the confirmed newspaper report that the Serious Fraud Office, at the request of the Swiss Bank, had opened an investigation into the fate of the First Tokyo portfolio. To the *Sunday Times*, more sceptical than others, he confessed, 'We never anticipated the Swiss Bank situation. It was the greatest surprise since Bob died.' In an article headlined, 'Boys on the Burning Deck', the impression given by the newspaper was of two young, innocent men gallantly fighting to salvage their unexpected inheritance: 'In the days immediately following Maxwell's death, they seemed to have brought some order to the threatened chaos.' A similar theme was reflected in the *Sunday Telegraph*, which reported that 'normality had returned' thanks to Kevin's 'resilient performance in adversity'. In a show of contempt for those faithful employees feeling increasingly bruised by the unfolding evidence of dishonesty, Kevin said, 'We are satisfied that after a full inquiry there will be no case to proceed with.' Ian was likewise afforded sympathy in the *Sunday Times* comment that he 'angrily denounces the "tasteless" attacks on his father. Sometimes, somewhere, one feels, he will want his revenge.'

The reality was precisely the opposite of what those journalists reported. Kevin needed to scrape the barrel for cash and, early on Sunday morning, 24 November, he appealed to two people who remained untouched by the saga.

Kevin's first call in Highgate, north-west London, was on Conrad Black. With his usual composure, the visitor outlined his problems to the majority shareholder of the Telegraph group: 'I wonder whether you would be interested in buying the *Daily News* in New York, the *Lady Ghislaine* and our stake in the *Independent*?' Black expressed interest in a voice that sounded like a polite 'no thanks' and bade him goodbye. Five minutes later, Kevin was nearby at Gerald Ronson's front door. The businessman was not a customer for anything Kevin offered, but was asked for advice about his conduct at a meeting that evening with bankers. Over a cup of coffee, Ronson advised Kevin 'to tell the truth. If you want to retain your credibility and want to keep your bankers' support, don't lie to them or they'll bury you.' Expressionless, Kevin gazed at the man. 'Be one hundred per cent honest' were Ronson's last words as he bade farewell at the door.

'Yes, I'll do that,' replied Kevin.

Driving back into town, Kevin resolved not to adopt Ronson's advice wholeheartedly. Fathered by a survivor of the Holocaust whose Ruthenian childhood had bequeathed a unique approach to 'the truth', Kevin interpreted Ronson's advice in his particular fashion. The moment, he decided, had arrived to adopt another strategy.

That afternoon, back in his office full of besuited people working as if it were a weekday, Kevin uttered a confession to Cook: 'Something's gone wrong, but I don't know the details. However, I think we've got a good chance of rescuing it all.' Once again, Cook felt reassured and dutifully noted down Kevin's suggestions for finding the pension funds' assets. Obediently, Cook began telephoning bankers. Their replies were unexpected. 'We'd like a deal,' said the bankers. 'We'll give you back the pension fund shares if you can give us cash.' Ruefully Cook was later to conclude, 'Kevin pointed me to go down blind alleys. He knew it was all rubbish.'

In the middle of the afternoon, Ian returned from a daytrip to Jerusalem. In their bid to find a saviour, the brothers believed that their father's fame and popularity in Israel might produce government help. Ian had travelled with David Vogel, the solicitor who had cautioned that any request for help, must be based upon 'full disclosure'. Ian had nodded. At Neeman's request, Ian was received by Yitzhak Modai, the minister of finance. After a short appeal for help which did not encompass 'full disclosure', the minister agreed that he would happily consider any proposal. It was typically a politician's gesture which promised nothing.

After visiting his father's grave, Ian returned to London to accompany Kevin to see John Melbourn in the NatWest Tower. 'We are sure that a major Israeli investor will inject £400 million into the group,' Kevin told the banker. Melbourn believed that assurance and then abruptly changed his tone: 'We have a grave concern about the apparent lack of integrity in the management of the Maxwell business.' Kevin stared blankly as Melbourn continued in a studiously understated manner, 'The Swiss Bank seems to have a problem with First Tokyo and there seems something amiss with Berlitz.' A chill enveloped the room. Kevin coughed to break the tension. As he spoke, Melbourn wrote, 'Both Maxwells say they cannot honestly deny they had been party to such transactions . . . Ian Maxwell [says] that he had signed one document for the Swiss Volksbank transaction.' Adopting the posture of the poor victim, Kevin launched into a tale of woe, complaining, 'Bob had a way of doing things and we just followed . . .' The banker listened in apparent sympathy although the following day, Linklaters, the bank's solicitors, would send a list of queries about diversions of shares and money to Titmuss Sainer 'raising questions about the integrity and probity of the brothers'.

At this point, Kevin's fate seemed to depend upon many people in many places, but it was sealed, unintentionally, by Philip Morgenstern. Over the previous years, the lawyer had provided advice and comfort letters which Kevin had welcomed. Occasionally, Kevin had asked his lawyer questions which had confused the issue. For example, only recently, he had asked whether MCC was entitled to pay £30 million to BIM to cover the payments to BPCC. The lawyer replied in the affirmative, but the real issue – that the £30 million was owed to BIM by RMG – was ignored. But over previous days, Morganstern had become concerned by Cook's disclosures about Kevin's unusual procedures to transfer the Teva shares from BIM to RMG, Lehmans and the Israeli banks. Moreover, on Berlitz, Morgenstern had direct knowledge of the facts and, having been asked by Hodes, the New York lawyer representing Macmillan, for his complete file, Morgenstern properly held nothing back.

To Hodes's surprise, Morgenstern had not queried his authority for the request. Still more astonishing to him, among the pile of documents which stuttered out of the fax machine at his Bedford home in New York on the morning of Sunday, 24 November – just as Kevin was returning from Ronson's home – was a copy of the document transferring 1.9 million Berlitz shares to Lehmans. The clear signature on the transfer was Kevin's. The date was September. Suddenly, all Kevin's accusations against 'Bob' crumbled. 'I wonder if Morgenstern knows what he's sent us,' Hodes thought as he telephoned Shaffer. Minutes later, Shaffer was passing on the dramatic revelation to Laister: 'Kevin's signature is on the transfer form of the Berlitz shares to Lehmans.' Laister was shattered. As he digested the news, Shaffer called again: 'Ian's signature is on the pledge of 2.4 million Berlitz shares to Swiss Volksbank. It's dated 12 November. After Bob's death.'

Baffled and outraged, Laister barged into Kevin's office. 'What's this?' he spat.

'I don't know what you're talking about,' cooed Kevin.

'But look at the facts,' spluttered Laister.

'I really don't understand,' replied Kevin calmly. 'I didn't realize what all that meant. My father must have authorized it and just told me to sign.'

Laister was incredulous: 'But you signed in September!'

'I didn't sign in my capacity as an MCC director,' said Kevin. 'I was under the impression they were a private holding.'

'You'll have to go!' shouted Laister, storming out. He now understood that MCC did not own Berlitz any more, so the £149 million lifeline from Fukutake was a hollow myth.

'Kevin is the problem,' Laister told his colleagues when they gathered in Holborn early on Monday morning, 25 November. 'He's lying and he knows we think he's a liar.' Appointed by Robert Maxwell for their pliability, none of the four directors had been sufficiently robust to outwit his son. Their predicament was agonizing. If their discovery was revealed to the world's bankers and accountants, MCC would be finished. But if they kept quiet to save the company, they allowed Kevin to exclude them from the continuing negotiations. 'Our problems won't be solved by Kevin's efforts,' said Laister despairingly, himself unable to propose a solution.

By then, the Swiss Volksbank bankers had come to understand their own plight. To their astonishment, Kevin had just told them that the Berlitz shares he had pledged a mere two weeks earlier at Zurich airport in fact belonged to MCC. 'Apparently they are not owned by the private side,' said the man who, in the same tone and with the same confident manner, had assured them that the shares were owned by the family. This was to be Kevin's defence, and those to whom his words were directed understood precisely their meaning. The effect was awesome.

Panic began to infect normally level-headed men and women to whom bad debts could be a death sentence for otherwise promising careers. In a bid to forestall that unpleasant fate, bankers began rushing to register their legal ownership of the Berlitz shares. Among the herd was Julie Maitland. Daily her bank had warned Kevin that the collateral for their loan was still insufficient. On the morning of 25 November, she received another reminder from the Bank of America that the shares which had been delivered over the previous two months belonged to pension funds.

All those bankers were among ninety of that calling who gathered at 10.30 a.m. that same morning in the Chartered Insurance Institute, a wood-panelled neo-Gothic edifice in the City, to ponder

Kevin's promises. Ian Maxwell, silent but oddly smiling, stood near Kevin. None of the bankers was aware that MCC's directors had discovered the diversion of the Berlitz shares or that about £454 million – the official total – was missing from the pension funds. 'I hadn't thought of the pension funds,' Richard Stone would complain. They would not correct the investigators' naive statement, 'BIM is a subsidiary of Headington Investments.' But many of them harboured their own secrets, possessing share certificates clearly showing 'Bishopsgate Investment Management' as the registered owner. So, as unwilling accomplices, they sat listening to an assessment of the private companies' assets by Colin Kier of Bankers Trust, appointed for that task by Kevin and Coopers.

The valuation had been completed earlier that week by Scott Wheeler, a senior Bankers Trust executive. Conveniently, he had found his task made easier by reliance upon Kevin. Among the private interests listed in the thick, blue-bound report (codenamed 'Project Sage') was Teva Pharmaceutical. Kier said that the Maxwell private assets were valued at between £946 million and £1.37 billion, while the family's debts were £850 million. Ripples of relief spread among the audience, although the debts were higher than previously stated. For Kier's estimate suggested that the loans would be repaid. Characteristic of his judgment, however, was his valuation of the *European* at £26.5 million. Six weeks later, the newspaper would be sold for about £2 million.

Richard Stone, Coopers' rescue specialist, made the second presentation, codenamed 'Russet'. Prefacing his comments with caveats, he voiced similar reassurance. His estimate – also based on fanciful information supplied by Kevin with his signed assurance that 'there are no material inaccuracies or omissions' – was that Maxwell's private companies owed £70 million to MCC and Mirror Group and another £70 million to the pension funds. Salvation and repayment of the loans, cautioned Stone, depended upon the banks' patience. The alternative was immediate bankruptcy of the Maxwell empire and the certainty of bad debts. Although some bankers among his audience had good reason to be sceptical about his sanguine approach, none was inclined to question his assessment and thereby expose his or her own culpability. Instead they accepted Kevin's assurances and his *mea culpa* when he rose to speak and, among a catalogue of causes, blamed his predicament on 'an over-ambitious expansion plan'. He continued, 'All the directors of the private group, including myself, must bear responsibility in part.' None even expressed either anger or disbelief when he added that 'all the Berlitz shares are owned by MCC', a strange statement in the circumstances. There was unanimous acceptance of John Melbourn's advice that Stone should be allowed another week's investigation with a bankers' 'standstill' for another three weeks. 'The alternative', cautioned the NatWest banker, 'is to lose everything.' In an echo of another banker's self-confident statement, it was agreed that MCC would be 'ring-fenced'.

Kevin left the meeting pleased with his display of nerve: the partitions erected by Robert Maxwell to compartmentalize his activities had only crumbled at the edges. His success in persuading Kier and Stone that the hole was no bigger than £70 million, with some questions about two Berlitz holdings, boosted his morale as he returned to Maxwell House, smiling at the television news cameras. Outside the citadel, he was still so free of suspicions that he had successfully drawn $3.8 million from a joint account shared with a Berlin newspaper without Bertelsman, his partner, realizing until too late. With luck, the banks' agreed standstill until 20 December would allow him to survive the new Coopers' audit due to be completed within two weeks.

As the two brothers walked out of the lift on the ninth floor, Laister met them with a challenge: 'Your signature is on the transfer of 2.4 million Berlitz shares to the Swiss Volksbank.'

'It's not as it seems,' grimaced Ian. 'I was wearing another hat.'

Uncertain and confused, Laister and Woods hurried to Geoffrey Rippon's chambers, where the lawyer was at work. 'Can we trust Kevin any more?' asked Laister, shattered by the sudden discovery of Robert Maxwell's crimes. 'The problems are massive. Money is missing. The banks know there's a gigantic hole and that the Berlitz shares are owned by banks. Kevin can't be telling the truth. We should get rid of him. But how?'

The three directors agreed to seek the help of Samuel Montagu, since MCC did not retain a permanent merchant bank. Driving into the City, they consulted Ian McIntosh. 'It would be suicidal,' they told him, 'if the truth leaks. Secrecy is vital to survival.' The banker did not disagree, but that did not provide sufficient reassurance.

At 11.45 Laister, Woods and Brookes returned to MacFarlanes, the solicitors. 'The whole of Berlitz has been lost,' revealed Laister. 'The whole 56 per cent, worth $270 million, has been pledged. We can't find any of the share certificates.' But he dismissed stories of pension fund losses of £400 million. 'It's more like £60 million.'

'Kevin's clearly a liar,' declared Derek Hayes, one of the lawyers.

In the early afternoon, Laister barged into Kevin's office: 'We've got a major problem, Kevin. Cook says that $77 million from the sale of Que has been committed to the pension funds.'

'He's wrong,' replied Kevin, feigning astonishment and calmly picking some papers off his desk. 'Cook's wrong about the debts and the agreements.' Laister, standing on the other side of the desk, exploded. 'You've lied to us. Our assets have gone. We don't trust you any more,' he shouted. 'You'll have to go.'

'That would be most unwise,' replied Kevin, gazing back at him. 'I've told the banks everything I know, but I don't understand everything. I've persuaded them to agree to a standstill on the private-side debts. If I go now, MCC will fold.' Laister was flummoxed, as the younger man asserted his indispensability: 'The banks know everything about the private companies' debts to MCC and about Berlitz.' Laister's life experience had not prepared him for such audacity.

But Kevin reserved his coup for the board meeting of six directors held minutes later: 'I've negotiated and confirmed the standstill with the banks.' He was now trying to distance himself from the earthquake and focus the blame upon his father: 'Bob acted *ultra vires*, so none of these transactions will be valid.' Then he resorted to an earlier ploy: 'I've been promised between £200 and £400 million from an Israeli source by the end of the week.' He said nothing about drawing on the family's fortune in Liechtenstein. Icily self-controlled, he stared at his audience. Thirty-two years of training by Robert Maxwell had inculcated in him an unusual disposition towards truth, morality and relationships. But his performance was decisive: Laister and the other directors were silenced. To force Kevin's resignation, they now believed, would be to inflict a fatal wound upon themselves and the company. 'We'll give it a go,' agreed Laister. 'It's in MCC's best interests,' he would say, 'to keep everything quiet.' Making no public announcement would avoid self-destruction. But as a sign of his distrust of Kevin, he moved his office away from the new chairman's, further along the ninth floor.

Still convinced that he retained control, Kevin welcomed his next visitors, Sir Michael Richardson and Colin Kier. Brokers, bankers and accountants had been promised unfettered and unprecedented access to all the records for their exhaustive audit. Altogether some forty bankers and accountants were combing through the empire to follow the money trail. 'Now Bob has gone, we need to find out the truth,' they sang, although not quite in unison. Of all the City's lions, it was Richardson who some thought was best placed to know the truth. But he denied any culpability and excused any bad judgment on the grounds of his gullibility. About Kevin he offered the opinion, 'His view of life was distorted by his father.'

Late that afternoon, at Kevin's request, officials from IMRO, the regulator, visited BIM's offices in Dorrington Street. Considering Cook's limited discoveries, Kevin calculated it wise to play the honest custodian, and he hoped to rely upon Stuart Carson, the compliance officer for LBI, to handle the visit judiciously. Carson presented an IMRO official with a list of shares held by LBI for stock lending by BIM on behalf of the pension funds. 'This is what I've been given,' he said.

The official was surprised. 'I didn't realize that LBI worked for BIM,' he said, revealing startling ignorance. He then walked over to Cook.

'I'm somewhat concerned about the situation,' said Cook, with his by then customary understatement. The official next asked Trachtenberg for the location of BIM's share certificates which had been handed over by Cook.

'RM', replied Trachtenberg, 'said I should leave all the collateral in his safe and we haven't been able to establish its whereabouts.'

The IMRO official turned to Peter Walsh, the senior Coopers auditor. His reply was hardly reassuring: 'Larry Trachtenberg told us that he physically checked the collateral at regular intervals'.

Carson's report from Cook's exchange with the IMRO official worried Kevin. The citadel needed to be re-fortified. 'You must never speak to regulatory authorities,' he wrote to Cook. 'Only Carson is authorized.'

London was still dark when Kevin arrived in his office at 6.30 a.m. on Tuesday, 26 November. The vibrations already reaching him from the teams of financial investigators sifting through the Maxwells' sensitive files suggested that his bluff was being called. Julie Maitland telephoned him early to explain that her superior at Crédit Suisse, Gerhard Beindorff, head of corporate banking, had confided his belief that Kevin did not own the shares which he had pledged, especially those from First Tokyo. This desperate situation, decided the Swiss banker, required desperate measures.

At 2.45 p.m., a delegation of Crédit Suisse bankers, including Maitland, arrived in Kevin's office. After brief pleasantries, the visitors proffered letters drafted by their lawyers. Kevin was to sign authorizations for the bank to register their ownership of all the pension fund and First Tokyo shares pledged as collateral. Another letter, drafted by the bank for his signature, attested that all those shares, even if registered in another name, were owned by RMG. Unflinching and unhesitating, Kevin signed all the documents. He also agreed that all the shares could be sold by the bank. (He asked that the shares of Teva, Berlitz and MCC be excluded from the sale.) Grateful for his co-operation, the bankers left the building at 3 p.m. and began selling the shares before the market closed that afternoon. Whether they believed Kevin's assurances was doubtful, but that was irrelevant compared to the stakes: their careers, their reputations and the bank's money. Their individual fates were still tied to Kevin's. Any dispute about title could be left to lawyers and courts, who could argue, so far as they were concerned, for ever.

Not everyone's nerves in Maxwell House were as steely as Kevin's. On the eighth floor, Trachtenberg was fretting. Cook had sent an unwelcome memorandum complaining that he had been deceived about the location of the Teva shares. 'I would be grateful', he wrote, 'if you could fully explain the position with Lehman Brothers.' That was precisely what Trachtenberg was unwilling to do since at that moment he was on the telephone with Mark Haas discussing Lehmans' requirement of a letter from BIM authorizing their registration of ownership of the Teva shares in Israel. 'I'm sitting in Robert Maxwell's old office and we're trying to get some bastard to sign the letter,' he told Haas. 'BIM is going to hold a board meeting to authorize the letter.' But Trachtenberg could not conceal that someone was causing problems. Nor could the American's temperament prevent his mask slipping. To one contact at the Bank of America he unexpectedly admitted, 'I don't know if the stock lending was collateralized.' Then he typed a letter to Trevor

Cook confirming that all BIM share certificates had been 'passed to RM'. He dated the letter June. Cook had never received the letter, but Trachtenberg would eventually hand his own copy to the Serious Fraud Office.

By contrast, Kevin was becoming cooler by the day. His survival depended, he knew, on astute housekeeping, and that required a visit to New York. The opportunity presented itself on Thursday, 28 November, when his father had been due to stand on the tribune in New York for Macy's Thanksgiving parade. Still toying with Maxwell's notion that the empire could be rebuilt around the *Daily News*, Kevin slipped out of Maxwell House, drove by car to Farnborough and boarded the G4 at 4 p.m. on the Wednesday. Persuaded by Pandora that he should take a break, he decided to abandon ship temporarily for an astonishing journey to join his wife, three children and a nanny at the Carlyle in New York. The hotel bill for two suites was 'over $10,000'. In London, no one was aware of his journey. Greeted in New York by John Campi, Kevin seemed in good humour, remarked in passing that all was well in London and on the 28th took his place near Mayor Dinkins. 'They're having a great time,' noted Campi. At noon, after Kevin had had a brief discussion with Aboff about the financial reserves in Ph(US)Inc., the Maxwell family drove to the airport and flew home in the Gulfstream. 'Children were everywhere,' recalled Captain Whiteman of what was to be his last flight for the Maxwells – bringing Kevin back not just to London but to reality.

In his brief absence, the jigsaw had become marginally more complete. Basil Brookes had been compiling his own schedule of loans based on information from the private companies, which he previously had not demanded or been allowed to see. He now realized that the Maxwells had borrowed substantially more from MCC than the £60 million claimed by Kevin. The missing amount was a staggering £297 million. Richard Davey, an investigating banker from N. M. Rothschild, only heard about Brookes's discovery indirectly on Friday afternoon. His source was Michael Stoney, the Mirror Group manager whose assistance in finding a route through the labyrinth had been valued by the bankers. 'We suddenly realized that a number of people must have known about those loans,' commented Davey, 'and it was the moment we realized that we needed to open up the pension can of worms.'

Soon after Kevin had returned to the building – without mentioning his dash to New York – he was asked by Richard Stone to explain how Swiss Volksbank had come to possess the Berlitz shares. 'I went with Bob to Volksbank for a loan,' he answered calmly, albeit with a sheepish look, 'and he pledged the shares. Bob told the bankers that the shares were privately owned because they had been transferred from MCC to BIT. I had no reason to doubt my father.' It was no longer possible to believe a word Kevin said.

That evening, control over the empire slipped from Kevin's grasp. His removal from the board of MCC required a unanimous vote (and he was unlikely to approve his own dismissal), so on Laister's initiative the other directors proposed to delegate all the board's powers to a sub-committee from which both Kevin and Ian would be excluded.

'That's totally improper!' stormed Kevin. 'I can't operate if there's this sub-committee.'

'We insist,' said Laister, and Kevin was outvoted.

Elsewhere in the building, Richard Stone for the first time came across the name Larry Trachtenberg, until then unknown to him. He was meanwhile attempting to meet Trevor Cook, but the pension fund manager was resisting invitations: he would answer questions only through Michael Stoney. 'He had known something was wrong,' said Stone later, 'but it never occurred to him what the mechanics were leading up to. He had the shock of his life.' Others were less charitable.

By telephone, Cook guided Stoney through his files, showing how he had passed the pension fund shares for stock lending to Trachtenberg at LBI. Trachtenberg had supplied sufficient details by Saturday night, 30 November, for everything to fall into place. Davey could conclude: 'We understood the rape of the funds.' Cook and Trachtenberg, the investigators concluded, 'knew they were sitting on a bomb'. After totting up the sums, Stone's previous estimate that MCC was worth about £200 million was drastically altered: the company in fact had net debts of over £1.9 billion. RMG's debt to BIM was estimated at £440 million. The private companies' debt was estimated to be an additional £758 million. 'It throws the total position into dramatic insolvency,' concluded Stone.

'This is awful,' stuttered Samuel Montagu's Ian McIntosh. 'My

God,' said Laister looking as if 'he'd been hit with a club'. White faces in dark suits sat slumped as the news spread. Even Ian Maxwell appeared 'shattered and uncomprehending'. Only Kevin remained composed. 'It's terrible what Bob's been up to,' he blithely told Andrew Galloway, the Samuel Montagu banker who had floated the Mirror Group. Even on Sunday morning, 1 December, Galloway was still not pointing a finger at the brothers, unaware that the directors of MCC, Mirror Group and the private companies knew precisely the nature of Kevin's involvement.

On Sunday night, Stone and Davey visited John Melbourn at the NatWest's headquarters to advise that Maxwell's private companies required £400 million to survive. At their frequent meetings throughout the previous week, Melbourn had sympathized with Kevin, not least because ever since the 1940s Robert Maxwell had built his business with the old Westminster Bank and had never defaulted. Melbourn had always trusted the younger son and now believed his assurances of an imminent £400 million investment from Israel. By then, the unknown investor – the White Knight – was assumed to be an Arab, because he could not be reached by telephone from Israel. 'Only God', it was quipped within Kevin's small sanctum, 'can reach him.' Kevin went further. 'God himself', he said, 'is being considered as an investor.' Given his cool self-assurance, he might have even believed that scenario when he had last spoken to the mild-mannered and gullible banker on the telephone.

'I'm unwilling to pull the rug,' Melbourn told his visitors. 'Let's give them time. They've still got a fifty–fifty chance of survival.' His optimism was based on the same lack of reality which had enabled Robert Maxwell to borrow money long after his insolvency. Unconvinced, Stone returned to Maxwell House determined to advise the banks that rescue was impossible.

As he returned, Shaffer called Laister with the result of some fast research in the company's registry. '10.1 million Berlitz shares have been pledged,' he reported. 'Crédit Suisse and a New York company called Advest are among the other owners.' Advest's director was Shelly Aboff, Maxwell's crony.

Laister's shock was redoubled. 'That's it,' he said through gritted teeth, recalling that both brothers had signed transfer forms for Berlitz shares, 'Kevin's got to go.' Once more bursting into Kevin's office, Laister's threat was vehement: 'If you don't go, I'll expose you publicly!'

'I'll think about it,' answered Kevin, taken aback.

The sanctuary provided by his father's enormous office was dissolving. Beyond, in the corridors on the ninth floor, the atmosphere resembled the quiet chaos familiar to those who have witnessed the dying days of an embattled regime in the Third World. Everywhere on Monday, 2 December, the 'suits' were huddled, conferring in whispers about their discoveries and the consequences. Richard Stone was suggesting that dealings in MCC and Mirror Group shares be suspended. Bankers and accountants spoke with lawyers about the procedures to be followed in applications for insolvency, only to be interrupted by Kevin, emerging from his office, to talk about a new agreement with the banks to allow an investigation of MCC by Price Waterhouse. Throughout that day, Ian Maxwell, the new chairman of the Mirror Group, expressed surprise that the City's reverence towards his family should be evaporating. 'These grey suits are crazy,' he told a poker-faced banker. 'We've got money coming on Friday which will save us.' He had been repeating that incantation ever since he returned from Israel one week earlier. 'Don't rock the boat,' he urged. 'Don't get in a flap.'

Later that night Ian told the Mirror Group board that among the company's previously undisclosed debts was £50 million owed to Bankers Trust. His informant, he explained, was Kevin. Even Sir Robert Clark, an admirer, was shocked when he understood the manipulation which Robert Maxwell had authorized. 'That's the last straw, Ian' he gasped. 'You'll have to go.'

Outside, Clark saw Kevin, who, although not a director of the Mirror Group, had clearly played a part in sanitizing the loan.

'It's just a trivial matter,' remarked Kevin of the £50 million. 'Just wait for the money from Israel.'

'I don't believe a word you say,' Clark replied.

'That's your misfortune,' retorted Kevin with studied aloofness.

'He thinks we're all fools,' Clark reflected later. 'He thought he could hide all this and get away with it.'

Late that night, John Melbourn of NatWest heard about the latest discoveries – the Berlitz shares, the £50 million loan from Bankers Trust and the massive inter-company debts. 'I'm shocked at the disclosures,' he confessed. 'The situation is slipping away.'

'We'll have further discussions with the banks tomorrow,' said Kevin. 'We'll continue the standstill.'

'Too late,' said the banker, convinced that the only hope of rescue was if the unnamed Israeli 'immediately put cash on the table'. In the meantime,' he said, 'the shares of MCC and MGN will have to be suspended.'

Late on that Monday night, sitting in the Mirror building to avoid the bedlam around their own offices, Laister consoled himself with Woods and Brookes: 'It's all hopeless.' Regarded as the elder statesman by the others, he confessed to having had 'a soft spot for Kevin'.

'My God,' said Brookes. 'What a mistake to trust Kevin. He was so plausible. I really feel he has raped me. He came across as so helpful, but he was in cahoots with his old man.'

Feeling somewhat sorry for themselves, they spoke to directors of three London clearing banks. 'Kevin must resign,' the bankers separately advised. Accordingly, at 10.30 p.m., Laister went to Kevin's office. 'You must go,' he said.

Kevin refused: 'I want to hear from each of the directors.' Pathetically, he then visited the two other directors one by one to face accusations from each.

'Two weeks ago I couldn't have said this, Kevin,' whispered Woods, who thought he was acting courageously, 'but too much has tumbled out of the woodwork. You must resign.'

The following day, Tuesday, 3 December, Kevin was formally told at a MCC board meeting by Laister, Woods and Brookes, 'We want your resignation immediately.' Ian sat quietly by his side.

Showing no sign of emotion, Kevin agreed, but with a caveat: 'I think Ian should remain.' Laister refused. Both brothers would have to go but, in a gesture which the directors would regret, they were allowed to leave quietly and with dignity. 'No one realizes what they did,' Laister reflected months later.

For the non-family directors there was momentarily 'a great sense of relief'. The past weeks had absorbed so much energy, as they had wrestled with a nightmare in a fog of ignorance. Kevin had been so clever, dealing with the bankers on his own, blocking the other directors and not revealing what was happening. His departure appeared to calm the storm, not least because all believed that they could still save the company.

By then, at 8.25 a.m., trading in the shares of both MCC and Mirror Group had been officially suspended. MCC's price was 35p and Mirror Group's 125p. That same morning, Lawrence Guest stepped into the lift to find Kevin standing in a corner. Kevin stared at him and Guest glared back. Neither man spoke.

Still displaying no emotion, Kevin arrived later that morning at the Chartered Insurance Institute to hear Stone's revised 'Russet' report to the bankers. Listened to in anguished silence, Stone revealed that the Maxwells' private debts had risen to a new total of £1.8 billion. His report concluded: 'Survival impossible.' Then Kevin spoke. During the previous night he had been urging Neeman to produce a fax promising that an Israeli investor would inject £400 million into the group. 'I urgently need this letter to show to people,' said Kevin. The author of the letter, but not the promise, would be David Kimche, the former director-general of Israel's foreign ministry and a former senior Mossad officer who boasted excellent contacts in Israel. The detail that the 'Israeli investor' was now possibly an Arab might have caused serious questions if the atmosphere had been calm. But the mood made it appropriate not to challenge Kevin's quip to members of his circle as they awaited written confirmation which might halt the slide towards insolvency: 'The hand of God will save us.'

Just after 5 p.m. Israeli time, Kimche approved Neeman's letter to Kevin: 'David Kimche has spoken to representatives of the investor who is still in London. . . . The representative will be happy to assist you as much as he can within his limitation.' The investor was described as 'very serious and prominent . . . and capable to make this size of investment'. The letter was identical to a draft prepared by Kevin two days earlier. The investor's identity was not revealed. 'Kimche', explained Neeman, 'is very discreet.'

Kevin naturally grasped at the straw. Flourishing Neeman's fax, he told the assembled bankers that new money would arrive from Israel and pleaded for three days' standstill. Since the bankers had only straws to clutch, his proposal could not be rejected, if only to save face. Only one banker, a Japanese, challenged him: 'You lied to us. Why?' Kevin said nothing – so much more convenient.

Just after noon, he returned to Maxwell House and announced his resignation from the board. To the press he explained that he wanted to avoid a conflict of interest between his loyalty to his father and his wish to co-operate with the impending investigation into the relationship between the private and public companies. In reply to a query whether any money was missing from the pension funds, he replied, 'I can't say.' All the transactions, he insisted, between the private and public companies had been authorized and properly recorded: 'My brother and I were board colleagues with my father for many years. But clearly we didn't know everything that was going on. My father had a style of business based on "need to know" rather than a sharing of information all the time.' Richardson was moved to remark that Kevin's performance on this occasion was 'brilliant'.

Ian still hoped to survive as chairman of the Mirror Group. His supporters included Joe Haines, the columnist who had denounced his father as a crook in 1984 but had asserted new principles after being offered money and status. Another sympathizer, albeit a more realistic one, was Ernie Burrington. 'Ian,' he said, 'if your name was Smith there wouldn't be a problem. But your name is Maxwell and I don't see how you can stay.' One hour later, Kevin's promise of an Israeli saviour was finally discounted. The Maxwell Communication Corporation, destined by its founder five years earlier to rank by 1990 as one of the world's top ten media giants worth £3 to £5 billion, was on the verge or being declared insolvent and placed under the control of administrators. Simultaneously, the Robert Maxwell Group and most of the 400 private companies were placed under administration. Shock spread throughout the capital.

That night, in a move which symbolized the new *Daily Mirror*, the editor who four weeks earlier had eulogized Maxwell as the saviour damned him as a fraudster. Richard Stott, Maxwell's willing toady, spewed out venom against his late employer. 'Maxwell the Crook' was succeeded by stories of 'Maxwell the Lover' and then 'Maxwell the Bugger' as Pole's microphones were discovered in the building. The journalist now pretended that his previous servility to Maxwell had been an invention of his rivals. Habits of allegiance were being shed across the world by those who had rushed to accept the late Publisher's invitations and pleaded for contracts. Many spoke with disdain of the man in whose outer office they had waited for hours and even days to win an audience.

Joe Haines confessed to his readers that he had suffered 'an awful week, the worst I can remember'. Demonstrating his capacity for self-deception, he continued, 'Bob Maxwell, the man who once genuinely saved the *Mirror*, has, through his manipulations of that [pensions] money, now delivered us into the hands of those whom he hated, the pinstripes of the City of London.' Even at the end, Haines understood nothing, for the truth was that Maxwell desired above all to be accepted by the City establishment. And, like all the other Mirror Group directors, Haines expressed no sense of responsibility for failing to safeguard the shareholders' and pensioners' funds. For he had earlier retired from the Mirror Group with a pension generously enhanced on Maxwell's orders.

The presence of the Price Waterhouse investigators – who would become the administrators – in Maxwell House disturbed the unreality which had prevailed for so long. It was like Berlin in May 1945, as the besiegers stormed through the security doors, ignoring the late dictator's decree. Like the Red Army entering Hitler's smouldering Chancellery, the administrators were hunting both for trophies and for evidence. Among the first to arrive was David Lee. Astutely, and thereby earning the gratitude of the army of investigators who would follow, he ordered that all the main frame computers be downloaded – their records copied before more incriminating files could be destroyed. Rushing through the building, he opened door after door, pausing only to establish the importance of the room's occupants. Finally, inside Kevin's office he found six lawyers sorting through Maxwell's files. 'Client confidentiality,' they chorused, forcing Lee to retreat. 'I'll be back,' he thought and went off, as the reality of bankruptcy was announced by the administrators of Headington Investments and RMG: Bob's toys were for sale. The *Lady Ghislaine*, the Gulfstream jets, the Rolls-Royces and the helicopters were all impounded to await bidders. On 8 December, a provisional liquidator was appointed to supervise BIM's affairs.

Kevin missed those momentous hours. He had flown by Concorde to New York, still pursuing his father's notion that the empire could be refounded upon the *Daily News*, although Maxwell had failed to extricate the newspaper from its registered owner, which was now among those companies controlled by administrators. 'Did you sign any documents diverting pension fund assets?' he was asked at Kennedy airport. 'I'm here on *Daily News* business,' he unblinkingly replied, pushing his way towards a limousine. Walking into the newspaper's headquarters as the owner, Kevin appointed Shelly Aboff and Ellis Freedman, his father's cronies, as directors and asserted his continuing proprietorship. The administrators in London were a world away.

Jim Willse, the editor, seemed unperturbed. The impact of events across the Atlantic had not fully percolated through and Kevin was still regarded as the proprietor, albeit of a company which had filed for protection under Chapter 11, a stage before what English law calls administration. Nearly one hundred international journalists had gathered in the basement of the *News* building to hear Kevin, who spoke from a podium surrounded by, for the most part, respectable executives. By his side were Shelly Aboff and Ellis Freedman. Neither was known to have previous experience of newspaper publishing.

Opening with confidence, Kevin announced that the newspaper was not for sale and that his family, after an investment of $25 million, would not forsake their property. The obvious objection – that this was a company owned by the administrators – was brushed aside with bravura: 'There's no conflict of interest. That's bullshit.' But the question, 'Was your father the crook of the century?' hit the target. Kevin's eyes darted from side to side before he jumped up and, accompanied by Aboff and Freedman, headed for the door pursued by television cameras.

On his return to London, 9 December, he found that his plight had worsened. After at first denying any interest in the Maxwell saga, the Serious Fraud Office had finally become suspicious and police officers had, three days earlier, marched into Kevin's headquarters to demolish the last traces of the Maxwell myth. Those documents, computer disks and records not yet taken by the administrators were seized in a succession of raids which were devastating to those who had devoted their lives to the 'Old Man'. Safes were opened, personal computers were downloaded, bags of correspondence grabbed before they could be shredded, and desks were systematically emptied. Officers would chuckle that the drawer in the desk of Kevin's secretary, Carolyn Barwell, contained an empty box of coloured Mates condoms. They would be less amused when they discovered that fifty cardboard wallets for 'private correspondence' had been marked SHRED capital letters. Unshredded, among the thousand crates carried from the buildings, were hundreds of condolence letters received after Robert Maxwell's death.

At noon on 9 December, Kevin stood in his old office with Detective Sergeant Robert Scott, a squat, bearded police officer from the Serious Fraud Office. His desk was stacked deep with files – 'higgledy-piggledy' according to Scott's non-police description. Scattered around on the floor were other bags marked 'SHRED'. The door of a wall safe was open; inside it was bare. As other police officers carefully scooped torn shreds of paper from waste-paper bins and dropped them into marked plastic bags, Kevin, Scott and a group of lawyers systematically sorted Kevin's files, separating the private from the public companies. Constantly over the following three hours they had to interrupt their chores as Kevin was called to the telephone or required to speak to a visitor. By the time they had completed the task, dozens of filled and tagged bags of Kevin's correspondence had been loaded into the lifts by the police.

Among the bags of tapes carried out to the vans was the cassette of a conversation between Larry Trachtenberg and a forex dealer on 4 November negotiating the $35 million deal with Salomons. Its existence would only be discovered one year later by a diligent police officer and would be used, after considerable legal argument, in the criminal trial.

To begin with, Kevin appeared to be trying to help the administrators and the SFO, but when the trail began to lead into uncomfortably sensitive areas he retained the services of Monty Raphael, an aggressive solicitor favoured by a number of those notorious executives accused of fraud, and was advised to refuse to answer pertinent questions. Silence was his safest ploy as policemen, administrators, accountants, bankers, journalists and politicians asked questions prompted by the growing avalanche of revelations. He needed all his resources to protect the family's assets. Unfortunately for the beneficiaries, as Kevin knew, the Liechtenstein trusts were by then completely worthless. Their assets, shares in the bankrupt MCC and the Mirror Group, were all pledged against debts to banks. The remaining cash deposited in banks in the Cayman Islands, Guernsey, New York, Germany and the Dutch Antilles, appeared safe.

Kevin, like his father before him, believed that a carefully cultivated and adroitly targeted image could successfully secure his acquittal if he were prosecuted. So the habitué of Concorde and the Carlyle posed for the *Sunday Mirror* with his family on board a London bus taking them from his Chelsea home to Piccadilly. This was to establish the image of miserable poverty for British eyes; yet in New York he took care to present himself as the newspaper tycoon on the *Prime Time* television show, to reinforce his control over the *Daily News*. 'I don't think anyone would ever describe me as being a member of the Salvation Army,' he replied aggressively to the interviewer, 'and I'm not in business just for the pleasure of it. I'm in business to make money.' The sneering boast was convincing. These were the words used by his father to the *Daily Mirror*'s employees on that fateful day in 1984 when he bought the news-paper group and threatened closure if they failed to obey his edicts. Looking neither shocked nor remorseful about the evident plight of 20,000 pensioners contemplating destitution, Kevin displayed all his father's ruthlessness, but without the occasional burst of char-isma or charity towards the less fortunate. His anger and his self-pity he reserved for his relations with the banks. He did not care about their losses, because they were big boys and knew the score. But there was one thing he did care about: he had broken his father's cardinal rule, not to disturb any bank's trust in himself.

Inevitably, the mask was also torn away in New York. Assailed by headlines, reports and constant speculation about Robert Max-well, Kevin was persuaded to resign from the *Daily News*. Looking surprisingly unruffled, he waited for the long, tortuous investi-gations to expose the ruins of his strategy for survival which, reassembled, would reveal what few outsiders could yet compre-hend the extent of Kevin's involvement.

The spreading odour exuded by the discoveries hardened the administrators against the efforts of Laister and the other directors to save MCC. David Lee of Price Waterhouse pushed for a court declaration that the company was insolvent, while others sought similar remedies against the Maxwell family. By 20 December, the administrators had succeeded. In London and Oxford, Robert Maxwell's possessions were being seized, itemized and crated for the auction rooms. In death, Robert Maxwell had cheated those who would have delighted in witnessing his ultimate indignity. Eighty guffawing journalists poured through his Holborn penthouse to preview the sale, an irony Maxwell might not have appreciated despite his oft-proclaimed assertion, 'Money means nothing to me.'

On 14 February 1992, St Valentine's Day, Sotheby's in Bond Street was packed with bidders and onlookers as every bed, curtain, kitchen utensil and item of office furniture, even Maxwell's personal towels, bathrobe and baseball caps, were offered for sale. Just as souvenir hunters would pay a premium for a chip of the Berlin Wall, competition was fierce to own a slice of Bob's life – even though they were testaments to awful taste, raising only £240,000. The 'Max Factor' had assumed an unexpected meaning, but the legacy remained unresolved.

At 7.30 in the morning of 18 June 1992, two police officers rang at the door of Kevin's Chelsea home. It was no coincidence that dozens of journalists and cameramen were gathered outside. For days there had been rumours of arrests, and finally the tip-off had been passed. The only people apparently unaware of the identity of the men standing at Kevin's front door at that hour were the house's occupants. A first-floor window screeched open. 'We don't get up until half-past eight!' shrieked Pandora down at the door. The window crashed down.

'I see,' said one of the besuited heavies, self-consciously pressing the bell again long and hard.

Once again, the bedroom window was yanked open. 'Piss off or I'll call the police!' screamed Pandora.

'We are the police,' said the officer with studied self-congratulation. The window slammed down. The show had begun.

After Kevin had been escorted from the house one hour later, he and his brother were taken before a magistrates' court later that day in handcuffs. The police swoop also netted Robert Bunn and Larry Trachtenberg. Offers by the lawyers for all the former Maxwell executives to arrange their clients' arrest in civilized circumstances had been ignored. The public, the police decided, wanted a target for their anger, and the ritual humiliation of a fallen tycoon's sons would whet the appetite for what was to come. Their challenge appeared to have been accepted. Walking from the court that afternoon, Kevin stood in the road to deliver an impromptu statement: 'I'm looking forward to answering all the charges and giving a full explanation.'

SEVENTEEN

The Trial

– 30 May 1995

Striding into the bright, air-conditioned courtroom in Chancery Lane three years later, on 30 May 1995, Kevin Maxwell's self-assurance suggested that little had changed. Dressed in a dark-blue suit, with his hands resting on his hips, elbows stuck out, the former chief executive and chairman of the multi-billion-pound empire behaved like a City prince, his whole posture proclaiming that his royal dignity was untarnished and his confidence undented despite the declaration in September 1992 of his personal bankruptcy, for the record sum of £406 million.

Indeed, as Kevin gazed across the neon-lit, converted office space, with its laminated wood furniture, blue-upholstered chairs and dozens of computer screens, at the seventy journalists corralled on the other side, the casual observer might have mistakenly surmised that the Lotus Eater had arrived at the annual general meeting of Maxwell Communication Corporation rather than to stand trial in Court 22 of an Old Bailey annexe, alias Chichester Rents, a new building in Chancery Lane.

Reality returned as Kevin edged closer to a large, black-gowned man wearing a wig. He began to banter with Alun Jones QC, a hard-working, committed but temperamental barrister whose interest in growing vegetables had been supplanted by a fervent desire to win Kevin Maxwell's acquittal. As Jones reached towards one of the dozens of red case files piled around him, his client walked self-consciously fifteen feet across the room towards his elder brother Ian. Thirty years earlier, the two boys had played on the lawn of their parents' Oxford mansion, conscious that their wealthy father was zealously trying to transform himself from a go-getter into an international statesman. Ten years later, at Marlborough

College, both teenage boys would confess to housemasters the rank fear aroused by their father's imminent arrival. 'I want you to push them. Show them no mercy,' Robert Maxwell would urge the boys' teachers, expecting absolute compliance with the customer's orders. That despotism had continued throughout their lives, evoking the sympathetic belief that their presence in Court 22 was the consequence of their father's oppression. In those first minutes, the mental image of those two small boys would recur as the brothers jocularly talked amid the anticipatory turmoil of what was widely billed in that morning's newspapers as 'The trial of the decade'.

Standing behind the brothers were two other defendants. Robert Bunn, the tall, grey-haired financial director of RMG, was nervously seeking a friendly face. Nearby was Larry Trachtenberg, the smaller, dark-haired, chubby American whose loyal management of the private empire's share deals had been rewarded in its dying weeks by his appointment as director of both BIM and RMG, and hence by the legal responsibilities exposing him to a criminal prosecution. Since his arrest, Trachtenberg had shaved off his moustache and cut his hair. Like Bunn, his only companion appeared to be a grey-suited solicitor financed by legal aid. Neither man spoke to Kevin, a reflection of the hint in their former employer's unpublished defence statement that he had relied on their judgment in pledging pension fund shares. For the moment, however, neither intended to give evidence in his own defence. Instead they had been persuaded to rely on Kevin's genius in the witness box and finally decide their strategy after his testimony. Until that moment, still months away, they would all sit, much to their relief, alongside their own lawyers rather than in a dock, and there was not a blue uniform in sight.

All four defendants had entered the building serenaded by the screams of more than fifty cameramen who, early that morning, had staked their ground across the narrow road opposite the courtroom. The most striking arrival in the warm sunshine had been Ian Maxwell's, walking hand in hand with Laura, his attractive wife. Both he and Kevin, who had arrived surrounded by lawyers (Pandora, it would be said, could not be in court because she was to be called as a witness), had remained grim-faced. Neither of the former directors of Mirror Group Newspapers showed much sympathy for journalists.

The brothers' itinerary since their arrest had not been as uncomfortable as that of others in their predicament, although their standards of living had noticeably diminished, suggestive of poverty. Hence, with proof of insufficient funds, they had applied for legal aid. While Kevin's bankruptcy clearly qualified him for help, Ian staved off BIM's petition for his bankruptcy by disputing his participation in the use of several of the pension fund assets. In an interim judgment, he was ordered to pay £500,000. His cheque was handed over to BIM's solicitors by solicitors based in Oxford and connected to Fivetell, the company used by Maxwell to control Derby County football club which in summer 1991 had collected £2.6 million profit after the club's sale. The money had disappeared long before the administrators began their search. Yet both were deemed eligible, though neither brother was homeless. Kevin had managed to secure a large house for his wife and his family, increased to five children, near his parents-in-law, in Moulsford, Oxfordshire; while Ian had moved from Eaton Square to Hackney. Speculation about their good fortune during the previous three years had been fed by publicized appearances at fashionable London restaurants and in the business-class sections of aircraft travelling across the world, and by their management of a profitable business.

Working under the umbrella of Westbourne Communications, a company with offices off Piccadilly whose director was Jean Baddeley, Robert Maxwell's former secretary, Kevin had developed a business in Bulgaria and Russia using his father's contacts. In Sofia, Kevin and Ian, with the help of Ognian Doynov, formerly employed by his father, performed services similar to those provided in 1991. In Moscow, besides publishing a small English newspaper, Kevin offered his expertise in finance and banking to Russians looking for investment opportunities in the West. Simultaneously, he had proffered his services to Western companies seeking contracts in the Soviet bloc. Among those prepared to collaborate with him were Salomon Brothers, Cable & Wireless and, especially, Nordex, an unusual trading company based in Vienna and employing former Soviet intelligence officers with access to millions of dollars released in the liberalization of the Russian economy. Kevin regularly commuted to Moscow, even during the trial: on a Sunday morning in June he would fly to the Russian capital carrying a heavy attaché case, returning on the same plane that evening empty-handed.

Among his lucrative successes was negotiating the finance for a preliminary study of a new telephone exchange for St Petersburg. His partner in that venture, which earned Kevin over $1 million in fees, was a former employee of Cable & Wireless.

The delay in starting the trial had allowed Kevin to create a multi-million-pound business which could survive regardless of the outcome. Indeed it was rumoured that Kevin's strategy was to take any blame from Ian, if only to allow his elder brother to continue their new enterprise. During the trial, Ian would fly to Sofia and regularly to Paris – by private jet from Northolt airport. His fluent French had helped the brothers establish a business among those unprejudiced by events in Britain. Since neither brother was allowed by the judge to travel to New York, Ghislaine would come to London for business consultations – flying by Concorde. (On 14 September 1995, she would be met at Heathrow by her brothers, who had absented themselves from the courtroom for that day.) Having recovered from their father's débâcle, an emerging family business was prospering.

During the intervening years, Kevin had often mixed his assignments. For example, during his trip to New York on 24 November 1994 with Keith Oliver, his tenacious solicitor, to seek evidence among the hundreds of crates of documents still held by MCC's former subsidiaries, he had sat in a Macmillan office working his portable telephone to negotiate business deals and had later visited bankers and prospective clients. While some would ponder the appropriateness of legal aid funding that journey, none could ignore Kevin's nerve.

Ever since the empire's collapse, the Maxwells had been dogged by allegations, rumours and speculation, not least about the real cause of their father's death. The Israeli 'state' funeral and the pathologists' inconclusive findings about the cause of death had been utilized by journalists, politicians and businessmen for a variety of motives to conjure a scenario in which Robert Maxwell had been murdered. While the obvious culprits for Ariel Sharon, the Israeli politician, were Arabs, others like Vladimir Kryuchov, the former KGB chairman, were convinced that Israelis were the murderers. The third group of suspects were KGB agents, a speculation fuelled by the experience of Yaakov Nimrodi, a wealthy Israeli businessman and former intelligence officer who had coincidentally bought *Ma'ariv*, Maxwell's Israeli newspaper, from the administrators.

During 1991, the Israeli had spent considerable time in Moscow negotiating the purchase of tons of gold worth $1 billion from KGB officers. Having spent $2 million in expenses, he amassed half the money for the initial payment, chartered cargo aircraft and arrived in Moscow to take possession of the precious metal. To his surprise, his contacts revealed that the gold was 'lost'.

After Maxwell's death, the details of Nimrodi's venture became richly embellished. The gold, it was said, had been stolen by KGB officers after the attempted August coup. Moreover, far from having been lost, the gold had allegedly been transported and stored in Israel as part of a conspiracy between KGB and Mossad officers. According to that scenario, Maxwell, the Mossad agent with good KGB connections, was said to have brokered the original deal, only to dip his fingers into the stockpile to relieve his financial problems. That allegation gained credibility from Maxwell's negotiations in June 1991 with the Soviet government as part of his bid to trade in the country's international debt. Then, Maxwell's double-cross had so outraged his KGB–Mossad contacts – and his knowledge of their affairs was so extensive and dangerous – that his elimination had become the conspirators' cleanest solution.

Inevitably, the epic was subject to further adornment. MI6, the British foreign intelligence agency, had surely monitored Maxwell's last telephone calls from his boat and had precisely reconstructed the countdown towards his murder by identifiable assassins. A leading German politician whom Maxwell frequently met had also been involved, it was said, because he was suspected by the CIA of being a former Soviet spy. Even Turkish intelligence agents were mentioned as co-conspirators because of Maxwell's attempted mediation during the Gulf war.

The account of his murder was colourful. The assassins, it was whispered, had boarded the yacht either in Tenerife or at sea during Maxwell's last, fateful night. Unseen by the crew, he had been seized, bundled on to a small boat, injected with an untraceable heart-stopper and later dumped in the water. By any reckoning, it was a perfect crime uncannily committed on the very eve of his return to face his financial crisis.

That whole scenario suffered a comprehensive flaw – not a shred of irrefutable evidence was ever produced to identify Maxwell's murderers, prove the motive or establish how two teams of pathologists and forensic scientists had been so thoroughly deceived.

Moreover, all the evidence had been investigated by those insurance companies liable to pay £21 million to the administrators on Maxwell's policies covering a personal accident. In the event of suicide, the policies were invalid. Most of the insurance companies had eventually agreed to pay the full amounts to the creditors on the ground that Maxwell's death was most likely caused by an accident or by a heart attack. Others still disputed their liability.

Yet, despite the lack of evidence, the murder theory had gained supporters, not least Kevin and his family. Having initially argued that Maxwell had died of natural causes, the Maxwells and their legal advisers saw an advantage in joining the murder-conspiracy theorists. The lawyers would then blame the misconceived suspicion among bankers on 5 November 1991 that the Publisher had committed suicide for propelling the empire into the financial abyss: the Maxwells' finances, they would argue, had not been as bad as the bankers had imagined.

Since November 1991, the empire's history and activities had been painstakingly dissected by hundreds of skilled professionals: accountants, lawyers and police officers. During hundreds of thousands of man-hours, the administrators had combed through millions of documents to reconstruct the paper trail and unravel the suspected frauds. In total, over £100 million had been spent by Price Waterhouse to investigate MCC's accounts, by Arthur Andersen in probing into the private companies, by Robson Rhodes in acting as BIM's administrator and by Buchler Phillips in realizing the assets of Maxwell's private estate.

The liabilities of the private companies, they established, were £3.8 billion, including £2.8 billion in inter-company debt – money taken from MCC, the Mirror Group and the pension funds. MCC's unsecured liabilities were approximately £3.2 billion, of which £1.3 billion could be recovered. The administrators' prime task was to find any remaining assets which could go towards meeting the creditors' claims. Overshadowing the normal victims of bankruptcy were the pensioners – over 30,000 people who feared that all of the Common Investment Fund, finally valued at £406 million, had been lost, many felt destroying their security in old age. Considering the enormity of their task, the administrators were indisputably successful in disentangling the web of Maxwell's finances, and their fees were commensurate with the earnings of the professions. More open to criticism was the administrators' disposal of the empire's assets, often done with unnecessary haste for prices which critics asserted were too low. None of those who bought the property, publishing and media businesses from the administrators – least of all Andrew Smith of LBII in New York, who was allowed by Andersens to write off Maxwell's original £10 million investment – ever complained about the sums they paid. Under political pressure to produce cash for the creditors and the pensioners, both Price Waterhouse and Arthur Andersen had accepted offers which at a more sedate time would have been spurned. Yet criticism of those administrators was too easy. Their activities were transparent and no one enjoyed paying the undertaker.

But in one critical area the administrators had failed. Their hunt for Maxwell's suspected secret fortune had proved futile. All four administrators would claim that their precise tracking of the billions which had moved through the Maxwell empire was persuasive evidence that hardly any money was unaccounted for. This was not a fraud, they declared, where the perpetrators had squirrelled away a pot of gold. On the contrary, true to his old pattern, Maxwell had poured his entire fortune into the furnace. But those explanations were never quite convincing. The administrators had gained access neither to the records in Liechtenstein (which clearly was not a repository of money) nor to his bank accounts in the Caymans and Dutch Antilles. Those accounts remained secret. The surfacing traces hinted that a clandestine fortune had survived. While pleading poverty, Betty Maxwell had nevertheless paid £152,000 in cash to the administrators for the flat jointly owned with her husband in Tignes, France, used for skiing holidays; she had deposited £900,000 for her sons' legal fees in 1992; and she possessed homes in London and Fraytet. More pertinent was Kevin's affluent lifestyle, a legal claim by Ph(US)Inc. that it had a £3 million interest in a German property, and the mysterious circumstances surrounding the payment in 1991 of $7.1 million by Advest, Robert Maxwell's private American company established with Sheldon Aboff to hold Berlitz shares, into Ph(US)Inc.'s account at the Chemical Bank in New York. Little of Ph(US)Inc.'s money had been recovered and no administrator could establish how much had flowed through the company destined for anonymous sources. Combined with his current business income, Kevin certainly enjoyed the comfort of a large sum of money.

All those financial investigations and the history of the pension funds had been considered in a series of authoritative hearings by the Social Security Committee of the House of Commons. Chaired by Frank Field MP, the Committee had summoned the professionals involved in the pension funds' management to explain their conduct. 'Pontius Pilate', the Committee reported at one stage, 'would have blushed at the spectacle of so many witnesses washing their hands in public before the Committee of their responsibilities in this affair.'

Responding to the MPs' pressure, the government had established a trust to organize the recovery of the pension funds' money from those banks, auditors and others who could be targeted for legal liability. Initially it had been headed by Sir John Cuckney, an industrialist and former MI5 officer; his role then passed to Sir Peter Webster, a retired High Court judge. Under Webster, the initiative languished. Yet in separate settlements prompted by the litigation launched by BIM's administrator, the Bank of America paid £25 million to the Mirror Group's pension scheme, Lehmans paid £27 million to the CIF, while Lehmans, Invesco MIM and Capel Cure paid another £32 million to the trust in pre-trial settlements. Other cases brought by Price Waterhouse as MCC's administrators against Coopers only started in 1995 while BIM's cases against Crédit Suisse and Bank of America, for £120 million and MGPT's case agaist Crédit Suisse for £70 million were settled on undisclosed terms in October 1995. Their outcome had been complicated by the fate of Macmillan's massive action, organized by Price Waterhouse, against Crédit Suisse, Lehmans and Swiss Volksbank to recover the Berlitz shares. In his lengthy judgment Mr Justice Millett after criticising the plaintiffs for their arguments, found in detail what he called 'the fraud', before finding in favour of the banks, allowing them to keep the shares on the ground that they had believed the Maxwells' claim to their private ownership. The judgment was a bitter blow to Macmillan, which lodged an appeal.

Soon after that unsatisfactory outcome for the American publisher, Webster resigned his responsibilities, having failed to extract

money in those cases where litigation had barely started. The task
was handed back to Cuckney who, emboldened by the administrators' thick, detailed statements of claim alleging negligence, resorted
to tough talk and efficiently negotiated a 'global settlement' of £117
million from Coopers and Lybrand, Goldman Sachs and Lehman
Brothers. Those compromise settlements, combined with a further
£53 million collected from the administrators of MCC and the
private companies and £102 million secured by BIM's administrators during 1992, were sufficient to guarantee all the pensions,
although the CIF would have been worth £587.5 million in 1995
had the borrowing saga never taken place.

Considering the numerous people, banks, partnerships and
organizations who by their questionable conduct had not prevented
the pension fund losses and the collapse of MCC, it was more than
surprising that official censure was so sparse. IMRO had reported
that Invesco MIM was found to have breached its rules on fifty-five
occasions; and Goldman Sachs was fined £160,000 by the Securities
and Futures Association for late registration of the purchase of
shares from Maxwell's companies, but the bank was acquitted by
the stock exchange of running a share-support operation for MCC
shares. Other than the resignation of IMRO's director, there was
no other official action, although two DTI chief executives, John
Thomas QC and Raymond Turner, were investigating the flotation
of the Mirror Group and their report would inevitably make criticisms – but after the trial and with predictable consequences.

The real casualties were those who had been personally duped
by the Maxwells or had become scapegoats for financial losses. For
those handful blamed in the banks and investment institutions –
Invesco MIM, Capel Cure, Lehmans, Goldman Sachs – it was hard
to find expressions of sympathy. But the resignations of Ernest
Burrington and Lawrence Guest as Mirror Group directors, forced
to depart by former colleagues who had either collaborated with
Maxwell or had not exercised the diligence for which they were
paid, rankled. Graham Bell, the Citibank dealer, was another scapegoat. Bell had reluctantly agreed to buy from Kevin Maxwell $40
million in New York on 21 October in what he thought was a
conventional forex deal. Instead, it became a personal nightmare.
Tormented by the pressure to recover the bank's money, Bell suffered a series of heart attacks and the breakdown of his marriage

before taking compulsory retirement. Thirty-two years of loyal service – 'I was married to the bank,' he would say – were ignored in the rush to assign responsibility, and the man at the bottom was the easiest target. The fate of Bell, Burrington and others was a familiar pattern: proud, loyal, hard-working, honest men were wilfully demeaned for having trusted the Maxwells.

Their fate did not appear to have troubled the brothers during the months before their arrival in Court 22. Immune to most objective emotions during their glorious era, their attention thereafter had been focused on their own survival rather than on the casualties of their actions. Kevin had been interviewed for twenty-two days under the insolvency laws by lawyers representing the administrators and by the Serious Fraud Office. For nearly four years, he had known that, unseen, a police investigation was inexorably collecting evidence from former colleagues and from bankers, lawyers and accountants who had served him on a basis of trust. Over sixty officers and accountants, supervised by three lawyers employed by the Serious Fraud Office, had spent £10.5 million in that investigation. Under the direction of John Tate and Michael Dury, they had sifted through 3 million documents weighing nearly forty tons and had travelled extensively across the world to take 843 statements from 485 witnesses, of whom many were implacably angered by the Maxwells' betrayal of their trust.

Burdened by a poor reputation following failures in recent big fraud trials, the SFO had been both thorough and fair, sharing its evidence and witness statements with the defence. Aware that what was at stake was not simply obtaining convictions but the very survival of the SFO and a host of professional reputations, its officers had conducted themselves with great delicacy. If the trial resulted in acquittals, the SFO would certainly not be to blame. The responsibility would lie if anywhere in the lawyers' presentation. Indeed, two of the defence silks had been the prosecutors who had floundered in earlier fraud trials.

Michael Hill QC, representing Trachtenberg, had failed to secure the conviction of 1989 of Kenneth Grob, one of the architects of a massive fraud within Lloyd's insurance market. In Grob's words, 'I knew after the first week of the trial that I'd be acquitted. Neither the prosecutor nor the judge gave the impression that they understood the technicalities of the case. Together, they successfully confused the jury.' In the Maxwell trial, Hill's natural charm would occasionally be submerged by his pseudo-dramatic style of questioning. Even his request to a witness to read a newspaper article would give the impression that he was leading towards an accusation of murder. Often it seemed that his exhaustive, confused questions were intended to infect the jury with similar confusion. Only occasionally did his verbosity discredit a witness's memory or establish that his client was possibly not present at a meeting.

Similarly, Robert Bunn's barrister, Peter Rook QC, a tall, thin, agonizingly slow advocate, had been prosecutor when George Walker, the former boxer, was acquitted of theft from his business empire. One juror afterwards revealed that their deliberations had not been helped by their confusion about the precise crime Walker was alleged to have committed. Similarly, during his truncated defence of Bunn, it was hard to understand Rook's arguments beyond his assertion of his client's ignorance. Past failures to secure convictions for fraud could clearly not be blamed entirely upon the inability of a jury to understand complicated financial matters; rather, the responsibility lay upon those who failed properly to explain those issues to jurors or where prosecutions were wrongly launched.

Not surprisingly, the Maxwell brothers had attracted more impressive advocates. Ian Maxwell was represented by Edmund Lawson QC, a beefcake with a bullying manner whose reputation as one of the most intelligent practitioners at the criminal bar said little for the standards of his brethren. Lawson's tactic would be to remain silent for the most part, reflecting his client's allegedly minimal participation. 'Ian Maxwell finds himself in the dock,' insisted Lawson's plummy voice, 'not because of what he did but because of what he is – a Maxwell and his father's son.' Ian, his advocate argued, utterly without experience in corporate finance, relied upon the guidance of his brother and advisers before signing documents. The SFO, continued Lawson, had produced only 'snippets' of evidence against his client – an opinion quietly shared by the prosecution, who admitted that there was only limited documentation pointing to Ian's criminal intent. That evidence, Lawson concluded, might prove that Ian did not 'properly discharge his director's responsibilities . . . but that does not make him a deliberate and dishonest fraudster'. The barrister's tactic would be to rise rarely, and then swiftly to secure, in withering style larded with pomposity, the agreement of an exhausted witness that Ian had been uninvolved in the empire's financial affairs; or to extract a valuable admission – 'I felt sorry for Ian,' Peter Laister would admit; or to obtain a witness's sympathetic acknowledgment that poor Ian had given an annual director's fee of £120 to charity – thus obscuring the reality of his £326,000 annual income.

For by the time the prosecution witnesses came to be questioned by Lawson, they had passed through the hands of Hill, Rook and – least tender of all – Alun Jones QC for Kevin. Bear-like and initially well prepared, Jones would exhibit flashes of wit and acerbity and spasms of pained embarrassment (spasms which he concealed from the jury by turning his back towards them) as he sought his intense, humourless client's acquittal. In that quest he had retreated with Kevin and his solicitors to an Oxford hotel for two week to brainstorm a cogent defence. He was supremely aided by Keith Oliver, a small, tidy solicitor whose dedication was assisted by a seemingly unlimited amount of public money. Their commitment to Kevin was shared by Clare Montgomery, an ambitious junior barrister chosen for her analytical mind but exuding the charm of an insensitive shrew. Montgomery's success would be to reduce an honest female witness to tears for failure of memory, but when confronted by intelligent bankers her crude attempts at entrapment would sometimes founder hilariously, resulting in several own-goals.

Unsuspecting witnesses would find that they, rather than the four defendants, seemed to be on trial. One after the other, the defence lawyers would rise to pick off among the seventy-two prosecution witnesses candidates for allegations of greed, dishonesty, deceit, forgery, negligence and complicity. Most commonly, they would be accused of suffering bad memories four years after the event by lawyers who could not even recall a page reference one minute after they had risen to their feet. In any debate about the suitability of the British criminal justice system for fraud trials, the most pertinent question would relate to the conduct of some defence lawyers in seeking to confuse the jury rather than establish the truth. But there was another side to the defence lawyers' conduct. Without exception, all were committed to their clients – not by token, but by seeming sincerely to believe their clients' innocence. Until the end, they would cocoon the defendants in optimism and would never betray any hint of doubt or cynicism. Utter professionals, they would fight, tooth and nail, to win.

One consolation urged upon the defendants by their lawyers was the approach of the prosecutor, Alan Sucking QC, a genial, uncombative pipe-smoker who had successfully prosecuted Peter Clowes. That conviction for fraud had broken the run of bad publicity suffered by the SFO, although one co-defendant had escaped with only minor retribution. But the achievement had not suppressed Suckling's reputation for timid presentations and for avoiding the jugular. No witness in the forthcoming trial would utter a fatal, emotional gasp of 'He lied to me!' to encapsulate the deception which the prosecution was alleging. Drama and colour were not ingredients in Suckling's honest style. Instead the prosecutor could be relied upon methodically to extract incriminating evidence for Kevin's cross-examination and for the judge to present to the jury at the end of the trial.

Richard Lissack QC, the junior prosecutor, was the jury's favourite. His late father Victor had been renowned in the legal profession for his successful solicitor's practice opposite Bow Street magistrates' court. With inherited charm, his son's intelligent, logical and friendly questioning of witnesses enhanced the prosecution's case.

The jury had been chosen the previous week from an initial pool of 700 summoned to the Old Bailey. The unprecedented number had been prompted by the Maxwells' strident plea that popular prejudice would preclude a fair trial. More than half of the pool were allowed to disqualify themselves by declaring their inability to sit for six months. 'I'll tell them I was on the boat with him,' quipped one potential juror seeking an excuse to avoid duty. The remainder were presented with a lengthy questionnaire to disqualify any who replied positively to an awareness of Robert Maxwell. The precedent for a similar questionnaire had been for the trial of the Kray twins in 1969.

To avoid trial, which it was estimated would cost £15 million, £1 million of public funds had already been spent on Kevin's behalf in an attempt to persuade the judge that the welter of publicity about Robert Maxwell's frauds had made a fair hearing impossible. During three weeks of unreportable legal argument in February

1995, Alun Jones QC had presented a catalogue of newspaper and television reports which had unconditionally asserted or assumed the criminality of both Robert and Kevin Maxwell. An opinion poll, commissioned at Kevin's personal expense and cited by Jones, revealed that about 50 per cent of those questioned believed that the Maxwell sons were guilty. In his own testimony on his thirty-sixth birthday, Kevin recounted how, eating at Joe's Café, a popular restaurant in Draycott Avenue, the waitress had thrown down his plate and shouted, 'I hope you choke yourself on it!' He also described the hate mail he had received and the public's automatic association of his name with the epithets 'devious, dishonest, untrustworthy and corrupt'. Above all, Kevin claimed that people who could give evidence in his favour had refused from fear of 'ridicule and opprobrium'.

Although persuasively argued by Jones, there was no chance that any judge would risk the public's obloquy by holding that a jury could not be found from among the ignorant who would reach a verdict based on the evidence rather than on preconceptions. After all, even on the basis of Kevin's own opinion poll, almost 50 per cent of those questioned were suitable jurors.

Such jurors had been those who were pinpointed by the questionnaire. Any who had replied that the name Maxwell had a connection with pensions were quietly excluded. The man who had loudly announced that it would be 'an honour to serve' on the jury disqualified himself. Those who admitted reading newspapers were questioned further. One who revealed himself as a *Sun* reader, and of the sports pages, was deemed a Maxwell virgin. The impression was given that the jury – seven women and five men of all ages – were healthy, unemployed and unintelligent. But that was not accurate. Several of the jurors read the *Daily Telegraph* and the *Daily Mail* and at least six were middle class. Among the women was an art historian, a former executive of Unicef, a colour designer and the wife of a retired police inspector. Despite the strange questions they were to pass to the judge in the early stages of the trial, the jurors appeared remarkably attentive, except during those periods of indigestible evidence when the reaction of any sane person was to meditate upon life's real pleasures. Each juror could claim up to £448 per week in compensation for loss of earnings.

Supervising the trial was Mr Justice Phillips, a suntanned

Cambridge graduate who had specialized in Admiralty litigation before his appointment to the bench. Considering that previous fraud trials had led to acquittals because the judges, sharing the prosecutors' affliction, had shown difficulty understanding financial intricacies and jargon, Phillips was an exemplary choice, especially after his successful management of the Barlow Clowes trial. Unusually intelligent for a judge, he would exude tact and charm while imposing an exceptionally efficient timetable upon a discordant gaggle of lawyers who, despite ample warning, would regularly fail to produce relevant documents for witnesses and complain of inadequate time for preparation. Unprecedently, Phillips, an enthusiastic self-disciplinarian, ordered that the trial would start daily at 9.30 a.m. and be completed by 1.30 p.m., allowing the afternoons free for legal arguments, a common disruption in fraud trials.

The case had been transferred to Mr Justice Phillips's care in December 1993. Briskly, he had decided that the trial should start at Easter 1994, but five times the defence had successfully sought postponement, claiming to need more time.

In that cause, Keith Oliver, Kevin's solicitor, had spent millions of pounds to formulate Kevin's defence, employing teams of accountants to sift the mountainous archives held by the administrators. At public expense, Oliver also flew with his client to New York. During the trial, the prosecution would complain of the defence's costs for the scanning of documents on to computer discs, which would reach £4,500 during one three-week period compared to the prosecution's £500. Oliver, it appeared, did not restrain the consumption of public money in pursuit of his client's interests. One witness, the president of a Canadian bank, would be summoned from Toronto at the defence's request, although three of his colleagues had already testified on the same issues. Two minutes after taking the stand, he was addressed by Jones on Kevin's behalf. 'Did you come to London especially for this trial?'

'Yes,' replied the banker.

'No more questions,' said Jones, to everyone's surprise.

The cost to the public of the banker's flight (business class), hotel (five star) and other incidentals (including telephone calls to Canada) for a three-minute appearance was, the SFO calculated, £5,000.

The task of the defence was certainly complicated by the nature of the charges. Since the original arrest, the charges of theft had been altered to conspiracy to defraud – an astute shift since it included Robert Maxwell among the defendants and was easier to prove. But, because Robert was also accused, the judge, at the request of Kevin's lawyers, sought to stifle any suggestion that the deceased had been criminal. On the lawyers' initiative, a musical had been banned, a House of Commons select committee had been criticized for prejudicing the trial by summoning the Maxwell brothers to give evidence, and Mr Justice Phillips had sent warnings to newspaper, television and radio editors not to prejudice the trial by referring to Robert Maxwell as dishonest. Even to mention his own letter, Phillips had added, would be condemned as contempt.

At the outset there had been ten charges against Robert Bunn, Michael Stoney, Albert Fuller, Larry Trachtenberg, Kevin and Ian. Mindful of the disasters which had befallen recent fraud trials, the judge had ruled in a 1994 hearing that the first case would concern only two charges, excluding evidence about Berlitz, First Tokyo, stocklending and the Mirror Group loan from Bankers Trust, and thus relegating Stoney and Fuller to a later trial.

In essence, the defendants were accused of using shares belonging to the pension funds to repay the Maxwells' private debts while aware that, because of RMG's insolvency, there was no chance of reimbursing the pension funds. That risk, the prosecution alleged, was dishonest and known to be dishonest when the defendants conspired to use the pension fund shares.

The first count charged Robert and Kevin with conspiring to defraud the pension funds of 5.4 million Scitex shares by dishonestly risking the proceeds of the sale to settle RMG's debts to the Nat-West Bank, knowing that RMG would be unable to repay BIM the £102 million owed.

The second count, against Trachtenberg, Bunn, Kevin and Ian, alleged that between November 5 and 21 1991 they had conspired to defraud the trustees and beneficiaries of the pension funds by granting NatWest Bank a charge over 25.1 million Teva shares, knowing that there was a risk that RMG would default and be unable to redeem the shares owned by BIM.

Although few of the seventy journalists crammed into the pen sixty feet opposite the jury understood the background to the charges, their hyperbole as they waited for the event to commence

raised its status to 'The trial of the century' in the hope that the
nation would be gripped by their reports, just as the American
public had been enthralled by the continuing trial of O. J. Simpson.
But their jocular speculation, not least about the imminent appearance of Cap'n Bob's ghost, began to evaporate the moment their
eyes fell on the courtroom's unusual technology. Great criminal
trials are associated with the Old Bailey's fusty atmosphere, not
with a soulless cavern accommodating dozens of screens spewed
across a low-ceilinged room. Some screens would show the thousands of documents scanned on to a computer, while others would
emit the stenographer's 'Live-Note'. Few journalists could complain
about that aid, but the judge's opening remarks insinuated that
the Fourth Estate was as unwelcome to lawyers as it was to the
defendants.

Dressed in splendid red robes, Mr Justice Phillips entered the
room, seated himself on the bench and uttered the first words of
the six-month trial: 'Am I live?'

'We can't hear a thing,' shouted the journalists, gleefully realizing
that the most simple piece of technology – a microphone – was
malfunctioning.

'I think I am live,' offered Suckling, although only the transcriber
heard as the prosecutor mumbled, 'I was switched on.'

Adding to the bathos, Michael Hill rose majestically to announce,
'My Lord, I know that I am not live.' The magic was vanishing,
hastened by Hill's further confession, 'My Lord, I am still dead.'

By then it had been discovered that the jury was waiting forlornly
at the Old Bailey, half a mile away. So an inaudible trial – thanks
to unrepaired microphones – would start two hours late. The anticipatory excitement was disappearing. At 11.30, with the jury finally
in place, the judge intoned, 'In this country, we do not have trial
by the media, we have trial by judge and jury.' His carping criticism
suggested that much of the publicity surrounding the Maxwell collapse had been 'objectionable and unfair', especially press comment
about the Maxwells' receipt of legal aid. Both Kevin and Ian, the
judge told the jury, 'have demonstrated to the legal aid authorities
that they are unable to meet the costs of their defence. There is no
justification for the suggestion that they should not be granted legal
aid.' The existence of the Maxwells' lucrative business had not been
investigated.

Finally Alan Suckling rose to spell out the prosecution case. Encouraged by television dramas and Hollywood, the preceding hours had not quite dampened the spectators' enthusiasm but Suckling's first remarks, 'Am I switched on?', greeted by yelps of 'No!', extinguished the last scent of drama. Hesitantly, the prosecutor launched into a two-day odyssey to explain the background of the misuse of £122 million of pension fund assets. As each name and detail of technical jargon struggled to be heard, Mr Justice Phillips's prediction that 'the trial will provoke a lot of public interest' was exposed as wishful thinking. Before the end of the first morning, the popular media's interest collapsed. Yet every day, over the following months, the atmosphere in that clinically immaculate courtroom never became sedate. On the contrary, tension prevailed from the moment when, punctually at 9.30, the jury entered the room without ever returning the fixed stare from Kevin Maxwell. Throughout those weeks, the twelve looked at the judge, at the eighteen lawyers and most of all at the witnesses, but rarely at the defendants, as the curtain was modestly raised upon the events masterminded in a ten-storey building (long since stripped of any resemblance to the Maxwell era), located just two hundred yards away.

For their part, the brothers' features soon began to reflect an appreciation of their reversal of fortune. The witnesses paraded directly opposite them were nearly all former employees, fellow directors, their professional advisers or bankers. Four years earlier, those witnesses had willingly danced to the Maxwells' tune. Earning high salaries, fees and bonuses, they had often compromised their integrity and in retrospect had been exposed as gullible fools, easy prey to the Maxwells' deception. But, however compromised they were, they arrived in court suffering an overriding emotion: anger. Anger that they, hard working and loyal, had been fooled. The auditors, bankers and lawyers had been well briefed before giving evidence. Feeds from the courtroom of the trial's daily transcript had been subscribed to by leading City solicitors to prepare their clients before they arrived in court. Invariably, those witnesses would answer some of the most sensitive questions with 'I can't recall.' But all the bankers could precisely remember Kevin's offers and assurances, if only because they had taken contemporaneous notes or because their conversations had been recorded. Their damaging testimony, describing Kevin's assurances about the forex deals, the ownership of shares, the movement of funds and the solvency of the companies, was rarely challenged.

As each witness entered the courtroom, the two brothers would stare. While Ian's embarrassment was patent – he flushed whenever his name was mentioned – his younger brother intuitively concealed his emotions beneath an expression of sardonic hauteur. Yet, when the witnesses' monotone syllables delivered succinct testimony about the Maxwells' deception, even cool Kevin would turn away from the jury or drop his head to hide the cracks in his mask. The contrast between his present predicament and the memory of himself four years earlier in Maxwell House, the dauphin attracting London's movers and shakers, vexed him. But that visible nostalgia surfaced only occasionally. With the jury seated just four feet away, his steely self-control compelled quick recovery. The only sign of a bad day was his rapid, baleful exit from the courtroom; but by the following morning Kevin would, right into September, again glide into the courtroom bidding 'Good morning' to everyone connected with the defence. In those early days, Kevin was the cheerleader, even congratulating Hill and Lawson on their cross-examinations.

The well-structured prosecution case was designed first to establish through Trevor Cook and Harold Abrahart, a BIM accounts administrator, the fate of BIM's 5.4 million Scitex shares after 4 July 1991 when Cook and Robert Maxwell had signed their agreement to transfer them to RMG. Robert Maxwell had proposed that the 7.1 million Scitex shares (that is, including the 1.7 million owned privately) would be sold in New York as a block. Under their agreement, RMG should have paid the proceeds of the 5.4 million shares to BIM on 4 August. According to the agreement's final sentence, the ownership of BIM's shares did not pass to RMG until the money was received.

The Scitex shares were sold on 18 October and it was not disputed that the $239 million thus realized were, with Kevin's agreement, immediately taken by NatWest Bank and the Bank of Nova Scotia to repay RMG's debts. BIM never received its share of those proceeds, which was nominally valued in July at £100 million and finally by Salomons on 5 November at £102 million.

The prosecution's success depended upon proving, through their witnesses, three facts. Firstly, that the defendants had deliberately deceived the bankers and others that all the Scitex shares were privately owned; secondly, that they had used the money from the Scitex sale as if it were their own; and, thirdly, that they knew that the empire was insolvent and therefore were dishonestly risking the pension funds' money.

The core of Kevin's defence, explained Jones, was his belief that he was entitled to use the Scitex shares (and similarly the Teva shares) for private purposes because they had been transferred from the pension funds to RMG: 'Kevin Maxwell's perception is his defence.' The source of that knowledge, according to Kevin, was his father's oral communications, for which there was, the lawyer admitted, no corroboration. Yet, Jones asserted, if Kevin believed that both sets of shares legally belonged to the Robert Maxwell Group, 'This is a complete and absolute defence to both charges.'

To compensate for the lack of corroboration, Kevin's second defence theme was that Robert Maxwell dominated the empire, moving shares around as if they were his personal property, demanding that everyone unquestioningly 'rubber-stamp' his decisions. Since Kevin was charged with conspiring with his father, Jones conceded that a successful defence depended upon proving that Robert Maxwell was also innocent. The empire's collapse, he argued, was caused not by insolvency but by the erroneous perception on 5 November 1991 that Maxwell had committed suicide because of imminent financial catastrophe. Considerable time would be spent arguing with the judge – out of the jury's hearing – whether the defence were entitled to produce evidence that Maxwell had been murdered.

In the jury's presence, the theme of Robert Maxwell's domination would begin to crumble by the end of the fourth week. Witnesses repeatedly testified to Kevin's central responsibility during the last year. By the time the summer heatwave settled upon Chancery Lane, Robert Maxwell's ghost had been expunged.

To counter the accusation that Kevin, knowing of the empire's insolvency, had risked the pension fund shares, Jones would seek confirmation from witnesses in cross-examination that Kevin had relied upon the sale of assets to repay debts, upon the continued support of the banks and upon his advisers, and so believed that there was no criminal risk in his activities. Bankers would be accused of knowing the true ownership of the shares or of collaborating with Kevin in their use, and blamed for suddenly and greedily withdrawing their support when the empire's fate was more precarious.

Finally, Jones claimed that Kevin was a scapegoat, the victim of a City conspiracy to heap the entire blame for the empire's collapse upon the defendants. The trial, Jones told the jury, was staged so that people could say, 'We were kept in ignorance of the true facts. We were deceived by the conspirators and we have no responsibility.' The real culprits, he said, were among the witnesses. Those, he predicted, who were liable to civil damages, professional censure and criticism by the DTI inspectors would lie to the court, 'to distance themselves from events and actions which they thought at the time were proper but which, with hindsight, look embarrassing'. The truth, Jones proclaimed, was that at thirty-two, with enormous responsibilities, Kevin had relied upon the banks and his advisers and had believed he was acting lawfully.

The result of the alleged frauds, continued Jones, was not that Kevin 'made any gain – there is no pot of gold', but that he was the victim. He was the victim not just of a City conspiracy but also of the disappearance of original documents – the result either of accident or of attempts to conceal and destroy self-incriminatory evidence. Repeatedly, Jones harped on the fact that vital files had gone missing after their dispersal to the three administrators of the companies and the SFO. In addition, he alleged, his client suffered because former BIM employees (Trevor Cook, Harold Abrahart, Jane Roberts and Jeff Highfield) had used their time employed by Robson Rhodes, the administrators, to rewrite documents in order to conceal their negligence and blame the conspirators. 'I am suggesting', Jones would accuse a witness, 'that documents have been rewritten and that the ones presented to us are in many respects misleading so that it is easier for a person in your position to face the world with greater confidence.' The truth, he said, was impossible to establish without the missing papers – an irony (unrevealed to the jury) given that in the last days Maxwell employees had been shredding documents and deleting computer records.

The 'missing-documents conspiracy' was launched by Jones against Trevor Cook, the first witness, who, blinking and nervous, took the oath and recounted to the jury the history of the Scitex agreement and his efforts to recover the proceeds. In those early days, Kevin's camp seemed eager, confident about the outcome of the forthcoming battle; and the BIM's former managers were, they believed, ideal candidates for destruction.

In his defence, Kevin claimed that he had seen an amended version of the 4 July agreement between his father and Cook for the sale of the Scitex shares. The last line of the contract, according to Kevin, had been crossed out, giving RMG ownership of the shares without payment. Unfortunately, said Jones, that copy could not be found and Kevin could not recall the initials on that contract. Trevor Cook would deny altering the contract and no subsequent witness could recall seeing an amended version. Neil Cooper, the BIM administrator, told Jones that despite questioning and a search, 'We found no trace, nor anyone else that can recall ever seeing such an amended contract.'

Kevin's second defence on the Scitex charge rested on an entry of £100 million in the inter-company account from RMG to BIM (named the Call Deposit Account or CDA), made on 4 July by Harold Abrahart, another BIM administrator. Jones elevated the CDA to the status of a holy tablet while simultaneously classifying it as 'bearing the same informality' as every other share transaction between RMG and BIM. Allegedly Kevin, a non-accountant, had read that schedule regularly until mid-November and believed that the entry of £100 million confirmed RMG's legal ownership of the 5.4 million Scitex shares, although payment for them was not due until the end of the year.

Following what Jones called a search for the 'footprints in the audit trail' of the Maxwell empire's pension fund, it was indisputable that Cook and Harold Abrahart, a slight and nervous man who seemed beleaguered in the witness box, had erred in making and then retaining the £100 million entry in the CDA. The significance of their mistake, alleged Jones, was revealed by the creation in November of a separate Scitex account. In his cross-examination of Cook (and subsequently of Abrahart, Jane Roberts and Jeff Highfield), the defence lawyer argued that the belated creation of that separate account proved that the BIM administrators had realized that a false impression had been given to the uninformed Kevin that ownership of the shares had passed on 4 July.

In support of that argument, Jones produced a note sent on 4 July by Abrahart to Jane Roberts stating, 'a cash movement on our call deposit account has taken place'. However Kevin's interpretation of Abrahart's confused RMG–BIM account was not supported by any other witness and was challenged by all four BIM administrators.

The testimony of these four witnesses, given in a noticeably faltering, even painful manner, showed only too clearly why they had been appointed by Robert Maxwell in the first place. They were vulnerable employees who, handicapped by Cook's chaotic direction and record-keeping, had unquestioningly obeyed the Maxwells. But unanimously they explained to the jury that the CDA entry on 4 July had been made purely for the calculation of interest pending the shares' sale and an official valuation. The CDA account, they pointed out, was an internal working document which bore no legal implications about ownership. Indeed, Cook claimed never to have seen the CDA. Inter-company accounts, testified Highfield, 'are not a mechanism for settlements, they are mechanisms for recording details of debit and credit transactions'. The documents, he insisted, showed that RMG had a liability to pay BIM after the proceeds from the sale of Scitex had been received on 18 October. 'I cannot agree', he told the court, 'that the account shows that the transaction has been treated as a deposit of monies.' One problem for the defence was that Maxwell's agreement with Cook stated that the cash would pass one month later, on 4 August, contradicting Abrahart's note to Roberts on 4 July.

Jane Roberts, a young woman out of her depth in the Maxwell empire, remained close to tears as she testified that 'the 5.4 million Scitex shares belonged to BIM'. But, clearly nervous, not least because Albert Fuller, her former superior, sat nearby throughout her testimony accompanied by two large lawyers, she could not withstand the defence lawyers' memory game. After she had finally broken down during her cross-examination by Clare Montgomery, her evidence was undermined by her repeated excuse, 'I can't recall,' in respect of documents which supported the defence arguments.

Highfield proved himself to both prosecution and defence an exceptionally honest witness, but unusually it was a question from the jury which pinpointed a critical issue. Their written question, passed to the judge, noted that the print-out of the CDA schedule bore no comment alongside the £100 million. While other entries were accompanied by the explanation 'Cash movement' and a 1990 schedule showed the comment 'Purchase of Scitex' alongside the sum of money, the space beside Abrahart's entry on 4 July 1991 was unmarked.

Understandably Jones was irritated by an observation that was apparently favourable to the prosecution, but to his gratification Highfield agreed that the creation of a separate Scitex schedule by Cook and Abrahart had occurred after 14 November, giving some sustenance to the defence suggestion of a conspiracy to conceal the consequences. Highfield's date contradicted the evidence given by Cook and Abrahart. Both had testified that the new schedule had been created on 6 November, the day after the shares' valuation by Salomons. The truth was elusive. In his statement to the SFO in March 1993, Highfield had dated the separation of the Scitex transaction from the CDA as 'late October', while, as Jones revealed, Abrahart had given the SFO contradictory statements about the date. In Jones's argument, the Scitex liability had only been placed in a separate account just before 15 November in antici-pation of a visit by the IMRO inspectors. That was rebutted by Highfield: 'I cannot recall any connection between Mr Cook's instructions for separate recording and any regulatory visit.' For himself, Cook admitted that when the IMRO inspectors had called on 15 November, 'I didn't say BIM had been swindled because I didn't know the whole story at that stage.' He added, 'I didn't think the shares' ownership was in danger.'

For the purpose of establishing Kevin's guilt, the CDA schedules and the dates of separation were irrelevant, not least because the judge, echoing Highfield's testimony, told Jones in the jury's absence that it was misleading to suggest that a CDA entry was proof of an actual payment. But the contradictions among the BIM employees somewhat discredited their evidence, sparking Jones's colourful allegory that the surviving schedules were 'edited history written in the camp of those soldiers who kept the documents at the end of the war'.

To support that argument, Jones's cross-examination produced another small discrepancy. Cook denied in court having seen a brief item on 18 October in the *Financial Times* reporting the Scitex sale in New York. 'I was not aware of the deal until later that month,' he added. In contradiction, Highfield testified that, having read the newspaper report on the same day, he had informed Cook: 'I made sure he was aware of it too.'

'When you spoke to him on the 18th did he appear to be aware of that?' asked Jones.

'Yes,' replied Highfield, adding that Cook had asked Robert Maxwell for 'urgent and immediate settlement of the debt' soon after 18 October. But that reply developed into a poisoned chalice, undermining an important defence argument: namely, that Kevin had expected to pay RMG's debt to BIM at the end of the year. 'I don't recall any discussion', said Highfield, 'as to the debt falling due for settlement at the end of the year.'

Cook stated that Kevin had certainly never suggested to him that RMG had paid for the Scitex shares. 'It was never questioned by Kevin,' he insisted, referring to his approach to Kevin on the first occasion they had met after Robert Maxwell's death. That evidence was supported by Kevin's undisputed offer on 6 November to pay for those shares from property owned by RMG, and then by his signing on 12 November of an 'irrevocable' pledge to BIM of $77 million from the proceeds of Que. Pertinently, Kevin would be forced to admit that the individual accounts of both BIM and RMG showed no deposit or withdrawal of actual money for the Scitex shares, and he had been a director of both companies.

Cumulatively, the unchallenged testimony from eighteen witnesses was that at the RMG board meeting on 23 July Kevin had seen listed among RMG's assets Scitex shares worth £48m (compared to £143 million for the whole block) and he had seen that there was no mention of a liability of £100 million from RMG to BIM for the 5.4 million Scitex shares. Similarly there had been no mention of that liability at RMG's second 'going-concern' meeting on 9 November. Moreover, nine bankers testified that Kevin had claimed to own all the Scitex shares. Firstly, to Brian Brown of Lloyds Bank Kevin had said on 30 July that 'after the Scitex sale the private side will have $220 million less debt', without mentioning RMG's liability to BIM; secondly, in August he had misled the four bankers representing the Bank of Nova Scotia about an earlier sale of 1.9 million Scitex shares (in July) but had pledged to repay a loan of £40 million from the proceeds of the Scitex sale in October; and, thirdly, he had later assured four NatWest bankers, including David Leal-Bennett, that all the Scitex shares were privately owned – without which assurance, the banker testified, 'the company would have gone under'. Representatives of Swiss Volksbank and

Bankers Trust also testified that he had pledged the shares. Kevin's misfortune was his inability to find independent corroboration for his defence. Even so, it was not certain that the jury would choose to believe those bankers and former Maxwell employees.

The evidence about the use of the Teva shares was less open to challenge. Indeed, one fact was indisputable: BIM had been the registered owner of those shares. According to the prosecution, all four defendants had known that the Teva shares were owned by BIM and had also known of the empire's insolvency; therefore they were guilty of dishonestly taking a risk. Kevin claimed that his father had orally authorized the shares' transfer to RMG but, as the judge established in questioning a witness, it had been Robert Maxwell's practice to confirm any change of ownership of shares between his own companies by a memorandum or a formal agreement. 'There would have been some documentary evidence of a transfer,' confirmed Cook, 'and receipt of money by BIM.' In the event, the only record of the transfer of the Teva shares to RMG was BIM's minutes of 8 November, signed by Ian Maxwell and Trachtenberg. To overcome that hurdle, Kevin claimed that when the 25.1 million Teva shares had been pledged by RMG to NatWest on 8 November his intention had been to organize their repurchase from the proceeds of Que ten days later.

Initially, the prosecution case was weakened by the exclusion from the trial of any evidence about the stock-lending agreements between BIM and LBI. The judge insisted that, to limit the scope of the trial, the stock lending was a separate charge which should be tried later. The jury would therefore not understand how BIM's shares could be used to secure private loans. Instead, the evidence was that somehow Cook had discovered that the Teva shares were being used by RMG after Robert Maxwell's death. That led to contradictions.

In court, Cook asserted that he had first asked about the location of the three Teva share certificates 'before 8 November'. He also claimed to have relied upon Kevin's assurance on 20 November that they were located in Israel. His testimony on the earlier suggestion prompted Jones's accusation, 'That is either a lie on your part or deliberately misleading.' Indeed the evidence on that point was contradictory. Mark Haas of Lehmans would testify to having heard on 5 November that Cook had protested about the bank's liquidation of the BIM portfolio, including the single certificate for 22.8 million Teva shares. Indisputably, on 13 November, Cook had been given a schedule of BIM securities held by Lehmans, which included the Teva certificate. The following day, he had noted in his diary, 'Teva subject to repurchase', which suggested that he had perfectly understood Kevin's intention to recover the shares from Lehmans. Yet in court he explained that the Lehmans list and Kevin's comments had caused him some surprise. 'I didn't know the position,' he told Jones. 'I jotted it down but I didn't know what it meant.'

Another entry in Cook's notebook on 25 November appeared to undermine his reliability further. After a discussion with Kevin he had written, 'Where is Teva?' Cook's explanation in court was 'I was trying to put together a jigsaw. I didn't know if it was a downright lie. I wasn't making value judgments.' But according to Jones, Cook had added the phrase in 'different ink' long after the 25 November discussion. Cook denied the accusation.

Jeff Highfield's testimony on Teva did not entirely buttress Cook's credibility. Highfield had seen the Lehmans schedule listing 22.8 million Teva shares among its collateral on 14 November. But six days later, as he began his search for the certificates in Israel, he had still been puzzled, not least because Cook had not told him about Kevin's intention to repurchase the Lehmans certificate. Subsequently, Cook would state that he had believed that Lehmans held the certificate in a conventional stock-lending operation and not as collateral for a loan; but that did not explain why he had initially believed Kevin's insistence that all the certificates were held in Yaakov Neeman's office. The one explanation which he did not offer in court was the most credible: 'I was fooled.' Just how credible that explanation was could be seen from a query added to Cook's notebook on 19 November: 'Teva is ours, why does RMG show it?'

The significance of the Lehmans certificate, which became clearer only weeks later, was that the transactions between the defendants and the bank concerning those Teva shares provided the evidence that the defendants knew that all the shares (including those pledged to NatWest, which formed the basis of the second count) were owned by BIM.

The question was whether Cook's alleged incompetence or negligence affected the defendants' responsibility for pledging the other

25.1 million Teva shares with NatWest on 8 November. For a time, Cook seemed vulnerable to Michael Hill's melodramatic cross-examination. Trachtenberg's defence was that he had believed that the Teva shares were owned by RMG. Playing with his glasses, raising and lowering his voice, demanding 'Will you concentrate on the question!', Hill would seek to establish through confusion and histrionics Cook's imperfection as BIM's compliance officer. Cook would be accused of lying about the background to the existing documents or of retrospectively creating new documents to improve his own position. Hill would insist that Trachtenberg had received only summary accounts describing the ownership and fate of BIM's securities. 'I do recall sending him a list of all the investments,' averred Cook, to an advocate whose eyes were flaming with indignation.

The weakness of Hill's onslaught was that he produced no documents or witnesses to corroborate Trachtenberg's claims, while in re-examination Suckling convincingly showed that Hill's allegation of forgery was false. Moreover Hill faced another herculean task in rebutting other apparently damning testimony. Several witnesses described his client as 'a key and influential figure in a large number of Maxwell companies', or the 'manager of investments for the private Maxwell companies'. As a director of BIM, RMG and LBI, and as the manager of the stock-lending operation negotiating with the banks, Trachtenberg needed to rebut the bankers' evidence that he had possessed detailed knowledge of all the shares' ownership in 1991.

According to Cook, Trachtenberg had claimed for the first time that RMG owned the Teva shares on 21 November, 'after I found a certified copy of the BIM minutes [of 8 November]'. Trachtenberg, insisted Cook, had not demurred about BIM's ownership at BIM's board meetings on 18 and 20 November. Nor had he properly replied to Highfield's request for information about BIM's securities after 15 November.

Pinned against the wall, Cook eventually came out fighting to save his reputation, claiming naivety and mismanagement and denying a conspiracy with the defendants or his own criminal negligence. But after his battering by Jones and Hill, Cook gratefully succumbed to Lawson's benign questions, which were designed to show that Ian Maxwell had had no financial role until after his father's death. 'Ian Maxwell was the messenger?' asked Lawson.

'That's reasonable,' replied Cook, conceding that Ian usually signed documents after asking advice and had even signed documents while not appreciating their significance. That suited Ian's defence that he had signed the transfer of the Teva shares from BIM to NatWest only because Kevin had been in New York. But on that one point Cook was emphatic: Ian had failed to contact him on 8 November to inquire about the legitimacy of BIM's transfer.

By the end of the BIM evidence, a numbness had spread across the courtroom, seemingly empty in the absence of any spectators. The prosecution's case, regardless of its virtues, now seemed confused. Alan Suckling and Richard Lissack expected their fortunes to change with the testimony of three former MCC directors: Laister, Brookes and Woods. After all, all three were honest and had been duped. Yet, although they gave sustained evidence about the Maxwells' deception on the inter-company debts, the attempted misuse of the Que proceeds, phoney board minutes and their 'shock, surprise and dismay' during the turmoil of August and November as the pension fund deficit came to light, they became vulnerable to Jones's remorseless questioning about their own failures, their willingness to trust the Maxwells rather than exerting their legal powers. 'I didn't want to argue with Robert Maxwell,' said Laister, admitting that he had never voted against his employer, 'because he had a much louder voice.'

Significantly, Jones was not challenging the former directors' allegations of deception but was criticizing them for timorously believing Kevin and his father. That unusual defence was understandable because these three men had been witnesses to many alleged lies, and Jones hoped to win the jury's sympathy for the argument that Kevin was the victim of a conspiracy. Hence Laister was led helplessly into a trap. The former non-executive director was shown a document of a $145 million forex deal. 'You approved that transaction?' asked Jones.

'I certainly did not approve it,' replied Laister.

The usher handed the witness another copy of the document. Laister's face flushed as he saw his initials, clearly scribbled by himself on 30 October in Kevin's office when approving a pile of forex deals with Brookes, albeit ones which the finance director declared would require further scrutiny. 'Clearly I was incorrect, sir,' said an embarrassed Laister.

'You forged this document after the event to save your own skin?' challenged Jones, suggesting that Laister had subsequently painted Tippex on the initials on the first page after realizing that it was an unauthorized transaction.

'That', replied Laister, visibly angry, 'is totally unwarranted and a wholly incorrect accusation.'

'You came to this court to put the boot into Kevin Maxwell?'

'I'm interested in seeing justice done,' replied Laister, coolly adding, 'You have no reason or evidence that I Tippexed the document. I take great exception to that. It's outrageous.'

Indeed, there was neither evidence nor motive for Laister's alleged deception. For, although Jones hinted that the document was the original, it was in fact a photocopy and several other copies of the same document with Laister's signature existed. Moreover, the Tippexed document had been found in Basil Brookes's file and there was no evidence that Laister had had access to it. The former finance director himself testified, 'I'm sure I didn't do it,' but Laister was convinced that it was done innocently by a secretary in Brookes's department. In any event, the Tippexed document was irrelevant to the charges which Kevin faced. But it was characteristic of Jones's strategy to destroy a witness's character without challenging his evidence. 'Is your reputation higher because you said "I was deceived by Kevin Maxwell"?' asked Jones of Laister, later suggesting that the former director had been motivated by greed: 'Your annual salary increased [after Kevin's resignation] from £30,000 to £300,000?'

'It was approved by the banks,' answered Laister, already wounded by the implication.

'Did you change your car?'

'I didn't have a company car' came the retort.

While both Brookes and Woods, delivering solid evidence of deception after July, were less vulnerable, neither felt tempted to accuse their former employers of 'lying' or of any malfeasance. That absence of emotive language aroused doubts that the prosecution could prove that a crime had been committed.

In theory, the evidence of the Coopers accountants should have supported the charge of deception by the RMG directors relating to the company's finances before the board meeting on 23 July. But the auditors' behaviour had rendered them targets for several of

Jones's themes. 'You had a meeting with Kevin a few days before the 23 July?' asked Jones.

'I have no recollection of such a meeting,' replied Stephen Wootten.

'Kevin and you had a meeting,' continued Jones, 'and Kevin Maxwell said, "What do we have to produce to consider whether RMG is a going concern?" Do you remember that?'

'No, I do not.'

In that way, Jones laid the trail for Kevin's defence. Firstly, that the auditors had been aware that Robert Maxwell moved money around the group and treated all the money as one; secondly, that Kevin had relied on the advice given by the auditors and had conducted himself accordingly; thirdly, that the advisers had approved of his conduct; and, fourthly, that the auditors had failed to make proper inquiries about RMG's debts to other parts of the group.

Both Peter Walsh and Stephen Wootten arrived with lawyers to testify in a manner which Jones alleged bore all the hallmarks of careful preparation in an attempt to minimize any liability and to deny any knowledge beyond the safe confines of their self-declared legal responsibilities. 'Nobody told us that there was an enormous debt due to MCC,' pleaded Walsh, referring to the secret inter-company debt. 'There was no reason to believe that suddenly out of the blue there would be an enormous debt due to MCC, far beyond what was normal.' Consistently, the two accountants refused to accept that it was an auditor's task to assume the existence of any inter-company debts which had not been revealed by the directors. The auditors, they insisted, had no responsibility for querying the information provided by the directors; nor were they liable to breach the Chinese wall between themselves and their colleagues auditing other parts of the group. Crucially for the prosecution, both auditors testified that the accounts which Bunn had presented under-estimated RMG's debts and that they would have expected to see the £100 million due to BIM for the Scitex shares included on the inter-company debts for the 23 July board meeting. Instead, Scitex had been listed as an asset worth £48 million.

After conducting a heated cross-examination, accusing the Coopers auditors of professional failures and of cunningly blaming RMG's directors to avoid their own censure by the DTI and their professional council, Jones spat, 'The prosecution of Kevin Maxwell suits you and Coopers. It suits Coopers if there was a small band of conspirators who lied to one of the big six accountants?'

'No, not at all,' answered Wootten.

Jones's attack shed a lot of light on the failures of Coopers and the accounting profession but provided no real excuse for his client. Kevin's problem was to prove that, although on 23 July he must have appreciated that RMG's undisclosed debts had rendered the company insolvent, he could still rely upon the auditors' statement that RMG was 'a going concern'. Kevin also had to reconcile three statements. On 17 September 1991 he said to Wootten that '$280 million is available to the private side' to buy Scitex while claiming that RMG's debt to MCC had been reduced from £300 million to zero (the repayments came partly from the sale of pension fund securities); and thirdly, he told his solicitors on 29 October that 'MCC owes RMG £80 million.' Whatever the failures of the auditors, they would claim to have been equally deceived at the second 'going-concern' meeting on 9 November, insisting that their advice not to declare the company insolvent had been based upon the banks' continuing support.

It was the defendants' good fortune that a potential Achilles heel was removed soon after the auditors' testimony. On Monday, 24 July, Robert Bunn was revealed to have suffered a heart attack. After doctors had agreed that he was unfit to continue, he was discharged from the trial, although the judge indicated that the jury should still consider the evidence against Bunn on the ground that it could establish the existence of a conspiracy. Given his evident nervousness during the trial, there had been every reason to believe that Bunn would eventually testify to his unease, and his evidence might have incriminated the others. Any blame thereafter placed upon Bunn by Kevin could not be challenged while tackling the next group of witnesses – thirty-three bankers.

The witnesses who were potentially the most vulnerable to Kevin's defence that his company had been plunged into insolvency by the City were the bankers from Barclays, Lloyds and NatWest. 'To see Kevin Maxwell in November,' said Jones, correctly, 'you had to fight your way through a crowd of bankers in various states of agitation.'

All the banking witnesses spoke of their 'concern', their 'serious concern' and the 'severe liquidity crisis' in the months before

November 1991. All testified that during that period Kevin had been 'the pivotal point of all financial activities' and 'the principal decision-maker', dismissing Jones's suggestion that young Kevin had been an innocent ingénu. More importantly, the bankers emphasized how 'very convincing' Kevin's behaviour had been at numerous meetings. Repeatedly they gave accounts of his 'comforting' assurances about the level of inter-company debts, about the ownership and disposal of shares and in particular about the private side's ownership of all the Scitex and Teva shares. They attested to the repeated thanks both Robert and Kevin Maxwell had expressed for the banks' support, contradicting Jones's assertion that the banks had conspired to destroy the empire.

The Lloyds and Barclays bankers proved invulnerable to Kevin's attack, clearly establishing that he had repeatedly offered the same Scitex shares to six different banks, and that he had assured each banker that they were privately owned. The NatWest witnesses, on the other hand, turned out to be susceptible. Successively they would be accused by Jones of 'making it up as you go along' and even of dishonesty, as they sought to rebut suggestions that they had greedily squeezed the Maxwells to reduce their loans. These bankers found that no help was forthcoming from the prosecution as they tried to justify the weakness they had shown in succumbing to pressure and the sense of responsibility they had felt when appointing themselves 'lenders of last resort' to the Maxwell empire and allowing the overdraft to exceed the agreed limit by £112 million in August. That £112 million, testified Bob Brown, who had 'left work one day suffering a toothache and returned to discover a heartache', was 'not lent, it was taken'. The bankers' 'incredibly frantic' attempts to provide money to save the group were not interpreted by Jones as charity – an interpretation that was in any case harder to accept after the revelation that the banks had charged a £1 million fee for organizing further loans.

Most woundingly, the NatWest bankers were accused of accepting the Teva share certificates, which quite clearly showed BIM as the registered owners, knowing that BIM managed pension funds. The source of their knowledge was the Cordmead deal in 1988, arranged to effect a bridging loan for MCC through BIM. Although John Melbourn denied the similarity between Cordmead and the loan against the Teva shares, the coincidence was too great to expunge the notion that the bank had known that BIM managed pension funds. 'I would be hard put,' agreed John Melbourn, 'if I were confronted with a replica transaction today, to agree to it.' Answering Jones's accusation that he knew of BIM's role, Leal-Bennett retorted, 'That is not true. That is not true. I have nothing to hide. If I had heard or thought that pension funds were involved I would have had that discussed within the organization.' Certainly, that was a healthy moment for Kevin's defence.

Repeatedly Jones pressed the bankers to admit that they had known the true ownership of the Teva shares. No less repeatedly he sought to establish that the shares had been pledged as a 'bridging loan' and that Kevin's intention had been to seek their recovery using the $160 million proceeds of the Que sale. That was rebuffed by David Ingham: 'It was not a specific bridging loan,' he repeated, as Kevin smiled at the banker's discomfort. For the defence believed that serious doubts about NatWest's behaviour had been aroused when the banker admitted that their original intention had been to use the Que proceeds to reduce RMG's debt. In the event, the $160 million had been paid, at NatWest's insistence, into MCC's account, reducing the company's unsecured debt to the bank. That had clearly been an advantage to the bank, an advantage which the defence also sought to exploit as an example of greedy bankers undermining the entire group's finances by seizing whatever money was available during the last days. Time and again, Jones tried to extract an admission from the bankers that on 18 November Kevin had attempted to reclaim the Teva shares; but the bankers' denials were confirmed by the written record of two meetings with Kevin. Nevertheless, the NatWest bankers did not convincingly deny that the Maxwell empire was viewed by them as one group, which Kevin believed strengthened his case that the family could lawfully use MCC's money and the Teva shares for their private purposes.

The balance of advantage, already tilted in favour of the defence, shifted further with the testimony of Ian Huntington, an accountant employed by Peat Marwick who between November 1991 and June 1993 had been attached to the SFO. Jones used the opportunity to establish that in 1988 one accountant in the partnership had written of the widespread knowledge that Robert Maxwell was using the pension funds for his own activities and that the trustees did not object. 'If the horse keeps on winning you do not break its leg,'

Jones read with relish from the report, which the witness had not known existed. Then the lawyer launched an attack on Huntington for having authorized the dawn raid by the police in June 1992, 'to inflict ritual public humiliation upon Kevin Maxwell by having him arrested in the full glare of the press'. Huntington's denial that he had been responsible or that he had tipped off the press was the last testimony when the court rose that day, 10 August, for a two-week break. As they streamed into the sunlight, both prosecution and defence believed themselves to be winning – and, since the prosecution needed to prove their case beyond reasonable doubt, the Maxwells were entitled to think that they had a good chance of acquittal.

The mood markedly changed soon after the trial resumed on 29 August. The unexpected reason was the Maxwells' most intimate advisers – their lawyers. A taste of their incriminatory evidence had been served before the break by the two Israeli lawyers, Michael Fox and Yaakov Neeman. Matter-of-factly, Fox had recited the confused and mysterious fate of the Teva share certificates. In Tel Aviv, he had received inquiries from Highfield hunting for the certificates even while Kevin was agreeing to buy one certificate back from Lehmans having pledged another to NatWest. No one in the courtroom could miss the implications of the contradictory messages coming from London.

By contrast, Neeman, who had known Robert Maxwell well, confirmed only the exchange of faxes concerning Kevin's plan to raise a loan in Israel in order to buy back the Teva shares from Lehmans. But Neeman was reluctant to volunteer more information than could be gleaned from the written records. 'What's the question?' he snapped at Jones after listening to a recitation of Maxwell's activities in Israel. The Israeli lawyer had no intention of obliging Kevin by endorsing Jones's attempt to establish Maxwell's status in Israel. 'That's a wrong assumption,' he growled when Jones suggested that Maxwell was a generous benefactor to the hundreds of Israelis writing for help. 'Ninety-nine per cent of those letters were refused,' snarled the lawyer. Neeman manifested the embarrassment felt by the whole court when Jones recited President Herzog's valediction at Maxwell's funeral; only the two sons, unsurprisingly, reacted with emotion. Jones's peroration about the deceased was cut short by the judge: 'I wonder whether we need to go into all the details.' Neeman departed in a huff, tarnished as the architect of Robert Maxwell's 'state' funeral and as a lawyer whose firm had reluctantly revealed Kevin's unorthodox use of the Teva shares. But his and Fox's evidence of double-dealing was unchallenged.

The more crushing lawyers' evidence was supplied by the three solicitors from Titmuss Sainer. Flushed and evidently embarrassed by their close association with Kevin, they offered recollections based largely upon their contemporaneous notes, frequently resorting to 'I cannot recall' when asked to describe events not recorded in writing. Across the courtroom, chewing hard, Kevin seemed initially bemused by their turmoil and lapsed memories, looking grave only when he realized that their evidence, even if restricted, was damaging. Despite their equivocation, the three solicitors revealed that they had been misled by Kevin about MCC's debt to RMG, about the fate of the £55.7 million owed to the Swiss Bank, about the £400 million owed to the pension funds, and about MCC's own money being used to buy MCC shares. Suggestions by Jones that Kevin had actually declared, 'RMG owes MCC money,' were limply rebuffed. 'I don't recall that discussion,' testified David Vogel, quietly asserting the opposite. 'It was an issue in my mind and I made a note ten minutes later.' His reaction when he discovered the truth had been, he said with considerable understatement, 'some surprise'. There was no easy rebuttal by Kevin of his own lawyers' harmful testimony. By the time Dick Russell, Kevin's brother-in-law, took the oath, Jones had decided that his interests were best served by silence.

Anxiety now infected the Maxwell camp. The prosecution threatened a parade of nine bankers to testify to Kevin's unfulfilled promises concerning unpaid foreign exchange deals. Jones sought to exclude their appearance or at least to confine their evidence to the reading out of statements. After all, he told the judge during one day's argument in the jury's absence, their testimony was admitted by Kevin and was prejudicial. The judge declined Jones's request. Over five days in the first week of September, clean-cut, sober bankers gave unchallenged accounts of a distasteful pattern epitomized by a reference in one bank's internal memorandum to the Maxwell group as a 'Potentially dangerous customer'.

'Presumably that does not mean that the customer might attack you?' asked Montgomery. 'No,' replied the banker, no doubt grateful that he had eventually recovered the £3.9 million which Kevin had suggested to his face was 'lost' thanks to yet another snafu. The gallows humour did not remove the chill.

By mid-September, smiles on Kevin's pale, puffy face were as rare as daffodils in the desert. There was overwhelming evidence from bankers, auditors and former personnel that the Maxwell group was unable to repay loans or even employees' wages. With the empire's insolvency established, the prosecution needed to prove that the defendants intentionally took a risk with the pension funds' assets.

To satisfy that requirement, two weeks of testimony in September produced a broadly unchallenged version of deception on 15 November 1991 regarding the Teva shares. The evidence from Jeff Highfield and five Lehman bankers confirmed that on that day, firstly, Kevin and Trachtenberg had signed a transfer on behalf of RMG to NatWest; secondly, Kevin and Trachtenberg had signed an agreement on behalf of BIM to repurchase the Teva shares from Lehmans, which was confirmed in a taped telephone call between Trachtenberg and Piers La Marchant, a Lehmans lawyer; and, finally, Highfield had asked Trachtenberg for the first time about the whereabouts of all BIM's Teva certificates, to which he had received 'no reply'. Not only was Highfield's testimony about his subsequent hunt for the Teva share certificates left unrebutted, but the reason he gave for first asking Trachtenberg about their whereabouts was damning: 'because he was most appropriate . . . as the man responsible for monitoring the stock-lending programme'.

Originally, the defence had hoped to expose the five Lehmans bankers, dubbed by NatWest as 'hostile', as responsible for plunging the empire into insolvency rather than allowing it a period of grace for survival. The evidence was certainly that Joe Gregory, among the witnesses from New York, had prompted the issue of a default notice immediately after hearing that Maxwell was missing and that Kevin had been 'angry' about the bank's breach of an understanding not to issue the notice. The bankers' admission that they had apologized to Kevin might have been exploited by Montgomery, but fearing that her insensitive questioning had already established that the bank rather than the Maxwells were the victims – Gregory spoke succinctly of seeking to 'avoid a larger-than-life calamity' – she retreated from attack.

To the prosecution's glee, the Lehmans evidence firmly established that Kevin and Trachtenberg had known before 8 November that BIM owned the Teva shares. Under the 1989 agreement with the bank, Kevin had pledged BIM's securities as collateral for loans of $77 million to the private side. The taped telephone conversations between the bankers and Kevin and Trachtenberg, combined with letters and agreements signed by the two BIM directors in October and November, established that both had known about BIM's ownership of the Teva shares.

In court, the contrast between the testimony of Highfield and Mark Haas relating to conversations during the period 25–27 November led to the first suggestions of a split between Kevin and Trachtenberg. On 25 November, Trachtenberg had called Highfield to say that there was 'confusion about the ownership of the Teva shares'. But in a call to Haas the following day he had said, 'I'm sitting in Robert Maxwell's old office . . . trying to get some bastard to sign a letter' authorizing Lehmans to register their ownership of the Teva shares in Israel. Clearly, Trachtenberg had lied to Highfield. In cross-examining the Lehman bankers, neither Jones nor Hill disputed their clients' knowledge of the shares' true ownership, but Trachtenberg's advocates suggested that he was merely Kevin's agent or a witness to Kevin's signature, 'just like in a will', and that he was confused about the roles of four Maxwell companies – LBG, RMG, BIT and BIM – in relation to the collateral's ownership. Kevin gave a pained glance towards Trachtenberg's corner as Hill sought reinforcement for that defence from a Merrill Lynch banker, who agreed that the Maxwells had 'conducted themselves as if they were in effect the owners of the [Teva] shares'.

The answer to Kevin's problems, according to Jones, would have been the white knight – the Israeli or Arab investor prepared to inject £400 million into the group. In Kevin's opinion the sum was sufficient to save the empire, but in fact it was scarcely enough to compensate the pension funds. He argued that the empire's collapse had been caused by the banks' greed and their unwillingness to wait for the investor's money. His first task was to prove that the offer had been genuine. Although Neeman testified that the fax he had sent on 1 December had been serious, his failure to identify the investor nullified his evidence. The attempts by the defence to extract favourable testimony from the bankers and lawyers about the investor only provoked statements about his inconsequence and their own bewilderment. An attempt by Montgomery to use a Lehmans taped conversation between Philip Howard and another executive in order to obtain Howard's agreement that the mysterious investor was considered a serious possibility by the bank was countered in re-examination by Richard Lissack reading a later transcript of Howard in conversation with Lehmans in New York: 'You won't believe this. It's almost the funniest thing in my life. They have an investor, unnamed and unsupported by any evidence, with £400 million who is going to rescue them, and they've given the guy until Friday to turn up with the money.' Howard's colleague replied that he should tell Joe Gregory, 'but without me here. All I'll do is laugh again.'

Lissack sat down smiling. Behind him, Kevin gazed gloomily at Clare Montgomery, who stared frostily at her files. By the following week, the barrister had recovered her nerve to take on a more important quarry, the police.

The topic was the police handling of the documents seized from Maxwell House, and Montgomery's focus was the alleged disappearance of the amended 4 July agreement critical to Kevin's defence. According to Montgomery, the pages were lost, possibly due to police incompetence. The target of her accusation was Detective Sergeant Robert Scott, the officer responsible for bagging the contents of Kevin's office. 'Can you find the agreement in that file there?' asked Montgomery, pointing at a lever-arch file numbered 894.

'I'm looking for it,' replied the bearded police officer.

'Just so you know this is not a trick question,' said Montgomery, 'I do not believe it is there.'

Scott looked up, 'I am sure you would not ask me if it was.'

Montgomery pulled up her gown, adjusted her wig and said, 'That is not very satisfactory.'

The police officer soberly agreed: 'It could have been handled better.' In the purest form, this was a theatrical re-enactment of the defence manoeuvres at the hugely popular O. J. Simpson trial. On the prosecution benches in Court 22, there was a flutter of activity. The fate of that document was critical to their case.

While Scott laboriously explained to the jury the police procedures for handling the documents, Lissack and SFO officers searched through the file number 894 where the 4 July agreement should have been and, just as Montgomery warmed to her theme of missing faxes, Suckling sprang to his feet. 'The agreement and that fax', announced the prosecutor, 'are in fact in the file.' Indeed, the agreement was on the very top.

'I was wrong,' admitted Montgomery unemotionally, as the jury conferred agitatedly among themselves and the prosecutors smiled. Kevin gave his lawyers a pained look. To his left, Michael Hill's face reddened and his head drooped. Corrosion had penetrated the defence case. On Kevin's insistence, a radical solution was adopted.

By the end of September, it was apparent that the defence's strategy was undergoing a complete metamorphosis intended to undermine the judge's original limitation of the trial's issues, which had excluded the other alleged crimes.

Kevin had always argued that he could mount a proper defence only if his trial covered every aspect including the stock lending, First Tokyo, Berlitz and the £50 million loan from Bankers Trust to the Mirror Group. As the trial progressed into the autumn, Alun Jones, under pressure from Kevin, began questioning witnesses about those previously taboo areas. Automatically, the prosecution were allowed to introduce evidence which had previously been excluded. By 28 September, the introduction of the unexplained controversies seemed to have complicated the picture for the jury. Yet, simultaneously, the central issue had become more defined – Kevin's private use of a whole swath of assets besides the Teva and Scitex shares. Bewilderingly, both the prosecution and defence appeared delighted by the development. To the former it seemed a bonus, a kamikaze tactic promising a glorious vista for Kevin's cross-examination; while Kevin's camp believed that they had created the opportunity to present his case in its most advantageous form. The atmosphere in courtroom noticeably changed towards an irreconcilable mixture of light-heartedness and concern. The countdown had begun towards Kevin's own testimony. Then came an upset.

At 9.20 a.m. on Friday, 29 September, before the day's proceedings had started, Kevin and his lawyers were anxiously standing by a tape-deck. The courtroom was filled with the sound of Larry Trachtenberg ordering the £20 million in exchange for dollars on 4 November 1991. His face twisted in anguish, Kevin was clearly concerned. It was the incriminating tape which Trachtenberg had extracted from Adrian Black on 18 November.

One hour later, Oliver Jefferson, the foreign exchange dealer who had taken Trachtenberg's order for the currency exchange, stepped into the witness box, having just arrived that morning from New York. Michael Hill, on Trachtenberg's behalf, ordered that the tape be played and then abruptly stopped when the recorded conversation paused and Trachtenberg's words became muffled. 'Can you hear another voice giving Mr Trachtenberg instructions?' asked Hill.

'No,' replied Jefferson, and repeated that answer when the tape was replayed.

'Surely you can hear Mr Kevin Maxwell giving instructions?' asked Hill angrily.

'I can't,' answered Jefferson unobligingly.

The implications were clear: Trachtenberg's defence had changed. He was claiming to have been acting under orders. Four months into the trial, a split had opened between the defendants. Kevin's camp looked grim. The prosecutors smiled. To them, it seemed to be good news. Even the judge smiled. The end of the trial was in sight. For most of those involved, the ordeal appeared to be nearly over.

As Kevin self-confidently took the stand on 16 October, the eighty-second day of the trial, his face was pale and his eyes appeared bloodshot. His hope was that his unshakeable self-confidence would not terminate in self-destruction. Watching nervously, Ian looked unusually ill. Over the previous weeks, the elder brother had sat silently, practically out of the jury's sight, reading colour magazines and occasionally dozing. Now, however, he showed intense disappointment that he was still in the courtroom. Until four days earlier, Edward Lawson, his counsel, had encouragingly spoken of persuading the judge that there was no case to answer and calling for Ian's acquittal. In the course of a two-day argument, ignoring his own promise 'to avoid hyperbole', Lawson had argued that Ian's silence in court, the absence of hostile cross-examination by himself, the uncertainty of the NatWest witnesses, Ian's non-involvement in the group's financial management and the absence of references to Ian by the prosecution witnesses had proved that his client signed the documents to transfer the Teva shares at NatWest only at some-one else's request and bore no responsibility for the circumstances and consequences of his action. By 8 November 1991, when Ian had signed, said Lawson, the share certificate had already been delivered by Kevin to the bank.

Lawson's suffocating speech, one year in preparation, was neatly demolished by Richard Lissack for the prosecution. Crisply, Lissack reminded the judge that in 1991 Ian had been acknowledged by everyone to be 'a consummate businessman, instrumental in turning around the fortunes of MGN and setting up and running the *European*'. Ian's knowledge, continued Lissack, stretched much further back than November 1991. As a director of BIM, MCC, RMG and Teva, he knew about the shares' true ownership and understood the Maxwell group's development financial crisis. His alleged non-involvement in the group's detailed financial management, argued the lawyer, was irrelevant given that after his father's death, on Lawson's own admission, Kevin had relied upon his brother (sug-gesting participating in the conversations necessary to sustain a charge of conspiracy) and had involved him in the crisis talks with the bankers and in the search for an investor. The crux, Lissack contended, was the lack of evidence that on 8 November 1991 Ian had said, 'I do not understand what we are talking about. These are pension fund assets.' As Cook had testified, 'Ian Maxwell always took care of all he was signing and regularly rang me to confirm and check on matters that I placed before him.' Significantly, at no stage had Ian ever told Cook about RMG's use of the Teva shares – proving, contended Lissack, that the elder Maxwell brother had conspired in the taking of dishonest risk.

At the end of the second day Judge Phillips said starkly, 'My conclusion is that there is a case to go to the jury,' and he then disappeared from the courtroom. Depressed by Lawson's failure and visibly strained, Ian watched with novel attention as his brother entered the climax of their trial. His best hope was for the jury to accept Kevin's insistence that he alone had assumed financial con-trol over the empire, excluding Ian.

In his short introductory speech to the jury, Alun Jones promised a 'forest of detail' to prove that, although the Maxwell group had been suffering liquidity problems, it had possessed sufficient assets which, if sold, could have repaid its debts. (Significantly, he never produced any independent evidence or challenged any witnesses to prove that assertion.) Displaying an exuberant certainty of his client's innocence, he suggested that the prosecution had failed to prove more than that Kevin had lied to banks – 'for which he deserves to be embarrassed'. But that, said Jones, was relevant only if Kevin was accused of defrauding banks. To demonstrate that his client was guilty of defrauding the pension funds, the barrister insisted, the prosecution needed to prove his intent and the existence of a conspiracy – and that had not been achieved.

Seated in the witness box, dressed in a grey suit and blue shirt, Kevin could console himself by reflecting on one piece of good fortune. Over the previous three years, there had been four private dry runs for that moment – the intensive, compulsory hearings for the three administrators and the interviews with the Serious Fraud Office. Thereafter, he had exhaustively discussed with his lawyers the replies he would offer to Jones' helpful questions and how he would rebut the inevitably hostile prosecutor. For months he had studied the thousands of documents on which the prosecution relied, as well as those which his own lawyers unearthed – weaving from their omissions, contradictions and qualifications a coherent explanation for his conduct. Painstakingly he had discussed with his legal team how best to present himself to the jury, agreeing that he should pose as the victim – of the City, of his advisers, of his former employees and most of all of Robert Maxwell.

In a bid to win that sympathy, in the opening moments of his testimony Kevin conjured an image of his tyrannical father, 'a frightening character' who demanded utter obedience and who contemptuously dismissed his son's suggestions with 'Are you comparing yourself with me?' But, incongruously, Kevin's cool demeanour hardly suggested a vulnerable man, liable to be overwhelmed by emotion. Even his observation that 'My father is dead. He is not here to defend himself. We are all living with the consequences,' barely raised the temperature.

Whatever sympathy had been won was quickly dissipated by his description of his meteoric career. After joining the business in 1984, he explained, he had risen from the bottom, overcoming prejudice against nepotism, to become engaged in dozens of multi-million-pound take-overs, receiving, amid ferocious rows with his father, a business education whose unorthodoxy conditioned him to accept that shares, assets and millions of pounds belonging to the public and private companies and the pension funds could be informally moved around the group at his father's unilateral, oral direction. To place the 'normality' of those complicated transfers in context, he repeated: 'I came to accept that the paperwork would follow.' Emphasising that the company's lawyers, auditors and pension fund trustees had knowingly co-operated with his father's unconventional transfers – 'going back and forth . . . unwinding transactions' – Kevin in fluent jargon expounded the intricacies of City finance, spewing out a complicated tangle of facts, figures, names and relationships, oblivious to the fact that his audience had occasionally been guided by himself and Jones towards incomprehension.

As Kevin spoke, his confidence rose: he was pleased to have set up a duet with his advocate, putting on a performance which, as could be expected of a Balliol College graduate, was immaculate. For his part, Jones, obsequiously punctuating his loaded questions (which often lasted a couple of minutes) with 'please' and 'thank you', sometimes twice in one sentence, had ushered himself into a belief that the mere complexity of facts would, if it did not prove Kevin's innocence, at least induce the jury into a state of reasonable doubt. In breach of custom, Jones even ended his long questions with a nod or grimace to elicit the answer, yes or no; and occasionally, as if the court were an Oxbridge seminar, Kevin was generously rewarded with 'Correct.'

By the end of the first day, Kevin had entered sensitive territory: he admitted ignoring the constant conflicts of interest which arose from his directorships of 'hundreds and hundreds of companies'. Instinctively, he suggested, he had adopted Robert Maxwell's practice of using the law as a weapon: 'My father would stretch the law as far as it would go to achieve his business ends. There was the letter of the law and the spirit of the law.' While the letter of the law was to be obeyed, the spirit could be broken. His father ran the business, explained Kevin, ignoring the board of 'rubber-stamp' directors who merely ratified what had already been done, and he 'hated' the 'tremendous irritance' of obeying the 'the minutiae of compliance'. An example of the Maxwells' unorthodoxy, said Kevin, was the habit of Alan Stephens, the company secretary, of 'accumulating hundreds of documents requiring signature and bringing them to my office for a grand signing session where I signed merrily away [with] no time to check'. But, since he was charged jointly with Robert Maxwell in the conspiracy, Kevin volunteered that there could be no doubts about his father's 'personal honesty and integrity. He loathed fraud in his own businesses.' The only problem was his father's behaviour: the 'spectacular risk-taker' had gambled his fortune away.

Kevin's next step, having asserted the legitimated unorthodoxy of the Maxwell finances, was to justify his lack of attention to the pension funds despite his trusteeship and his directorship of BIM. Referring to the IMRO guidance manual he told Jones, 'I certainly did not take the time or trouble to open such a document and was not aware of its content,' although he 'regretted' that pension fund trustees were not bound by statue to be trained. To underline his detachment, he added, 'I did not believe that my duties were any more onerous or different to the duties of a director. . . . I would be very surprised if I spent more than thirty minutes a week considering the affairs of BIM.' His reason was plain. The pension fund trustees he insisted, until 1991, accepted Robert Maxwell as the sole 'investment manager' and dared not interfere with his unholy *diktat* that the pension of funds were to be used to 'support the group'. What was good for the group, pouted Kevin, was good for the pension funds and vice versa. Shares would be transferred by his father to generate profits at the end of the financial year and cash moved into accounts for a matter of hours to 'zero' intercompany debts – all with Coopers' approval. Any retrospective condemnation, he urged, was vindictive.

The next stage was to introduce the predominant thread of the defence: blaming others for Kevin's misfortune. Vitriol filled the courtroom. Since Robert Bunn was no longer a defendant, he was an easy scapegoat for a spate of embarrassments. 'I relied upon Bunn and Stoney.' Kevin would say of a tricky financial issue, while associating Bunn with a lie told to Citibank. The next scapegoat was Richard Baker, the former managing director of MCC, whom Kevin accused of conceiving a ruse to hide the group's enormous debts. Then Kevin attacked Coopers, who knew everything and were responsible for RMG's 'going-concern' meetings – 'Nobody from Coopers ever raised any complaint, any reproach.' Peter

Walker was tarnished as a man who had been 'basically fired' because 'my father changed his mind'. The public statement about the demerger of MCC, sniped Kevin, was merely 'a peg for public consumption'. Like so many other denunciations irrelevant to the case, it skirted the truth, not least by suggesting that Walker had received only £150,000 in compensation. Kevin's personal lawyers were another target: David Vogel's notes and his testimony about inter-company debts, said Kevin, were wrong, while Philip Morgenstern was a fabricator who had betrayed the family's friendship.

Few former advisers were besmirched more than Eric Sheinberg of Goldman Sachs. In preparing for his defence, Kevin had been allowed to read a 150-page statement submitted confidentially by Sheinberg to the SFO about his relationship with Maxwell. Although, to the satisfaction of Sheinberg's diligent lawyers, the SFO had taken no further action, Kevin used the document to assert that the American had contrived with his father to purchase MCC shares through Liechtenstein in a covert support operation. Warming to his theme, he accused Sheinberg of double-crossing his father by encouraging his belief that unknown speculators were involved in a bear raid to drive down MCC's share price. 'My father,' said Kevin, 'agreed to follow the advice of Eric Sheinberg and to engage in a concerted and sustained pattern of purchasing shares in MCC to force the bears out of the market.' In reality, he claimed, the bear was Sheinberg himself – 'the principal seller of shares'. In New York, meanwhile Sheinberg was outraged but helpless as Kevin went on to defend the legality of the operation: 'I would say it was an example of pushing the law to the limits,' but 'a terrible waste'. The legality, said Kevin, kicking out, was provided by Morgenstern's advice that the private use of MCC's money was legitimate.

Those whom Kevin blamed were also accused of lying. Among the most brutally castigated of these 'liars' were the MCC directors – the 'rubber-stamp' directors in Kevin's phrase – whose protest in August 1991 he derided as 'a storm in a teacup', although he pleaded, 'I was under tremendous pressure to contain [my father's] anger in this period. It was very, very difficult.' The directors' evidence that they had opposed what was going on he simply dismissed as irrelevant on the ground that until that August, they had unquestioningly approved Maxwell's use of MCC's money. Yet Kevin's testimony was contradictory. Although saying that he had 'encouraged' the directors' confrontations with his father, he was also claiming to have been 'very upset about the same directors' disloyalty and lack of confidence' when they consulted MacFarlanes and telephoned him on the *Lady Ghislaine*. Revealingly, his anger had not dissipated: 'I am still upset. I could not understand it.' His concern for himself remained paramount.

Bluntly, Kevin felt no shame, either in 1991 or in 1995, for relying upon the 'rubber-stamp' directors' gullibility to establish his right to take without authorisation and for his private use the proceeds of the Que and Directories sales and the Berlitz shares, which all belonged to MCC. Not only were the directors' mistakes exploited for their common denigration, but even their belated remedial efforts were damned. Encouraged by Jones, Kevin denounced a polite memorandum by Laister written in October 1991 complaining about the failure to observe the agreed procedures on inter-company debts as 'genuine balderdash', and he constantly referred to Laister painting Tippex over his initials, which was an unproven allegation.

Yet these were the same people who, Kevin believed, after his father's death 'would do whatever was in their power to help me in this crisis'. After all he scoffed, they had never previously condemned the use of MCC's money as 'unlawful'.

'You had not told them about your liability to the pension funds, had you?' retorted Suckling, when Kevin repeated the lament in cross-examination.

'No,' replied Kevin. 'That is common ground between us. . . . They would have run a smile.'

To neutralize the effect of such unpleasant exchanges, Kevin's defence was interspersed by his reading of condolence messages from bankers and politicians such as James Callaghan and Margaret Thatcher – exploitation of private politenesses was apparently customary for Kevin – and by telling the packed courtroom about the events on the day his father died. Unexceptionally, even his account of those uncontroversial events contradicted other recollections. According to his version, he learnt of his father's disappearance from the switchboard at Maxwell House: 'They said the captain said he was not on the boat. That struck me as bizarre.' Continuing, Kevin recounted how *he* had telephoned Gus Rankin, who after prevarication had revealed that 'they were cruising and that my father was lost overboard'. By contrast, Rankin and the managers at MAMI insist that the alert came from the *Lady Ghislaine*. A similar contradiction lay in Kevin's testimony that he had heard about the discovery of his father's body 'as I arrived home around 10 o'clock'. In fact, he had heard at 12 p.m. in his office. Even on such straightforward matters, Kevin's memory seemed faulty. The murder theory, however, had been abandoned. The cause of death, he said, was that his father, a light sleeper, had in the middle of the night relieved himself near a lifeboat and, unhindered by two thin pieces of wire, had fallen overboard. The possibility was later raised that Maxwell might have fainted while urinating.

The first public description of Kevin's reaction to the death was heard politely: 'It was the physical loss, it was a terrible burden. . . . I found myself almost unable to control myself physically and I realised that, if I did not get a grip, I would probably suffer some kind of breakdown.' With MCC shares pushed 'into free-fall', and lacking his father's forty years' experience, 'I missed him, his presence and his ability to dominate.' Even a hardened cynic suspended judgment as Kevin described the 'powerful effect and . . . tunnel vision, focusing at the end of the week, to go to the funeral and bury him in peace. I could not think properly until after that.' But the cynicism returned to some when the generosity and goodwill of the 'state' funeral in Israel was used by Kevin to attest to his own honesty: 'I was genuinely amazed and heartened by the depth and quality of support from the financial institutions connected with us. They were very, very supportive. I derived great personal comfort from a business point of view, as well, from those indications of support.'

That introduced the next stage of Kevin's defence. The group's financial position, he claimed, was actually improving in 1991: 'I saw the illiquidity as a temporary problem.' His assertion highlighted the nub of the prosecution's problem: the jury would remain unaware, because the prosecution had not produced the evidence, that after 1988 MCC's annual accounts had been contrived; meanwhile Kevin could vehemently claim that the group was solvent so long as the banks remained supportive.

The banks' attitudes placed Kevin in a quandary. On the one hand he wanted to show how the banks had happily given loans despite the group being 'under severe pressure' when 'survival was questionable'. On the other hand, the Maxwell group did collapse because the banks had withdrawn their support after his father's death despite Kevin's own insistence that there were more assets than liabilities. That decision, he knew, was associated with their receipt of information about the pension funds – and that knowledge determined his strategy.

Bankers, he decided, were to be cast as villains harassing an honest and grieving young man regardless of their rights to recover loans. Hence Mike Moore of Bankers Trust was denounced as a liar for denying that the switch of the £50 million loan was linked; Richard Pelly of Barclays was damned for threatening 'commercial blackmail'; Bob Brown of NatWest was castigated as a 'hatchet man' for wanting to 'reduce the bank's exposure to the Maxwell connection'; John Melbourn was accused of 'threatening' behaviour on 18 November 1991 and damned for 'swiping' £65 million from the Directories sale to reduce MCC's debt; and Lehmans were cursed as 'an exceptionally aggressive and hostile institution with no motivation beyond their own self-interest' when they issued their recall notice the day his father died: 'They said they could not stop the wheels of justice, they were a large business, they were responsible to their shareholders, they wanted the money and they couldn't give a stuff about my father.' In a familiar pattern, those claims had not been put by Jones to the five witnesses from Lehmans.

What emerged clearly from his early testimony was Kevin's approach to business, apparently the product of his father's education. In Kevin's world, to mislead bankers was acceptable if they did not ask the right questions. 'I misled all the banks,' he told the court. 'If they didn't ask, they didn't get.' Omitting to correct 'a misapprehension', he said, was not dishonest. In his enterprise culture, not repaying bank debts on time was merely 'technical'; when the forex deals failed, that was 'a temporary hiccup that had to be solved before asking the banks for more money'; board minutes, prepared before meetings and then signed, could still be 'nonsense, a load of tosh'; offering to banks as collateral shares which he did not possess was acceptable because 'that's different than a legally binding commitment'; RMG's debt to BIM was in his world 'A BIM asset' even if RMG was insolvent; while, even on his own confession, his lie to the Bank of Nova Scotia (BNS) 'was not dishonest' because the bank eventually received its money, albeit from the sale of the pensions' Scitex shares. Kevin's representations to BNS about the fate of 2.6 million Scitex shares pledged against a £40 million loan had been false. As Jones observed, it was 'a bit like being in the dentist's chair for us'. The barrister had desperately but unsuccessfully sought to exclude from the trial the evidence of the banker's memoranda of a conversation with Kevin in August 1991, supported by four witnesses. Now, he advised his client, there was no alternative but to admit to that single deceit.

To minimise that weakness, Kevin would describe, to the judge's bemusement, the failure to honour the commitment to repay BNS as 'a technical default', which was 'not a dream' and 'not a disaster'. First he blamed Bunn for the agreement, and then his father, who when contacted on the satellite phone to the yacht was 'extremely short and sharp' in his instructions to lie to the bank. Back in London according to Kevin, Maxwell 'was angry and thumped the table', exploding and again demanding that his son lie. That account to the court led Kevin to an outpouring of remorse about what he claimed was the single, dishonest, 'fateful decision' which he had committed: 'My feelings of embarrassment and even shame about the conduct are not any different today in this public courtroom than I felt at the time; and I did feel very bad about misleading, at best, and lying to the bank, at worst.'

By the end of the third week, Kevin seemed harassed. Notably absent during his exhausting, solitary battle for survival was the supportive presence of his five other brothers and sisters, while his mother and wife had been advised that as witnesses they were barred from the courtroom. The only friendly faces were those of John Warnford-Davis, his suntanned father-in-law, and occasionally Dick Russell, his brother-in-law. The jury's reaction was still impossible to determine. Even the lawyers, experienced in criminal trials, were uncertain. Would the twelve men and women be swayed by sentiment or would they find the evidence simply unconvincing? The flickers of emotion on their faces were always noted, but defied accurate interpretation. So much depended, everyone agreed, on Kevin's greatest test – the cross-examination, which started on 1 November.

Throughout Kevin's testimony, Alan Suckling, having moved to a chair directly opposite and underneath the witness, had sat watch-

ing his quarry with increasingly narrowed eyes, reflecting disbelief
and dislike. Although his questioning of some prosecution witness
had been disappointing, the unaggressive Suckling had been persuaded, temporarily, to transform himself. In his view, Kevin and
Jones were planting so many landmines that his prey was ripe for
destruction. The sympathy which Kevin would seek from the prosecutor – 'You were not in my shoes. You were not behind my
father's desk in the immediate aftermath of his death. You should
take into account a primordial desire to have my father buried . . .
You show a lack of sympathy or empathy for the situation' – would
have carried more weight had, he claimed, Kevin not continued to
lie after his father's death, after his burial, after the collapse of the
group and until his trial – four years after the crash. By his own
conduct, Kevin had forsaken the prosecutor's sympathy.

Robustly, Suckling launched his cross-examination by demanding
to know whether Kevin understood his duties as a pension trustee.
Either through misapprehension or fear of being led into a trap,
Kevin faltered, reluctant to give a direct reply. The tension rose as
Suckling pressed for confirmation that Kevin admitted spending no
more than thirty minutes a week dealing with BIM's affairs.

'That's my evidence,' replied Kevin.

'That is less than you were spending watching Oxford United.
Do you regard that as disgraceful?'

'I do not,' replied Kevin, asserting that he had delegated his
duties. 'Do I wish I could turn the clock back? Of course.'

In presenting the image of a victim of circumstance, Kevin had been
briefed to offer seven standard replies: 'I was acting under my father's
instructions', 'the prosecution witnesses are lying', 'you will have to
take me to the documents', 'I cannot recall', 'I have no independent
notes of that meeting so I cannot recall what occurred', 'I have been
denied access to vital documentary evidence and witnesses' and,
finally, 'I am being bullied by the prosecution'. When all else failed,
he was to adopt his father's technique when discomfited by an irrefutable truth: speak at length with apparent frankness and likely cause
the listener to be confused but too embarrassed to mention his or her
inability to understand the answer without engaging in a lengthy
and unprofitable discussion. His deflecting ploys usually succeeded
when the issues which Suckling raised were complicated, and
occasionally succeeded on issues of truth. But Jones had allowed so

many landmines to be laid that Kevin's bitter fight for survival could only be hampered by unavoidable explosions.

'Did you say it,' asked Suckling, referring to Kevin's admitted lie to BNS, 'straight-faced and in a sincere manner?'

'I conducted the meeting in a businesslike way and I told the lie and the various misleading statements to them, and they accepted it.' In the hope that a confession would mitigate the transgression, he added: 'The moment you embark on path which is not straight, then you often find yourself in a position where the lies get bigger. I make no bones about it, that this is one of those occasions where a small lie gets larger.'

Moving to exploit that admission, Suckling asked: 'You never told a single bank that RMG had to pay BIM £250 million by the end of the year?'

'No, I didn't,' agreed Kevin. 'It was none of their business . . . I was trained not to volunteer information.' In 1991, he insisted, the banks 'did not care' to whom they lent money as long as it was secured.

'The reason for telling lies was because you couldn't pay?'

'I agree,' replied Kevin.

'Lies' was not Kevin Maxwell's favoured word. He preferred 'misleading'. After a succession of admissions that he had 'misled' people, Suckling asked, 'I do not know into what category that sort of misleading comes. Does it class itself as a lie?'

'That is obviously going to be in the eye or ear of the listener,' replied Kevin, appealing to the jury.

Fortunately for him, as the pressure increased the spreading flushes across his face and the prevailing redness of his eyes could not be seen by the jury. Separated from him by over sixty feet of courtroom clutter, they were watching his testimony on television screens whose flat image obliterated his shifting colour.

By the third day of cross-examination, Kevin's most favoured phrase had become, 'I cannot recall'. Over one hundred times, he had pleaded a bad memory about meetings, conversations and his own alleged representations which bankers had recorded in written memoranda. On 3 November, Suckling asked, 'Mr Maxwell, how is one to tell when you're telling the truth?'

Kevin's reply was an appeal to the jury: 'Whether I am telling the truth or not is a subjective decision based on all the answers I give, my conduct in this box, and how people judge it . . . I am not happy about what I did in the summer of 1991. It is a huge millstone around my neck. It is one of the very great mountains I personally have to climb to convince people that I am a truthful witness.'

Suckling's first task was to prove that the Maxwell group's financial plight was dire. One example he offered was RMG's method of settling a $36.5 million debt to Banque Paribas in October. RMG had curiously paid only $3.65 million. 'Is this some dodge,' asked Suckling, 'so you can say you made a little mistake with the decimal point?'

'From the misery-guts school it is presumably a dodge. From the optimist's, yes.'

A second example was RMG's 'going-concern' meeting on 23 July 1991. That was dismissed by Kevin as 'not a very serious meeting', one to which he had given little attention. He blamed Bunn (to whom he admitted lying) and the auditors for the mistakes, concealing debts of £435 million and valuing the Scitex holding at £48 million. Even his signature confirming the RMG accounts as true was apparently irrelevant: 'I don't recall sitting down and reading this with care.'

That sparked Suckling's controlled anger: 'You're inventing a story!'

'We are opponents,' snarled Kevin. 'I am telling a consistent story which is the truth. You are the prosecutor who wants to send me to jail. I am not going to help you.'

A third example was the suspicious use of MCC's and BIM's cash to buy MCC shares. Kevin admitted only that he did not tell Morgenstern, his lawyer, all the details. 'Why not? asked Suckling. 'You would not dare, would you? Did you have something to hide, Mr Maxwell?'

'On the contrary,' replied Kevin, 'you do not go to a lawyer to seek advice about what you should be disclosing, if you are worried about something.'

'You never told him all these details?'

'Mr Suckling, I have not come here to pull the wool over your eyes or anybody's eyes.'

That, alleged Suckling, was precisely Kevin's intention, but it was not easy for him to prove that the accused knew that the group was in irretrievable financial straits. Understandably, Kevin argued that so long as the banks gave credit, regardless of their anger about failed forex deals and his lies, there remained the commercial reality of continued support: 'A failure to pay a debt is a technical term which does not automatically transfer into insolvency.' The group, he repeated, was in 'choppy waters' but that was not desperate. Kevin argued that it was not incumbent upon him or his father to volunteer information about the inter-company debts, especially if the banks did not pose the right question. 'If they didn't ask, they didn't get' was his guiding principle. Pressed, he finally uttered serious admissions about financial risk: 'On 5 November, probably ten different facilities were capable of being in default.' He added, 'I am certain that my brother . . . was aware that there was a real crisis,' and he ascribed the same knowledge to Bunn and Trachtenberg.

'NatWest were not the lenders of last resort,' retorted Suckling in reply. 'The pension funds were.' Here the prosecutor entered the heart of his case, where he hoped Kevin's emotional appeals could not gloss over the defence's vulnerability.

In the first place, there was the Scitex agreement of 4 July 1991 between Maxwell and Trevor Cook which had allegedly been amended. In February 1992, Kevin had told lawyers acting for the administrators that his father had shown him 'at the end of July' the agreement with the last sentence (transferring ownership of the shares from BIM to RMG only after receipt of £100 million) crossed out. There were 'two initials' besides the deletion, he had testified.

That explanation, Kevin's trial lawyers realized, caused problems. First, Cook denied initialling any change to the agreement; secondly, Kevin had begun pledging the Scitex shares in repayment of private loans on 8 July 1991; thirdly, he had never mentioned the amended agreement to anyone before 1992; and, fourthly, the amended agreement had not been found.

Kevin seemed to change his story. 'Over the years,' he told Jones, 'I have had my memory jogged.' His father, he said, had shown him a fax copy of the contract which was on shiny paper. About the signatures, he suggested an earlier mistake: 'I can't recall if there were two initials. It might have been one.' He also changed the date which he had seen the amended document. His father, he explained, had summoned him on 5 July, the day after the agreement was signed, had shown him the fax and had said that the contract 'is a nonsense and has been altered'.

Suckling was sceptical: 'Was it not a question of shifting back the deal when some awkward documents came later?'

'You're a professional prosecutor doing your job,' replied Kevin, adopting a powerless pose, 'but I resent that.' Then he made a critical admission. Having not read the contract when it was signed on 4 July, he volunteered that the following day 'I did not actually study it. I did not look at it specifically.'

Suckling's response was blunt: 'It obviously stank, didn't it?'

It fell to the judge to understand the true import of this. In his charming way, Phillips asked Kevin to describe his father's desk. 'The desk was huge,' Kevin replied, and his father was seated on the other side. 'Did you recognise', asked the judge, 'what the document was from there?'

Kevin paused, realizing the implications: 'All I can recall is seeing a deletion, some initials, and that is the fleeting memory that I have left.'

'From that description you could have had no idea what had been altered, or indeed what the contract actually said?'

After another pause, Kevin admitted that the first time he had actually read the contract and identified the allegedly deleted lines was in February 1992.

'What happened to the fax?' asked Suckling.

Exploding in anger, Kevin's face blackened and his eyes reddened: 'I cannot believe you're asking me that question. I have been denied access to papers.' To counter the suggestion that the amended contract did not exist, the defence relied on their claim of a denial of access compounded by the negligent storage of Maxwell documents by Arthur Andersen.

In support of his allegation that Andersen's negligence had caused the loss of that critical document, Jones had melodramatically produced photographs of archival chaos taken in the presence of his second junior, Leah Saffian, an American, at Rockall's storage depot in Sittingbourne, Kent. The photos showed bursting boxes of Maxwell documents piled to the ceiling, with papers spilling on to the floor. 'I want to suggest', said Jones, 'this is how we found them ... This reflects the position in which documents were kept in Rockall when we asked to look at them.' Unfortunately for Jones, Saffian and Keith Oliver, their attack misfired. Stephen Bennett, a storage employee, was rushed to court from Sittingbourne to testify that Jones' photographs did not show Andersen's general storage area, but were taken in Leah Saffian's private inspection room. On the last day of Saffian's inspection, Bennett had discovered that the barrister herself was the cause of the disorder, breaking, he claimed, Andersen's rule of stacking boxes more than two high and leaving files on the floor: 'We found loose files on top of boxes, badly damaged boxes and inventory lists, mainly documents that were not in the boxes.' Rockall's managers had complained about their discovery. To observers it seemed that the defence's claims about of lost documents were not crystal clear.

'Did you ever tell anyone that the agreement had been amended?' Suckling asked Kevin.

'No,' the defendant replied, aware that he was back on slippery ground. 'I am not the keeper of documents.'

The prosecutor moved to challenge Kevin's assertion that RMG had paid for the shares by a movement on the Call Deposit Account. By then the much discussed CDA had lost its previous importance. While being examined by Jones, Kevin surprisingly admitted that he had not seen the CDA showing RMG's debt to BIM. Instead, he assumed that payment would be made by RMG on the inter-company account on 31 December. Suckling proffered documents which he claimed weakened Kevin's assertion. On the courtroom screens, two letters appeared dated 11 and 19 July 1991, both from Kevin to his father, reminding the Chairman to arrange for a valuation of the Scitex shares, reminders which seemed consistent with the timetable set on 4 July. Naturally, Kevin had spent months preparing his reply to Suckling: 'I have no recollection [and] regrettably with the passage of time I cannot call to mind' those reminders. Nor, he added, could he 'recall' receiving on 14 August Cook's memorandum asking for the Scitex payment to which an unamended copy of the 4 July agreement was attached. 'It is', he lamented to the court, 'simply impossible for me to say that I can recall receiving a specific fax.'

Calmly he continued that when, after 5 July, he pledged the Scitex shares, 'I did not address the specific issue of the need to protect the pension fund shares . . . nor consider that the pension funds were at risk.' That went to the heart of the criminal charges: the need to prove Kevin's knowledge that he was taking a dishonest risk.

'No sane, independent, honest director', charged Suckling,

'would loan a quarter of the Common Investment Fund to RMG in its financial condition in July?'

'I was sane and honest,' Kevin replied, pointing out that no one else had objected – 'but conflicts of interest had been allowed to develop'. His stand was partially weakened by his repeated insistence that the public and private assets all belonged to 'the group', rejecting any distinction between BIM's assets and the rest.

'Was the removal of the last sentence in the interests of the pension funds?' asked Suckling, pressing the point repeatedly.

'On 5 July, it was not a thought that occurred to me . . . I was honest . . . There was no intention to deprive.'

'The jury have seen that you are very intelligent,' said Suckling, enjoying an opportunity to rebound on the accused his displays of financial mastery 'Are you saying that the removal of the last sentence did not put the pension funds at risk?'

'That did not go through my mind,' replied Kevin.

'Effectively, it was an unsecured loan by the pension funds to a company in a shaky condition?'

Suckling's persistence paid off as Kevin abandoned his insistence that the debts to BIM could be repaid. 'I agree they were making an unsecured loan.'

'No sane trustee would lend to such a company as RMG? . . . You would have to be a dishonest man of pure self-interest to do it?'

'I agree with you,' replied Kevin, 'armed with the knowledge of the crash . . . but my motivation was honest.'

RMG's public announcement on 18 October 1991 that it had earned for itself all the Scitex profits, Kevin agreed, was 'an example of my father stretching things', but in the Maxwells' opinion it was not misleading. Rather, it was just 'casting the transaction in the most positive way'.

Blame was heaped by Kevin on to Cook: 'He never voiced his concern about the Scitex proceeds.' Asked about Cook's letter of 11 November requesting £102 million, Kevin replied: 'I have simply no recollection. . .

By 8 November 1995, his eighteenth day in the witness box, Kevin appeared haggard, weary and distressed. Even the judge looked pale. By contrast, Suckling and the prosecution team were pictures of health. The day previously, Kevin had volunteered to the pressing prosecutor, 'I was probably one of the most arrogant people you will ever meet. I could not imagine failure. With hindsight, bloody arrogant,' and now Suckling had extracted a further confession: a lie to Citibank involving the $40 million forex deal which Bunn pretended came from the Scitex sale. Kevin justified his lie about the inter-company debts: 'I was not prepared to go through the hassle of dealing with those inquiries.'

'You were leading them up the garden path?' scoffed Suckling.

'After 14 November, I was not being frank with them,' agreed Kevin.

Now the landmines – in his testimony and replies to Alun Jones' examination – began exploding. His rotund defender watched in some anguish, his face, in unedifying contrast to his wig, beetroot red.

The fuse was the Teva saga. No one disputed that, until the end of October 1991, the 25 million shares pledged on 7 November by RMG to NatWest belonged to BIM. Kevin's initial story had been that, at a meeting with his father 'late at night' on either the 29 or 30 October – 'I cannot now be precise' – and over a long drink, he had been told that all the Teva shares had been transferred to RMG. The lack of corroboration or paperwork, said Kevin, was normal: 'I relied on what he said to me.' The following day, Kevin told the court that the conversation had occurred on 30 October – allegedly his last conversation with Robert Maxwell. According to him, Maxwell physically possessed the certificate for 25.1 million shares (presumably received from Trachtenberg, who had retrieved it on BIM's behalf from Crédit Suisse) and said, 'I'll take it to Israel to have it re-registered in RMG's name.'

Do you mean, asked the judge, that your father could transfer ownership of shares in his head without mentioning his decision to anyone and that would be legally effective? Precisely, replied Kevin, grateful that someone understood his defence. Suckling naturally sought to exploit an intervention which had revealed a flawed understanding of the law by a man who had boasted involvement in eighty multi-million-pound acquisitions.

'I have nothing more to add to that,' said Kevin abruptly, but the prosecutor continued mockingly to conjure the image of Robert Maxwell going personally to register one share certificate with Teva's chairman. Kevin's temper snapped: 'You can be as surprised or amazed as you like . . . I accept it beggars belief.' But, when pressed, even he conceded that such transfers were 'simply not in the interests' of the pensioners.

Feigning amazement, Suckling encouraged Kevin to describe how he had adopted his father's practice of cerebral transfers of pension fund property when attempting to recover the 22.8 million Teva shares from Lehmans in BIM's name. After 7 November, Kevin said, he had 'reversed' the ownership from RMG back to BIM – simply in his own mind.

'So you say,' asked Suckling, 'I'm reversing it and that does it?'

'Yes,' replied Kevin po-faced, recognising the farce and the contention that the transaction was invalid in law.

'And if you say it belongs to RMG, it belongs to RMG?'

'Yes. I had the powers and the best interests of the group as a whole in mind.' To cognoscenti, the performance bore an extraordinary similarity to Robert Maxwell's defence of himself twenty-five years earlier before Lord Shawcross at the Take-Over Panel's inquiry into the Pergamon–Leasco affair.

The certificate for 25.1 million Teva shares, Kevin said, was found by his mother on the *Lady Ghislaine*: 'She said she had found it in the safe.' That nearly corroborated Kevin's quip to the NatWest bankers, 'I found this in Bob's safe.' But, three weeks after that testimony, Kevin's lawyers heard that Gus Rankin and Spanish police officers had watched Betty Maxwell open the safe to find it empty. When she eventually gave evidence, Betty would tell the court that she had found the certificate 'in a briefcase . . . near the safe'. According to Kevin, the piece of green paper was flown to London and handed to NatWest.

Until Kevin's testimony, it had been assumed that no one else knew about Robert Maxwell's oral transfer. Emphatically, Kevin had insisted that he had not told either Ian or Trachtenberg, so when they had signed the transfers to NatWest both men had believed that the shares belonged to BIM. But Kevin had unexpectedly revealed to Jones that, though Titmuss Sainer believed that Teva belonged to BIM, two other lawyers – Morgenstern and Neeman – had been told that the Teva shares had been transferred to RMG. 'Why didn't you put that to them when they gave evidence?' asked Suckling, amazed by the disclosure. Morgenstern, replied Kevin, was untruthful. The judge, also perplexed that the defendant was accusing so many lawyers of lying, asked if Neeman was dishonest. Kevin's answer was long and inconclusive, but he did reveal that Robert Bunn and Cook were also told about the change of ownership. 'Is this something you have invented in the witness box, Mr Maxwell?' smiled Suckling.

'Not sitting here,' replied Kevin, exhausted. It had germinated over the previous days.

Cook had also not been asked by Jones about that transfer, said Suckling.

'If that is a criticism of my counsel, then I am sure they are listening,' reported Kevin, finding a new target to blame.

Both Cook and Highfield had testified that on 20 November 1991 they had been told by Kevin, 'The Teva certificates are in Israel.' Kevin's response was simple: Cook's testimony was 'completely untrue' and 'a fabrication'. In anxious anticipation of the visit by the IMRO inspectors on 25 November, said Kevin, Cook had been 'a progressively extremely rattled individual . . . exhibiting signs of stress' and had dishonestly created a paper trail to prove his innocence. Cook's testimony that his anxiety had sprung from his discovery that £296 million of pension fund assets were unsecured or missing was derided by Kevin: the gap would have been filled by the end of the year.

Then Kevin lost his cool. What was the benefit to the pension funds, asked Suckling, of providing the Teva shares to NatWest as collateral for a loan to MCC? It was not the action of 'a sane, independent director'. Kevin exploded: 'I know you will find this incredulous [sic]. I was not acting in an insane manner. Not once but on more than ten occasions his temper snapped during that day as he attacked Suckling for doubting his honesty while he himself accused Cook, as he accused practically all the seventy-two prosecution witnesses, of lying.

'To save their skins?' asked Suckling.

'Yes,' replied Kevin.

'Isn't that what you're doing,' retorted Suckling, 'not telling the truth to save your skin?'

Kevin's face flushed. 'If you don't get the answer you like,' he snarled, 'you smear someone.' Tension pervaded the courtroom. After two other accusations of lying, Kevin accused the diminutive Suckling of 'bullying' – a comical suggestion.

'You've admitted lying,' retorted Suckling.

'Are you thinking I'm going to suddenly trip up?' asked Kevin with a scowl.

Suckling wryly homed in on his target, flourishing Kevin's failure to tell Richard Stone of Coopers about the £400 million owed to the pension funds: 'You could have tipped the wink to help them on their way?'

'What you're ignoring', replied Kevin, his voice rising, 'is how the business was conducted . . . I cannot reinvent the wheel. I wish to Christ we had changed the priorities.' On the other side of the courtroom, Keith Oliver, Kevin's ultra-loyal solicitor, looked concerned. In front, Clare Montgomery dropped her head into her hands. Jones, however, believed that his client's saviour was at hand.

The 'white knight' had been trailed by the defence from the outset as their mystery ace whose credentials and intention to invest £400 million in the stricken group would prove that Kevin had not taken a dishonest risk. Kevin's evidence had been succinct. Relying upon his father's lawyers, especially Sam Pisar, he had 'turned to the Jewish community for support at a moment of crisis' because of Maxwell's close links with Israel and the Jewish community in New York. For Kevin, a Protestant, to play the Jewish card in his circumstances was intriguing. Among those who had been unsuccessfully petitioned by him was Edmund Safra, the president of the giant Republic National Bank and a close friend of his parents. In parallel, Kevin had hoped that Yitzhak Modai, the Israeli finance minister, would deliver a saviour. The intermediary had been David Kimche. It was the revelation of and evidence from the mystery multi-millionaire which Jones expected to tip the balance.

Kevin had revealed that his 'white knight' was Roger Tamraz, an Egyptian whose credentials as an international tycoon seemed impeccable. Educated at Cambridge and Harvard, employed by Wall Street's finest and involved in mega-million buy-outs of stricken empires, Tamraz explained on the hundredth day of the trial his attraction towards the Maxwell investment: 'An empire which took thirty years to build, you could buy in three months.' Tamraz, operating through Oil Capital Limited, had met Kevin on 28 November 1991, just five days before the collapse. According to Kevin, he was told about BIM's problems. 'I was extremely encouraged,' said Kevin, 'he had no problems to get the money.'

Kimche endorsed Tamraz's credibility but admitted that, after hearing about the pension funds' problem, he had run: 'I wanted no more to do with it.' Frankly, Kimche had also recounted how Ian had spoken of the need for £400 million 'very soon after his father's death', suggesting a knowledge of the pension fund hole. Unconcerned, Jones extolled Tamraz's many commercial achievements, mentioning in passing a bank called Intra.

By then, relations among all the lawyers in Court 22 had soured, not least between the emotional Jones and the cool Lissack. Much had changed since Phillips's promotion to the Court of Appeal at the beginning of October when, in thanking Michael Hill for his congratulations, the new Lord Justice (now dressed in sombre black) had replied that the trial 'exemplified the highest standards and the best traditions of both branches of the profession'. In the ensuing weeks, that lofty self-praise had crumbled. There had been too many unsubstantiated allegations by Jones against prosecution witnesses for dishonesty.

In cross-examination, Tamraz's account of his promises to Kevin became less impressive. When he had met Kevin, he told Richard Lissack, on the single occasion, 'I only listened,' and he suggested that due diligence over the following weeks would have revealed the group's true value. He had, he said, received the first Russet report (compiled by Coopers on 25 November 1991 to assess the group's value) that same day, contradicting the later submission by Kevin's lawyers that Tamraz had read the second report published on 3 December which mentioned the debts to the pension funds. But the Arab was honest about his approach. Under his plan, said Tamraz, all the creditors would have taken 'a haircut' – reduced their claims – including the pension funds. With his experience, concluded the Arab, a rescue operation was realistic whatever the price. The beam returned to the faces of Kevin, Oliver and Jones.

Lissack's tone changed. Tamraz was asked to confirm that his relationship with the Intra Bank had culminated in a two-year sentence of imprisonment in Jordan for 'fraudulent conversion, embezzlement and fraud' of $200 million from the bank. There was also, mentioned Lissack, an order by a French court against Tamraz to pay $56 million after another bank's collapse. And there was an outstanding warrant, issued in March 1995 in Beirut, for his arrest. Fifteen feet away, Kevin and his lawyers squirmed. Their faces froze as the witness acknowledged the list of accusations, lamely explaining that they were motivated by his political enemies in the Lebanon.

For the defence, the exposure was a deadly embarrassment. In front of the jury, unable to contain his anger, Jones indignantly accused Lissack of lacking 'the guts to tackle the issues', meaning that the witness had been truly smeared, and after the jury departed the lawyer intensified his attack. Fuming and red-faced, he accused the prosecutor of 'unprofessional, improper and disgraceful behaviour'. The lawyers, as the judge commented when overruling Jones' complaint, had lost their cool. This was too much for Jones. The apoplectic advocate requested that the court rise early. With only Betty and Pandora Maxwell to appear as defence witnesses, his case was suffering. Peter Jay, once willing to attest on Kevin's behalf, had withdrawn but then agreed to appear, only to be disinvited. Considering the evidence available to the prosecution about Jay's duties on Maxwell's behalf, the defence took a strategic decision. Others, according to Kevin, had also forsaken the 'aggravation', including Geoffrey Robinson MP and Eve Pollard, the journalist, both former Maxwell employees.

The two most important women of Kevin's life contributed nothing towards denying the criminal charges, while commendably restraining their natural emotions. Pandora recalled that her father-in-law had been a daunting man whom she had met rarely. Kevin's father, she said, would call him at any time of the day or night. 'There appeared', she told the court, 'to be a strain in the relationship.' Betty spoke of how Maxwell had resented handing control of his business over to his sons, despite grooming them for the inheritance. Kevin, she said, was the 'heir apparent', although her late husband 'could not bear to have any power taken away'. Her anticipated testimony about her husband's tyranny towards Kevin as a boy did not materialize. Wiser counsel had suggested that it might reflect none too well upon her own conduct.

So Kevin's testimony closed with the memory of his earlier invitation to lament his fate. In mid-1991, he had been aware that his father's empire was doomed in dismemberment: 'I did not foresee MCC surviving by March 1992.' Everything except the Mirror Group and the *New York Daily News* would have been sold off, he said, with his own future elsewhere. Instead he had fought to save the empire and had lost. 'What sane person,' he asked, 'would want to be in the Central Criminal Court on trial? . . . There must have been a moment when one could and should have abandoned the ship.' Blaming his 'complicated relationship' with his father, he said unemotionally, 'I could not abandon him when there were problems.' Conceding that the 'losses have been on a huge scale' he launched into a plea of explanation, brooding on 'my business education' in his father's circle, where the 'culture was evasive', laws were stretched to the limit, accounting standards were exploited to show increased profits and board colleagues did not stand up to their Chairman. But, he concluded, 'ultimately our motivation was not, putting it crudely, to conspire to defraud pensioners. It was to save this one group. I suppose that my greatest regret, at the end, is that we failed.'

At the conclusion of his testimony, there was not a moist eye in the courtroom. Along the prosecution bench, there were smiles. Among the defence ranks, Jones stood beaming in admiration. Other lawyers looked bemused. Kevin had given his best in his fight for survival, both for himself and for his father.

Since neither Ian nor Trachtenberg, to avoid such a rigorous cross-examination, gave evidence on their own behalf, Suckling rose again on 21 November to sum up the case for the prosecution. All three defendants, who six months earlier had entered the courtroom with some confidence, began nervously counting the days to the moment when they would hear whether the jury had accepted Kevin's account.

To Kevin's glee, Suckling inexplicably reverted in his closing speech to his previous dislocated and unpersuasive style. Although the prosecutor's language to the jury sounded condemnatory – 'a laughable story', 'persistent bare-faced lies' and 'they didn't care tuppence about the pensioners' – the effect upon the audience in the suddenly overheated and uncomfortable courtroom seemed negligible. Over three days, the jury's attention waivered from a man who increasingly attracted criticism for his failure to sound convincing about the defendants' guilt. Even the judge voiced his bewilderment about the prosecution case against Trachtenberg but Suckling practically ignored the criticism. 'You'll be happy to know that's the last you'll be hearing from me,' he smiled, sitting down. The dearth of plaudits reflected new uncertainty about the outcome. Looking at the impenetrable jury, new doubters speculated about the prosecution's weakness. Suckling, said the critics, was relying on the jury's forgetfulness of his performance and on the judge's presentation of the prosecution's case in his summary.

For the first time in weeks, the defendants relaxed. Trachtenberg smiled. Successively, their advocates, engaging the jury's attention by forceful delivery, propounded seemingly convincing cases which might lead reasonable men and women to afford their clients at least the benefit of reasonable doubt. Attentively, the jury noted the defence lawyers' contentions that the prosecution had failed to prove its case and that the prosecution witnesses were unreliable. Buoyed by these appealing arguments, all three defendants looked to the judge for a balanced summary.

They were soon disappointed. From the outset, Phillip's well-honed words suggested balance but as the faces of the defence lawyers and their clients fell, then flushed and then reddened, Phillips gradually exposed the frailties of Kevin's defence. Quoting at length Kevin's own testimony, the judge suggested to the jury that they should consider the contradictions in the witnesses' testimony, the allegations and confessions of lying by Kevin, and accept his direction that Kevin's description of how the Scitex and Teva shares had been validly transferred from the pension funds by his father was legally impossible. By Friday afternoon, it seemed that everyone in the courtroom acknowledged that the judge's fluently delivered summary had shifted the balance against the defendants. 'He's done the prosecution's job,' complained more than one defence lawyer. The prosecution believed that he had merely exposed the weaknesses in the defence. The remaining issue was whether the jury would accept the judge's interpretation.

On Monday 8 January, thirty-two weeks after the trial began, the five men and seven women filed out of the courtroom, their familiar faces revealing no final clue about their sentiments, to begin their ritual task. Four women, it was believed, would lead their deliberations.

When the jury returned, over one hundred tense faces searched forlornly for an insight. After the well-known phrases were exchanged confirming that a unanimous decision had been reached the foreman of the jury solemnly announced their verdict. Robert,

Kevin and Ian Maxwell, and Larry Trachtenberg were all found innocent.

Emotions raged across the courtroom. In the turmoil, heads craned to witness the defendants' reactions. Unsurprisingly, Kevin was beaming, vigorously shaking hands with loyal lawyers, pouting at the spectators of his glorious vindication. Behind him, Ian was gleefully embracing his advisors, elated by the triumph of justice and relieved that his ordeal had passed. Above them, the ghost of Robert Maxwell bellowed in laughter.

The jury's verdict was that frauds had not been perpetrated and that those allegedly unsavoury accomplices in so many high places – naive, greedy or negligent – did not require censorship. After all the sensational exposures, the cynic might reflect that similar operations would be repeated in the future.

Robert Maxwell's life suggests that any successor's fortunes will depend upon whether self-regarding professionals have learnt lessons from the past and the omens are not encouraging. The billions lost and thousands spent to investigate Maxwell's financial dealings have been in vain. For Robert Maxwell established that human weaknesses and vanities smother the independent judgment of all except the strongest individuals and his life demonstrated the paucity of independent spirits in our midst.

Notes and References

The sources for this book, besides over one hundred new interviews, were the material I gathered for *Maxwell the Outsider* and voluminous original documents from the archives of the Maxwell group of companies. Several of the participants made notes as events unfolded. The most important were those of Ron Woods, referred to as Woods Memorandum. Other gave long statements to lawyers supported by contemporaneous correspondence and memoranda. I also relied upon the statements of claim and defence statements (after checking their veracity) of those many legal proceedings which followed the Maxwell collapse. The principal suits were initiated by the administrators of Bishopsgate Investment Management (BIM) against Crédit Suisse, Bank of America, Lehman Brothers and Coopers & Lybrand; by MGN against the *Daily News* (in New York). Finally, I attended daily the trial of Kevin and Ian Maxwell and Larry Trachtenberg. Citations of testimony, unless otherwise indicated refer to this trial.

THE SECRET — 5 NOVEMBER 1990

11 'Either I was'. TB/Shaffer
11 'Maitland had eagerly'. *Crédit Suisse* sources.
13 'Speculative characteristics' were. BIM st. of claim, p. 29.
13 Businesses worth $500 million. *Guardian*, 1 October 1990.
14 On 7 September. On 17 September, Kevin asked for the first £10 million; the remaining £40 million he would demand in stages up to 8 November. BIM st. of claim, p. 19.
15 With each share. The first certificates sent to Maitland's office were for shares in Ansbacher Bank, CCM, Invesco MIM (an investment fund manager) and Crown Communications, as well as Japanese shares owned by First Tokyo.
15 Indeed, when on. BIM st. of claim, p. 26. Returned to Bunn.
16 'Robert Maxwell of'. TB/Laister.
16 Later that week. Maxwell and Ron Woods signed as directors of BIT. Macmillan's accounts department in New York believed that the nine share certificates were held by BIT and accordingly paid Berlitz's dividends to BIT rather than MCC, providing Maxwell with more unauthorised funds. TB/Woods.

18 'You are a'. Joe Haines, *Maxwell* (MacDonald, 1988), p. 448.

20 'Plays him like'. Tom Bower, *Maxwell the Outsider* (Heinemann, 1991), p. 408.

20 'Maxwell had no'. Ibid., p. 403.

24 Since 1989 he. BIM st. of claim, p. 27.

25 In return for. For the parallel sale in 1990 of Maxwell Graphics – twelve American printing plants – at a loss, see Bower, *Maxwell the Outsider*, p. 507. This was the background to Maxwell's sale of Pergamon.

26 Maxwell had channelled. His other Liechtenstein trusts were called Alandra, Kiara, Jungo, Boccano and Akim.

27 'hoovered up all'. Bower, *Maxwell the Outsider*, p. 498.

27 'besotted by Andrea'. TB/Harrod.

28 'We need to'. TB/Pole.

30 'I knew my'. TB/Cheeseman.

31 'I stayed and'. TB/Cowley.

32 'he always became'. TB/Hull.

32 Captain Hull had. Ibid.; TB/Whiteman.

33 'Where am I?' Roy Greenslade, *Maxwell's Fall* (Simon & Schuster, 1992), p. 344.

35 'a friend – a'. TB/Sharon.

37 'sadistic pleasure' in. Betty Maxwell, *A Mind of My Own*, (Sidgwick & Jackson, 1994), p. 450.

38 'My love for'. Bower, *Maxwell the Outsider*, p. 273.

39 'If only I'd'. TB/Vladina.

44 'I could order'. TB/Pelley.

45 'a fairy tale'. TB/Anselmini.

45 'We needed myths'. Confidential information.

45 'hero and father-figure'. TB/Woods.

45 'Only Woods could'. Walsh testimony, 3 July 1995.

49 Only after his. Mr Justice Vinelott, *Law Debenture* case.

50 'Maxwell regarded his'. TB/Cook.

52 was a 'shambles'. Huntington testimony, 10 August 1995.

53 'Go and talk'. TB/Cook.

54 called 'erroneous figures'. Larry Trachtenberg file, LBI.

56 'I had no'. TB/McInroy.

56 Unfortunately, however, he. TB/Shaw.

56 'That wasn't my'. TB/McInroy.

57 For more than. TB/Cook.

58 'purely a funding'. Haas testimony, 18 September 1995 and Lehmans interviews.

58 'purely a funding'. BIM st. of claim, p. 113.

58 Indeed, Trachtenberg said. Ibid., pp. 128 and 131.

58 At the end.

In the event, in return for pension fund shares Lehmans paid $52 million into the account of Pergamon Holdings. From there the money went to Pergamon Holdings (US) Inc., another private Maxwell company, registered in New York, where it was used to buy MCC shares. Throughout 1990, LBI extended or 'rolled over' the arrangement without the bankers raising any queries. TB/Cook.

59 He remained unsuspicious. That loss occurred after an unusual transaction on 21 December 1989. Kevin directed Cook that BIM should sell 5.8 million MCC shares for $22.4 million to IBI, a company privately owned by the Maxwells. (The shares were registered in the name of Pergamon Holdings, a privately owned company.) But BIM was not to demand any money. Instead Cook agreed with Maxwell that he would merely accept a credit note. Yet simultaneously BIM was to buy for real cash shares in IBI for $22.9 million (*BIM v Coopers & Lybrand*. st. of claim, p. 124.) In that way, Maxwell could use $22.9 million of pension fund money, interest free. When the deal was reversed on 21 June 1990, BIM lost £150,000, but the whole arrangement had been successfully concealed. Cook did not protest about the losses.

59 'I didn't realise'. TB/Cook.

59 Days before the. *BIM v Coopers & Lybrand* st. of claim, p. 123.

59 The option, exercised. Ibid., p. 119.

59 By 29 June. Ibid., p. 112.

60 To settle that. The debt settlement occurred one day before the end of Headington Holding's financial year (ibid., pp. 121 and 152–4). The ownership of the Scitex shares was registered in BIT, while the 48 million Invesco MIM shares were owned by HHL (ibid., p. 81).

60 He listed the. Ibid., p. 81.

60 But he failed. Ibid., p. 113.

61 'We're doing it'. TB/Tapley.

63 On 8 October. MGN st. of claim, p. 43.

63 Capel Cure's covering. Ibid., p. 83.

63 The reason for. Ibid., p. 70.

63 He would only. Ibid., pp. 23 and 39.

64 'to taste the'. TB/Daily.

64 'Daily found Haas'. Ibid.

64 Daily decided to. MGN st. of claim, p. 24.

64 Haas knew that. BIM st. of claim, p. 45.

64 His superiors, after. Lehman Brothers interviews.

65 'I don't like'. TB/Daily.

65 Southgate's reaction was. MGN st. of claim, p. 27.

65 Yet in Lehmans'. Lehman Brothers interviews.

65 'I trusted Donoughue'. TB/Cook.

66 So, on 19 October. In formal terms, Cook 'lent' the pension fund portfolios to Robert Maxwell Group (RMG), Maxwell's private holding company, through LBI. In return, he was given security or collateral, principally MCC shares. Maxwell then delivered BIM's shares (through LBI) to Lehmans in return for Treasury bills, which were exchanged for cash.

66 Although dated 1 October. TB/Cook.

66 It allowed both. TB/Cook.

66 'I just got'. TB/Cook.

HUNTING FOR CASH – 19 NOVEMBER 1990

69 For all of. TB/Laister.
69 'behaviour around the'. Ibid.
70 In 1990, 43. *MCC* v *Coopers & Lybrand* st. of claim.
72 Whenever the Maxwells. TB/Woods.
73 He ignored any. Ibid.

MISERY – DECEMBER 1990

75 'A bit of'. TB/Highfield.
75 Since the last. *BIM* v *Coopers & Lybrand* st. of claim, p. 113.
75 In 1991 Walsh. Walsh testimony, 30 June 1995.
76 'I never spoke'. Ibid., 4 July 1995.
76 That self-denying ordinance. Wootten testimony, 4 July 1995.
76 Maxwell's £49 million. Bower, *Maxwell the Outsider*, pp. 471 and 509.
77 'a high-risk company'. *BIM* v *Coopers & Lybrand*, st. of claim, p. 42.
77 An internal Coopers. Ibid., pp. 43–5.
77 After all, Cook. Trachtenberg's memoranda mentioned that the collateral LBI had pledged for BIM's shares was higher than their value.
77 Nevertheless, within days. *BIM* v *Coopers & Lybrand* st. of claim, p. 52.
77 He also discovered. Ibid., p. 97.
78 To comply with. Ibid., p. 147.
78 Unable to persuade. Hansard, House of Commons, 8 July 1993; *BIM* v *Coopers & Lybrand* st. of claim, p. 509.
80 'What?' exclaimed Maxwell. Greenslade, *Maxwell's Fall*, p. 227.
83 'A phobia about'. TB/Wheeler.
84 Her husband was. Betty Maxwell, *A Mind of My Own*, p. 495.
85 Both were handed. Lehman Brothers interviews. The loan was through Treasury bills, which were paid to Maxwell's private company Pergamon Holdings, and the cash used to repay loans and to buy shares.
85 The Maxwells' total. BIM st. of claim, p. 54.

FANTASIES – JANUARY 1991

86 Over the previous. TB/Capitman.
87 Once again the. BIM st. of claim, p. 19.
89 Unknown to Cook. TB/Cook.
90 He had not. *BIM* v *Coopers & Lybrand* st. of claim, pp. 57–8.
90 (Haas would subsequently. TB/Cook; TB/Daily; Lehmans interviews.
90 'Can you put'. *BIM* v *Coopers & Lybrand* st. of claim, p. 98.
90 'The Treasury bills'. Ibid., pp. 96–7.
90 Cowling later received. BIM st. of claim, p. 57.
90 By then, other. *BIM* v *Coopers & Lybrand* st. of claim, pp. 110, 111 and 129–33.

91 Cowling's only caveat. Ibid., p. 52.
91 He noted a. Ibid., p. 106.
91 His conclusion was. Ibid., p. 89.
91 'this should please'. Ibid., p. 62.
91 The audit was. Coopers' work on the accounts would be completed on 11 March (ibid., p. 147).
92 By the second. TB/Perpich.
95 On a recent. Bower, *Maxwell the Outsider*, p. 430.
95 was 'squeaky-clean'. TB/Richardson.
97 No one, he. TB/Lamont.

VANITY – MARCH 1991

101 'a great family'. TB/Hoge.
102 'We were looking'. TB/Brombach.
103 'I'm not so'. *International Herald Tribune*, 18 March 1991.
105 'lived like a'. TB/Shaffer.
106 'not the best'. TB/Mcdonald.
106 'He was so'. TB/Ratner.
111 'I was totally'. TB/Laister.
111 'TIB Corporation'. TIB was a nominee of Akim Stiftung, a Maxwell Liechtenstein trust. Through TIB, Maxwell paid $21.4 million to Goldman Sachs to buy Mirror Group Newspaper shares.
112 Brookes agreed and. Bower, *Maxwell the Outsider*, p. 524.
112 'had long owned'. Credit Suisse defence (against BIM), p. 39.
112 Naturally Kevin did. Included stock from Capel Cure, with signed transfers from Capel Cure to Crédit Suisse.
114 'My reaction could'. TB/McInroy.
114 Later, asked about. TB/Tapley.
116 'Is there something'. TB/Brookes.
116 One chunk, bought. *MGN* v *Goldman Sachs* st. of claim, p. 7.
117 Those who witnessed. TB/Woods.

FLOTATION – APRIL 1991

120 'My job was'. TB/Richardson.
120 'You were in'. TB/Clark.
121 'This one's okay'. Ibid.
122 'looks too good'. Walsh testimony, 2 July 1995.
123 Robert Maxwell, he. Ibid., 30 June 1995.
123 'I have a'. Ibid., 2 July 1995.
123 'Expediency was the'. TB/Burrington.
125 'I have no'. TB/Pittaway; Bower, *Maxwell the Outsider*, p. 531.
125 Indeed, Guest could. TB/Guest.
126 'I've physically checked'. TB/Cook.
128 From his desk. TB/Tapley.
129 No unauthorised bug. TB/Pole.

130 Still unknown was. Greenslade, *Maxwell's Fall*, p. 243.
130 hosted a dinner. On 10 April, 1991.
133 'we do not'. Brian Brown testimony, 10 July 1995.
134 'I realised that'. TB/McInroy.
135 'It's a fairly'. Ibid.

A SUICIDE PILL – MAY 1991

137 'He flittered around'. TB/Richardson.
138 'He was surprised'. Ibid.
141 At 11 a.m. The plan had started on 2 April when BIT 'bought' 12.5 million
     MCC shares from MGPT at £1.73, and another 12.5 million shares from an
     MCC pension fund. Acting as BIM's finance director, Kevin informed IMRO
     that the reason was 'to reduce self-investment'.
142 Sheinberg was told. *MGN* v *Goldman Sachs* st. of claim, p. 4.
142 'We can't get'. Affidavit Jonathan Leslie.
142 In a recorded. For Goldman Sachs' denials of their knowledge of the secret
     inter-company deals, see Bower, *Maxwell the Outsider,*, pp. 524–5. Shein-
     berg knew that BIT was controlled by the Maxwells because in August 1990
     and January 1991 he had sold put options for MCC shares to BIT.
143 'certainly the possibility'. Bankers' Trust memorandum.
143 'My offer is'. TB/Shaw.
144 'behaving like that'. TB/Clark.

TWO HONEYMOONS – JUNE 1991

146 'I relied on'. TB/Brookes.
148 If the property. BIM st. of claim, p. 40.
148 Over the previous *MCC* v *Coopers & Lybrand* st. of claim.
148 The Maxwells would. Ibid., p. 60.
149 'Can I see'. TB/Shaw.
149 'lapdog who did'. Ibid.
149 'Did you know'. Ibid.
151 'You are the'. Betty Maxwell, *A Mind of My Own*, p. 499.
151 'Everyone was so'. TB/Cheeseman.
152 'It took us'. TB/Jacobs.
152 'Maxwell was puffing'. TB/Harry.
153 'How can Bob'. TB/Shaffer.
153 'Listen,' McDonald said. TB/McDonald.
153 'The mice are'. Ibid.
153 'I was expecting'. TB/Hoge.
155 BIM was not. Lehman Brothers interviews.
155 To cover themselves. Ibid.
155   Fearing that the. BIM st. of claim, p. 64.
157 'He was sincere'. TB/Kryuchkov.
157 In their several. Ibid.

157 'We would try'. TB/Shebashin.
157 'I feel a'. TB/Kryuchkov.
158 At some stage. Bower, *Maxwell the Outsider*, p. 35.
159 'He did produce'. TB/Bristow.
159 'I was ordered'. TB/Gradov.
160 Showing neither surprise. TB/Litvin.
161 He would be. TB/Shebashin.
163 'so struck that'. TB/Vladina.
165 Naive about the. TB/Shebashin, who saw transcripts of the conversation.

BUYING SILENCE — JULY 1991

168 'I understood that'. TB/Harrod.
169 Aware of Maxwell's. Letter, Deborah Maxwell to Alan Stephens, 10 October 1990.
170 To the benefit. Hansard, House of Commons, 8 July 1993; *BIM v Coopers & Lybrand* st. of claim, 510.
170 'Nothing clicked. I'. TB/Woods.
170 'Have you ever'. Ibid.
171 'If the directors'. TB/Laister.
171 'deadpan, poker faces'. TB/Brookes.
171 'didn't question anything'. TB/Laister.
173 'Peter agrees to'. TB/Richardson.
176 Even his father's. Leal-Bennett testimony, 20 July 1995.
177 'The result', he. Bob Brown testimony, 7 July 1995.
178 This discussion was. TB/Laister.
180 'the effect of'. TB/Brookes.
180 'Peter Walker had'. TB/Laister.
180 Stoddy departed to. *Financial Times*, 17 July 1991.
182 Brookes knew that. TB/Brookes.
182 'He was also'. TB/Richardson.
183 'Very tired, overweight'. TB/Kay.
183 Although it included. BIM st. of claim, p. 40.
184 'it does raise'. Ibid., pp. 36 and 42.
184 'They complain of'. SVB interviews.
185 When they met. Walsh testimony, 3 July 1995.
185 The MCC shares. Ibid.
186 That those millions. Wootten testimony, 4 July 1995.
186 The auditor knew. Walsh testimony, 30 June 1995.
186 Neither considered consulting. Ibid.; Wootten testimony, 5 July 1995.
186 Their sole interest. Walsh testimony, 3 July 1995.
186 They reflected Coopers'. Coopers memorandum, 24 June 1991, cited in ibid., 30 June.
186 In Walsh's opinion. Walsh testimony, 3 July 1995.
189 To his surprise. MGN st. of claim, pp. 47 and 74.
189 Boucher summoned. Ibid., p. 75.

189 'just let Larry'. TB/Cook.
190 'I expect the'. MGN st. of claim, p. 85.
191 'Just more chaos'. TB/Highfield.
193 But he was. TB/Burrington.
193 'You're to live'. TB/Guest.

SHOWDOWN – AUGUST 1991

196 Unaware that Maxwell. TB/Brookes.
197 'It was horrific'. Bob Brown testimony, 2 August 1995.
197 'Give me three'. BIM st. of claim, p. 70.
198 Trachtenberg was offering. Ibid., p. 79.
198 It stated that. Ibid., p. 73.
198 'This is all'. TB/Anselmini.
199 'MCC's problems,' he. After 2 August, Ron Woods kept a detailed diary of the directors' meetings with the Maxwells and with their own advisers.
201 Yet, for all. TB/Brookes.
203 'We followed Laister'. TB/Brooks.
203 For the first. Ibid.
205 He then added. Marlatte testimony, 4 September 1995.
205 'For a start'. Marlatte and Kluge testimony, 4 September 1995.
206 'filial love remained'. TB/Woods.
206 The rows, he. TB/Laister.
207 'Stop taking notes!' Woods memorandum 1991.
208 'implored Kevin to'. Leal-Bennett testimony, 20 July 1995.
208 'the breakdown in'. Pelly testimony, 27 July 1995.
211 'satisfied by the'. TB/Laister.
212 He telephoned Trachtenberg. MGN st. of claim, p. 34.
212 Meanwhile, John Di. BIM st. of claim, pp. 79 and 81.
213 In fact, by. Ibid., p. 17; MGN st. of claim, para. 81, p. 42, and p. 51; letter; Ro3ert Bunn to Julie Maitland, 23 May 1990.
213 'I relied upon'. TB/Cook.
214 'I didn't think'. Ibid.
214 First, to allay. MCC, the lawyer wrote, 'is a subsidiary of Headington Investments Limited' and MCC could give loans to HIL since they wre not Class 4 transactions (i.e. transactions between related parties where there is a potential conflict of interest).
214 Brookes would dispute. TB/Brookes.
216 Once the last. TB/Woods; TB/Laister; TB/Brookes.
216 'fits in with'. TB/Laister.
216 The very next. Woods memorandum, 22 August 1991.
217 'heading towards bankruptcy'. Lehmans source.
217 During that same. MGN st. of claim, p. 76
217 'I'm learning as'. Bunn testimony, 25 July 1995.
218 'All of a'. Betty Maxwell, *A Mind of My Own*, p. 499.
218 'I trusted Maxwell'. TB/Burrington.

218 Burrington, like others. Mirror Group, Chairman's Review, 1991.
220 'What's going on?' TB/Brookes.
220 The Swiss Bank. BIM st. of claim, p. 84.
221 The negotiations were. TB/Pole.
222 'I never quite'. Ibid.
223 Nor did he. Ibid.
223 'He had all'. TB/Cook.
223 'I didn't see'. TB/Cook.
224 The £38 million. Maxwell had paid £11 million to Goldman Sachs, £1 million
     to Lehmans, and £26 million to other banks through LBG.
225 'I thought it'. TB/Burrington.
228 The bank had. Haas testimony, 14 September 1995.
229 His ploy worked. BIM st. of claim, pp. 83–9.
229 Why, he was. Ibid., pp. 95–6.
229 'I'm sort of'. Ibid., p. 97.
229 'I'm fed up'. Charles Bingham testimony, 11 September 1995.
230 On the eve. Letter, Robert Maxwell to Mark Thompson, 17 September 1991.
230 'a very good'. TB/Cook.
231 'I was completely'. TB/Jacobs.
232 'to protect your'. Brian Brown testimony, 10 July 1995.
234 'reached the limit'. Leal-Bennett testimony, 28 July 1995.
234 'Kevin seemed quite'. Wootten testimony, 5 July 1995.
234 Trachtenberg's rapid solution. MGN st. of claim, p. 51.
237 Maxwell's legal ploy. In 1987, at the height of his fame, Maxwell had sold
     the rebuilt Pergamon to MCC to increase MCC's size and come closer to his
     aim of creating a £5 billion corporation.
237 'the exodus transaction'. Before PPI was sold to MCC for $200 million,
     PHUSI was established in December 1987 as a nominee of Swico Anstalt to
     inherit PPI's non-publishing assets, alias the 'Twilight Assets': Artgraphtel
     Holdings, Anco Engineers, ITASCA Consulting, Microforms International,
     European Publishing Corporation and Fivetell. On Robert Maxwell's instruc-
     tions, PHUSI maintained two unreconciled sets of books – in the UK and the
     USA.
238 'a walking case'. TB/Rosenbaum.
239 'I haven't seen'. New York Observer, 28 October 1991.
239 'tell about my'. TB/Burrington.
239 'That's all ridiculous'. TB/Galloway.
240 'It's all being'. TB/Galloway.
240 He did not. SVB interviews.
241 No eyewitness recalls. Ibid.

WHIRLWIND – OCTOBER 1991

243 The pittance which. MGN st. of claim, p. 52.
243 'the guy is'. BIM st. of claim, pp. 97—8.
243 Kevin was clearly. TB/Brookes.
244 a 'unique' relationship. Marlatte testimony, 4 September 1995.
245 For the obfuscation. House of Commons Social Security Committee, 2nd Report, 4 March 1992, para. 166.
246 'There's a final'. Letter, Sir Michael Richardson to Kevin Maxwell, 2 October 1991.
248 He's a distressed'. BIM st. of claim, pp. 102–3.
250 'all smiles. Happy'. TB/Featley.
250 Overnight he had. Genger papers.
251 Anyway, he liked. TB/Bogni.
252 Another telephone call. Lehmans source.
252 To placate her. Roberts testimony, 27 June 1995.
253 It would say. Betty Maxwell, *A Mind of My Own*, p. 500.
254 'I have a'. Ibid., p. 500.
254 'it's zero'. TB/Laister.
256 He assured Kevin. TB/Brrington.
256 'There's something radically'. TB/Wheeler.
258 'relive the experience'. Leal-Bennett testimony, 21 July 1995; Brian Brown testimony, 14 July 1995.
259 'Musical-chairs scenario'. Moore testimony, 28 September 1995.
259 'Of course'. *MGN* v *Daily News*, post-trial memorandum, Stroock, p. 4.
259 'is not a'. Genger papers.
260 The transfer was. TB/Clark.
261 But, for him. TB/Genger.
262 'What's gone wrong?' Ibid.
262 'Deal, deal, deal'. Bell testimony, 5 September 1995.
265 'a man who'. TB/Hoge.
266 Her confusion was. Credit Suisse sold shares from the Thornton investment fund owned by the pension funds in order to settle a £6.9 million debt to Chase Manhattan. The cheque, issued by their agents Salomon Brothers, was for payment to 'Bishopsgate I M', but some money left over was handed to RMG.
266 'LBI a/c AGB'. Letter, Matthew St Paul to Credit Suisse, 23 October 1991.
267 'farrago of falsehoods'. Crédit Lyonnais interviews.
267 'Bob was squeaky-clean'. TB/Richardson.
267 Robert Katz, one. Katz testimony, 22 September 1995.
271 'the worst case'. TB/Featley.
272 and 'utter surprise'. Bell testimony, 5 September 1995.
272 His bank, convinced. BIM st. of claim, p. 104. Technically, Lehmans were asking BIM to repurchase the Treasury bills, which had been cashed by LBIIM. Originally, the Treasury bills had been given in exchange for BIM's shares.

272 The outflow of. Woods memorandum 1991; TB/Cook.

273 'I didn't know'. TB/Cook.

273 In the meantime. Aboff was nominated by Kevin as an authorised BIT officer 'until further notice' to handle the Berlitz shares and to open a margin account for the proceeds of their sale at Paine Webber. On Kevin's authority, Robert Bunn sent a letter which authorised the brokers 'to transfer any or all Berlitz shares owned by BIT to Sheldon Aboff'. To allay the brokers' suspicions, Alan Stephens also wrote to Geoffrey Bloch at Paine Webber confirming the letter's legality.

274 'very authoritative and'. Fairfield testimony, 20 August 1995.

275 'I'd fall into'. TB/Clark.

276 'a difficult conversation'. Gregory testimony, 19 September 1995.

276 His leniency surprised. Haas testimony, 15 September 1995.

276 He turned to. MGN st. of claim, p. 50.

277 'I cannot accept'. BIM st. of claim, pp. 106–7.

279 The sheet given. Roberts testimony, 27 June 1995.

279 'Are you happy'. Brookes statement.

283 He had read. Haas testimony, 14 September 1995.

284 'A file is'. TB/Bogni.

DEATH – 2 NOVEMBER 1991

286 'an unpleasant place'. TB/Rankin.

286 Haas seemed placated. Haas testimony, 14 September 1995.

291 At 6.10 p.m. BIM st. of claim, p. 108.

292 'because he was'. TB/Rodriguez.

300 'He was squeaky-clean'. TB/Richardson.

303 'It is absolutely'. TB/Lamela.

303 To their surprise. Betty Maxwell's subsequent description of her relationship and conversation with Rankin was vehemently disputed by the captain, who was supported by other members of the crew.

303 If any clues. Mrs Maxwell's later suggestion that she had found her husband's wet bathing costume on the bathroom floor was disputed by the crew, who said that it would have been removed while he ate dinner: Betty Maxwell, A Mind of My Own, p. 9; TB/Rankin.

DECEPTION – 6 NOVEMBER 1991

308 'He must have'. TB/Anselmini.

309 'a pool of'. Marlatte testimony, 5 September 1995.

309 'This is all'. Haas testimony, 15 September 1995.

309 'half the Que'. Letter, Kevin Maxwell to Rudolph Bogni, 7 November 1991.

309 Kevin's voice, Bender. TB/Bender.

309 filed an interest. Formally, a section 13D, which protects ownership. The bank also transferred the shares to another company.

310 'It didn't dawn'. TB/Laister.

311 'I found no'. TB/Lamela.

311 'assured that Mr'. Ibid.

312 'It was a'. TB/Hull.

314 'I found this'. Leal-Bennett testimony, 1 August 1995.

314 All they knew. Ibid.

315 In his opinion. Ingham testimony, 4 August 1995.

315 Since August, both. Bob Brown testimony, 2 August 1995.

315 Opposed to Leal-Bennett. Ibid., 3 August 1995.

315 The bankers had. The bankers would admit believing that BIM risked losing some money during that brief period (Melbourn testimony, 8 August 1995). They were, however, mistaken. The Cordmead agreement (albeit unsigned), as the prosecution subsequently showed, expressly provided that MCC would compensate BIM for any losses suffered (Morgenstern testimony, 29 September 1995).

316 'We must have'. Wooten testimony, 4 July 1995.

317 'We have hundreds'. TB/Rankin.

320 £5,000, retaining £10,000. Betty Maxwell later claimed (*A Mind of My Own*, p. 14) that she herself had brought £30,000 and had handed over £10,000. This is disputed both by Rankin and by the MAMI accountants.

321 'That would be'. Katz testimony, 22 September 1995.

322 'I was unaware'. TB/Cook.

322 'I had no'. Bob Brown testimony, 3 August 1995.

324 'Considering the circumstances'. TB/West.

325 The first to. TB/Herzog.

325 Betty Maxwell was. Betty Maxwell, *A Mind of My Own*, p. 34.

327 'It was champagne'. TB/Whiteman.

327 Seven Liechtenstein trusts. For example, Isabel was the sole beneficiary of Alandra and Corry Stiftungs, and Anne the sole beneficiary of Akim Stiftung.

328 'The Swiss bank'. SVB interviews.

329 The sole question. Hennessey-Brown testimony, 7 August 1995.

329 'He's very upset'. Covell testimony, 5 September 1995.

329 One solution was. TB/Laister; TB/Brookes; TB/Shaffer.

329 'I was fooled'. TB/Cook.

332 None of the. Hennessey-Brown testimony, 7 August 1995.

332 Laister was puzzled. Laister testimony, 21 June 1995.

334 'We've got a'. La Marchant testimony, 19 September 1995.

334 With the Sabbath. By then, all the 49 million Teva shares had been pledged: 1.1 million to Credit Suisse; 25.1 million to NatWest; and 22.8 million to Lehman Brothers. 1 million had been sold earlier that year.

336 Unfortunately, NatWest managers. Hennessey-Brown testimony, 7 August 1995.

336 'I can't imagine'. Katz testimony, 22 September 1995.

337 offer $35 million. Salomons paid the £20 million to Swiss Volksbank, who in turn paid $35 million to Salomons. SVB's guarantee meant that RMG owed the money to SVB and the debt would eventually be 'covered' by Kevin pledging Berlitz shares.

337 'forex line with'. Black testimony, 7 September 1995.

338 'We've received notice'. TB/Shaffer; TB/Laister.
339 'Can you tell'. Covell testimony, 5 September 1995.
339 The bankers noted. Gary van Lehmenden testimony, 7 September 1995.
340 'I'm absolutely shocked'. TB/Hodes.
340 'My father improperly'. Interview with Laister, Brookes, Woods and Shaffer.
341 'concern at the'. TB/Woods.
342 'I'm feeling very'. TB/Pirie.

MELTDOWN – 21 NOVEMBER 1991

343 'extremely odd'. Fox testimony, 13 July 1995.
343 'Look at this'. TB/Highfield; TB/Cook.
344 'The Maxwells have'. TB/Cook.
344 Highfield had also. Highfield testimony, 11 September 1995.
344 'Keven appeared honest'. TB/Stone.
345 'passed the information'. TB/Guest.
347 'I don't think'. Ibid.
347 That morning, Julie. BIM st. of claim, pp. 32, 76 and 62.
347 'All the allegations'. BIM st. of claim, p. 61.
347 'I don't think I am'. TB/Guest.
348 'We never anticipated'. *Sunday Times*, 24 November 1991.
348 'In the days'. Ivan Fallon in ibid.
348 'angrily denounces the'. Fallon in ibid.
349 'Something's gone wrong'. TB/Cook; Melbourn testimony, 9 August 1995.
351 'Kevin is the problem'. TB/Laister.
354 But Kevin reserved. Memorandum of meeting, 4.10 p.m. on 25 November 1991, at MacFarlanes.
355 'His view of'. TB/Richardson.
355 'This is what'. TB/Cook.
355 'Larry Trachtenberg told'. CL report by Peter Walsh and Steve Wootten, 3 December 1991.
356 Julie Maitland telephoned. BIM st. of claim, p. 63.
356 He asked that. Crédit Suisse source.
357 'They had a'. TB/Campi.
357 'We suddenly realised'. TB/Davey.
357 Among Ph(US)Inc's assets was a $2 million mortgage; dividends worth $304,483; $3 million owed by Sphere Inc., a Maxwell software company; $2.2 million owned by Microforms International; $1.5 million loaned to David Shaffer of Macmillan as a mortgage; and about £3 million by Robert Fraser. Sphere employed ninety people in Alameda, California to market computer software. Among PHUSI's liabilities was $50 million to Swico Anstalt; $8.2 million to Pergamon Holdings Ltd; and an unquantifiable number of millions connected with the transfer of the 'Twilight Assets'. In other words, the Maxwell family Liechtenstein trusts 'owned' over $58.2 million of credit held by PHUSI. What remained unclear were PHUSI's liabilities in the UK.
   In August 1991, PHUSI had wrongly deposited a $2.3 million tax refund

that belonged to Macmillan. The money was passed on to members of the Maxwell family and private Maxwell companies. On 5 December 1991, a further $50,736 owed to Macmillan by the US Revenue was erroneously paid into PHUSI's account.

358 After totting up. CL BIM draft report, 30 November 1991, started on 28 November by Peter Walsh and Steve Wootten; House of Commons Social Security Committee.

360 'He thinks we're'. TB/Clark.

360 'I'm shocked at'. Woods memorandum 1991.

366 'higgledy-piggledy'. Scott testimony, 28 September 1995.

TRIAL – 30 MAY 1995

372 While the obvious. TB/Sharon.

372 others like Vladimir. TB/Kryuchkov.

372 The third group. TB/Nimrodi.

374 At least £100 million. House of Commons Social Security Committee, Fourth Report, 13 July 1993.

375 Their activities were. The only criticism that might have been valid was directed in October 1992 against Buchler Phillips, which had suggested that Maxwell's private fortune was worth more than £8.7 million. In the event, the firm discovered assets worth £1.2 million, yet charged fees of £1.1. million. That discrepancy between estimate and actuality was condemned by the House of Commons Social Security Committee as 'misleading'. Buchler Phillips was accused of taking the opportunity to 'maximise its fee income and to garner more publicity opportunities'. House of Commons Social Security Committee, Third Report, 16 March 1994.

376 Webster, confidential source.

377 although the CIF. Cooper testimony, 25 September 1995.

377 Considering the numerous. House of Commons Social Security Committee, Fourth Report, 13 July 1993 p. vi.

378 'I knew after'. TB/Grob.

380 but when confronted. For example, Howard testimony, 19 September 1995.

388 Jones conceded that. A conspiracy requires an agreement between at least two people. The prosecution's inclusion of Robert Maxwell in the first charge was therefore necessary. Moreoever, because he had signed the 4 July agreement and had told Kevin that it had been amended, it was advantageous for the prosecution to place the burden upon Kevin to prove that his father had acted innocently as well. Finally, it undoubtedly satisfied the public's desire that Robert Maxwell's deeds should not be ignored.

389 'We were kept'. Court proceedings, Kevin Maxwell trial, 2 June 1995.

390 'We found no'. Cooper testimony, 25 September 1995.

390 'bearing the same'. Court proceedings, Kevin Maxwell trial, 12 September 1995.

391 'are not a'. Highfield testimony, 14 September 1995.

391 'the 5.4 million'. Roberts testimony, 27 June 1995.

392 Highfield agreed that. Highfield testimony, 12 September 1995.
392 'I didn't say'. Cook testimony, 8 June 1995.
392 'I was not'. Ibid., 7 June 1995.
392 'I made sure'. Highfield testimony, 13 September 1995.
392 'urgent and immediate'. Ibid., 12 September 1995.
393 'It was never'. Cook testimony, 14 June 1995.
393 'the company would'. Leal-Bennett testimony, 20 July 1995.
394 Robert Maxwell's practice. Highfield testimony, 14 September 1995.
394 In the event. Cook testimony, 14 June 1995.
394 In court, Cook. Ibid., 8 June 1995.
394 Mark Haas of. Haas testimony, 15 September 1995. Cook subsequently
     denied that he had spoken to Haas on that day: TB/Cook.
395 'I didn't know'. Cook testimony, 8 June 1995.
395 Subsequently, Cook would. TB/Cook.
396 'I do recall'. Cook testimony, 9 June 1995.
396 'a key and'. Black testimony, 7 September 1995.
396 'manager of investments'. Foster testimony, 11 September 1995.
396 'after I found'. Cook testimony, 13 June 1995.
396 Trachtenberg, insisted Cook. Ibid.
397 But on that. Ibid.
397 'shock, surprise and'. Laister testimony, 19 June 1995.
398 'You approved that'. Ibid., 21 June 1995.
398 'You had a'. Wootten testimony, 4 July 1995.
399 'Nobody told us'. Walsh testimony, 4 July 1995.
400 '$280 million'. Wootten testimony, 5 July 1995.
400 'To see Kevin'. Vogel testimony, 31 August 1995.
401 'left work one'. Bob Brown testimony, 3 August 1995.
401 'I would be'. Melbourn testimony, 8 August 1995.
401 'That is not'. Leal-Bennett testimony, 31 July 1995.
402 'It was not'. Ingham testimony, 4 August 1995.
403 Matter-of-factly, Fox had. Fox testimony, 13 July 1995.
403 By contrast, Neeman. Neeman testimony, 17 July 1995.
404 'I don't recall'. Vogel testimony, 31 August.
404 'Potentially dangerous customer'. Christopher Stamford testimony, 7 Sep-
     tember 1995.
405 'because he was'. Highfield testimony, 11 September 1995.
406 'just like in'. La Marchant testimony, 20 September 1995.
406 'conducted themselves as'. Anders Bergendhal testimony, 12 September 1995.
407 'You won't believe'. Howard testimony, 19 September 1995.
407 'Can you find'. Scott testimony, 28 September 1995.
409 'Can you hear'. Jefferson testimony, 29 September 1995.
409 'Ian Maxwell always'. Cook testimony, 14 June 1995.
411 'My father is'. Kevin Maxwell testimony, 6 November 1995.
412 Emphasising that the. Ibid., 17 October 1995, when he mentioned Cordmead,
     Marceau, Reuters and Philip Hill.
413 'accumulating hundreds of'. Ibid., 26 October 1995.
413 'I certainly did'. Ibid., 17 October 1995.

413 Shares would be. Ibid.

413 'Nobody from Coopers'. Ibid., 20 October 1995.

414 David Vogel's notes. Ibid., 27 October 1995.

414 while Philip Morgenstern. Ibid., 8 November 1995.

414 'My father', said. Ibid., 18 October 1995.

414 'I would say'. Ibid., 26 October 1995.

414 'a terrible waste'. Ibid., 1 November 1995.

415 'I am still'. Ibid., 26 October 1995.

415 'genuine balderdash'. Ibid., 6 November 1995.

415 'would do whatever'. Ibid., 7 November 1995.

415 'They said the'. Ibid., 20 October 1995.

416 The possibility was. Dr Jane Ward testimony, 14 November 1995.

416 'It was the'. Kevin Maxwell testimony, 18 October 1995.

416 'powerful effect and'. Ibid., 20 October 1995.

416 'I was genuinely'. Ibid., 26 October 1995.

416 On the one. Ibid., 23 October 1995.

417 Hence Mike Moore. Ibid., 26 October 1995. Kevin was asked by the judge to explain why MGN would first want the money and then route it through New York back to London, incurring extra costs. 'The Mirror group', he answered, 'wanted to buy an option on the *Daily News*.' It was a bizarre explanation because, on his own admission, no one else knew about that decision and he admitted that he wanted the option reversed after his father's death. 'A pointless exercise,' said the judge, looking puzzled – although he understood the truth. (Ibid., 6 November 1995.)

417 'commercial blackmail'. Ibid., 27 October 1995.

417 'reduce the bank's'. Ibid., 23 October 1995.

417 John Melbourn was. Ibid., 24 October 1995.

417 'an exceptionally aggressive'. Ibid., 30 October 1995.

417 In a familiar. Jones fed questions to elicit Kevin's disingenuous answers. On the failed $35 million deal with SVB on 4 November, Kevin was prompted by Jones' smiling question, 'Repaid again with interest?', to tell the jury without mentioning that Berlitz shares were the source of repayment: 'Again with interest' (Ibid., 27 October 1995). Similarly, when Jones asked about the discussions with the Bank of England and John Melbourn concerning the £55.7 million owed to Swiss Bank after the misappropriation of the First Tokyo shares, the jury, unaware of the background, were told by Kevin that the £55.7 million owed to Swiss Bank was a 'loan which did not expire until May 1992' (ibid., 7 November 1995). The same balm was applied to the stock lending. Kevin simply mentioned his 'comfort' that 'stock lending was legal' (ibid., 30 October 1995).

418 'a BIM asset'. Ibid., 2 and 3 November 1995.

418 'a technical default'. Ibid., 24 October 1995.

419 'You were not'. Ibid., 7 November 1995.

419 'That's my evidence'. Ibid., 1 November 1995.

420 'Did you say'. Ibid., 3 November 1995.

420 'I do not'. Ibid., 3 November 1995.

420 'Mr Maxwell, how'. Ibid.

421 'Is this some'. Ibid.

421 'Not a very'. Ibid., 2 November 1995.

421 He blamed Bunn. Ibid.

421 'You never told'. Ibid., 2 November 1995.

422 A failure to. Ibid., 1 November 1995.

422 'If they didn't'. Ibid., 3 November 1995.

422 'On 5 November'. Ibid., 7 November 1995.

422 'I am certain'. Ibid.

422 'Over the years'. Ibid., 18 October 1995.

422 'I can't recall'. Ibid., 2 November 1995.

423 'The desk was'. Ibid., 14 November 1995.

423 'I want to'. John Talbot testimony, 6 October 1995.

424 'We found loose'. Bennett testimony, 16 October 1995.

424 Kevin surprisingly admitted. Kevin Maxwell testimony, 18 October 1995.

424 'I did not'. Ibid., 2 November 1995.

425 'No sane, independent'. Ibid., 2 and 6 November 1995.

425 'No sane trustee'. Ibid., 3 November 1995.

425 'casting the transaction'. Ibid., 6 November 1995.

425 'I have simply. Ibid., 30 October 1995.

426 'I was probably'. Ibid., 7 November 1995.

426 a lie to. Ibid., 27 October 1995. Kevin's story was that, on his father's instructions, Bunn had unfortunately been 'confused', entering the deal and mistakenly mentioning Scitex: 'It didn't have anything to do with Scitex in my mind. It was a private-side transaction.'

426 'You were leading'. Ibid., 8 November 1995.

426 'late at night'. Ibid., 19 October 1995.

426 'I'll take it'. Ibid., 20 October 1995.

427 'simply not in'. Ibid., 7 November 1995.

427 'So you say'. Ibid., 8 November 1995.

427 'She said she'. Ibid., 20 October 1995.

427 'in a briefcase'. Betty Maxwell testimony, 14 November 1995.

428 'Is this something'. Kevin Maxwell testimony, 8 November 1995.

428 'If that is'. Ibid.

428 'a progressively extremely'. Ibid., 31 October 1995.

428 'I know you'. Ibid., 7 November 1995.

429 'turned to the'. Ibid., 30 October 1995.

429 Kevin had revealed. Ibid., 31 October 1995.

430 'An empire which'. Tamraz testimony, 9 November 1995.

430 'I was extremely'. Kevin Maxwell testimony, 31 October 1995.

430 'I wanted no'. Ibid., 9 November 1995.

430 'exemplified the highest'. Trial transcript, 3 October 1995.

432 'I did not'. Kevin Maxwell testimony, 31 October 1995.

Maxwell Foundation Group – Detailed Family Tree – at 31.03.91

(Apart from PHL – only main operating/holding companies shown)

Maxwell Foundation

Pergamon Holding Anstalt

Mirror Group

100%	100%
PHL	**MH**

	100%	51%	80%
	MMR	**MGN Ltd**	

All votes 100% | PREF | 65% | 35% | 100% | 100% | 100% |

| **PHA[I]** | | **AGB INT** | **SDR** | | **BIH** |

'Other' subsidiaries
of PHL
SEE BELOW

MCP

MGInc

MInc

Key for Mirror Group Companies

AGB INT	AGB International	plc
B/VER	Berliner Verlag	
BIH	British International Helicopters	Limited
BPL	Bishopsgate Property	Limited
EURO	The European	Limited
LBG	London & Bishopsgate Group	plc
LBI	London & Bishopsgate International	Limited
MCP	Mirror Colour Print	Limited
MCS	Maxwell Cable Services	Limited
MEG	Maxwell Entertainments Group	plc
MH	Mirror Holdings	Limited
MGInc	Mirror Group	US Coy Inc
MGN	MGN	Limited
MGN(NA)	Mirror Group N/Papers N/America	
MInc	Mirror	US Coy Inc
MM	Metromode	Limited
MMR	Maxwell Market Research	Limited
MNInc	Mirror Newspapers	US Coy Inc
MTV	MTV Europe	Partnership
M/HIR	Magyar Hirlap	
PFT	Pergamon Financial Trust	Limited
PGH	Pergamon Group Holdings	Limited
PG	Pergamon Group	plc
PGFS	Pergamon Group Financial Services	Limited
PHL	Pergamon Holdings	Limited

Key for Mirror Group Companies Cont.

PHA[I]	PHA [Investments]	Limited
PMT	Pergamon Media Trust	plc
SDR	Scottish Daily Record	Limited

'Other' Active Subsidiaries of PHL

Allcentre Properties	100%	Limited
Balmpower	100%	Limited
Balmtech	100%	Limited
Bishopgate Property	100%	Limited
Infoline	100%	Limited
Information Management Techniques	100%	Limited
Maxwell Building Enterprises	100%	Limited
Maxwell GED International	100%	Limited
Maxwell Microform Publication	100%	Limited
Newman Neame	100%	Limited
Newport & Robinson	100%	Limited
Pergamon Fleet Services	100%	Limited
Pergamon Group Services	100%	Limited
PHL Estates	100%	Limited
Science, Engineering, Medical and Business	100%	Limited
The Nuffield Press	100%	Limited
Thomas Cook	US Coy	100%	Inc
TMTR Investments	100%	Limited

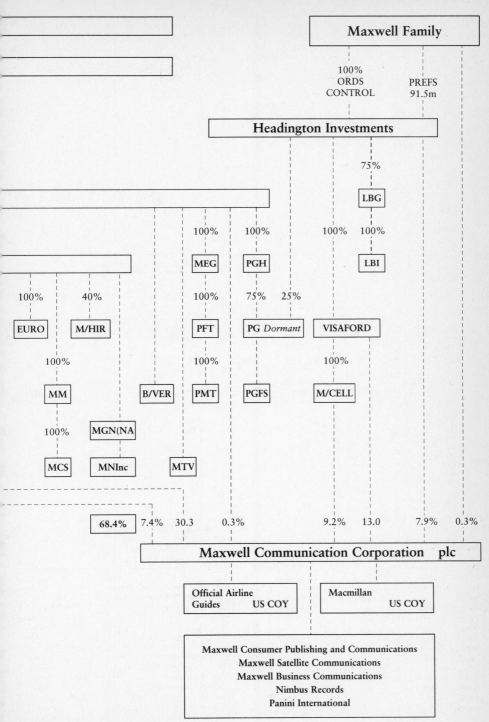

Maxwell Family

100%
ORDS
CONTROL

PREFS
91.5m

Headington Investments

75%

LBG

100%   100%   100%   100%

MEG   PGH   LBI

100%   100%   75%   25%

EURO   M/HIR   PFT   PG *Dormant*   VISAFORD

100%   40%   100%   100%

100%   100%   100%

MM   B/VER   PMT   PGFS   M/CELL

100%   MGN(NA

MCS   MNInc   MTV

68.4%   7.4%   30.3   0.3%   9.2%   13.0   7.9%   0.3%

Maxwell Communication Corporation   plc

Official Airline
Guides   US COY

Macmillan
US COY

Maxwell Consumer Publishing and Communications
Maxwell Satellite Communications
Maxwell Business Communications
Nimbus Records
Panini International

Maxwell Foundation Group – Detailed Family Tree – at 20.05.91

(Apart from HHL – only main operating/holding companies shown)

Maxwell Foundation

Swico Anstalt

CONV
LOAN
STOCKS

ORDS
27.5%
24.8%

Robert Maxwell Group

100%   100%

HHL   **RMH**

100%   51%   80%

MMR   **Mirror Group Newspapers   plc**

All
votes
100%   PREF   65%   35%   100%   100%   100%   100%

PHA[I]   **AGB INT**   **SDR**   **MGN**   **BIH**

'Other' subsidiaries
of HHL
SEE BELOW

MCP   **MGInc**

MInc

Key for Robert Maxwell Group Companies		
AGB INT	AGB International	plc
B/VER	Berliner Verlag	
BIH	British International Helicopters	Limited
BPL	Bishopsgate Property	Limited
EURO	The European	Limited
HG	Headington Group	plc
HGFS	Headington Group Financial Services	Limited
HHL	Headington Holdings	Limited
LBG	London & Bishopsgate Group	plc
LBI	London & Bishopsgate International	Limited
M/HIR	Magyar Hirlap	
MCP	Mirror Colour Print	Limited
MCS	Maxwell Cable Services	Limited
MFT	Maxwell Finacial Trust	Limited
MGH	Mirror Group Holdings	Limited
MGInc	Mirror Group	US Coy Inc
MGN	MGN	Limited
MGN(NA)	Mirror Group N/Papers N/America	
MInc	Mirror	US Coy Inc
MM	Metromode	Limited
MMP	Maxwell Media	plc
MMR	Maxwell Market Research	Limited
MMT	Maxwell Media Trust	plc
MNInc	Mirror Newspapers	US Coy Inc
MTV	MTV Europe	Partnership

Key for Robert Maxwell Group Companies Cont.		
PHA[I]	PHA [Investments]	Limited
RMH	Robert Maxwell Holdings	Limited
SDR	Scottish Daily Record	Limited

'Other' Active Subsidiaries of HHL		
Allcentre Properties	100%	Limited
Balmpower	100%	Limited
Balmtech	100%	Limited
Bishopsgate Property	100%	Limited
Headington Fleet Services	100%	Limited
Headington Group Services	100%	Limited
Infoline	100%	Limited
Information Management Techniques	100%	Limited
Maxwell Building Enterprises	100%	Limited
Maxwell GED International	100%	Limited
Maxwell Microform Publication	100%	Limited
Newman Neame	100%	Limited
Newport & Robinson	100%	Limited
PHL Estates	100%	Limited
Science, Engineering, Medical and Business	100%	Limited
The Nuffield Press	100%	Limited
Thomas Cook	US Coy	100%	Inc
TMTR Investments	100%	Limited

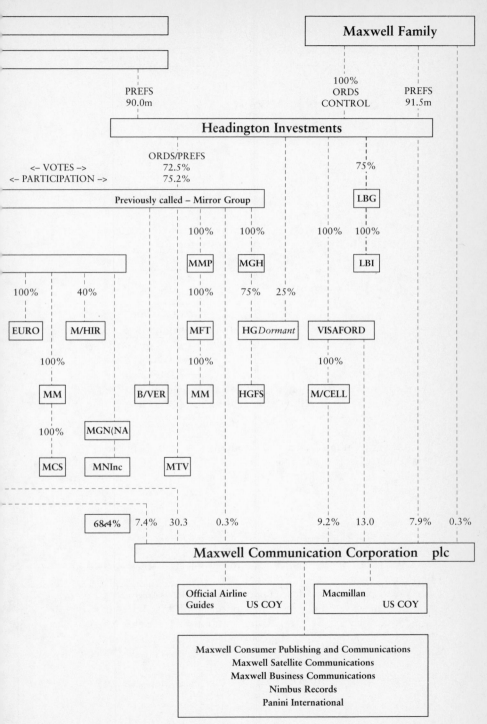

Maxwell Family

PREFS
90.0m

100%
ORDS
CONTROL

PREFS
91.5m

Headington Investments

ORDS/PREFS
72.5%
75.2%

75%

<- VOTES ->
<- PARTICIPATION ->

Previously called – Mirror Group

LBG

100%   100%   100%   100%

MMP   MGH   LBI

100%   75%   25%

100%   40%

EURO   M/HIR   MFT   HG *Dormant*   VISAFORD

100%   100%   100%

MM   B/VER   MM   HGFS   M/CELL

100%   MGN(NA

MCS   MNInc   MTV

68.4%   7.4%   30.3   0.3%   9.2%   13.0   7.9%   0.3%

Maxwell Communication Corporation   plc

Official Airline
Guides   US COY

Macmillan
    US COY

Maxwell Consumer Publishing and Communications
Maxwell Satellite Communications
Maxwell Business Communications
Nimbus Records
Panini International

List of illustrations

Index

Montgomery, Clare 380, 391, 404–7, 429
Montgomery, David 127
Moon, Rev. Sun Myung 98
Moore, Michael 80–1, 143, 206, 258–62, 307, 345, 417
Morgan, Charles and Jane 209
Morgan, John 51
Morgan, Sir John 93–4
Morgan Stanley 44, 201
  and Berlitz shares 236, 273, 329; and BIM shares 223–4; missing share certificates 114, 149, 240; and stock lending 56, 60–1
Morgenstern, Christian 166
Morgenstern, Philip 79, 125, 214, 287, 334, 338–9, 350, 414, 421, 428
Morton, Sir Alastair 103
Moscow 156–65, 169, 215, 293, 371, 372–3
Moscow News 162
Mossad 263–4, 267, 270, 274, 305, 325, 362–3
Moulsford 371
MTV 83
Müller, René 183, 214, 235–6
Muracciole, Odile 346
Murdoch, Rupert 19, 20, 23, 27, 80, 83, 92–3, 100, 110, 120, 210
My Gail 189

Nadir, Asil 314
National Enquirer 98
National Westminster (NatWest) Bank 111, 142, 174, 205, 315, 332
  corporate risk department 314, 331; critical of managerial integrity 349; and foreign exchange deals 201; Leal-Bennett at 183, 200–2, 208, 261, 322; loan refused 175–6, 227, 313–14, 341; loans 120, 133, 202, 208, 258, 267, 322, 331; overdraft 196–7, 200, 202, 248, 336, 401; relations with Maxwells 20, 75, 217, 229, 249, 330, 359; and Scitex shares 384, 387, 393; settlement demands 177, 208, 234, 248–9, 257, 271, 307; siezes assets 336, 346; sympathetic to debt situation 359; and Teva shares 314, 322, 334,

336, 341, 384, 394–6, 401, 403, 405, 410; trial evidence 400–2, 409
Neeman, Yaakov 310, 336, 342
  funeral arrangements made by 319, 325, 403; and Israeli loan 324, 341, 349, 362, 403, 406; Maxwell's lawyer 117, 155; and Scitex shares 156, 265; and Teva shares 156, 178, 346, 395, 403; trial evidence 403
Neil, Andrew 81, 140
New York 42, 68, 84–5, 118, 140, 145, 148, 233, 252–3, 269, 331–2, 357, 367
New York Daily News
  acquired by Maxwell 99–111; administration threat 365, 432; and bank loans 260–3; financial situation 140, 153–4, 185, 265; Kevin Maxwell takes over 320, 332, 357, 364–6; Kevin's resignation 367; Maxwell's management of 115, 117, 130; offered as collateral 321; ownership of 237; property development 259; sale offer 348; staff 134; trade unions 153, 179, 265, 328
New York Post 100, 301
New York Times 98
News of the World 93, 120
Nicholson Graham and Jones 79, 125, 204, 230
Nimrodi, Yaakov 372–3
Nordex 371
Nurse, Sarah 306

Official Airline Guides 19, 20, 47, 116
Official Receiver 131
Old Bailey 369, 381, 385
Oliva, Isabel 316–19
Oliver, Keith 372, 380, 383, 424, 429
Olmert, Ehoud 35, 326
Oil Capital Limited 430
Oxford United 43, 419

Palma 188–9, 191, 193–4
Panini 96, 116
Pankin, Boris 103, 232
Panorama 221, 230–3, 234–5, 247, 267, 288
Paramount Pictures 35, 104
Paris 137, 229, 328, 372